Travels of a Hard-Rock Mining Engineer

TRAVELS OF
A HARD-ROCK MINING
ENGINEER

Martin Stoakes

YOUCAXTON PUBLICATIONS

OXFORD & SHREWSBURY

Copyright © Martin Stoakes 2014.

The Author asserts the moral right to
be identified as the author of this work.

ISBN 978-1-909644-44-1
Printed and bound in Great Britain.
Published by Martin Stoakes 2014.

All rights reserved. No part of this publication may be reproduced, stored in a
retrieval system, or transmitted in any form or by any means, electronic, mechanical,
photocopying, recording or otherwise, without the prior permission of the publisher.

This book is sold subject to the condition that it shall not, by way of trade or otherwise,
be lent, resold, hired out or otherwise circulated without the publisher's prior consent
in any form of binding or cover other than that in which it is published and without a
similar condition including this condition being imposed on the subsequent purchaser.

Heartfelt thanks

to my Editor, Bob Fowke, for his patience

and to my wife, Gillian, for her support.

For Sproggs

1

Clunk! The sound of the trap window banging shut as a consequence of the reverberations of an aircraft passing over at rooftop height. That was my earliest recollection as a four year old in 1940 as the Battle of Britain unfolded over the skies of west Kent. The peace and serenity of Royal Tunbridge Wells now shattered by the sound of an aerial dog-fight and the continual thump, thump of the anti-aircraft batteries situated up on the Common at Mount Ephraim.

As soon as the air raid all clear sounded we scuttled out onto the street looking for bits of shrapnel. That continued for several weeks until our house received a hit and a near miss from incendiary bombs. The next thing I can recall was helping to pack up a few clothes and toys, heading down to Tunbridge Wells West station and taking the steam train to Reading. There were four in our party my parents and my elder sister Judy. At Reading we were met by an Uncle Joe & Aunty Molly. My parents handed us over, so to speak, and caught the next train back to Tunbridge Wells - my sister and I had become evacuees.

Uncle Joe, with a gammy leg from a motorcycle accident, loaded Judy and me into an upright Austin 16 car for the journey back to Harlesford Farm at Tetsworth in Oxfordshire. Running a 300 acre farm he had a petrol allocation which enabled him to run the car. The farm seemed very isolated and quiet after the hurley burley of the Battle of Britain in Kent.

Uncle Joe and Aunty Molly had three children, oldest Betty, middle Bill and youngest Mu ranging from circa nineteen down to thirteen years. Betty basically organised Judy and me and took us on our first visit to the local school in Tetsworth village. We walked over the farm's fields - it was all very rural. At school we were treated as "southern oddities - evacuees from London".

The farm, in fact, was still worked mainly by draught horses; there were six or eight carthorses, although later in our stay at the farm a yellow-reddish tractor, a Fordson Major appeared and was greatly admired by the ten farm hands. The farm buildings, stables and barns were arranged around a central courtyard where there was a large tump of horse manure and semi-rotted straw. Chickens wandered everywhere scuttling out of the way of several farm cats. There was a sizeable herd of milkers as well as bullocks (for beef) kept up at the higher, more remote part of the farm called Killases.

Few things stick out in my memory. I really enjoyed the farm life (of course we had much better food than most of wartime Britain - fresh eggs, butter, milk etc) with its great sense of space, daily rhythm, peace and almost complete absence of outside influences. I was quite frightened of Uncle Joe as he ran the farm with a rod of iron. My best mate was their son Bill, although more than ten years older, he was my hero. He was mad keen on horse riding and hunting and in my eyes seem capable of doing anything. He teased me unmercifully - ran the yard broom through my hair and dunked me upside down into the Brook, which ran along the lower boundary of the farm. He was always trying to get me out of trouble with Uncle Joe when I did something stupid, such as leaving the molasses tap running in the cowshed!

Of course all windows had black-out curtains, but one clear moonlit night a German bomber returning from raids in the Midlands was in a hurry to get back home, spurred on by night fighters from RAF Benson he spotted the light-coloured cowshed roof. He jettisoned his remaining bomb which exploded about 100 yards from the main farm buildings with an enormous crump that had us all out of bed in a flash. Next morning all the farm hands were up on the cowshed roof painting it matt black. We thought it great fun but Uncle Joe was not amused, it disturbed the farm's rhythm.

One thing did leave a permanent impression (literally) on me. I was with Uncle Joe in the horse and two wheel trap coming down from inspecting the bullocks up at Killases when the horse bolted, spooked by something. We hurtled down the field at a full gallop with Uncle Joe struggling to rein the horse back. No luck, at the bottom with a sharp turn right into an adjacent field the trap overturned and we were both catapulted out. I fell on my left side shoulder and received a "greenstick" fracture of my collarbone. That has left me with a marked bump on my left shoulder. Uncle Joe, knowing how to fall, was unhurt physically, but more than a little irate with the horse. Our absence was eventually noted and we were both carted off to the nearby Thame hospital. No harm to Uncle Joe and I was merely heavily bandaged up to keep the shoulder immobile.

Towards the end of 1945 my sister, Judy, and I headed back to the parental home in Culverden Park, Tunbridge Wells. My parents had moved from Birch

Cottage (No. 21) a few yards up the street to No. 11, which was promptly renamed Harlesford after the farm. I was sent as a day boy to St Georges School near Pembury Road in Tunbridge Wells. My only recollection of that school (I was only there for two terms) was the swimming lessons at the indoor Monson Road Baths. I really loved learning to swim. My parents then decided to send both of us off to boarding schools - Judy disappeared to a school at the back of Hastings and I went to Fonthill School a few miles outside East Grinstead.

Fonthill, a boys only prep school, was very spartan, similar to an Outward Bound school. We slept in seven-bed dormitories, with individual large porcelain basins and a jug of ice cold water. After games there were no showers but communal baths with (some) hot water. The school had a small outdoor, unheated swimming pool, which we used at least twice a week, usually throughout the year. However the winter of 1947 was the coldest on record (the pool was well frozen) and for the only time in my life I experienced chilblains. We seemed to do a lot of outdoor physical exercise, particularly long distance running chasing "trail layers". My great sporting achievement (!) was winning a "Diving Cup", no idea how, I just seemed to flop in head first. At half term my mother generally came across from Tunbridge Wells by train to "take me out".

During holiday time I was at home at Harlesford. Outside activities were playing in "The Park", which abutted the bottom of our garden, with the Helm boys building a rickety boat for the pond, constructing a hide and in the evening kicking a football with my dad. Inside (on wet days) my pride and joy was a Meccano set. At the age of twelve (1948) my dad bought me a Hercules bicycle. That really changed everything for me because it gave one freedom to move around and explore. Both my sister and mother had bikes and all three of us used to go off on quite long rides. I don't think my dad cycled, he was very busy with his surveyor/estate agents business. Both he and my mother were sporty, playing golf and tennis and my dad additionally played cricket and football for local club sides. Both of them were musical, my mother an excellent pianist, whilst my dad played violin and sang (tenor). They formed a musical quartet (piano, singers - alto, tenor & bass) and used to visit "grand houses" around Tunbridge Wells and entertain the owners and guests (eg Hever Castle, near Penshurst). Obviously that was before the advent of television, computers, the internet and smart phones.

I left Fonthill at the end of 1948 and in January 1949 went to Tonbridge School at Tonbridge in Kent. That was a well-known public school, founded in 1553, run by the Worshipful Company of Skinners. My father had attended Skinners School in Tunbridge Wells. I attended as a day boy assigned to Smythe House. I travelled daily on the No 98 Maidstone & District double-decker bus, which picked up several other Tonbridge School day boys in Tunbridge Wells and Southborough. We monopolised the front of the upper deck. We were all required to wear the School straw boaters much to the delight of local "youths" who taunted us with cries of "strawberry baskets".

I started in form one and at the end of my first term came 12th out of 14. My father was not best pleased; after all he had opted to send me to a "good public school", which was costing him close to £500/year, a small fortune in 1949. I tried to buck up my ideas, but was a slow starter on the academic side and never managed to get into the top half of any subsequent classes. I enjoyed most sporting activities and by 1952 was in the Smythe House team for cricket, rugby, squash and fives. I disliked all athletics. However we were obliged to do either cross country running (3.5 miles juniors, then seven miles seniors) or boxing. I reckoned cross country running was like drawn-out suicide whereas boxing was short, rapid murder. I opted for boxing and also represented the House in that sport. I was not good enough to represent the School at any sports. (M C Cowdrey dominated cricket and R W Marques rugby, both eventually played for England)

We were also obliged to join the Combined Cadet Force (CCF). I opted to join the army section, as opposed to air or navy and additionally joined the School's military drums and pipe band as a side drummer. That sparked my later interest in and love of beat music and traditional jazz. In 1952, when I was 16, the army CCF went by train to tented field barracks just outside Folkestone. Those were run by The Irish Inniskillin Guards, who were a really tough lot. The toilet "facilities" comprised a long trench with water running through it, whilst alongside was a 6" log supported on two trestles, so that the log was about 18" above the ground. It was a precarious and exposed position to be in when about ones' business as certain jokers would send lighted "candle boats" down the ditch!

I had a good bunch of mates from Smythe House and we used to go pub crawling in Kent when one of the older lads borrowed his dad's car. Shortly after my 16th birthday I acquired a French Gnome-et-Rhone 250cc side valve motorbike from Count Vonovych. At that time my sister Judy was working for Womans Own magazine in London and the Count, a minor "noble" from Yugoslavia, was a professional court photographer. Visiting the Womans Own offices he spotted Judy and asked her to model for him. She 'appeared on many magazine covers etc and eventually joined the Count full-time as personal assistant; that was the motorbike connection. The Gnome was grossly underpowered with a pressed steel frame and "rubber band suspension". However together with Dave, a Tonbridge school friend who had a 1928 Raleigh motorbike, we spent the summer holidays motorbike camping through the Peak District, Yorkshire Dales and Lake District. We climbed all the main Lake District mountains from our campsite between Lakes Crummock and Buttermere. Later that year I ditched the GetR and purchased (with help from Dad!) a 1935 OK Supreme 250cc OHV JAP, three speed foot-change Burman gearbox motorbike. That was a dream machine after the GetR to the extent that I took it up to the Brands Hatch motor circuit to "try out" on open days. Judy's boyfriend, Bob, had a Leonard MG two-seat sports car that he used to race at Brands.

About six or seven of us from Smythe House went up to the Norfolk Broads for a boating holiday. A Mr Wheeler, who had a specialist garage in Tunbridge Wells and was a friend of my father drove us up in a supercharged saloon Jaguar. We were all pretty quiet on the trip as Mr Wheeler was no mean saloon car racer! We'd hired three boats, two 2-berth boats and the one I was on a gaff rigged sloop called Morning Calm. As I was the tallest I ended up on the floor between the two side bunks. The most memorable activity of the holiday was quanting the boat under low bridges when the mast had been lowered. Of course nearly everyone either lost the quant pole or fell in trying to retrieve the pole as the walk/push came to an end at the boat's stern.

In 1952 I was in the Upper Fifth form at Tonbridge taking a History course. My father suggested it was time I thought about what I wanted to do with my life. All I knew was that I wanted to get out of Tunbridge Wells and see the World. I really wanted to see Rio de Janeiro. I thought I might like the Merchant Navy (Norfolk Broads influence?), whilst my father, who was a chartered surveyor and estate agent, thought I might be interested in the Ordnance Survey. He never made any attempt to press gang me into his estate agency business in Tunbridge Wells. So off we went to Southampton. The OS offices were a bit dingy and daunting and a far cry from "seeing the world", so for a while we concentrated on Merchant Navy bumph. At that time, early 1953, numerous career people visited the school. From London a gentleman appeared offering Metalliferous Mining Scholarships for a three year degree course at the Royal School of Mines (RSM), part of Imperial College. He stressed the opportunities to "see the World" with a career in hard rock mining.

I attended an interview at the RSM in London (no exam) and much to my and everyones amazement at Tonbridge I was offered a Scholarship, although at that time I had no GCSE A Levels and only seven O Levels. However the RSM said that they would support me for a "pre-year" at Battersea Polytechnic doing A Level Maths, Physics and Chemistry before going on to the three year mining course at the RSM. My parents were very pleased and we contacted Battersea Poly to enquire about student accommodation. We eventually settled on a house at 14 Loxley Road, off Trinity Road in Wandsworth. The number 19 bus from Tooting Bec went along Trinity Road towards Clapham, Battersea and the West End and was thus very handy for the commute from digs to Poly and return. There was one other student at the digs, a Scottish lad, Dougal, who was sponsored by Tube Investments in Corby.

During those last school holidays, July 1953, my mother was taken ill and went to Switzerland to recuperate. I went to stay with Dave's family in Paddock Wood for about six weeks. Dave's father was a practicing C of E priest in the local parish, but to my delight also an excellent practical motor mechanic. I was having a few problems with clutch slip on the OK Supreme motorbike, which greatly worried the Rev Nightingale. So with no more ado he taught Dave and me how to completely strip down the engine, clutch and gearbox! In particular relining the clutch with cork inserts obtained from medicine bottle corks from the local chemist left a lasting impression.

In early September 1953 I caught a steam train from Tunbridge Wells West to London Bridge and thence by bus to the Loxley Road digs. There were three other pre RSM mining students at the Poly also doing A level maths, physics and chemistry. Unsurprisingly we tended to stick together. As a 17.5 year old youngster I found London attractions (and distractions!)

hard to reconcile with applying my mind to fairly turgid science lessons. The old CCF side-drumming came to the fore and I became one of the drummers for the "Polgonaires" jazz group formed by Battersea & Chelsea Polytechnic students. We had great fun, not only practicing but playing at student dance nights. In addition we used to go up to the Cy Lawrie jazz club in Great Windmill Street. If we could scrape up some money we'd also go to Ronnie Scotts Club as well. In 1953 trad jazz was all the rage so the (rather basic) Polygonaires were much in demand for "sessions" around south London suburbs.

I also discovered the delights of the female sex and in pursuit of that interest used to go down to the Richmond Ice Skating Rink with some mates from the Poly. We had learnt that that was a good place to meet young ladies. If we drew a blank on the primary interest there was always the attraction of learning to skate, which in itself might impress some of the female onlookers. All in all the jazz band, ice skating and chasing girls did not assist my science studies at the Poly.

The winter of 1953 produced the most amazing London smog. One could not see the other side of the road. Transport came to a standstill and the only way to get to the Poly was to walk. Even that was quite tricky as it was very easy to lose ones way in the thick smog trying to cross Wandsworth Common. The spring and summer terms at the Poly passed in a flash interspersed with many jazz band and ice skating outings. That latter routine was shattered by A Level exams in June in which I felt I had not excelled.

By early July 1954 I was established in digs in the middle of Deal on the east coast of Kent as part of the RSMs practical introduction to mining. The National Coal Board (NCB) bus used to pick me up in Deal at 4am and take me to Betteshanger colliery, where as new trainees we had to be suitably clothed ready to go underground with the 6am shift. Betteshanger was a large, 3000 tonnes/day, deep, 3000ft unmechanised colliery, by far the largest of the four Kent collieries. It had a magnificent bi-cylindro-conical 28ft diameter steam winder that used to hoist coal in triple deck cages at the astonishing speed of 6000 ft/min. The hoist drivers used to brag that they could "get the chains slack on the top of the cage" when they sent the empty cage back underground. Certainly standing on the pit bank when they were winding coal would turn ones stomach over. Fortunately when hoisting men the winder speed was limited to 3000 ft/min.

That first introduction to underground mining I found fascinating and challenging. I was impressed with the comraderie of the miners and the way they looked after each other. However I did not relish the cramped conditions on the low, 3 to 4ft seams where the coal was won by hand in the longwall fashion, shovelling the hewn coal onto a scraper chain conveyor. Also, at that depth the mine was very hot and humid. The experience put me off coal (or soft rock) mining but not mining in general. The NCB trainee course finished in mid August and I went back to my parents house in Tunbridge Wells to learn that I had failed all three A level subjects. On reflection it was unsurprising since I had been larking around enjoying myself in the "Big Smoke" doing a minimum of studying.

After much soul searching and discussions between my father and the RSM it was agreed that I could enter the RSM in September 1955, provided I had the requisite science A levels. Apparently I had had a good report from the Mine Manager at Betteshanger colliery who said something to the effect that "the lad seems to have a natural aptitude for underground work". My father realised that I was too immature to handle the London scene and thought it better for me to have private coaching at home. I duly battled with that but only made poor progress by the end of 1954.

A few doors away from where my parents lived in Tunbridge Wells was a certain Mr Jasper Kell whom my father faintly knew. Mr Kell was a director of the firm of Mott, Hay and Anderson, who specialised in underground civil engineering and were currently doing tunneling work on the London Underground. My father duly arranged for me to have a chat with Mr Kell who said that if I really liked the practical side of underground mining why didn't I try the Camborne School of Mines (CSM) in Cornwall, after all the RSM was more academically inclined? I duly contacted the CSM in Camborne, who said I would have to sit their Entrance Exam in May/June, plus the additional requirement of a Foreign Language at O level.

Mad scrum around for a local French language tutor together with studying past CSM Entrance Exam papers. I finally managed to get a grip on all this studying and passed the CSM Entrance Exam with no problems together with a GCSE pass in O level French. To keep up the practical element of mining either the RSM or CSM (I can't remember which) arranged for me to have practical training during the forthcoming summer holidays at the large opencast iron ore mines operated by A/S Sydvaranger in northern Norway. Thus in early July I caught the train (steam, Southern Railway "Schools" class) to London, then train from Kings Cross to Newcastle-on-Tyne where I embarked on the North Sea ferry to Bergen in Norway. Here I transferred to the Norwegian Coastal Steamer, which took six days to cover the 1200 miles to the end of the line at Kirkenes.

Those Coastal Steamers were mixed cargo/passenger/mail boats of a few thousand tonnes that sailed all year round and were the lifeline for the people of northern Norway. I was the sole Englishman in a small four-berth cabin, but everyone seemed to know some English. The arrival of the coastal steamer at a port was the "event" of the day with dozens of people coming down to the quayside. Passengers, cargo and mail were disembarked and new passengers, cargo and mail loaded in very quick time. Often the boat was turned around in less than two hours.

The Norwegian fjord scenery was very spectacular. The Lofoten islands with their huge racks of drying fish were very memorable as was the Midnight Sun as we passed North Cape. The port of Kirkenes on the mouth of the Pasvik river was dominated by the concentrator and pelletising plant of A/S Sydvaranger. Here the silica rich magnetite ores (known as taconite) were enriched by magnetic separation and then formed into pellets for shipment to steel plants in the UK and elsewhere in Europe. Those enriched pellets were some of highest grade sources of raw iron available in Europe.

However my final destination was Bjornevatn where the huge magnetite deposit lay some seven miles south of Kirkenes. A room in the single mens bunkhouse was my home for the next eight weeks. I was assigned as a driller's helper on a Bucyrus Erie 42T churn drill putting down nominal 9in diameter holes in the exceptionally hard taconite rock. The mine was worked as a conventional shovel-truck open pit with 15m benches. The blasted ore was delivered to a primary crusher and the subsequent crushed ore hauled by a standard gauge railroad to the concentrator in Kirkenes.

Everyone at the mine was very friendly to me and keen to try out their English! I was the only Englishman at the mine and treated almost as a celebrity. I found that puzzling until someone explained that during WW2 the area had been occupied by the Germans and many of the locals sheltered in parts of the underground workings when, later in the war, the Allies attacked then liberated the area. There was no love lost on Germans!

On two or three occasions I witnessed the curious sight of reindeer wandering through the periphery of the open pit seemingly unworried by the mining work. A few miles to the east, in what is now Russia, one could see the tall stack of the Petsamo nickel smelter, which, of course, prior to WW2 used to be part of Finland. The countryside surrounding Bjornevatn was typical arctic tundra. At weekends we would take the works bus into Kirkenes for a little R & R, which mainly comprised downing an unpronounceable drink of half a glass of raw alcohol topped up with warm water and dancing with any and everybody to a duo playing double bass and piano accordion.

I got friendly with the Mine Manager's daughter, Inga, and she knitted me a huge Nordic style sweater. That I kept/used for circa twenty years. My wife, Gillian, then wore it for a further thirty years. They certainly knitted sweaters to last. All too soon it was the coastal steamer back to Bergen, the ferry to Newcastle and train to London and on to Tunbridge Wells. At home finally there was good news on the academic front; I had been accepted for the mining engineering, three year course at the CSM.

2

Early in September 1955 I took the GWR Castle class steam train from Paddington to Camborne. The CSM had arranged digs for me in Park Street, Camborne a short distance from the School Club, run by a guy called Skipper. There was another CSM student in the digs, but he was second year and didn't have much to do with "freshers". I teamed up with Arthur (like me first year) and in the following January term we moved to fresh digs at 6 Bellevue Terrace, Tuckingmill. The landlady's husband, a mining engineer, was working for Cerro de Pasco in Peru. The digs on Tuckingmill hill were sited just opposite the South Crofty mine's stamp battery, which was on the other side of the main road. The considerable rumble of the Cornish stamp battery continued round the clock for six days/week. The mine did maintenance on Sunday, the only night one couldn't sleep - it was so quiet!

Both Arthur and I had brought our push bikes back for the second, January, term as it was a 2.5 mile cycle into the CSM, just off Trelowarren Street, behind the Tyacks Hotel. It was more like a five-mile cycle "up Camborne Hill" to the King Edward Mine (KEM) in Troon. At the KEM we undertook practical work such as assaying, surveying, rock breaking and mineral processing. Arthur was a heavy smoker and always started the day, from bed, with a fag. Although we both played rugby for the CSM 2nd fifteen and kept fairly fit we both agreed we needed to save up for a "motor" to help the three or four times a week commute to the KEM.

Money was always in short supply so most students tried to supplement this from paid holiday work. Thus in April 1956 I worked for British Gypsum at their Mountfield underground mine in East Sussex. It was only for about ten days but, apart from the pay, provided further useful practical underground work with drilling (dry - very dusty!); blasting; operation of Huwood slusher/loader and conveyor belt haulage. I lived at my parents home in Tunbridge Wells and commuted daily in my mother's little Standard 9 soft-top. I only had to pay for petrol so there was something left over from the wages.

During the summer vacation in July 1956 we attended a CSM survey course at the KEM both surface and underground. This lasted for three to four weeks. We formed survey teams of four and ours comprised Cheong, Cyril, Arthur and me. Arthur was an absolute whizz at mathematics so did most of the calculations, whilst Cyril and I did most of the instrument work. Cheong, who had a car (unlike most first year students) kept us supplied with beer and pasties and generally kept look-out!

After this survey course finished most of the students headed for home prior to setting out for additional practical mining holiday work. In my case in early August I took the train to London then the tube to somewhere near the A1 and commenced hitch-hiking to Scotland, where I had landed a job with Lowland Lead Mines, a subsidiary of Siamese Tin Syndicate. I got a really good ride up the A1 to Scotch Corner and then another truck going west on the A66 and finally north on the A6/A75/A76 for Dumfries and Kilmarnock. The trucker dropped me off just before Sanquhar at Mennock by the B797 for Wanlockhead/Leadhills. It was around midnight and I spent the rest of the night propped up in the lower branches of a tree! I picked up a lift in the early morning to travel the remaining nine miles into Wanlockhead.

For the next six weeks I was mainly involved in rehabilitation work of an old incline shaft. This involved hitch cutting by hand and jackhammer; installing shaft timbers and bearer sets together with sleepers and skip rail track. It was very hard, physical work and I was glad to get back to the single mens bunkhouse at the end of shift. Two aspects of this holiday work stick out in my memory. Firstly, the Saturday night dance in the local village hall, where all the guys lined up on one side and the (fairly few) girls lined up on the other. As the music, supplied by a piano accordion, struck up one had to dash across the hall to approach a girl and ask her for a dance. If one was a bit slow there was no one left to ask and one was a wallflower until the next dance began. Secondly, on Sundays there was the curious activity of all the Wanlockhead based miners walking to Leadhills and the Leadhills based miners walking to Wanlockhead. This was on account of the quaint Scottish law that you could only get an alcoholic drink on Sunday if you were a bona fide traveller. There was much hilarity as the groups passed each other on the road, staggering back to their respective bunkhouses after a days steady drinking.

There was good news at home where I learnt that, finally, I had achieved a "first-class pass" on the first year of the CSM course. Back at Camborne

Arthur and I had to move digs from Bellevue Terrace on the return of the landlady's husband from Peru. We found very good digs at 159 North Roskear Road, Tuckingmill, just opposite the Bickford-Smiths safety fuse factory. At first we both missed the rumble of the South Crofty stamp battery, but not for long. At this time in the mid '50s Camborne-Redruth was a major centre of engineering (eg Holman Bros, Climax Rock Drill & Engineering) and underground tin mining (eg South Crofty, Tincroft, East Pool & Agar, Dolcoath, Pendarves, Wheal Jane) as well as tin streaming alluvial plants down the Red river valley below Tuckingmill. Many Malaysian tin mining companies had their head offices in Redruth. Lunch time in Camborne was dominated by the green overalls and yellow H of Holman Bros workers outside the Works eating Cornish pasties.

Both Arthur and I were still playing rugby for the CSM second fifteen, which involved matches on most Saturday afternoons during the winter and spring terms. Additionally I had taken up squash again and started to represent the CSM, playing at number four or five in a five-man team. We played several service clubs - RAF St Mawgan, RAF St Eval & RNAS Culdrose both home and away. The CSM court was curious in having a concrete floor and wooden walls rather than vice versa as was normal. Unsurprisingly we generally won our home fixtures and had about a 50% success rate on away matches. However our nemesis was always the Falmouth Squash Club who regularly used to beat us 5-0, home and away. For more "serious pursuits" on Saturday evenings we used to cadge a lift from one of the few car owners for a run up to Newquay, where the Blue Lagoon dance/night club attracted some unattached young ladies. In summer, of course, the Blue Lagoon became a Mecca for single tourists and CSM students!

At one of the CSM club/dance nights I had become friendly with Louise, a student nurse from the Royal Cornwall Infirmary (RCI) in Truro. Louise had been brought to the CSM club by another student. To pursue my interest I had to take the train or bus to Truro, where our activities were restricted to walking around and sitting in pubs, brought to an abrupt end by my need to catch the last train/bus back to Camborne. I talked this over with Arthur who agreed it was time to get "the motor". In fact he was not so worried as he had a regular girlfriend who lived in Troon, much closer to Tuckingmill. We agreed we'd try and find a "reasonably priced car" in the Spring holiday.

In January 1957 the whole CSM second year attended a ten day course at Holman Bros underground test mine at Troon. This was great fun and involved jackleg drilling of an underground face, charging up and blasting and, after ventilation, mucking out the round with an Eimco 21 rocker-shovel. Just to keep us fit we also had to hand tram the muck cars. We also did penetration testing of the Holman Silver Three jackhammers whilst hand held drilling of large granite blocks. This practical course ended with a tour of the huge Holman Works in Camborne. One of the Holman guys told me I could pick up a really cheap motor at Trevaskis Motors in Trelowarren Street. After much soul searching I became the proud owner of an early 1930s Austin Seven for the eye watering price of £15! It had a lovely fixed brass starting handle and to be fair it started easily and ran well although it struggled with four passengers when the rear bodywork sank onto the rear tyres and restricted forward progress. However, importantly with two occupants it could manage most of the local hills.

On my next Saturday night free I drove over to Truro to show off my new set of wheels to Louise. However she was distinctly underwhelmed by the Austin Seven having imagined from my enthusiastic telephone call about my impending trip to Truro to "take her out for a drive" that I had at least purchased a sports Riley or Fraser-Nash. In a forlorn attempt to retrieve the situation I suggested we take the Scillonia ferry to the Isles of Scilly on the first sunny weekend in Spring. This we duly did, but both the weather and Louise were in a "changeable" mood and the visit was not an unqualified success. However we both enjoyed the ambience of St Mary's and at least we had our own transport for the return journey from Penzance back to Truro. In truth the Truro - Penzance return trip was probably the longest journey I made in the Austin. Nevertheless the car gave valiant service to Arthur and me on the four times a week commute from Tuckingmill to the KEM, as well as providing essential weekend service over to Truro for R & R.

The CSM annual dinner/dance, a formal (well initially) black tie affair came up in early May. Louise had agreed to come and also wished to bring another student nurse from the RCI. Mindful of the suspect reliability of my Austin Seven and the difficulty it had of moving with more than two people on board Cyril agreed to lend me his modern Morris Minor 1000.

This was a "proper" modern car and seemed entirely suitable for a formal dinner/dance. I duly motored to Truro to pick up Louise who lived in digs just up behind the Daniel Arms. There Louise introduced me to Gillian and the three of us set off for Camborne. My recollection is that we had a good time and I dropped the girls back in Truro in the early hours, Louise to her digs and Gillian to somewhere on Princes Street.

On Sunday as I reflected on the previous evening I realised that Louise and I were not really compatible, whereas Gillian seemed much more my ideal girl. I duly wrote a note to "Nurse Gillian", 23 (?) Princes Street, Truro, saying I would like to see her again. After quite a while (Gillian, I think, had gone home to St Mawgan, north Cornwall with flu) I heard from her. We met up again and started a steady relationship. We used to walk around Truro a lot and along the river towards Malpas. However I had to concentrate on the second year CSM exams coming up in June 1957. I felt they went OK as I was really settled, enjoying life at the CSM with a lot of good mates and now a steady girl friend. In addition the CSM had obtained for me a summer vacation job at the Algom Quirke Mine in northern Ontario, Canada.

In early July 1957 I caught the train from Tunbridge Wells to London then on to Liverpool where I embarked with a steerage ticket on the Cunard liner Saxonia. About six days later the ship made its way along the St Lawrence Seaway to Quebec and Montreal where I disembarked. There I caught a Canadian Pacific (CPR) train headed for Sault Ste Marie, passing through Ottawa, North Bay and Sudbury before detraining at Spragge on the North Channel of Lake Huron. Here a local bus took me about twenty miles north to the uranium boom town of Elliot Lake. I checked into the offices of Rio Algom Uranium Mines and was duly allocated to a single mens bunkhouse. The Algom bunkhouse served two underground mines, Quirke, a conventional tracked mine and the newer developing Nordic mine which was trackless. The bunkhouse was operated by Crawley McCracken, a well-known Canadian accommodation and catering operator. There were communal ablution blocks and a large self-service mess hall. The sleeping facilities comprised five double-deck bunks in a room about 20ft by 20ft. Quiet it was not.

Elliot Lake was a real mining boom town with construction going on everywhere. Besides Rio Algom's two mines, the huge Dennison mine was under development as well as eight or ten other mines whose names I cannot recall. The Algom works bus took us eight miles north to the Quirke mine. Here I initially worked as an underground helper to both the geological and sampling crews and then had a fortnight with an underground survey crew. Although fairly well paid (by UK standards) these were day-wages jobs. However I was extremely fortunate to become a contract miner's helper for about six weeks undertaking breast stope drilling with a Joy AL-47 jackleg, rock bolting with an Ingersoll Rand stoper, charging up, blasting and stope mucking with a 50 HP Joy 3-drum slusher. For me not only was the practical experience great, but the contract wages, based on tonnage broken, were beyond my wildest dreams. At this time the Quirke mine was in full production delivering 3,000 tonnes/day crude ore to the acid leach concentrator.

Elliot Lake was located in virtual virgin forest. In summer it was hot and fairly humid on account of the numerous small lakes in the area and the swarms of mosquitoes were voracious. It was always noisy in our bunk room, as the guys were from both Nordic & Quirke mines and both mines were working three shifts/day. In the evening the day shift guys liked to play black-jack whilst sitting on cases of rum or coke. Of course they used to take me to the cleaners at cards, but it was all very amicable. I drank rum & coke with them as well, but to this day I've never really enjoyed the smell of rum (brings back memories of losing too much money at black-jack!). There were very few women in Elliot Lake at that time, and the Crawley McCracken catering "ladies" were universally known as the Crawley dollies; they were much in demand by the mining & construction crews.

I left Elliot Lake around the 20th September taking the bus down to Spragge on the main CPR line. Here I picked up an east bound train for Sudbury and then south down to Toronto and a short run around the western edge of Lake Ontario to Niagara Falls. I stayed overnight to have a good look at the Falls, which were obviously many many times larger than any falls I had seen before - very impressive, but not really "wild" as there was man-made development all around. The next day I caught a Greyhound bus to Buffalo and crossed into the USA. The Greyhound bus was very luxurious and comfortable as it headed for New York passing through the grim, dirty steelmaking town of Scranton. In New York, I stayed in the Cornwall Hotel (I wonder why?) somewhere in downtown Manhattan. I spent a couple of days in New York looking around the major tourist attractions such as the Empire State Building, Broadway, Statue of Liberty and the jazz area down near the Brooklyn bridge. Then it was a steerage cabin in the bowels of the Queen Mary and a five day crossing to Southampton.

Back home I was really pleased to learn I had obtained a first-class pass for the second year at the CSM. With my dad we scoured motor magazines and located a 1932 MG, two seater sports L-type Magna, 6 cylinder, single OHC 1100cc machine in south London. This I bought for £100 from my Algom Quirke wages. Fortunately the car included an MG Workshop manual, which was my bible for car maintenance over the next two years. So, in great triumph, I set off on the long drive to Cornwall. I wasn't very popular with the CSM staff as I had missed the first week of the term, but my room mate, Arthur, was very happy and the old MG looked really smooth outside 159 North Roskear Road in Tuckingmill. The commute up to the KEM in Troon with the MG became something of a battle with the GWR at the Camborne station level crossing. If the train was late and the gates closed we were bound to be late at the KEM. (This didn't affect bicycles as one could cross the tracks through the pedestrian gate). Happily Arthur and I were not the only ones late at the KEM. Several other CSM students had bought dilapidated sports cars with their summer vacation practical work experience wages. However the MG really came into its own on the weekend run into Truro to see Gillian.

I think Gillian was quite impressed with the MG, she certainly liked the registration number ALO 5. We managed to extend our Truro walking range to places like Feock, Falmouth and the north Cornish coast. Much to my delight Gillian offered to type up my Algom Quirke report for submission to the CSM. Before becoming a 'student nurse at the RCI Gillian had worked for a furriers in Newquay where she had acquired typing skills. One weekend on a visit to see her in Truro I was introduced to her parents (unexpectedly for me) in the Red Lion pub/hotel. When asked if I'd like a drink by Lofty (her dad) I said "a whisky", thinking it would sound a bit more sophisticated than "a beer". What a mistake, Lofty was a regular beer drinker. Fortunately I made amends by saying I played rugby for the CSM seconds, not knowing, of course, that Lofty had played rugby for the RAF. That was the first & only time I ever drank whisky with Lofty. On visits to Gillian's parent's home in St Mawgan I used to accompany

Lofty to the Falcon Inn for a beer or two often accompanied by Stinker, Lofty's semi-tame pig! Sometime during the Spring term, on a visit to St Mawgan, I asked Lofty if I could marry his daughter. Fortunately he was in favour as was Gillian and we agreed to get married after I had qualified with my ACSM and secured a professional job.

The third year at CSM seemed to pass very quickly. In spite of the attractions of Gillian, the MG, rugby and squash I really managed to get my head down and put in some serious studying at last. In the Spring term I became joint editor with Cyril of the CSM Magazine, published in June 1958. It certainly proved difficult to get mining students to contribute written technical articles. I guess that's typical of engineering people who prefer "doing" to "writing". During the final term a number of major companies had visited the CSM looking to recruit final year students (subject, of course, to qualifying with an ACSM). Companies such as Anglo American & Roan Selection Trust from Africa; International Nickel & Falconbridge from Canada and several from the UK. I was offered a post as assistant engineer with The Cementation Mining of Doncaster on shaft sinking contracts for the National Coal Board (NCB). As a 22 year old I was liable to be called up for National Service on completion of my studies. However one had the option of working for the NCB or companies contracted to the NCB. This came about as an extension of the "Bevin Boys" scheme operated during WW2, whereby youngsters did "National Service in the Pits" to maintain all important coal output to sustain industrial production. I felt it was preferable (for a budding mining engineer) to get practical, professional mining experience rather than two years in the armed services.

I received my First-Class ACSM on the 10th July 1958, together with a British Ropes "Principles of Mining" prize. Needless to say Gillian & I and my parents were very pleased. I immediately accepted the offer from Cementation as assistant engineer on shaft sinking contracts for the NCB at the huge salary of £55/month and the relevant National Service authorities were informed of this decision. We arranged to get married at St Mawgan church on Saturday 4th October 1958. In early August I visited Cementation Mining in Doncaster for several days to familiarise myself with various head office functions - design/drawing office; plant park; transport; accounts; personnel etc. The company confirmed that I would be placed as assistant engineer at the Florence colliery contract in the Stoke-on-Trent area.

However on or about the 27th August a policeman turned up at my parent's house in Tunbridge Wells and served me with papers to report, within 48 hours, to the Royal Engineers barracks in Worcester - I'd been called up for National Service! Before I left for Worcester by train on the 28th August I phoned Cementation Mining to tell them the news and ask them to make representation on my behalf (not a great way to start a new job), whilst my dad approached our local MP. I also broke the news to Gillian who was still working at the RCI in Truro. Thus by the 28th evening I was enrolled as 23572898 Sapper Stoakes in the Royal Engineers regiment. Both the local MP and Cementation, who said they were very short of trained engineers (the UK coal industry was developing a large number of new deep mines in the late 1950s) must have spoken to the "right people" because I received my discharge papers on the 13th September after "16 days with the colours"! I returned to Tunbridge Wells a civvi again. Here I spent a great deal of time with the MG Workshop handbook attempting to get the old car, already 26 years old, in fine fettle for the fast approaching wedding. Then it was back down to Cornwall again in the MG to put my motor fettling to the test.

My old CSM mate, Arthur, had already gone abroad to West Africa so I asked Chris from Tonbridge School days to be best man. He agreed and a group of about six old Smythe House lads came down for the wedding plus several from the CSM. With Chris I stayed at an hotel at Watergate Bay and on the wedding morning I created a bit of a stir for the best man by vanishing. In fact I realised I forgotten my shirt and went back to St Mawgan to collect it. The wedding was at 11am in St Mawgan church followed by a simple reception at the Bristol Hotel in Newquay. I was worried about the extreme vulnerability of the MG (to the ministrations of the "lads") so decided to use a small, inconspicuous hire car parked out behind the Bristol Hotel. The MG meanwhile was parked at a Chacewater garage (from where the hire car had been obtained) fully fuelled for the honeymoon getaway! After the reception Gillian and I doubled back around the hotel to the hire car but were not quick enough to escape attention. The lads pursued the hire car around Newquay and then followed us all the way to Chacewater, where lo and behold the old MG was standing proudly outside. I dared not stop, kept straight on for Truro and fortunately neither of Gillian's sisters (who were with the lads) recognised the MG as they flashed past the garage. Our superior local knowledge of Truro's one-way road system enabled us to throw off the pursuers and we hared back to Chacewater, switched from the hire car to the MG and took off for Castle Carey, where we stayed the night.

The next day we made our way steadily north to Stoke-on-Trent. Here we stayed in the Old Vicarage Hotel, situated between the Potteries towns of Fenton and Longton. After a few days R & R I checked into Cementation Mining's site office at Florence colliery. Seoras was the Resident Engineer and Joe the Master Sinker, both of whom were experienced shaft sinking people. Seoras was just in the process of moving to a new house a few miles away at Muir Heath and he suggested we take over their furnished rented flat in Dresden. This was very handy, a mere ten minutes walk from Florence colliery. We thus moved in to No 6 Parkfield Avenue, Dresden, a quiet tree lined street overlooking the park. The flat was very small, a single Victorian room divided up into bedroom, living room & tiny kitchen. There was a communal bath/loo facility down the corridor. Out the back there was room for the MG alongside some old barns and a huge chestnut tree.

A week or so later Gillian had to return to the RCI to complete her contractual hospital work following qualification as a SRN. I took a great deal of ribbing at work that my new bride had walked out on me. Cementation's work at Florence colliery comprised widening the old brick lined No 1 Shaft from 16ft diameter to 20ft concrete lined as well as an inby deepening of the No 3 Shaft, also 20ft concrete. Florence at that time was a fully producing pit. We also had to first excavate and then construct massive reinforced concrete foundations for a new tower headframe. Seoras was an excellent, experienced boss and left me to get on with day-to-day engineering supervision. If I didn't know, or was unclear what to do he expected me to ask him, which I did. Both Joe, the Master Sinker and Bill, the Concrete Foreman were great people to work with. They appreciated I knew very little about shaft sinking activities, teased me unmercifully, but always rallied round if there was a serious problem.

My main duties involved ensuring both shafts stayed truly vertical (controlled by a central plumb bob when levelling up for a concrete pour), the minimum concrete wall thickness of twelve inches was maintained and that the concrete met the NCB specification. We prepared all our concrete on site in our own batching plant from cement, sand and aggregate. There was also the problem of reading and interpreting the complicated steel reinforcing drawings provided by Cementation's design office in Doncaster for shaft insets, curb rings, water garlands and the huge foundations for the new tower headframe. Here I often had to ask for Seoras's help.

Gillian returned to Dresden after three months, much to my delight. We found it very tight to make ends meet on my salary. Gillian immediately put her SRN skills to use in the nearby Longton Cottage Hospital (20 minutes walk), mainly patching up injured/ill coal miners. Longton itself, one of the "Five Towns" was a pretty grim, dirty place dominated by the stinking, smokey bottle kilns used for pottery making. The kilns were shut down on Saturday night and refired on Sunday night when the whole town was covered in dense yellow smoke. The shaft widening/sinking continued for three shifts/day, six days/week. On Sundays Gillian and I would drive down to Stone for a drink & pub lunch or drive out to The Roaches or nearby Lud Church on the edge of the Peak District. However this ceased for a while after I took off the MG cylinder head and took it to the colliery workshop for skimming to raise the engine's compression ratio and increase performance. This wasn't entirely satisfactory as I then had to reduce the shim packing on the vertical cam shaft drive, which upset the overhead camshaft oil drainage which...... For a good few weeks Gillian became known by our neighbours as the "MG Widow".

In the Stoke-on-Trent area Cementation Mining had numerous contracts at other NCB collieries, eg Hem Heath, Holditch, Stafford, Sneyd and Wolstanton, where they broke the existing UK shaft sinking speed record. At Florence the inby deepening No 3 Shaft sinking proceeded at about 120 ft/month finished and the No 1 Shaft widening at about 150 ft/month finished. One night I had a phone call from Joe - a major incident at No 1 Shaft. He sent the Cementation van to collect me (the MG was still in bits!). I met Joe on the pit bank and he told me that the tubular shield, which fitted inside the old shaft brickwork had been detached (by the shift charge hand, against standing instructions) from the sinking scaffold and fallen down into the existing shaft sump fouling the existing guide ropes and cheese weights. Joe and I got putlogs and planks together, placed them in the cage and we then descended the shaft on "slow", with Joe running the rapper line through his hand for an instant stop to the winder driver.

We arrived at the "widening" face (about 900ft down) to be met with a circle of seven cap lamp lights from the night shift crew now marooned on an annular bench, some 3 to 4ft wide surrounding an open 16ft diameter shaft - quite scary. We got the putlogs and planks out onto the "bench" and one by one the crew came into the cage. Putlogs and planks cleared, we were hoisted to the pit bank. Joe and I then went back down the shaft, past the "bench" and slowly down into the old shaft sump, past the ventilation drive to where the tubular shield was resting on the guide rope bearer sets. Amazingly the guide ropes were still hanging true, although the tubular shield was damaged.

There was a big NCB enquiry involving Seoras, Joe, the shift charge hand and me. When it was firmly established that nothing had broken, but that the "incident" had been caused by gross negligence of the charge hand in removing the tubular shield's safety chains from the scaffold, in contravention to Cementation standing instructions, the company was exonerated and the charge hand sacked forthwith. Nobody had died, fortunately, but it certainly showed me how dangerous shaft sinking/widening could be. The tubular shield was recovered, repaired and the No 1 Shaft widening contract was underway again in two weeks.

For our annual holiday in September 1959 Gillian and I hired a small cabin cruiser from a boatyard in Tewksbury, spending the next week cruising the river Avon. The cruiser also towed a small dinghy with sail, which provided additional amusement. We paid for the holiday from a jar of half-crowns saved throughout the previous ten months. We moored just above Breedon and climbed the nearby Breedon Hill. We only made slow progress up the Avon as I spent quite a bit of time mucking about in the sailing dinghy. I think we got about as far as Pershore before returning downstream to Tewkesbury. It was a very pleasant relaxing week.

A few weeks after returning to work there was a Florence site meeting with Arthur, Cementation's Stoke area manager, Seoras and myself. Arthur announced that Seoras was moving to a new major shaft sinking contract and another Cementation engineer, named Dick, would take over as Resident Engineer (RE) at Florence. Although I was only 23 and had had only a little over a years experience with the company I was extremely disappointed not to be offered the RE's job. Dick, the new RE turned out to be a very different type of boss to Seoras, rather disinterested in the job and preoccupied by personal problems relating to his recent divorce. After discussion with Gillian I decided to look for another job. Perusal of the mining press and daily papers produced few suitable opportunities for someone of my limited mining experience. However an ad in The Telegraph for a mine surveyor in Tanganyika sounded promising. I duly applied.

The company, Colonial Development Corporation (CDC) of Hill Street asked both Gillian and me to attend an interview in London during December 1959. CDC were looking for an assistant mine surveyor for their joint venture (with Consolidated Goldfields of South Africa) underground gold mine near Musoma close to the eastern side of Lake Victoria. We, apparently, fitted the bill and after full medicals a job offer of a 24 to 27 month contract at £1200/year was offered, starting as soon as possible. The one major drawback was that it would be single status for first three months until a suitable house was available. We agreed to go for it; I gave one months notice to Cementation Mining and we packed up our bits and pieces and Gillian went back to Cornwall and some more nursing work at the RCI in Truro.

3

I flew out at the start of February 1960 by a BOAC Bristol Britannia to Entebbe in Uganda. There I transferred to an East African Airways (EAA) DC3 which trundled anti-clockwise around Lake Victoria landing at Bukoba and Mwanza before arriving at Musoma. Here I was met by a Tangold Mining Company (TMC) Land Rover for the 22 mile drive, over rough laterite roads to the mine. The mine employed about forty expat staff split 50/50 between Brits and South Africans. About twelve of the staff were on single basis and I initially joined them in the single mens quarters. As expected there were communal washing and eating facilities. The quarters were only a short distance from the Mine Club an attractive open-sided thatched building including a well stocked bar. Alongside there was a single laterite tennis court.

The Kiabakari mine of TMC was a 1000 tonnes/day low grade (c. 4 dwt) underground gold mine worked by blast-hole open stoping. Ground conditions were strong, a minimum of support being required in the conventional tracked layout. My main duties covered all regular mine underground, surface and exploration surveying. It also involved various one-off survey needs (new houses, rondavels, roads, sceptic tanks and long-drops etc). I also assisted the mine geologist with logging of underground diamond drill core. A major part of my work entailed the preparation of ring drilling layouts for the underground blast-hole stoping, both conventional vertical ring drilling off sub-levels and the newer Horodiam stoping or horizontal drilling off vertical raises. The long-hole drilling rigs were Holman SL16 4in drifters, which I had seen in use at the Holman Underground Test Mine in Troon.

My boss, the Chief Surveyor Alan, a Brit, was an old East Africa hand, who spoke fluent Swahili and was thoroughly used to working with the local Lake tribe, the Luo. He was an excellent boss, very meticulous (as any surveyor should be) in keeping records etc. He was also an excellent instrument man and taught me how to use the old theodolites and levels. Nearly all the mine, mill and engineering equipment (including survey gear) was second hand having been shipped over from the Tarkwa & Oboso mine in Ghana.

During my first three months "single status", one incident sticks out in my mind. It was a Friday or Saturday night around midnight following a few Tusker beers in the Mine Club. Although not drunk, but definitely very cheerful, I weaved my way back to the single mens quarters. I opened the door to my room and switched on the light, to see this huge snake which stretched right across the room floor, ten feet or more in length. I staggered back out of the room, quite aghast, only to hear badly suppressed guffaws of laughter from some of the other single guys who had, apparently, been lurking nearby. The snake, a python, was dead, shot that afternoon by Angelo, Vic and others who had been out hunting on the Kabassa plain. It was the largest snake I had seen. Unfortunately it was not the last snake I encountered around Kiabakari, the scariest being a puff adder, lying in the bottom of an exploration trench. The survey crew boys also had a good laugh when Bwana Footi Sabe (me, Mr Six Foot) leapt out of the trench breaking the East African high jump record!

Around late April Gillian flew out from England to Entebbe and then transferred to the old EAA DC3 for the flight around Lake Victoria. It was touch and go whether the DC3 would manage to land on the Musoma dirt strip as the annual rainy season had started and the strip was quite boggy. It did and we set off for the hairy drive to Kiabakari over the rain sodden laterite road. We had been assigned, temporarily, the Underground Manager's bungalow as he, Peter and his wife, Terry (Gillian's life long friend) & two young daughters were on three months leave. This bungalow was quite a distance from the main mining/mill complex and Alan used to pick me up in his VW Beetle in the morning. If I was going straight underground the Mine Land Rover would collect me.

We only stayed in this bungalow for about six weeks and then moved into our "own" bungalow just across the road from the Mine Club. It was a one bedroom, concrete block wall and galvanised iron roof bungalow with a stoop and red polished concrete floors. There was a wood burning cooker and paraffin fired fridge. There was electricity (from the Mine Power Plant) and water pumped straight from Lake Victoria to a mine holding reservoir and then into the houses. The water was crawling with livestock (made for an interesting bath!) and, for drinking purposes, had to be boiled for at least ten minutes and then, when cool, passed through a large candle filter and finally into bottles in the fridge to cool down. Being so close to Lake

Victoria, mosquitoes were a major hazard. Although doors & windows were meshed it was essential to use plenty of Flit spray everywhere and burn mosquito coils under the bed at night.

We had two servants, a cook/houseboy and a shamba boy who looked after the small surrounding garden (tough couch grass, hibiscus, frangipani, canna lilies and a papaya tree). The cook used to work miracles with both the local meat from the Somali butcher and the vagaries of the wood burning cooker. He also did the laundry and house work and in effect ran the bungalow. He really made our domestic life simple. He lived up in the domestic servants quarters which were part of the "Native Compound". (One has to remember that this was still colonial times and it would only be next year when Tanganyika obtained independence and became Tanzania). If one had to visit the kitchen at night putting on the light disclosed dozens of cockroaches everywhere.

From the previous occupiers of this bungalow we acquired a magnificent black Alsatian dog, Kim. He was young (three or four years) and took only a little while to get used to us. Gillian used to take him for a walk, early in the morning before it got too hot, with another lady, Mary and her dog, along the side of the airstrip, which we could see from our bungalow. The mine had a Piper Tripacer light aircraft in which the General Manager (GM), piloted by the Mill Manager, John, used to fly to Nairobi and other mines around East Africa such as Macalder-Nyanza, Kilembe and Mwadui Diamonds down near Mwanza. If the Tripacer was indisposed for any reason a charter Cessna 172, flown by Jimmy, came up from Mwanza. Jimmy was a great "bush" pilot and could get the old 172 airborne in about 150 yards!

We had no car, so relaxation was all "mine based". Gillian joined a group of ladies who taught her to play mahjong and both of us learnt to play bridge. For physical exercise it was dog walking along the airstrip. Peter, one of the mine accountants, taught me to play tennis on the single laterite court alongside the Mine Club. Later, in my role as surveyor, I set up, prepared and marked out a second tennis court. The major, regular social event was the 8mm film show in the club, one Friday in the month. Everyone came feet/legs shoved into pillowcases to ward off the voracious mosquitoes. On film nights the club bar did a roaring trade. On most other days the club bar was open from about 6.30 until 10.30 with the usual bunch of regulars. On Sundays the bar staff arranged for a Curry Lunch at the club, where the usual Tusker beer was augmented with Pimms. The bar boys used to come over into our garden looking for papaya (our bungalow was the closest to the club).

During June 1960, as the rainy season drew to a close, the entertainment committee, led by Victor (Chief Geologist) and his wife Peggy decided to put on a cabaret at the club - the Tangold Follies. Five or six weeks of intensive rehearsals took place in Peggy's bungalow and by mid July the "show" was set for a Saturday night. Bob (Garage/Transport Manager) was MC and I was his stooge for a number of capers. We sung a few ditties about Mac's mine accompanied on a piano and me playing a few notes on the alto sax. However the highlight of the evening was the Can-Can danced by Gillian, Maureen, Shirley, Corrie and Gwyneth. How they cheered. People had come in from Musoma and the nearby small gold mine, Buhemba. It was a great night ended by the 6am mine hooter as the men were playing Bok-Bok (a type of free for all rugby!) with yet another paw-paw (papaya) snitched from our garden.

The Kiabakari mine was situated on the edge of the Kabassa plain which on the southern side adjoined the great Serengeti game reserve. There were plenty of wild animals close by and, apparently some of the Askaris (mine police) patrolling around the mine perimeter had been spooked by hippos cooling off in the mine's tailings dam! A number of the younger mine staff, who had Land Rovers, would often go on safari into the surrounding bush. Later that year Mac (GM) had a BBQ on the edge of Lake Victoria, where he kept a cabin cruiser. Water skiing was the attraction. I had a go, took for ever to "get up" onto the skis and promptly flipped off. Apart from the difficulty of getting "up" (the small outboard motor tow-boat was not really fast enough) my arms very soon got tired and the easiest way out was to let go! It was not very sensible swimming or water skiing in the Lake as bilharzia was endemic. We also foolishly slept out on the deck of the boat when moored near the mouth of the Mara river. This was almost certainly the source of my subsequent malaria attacks as one ended up with mosquito bites on top of mosquito bites. All the expats took paludrine every day, but malaria was a major hazard. Another mosquito-rich place was the old WW1 German lake steamers. These used to trundle around the lake, anti-clockwise Kisumu, Entebbe, Bukoba, Mwanza, Musoma and back to Kisumu. On a few occasions at the weekend we would go to Musoma to have dinner on the open deck at the back of the steamer - swarms of mosquitoes in attendance.

Sometime in early 1961, before the annual rainy season, Gillian and I flew up to Nairobi for our two weeks "local" leave. We stayed at the very pleasant colonial hotel - The Norfolk. We had our own stand-alone bungalow, very colonial. After a good wander around the city we hired a little Morris 1000 car. It took me a little while to get used to African roads and driving styles and in the Nairobi suburbs I even succeeded in driving straight up and over a small roundabout to Gillian's alarm after she'd said "straight on"! After three days or so in Nairobi we headed due south for about 160 miles on a sealed road to Arusha, crossing the Kenya - Tanganyika border on the way, seeing plenty of game, in particular giraffes. In Arusha we stayed with Simon (an old school friend from Tonbridge) and his wife Jill. Simon, a biologist, was working for The Colonial Pesticide Research Institute. Arusha is sited on the southern side of Mt Meru (+4500m). With Simon and Jill in their VW Beetle we set off due east for a couple of days in the Tsavo National Park, staying in typical thatched rondavels. The main park is less than twenty miles from the snow covered Mt Kilimanjaro (+5895m), which dominated the horizon to the NE. We saw masses of game, lion, rhino, buffalo, elephant, zebra, antelope, giraffe, gnu and dozens of wild pigs. It was certainly the "African Travel Brochure" come true. We returned to their house in Arusha for one more night and then headed back north for Nairobi.

From Nairobi we then headed NW in the Morris 1000 into the Great Rift Valley first stopping at Lake Naivasha to look at the huge wading flocks of pink flamingoes, a really amazing sight. Then further NW where we spent the night in the centre of the town of Nakuru. Here we stocked up on emergency supplies and headed for Thompson Falls in the White Highlands. This was a beautiful peaceful spot, lovely falls and a superb ranch style hotel, cool enough in the evenings (because of the altitude) for a roaring log fire. We stayed a couple of days and then turned east, the old Morris 1000 struggling up to 9000ft as we crossed the Aberdare Mountains on a narrow dirt road. There were a few scary moments as we passed several elephants on the narrow road with an impenetrable bamboo forest immediately below the road on the north side. On reflection it was a pretty foolhardy trip to take as there were still active Mau Mau units operating in the Aberdares. However we made it through to Nyeri, situated at the foot of Mt Kenya (+5200m). This is my favourite East African mountain as it stands alone and is a regular steep sided cone shape. From Nyeri we turned SE then south towards Thika (flame trees thereof - and they are spectacular) and eventually back to Nairobi. The little Morris 1000, a bit dusty, did a valiant job and never let us down over some fairly rough, steep, rutted dirt roads; a good, solid piece of British engineering. From Nairobi we flew back to Musoma and the final 22 miles by Land Rover on to the mine at Kiabakari.

Alan, the Chief Surveyor, went on three months long leave, which meant that I was in charge of all survey work. I was a little nervous, but the survey crew boys were very supportive. There were no major survey problems in the mine apart from a tricky major winze plumbing job to transfer coordinates to a new level. Here the old CSM practical work was put to good use as I used the Weisbach triangulation method on the lower, new, level. It was slow, painstaking work, but proved worthwhile as some six months later the mine, having driven this level about 250m, holed through to the stub drive off the other winze bang on line and only a few mm out on level - sighs of relief all round, not least from me. However there was a major problem in the camp's Power House. Two of the ancient, 1926, flat four, Crossley HFO diesel engines (ex Tarkwa & Oboso) broke their main crankshafts. The Chief Engineer, Harry, believed this was caused by poor, hurried installation when the Kiabakari mine was commissioned several years earlier. As a consequence the mine now had no standby generating capacity. The immediate fix was to borrow a V16 English Electric unit from Nairobi Light & Power and a Ruston gas turbine from Mwadui Diamond Mines. My job was to survey in the new foundations for these units, as well as redo the foundation levels for the old Crossleys. Reading the foundation drawings was OK but the big problem was the instrument work inside the Power House, where the heat from the on-load generating engines caused extensive air shimmer making it very difficult to read the Level figures.

The engineering crews used quick setting cement on the foundations & hold down bolts and inside three weeks both temporary engines were commissioned. The English Electric unit seemed to burn more lubricating oil than diesel, producing clouds of black smoke. Dick, a commissioning engineer from Rustons, Lincoln had the gas turbine up and running very quickly. The Ruston was an amazing contrast to the heavy, old slow running

Crossleys (216 rpm!) as it could pick up the load very quickly, but it did produce a banshee howl heard all over the camp as it came on to full load.

I managed to break my lower left leg when falling awkwardly on the tennis court. Hard to believe on a perfectly flat tennis court! The ride in to Musoma Hospital in a bucking Land Rover over the rutted, dirt road was extremely painful on the strapped leg, but the local doc did a good job, setting and plastering from just below the knee to my toes. I was confined to office work (survey calcs, plan drawing & ring drilling layouts) for a month or so and Alan, back from leave, did all the instrument work. The biggest problem with my plastered leg was that the leg used to itch terribly in the heat. Fortunately some of the ladies did knitting and I borrowed knitting needles to scratch the annular space between the plaster and my leg as my leg steadily "wasted" through lack of use. Gillian was (literally) very supportive and her professional nursing work at the Mine Hospital continued at our bungalow.

The club put on a traditional Christmas lunch in 1961 with all the trimmings. Father Christmas (Ben, with beard) turned up at the club with a sledge (small wheeled cart), pulled by a reindeer (our dog Kim, led by Gillian), loaded with presents for the children. It was a great way to spend Christmas Day, but everyone wished we had a swimming pool.

During the later half of 1961 there was a lot of trouble in the Congo when Katanga Province tried to secede under Moise Tshombe. Belgian paratroopers were sent in and there was some heavy fighting. Some refugees fleeing the Congo started to appear in western Tanganyika. At the same time the independence movement in Tanganyika was getting ready for Uhuru, when an independent Tanzania would come into being. All in all the expats at Kiabakari were feeling a bit jittery. My two year contract finished in February 1962 and CDC offered me a further two year contract after our three month long leave. However with the deteriorating political situation in the Congo & Tanzania, we felt it was time to leave and try something new, somewhere else. We packed our personal bits and pieces into a crate, which went by steamer to Kisumu, then rail to Dar es Salaam and finally ship to Tilbury Docks, London. We arranged for Kim, the Alsatian, to join an expat farmer in Kenya. We flew to Nairobi, stayed at the Norfolk Hotel and saw "Ben-Hur" at a new wide screen cinema, quite a change from the buzzing, shaking 8mm film in the Kiabakari Club. A day later we flew from Nairobi to London on a BOAC VC10 - what a lovely plane.

4

From Heathrow we went to my parents house in Tunbridge Wells. We stayed a couple of weeks whilst we looked around for a car. We found a very nice little second-hand red bug-eyed Sprite two seater at Wards Garage in Southborough. It was a great fun machine. My parents were still very busy with the Estate agency business and suggested we move in to their "holiday cottage" in Northiam, East Sussex whilst I telephoned around & wrote letters looking for a new job. My parents lent us a typewriter and Gillian, again, was the maestro on the keys. Towards the end of March 1962 I received an offer from Zinc Corporation of a post as Technical Assistant at Titanium & Zirconium Industries (TAZI) dredging operations on North Stradbroke Island, Queensland, Australia. The offer suggested travelling to Australia under the assisted passage scheme (Ten Pound Poms!) to take up duties in August/September. After much discussion I accepted the offer.

However this new professional job was still five or six months away so we decided to go to Cornwall, live in St Mawgan with Gillian's parents whilst we took on local holiday work. Gillian got a job working in Doney's Beach Cafe at Watergate Bay selling ice cream and beach gear. Gillian was the registered First Aider as well. I also worked for Doney driving his boat-like Land Rover on the beach at Mawgan Porth also flogging ice cream to holiday visitors. I found Doney a difficult person to work for (nothing I did was ever "right" to his mind) so after a couple of weeks I quit and went to work for Ma Kelly at Lusty Glaze beach in Newquay. There my main job was flogging deck chairs to visitors and helping Joe, Ma Kelly's manager, to transport stores/supplies from the top of the cliff to the beach cafe by a simple zip-wire. It was a happy, cheerful environment and I thoroughly enjoyed the "paid holiday". All too soon it was goodbye to Cornwall, motoring back to Tunbridge Wells in the Sprite. Then up to Wards Garage to sell the Sprite (at a considerable discount from the purchase price!). By then we had all the necessary emigration papers etc for Australia and were booked on a late August Qantas flight to Brisbane. We spent a few days in my sister Judy's flat off Gloucester Road in London. I managed to see Arthur, my old CSM mate who was off back to Ghana and we joined my parents on a trip up to Cambridge for my cousin Michael's son christening. Then it was out to Heathrow as a couple of "Ten Pound Poms" to board a Qantas 707 for the long flight to Brisbane.

Darwin was our first sight of Australia and it was not very encouraging. The Terminal building was a small shack abutting a rusty barbed wire fence intermingled with broken bottles. Fortunately it was a short refuelling stop. Brisbane airport was a huge improvement and after clearing Immigration & Customs we caught a cab down to Cleveland to catch the ferry for Dunwich on North Stradbroke Island. It was only a short 45 minute trip and at Dunwich we were met and taken to the GM's house for lunch! (This was directly after over thirty hours travelling, we were both knackered and didn't eat very much!) Someone then drove us across the island to "our" house in Herring Lagoon on the Pacific coast side of the island. It was a corrugated iron clad timber frame house set up on five-foot-high support posts. We accessed the house up open timber steps. Apart from an electric cooker and fridge the house was empty. My job spec had stated a "furnished house", but I guess no one had told the Aussies. It was the only time that Gillian sat down on our suitcases and had a little cry. However help was at hand and a very nice Scottish engineer (also living in Herring Lagoon) ran us back to the TAZI offices in Dunwich to collect essentials (beds, cooking gear, cutlery, curtains etc) from the company store. All in all it was not a great introduction to the "Lucky Country".

TAZI operated two 4000 tonnes/day suction dredges working the coastal sand dunes. These coastal dunes were separated from the main island high dunes (circa 700ft high!) by a fresh water swamp up to 300ft wide, running the length of the beach. The dredges operated in their own pond, where the fresh water level was maintained by large centrifugal pumps extracting water from the swamp. The dredges had on-board concentration equipment of Humphrey Spirals for the recovery of the heavy minerals and the barren tailings were pumped out the back of the dredge into the previously dredged area. In this manner the dredges with their respective ponds slowly moved along the beach. As Technical Assistant my main job was laying out the Banka (type) grid drilling of the coastal dunes ahead of the dredges. The sand drill samples were duly assayed for heavy minerals (rutile, ilmenite, titanium, zirconium etc) and mineral value profile lines, at 50ft interval, were run across the beach. From this I had to determine the dredging depth from a specific pond elevation together with the width of the "cut". It was pretty boring repetitive work, not helped by a really bolshie Aussie foreman, Buck.

To get to work I used to walk, maybe 300 yards to the inland edge of the swamp. There I'd join Hans, the electrical engineer and Jimmy the mechanical engineer. We then embarked in a small boat powered by a temperamental single cylinder diesel engine. This engine was hand cranked as fast as one of us could manage whilst someone else closed the decompressor valve - with luck, or persistence the "beast" started. It was a short trip, 100 yards or so across the swamp to the inland edge of the coastal dunes. Here there was a Mercedes Unimog. Generally I used to drive dropping Hans & Jimmy off at one or other of the dredges. I then drove further up the coastal dunes to see how the sand sampling crews were getting on. Here I collected sample bags, suitably tagged and also any worn or damaged drill pipe and cutting bits. These were later taken back to the "boat station" for collection and transport to the Dunwich assay lab and workshop. The rest of my day was spent running survey lines across the dunes and spotting drill locations for the drilling crews. I also had to visit each dredge and check the pond levels. Frequently this required an additional pump in the swamp to be started up to maintain the requisite pond level. Generally in the afternoon I took one of the boats back across the swamp and then walked to TAZI's Herring Lagoon office. Here I would plot new sand sample values on the cross-dune sections and calculate tonnage and grade values. It was all pretty uninteresting.

However, Jimmy, the mechanical engineer, went on two weeks leave and I had to assume responsibility for that function. There was a team of tradesmen (mechanics, welders, painters etc) on each dredge carrying out regular repair/maintenance work on dozens of pumps, pipes, spigots, chutes and Humphrey Spirals, as well as an army of painters, de-scaling and covering the dredge structure and fittings with a tar-epoxy paint against the ravages of the Pacific salt spray. These guys knew what to do and my "engineering supervisory role" was mainly making sure they had the necessary supplies. There was also the problem of repositioning the swamp pumps as the dredges worked their way along the beach. These swamp water pumps were hefty Harland centrifugal units with an 8in diameter suction line attached to a foot valve and mesh grid. Having unbolted the pump itself it was necessary to wade into the swamp to recover the suction line and foot valve, in itself no big deal as the water depth was no more than 4ft, but there was an unseen enemy - leeches. There were dozens of the blighters and they attached themselves to all parts of ones anatomy below the waist! A session of moving the swamp pump was always followed by using lighted cigarettes to "persuade" the leeches to let go, not always successful, whence an infected bite occurred.

Relaxation in Herring Lagoon comprised card playing (pontoon, poker or bridge) plus heavy drinking in one or other of the staff houses. Although Stradbroke Island is almost entirely composed of sand dune these have been fixed with marram grass and eucalyptus trees, which came right up to the back of the house. Like everyone else we had huge problems with goannas (large lizards, 5ft long weighing up to 35 Kg) which would raid the dustbins, climbing inside and heaving everything out. It was necessary to slide the dustbins under an overhang to prevent lid removal. Here we also saw our first kookaburras, beautiful birds and very, very quick on zapping unwary small snakes. On Sundays we would bum a lift off somebody and go up to Point Lookout at the northern end of the island, where there was a decent hotel/pub. On a two day break we went over to the mainland and took a taxi up to the Lone Pine Koala sanctuary and had the regulation photo holding one of these delightful bears. For me the biggest surprise of the koalas was how rough and coarse their hair is and how sleepy they are.

This surface dredging was not for me, so at the TAZI GM's Christmas party I committed the unpardonable sin of button-holing the visiting Zinc Corp director from Melbourne, Russ, requesting a transfer to their underground mines in Broken Hill, New South Wales. His, unsurprisingly brusque, response was "you've only just arrived, take it (my current job) or leave". So I decided to leave, or rather, start to look around for another job in underground hard rock mining. Fortunately for us, in early 1963, the Australian mining industry was expanding and there was a severe shortage of trained engineers. I responded to a number of job adverts for mining engineers in Queensland, NSW, Western Australia and Tasmania and we awaited replies with bated breath. I received several "expressions of interest", but that from Electrolytic Zinc (EZ) in western Tasmania sounded the most promising. Very surprisingly EZ did not stipulate an interview, but asked me to contact their Underground Manager, Wyn, by phone. This I duly did and Wyn briefly described the operation, what my duties would be and what was covered in the job offer - salary, housing, medical, travel expense etc. It all sounded OK, I accepted on the phone and EZ said they would confirm by post and when could I start? On reflection we were amazed that EZ did not interview me but, unbeknown to us Bob, a senior accountant in the TAZI Dunwich office, had just joined EZ Rosebery and, apparently, had said I was "OK", but unhappy working in surface dredging. Anyway by the end of March 1963 we left TAZI and Stradbroke Island and flew down to Melbourne.

5

We were booked into the London Hotel in Melbourne and scheduled to fly out to Wynyard in north-western Tasmania the next day. Arriving at the hotel in early afternoon it seemed very quiet. However when we went out of the hotel a little before six, the bar was absolutely heaving - the notorious six o'clock swill! All the drinkers lined up a number of glasses on the bar immediately ahead of the six o'clock bar closing time It had to be seen to be believed. As we wandered around central Melbourne another oddity appeared, no Asians or blacks were about - the White Australia Policy was still in full swing. At least the hotel was quiet and peaceful in the evening on account of the bar being closed. However if you sat down and had a meal you could still get an alcoholic drink.

The flight from Melbourne to Wynyard only took a little over an hour. From there it was a short drive eastwards along the coast to the town of Burnie. Here we embarked on the Emu Bay Railway (EBR) for Rosebery. The EBR, a mineral railway was operated by an EZ subsidiary. In 1963 there was no road access from the west coast mining areas of Queenstown, Zeehan and Rosebery to the north-west coast at Burnie. The EBR 3ft 6in gauge line passed through some spectacular mountain scenery on its tortuous way to Rosebery some 75 miles due south, reaching a high point of over 2200ft near Waratah. The mineral trains were hauled by British built Beyer-Garratt articulated 2-8-8-2 steam locomotives, eminently suitable for this twisting railroad with very tight curves. The EBR also ran a daily passenger service hauled by the steam locos Heemskirk or Murchison. The train journey was fascinating as the route winds through pristine, sub-tropical dense jungle. We wondered where on earth we were going!

Rosebery lies in the shadow of Mount Murchison (4400ft) at the foot of Mount Black (+ 3000ft) surrounded by dense rain forest. The passenger train dropped us at Rosebery and continued on about twenty miles to the town of Zeehan. The Underground Manager, Wyn, met us at the small station and drove us to our new (not yet lived in) house in the developing "suburb" of Primrose. The house was of modern, coloured corrugated iron sides and roof over a timber frame on short wooden posts, surrounded by cyclone wire fencing enclosing a small "garden" comprising general building rubble. We were amazed to find that Bob, the TAZI accountant, was living right next door in a similar house to ours.

Rosebery was an EZ company town with a population of about 2300 people. It had two hotel/pubs, an RSL Club (ex Services), a small cottage hospital, a newsagent/general store, furniture store, two garages and a community hall. It had a real bush, Wild West feel about it. Apart from a little tarmac in the main street, everywhere else was served by dirt roads. A dirt road connected Rosebery to Zeehan and further away the major copper mining/smelter town of Queenstown. From there a dirt road continued up in to the interior by the Great Lake and from there eventually south to the capital, Hobart. It was a good eight hours drive to reach Hobart from Rosebery. The closest "civilisation" was Burnie on the NW coast, but that could only be reached by the EBR.

The EZ operations comprised a 1000 tonnes/day underground lead/zinc mine on the flank of Mount Black accessed through an incline timbered shaft starting at 33 degrees then steepening to 45 degrees. It was a conventional tracked mine using cut-and-fill and square-set stoping. Broken ore was hoisted in five tonne skips to surface mine cars for transfer to the concentrator. Here lead, zinc & copper concentrates (containing gold & silver) were recovered by differential flotation, the waste, or tailings (after thickening) being sent back underground as fill for the cut-and-fill stopes. The individual concentrates were loaded into special rail cars for haulage by the EBR to Burnie docks. From there the concentrates were shipped around the Tasmanian coast to the EZ electrolytic smelter sited at Risdon just north of Hobart. In addition to the Rosebery Mine the company also operated the small, but high grade Hercules underground mine situated at 2500ft up on the adjacent Mount Read. This 100 tonnes/day mine was worked entirely through adits. Stoping was by incline (or rill) cut-and-fill using surface waste rock as the fill medium. Underground tracked haulage was powered by one of three draught horses. The full ore trains exited the mine by gravity, controlled by a brake car and the horses pulled the empty rake (ten one tonne capacity, side dump wagons) back upgrade into the mine. On surface the broken ore was transferred to a balanced haulage system, which carried the ore down the mountain to a large storage bin at the small village of Williamsford. From here a four mile aerial ropeway carried the ore to the crushing plant at the Rosebery concentrator. Due to the isolated location the EZ Rosebery operations were very self contained. There were full central engineering facilities to handle all and any repairs or maintenance. The only "bought in" service was power from the state Hydro-Electric Commission.

I was one of several mining engineers. My specific duties, reporting to the Assistant Underground Manager, was development and in particular the sinking of a 45 degree inclined winze from the lowest mine level. This winze was to provide access beneath the existing main incline shaft so that it, in turn, could be extended by raising. I took over engineering responsibility from Clive, who was leaving within a couple of weeks, to take up a new post in Western Australia. (This was the reason EZ were in a hurry for me to start). Sinking of the inclined winze was by conventional drill & blast but mucking was achieved by a wire rope wound onto small drums on the rear wheels of the track mounted Eimco rocker-shovel. This was a tricky, slow operation made possible only by excellent mucker operators. Other mine development was all tracked, 7ft by 7ft size, using hand held air legs, Eimco shovels and muck hauled in small side tip cars. Occasional back support used split set rock bolts. All fairly straightforward.

My duties also included a weekly visit to the Hercules Mine. I used to drive a large Willys jeep loaded with supplies (drill steel, pipes & couplings, timber, rock bolts etc) over to Williamsford and then up the zigzag dirt road to the Hercules Mine site. Fred, the Hercules Mine Foreman was a really nice guy from whom I learnt a lot about rill stoping and waste filling from surface glory holes. Besides the usual mining gear for repair/renewal that I took back to Rosebery there was a "special" delivery for the Rosebery GM. Three sack loads of horse manure! Yes, Ted, the GM was a really keen gardener and grew the best roses in Rosebery thanks to the three Hercules horses. The horses lived in a surface stables close to the No 6 adit portal. Louis was the regular horse minder and they were very well looked after. In August the horses were led down the mountain to a nice paddock in Williamsford for a two week "holiday". It was quite a sight to see these big draught horses galloping around and having a good roll in the rich grass.

Tasmania lies in the Roaring Forties and Rosebery lying at the foot of the western mountains thus received a lot of rain. The surrounding dense sub-tropical rain forest included considerable areas of amazing horizontal scrub and giant tree ferns seven or eight feet tall. One of our first acts was to buy a second-hand car and the dirt/gravel roads dictated a rugged 1200cc VW Beetle. There was a little winter snow in the town, although, of course, Mounts Murchison, Black and Read would be snow covered down to 1000ft above sea level (ASL) for a couple of months. A small river, the Stitt, ran through Rosebery and joined the major Pieman river immediately west of the EBR line, a little to the south of the town. The EBR main line passed a mere fifty yards behind our house with a steep drop into the Pieman gorge a further 100 yards away. Having bought the car, the next thing was to buy a 'galvanised iron (GI) garage from someone who was leaving. Rather short sightedly the EZ company had not included garages with the new houses so a real hotch potch of custom built garages appeared. One could obtain virtually any DIY stuff one needed from either the EZ Company Store or the town's general store, The River Don Trading Co. So we set to preparing a low concrete foundation wall including some hold down bolts. With help from a neighbour we soon had the timber framework up, followed by cladding with good, bad and rusty GI. We then finished the edifice off with a coat of shocking pink paint! It looked awful, but did the job and in particular provided a space to string some clothes line for clothes drying on (the many) rainy days. The garage was also useful in providing a structure on which to attach a tall pole to carry an aerial extension. Obviously there was no TV, and radio reception in Rosebery was poor on account of the surrounding mountains. However the "garage" extension aerial plugged in to our old Blaupunkt (ex East Africa) short wave radio maintained a listening brief on the outside world!

The VW Beetle was mainly used for shortish trips around town for shopping or visiting other staff houses. Relaxation was reading, listening to vinyl records, playing bridge and of course the inevitable round of staff parties. Heavy drinking seems to be the norm for mining camps and Rosebery was no exception. There was always a good queue of ladies outside the Mine entrance gates on Friday, pay day, hoping to get their hands on some cash before the EZ miners disappeared into either of the two pubs or the RSL Club. Both pubs were surrounded by wooden covered walkways (as in Wild West films, but no horses hitched there!) and numerous drunken brawls were guaranteed. One tended not to walk around the centre of Rosebery on a Friday evening/night. The two Tasmanian brewers, Boags and Cascade, must have made a lot of money out of the Rosebery and

Queenstown pubs and RSL Clubs. We became friendly with the English dentist, Fred and his Danish wife, Bodil; they also lived in Primrose. The four of us played a lot of bridge and also used to walk along the EBR track over the Stitt river bridge.

Poor Gillian had to have driving lessons from me, not the most patient person. Nevertheless she progressed very well and after a couple of months she approached the local Rosebery copper to see about a driving test. This she passed with flying colours as the "test" consisted of the copper saying "yes, I've seen you driving around town whilst you've been learning - seemed OK, here's your licence"! So having obtained her driving licence Gillian began working at The Rosebery Hospital, initially as a Staff Nurse and later as a Sister. She worked both day and some night shifts so the car was essential. I used to walk to and fro to the mine, it was only about a mile distant.

We made a few weekend trips out to Zeehan, Strahan or Queenstown, with the occasional longer journey to Launceston or Hobart over an extended holiday weekend. The dirt roads were quite punishing, but the VW Beetle coped well. I had a couple of memorable "boys only" trips. One, a fishing trip on MacQuarie harbour out of Strahan, where, being of a tidy nature, I was sinking the empty beer cans. The Rosebery lads preferred to leave them floating so they could find their way back to Strahan when we turned for home! The second was a strenuous hike with Bruce, back-packing, from Cradle Mountain in the north to Lake St Clair in the south. There was a very crude trail with log cabins spaced fifteen to twenty miles apart. Being Tassie the route was often very wet, with deep torrents to ford as well as frequent rain. This walk re-introduced me to the delights of Australian leeches. The first job after arriving at the log cabin was to get a fire going (there was a basket of split wood available), the second job was burning off the damn leeches with a lighted cigarette. One replaced the wood burnt by splitting logs the next day and re-filling the dried wood basket. We attempted to climb Mt Ossa (1617m), the highest peak in Tassie, but heavy misty rain prevented us; we could see nothing. We took about seven days through to the Great Lake where somebody picked us up at Derwent Bridge on the central highway to Queenstown. I hadn't shaved during the weeks hike, no point carrying unnecessary clobber. However there was quite a shock when I got back to Rosebery and spied, in the mirror, this ghastly, wispy, gingery beard. It came off post haste and explains why I have never, ever grown a beard again.

During the summer of 1963-64 I took up tennis again, playing on the hard courts of The Rosebery Tennis Club, sited out at the suburb of Barkers Crossing. The club championship tournament took place in March. The less said of my singles endeavour the better. However I joined Geoff, a regular Aussie Rules footie man, in the doubles. Geoff was very fit with quick reactions, a natural net player. I on the other hand, with long legs and arms could, sort of, cover the baseline. Anyway to everyones surprise we won the club Mens Double title - definitely the zenith of my sporting life.

Later that year as the southern Spring approached, my parents visited us for a couple of weeks. My dad, now aged 60, had brought two younger men into his Tunbridge Wells business and felt he could take some time off. They came out by sea, sat at the captain's table, and had had a really enjoyable, pampered cruise. The mining town of Rosebery was quite a culture shock. We put on a "cocktail party" at our house for my parents to meet our friends. My dad was quite non-plussed that we dispensed beer from a firkin (or two!). He correctly surmised that in this sort of environment everybody drank like fishes. A day or so later all four of us crammed into the VW Beetle and we did a tour of Tasmania taking in Zeehan, Strahan, Queenstown and the central Great Lake. Thereafter we headed for the north coast, Burnie & Devonport before turning south again to Launceston. Then out to Bicheno on the east coast before finally south to Hobart and Port Arthur. It was great fun and passed much too quickly. All four of us then flew to Melbourne and then on to Sydney where we stayed in the very posh Wentworth Hotel. Gillian and I only stayed a couple of nights before flying back to Melbourne then Hobart (to pick up the car). My parents left the next day by air for Honolulu, the USA and home.

We were now well past our two year stint in Australia as proscribed by the terms of the Ten Pound Poms deal. I requested the return of our passports from the Immigration Department, who duly obliged. We hadn't yet decided on moving, but obviously my parents visit had proved somewhat unsettling. We talked about going to New Zealand, but Gillian felt it would be good to get out of Australasia where she felt, quite correctly, that we lacked exposure to any culture and, besides that, were drinking too much! So in the end we decided to head back to the UK and see what turned up. I sold the old, trusty VW Beetle to a new Rosebery arrival without any bother. We then booked a cabin on the ss Fairstar of the Italian Sitmar Line sailing from

Melbourne. After the usual round of farewell parties we left from Primrose station on the old EBR for Burnie. We stayed that night at a hotel in Burnie. Whilst we were having dinner that night a Burnie policeman appeared at our table and asked me to accompany him as "there was some problem with unpaid bills in Rosebery". I was totally discombobulated and more than a little worried as we were due to fly to Melbourne next morning to join the Fairstar. He was quite a friendly copper and after a while he couldn't keep a straight face and admitted he'd been put up to the lark by Rod of the Rosebery Garage. It was a really good leg-pull and I'd swallowed the bait. I was very relieved to return to the dining table and tell Gillian we could still make the flight to Melbourne tomorrow.

6

The Fairstar was about 26,000 tonnes dwt and was a civilian conversion of the British troopship Oxfordshire. She had an Argentinian captain and a mainly Chinese crew. We had an outside, small two berth cabin. The first stop was Sydney, where the ship filled up with many returning Europeans. As she started to pull away from the quay many paper streamers were thrown on board by the watching shore crowd. I caught one of the streamers and held it until it finally broke; Gillian very presciently said that this meant we would return. The next scheduled stop was Singapore, but in fact we hove to off Cooktown in northern Queensland, where a seriously ill passenger was taken off by tender. Unfortunately we were on a table for two, but got very friendly with a group of Brits and Latvians who were on a nearby table. Aldis & Ruta (the Latvians) were very lively and over the next few weeks we got to know them well. We used to play deck quoits and ping pong a lot as well as chatting, drinking and lazing in the sun. The captain suggested that we shouldn't spend all our money in Singapore, but save some for Aden, where the duty free bargains were even cheaper (apparently). The ship only stayed in Singapore for 24 hours but it gave us our first chance to experience the orient. In 1965 Singapore was still the exotic, mysterious, undeveloped Far Eastern trading port. Change Alley had to be seen, smelt and heard to get an appreciation of this great port city.

We headed NW up the Straits of Malacca and across the Indian ocean to Colombo in Sri Lanka. We took a taxi out to the beautiful cliff top Mount Lavinia Hotel a few miles south of the city. Next day we started the long haul to Aden. Things really livened up in the dining room one day when a huge fight broke out amongst the Chinese waiters. It was very spectacular, soup tureens, serving dishes of all sorts were hurled at each other whilst trolleys were overturned and plates smashed on any nearby head. The dining passengers took evasive action moving away from the kitchen entrance. Eventually some senior deck crew came in and restored order. At breakfast, the following day, most of the Chinese waiters had numerous head and arm bandages! (The Fairstar, "waiters fracas" made quite a splash in the UK popular press). It was the highlight of the Indian ocean crossing. There was more bad news at Aden. Apparently there had been a recent armed uprising, which British forces were attempting to put down. The captain was thus advised not to dock and we headed straight on into the Red Sea and up to El Suez at the southern end of the Suez canal. Along with many other passengers we decided to leave the ship at El Suez, travel overland through Egypt and rejoin the ship at Port Said on the Mediterranean coast.

The first night the four of us, Gillian, Aldis, Ruta and I had been out for dinner in El Suez and were making our way back to the ship. Foolishly we strayed onto some back streets and were whistled and jeered at by a crowd of Egyptian youths, which turned nasty as stones were thrown. The girls scuttled off as fast as they could run, whilst Aldis and I beat a steady retreat trying not to look too nervous. I guess Brits were still not very popular after the 1956 Suez landings. The next morning the "overlanders" buses took us westwards to Cairo. We stayed for two nights in a very pleasant central hotel. Of course we had a trip out to the pyramids and the Sphinx, complete with the mandatory camel ride. My overriding memory of camels is that they have very strong halitosis, seem bad tempered and are incredibly uncomfortable to ride. Certainly not my favourite means of transport. In Cairo we also visited the Tutankhamen exhibition at the main museum - it was stunning. The next day we bussed north-east about 140 miles to rejoin the Fairstar at Port Said.

We now had three to four days steady Mediterranean cruising until we docked at Naples. There we found a lovely little Italian restaurant and thoroughly enjoyed the food, wine and ambience. It felt as if we had arrived back in the civilised world after the rather rough and ready, albeit friendly, west coast of Tasmania. That was a definite high point as we had now been on the Fairstar for four and half weeks and couldn't wait to get off. However, half a day out of Naples I went down with a bad bout of malaria. I was confined to the ship's isolation sick bay and when we finally arrived at Southampton the Port Authorities would not let me disembark! Poor Gillian had to handle all the disembarkation formalities & sort out the luggage. Finally the Port medical guys came and had a look at me, did some blood tests and after half a day allowed me off, with the proviso that I had to be checked out by The Hospital for Tropical Diseases in London. All in all not a great homecoming.

We headed for my parents house in Tunbridge Wells. Then up to Wards Garage (again) in Southborough to take delivery of a new MG-B. (I had ordered it shortly before we left Rosebery). It was a rather awful pale blue - goodness knows why we chose that colour. I did a fair amount of phoning around and perusing the national press looking for mining jobs. There weren't that many in the UK, unlike Australia. The newly formed Amalgamated Roadstone Corporation (ARC) was looking for trainee quarry managers and I attended an interview with ARC in London. The job sounded interesting, a six month training program at Penlee Quarry, near Mousehole, followed by a permanent position as Assistant Quarry Manager (AQM) at Hingston Downs Quarry near Callington complete with a local assistant managers house. Both quarries were based in Cornwall and this suited us fine with Gillian's parents house nearby in St Mawgan. Although the salary wasn't brilliant, the provision of a nominal rented house was a great attraction. We packed up the MG-B and headed for Gillian's parents house.

I had a quick run around both Penlee and Hingston Downs quarries and noted that although long established quarries ARC were in the process of re-equipping and modernising them. All in all it looked promising and I accepted ARC's job offer. Next Gillian and I looked around for somewhere to rent for six months close to Penlee. We found a lovely little place in Mousehole, just back from the quay - Pilot's Lookout. We moved in our few bits & pieces and browsed our local town of Penzance-Newlyn. The poor old (new!) MG-B had quite a tough time with the salt spray/air at Mousehole, where the car was parked on the quay and the dust at Penlee, where the car was parked close to the crushing and screening plant.

As a trainee quarry manager I worked through the quarrying, roadstone production route, ie, drilling, blasting, loading, haulage, crushing, screening, storage and load-out. There was also a coated stone plant (tarmac & asphalt). The roadstone products were shifted by road, for local deliveries, and both by train and boat for other UK destinations. These "stone boats" had a capacity of 2,500 to 3,000 tonnes and were loaded by conveyor from Penlee's own jetty. They used to deliver stone to ARC distribution centres in Liverpool, Bristol, Southampton and Thames Estuary. I was particularly interested in the quarry drilling rigs - Down-The-Hole (DTH) units, a Halco and Holman Voltrac. They were used to drill a nominal 6in diameter blast-hole up to 12m deep. The rigs were self propelled towing their own compressor. Their penetration rate was not very rapid (the actual hammer was only 2.5in diameter) in the hard diorite, but the penetration rate did not drop off with increased hole depth. Conventional, rope face shovels were used to load 25 tonnes capacity Foden dumpers. The crushing plant comprised a primary jaw crusher followed by secondary cone crushers in closed circuit with various screens. The actual screening circuit was adjusted according to the stone size/quantity required. The quarry was self draining being, in essence, a side-cut into the rapidly rising ground from the sea shore. Again very straightforward.

Our relaxation was mainly provided by some lovely old pubs/restaurants in Mousehole and Newlyn. Over Christmas 1964 we got involved in the preparation for nighttime carols at the Newlyn Lights festival. Otherwise at weekends we generally drove up to north Cornwall to see Gillian's parents in St Mawgan or her sister Pat at Mawgan Porth. We also visited Lands End, the Lizard, Kynance Cove, St Michaels Mount etc.

After three or four months ARC management asked me to move to Hingston Downs quarry to take up the AQM's position. The promised house was not yet available and I had to stay in a Callington pub, whilst Gillian returned to her parents at St Mawgan; it was not ideal. Worse was to follow when ARC said that I would not be paid the AQM rate as I hadn't finished the six months trainee course. I was really pissed off. I argued that they (ARC) had thought I was ready to take up the AQM position and therefor they should pay the rate agreed for that role and provide the promised house. They wouldn't budge so I resigned forthwith seeing no future with a company like that and gave the agreed one months notice. What a mess. So back to St Mawgan (good old parents) to look for another job.

A mining friend mentioned that Silvermines in Ireland were looking for staff. I phoned the company and they invited me over for an interview. Gillian and I decided to make the visit to Silvermines into a small holiday. We took the MG-B using the Fishguard-Rosslare car ferry. From Wexford we drove west and north-west along almost deserted roads (apart from the occasional donkey drawn carts) to Nenagh, where we'd booked in to the local pub for three nights. The next day I drove to the mine about ten miles due south. It was a fairly recent underground development of an old lead-silver mining area. They were looking for mine planning engineers, but the terms and conditions were not attractive, so I did not proceed. Gillian was disappointed that no job was secured but was greatly cheered the next day when we were press-ganged into joining an Irish wedding that was underway in the pub! It was great fun, everyone very friendly helped along with lashings of alcohol. No one could sleep in the pub that Saturday night. After a very quiet Sunday (!) we drove NW to Galway so that we could see "the the sun go down on Galway Bay". It was a glorious evening and quite spectacular. Next day we drove back to Rosslare, took the ferry to Fishguard and on to Cornwall to continue the job search.

I was very fortunate. Associated Portland Cement Manufacturers (APCM) were looking for an Assistant Quarry Manager for their Dunbar Cement Works in Scotland. I applied by letter and was invited to attend an interview at their Head office in Hull. I accepted the offer (better paid than Silvermines and ARC, but no house) and went back to Cornwall to tell Gillian we were off to Scotland asap. So we packed our stuff into the back of the MG-B and set off for the long drive north. Dunbar was a small seaside town in Lanarkshire, about thirty miles due east of Edinburgh. The cement works was a few miles south of the town. APCM had booked us accommodation in the local hotel. This was fine as we were right in town and after a long search we found a suitable place to rent. The place was, in fact, an old bank and our wardrobe was the old walk-in vault - very secure!

The limestone quarry and shale workings were about a mile and half from the cement works and connected to it by a 3ft 6in gauge railway. The quarry manager was a formidable Scot - Mr Hamilton, I never knew his first name - who had the quarry very well planned and ran it with a rod of iron. My duties mainly comprised extensive surveying of the drilling lines and preparing blast-hole loading patterns. This was my first experience of pre-split, precision rock breaking to maintain a dead straight, clean-cut quarry face. This was required to ensure that the huge (450 tonnes weight) tracked overburden conveyor transporter was always the correct distance from this face. The transporter carried the stripped overburden waste right across the working quarry face and adjacent load-out rail track to discharge the waste into the previously mined area. Here the waste was spread by dozers and then finished off with top soil for re-seeding.

Drilling was carried out by self contained Gardner-Denver Airtrak rigs mounting a PR123 4.5in drifter. Air was supplied from a towed GD compressor. The penetration rate of these drifter rigs was much faster than the DTH rigs at Penlee. This was obviously due to two main factors. The Dunbar limestone was much softer than the Penlee diorite and the drifter's piston at 4.5in diameter was a full 2in diameter bigger than the DTH rigs. It was apparent that DTH rigs would only come in to their own (penetration wise) with blast-hole depths considerably greater than 10m. (This was on account of the effective power loss of 10% over each drill rod coupling of the drifter rig). The 4in diameter pre-split drill holes were placed 2ft apart and drilled to a depth of 11m for the 10m working face. A light blast using continuously decked 60% gelignite ensured the development of a longitudinal crack along the full face length. In front of this pre-split "crack" normal production drilling used either 4in or 6in holes on a 2 to 2.5m square pattern. Loading off the quarry floor direct to the rail wagons was handled by Ruston Bucyrus rope face shovels. Fragmentation was good, there was very little secondary blasting and the train wagons delivered the run of quarry stone direct to the primary crushing plant alongside the cement works. A certain quantity of shale (required for the cement process) was also quarried.

I found the survey work relatively simple (after underground survey work) but one had to keep a close eye on the drilling rig operators to "spot" the holes accurately. Mr Hamilton would not countenance a "ragged" quarry face and, of course, the quarrying method did not allow this. The Scots quarrymen were not unfriendly, but operated in a semi-feudal manner, which I found unsettling. They referred to me as Sorrrr (at least to my face!) and were unnerved if I attempted to have a drink with them in the public bar. As part of "management" I was expected to drink in the saloon bar. All in all, not just at the quarry, both Gillian and I found Dunbar a very unfriendly place, certainly for us English.

Dunbar itself had a nice little harbour and beach surrounded by low red sandstone cliffs. Here there were dozens of sand martins nesting in holes in the cliff face. However when the wind was in the east Dunbar became a very cold place indeed. At weekends we used to drive the thirty miles west to Edinburgh, which we both liked. It was a scenic city with fine imposing granite buildings and plenty of interesting pubs, restaurants and art galleries. We were fortunate enough to attend the Tattoo in December 1965, very moving. We also used to drive off into the nearby Lammermuir Hills to find a byroad ford in which to wash down the old MG-B. These hills were magnificent rolling country echoing with the plaintive cries of curlew and lapwings. Gillian's sister Pat came up to visit us. We picked her up at Edinburgh station, fitting the third person in by squatting on the transmission tunnel behind the front seats. Although not the most comfortable, we rotated drivers and managed to make a long trip up by Loch Lommond north through the highlands to Glen Coe and Fort William. The spectacular scenery was easy to appreciate from an open car on a fine day and even the numbness in one's bottom, when "seated" on the transmission tunnel, seemed less intense.

We had been in Dunbar for about seven months when, out of the blue, I received a telegram from EZ Rosebery offering me a new job as Assistant Project manager for a brand new shaft project to double production at the Rosebery mine to 2000 tonnes/day. Gillian was not very happy on the idea, but EZ offered a good house in the senior management area of Barkers Crossing, together with a good hike in salary and fringe benefits. We talked it over with both families and the general consensus was that opportunities in the hard rock mining industry in the UK were mainly restricted to open-pit coal or quarrying. I much preferred the challenge of underground operations and felt this was a great chance to further my career (a tad selfish perhaps?). However it was also apparent that Gillian could get a job as nurse at the doctor's surgery in Rosebery. I accepted the offer and gave notice to APCM. Although I had learnt a lot about "smooth-wall blasting", my basic day-to-day job was really as a surface surveyor, which I did not find particularly stimulating. The attraction of project engineering for a new shaft was really enticing, added to which we knew the working/living environment well. Certainly neither Gillian nor I were sorry to be leaving Dunbar - it was not a happy place and one felt the "natives" would be glad to see the back of us.

We returned to Cornwall (patient parents again) and sorted out our bits and pieces, whilst getting the necessary travel, visa and work permits organised. Then it was up to Kent (my parents again) to sell the MG-B back to Ward's Garage at a still greater loss than before. It is obviously a financial disaster to keep changing ones job, but I was very slow on the uptake. EZ provided funds for air tickets and luggage transfer so we could arrange flights to suit ourselves. A welcome change from the original Ten Pound Poms experience when you had to go when the Australian government said so. We flew Qantas to Perth, Western Australia then on to Melbourne, overnight and then next day to Wynyard, north-western Tassie. Here there was a big surprise as an EZ car was waiting to collect us and drive to Rosebery. The driver explained that the brand new Murchison Highway from Rosebery to Burnie had been opened just three months ago, thus no trip on the EBR necessary. It was old sealed roads through Burnie suburbs and then the new dirt road commenced, passing through Waratah and Tullah on the way to Rosebery. This new dirt road was quite hazardous with loose gravel everywhere, tight bends in the mountains and everyone - trucks, logging units and private cars - traveling way too fast. It was a relief to reach Rosebery in one piece.

Our bungalow in Barkers Crossing (BC) was an old (by Rosebery standards - twenty years) timber frame, painted GI clad house set in a lovely mature garden overlooking the Rosebery sports ground. There was a beautiful nectarine tree alongside the gravel drive. Compared to Primrose it was quiet and (almost!) exclusive. An interesting feature was the outside loo (or dunny) on the side verandah leading to a utilities room. One used to check carefully for local wildlife presence before using the facility. BC was a little further from the mine than Primrose and with the rainy west coast weather a car was essential. I placed an order for a new 1200cc VW Beetle with Burghel, the local agent. These VWs were now built in Australia, but they proved much less reliable than our previous second-hand Beetle, which was an original German import. These new Aussie built VWs could not handle the cold, wet conditions at Rosebery. The short runs from BC to the mine or return required plenty of choke, now an automated device, and had the nasty habit of dumping condensed moisture into the engine sump introducing water into the lubricating oil - really bad news. Burghel, had plenty of unhappy new VW owners, to the extent that someone from VW (Aust) came down to check cars and eventually a modified carburetor was fitted. (There were similar problems with new VWs in Renison Bell, Zeehan, Strahan and Queenstown).

I shared a new shaft project office with Daryl, the project engineer, alongside the main mine engineering/surveying/geological offices. Our job was to determine the best means of doubling daily ore hoisting capacity from the new, lower levels of the mine. This also included, manhandling, ventilation, power, air, water and pumping requirements. Our first investigations, of course, concerned geology - where was the ore centre of gravity on successively deeper levels. We also needed geotechnical data concerning hangingwall and footwall rocks and predicted ground-water statistics. It was necessary to consider the mine's major mining methods of shrinkage, cut-and-fill and square-set stoping together with the number and size of various types of stope equipment. The mine's deep diamond drilling programme was outlining the physical limits of the ore zone(s) and we soon had key information of orebody dip and plunge into the flanks of Mount Black.

Traditionally the Tasmanian west coast mining region had used long rectangular timber lined inclined shafts, generally sited a short distance from the orebody footwall. The Rosebery orebody was steepening up to 55 degrees at depth and a hangingwall vertical shaft seemed to be the logical alternative. However, as the orebody dipped into the flank of Mount Black the shaft sinking distance from surface increased rapidly. Our solution was to develop a major crosscut into Mount Black, some 100ft above the existing main haulage adit. From the end of this crosscut the necessary headworks for an internal shaft would be developed in solid hangingwall rock at the desired coordinates. Then the major investigation was what type of shaft? The obvious choice was a monolithic concrete lined vertical circular shaft. But this type of shaft was unknown on the west coast. Daryl and I therefore set off to visit Mt Isa, Broken Hill, Cobar and Kalgoorlie to investigate major metal mine shafts in Australia. Without exception all these major metal mining areas were using circular, concrete lined vertical shafts, no matter what the dip of their respective orebodies. In addition there had been huge changes in the type of hoisting gear operating in these shafts. The conventional double-drum winder had been replaced by the modern friction winder with either Ward Leonard or thyristor converter/inverter control. We took this information back to the EZ Rosebery management, who eventually accepted this approach.

Over the next few months we refined all the conflicting design parameters to arrive at an overall mine hoisting concept. An overriding consideration to the size and shape of the "sinking bank crosscut" (SBC as it was subsequently named) and the internal shaft itself was the mine's ventilation requirements. Both the crosscut and internal shaft were to be the mine's main ventilation, fresh air downcast. The crosscut was to be developed with a semi-circular back formed by pre-split and smooth-wall blasting, where my experience of such techniques gained from APCM's Dunbar Quarry in Scotland was useful. Again to meet ventilation needs the shaft was sized at 22ft diameter equipped with aerofoil buntons and guides to accommodate two friction winders, one pulling balanced side dump skips and one pulling a large single cage and counterweight.

The EZ management decided to undertake the development of the crosscut with its own in-house mining crews, but the sinking of this major sub-vertical shaft (projected depth 2400ft) and the provision of two winders and associated electrical control equipment was to be put out to international tender. Thus Daryl and I spent a further six months preparing detailed tender specifications for firstly a shaft sinking and equipping package and secondly a winder supply package, including all mechanical and electrical control systems. We also had to draw up potential bidders lists for both tender packages.

Relaxation activities changed somewhat from our first Rosebery visit. However the regular round of house parties with too much beer continued apace. The big change was direct road access to Burnie and the NW coast with the completion of the Murchison Highway. Thus most Friday evenings (Friday was pay day) there was a continual stream of Rosebery cars heading up to Burnie & civilisation! In fact we used to go up to Burnie and the coast about every third week. This was mainly to stock up with essential supplies (unobtainable in Rosebery) and, of course, beer and wine. With a new gravel/dirt road and a lot of "enthusiastic" drivers going too fast we suffered the inevitable smashed windscreen on the VW Beetle. No serious harm, we punched out the rest of the glass and continued, arriving in Burnie covered in road dust and flies, whence everyone knew you had just driven up the Murchison Highway. It was another good, practical reason to drive a VW Beetle, since the garages in Rosebery and Burnie always had a huge supply of VW windscreens, which were cheaper than the ubiquitous Holdens. We seldom spent the Friday night at the Burnie Hotel since Gillian often had Saturday morning work at the doctor's Rosebery surgery.

The new road also allowed me to drive up to Wynyard Airport on the occasional Saturday or Sunday to take flying lessons in a Cessna 150 high wing monoplane. The lessons were relatively cheap and the Wynyard airspace uncluttered for nervous beginners. I also started an economics correspondence course with the Wolsey Hall organization of the UK. All necessary books were specified and these were then obtained by post from a university bookshop in Melbourne. It was something else to do on the interminable wet evenings. Annual rainfall was plus 50 inches. There was another English mining engineer, Bob, in Queenstown working for The Mount Lyell Company who was also doing an economics course and we often compared notes. Both Gillian and I took up badminton and joined the Rosebery Badminton Club. We played in the town's Memorial Hall on a regular basis as well as trips to other clubs in Renison Bell, Zeehan and Queenstown. There were also regular Aus IMM technical meetings in Rosebery and Queenstown as well as social events. For our annual leave we spent a few days in Launceston followed by a week or so in Hobart, a port town, which had a good feel to it and although not a big city was quite lively. There was a large boating community with excellent sailing in the steady westerly winds out on the bay. There was a very popular casino at the Wrest Point Hotel. This was surprising as there were very few casinos on mainland Australia at this time. The England cricket team were in town, staying at the Wrest Point. With Rod's son we approached Ian Botham & Bob Willis for autographs at breakfast time. They were both grumpy & hung-over and reluctant to oblige. Who would wish to be famous when all the world wants a piece of you? Much better to be a minor miner and remain anonymous.

We received several bids for the shaft sinking contract from firms such as Shaft Sinkers & Roberts Construction, both from South Africa; Thyssens from West Germany; Cementation from the UK; Thapur Intrafor from India; Fry and Harrison, both from Canada. The only Australian bidder was Dillingham Construction, who were a major civil engineering contractor on the Snowy Mountains (SMA) scheme in NSW. Our short list for initial interview was Harrison, Thyssen and Cementation. The others were rejected as non-conforming bids. On the winder side the leading bidders were GEC of the UK; ASEA of Sweden; Siemens of West Germany and Ingersoll Rand of the USA. With the help of the mine's engineering department it soon became apparent that the GEC bid was superior on technical grounds, delivery time and price - no contest. However EZ management were unhappy that there was no local, Australian involvement in a potential shaft sinking contract and we (Daryl and I) were instructed to examine Dillingham's Snowy Mountain activities in more detail before "closing off" the initial short list. Consequently the bid submission date was extended and Daryl and I flew up to NSW to examine Dillingham's shaft sinking credentials on the SMA project. They only had experience of 100ft deep surge shafts, excavated with typical civil engineering methods. We duly reported back that Dillingham's lacked basic shaft sinking experience and had no suitable plant or experienced project engineers for the major Rosebery shaft.

EZ management then contacted Dillinghams and requested they submit a JV bid with Shaft Sinkers of South Africa. All four companies Harrisons, Thyssen, Cementation and now Dillingham-Shaft Sinkers were invited to rebid. Both Harrisons and Thyssen declined to rebid (the shaft sinking grapevine was buzzing!) and Cementation resubmitted their original bid, unchanged. Daryl and I did a rigorous evaluation of the two bids and firmly recommended Cementation as preferable in every way, including price. We were over-ruled and the contract was awarded to Dillingham-Shaft Sinkers. This was a complete slap in the face for all the work Daryl and I had carried out over the past eighteen months. We had been used as frontmen in the discussions with all the shaft sinking firms. All the firms were aware that there were common share holders in EZ and Shaft Sinkers, but we had stressed that the bids would be evaluated on technical merit, price and completion date alone. That now was patently untrue. After one nights reflection I resigned forthwith. One has to have integrity in commercial dealings as with other aspects of life.

Gillian was upset on one hand, but not too upset that we might, finally (!) be leaving the west coast of Tasmania. A few days after the shaft contract was awarded to Dillingham-Shaft Sinkers I received a telephone call from the Melbourne Office manager of Cementation who opened by saying "I hear you may be looking for a job". I agreed and he invited me over to Melbourne for an interview. We agreed a date. A couple of days later I drove to Wynyard and flew from there to Melbourne. Cementation made me a good offer of a position as Resident Engineer on a new shaft sinking contract. I assumed this would be somewhere in Western Australia where the new nickel boom was underway and Cementation had several shaft/mine development projects in hand. I was more than a little surprised when they said Chasnalla No 4 Shaft, near Jharia in Bihar, India. The terms and conditions were good but India? I said I'd have to consult Gillian. I stayed overnight in Melbourne and flew back to Wynyard the next day. Arriving home in Barkers Crossing Gillian said "well"? I said they'd offered me a good job as Resident Engineer on a big shaft sinking project. She said "good, where?" I said "India". Gillian replied "well....(pause)... we haven't been there yet, so why not", which I thought was a fantastic supportive response.

7

The mine carpentry shop made us some crates and we packed up our bits and pieces again. I sold the new(ish) VW Beetle through Burghel and we said goodbye to Rosebery friends and took the old EBR passenger train back to Burnie for the last time. Flew from Wynyard to Melbourne, stayed overnight and flew the next day, with minimum baggage, to Bangkok, Thailand. I had agreed with Cementation that we would take five days holiday en route to India. We stayed at the Erawan Hotel in Bangkok, which seemed very luxurious after Australian hotels. By contrast Bangkok city itself was mysteriously eastern, exotic and chaotic. The traffic in late 1967 was totally anarchic and one held one's breath as the tuk-tuk driver joined the maelstrom. We thoroughly enjoyed Bangkok visiting the large floating market; the main Buddhist temple; the girly bars down Patpong Road and several excellent Thai restaurants. All too quickly this R & R was over and we flew on to Calcutta's Dum Dum airport. We took one of the ubiquitous Ambassador taxis (Morris Oxford car, Indian version) to The Great Eastern Hotel, where Cementation (India) had booked us a room. The semi-mayhem of Bangkok proved a good intro for the seething mass of pedestrians, cyclists and Ambassador taxis which continually sounded their horns. Peaceful it was not, but exciting yes and more was to come.

Cementation had left instructions at the hotel for us to catch the "Coalfields Express" from Howrah Station to Dhanbad, a short rail trip of about 180 miles. We took a taxi to Howrah Station and thereafter were swept up in the madness of this famous station. Two red coated porters each placed one of our suitcases on his head and, having said we wanted the Coalfields Express, set off at a pace into the seething crowd. We charged along behind desperately trying to keep our suitcases in sight. Goodness knows how many people actually live and sleep on this huge terminal station, but every facet of human existence appears to take place there. There were dozens of hawkers selling drinks/snacks/anything you might want for a rail journey. Howrah was Calcutta's main terminus and long distance trains departed for every corner of the subcontinent. It seemed to us to be one of the great sights/experiences of the world. Our porters located the Coalfields Express with no trouble and we settled in to a busy first-class carriage, whilst metaphorically beating off the myriad hawkers who smelt business from Europeans.

Immediately leaving Howrah the train crossed the wide, muddy Hooghly river. Thereafter the train lived up to it's express moniker, stopping only at Asansol, arriving at Dhanbad in three and half hours. Needless to say the train was steam hauled. Dhanbad was a major coal mining centre lying close to the Damodar river on the southern flank of the Ganges river basin. The area was thus hot and very humid. At Dhanbad station CemIndia's (CI) site agent, Marcus, met us. We drove SW through Jharia to the Indian Iron & Steel Corporation's (IISCO) compound at Chasnalla. The driver, in fact was Indian, since CI's European staff were not insured for driving in India. We had our own two bedroom, concrete block built, flat roofed bungalow. There were individual air conditioner units for the living room and one bedroom. The bath was made of concrete, but there was running water and electricity. Three servants were provided, a cook, housekeeper, and driver (for the ever present Ambassador car).

CI's client IISCO was the main coal mining company in the Jharia region. The area was dotted with pit headgears and an enormous network of aerial ropeways handling both coal to central washing plants and dredged sand (from the nearby Damodar river) for use as mine backfill. Part of the region was covered by acrid smoke from numerous fires in the old shallow mined-out areas (the goaf). CI's Chasnalla contract comprised sinking five concrete lined circular shafts to varying depths around 1500ft All the shafts required pre-cementation injection since the overlying coal measure strata were heavily water bearing from the adjacent Damodar river. The shaft contracts specified maximum water inflow rates for the completed shafts and it was thus necessary to carry out backwall injection to dry off the shaft after completing every concrete walling length. Each shaft had a European complement of a Resident Engineer, a Master Sinker, three Chargehands (ie Shift Bosses), a Mechanical Engineer, an Electrical Engineer and a Concrete Foreman. The local workforce comprised thirty miners, about eighteen tradesmen (mechanics, electricians, welders, carpenters, fitters, riggers) and a similar number of tradesmen's helpers. CI supplied all the shaft sinking plant - headframe, winder/winder house, compressor plant, electrical substation, concrete batching plant, changing room, mine store/

timekeepers office, ventilation fans, pumps, injection equipment, drilling and mucking equipment, cable reels etc. Apart from HV electrical supply to the substation and a piped source of water, each shaft site was completely self contained. The Master Sinker had an Indian jeep and another jeep was available to the shift chargehand. All shafts worked three shifts/day, six days/week with Sundays used for plant maintenance and statutory plant and shaft and winder rope inspections. Because the ground was so heavily water bearing these sinkings were technically demanding and required really close supervision and planning. Fortunately for me Charlie, my Master Sinker, was a very experienced, long time employee of Cementation Mining, Doncaster and had worked all over the world. He was a marvelous, straight-talking Geordie, who knew I knew nothing about wet sinkings, but if push came to shove as Resident Engineer I carried the can!

The Chasnalla No 4 Shaft was 20ft diameter, concrete lined (nominal wall thickness 18in). Sinking was by a conventional drill/blast/muck routine inside an annulus of pre-cemented ground of approximately 110ft vertical extent. When we arrived at Chasnalla the shaft was down about 450ft and the last 20ft lift of concrete lining had just been completed to the shaft sump. A combination of centrifugal and sludge pumps kept the shaft bottom relatively dry. The next phase was drilling a spin pattern of sixteen pre-cementation injection holes. First 4in diam holes were drilled 12ft deep. Then a 3in diam mild steel (MS) tube with a full-flow valve was inserted into each of these holes and, in turn, injected with a quick setting cement grout. After this grouting, each MS steel tube was drilled out and pressure tested for fixture. Then Holman SL16 drifter rigs drilled 2.5in diam holes up to 110ft deep (drilling through the full-flow valves) in opposite pairs. When water was intersected the drill string was withdrawn and the valve shut. The opposite hole of the pair was drilled to a similar depth and likewise stopped and shut off when water intersected. Both holes were then connected to high pressure ram pumps and a thin grout, becoming progressively thicker, injected until the desired pressure was reached and the hole(s) would not accept any more grout. The next pair of holes, at 90 degrees to the first pair, would then be drilled under the same procedure. This opposite pairs routine continued until all sixteen holes had intersected the water horizon and been successfully grouted off. Opposite pairs of holes were then drilled out and deepened until the next water horizon was met and the grouting procedure repeated or the hole completed at a depth of 110ft In this manner an annulus of pre-cemented ground was prepared ahead of the actual shaft sinking activity.

Shaft sinking itself was conventional. 7ft deep holes 1.5in diam, were drilled by Holman Silver Bullet pluggers. The full round was fired electrically with AN60 gelignite. Mucking was by a cactus grab from an air driven traverser unit slung on the underside of the sinking scaffold. The muck was hoisted in two balanced hoppits to a headframe bin for removal by fifteen to twenty tonne capacity Tata trucks. Temporary shaft wall support was by expansion shell rock bolts and straps. Walling lengths were set at 20ft or five walling lengths per 110ft pre-cementation depth, giving 10ft safety overlap. Backsheets were held against the shaft wall by relief pipes bolted to the shaft tubbing. These relief pipes were used when "drying off" a walling length by injecting grout into them to seal the ground tight behind the backsheets. Both sinking and concrete walling were straightforward cyclic processes and well handled by the experienced crews. When the shaft was walling the surface crews had to closely monitor the concrete batching plant and water content of the concrete being pipelined down the shaft to a drop-box before distribution behind the tubbing. The really tricky part of the work was the pre-cementation drilling and grout injection. The long-hole drilling had to be very accurate for both inclination and spin angle and the grout injection pressure a reflection of increasing ground-water pressure with increasing shaft depth from surface. Charlie and his chargehands were experienced in this and my contribution was the accurate surveying of the pre-cementation holes. It was a slow process, but actual sinking rates were over 100 ft/month of finished shaft.

In the walled compound there were both IISCO and CI staff. The CI staff wives used to get together and have coffee mornings and a natter and at least once a week used to be driven into the Jharia market for food shopping. It was very hot (+100F) and humid so there was little activity in the daytime. In fact I couldn't get down the shaft quickly enough for although wet(ish) it was cooler than on surface. Most evenings our driver would drive us to the Jharia Club for a few beers and a chat with other IISCO and CI staff. There was an outside corner of the club where badminton could be played. After our Tassie experience both Gillian and I enjoyed the chance to take up badminton again. The club also supplied a limited number of paperback books which were much in demand. People also played bridge, rummy and chess and, of course, gossiped and drank. There was also a small outdoor swimming pool. With the general shortage of transport we often picked up the off duty chargehands and Charlie, when he didn't have the No 4 Shaft jeep.

In November there was the Indian festival of colours, Diwali. That day Charlie had walked across to our bungalow to hitch a ride to the shaft (or so he said). In fact I think it was a set-up. Charlie and I were waiting for my car to turn around when a group of CI miners appeared from nowhere and we were pelted with numerous bags of brightly coloured fine dust - the colours. Startling, at first, it was a good laugh as we both became bedraggled, brilliantly coloured clowns. It must have been arranged with the agreement of the IISCO compound guards. There were even more "colours" thrown when we got to the shaft site. At weekends we had a few trips out to local places of interest. One of these was a Jain temple atop a small hill some miles to the NW of Dhanbad. Gillian also visited a leper colony with one of the IISCO wives. One Sunday, as Christmas 1997 drew near, Marcus's wife Mazie, put on a drinks/lunch party in the garden of her (senior staff!) bungalow for CI staff. The five Resident Engineers and wives came bringing some of their respective chargehands and European engineering staff who could not squeeze into the sites jeeps. Charlie was nowhere to be found. The party was well under way when around the corner came a very merry Charlie riding an elephant, which proceeded to plod straight across Mazie's prize rose beds. It was, of course, Charlie's way of making a point to senior management about the lack of transport. I had to soothe the ruffled feathers of Marcus & Mazie, but to their credit, they saw the funny side of things.

In the new year Marcus asked me to visit a cement works and associated limestone quarry up near the Bihar State capital, Patna. The quarry, alongside the Ganges, was experiencing de-watering problems. Patna was about 160 miles NW of Dhanbad. I suspect Marcus selected me to go on account of my quarrying experience with both ARC and APCM. We planned a four day visit, two days travel, there and back, and two days investigating the quarry workings and local hydrology. Gillian came with me and Singh, our driver, drove the faithful Ambassador. This was our first real drive outside the immediate Jharia area and driving or rather being driven in India was definitely not for the faint hearted. As in the UK one drives on the left, but in India it had the appearance of being voluntary. Apart from local farmers, various livestock, countless bicycles, Ambassador cars, Royal Enfield 350cc Bullet motorbikes, Tata trucks and (overloaded) Tata buses there were the ubiquitous holy cows, where the key decision was whether to pass in front or behind the animal, irrespective of which part of the road that led one to. We were glad to arrive at the quarry manager's house in one piece, but then Singh was a very good driver for Indian conditions. We stayed in the cement company's guest house. It was of similar cement block construction to those a Chasnalla. However instead of a concrete bath there was a shower with an open hole in the concrete floor. The house seethed with mosquitoes and we spent a torrid night under a framed mosquito net, which unfortunately was more hole than mesh.

The next day I went to the large limestone quarry with the manager. It was a conventional blast-hole drill, shovel, truck operation with 40ft high benches with the long axis of the quarry parallel to the Ganges river. The river was approximately 600ft away. The manager wanted to know if it was possible to put in a cementation "curtain" between the river and the quarry to reduce the considerable ground-water inflow. I explained that this was not really practicable. They were quarrying a very permeable limestone and the simplest way to minimise ground-water inflow was by re-orienting the quarry through 90 degrees and to carry a decent sump ahead of the lowest production floor and equip this sump with large low-head centrifugal pumps. He also asked me to look at their drilling and blasting patterns as they were carrying out a lot of secondary blasting of oversize boulders from the primary bench blast. We agreed that the burden/spacing pattern was OK but I felt better explosive distribution within the holes, by some form of decking, to concentrate the explosive in the notably harder bands within the limestone would help. After these two days around the quarry and engineering offices Singh drove us back to Chasnalla. The visit gave us a good opportunity to see a large part of Bihar State.

By early 1968 we both felt we'd like to return to the UK and catch up with friends and family. Cementation Mining in Doncaster were very understanding and appreciative that we had "filled in" an unexpected RE vacancy at Chasnalla No 4 Shaft. We then heard from Gillian's elder sister Pat that she was coming to visit us in April! This was a lovely surprise and Gillian and I took the train from Dhanbad to Calcutta. There, we again stayed at The Great Eastern Hotel. On the expected arrival day we took a taxi to Dum Dum airport to meet Pat. We waited until everyone appeared to have left the plane only to observe Pat, ensconced in a wheel chair, being carried off the plane. Of course, we assumed she had imbibed a little too much on the flight (uncharitable thought!). In fact she had badly strained her ankle playing badminton at school a couple of days ago, but no way was Pat going to miss out on an Indian visit. We piled into a taxi, complete with Pat's crutch and headed for The Great Eastern Hotel. On arrival I forgot Pat's cases in the taxi whilst busy trying to ensure that she could hobble into the hotel. At reception we all looked at each other when the porter asked if he could take the luggage. No luggage - panic! Fortunately I remembered the name of the taxi company, hired another taxi from outside the hotel to take me there and eventually, after a little baksheesh, recovered the luggage - phew, vowed from now on to sharpen up and get my brain in gear. With Pat's injured foot and the heat and humidity we took things quietly for a couple of days before taking the Coalfields Express from Howrah to Dhanbad.

It was great company for Gillian to have Pat staying. They sampled the usual Jharia Club coffee mornings and evening drinks, but no badminton! I moved out of our bedroom and slept in the living room where the air conditioner made it tolerable. As it was now approaching the monsoon season it was very hot and sticky. An unexpected consequence of Pat's arrival was that I soared in the estimation of the No 4 Shaft Indian workers; the engineer Sahib had two wives! Charlie and the crew put on a great farewell lunch for us at the shaft offices and the "Sahib & two wives" were given flower garlands. Later that night Singh drove us to Dhanbad station to catch the midnight Kalka Mail Up express. Charlie and some of the No 4 Shaft chargehands turned up followed by a large group of turbaned Sikhs from the local contractor who supplied No 4 Shaft with sand & gravel. They all had bottles of Kingfisher beer shoved down their trousers, skirts or dhoti. A very lively platform party ensued, which was a great send off for us. We travelled air-conditioned class (ACC) on the express through to Varanasi (Benares), a distance of about 270 miles arriving in early morning. We detrained and checked into a local hotel and after a tidy up and late breakfast took a taxi to visit the Burning Ghats on the Ganges river. Then a taxi took us north to Sarnath to visit Buddha's sacred banyan tree at Bo'd Gaya. It was a very large tree! The next day we took another express to Agra, a journey of about 500 miles. The ACC train compartment was excellent and included ones own washing facilities and a steward to make innumerable cups of chai. We detrained at Agra and stayed at the Clarks Hotel overlooking the Taj Mahal. Viewed from the hotel, by moonlight, it looked quite ethereal and haunting. Next day, a close visit, was slightly disappointing, as this marvelous structure covered in mosaic, was in need of repair. The following day we boarded our final train for the 150 mile run into Delhi. Here we stayed in the old-fashioned, colonial style Janpath Imperial Hotel - hot and humid with no air conditioning.

Over the next few days we "did" Delhi. Coffee and drinks in Connaught Place; a tour round the colonial (Lutyens design) New Delhi government buildings; a visit to the huge Jama Masjid mosque; drinks at the swanky Oberoi Intercontinental and a trip out to the Red Fort where, unfortunately, Gillian suffered from heat-stroke and had to return to the hotel for a lie down and plenty of water. Next we went to Delhi airport and from there flew in an ancient Indian Airlines plane to Srinagar in Kashmir. The cool, clean mountain air was invigorating after the mugginess of Delhi. We stayed in The White Palace overlooking Dal Lake, an idyllic spot. Of course we took a shakira, water taxi, on the lake with their memorable heart shaped paddles. We wandered around the magnificent Mughal gardens with their numerous fountains and water features. Gillian and Pat did lots of shopping in the care of number-one guide! We took a taxi west to Gulmarg, past fields of dazzling saffron. Another day we drove east about thirty miles and from there hired three ponies for a trek up towards the Kolahoi glacier. We were glad the ponies were doing the hard work as we were at an elevation of well over 12,000ft To the north, maybe 75 miles away, the mountain Nanga Parbat dominated the horizon. After six days we flew back to Delhi, stayed one further night in the Janpath Hotel and the following day flew with Air France to Paris.

From Orly Airport the taxi took us on a very roundabout way into the centre of Paris. I attempted to remonstrate with the driver in my schoolboy French, to no avail. However he explained, in franglais, that several central Paris roads were blocked by rioting students. Welcome to Paris in May 1968. Eventually we reached our hotel, the quintessentially French, Hotel Littre near the Montparnasse tower. In the following days we "did" central Paris, including the Eiffel Tower, Louvre gallery, Isle de Cite, Champs

Elyse, Arc de Triomphe, the Bastille, Montmartre, Luxembourg gardens and used the carnet (of tickets) on the Metro. The student riots by then were winding down and we were able to enjoy the Paris Spring sunshine in a fair selection of outside cafes, bistros and restaurants. Then one final short hop to Heathrow. From there by taxi to Paddington, then train to Cornwall to visit Gillian's parents in St Mawgan, whilst Pat went home to Mawgan Porth. We stayed a week or so then Gillian and I headed for Tunbridge Wells, Kent, where we stayed with my parents. They had bought a weekend cottage at Northiam in East Sussex and after a while suggested that Gillian and I move in there, complete with phone and typewriter to begin the inevitable job hunt. But first we agreed we needed some wheels of our own rather than borrowing my Mum's car. We eventually found a second-hand, cream coloured Triumph GT6 in a garage just inland from Rye. It had had only one owner, had a low mileage and the price came under our budget. We duly purchased it and returned my Mum's car to Tunbridge Wells

8

I had, of course, been looking in the Mining Journal, EMJ, IMM Bulletin etc for a job in the UK as we had both decided that we'd like to settle back in England. Unsurprisingly most hard rock mining jobs were connected to the indigenous quarrying industry, but my brief exposure to this surface mining sector with both ARC in Cornwall and APCM in Scotland had convinced me that underground hard rock mining was more my forte. After several phone calls and a meeting at their London offices I was invited for an interview with the head of mining of the consulting firm of Robertson Research Co Ltd (RRCo) in Llanddulas, North Wales. We drove to North Wales and stayed in the small resort town of Colwyn Bay. It was wet, grey (slate) and depressing, but the interview seemed to go well and they said they would write with a firm job offer. When we got back to Brendon Cottage in Northiam there was a letter from RTZ Consultants Ltd (RTZC), inviting me for interview in their London offices in St James. A couple of days later I took the train to Charing Cross and walked to St James Square for an interview with Les, mining director of RTZC. He was an RSM graduate, but in spite of that (!), the interview went OK. As we finished up close to one o'clock Les asked me what I was doing for lunch (nothing), so why not join him at the Crown pub in Babmaes Street, next door to RTZ's back door. We went to the pub, found we had a common interest in decent bitter, rugby and women and got on like a house on fire. I don't recall eating anything, but we fell out of the pub about 3.30pm and Les said they would write with a job offer.

The following week I received job offers from both RRCo and RTZC, with similar salaries and fringe benefits. RRCo seemed the safer bet, besides it wasn't in London which I didn't fancy and RTZC was (then) predominantly a management consultancy, rather than an engineering consultancy. However the parent company, RTZ, was always in the news opening up new mining projects in South Africa, Canada, South America and Australia and was bound to need some engineering input (or so I convinced myself). Anyway after much discussion, including my parents, I accepted the RTZC offer with an agreed start date of 1st July 1968 (phew, big sigh of relief).

We then began an intensive look for somewhere to live. As I knew the south-east from London (Tunbridge Wells home) we decided to look for places to rent in the Tonbridge, Sevenoaks, Orpington area as trains from there go in to Charing Cross station and then it was an easy ten minute walk to the RTZ offices. Finally we found a smallish flint built cottage at Badgers Mount, a short distance from the top of Poll Hill on the North Downs. Knockholt station was only 1.5 miles away. The cottage, Molly Ash, was set on its own, alongside a field off a quiet lane with a simple garage for the GT6. Gillian obtained a job as a SRN at Sevenoaks hospital. Sevenoaks was only five miles further south and Gillian was able to make the 9am start having dropped me off at Knockholt station. I'd let her know what time I expected to be back and she would pick me up. I had become a commuter, something I said I'd never do. The stopping train from Knockholt took about forty minutes to Charing Cross. It was often a scrum to get a seat and I really didn't enjoy commuting at all having got used to living near the mine or shaft site. Another thing I didn't enjoy was wearing a collar and tie together with a suit. Gillian had to persuade me to go to Austen Reeds to purchase the required "consultant's business ensemble".

My first job at RTZC involved checking ore reserve calculations for Mary Kathleen Uranium (MKU) mine in Northern Territory, Australia. John, another RTZC consultant, was currently at MKU preparing a new optimised open-pit design. A lot of my checking work involved going to the CSC computer offices in Shaftsbury Avenue and feeding punched cards into the machine's maw. I had very little idea what I was doing and felt if my work continued in this vein I would either be given the sack for incompetence or would quit because I couldn't hack it. All in all the first few months at RTZC were not enjoyable. I shared an office with two Rogers, both management whizz kids, computer literate and very bright. They used to help me with the computer punched cards and basically kept me afloat in meeting the deadline for recalculating the MKU ore reserve. I had met Ken, the Managing Director of RTZC, who was a hot-shot mathematician and singularly unimpressed by practical mining engineers. Oh dear my future did not look very rosy, since the bulk of RTZC's work was management consultancy for RTZ group companies (eg the open-pit design study for MKU). Just in time (for me at least) the Tanganyika Concessions (TC) company asked RTZC to undertake an appraisal of the Benguela Railway, which runs from the southern Congo/Zambian copper belt region to Benguela on the Angolan Atlantic coast. With a booming demand for finished copper out, and mining supplies in TC wished to expand the capacity of the single track railway. TC wished RTZC to carry out a financial evaluation of their project, the Cubal Variant, which comprised double tracking the line as it climbed from the coastal plain. It was a fairly straightforward linear programming exercise initially with a discounted cash flow (DCF) financial evaluation tacked on at the end. With major help from the two Rogers (on the computer programming) I managed to complete the task and the client, TC, seemed happy. At last I felt I'd contributed to RTZC.

The next assignment was really interesting and from my point of view a doddle. The owner of Swanworth Quarries, sited on the Isle of Purbeck, wished to sell the quarry as a going concern. Again this would be a DCF valuation based on future earnings. I set off to the quarry with a young geological assistant from Riofinex, an RTZ head office exploration company. First we undertook a plane table and levelling survey of the quarry property. We followed this with geological mapping and then an inventory of all quarrying, crushing, screening, haulage etc plant and equipment. We then collected operating cost data as well as sales data for the various quarry products. Finally we asked the quarry to drill four vertical holes (with a compressed air Halco DTH rig) at the extremities of the lowest bench through the Portland stone until they reached the Kimmeridge Clay. This was very easily identifiable since it contained tar. In this manner we determined the vertical extent of the Portland stone (the main quarry product) which together with the surface survey and geological interpretation enabled us to calculate the total remaining stone reserve. At this time a new Roll-On Roll-Off ferry terminal was under construction in Poole harbour. There was a huge demand for low quality fill (LQF) and Swanworth had a huge dump of this overburden material stripped to uncover the Portland stone. As the closest major quarry to Poole harbour this LQF added considerable (immediate) value to the quarry. Anyway our valuation was much higher than the owner anticipated and later that year the quarry was successfully sold. I really enjoyed this job as it was hands-on and not just a paper exercise.

During 1967/68 the Australian arm of RTZ, CRA had explored the huge Panguna copper/gold deposit on Bouganville Island in Papua New Guinea

(PNG). It was now under evaluation and detailed project engineering was being undertaken by an American joint venture, Bechtel-WKE, out of their San Francisco (SF) offices. RTZ were now establishing an Owner's Team in SF and much to my amazement Ken and Les put my name forward as the mining member of this team. It was accepted and Gillian and I scurried around in Molly Ash collecting our things to be packed into store. I was pleased to be out of commuting and as before Gillian's response had been "well we haven't been there". We whizzed down to Cornwall in the car to see Gillian's parents and then I headed back to Tunbridge Wells to see mine. Gillian stayed in Cornwall initially and I once again headed for Heathrow having also put the GT6 in store.

CRA's "man in SF", Ron, had booked me into the Clift Hotel in downtown SF. He was very helpful, introducing me to the Bechtel-WKE project team as well as other engineering staff in the main Bechtel offices on 50 Beale Street. Both Ron and the personnel people at Bechtel helped me to find a small, one bedroom apartment at 1204 Crystal Towers, 2140 Taylor Street, about five blocks back from Fishermans Wharf. From the apartment it was a twenty minute walk to the Bechtel-WKE project offices. Once established in the apartment, now complete with telephone (installed in one day! what a change from the UK, where one had to wait weeks) it was all clear for Gillian to join me asap. The buzz and modernity of SF was a huge change from staid London, notwithstanding the Swinging Sixties. We experienced our first supermarket, Safeway, close to the apartment on the junction of Columbus and Taylor. The choice of just about everything was mind blowing. It certainly made food shopping easy and exciting. The central, downtown, location of the apartment meant that we had no need for a car. We walked everywhere or used the marvelous cable cars, which criss-crossed the city. Our apartment, up on the 12th floor, provided a great view over Fishermans Wharf to Alcatraz island out in the Bay. We bought a "Stack Chart" so that we could identify the funnel markings on numerous freighters and passenger liners who docked just by the Embarcadero Freeway.

The RTZ/CRA Owners team rapidly expanded to six people. Reini, a Canadian, was The Owners Representative and his SF team comprised four Australians (all from CRA group companies), Ron the project engineer, Brian a mechanical engineer, Ken an electrical engineer and Colin a financial analyst. As the mining input I was the only Brit on the team. The ultimate client operating company was Bougainville Copper on Bougainville Island in PNG. The mining project team developing the open-pit design for a 100,000 tonnes/day operation was based in CRA's offices in Melbourne, Australia. My initial job was to check and monitor Bechtel-WKE's tender specifications for blast-hole drills, rope face shovels, diesel &/or diesel-electric haul trucks, motor graders, track dozers, wheel loaders, blast-hole pump trucks etc that these met the design requirements of the Melbourne mining project team. Their design indicated a stripping ratio of circa 1 to 1.5 so that the mining operation needed to shift 250,000 tonnes/day, an enormous earth moving exercise. Obviously both Brian, the mechanical engineer and Ken, the electrical engineer were very involved in these technical tender specifications. Later I became heavily engaged in ascertaining the merits or otherwise of several slurry explosive suppliers bids, whilst Colin, the financial analyst was much in demand determining the capital, operating and replacement cost implications for the various items of plant and equipment.

After three months the Melbourne project mining team suggested it would be beneficial for me to visit the island to appreciate at first hand the working conditions. I thus flew to Sydney, changed planes and flew on up to Port Moresby, PNG. There I switched to an old DC3 for the flight to Lae, Buka Island and Bougainville. Everything went OK until we took off from Buka when there was a "minor fire" in one of the engines and the pilot very rapidly put us back down onto the Buka strip. No harm done we all deplaned safely and there we were stuck for 48 hours until a replacement DC3 from Moresby could be found. We all stayed in the airstrip hut, about eight of us, and someone found a source of local beer so we celebrated ANZAC day in style. The activity on Bougainville Island was manic. Bechtel-WKE had more than 7000 workers building a 35MW power station; developing a deep water port; building a road from port to mine site over a rugged 2500ft mountain range; erecting a 100,000 tonnes/day copper/gold concentrator and pre-stripping the mining area of tropical jungle and glutinous lateritic overburden. Every day at around 2 pm the tropical rain steamed down for around 2.5 to 3 hours, during which visibility was greatly reduced and mine site roads became mud-runs. It was easy to see why the Melbourne project mining team had specified mechanical drive haul trucks rather than the more modern diesel-electric wheel units. I also spent time in the exploration crews helicopter getting a good aerial view of how the whole site fitted together. After this site familiarisation week it was back to SF via Port Moresby and Sydney.

This first hand evidence of the very heavy tropical rainfall at the mine site indicated that in-pit drainage would be a major design consideration. I had to estimate total quantities of rainfall run-off to be handled in operating years one through five to ten years and beyond. Basic rainfall data, including Intensity-Duration-Frequency (IDF) curves, was provided by PNG meteorological station in Lae and limited river gauging data on the Kaverong river which ran through the Panguna mine site. How to handle these huge water volumes once the side-cut pit was below river level? Basically there were two solutions; either pump it through a pre-developed drainage shaft or develop a low level drainage tunnel beneath the ultimate pit outline. I collected all the necessary costs (capital, construction, operating, replacement) for shaft sinking, tunneling and pumps etc and Colin "tumbled the numbers" to arrive at Net Present Value (NPV) for both alternatives at various time periods. This clearly indicated the shaft/pumps alternative as the way to go, albeit based on the somewhat limited hydrological data we had available. It was a fascinating exercise and stimulated in me a lasting interest in rainfall, ground-water and natural hydrological phenomena.

On the social/leisure side SF kept us very busy. We went around dozens of art galleries and saw a Royal Ballet performance danced by Fonteyn & Nureyev. We ate at Fishermans Wharf and Ghiradeli Square. Visited Macys and the Top of the Mark hotel. Tried plenty of different cocktails but settled on a dacquiri for her and whisky sour for him. I initially hired a VW Beetle (European & familiar) but soon found it a real pain to drive on the numerous, steep SF hills. Rapidly moved on to an automatic iconic Ford Mustang, which was great. We drove north over the Golden Gate bridge into Marin County and visited the Muir Woods reserve to see the giant Redwood trees. Then down to the Sausaulito Yacht Club where one of the Bechtel guys took me sailing (as crew) out on the Bay. I couldn't believe how cold the Bay water was. We drove across the Bay Bridge to Oakland and drove around Berkley Uni. Then through the tunnel and out into the hot dry country towards Sacramento. Another time the old Mustang carried us out to the vineyards of the Napa valley. We also had a great trip south down the coast through Big Sur, Salinas, Monterey (John Steinbeck country) and Carmel, which was very attractive. In SF itself it was just the end of Haight-Ashbury and Flower Power, but the topless/bottomless revolution was in full swing up around Broadway. There was Carol Doda's (the biggest pair in the west), Finnochios (Gay bar/club) and a whole host of very bare strip clubs. When Gillian's sister Pat came to stay we even had a Topless Breakfast with nude dancers in high heels on the table! It all seemed very avant garde in 1969. An interesting sideline developed in my work for Bougainville Copper. When various senior metallurgists, miners and engineers from CRA, Melbourne appeared for discussions with Bechtel-WKE, I was often deputed to take them around the more raunchy strip clubs. A young English lass living in the Crystal Towers worked as a stripper (complete with blonde wig) in one of the clubs. She and I had a deal. I would bring the visiting Australian "firemen" to her club (it put her in good stead with the club owners) if, at the end of her "strip", she would run down the aisle and leap onto my lap. The "firemen" were very impressed by this and didn't ask me too many awkward questions about mining aspects!

We had a very memorable evening with Ron and his wife at their nearby apartment watching a clear moon as Neil Armstrong stepped out onto the lunar surface. It was surreal looking at the moon and imagining these guys walking on it as we looked on. Sometime in our ten months stay in SF we experienced our first earthquake, which was very scary. It was about 10.30 pm, Gillian was washing in the bathroom and I was sitting on the sofa looking out at the lights of Alcatraz beyond Fishermans Wharf. All of a sudden the apartment's floor began rippling and one could feel the whole building sway and tremble. The movement slopped the water out of the washbasin onto the floor. We huddled on the sofa not sure what to do, listening to the local radio DJ giving a live broadcast on the quake. Apparently it was "only" a 5.6 magnitude on the Richter Scale with an epicentre at Santa Rosa about fifty miles north of SF along the infamous San Andreas Fault. The shaking of the building abated after about five minutes and we ventured onto the exterior access passageway to exchange comments with our neighbours from adjacent apartments. I certainly thought it was quite a significant quake, but the locals were much more sanguine and said they'd get one or two similar ones most years.

With the award of all major mining equipment contracts my work at Bechtel-WKE's offices was winding down and a recall to RTZC, London seemed imminent. However the CRA project mining team in Melbourne requested my presence there to continue discussions on the slurry explosive supply contract and the integration of my hydrological findings into their detailed open-pit design. RTZC, London agreed and so we were on the move once again after a very stimulating stay in SF. We arrived in Melbourne, via Sydney and the old chestnut of "put your clocks back twenty years" as you arrive from San Francisco seemed fairly apposite. Someone on the CRA project mining team had found us rented accommodation at Flat 4, 372 Orrong Road, Caulfield, a north Melbourne suburb. It was quiet and for me an easy No 64 tram commute into CRA's offices on Collins Street. I had met Dick, the project mining engineer and Ron, the Bougainville mine site manager, on their visits to Bechtel-WKE's offices in SF, so there were some familiar faces. Mike, another RTZC consultant, was the chief open-pit design engineer. He was working closely with Ken (RTZC's MD) who had developed a variable cut-off grade strategy to drive the open-pit design computer program. This computer design stuff was quite beyond me, but we had some fierce discussions on the slurry explosive supply contract, since an RTZ group company, IRECO Chemicals, had been lobbying senior RTZ and CRA management to get the contract. I was not popular, since, with the Bechtel-WKE mining guys, we had recommended an ICI-Nobel supplier. I thought "here we go again as at EZ on the shaft contract". I was summoned to see the head Bougainville Project honcho, Frank. He said we had to award the contract to IRECO. I said their product/cost was quite inferior to ICI-Nobel. I was instructed to tell IRECO to rebid on similar slurry specifications to ICI-Nobel and cut their price a significant percentage. Of course, IRECO got the job (apparently huge pressure from RTZ, London) and once again I was the sacrificial stool-pigeon, not a side of big business I like. With the slurry explosive contract out of the way I had a much more rewarding time scheduling the shaft/pump pit drainage scheme into the open-pit design.

Melbourne was a pleasant, somewhat staid city. Gillian and I enjoyed the serenity of the nearby Botanical Gardens. We had no car, but Melbourne with an extensive tram system made getting around easy. There were the usual Friday night get-togethers with the project mining team in various pubs and restaurants in the city. Over Christmas 1969 we met up with Fred (the English dentist) and his Danish wife, Bodil. They had been good close friends during our time at Rosebery in Tasmania. They were moving to New Zealand to be close to one of their sons. In many ways it was a highlight of our short stay in Melbourne, reminiscing about the west coast of Tasmania. Like us I think they were glad to move on to new pastures.

I received a telephone call from Ken, RTZC's MD asking me to go up to the Philippines where RTZC had recently been engaged to sort out a grade control problem at the Mankayan mine of Lepanto Consolidated Mining Company (Lepanto). John, the RTZC consultant who had been working at MKU was now up in Manila having taken over from Ken as RTZC site representative. Gillian, as usual, was quite relaxed and in truth glad to leave Australia for the third and she hoped, last time. Thus around late February 1970 we flew to Sydney and then on to Manila International Airport (MIA). After the relative calm and organisation of Australian airports MIA was completely mad. Outside the terminal the forecourt heaved with greeters & meeters and of course it was hot and humid. Someone from the Lepanto office picked us up and took us to the Intercontinental Hotel in the new Makati business area. We were booked in there for three nights. The air-conditioned Intercon was very pleasant with a lovely, peaceful piano bar. Later John, the RTZC consultant, turned up and we had dinner together in the hotel. The next day John and I visited the Lepanto offices on Roxas Boulevard in downtown Manila alongside the bay, where I met Dave, a CSM graduate who was now a Lepanto Exec VP. I had known Dave at Camborne, (he graduated in 1956) and he had already spent several years working in the Philippines at Altlas Consolidated on Cebu Island. He confirmed my visual impression that Manila was a crazy, vibrant but violent city. He also said that (President) Marcos presided over a thoroughly corrupt government with the police and military all taking bribes (surprise, surprise). He arranged for us all to fly up to the mine the next day in Lepanto's Beech King Air plane and made Ponciano, the Lepanto driver, available for us to look around Manila that night. Together with John we decided to go and watch the Hai-a-lai (similar to Spanish pelota) and have a meal at the stadium restaurant. It was quite an education. The city had a real Wild West feel with many Filipinos openly carrying guns. Ponciano's presence was reassuring and we could see at first hand how he handled the police at road intersections with a five or ten peso note tucked inside his driving licence. He always replaced the "licence inspection fee" before driving off again. The colourful Jeepeneys and huge 3ft deep storm drains alongside the roads were also memorable.

We left the Intercon early, Ponciano driving us to the private plane terminal at MIA. The Lepanto King Air plane was very luxuriously equipped with balut shakers & dice as well as a bar. Vic, ex Philippines Air Force, was the pilot on the 150 mile flight due north to Lepanto. Once clear of Manila he climbed to 10,500ft thus ensuring he would clear the Philippines highest peak, Mt Pulog 9600ft which was just to the east of the Lepanto mine. The mine itself was situated on the western flank of Mt Pulog at an elevation of 3800ft The airstrip was short (500m only) and cut into a mountain spur, one end being a sheer rock face! Vic took the plane well down the western valley before turning through 180 degrees to make a perfect (albeit for first time passengers heart-in-mouth) landing, stopping 100 yards before the rock face at the end of the airstrip. Welcome to Lepanto; little did I realise that this would be my home, on & off, for most of the next two years as well as regular visits over the following ten years.

Lepanto was a 3,200 tonnes/day underground copper/gold mine accessed through a series of adits driven in from the side of a steep valley. It was a completely self contained operation comprising the mine itself, crushing and screening plant, a flotation concentrator, thickeners, backfill plant, 14MW diesel power plant, full mechanical/electrical/fabrication/timber/and paint workshops. A fleet of 15-tonne capacity Peterbilt trucks hauled the 31% grade copper concentrate a distance of 163km to the west coast port of Poro Point, San Fernando, La Union. The Peterbilt trucks took a tremendous hammering on the Halsema Mountain Trail, as it rose to 7400ft on the Mankayan-Baguio section. From Poro Point the concentrate was loaded onto freighters for the long sea voyage to the American, Smelting & Refining Co (ASARCO) smelter at Puget Sound, Seattle, USA. The Lepanto copper concentrate largely comprised enargite, a copper/arsenic mineral and ASARCO's Tacoma, Seattle smelter was one of the few that could handle the toxic arsenic content. Of course Lepanto was penalised for the arsenic content but, in fact, ASARCO was reputed to be the largest supplier of arsenic compounds (eg for weed killers) in North America. The senior management at the mine was American with, of course, a Filipino workforce.

The mine had standardized on two basic methods of stoping. Flat-back cut-and-fill and square-set. The former method, used de-slimed mill tailings for fill and was used as the normal virgin ground method whilst conventional square-setting was used for pillar recovery and heavy ground conditions. The general application was that flat-back stopes were cut longitudinally (ie along the strike) if the ore width was less than 10m and transversely, with intermediate rib pillars, if the ore width was greater than 10m. Horizontal 2m thick stoping slices were taken by breasting with Holman Silver 303 jacklegs drilling 38mm diameter 2.2m depth holes. These were charged with 45% gelignite or, increasingly, ammonium nitrate/fuel oil (ANFO) fired with millisecond electric delays. Stope mucking was done by 25/40 HP two-drum electric scrapers pulling a 1m bucket. The scraped ore passed through 25 to 30cm gauge grizzlies to conventional ore passes or stope chutes. The mine was tracked, 24in gauge, and main haulage was concentrated on the 900 Level where 6, 8 and 10 tonne trolley locos hauled rakes of twelve 120 cu ft rotary dump cars. An annual lateral development of 3500 to 4000 metres of 3m x 3m size, maintained an ore reserve depletion rate plus 10%. The development was conventional with jackleg drilling, blasting with gelignite and half second electric delays. Mucking was with overshot loaders to side dump cars hauled by 4 or 6 tonne battery locos.

My main task was to appraise the whole mining process to see where improvements and cost savings could be made. Firstly this necessitated the re-classification of the ore reserves by individual ore lens and by each mine level. These new classifications also incorporated an Ore Reserve Factor (ORF) and Mine Call Factor (MCF) which had recently been determined by RTZC during their statistical analysis of sampling methods and assaying techniques. Next a comprehensive deep diamond drilling programme below the mine's lowest level, 900, was extended to locate and prove new reserves down a further 200m to the 700 Level. A full mine ventilation survey was also instigated as it was apparent that working conditions inby on the 900 level were poor with high virgin rock temperature (VRT) and slow blasting smoke clearance. A start was also made on geotechnical rock classification of individual ore bodies as well as host hangingwall and footwall rocks. All of these investigations required a strengthening of the Lepanto mining engineering department and both the mining and geological local staff were very supportive and enthusiastic.

On the personal side Lepanto had provided a very nice "ranch style" guest house for use by RTZC staff. The climate was pleasantly warm and not humid (unlike Manila) at this altitude and cool enough in the evenings to often warrant an open log fire. Most of the steep surrounding slopes were covered with pine trees; it was a very pleasant mine site! Although the mine had a sizeable timber cutting concession (for square-set mining) most of this was sited higher up the flanks of Mount Pulog. Social activities comprised bridge playing evenings with some of the American staff and weekly attendance at ten-pin bowling nights at the rink located near the concentrator. Lepanto had also provided a car for use by RTZC staff so that they could drive to the Chinese general store located just outside the mine security gate. Another RTZC member, James, joined John and me, but Gillian was the only RTZC wife present. There was a social club, with a well stocked bar, and the Filipinos seemed to organize some music and a dance at any and every opportunity. They were very cheerful, happy-go-lucky people. At one of the club social nights John and I "performed" the Beatles number Yellow Submarine, bobbing up & down making strangled buzzing sounds - it went down a storm. The Filipinos love to see you relaxing and making a bit of a fool of yourself.

Gillian and I "borrowed" the car over one long weekend and drove to Baguio City, staying at the lovely Pines Hotel, which was splendidly relaxing after the heart stopping drive over the Halsema Mountain Trail. Meeting a returning Lepanto Peterbilt concentrate truck on a blind bend against a sheer rock face with a 1000ft drop on the other side was definitely interesting. Baguio was a very pleasant city (the government moves offices up from Manila to Baguio in the typhoon season) and there was plenty to see and do. After that we drove down to the west coast at Poro Point. Here the immediate dock/wharves area was surrounded by stunning tropical beaches whilst offshore the "Thousand Islands" sparkle in the Lingayen Gulf. It was a beautiful peaceful unspoilt area so different from the hurley burley, heat and humidity of Manila. On another trip from Lepanto we drove north along the Cordillera Central towards Bontoc and the famous Banaue rice terraces. They are truly amazing climbing thousands of feet up the very steep sides of the Cordillera. They must have taken thousands of years to develop by hand. The only non-human power in their cultivation was provided by the ubiquitous water buffalo. Often there were small wooden carved "Rice Gods" placed on the edge of the terraces. On the drive back to Lepanto we stopped at the Sagada Caves in an area of limestone. The caves were very extensive and contained huge numbers of ancient skeletons, which had religious significance to the local people.

On arrival back at Lepanto we had a letter from my father saying he had found a suitable old farmhouse for sale in the village of Woodchurch, about three miles from where they now lived in High Halden, Kent. My father had responded to our recent request to look for an old farmhouse that we could "do up". He enclosed detailed plans of the house set in 1.5 acres with an attached 3.5 acres of old apple orchard. We trusted the old man, he was after all a chartered surveyor and had been in the estate agency business for years. We sent a cable back saying go ahead buy it (sight unseen by either of us - amazing!). Vic flew us down to Manila in the other Lepanto plane, a twin engined Beech Baron, and after a night in the Intercon, Gillian flew off to the UK. I went back to Lepanto for a further couple of weeks to tie up some loose ends in our mining investigations. Then Vic flew me back to Manila and I also flew back to the UK wondering what our very first house purchase would be like.

So after twelve years marriage and setting up home sixteen times from Stoke to Tanganyika then Cornwall, Queensland, Tasmania, Kent, Cornwall (again), Scotland, Tasmania (again), India, Sussex, Kent, California, Victoria and the Philippines we were finally to get a place of our own. It was quite a shock. The farmhouse, Beales, was completely run-down, full of junk and surrounded by tatty, half tumbled-down corrugated iron sheds. However my father assured us that the basic building, a fifteenth century, balloon-frame timber house with later brick cladding and tile hanging was quite sound - phew, well that's alright then! Seriously if either Gillian or I had seen it we would have run a mile, but my father could see the potential and he was right. As we had been away in San Francisco, Melbourne and Lepanto successively for sixteen months RTZC allowed me to immediately take three weeks leave and more importantly arranged a 90% house mortgage through the RTZ group. We collected our bits & pieces from store along with the old Triumph GT6. My father, who was renovating another property in Sussex, arranged for his gang of tradesmen - carpenter, brickie, plumber and decorator to come over and size up the job of renovating Beales. In the meantime Gillian and I, assisted by my parents, began to tear down the corrugated iron sheds and clear the house of mountains of junk. This was moved in numerous skips with a final clean up by a group of gypsies. The house stank of cat's piss so extensive fumigation was the order of the day. Needless to say Beales resembled a building site for the next six months or so. The professional tradesmen were a great gang - can do - and I learnt a great deal about renovating an old house. However the experience of owning ones own dilapidated farmhouse very quickly introduced me to the delights (!) of DIY.

All to soon I had to go back to work with RTZC. I used to drive the eight miles to Ashford station and catch the 8.10 train to Charing Cross. This was due in at 9.20 followed by a ten minute walk to the RTZC offices in the RTZ head office in St James's Square. Once again I had become a (long distance) commuter. At the same time Gillian became an Agency Nurse at the nearby Benenden Chest Hospital (for Post Office employees). This required another set of wheels and we purchased an ancient blue Ford Anglia van from the garage in High Halden. We also decided that Beales definitely needed a large dog to complete the rustic image. We located a pedigree Old English sheepdog puppy (pedigree name Halsall Jolly Roger) and Gillian collected a terrified mutt in a wire sided crate from Euston Station. He (the puppy) travelled on the train from Charing Cross to Ashford peering out of Gillian's shopping bag! Our logic for getting the puppy (now named Matt) so quickly was that with Beales as a building site, puppy training would be finished before renovations were complete. In fact Matt was amazingly easy to house train. He grew at a tremendous rate and really enjoyed human company. An interesting feature of the Old English sheepdogs is that they do not roam and Matt in particular seemed to have little interest in other dogs or bitches. Matt's presence ensured that I had plenty of exercise taking him around the orchard morning and evening (when daylight allowed) together with longer treks at the weekend. It was the start of becoming "dog people" for the next 38 years. Matt quickly came to love Gillian's Ford van, which in effect became his mobile "basket".

On returning to work at RTZC my first job entailed developing an organisation study for Yorkshire Potash. Obviously not a "hands-on engineering" job, more in the nature of a management consulting activity.

However I found that my project experience at both Rosebery and San Francisco was helpful. This job also introduced me to the City for the first time. One of the client company's directors was also a director of the bankers Kleinwort Benson (KB) and my first meeting with them took place in KB's private dining room in the City. This was very luxurious and a far cry from my experience of mining camp single mens bunkhouse mess facilities. But hey, variety is the spice of life and anyway I had to get used to wearing a collar/tie and jacket, never my favourite form of apparel. I had plenty of discussions with their project team in Yorkshire, most of which hinged on their desire to handle project management in-house as opposed to the use of an external engineer-constructor such as Davy McKee, Bechtel or Fluor. The latter approach had the considerable advantage of providing large numbers of experienced project engineers at short notice. They are then "off" the client company's books when the project is complete. I guess nowadays this would be called outsourcing!

Another "desk-job" followed. The client was British Steel (Tubes Division) and they wished to promote the use of structural hollow section (SHS) steel in mining. An obvious application to this type of structural steel section was for buntons and guides in deep mine shafts passing large volumes of ventilation air. I developed a brochure entitled - SHS in Deep Mine Shafts. Obviously all the technical specifications of the various SHS sizes were provided by British Steel whilst I outlined the structural loading requirements for fixed buntons and guides handling large skips (up to thirty tonnes capacity) hoisted at speeds of up to 3000 ft/min from depths of 8000ft A typical large concrete lined circular shaft was illustrated handling a large cage and counterweight together with twin balanced bottom dump skips. The reduction in overall steel weight (compared to regular RSJs and top-hat style guides) greatly favoured the use of SHS buntons and rectangular hollow section (RHS) guides. Another major plus point for this type of fixed shaft steelwork was their smaller frontal area, which reduced ventilation friction losses. My old employer, Cementation Mining, assisted with photographs of their SHS fabricated Tynagh Mine Headframe in Ireland, as well as a seven deck sinking scaffold.

On the social side we got to know several of our neighbours in and around Woodchurch and used to repair to the Six Bells pub in the village.

Peter, the Underground Manager from the Kiabakari mine in Tanganyika, by chance, happened to live nearby. We used to play bridge with him and his French wife Terry and often on a Saturday morning Peter and I would go for a pint or two in the Eight Bells pub in Tenterden to be joined for lunch by Gillian and Terry. The publican, Jack, was a really convivial guy and used to sit on the customers side of the bar and join in the chit chat. To help maintain the 3.5 acre orchard at Beales Gillian bought an ancient Villiers 2-stroke Allen Scythe from Ashford Cattle Market and that same day I bought Gillian a fancy hat in London - no gender type casting then! The Allen Scythe was a pig to start, but once running made short work of the long grass in the orchard - it was certainly easier, quicker and much more effective than the traditional scythe I had foolishly imagined I could manage. Charles, a near neighbour, had a large paddock for horses and he and I agreed to buy an old grey Ferguson tractor to assist with our respective land jobs. The Fergie had a four cylinder TVO engine that required warming with burning paraffin on the cylinder head, a forerunner to modern diesel glow-plugs. We both appreciated the little tractor's power take-off and soon understood how this early, pre WW2 tractor was the start of the mechanisation of farming.

Very soon I had to head back to Lepanto in the Philippines. The local mine engineering staff had just completed basic geotechnical and ventilation surveys of the mine. Each survey had identified a new, key factor. The geotechnical survey had identified a major section of the mine with good, strong Class 2 ground suitable for open stoping and the ventilation survey that heat-stroke conditions were predicted on the new, deeper 700 Level. Additionally the mine was dangerously short of jackhammer spares for the Holman Silver 303 machines. We had extensive discussions with the Manila representative of Holmans, but it was apparent that Holmans' Cornish factory was unable (or unwilling) to guarantee the required quantity of consumable jackhammer spares. We had crisis talks with other mining equipment manufacturers (eg Ingersoll Rand, Gardner-Denver, SIG etc) but it soon became evident that only the Japanese firm of Toyo could deliver both new jackhammers in our time frame and support them with consumable spares. Toyo also indicated that they could immediately supply a new, compact wagon drill rig mounting a 4in drifter, which appeared suitable for trial underground blast-hole stoping at Lepanto.

Armed with a Lepanto Letter of Intent (LoI) I flew from Manila to Tokyo, Japan for a meeting with the Toyo Rock Drill Company. I was taken around their manufacturing plant and spent considerable time at their test mine. The Toyo TY-280 jackleg (based, I believe, on an Ingersoll Rand JR-38 drill) was a simple, robust machine with good penetration rates in medium to hard ground. It seemed an ideal replacement for the Holman Silver 303 and on behalf of Lepanto I confirmed their order for 100 units for immediate delivery. Toyo also demonstrated their new TYW3 wagon drill mounting a TY-150B drifter. They agreed to make one of these units available to Lepanto for testing underground and to provide the necessary after-sales service with a new local Manila representative. The visit to Toyo was all very amicable and efficient. Unfortunately because of time constraints I only had one afternoon to have a quick look around Tokyo. The overriding impression was (unsurprisingly) of a densely crowded city with frenetic traffic, huge garish neon signs and everyone very polite, helpful and wanting to try out their English. I headed back to Manila with the good news of the immediate supply of Toyo rock drills.

Up at the mine again, courtesy of Vic and the Beech Baron, we had a senior management review of predicted ventilation conditions for the new, deeper 700 Level. The steep topography on the flanks of Mount Pulog had, of course, determined that the Lepanto mine was developed through adits, which, also provided gravity drainage of any ground-water or introduced mining water. Thus Lepanto had instigated the development of this new, deeper 700 Level. This adit was being driven by an American contractor from Tucson, Arizona. At this time the adit had been driven about 3Km of a total projected length of approximately 8Km required to reach the projected ore position on the 700 Level. The adit cross section was nominally 4m by 4m unlined. It was immediately apparent that this new 700 Level adit would be quite incapable of in-casting the required quantity of fresh intake ventilation air. Additionally the long intake length (8Km) would ensure that this intake air was anything but fresh, obviously approaching the high ambient VRT at this mine depth. What to do? The obvious solution was to stop the 700 Level adit and compensate the American tunnelling contractor.

Then immediately plan a new surface shaft sited close to the coordinates of the centre of gravity of the orebodies on the 700 Level, suitably modified by geotechnical considerations of the hangingwall and footwall rocks.

I spent the next few months working closely with Lepanto's mine engineering guys designing this major shaft installation. The major design parameter was ventilation; the need to intake and exhaust 425,000 CFM.. The final design comprised a 22ft diameter concrete lined shaft of overall depth from surface of 731m, or just under 2400ft. From surface to the 950 Level the shaft would be divided by a brattice wall to enable downcast (fresh air) to enter the mine below the 900 Level and also enable vitiated (exhaust air) from the 700 Level to 900 Level mining block to rapidly exit the mine. The downcast, intake air would arrive at the planned stoping areas by the shortest possible distance (less than 800m) and thus combat heat-stroke conditions when ambient temperatures exceeded 95 degrees F. An internal winder chamber was designed to enable ore hoisting/man handling/equipment etc for the 700 - 900 mining block. Obviously we also had to incorporate extensive pumping facilities, below the 700 Level, to deliver mine water to the 900 Level main haulage and drainage adit.

The mine management decided that this major specialist underground development could not be handled in-house but must, necessarily, be put out to contract. Thus on the basis of our overall design criteria I developed two contract packages, one for detailed design and one for construction. Enquires in Manila indicated that there were no suitable Filipino firms to carry out either of the proposed contracts. Lepanto then issued me with a LoI to negotiate with Cementation Mining (CM) for the execution of both the design and construction contracts. Because of the numerous unknowns these were essentially Schedule of Rates contracts with time based bonus/penalty clauses. Armed with the LoI I returned to the UK and spent the next few weeks in Doncaster in detailed discussions with CM. Having agreed an outline design contract Schedule of Rates CM immediately sent a team of shaft sinking project engineers to Lepanto to ascertain all the relevant local conditions/supplies etc before returning to Doncaster to complete detailed design of the shaft and associated facilities. CM also drew up a subcontract with GHH of West Germany to design/supply internal shaft brattice, steelwork, loading & unloading stations, cage and counterweight and twin bottom dump skips. All CM's designs were passed through me at RTZC's London office for vetting/comment before airmailing to Manila for Lepanto's ultimate approval. The mine had set up a dedicated new shaft unit, so that appraisal and approval/change comment was made quickly. My work at RTZC was completely taken up by the Lepanto/CM Tubo Shaft project. (Lepanto had named the proposed new shaft - Tubo - after the Filipino for tube). Final designs were approved after four months and CM immediately mobilised their shaft sinking plant and equipment from Doncaster to Manila. Unsurprisingly the most difficult part of the mobilisation was the transport of the main sinking double-drum winder and air compressors on the Halsema Mountain Trail between Baguio and Mankayan/Lepanto. After my intense work for Lepanto over the past nine months, the mine management requested a "pause" so that their own Tubo Shaft project team could work closely with the CM shaft sinking crew. I was back in the RTZC fold again.

9

Work came thick and fast. As a consequence of my "SHS in Deep Mine Shafts" brochure for British Steel, the Finnish State steel company, Rautarruukki Oy, requested RTZC to undertake an engineering review of shaft steelwork problems in their Vuonos Shaft near Rautavaara, some 260 miles NNE of Helsinki. As the RTZC (self appointed!) shaft guru I got the job. I flew from Heathrow direct to Helsinki, expecting to stay overnight and then fly up to the mine next day. It didn't quite work like that. To my (naive) surprise the Vuonos Shaft project crew had flown down to Helsinki for a little R & R before the serious engineering bit (they'd obviously used my arrival as an excuse to come down to Helsinki). Six of them turned up at my hotel as a "welcome party". Well, we hit the town and boy can those Finns drink and party! Apart from never ending beer and hard liquor there was a steady flow of Finnish girls who were eager to join the fun. I've no idea what time I eventually crawled to bed, but consoled myself that the Vuonos crew would feel as hung-over in the morning as I would be. Wrong. A different lot, bright eyed and bushy tailed, appeared at the Rautarruukki Helsinki offices ready for a detailed discussion on shaft steelwork design. I don't know how I got through the morning, but I was very pleased to learn that we were flying up to Rautavaara after lunch. It was a very well organised mine site, clean and tidy. The Vuonos Shaft primary job was skip hoisting run-of-mine (rom) iron ore with a secondary requirement for downcasting a considerable volume of ventilation air. The use of SHS buntons and RHS guides would greatly reduce the friction loss caused by conventional shaft steelwork, hence the mine's interest. The main technical discussion covered the overall beneficial effect of rigid guides and flexible buntons, rather than vice versa, to minimise the shock loads imposed on the shaft steelwork by the rapid hoisting of fully loaded skips in a shaft equipped with fixed steelwork. Why use fixed steelwork? The use of rope guides would be impractical because of the high downcast ventilation air velocity. With details of the hoisting cycle time (acceleration, full speed, deceleration), skip tare & payload weights together with vertical bunton spacing and length of buntons it was a simple calculation to select the correct sizes for RHS buntons and SHS guides. The Vuonos Shaft guys seemed happy with the results since these buntons and guides reduced the overall weight of total shaft steelwork by 18% and reduced the ventilation friction loss by 7%. After three days at the mine it was back to Helsinki (quiet this time!) and an onward flight to Heathrow.

There was a noticeable change in the RTZC workload from management consultancy to technical mining consultancy. A number of RTZ group staff from CRA (Australia) were transferred to RTZC in London, one of whom was Dick, the Bougainville Copper Project Mining Engineer who I had met in both Melbourne and San Francisco. Initially Dick was heavily involved in the RTZ Paragominas bauxite project in Brazil and the Coed-y-Brenin copper project in Wales, both open-pit projects. However my next (major) project was for the Indian state owned company Hindustan Zinc Ltd (HZL), whose lead, zinc mining operations were based at Udaipur in Rajasthan. The RTZC brief was to produce a full feasability study for the development of their new Rajpura Dariba lead/zinc project situated in an ancient mining area about forty miles from Udaipur. This required a full site project team of eight consultants with various back-up specialists. Initially a mining geologist, in this case Arthur (subcontracted from Riofinex), and I set out to appraise the exploration data which had been carried out by the Geological Survey of India (GSI). We flew direct to Delhi by BA and then transferred to an Indian Airlines Corp (IAC) Vickers Viscount for the flight to Jaipur and on to Udaipur. HZL were in the process of preparing a "RTZ Bungalow" in Udaipur, a short walk from their Head office, for our team use. However the "RTZ Bungalow" work was not yet complete so Arthur and I were put up in the HZL guest house, which was very comfortable and fully serviced.

Most of our days were, obviously, spent out at the Rajpura Dariba project site. HZL provided us with a driver complete with one of the ubiquitous Mahindra jeeps. GSI field staff, including diamond drilling (DD) crews as well as HZL project geological staff were on site and using temporary and portable facilities. Everyone was very helpful and we were submerged beneath a wealth of exploration data. There was also a small hangingwall decline and some restricted strike development on two levels. We were thus able to examine the ore zone and foot and hangingwall rocks at first hand. There were many boxes of diamond drill core to physically examine as well as the core splitting and sample preparation plant on site. This was very important to ensure no sampling bias had been introduced. Bagged samples were tagged and sent to HZL's main analytical laboratory at the Zawar mine, close by Udaipur. HZL project geologists had also taken underground channel samples from the two underground development drives. It was thus possible to compare ore grades calculated from diamond drill core values to those from the underground channel sampling. We spent time in HZL's Udaipur engineering office analysing and checking all the relevant GSI exploration data. We also took a selection of split drill core samples to be check analysed at RTZ's main analytical laboratory in the UK.

By the start of December 1971 we had nearly completed the initial geological/ore reserve evaluation when everything changed - the second Indian/Pakistan war. On the 3rd of December Pakistan launched a number of pre-emptive strikes on several Indian air bases. Although Udaipur was 150 miles from the Pakistan border, just north of the Rann of Kutch, the city immediately went onto a war footing. There was a complete black-out and air raid sirens sounded every time an aeroplane (friend or foe) was spotted. There were also fuel restrictions on non-essential motor transport (eg jeep travel to Rajpura Dariba). HZL agreed that it would be best to put the RTZC project on hold so we decided to head back to London. However for Arthur and me there was no flight out since IAC had cancelled all internal Indian flights. Thus we took the narrow gauge railway from Udaipur to Ahmadabad in Gujarat (140 miles) and then a further 300 miles south to Bombay. Here we were stuck for a few days since all UK bound flights were fully booked. We eventually got seats on an Air Egypt flight to Cairo, where we transferred to another airline for London. En passant it was in Cairo that I cursed the RTZ's travel department for issuing me with sterling travellers cheques, they were not wanted by anyone in Cairo. I never used sterling traveller cheques again. For future trips I always took US dollar traveller cheques and an American Express charge card. The Amex card was essential for hassle free international travel for buying airline tickets, paying for hotels and hiring cars. Anyway thanks to the war Arthur and I spent Christmas at home.

In fact the Indo-Pakistan hostilities were very short lived and a cease fire was announced around the 17th December. Nevertheless HZL suggested we recommence the Rajpura Dariba feasibility project in early January 1972 by which time they expected to have completed the "RTZ Bungalow". This suited me fine as I now had a couple of weeks at home over Christmas and the New Year. We had a family Christmas with my parents from the nearby village of High Halden. My father had made Matt, the sheepdog, a magnificent wooden kennel, which would have made quite a packet on the housing market! Matt was not that keen on it, however, preferring to get soaking wet sitting outside the kitchen door, waiting for Gillian to come back from nursing work at Benenden Chest Hospital. Eventually, with a large amount of food bribery, Matt took up daytime residence when it was raining.

Beales had two largish ponds, each about 120ft diameter and we had started to keep a few Khaki Campbell ducks on the pond nearest the house. The ponds attracted moorhens and the occasional visit from a heron. We fed the ducks close by the little stream that drained out of the house pond towards the orchard. One day looking through binoculars I noticed a heron standing close by the duck feeding bowls. I then became aware of some rats feeding on the duck food. As quick as a flash the heron repeatedly stabbed a nearby rat then swallowed it whole head first. You could see the "rat bump" moving down the heron's neck - spectacular nature in action. Only a few minutes later the same heron, still standing perfectly still, stabbed another rat and swallowed it as before. After a few more minutes it moved into the pond and then lazily flapped away with a fairly slow height gain on account of the heavy lunch (?). Our next home project was building a small boat from a kit. Here my father was very helpful as he was a dab hand at woodwork. Our biggest problem was steaming the side timbers to get the required curve. It took us a few weekends altogether, but finally we had a watertight, two-person, flat-bottomed dinghy, equipped with straight blade oars and a paddle. We kept the boat on the orchard pond so we didn't disturb the ducks. We looked forward to spring and summer and lazy days lolling about in the dinghy.

By mid January 1972 the full RTZC project team flew out to Delhi and on to Udaipur. Here we moved in to the RTZ Bungalow, which HZL had now finished. My recollection was that there were four or five double bedrooms and a large dining-living room. There was the usual Indian shower, or wet room with an overhead faucet and a sloped floor to a large hole in the floor. However the loo was the pièce de résistance. This was a western style toilet perched atop a three foot high plinth built over a typical Indian squatter hole-in-the-floor loo. One felt exceeding precarious and vulnerable when ensconced on the loo about one's business. This was particularly so as there were several "jokers" on the RTZC team; it was definitely much more stimulating than going underground at Rajpura Dariba! During mid December and early January Arthur had come up with an ore reserve so for me it was a case of preparing a three-D picture of this ore reserve. From that it was evident that an open-pit operation was unfeasible and the correct means of ore access and extraction was via a hangingwall vertical shaft. This would obviously tie up some ore in a shaft pillar but the relatively flat dip precluded the use of a footwall location because of increasingly long shaft access crosscuts at depth. Having located the main shaft coordinates Dave, the metallurgical engineer and David, the civil engineer, could start planning the position of the secondary crushing/screening plant and main differential flotation concentrator. All the ancillary plant (workshops; changing rooms; stores; garage; timekeepers; offices; load-out; tailings dam; substations etc) were meshed in with the main shaft and concentrator positions as well, of course, as the prevailing topography and presence of ancient mine workings allowed. With limited geotechnical and hydrological data available I closely examined the underground development in order to devise an appropriate mining method. A variation of conventional longitudinal cut-and-fill stoping, using de-slimed mill tailings as fill, seemed to be a suitable approach. Arthur's ore reserve indicated an ore expectancy of about 35,000 tonnes/vertical m (t/vm) for the main orebody, with an average width of 9m. Using the old Stoakes 10% rule (see page 94 for definition/explanation) for tabular ore deposits this indicated a sustainable mining rate of 3,000 tonnes/day and the project was sized and costed on this basis.

The overall project scope was discussed in detail with the HZL project staff and, where required, adjusted to meet local desires, conditions and customs. When this accord was reached it was agreed that the HZL project team would return to London with the RTZC project team to finalise designs, layouts, costings etc. Before leaving Udaipur we had a joint HZL-RTZC project team formal dinner. As honoured guests we were given special silver foil wrapped betel nut wads to chew. When the silver foil connected with a dodgy tooth filling in metallurgical Dave's mouth he received an electrical jolt that caused him to rise several feet off his chair. Of course little sympathy from any of the RTZC project team, but it was a definite project high point in more ways than one.

Back in London the combined HZL-RTZC team rapidly completed project design criteria and detailed layouts. Work then commenced on preparing the so called "bankable" feasibility study. This entailed a comprehensive write-up of the project description together with a detailed financial analysis of the project construction costs and subsequent cash flow generated by the operation. RTZC back-up staff prepared full drawings of the major elements of the project and the secretarial staff undertook all typing and report presentation; it was a good team effort. This London based work took about six weeks. As RTZC project leader it fell on me to entertain the senior HZL project staff on their mid-visit long weekend. Two of them, Hari and Ali, travelled down to Kent to stay with Gillian and me. Both were vegetarians so Gillian altered our home cooking accordingly. The only mildly discombobulating aspect was the extremely loud belching that took place after eating. Of course I should have remembered that this was a normal Indian expression of great satisfaction with the meal. I'm not certain Gillian believed me. We also took them to a Chinese restaurant in Tenterden and a visit to Rye Pottery where Ali took a great interest in the gas-fired kiln. Back in London we had a final project dinner in Veeraswammy's Indian restaurant in Swallow Street, which was a great success.

My next job was a short technical evaluation of an underground lead/zinc mine at Srebrnica in Yugoslavia. The objective was to determine whether this mine could provide additional lead/zinc concentrate for RTZ/CRA's Avonmouth smelter. Keith, a geologist from Riofinex and I joined Ken, the RTZC MD for the trip. This really showed me one of the benefits of working for an international company like RTZ. None of the - taxi to Heathrow followed by a long wait and then scheduled flight by YAT to Sarajevo - no sir, with Ken as team leader this produced a chauffeur driven limo to the private terminal at Heathrow followed by a very relaxed flight on RTZ's own plane, an HS125 executive jet, fully equipped with cocktail bar. It was hard to believe how quick and easy it was to pass through Heathrow Immigration & Customs etc at the private terminal. In Sarajevo we took a local hire car for the fifty miles drive north-west, through hilly country, to the town of Srebrnica, where we stayed. This town, of course, became infamous for the slaughter of 8,000 muslims by Serbian militia in the 1990s Bosnian war. At the time of our visit, May 1972, everything was peaceful. The mine was developed through a series of adits into the flank of a steep hillside. It was a typical tabular, steep dipping deposit, but of fairly limited strike length and, at that time, unproven in depth. Both Keith and I rapidly came to the conclusion that it had limited ore potential. In addition the flotation concentrator was somewhat dilapidated and produced a relatively low grade concentrate. All in all we did not see it as a reliable, major supplier of lead/zinc concentrates to Avonmouth. We only stayed for three days at Srebrnica before returning to Sarajavo and the onward flight by the RTZ HS125 jet to Heathrow. Without doubt this was the quickest, most hassle free overseas mine appraisal I had ever undertaken.

Amazingly this first flight in the RTZ jet was followed a couple of weeks later by another. This time it was led by Les, Deputy MD of RTZC and together with a five man RTZC team we flew from Heathrow (private terminal, of course!) to Bardufoss in north Norway. From this air force base we drove north-west 25 miles to the port of Finnsnes before boarding a boat for the short trip to the island of Senja (Norway's second largest island). On Senja the large underground graphite mine (the largest in Europe) of Skaland Grafitwerk was situated. RTZC had been retained by EverReady UK (a large consumer of graphite for battery manufacture) to appraise Skaland's expansion plans for the mine and concentrator. Although Senja is 69.3 degrees north (inside the arctic circle) just south of Tromso, in mid year it was surprisingly warm thanks to the effect of the Gulf Stream. The Norwegians were likewise warm and very, very hospitable and did everything possible to assist our review of their expansion programme. In fact there after work-hours hospitality threatened to derail the team's timetable with many glasses of their home brewed alcohol.

The graphite deposit comprised a massive dissemination in a contact metamorphic zone of schists and gneisses. The known ore reserve was large with considerable potential and, importantly, the ground conditions in the mine were good. The mining method was fairly conventional blast-hole open stoping with intermediate rib pillars. It soon became apparent that the constraint to expanding production was neither the ore reserve base nor the underground mine - it was the concentrator. It was already working at full capacity and required major modification and expansion to meet the proposed new output. This was, of course, good news for EverReady UK, who were prepared to finance Skaland's plant expansion to meet their own rising demand for graphite, but needed assurance that the ore reserves existed and that the mine could produce the required tonnage. Additional power could be obtained from Norsk Hydro and Skaland were confident they could obtain additional workers for an expanded operation from Finnsnes on the mainland. Having checked that the ore reserve and mine production scheduling was OK the spotlight fell on Umit, the metallurgical consultant and Derek, the construction consultant to sort out a concentrator expansion programme. After four weeks on site we left Senja for Finnsnes and drove north fifty miles to Tromso for the flight south to Oslo and on to Heathrow. An appraisal of the ore reserves and mine expansion plan was presented to EverReady UK. Umit, the RTZC metallurgist then began a long association with EverReady as, their man, overseeing the design of the Skaland concentrator expansion

Work continued apace at RTZC and much to Les's annoyance I was deputed to go on a visit to Bolivia in an attempt to locate potential sources of tin concentrate for the RTZ subsidiary of Capper Pass, who operated a tin smelter on the north side of the Humber estuary. It was a standing joke in RTZC that the deputy MD, Les, always went to suss out new clients/countries as he loved overseas travel. For some reason he was unable to go to Bolivia this time. The visit was led by Nick, a director of Capper Pass, with geological input from Keith of Riofinex and mining from me. We flew first to Rio de Janeiro, where we stayed overnight at a hotel on Copacabana beach. For me it was a dream come true as I had always wanted to see Rio. The beach was every bit as glamourous as I'd imagined and the only thing missing (bad timing here!) was the February Rio Carnival. The next day we flew to La Paz, Bolivia landing at El Alto airport. At over 3Km length this must be one of the world's longest civil runways, required on account of the 12,000ft altitude. The drive from El Alto down into La Paz was very spectacular. The steep descent zigzags down the side of a bare yellow silty landscape completely devoid of any vegetation. Away in the distance, looking across the La Paz city bowl, the huge mass of the 6,400m (21,000ft) Illimani massif looms. I was aware of a shortness of breath and the expected siroche, or altitude headache, duly appeared. This lasted for a couple of days during which time I refrained from drinking alcohol.

For the first two days we stayed in a La Paz hotel and visited the head offices of the major Bolivian "Medium Miners" companies such as COMSUR SA and EMUSA SA as well as the state mining concern of COMIBOL. However this was the lull before the storm. For the next three weeks we charged around the altiplano and high Andes in a Toyota Land Cruiser visiting a dozen or so small tin mines, most of which were situated at over 4,500m above sea level. Nick had been to Bolivia before and knew his way around a number of these isolated mine sites. Once out of La Paz/El Alto the roads were dirt, ranging from well graded to non-existent in the south of the country. About ninety minutes from La Paz on the flanks of Chalcaltaya mountain was COMSUR's well established Milluni mining complex. We spent a full day there, obviously going underground into various stopes (cut-and-fill) and development ends. We also visited the concentrator, compressor plant and other surface facilities. This 600 tonnes/day operation was of prime interest to Capper Pass as it had a strong ore reserve base, produced relatively clean tin concentrates and appeared well organised and run. Little did we know that this was to be by far the most suitable property visited. However, close by, in an adjacent valley, the Kelluagni project, a new trackless operation currently under development through a ramp-decline showed considerable potential, but, of course, no concentrates would be available for at least two more years. We then headed 100 miles SSE on a sealed (whoopee!) road to the smelter town of Oruro and visited a number of COMIBOL mines in the area. Most of these mines and mining facilities were in a woeful state, obviously starved of capital and a modicum of management - it was very depressing.

We drove a further 150 miles SE on poor dirt roads to the old mining town of Potosi, home of the famous Cerro Rico, or silver mountain. Here one of the underground COMIBOL mines on the flanks of the Cerro Rico showed some promise with reasonable reserves and mining conditions, but the concentrator was in a state of disrepair - short of investment again. We moved on to investigate some small private mines around the old state capital of Sucre, but again these had little potential. We then headed SW towards Pulacayo , some 120 miles away across atrocious dirt roads. In some small village (I forget the name) where we arrived late in the day the only accommodation available was the small Spanish built church! It was the first and only time I spent a night sleeping in an RC church. Stiff and grouchy in the morning, we headed SSW, across the salt flats of the Sala de Uyuni towards the remote settlement of San Antonio de Lipez, which was only forty miles from the far NW frontier of Argentina. In many ways the visit to the small mine at San Antonio summed up the difficulties of looking for tin concentrates in Bolivia. The long, tricky drive across the Sala de Uyuni and Cord de Lipez, often with no identifiable road or track, meant that we navigated by compass and finally arrived at the San Antonio mine at around 10 pm in complete darkness. Here Nick had the "bright idea" that we should go straight underground and do "the due diligence" on the geology/reserves and mining conditions. This he said would enable us to have an early start the next day for the long drive back to La Paz, now approximately 500 miles north over non-existent roads or at best poor dirt tracks. His suggestion was met with incredulity by Keith and me, but Nick called the shots (he was, after all the client), so we lit up the carbide lamps and clomped underground in stoney silence. Fortunately for us, but not for Capper Pass or Nick, the mine was much smaller than they had been led to believe. Although fairly high grade it had a very small ore reserve and virtually no potential. Somebody had done a good marketing job on the mines' (non-existent) potential. Thus we were out of the mine again shortly after midnight. The Mine Manager, who had accompanied us underground, arranged for some "interesting" (don't ask!) soup to appear after which we slept on crude bunks in the mines' store. As expected Nick was bright eyed and bushy tailed by 7am and we were underway before 8am. It took us twelve hours to drive the 300 miles back to Potosi. Here an ancient hotel was very welcome, especially the shower to remove days of grime and road dust and plenty of local beer to lubricate parched throats. Next day we drove back through Oruro to La Paz, staying a further two days to debrief the Medium Miners companies and COMIBOL. Then a flight from El Alto to Rio. One's first take-off from El Alto airport is somewhat disconcerting. Most commercial jets from rolling to lift-off take 35 to 40 seconds, depending on overall load. Not at El Alto they don't. I thought that Lloyd Aero Boliviano's (LAB) Boeing 727 would never lift off; it finally became airborne some fifty seconds from rolling and it's slow rate of climb evoked a comment from an American passenger - "Jeez this guy's got a crop-dusting contract!". It was, of course, the effect of thin air at the 12,000ft elevation. From Rio it was an eleven hour flight back to Heathrow by the new 747 Jumbo, which I really liked and became very friendly with over the next 25 years.

Footnote -
Stoakes 10% rule for tabular orebodies mine output.
Ore Expectancy (OE) is defined as the deposits tonnes/vertical m (t/vm) obtained from strike length (m) by average horizontal width (m) by bulk density by payability.
10% of the OE = sustainable daily mine tonnage output.
It is extremely simple to calculate and always closely matches the results obtained from the long established Taylor's Rule which states:-
6.5 x 4th root of the Ore Reserve tonnage (in millions) = mine life (years)

10

It was again soon apparent why I should never buy a rail season ticket longer than a weekly, Ashford to London, as the following week it was an extension of the search for tin concentrate supply for RTZ's subsidiary, Capper Pass. No flying involved this time, but a longish rail trip to Truro in Cornwall. The tin mine in question was Mount Wellington lying six or seven miles SW of Truro. It was located in an old heavily mined area, drained by the lengthy County Adit which discharged into Restronguet Creek, which in turn drained into Carrick Roads above Falmouth. A new operation had been set up by a Canadian company and the mine had now reached its planned output of 600 tonnes/day of rom ore to the gravity concentrator. Although the mine had only been in production for less than two years it was already proving difficult to sustain the rated throughput. Again with the Riofinex geologist, Keith, we made a rapid trip underground to examine at first hand the nature of the tin lode, wall rocks and working conditions. The major surprise was the limited strike extent of all the four levels already fully developed - circa 850m. With an average lode width of only 1.35m, an indicated payability of 70% this implied an ore expectancy of a little over 2200 t/vm, which on the old Stoakes 10% rule would indicate a sustainable mining rate of 200 tonnes/day. Unsurprisingly at the planned 600 tonnes/day rate the mine had very rapidly run out of developed ore reserves. The mine was quite incapable of delivering 600 tonnes/day to the concentrator. This was obviously a blow to Capper Pass's wish to obtain a new supply of tin concentrates for its Humber smelter, but an absolute disaster for the mining operation. In fact the Mount Wellington mine closed less than a year later.

Back at RTZC offices in St James's Square I received a call from the front desk at No 6 saying there was a "Mr Russell" here to see you. I replied saying I was not expecting any Mr Russell only to hear a mild altercation over the phone, followed by a deep brown Geordie voice "it's me, Charlie from Chasnalla" and so it was. I went down to the RTZ front door reception to meet him - just the same, brown as a berry, great big grin and full of fun as ever. We went back up to my office on the fourth floor, where Charlie's bon homie caused mild consternation amongst the female support staff. Charlie, although of short stature, was definitely larger than life. After upbraiding me for the collar & tie and swanky office surroundings we quickly repaired to the Cockney Pride pub off Lower Regent Street and proceeded to shoot the breeze whilst downing several pints. Charlie told me he was still with Cementation Mining, on holiday at present, returning to Doncaster next week before taking on a master sinkers job at a new shaft in NW Spain. He'd been back at home in Doncaster for a month, "but that's long enough", and wanted to get on with a new job. On return from India to Doncaster he had learnt that I had set up the Tubo Shaft design/sinking contract for Lepanto in the Philippines whilst working for RTZC out of London, which was how he'd found me. He said that all the Chasnalla shaft sinkings and furnishings had been completed on time, but Cementation's scope of work had been increased to do a lot of off-shaft development with the existing sinking crews. He said he'd quite fancied the Lepanto, Philippines job ("never been there!"), but it was a dry sinking and Charlie's expertise in wet, pre-cementation sinking would be wasted. I told him what I'd been doing with RTZC since returning from India, to which he replied "blimey you'll be having as much trouble with the missus as me, away all the time". It was great to see him again, a real mining industry character, one of the best people I was fortunate to work with and learn from.

Charlie's talk of new shafts in NW Spain was followed, by sheer coincidence, with a visit from ERT Consultores SA (ERTC) from Madrid. This was a mining/business consultancy a wholly owned subsidiary of Explosivos Rio Tinto (ERT), which operated huge pyrites mines at Minas de Riotinto in Huelva Province, Andalusia, southern Spain. Their MD, Anaya, had been approached by ERT for assistance in planning a new underground copper mine alongside the huge Atalaya pyrites open pit. Anaya was aware of RTZC's mining consulting work and wanted us to undertake a full feasibility study of this proposed copper mine known as Masa San Dionisio (MSD). Once again we had to request the loan of a geologist from Riofinex and this time Malcolm joined our team of metallurgist Umit, civil/project engineer Brian, financial evaluation Ron and me mining and project leader. We flew to Barajas Airport, Madrid and changed planes for the flight to Seville, where we were joined by two consultants from ERTC, one a mining engineer and the other project scheduling/costing. Both these ERTC people were very helpful in their own fields, but their major input, unsurprisingly, was speaking Spanish

(!) and a detailed knowledge of ERT's Minas de Riotinto's operations. We drove NW from Seville airport in two Seat saloons stopping at El Castillo de las Guardas where we turned off the main road to Cortegana and the Portuguese border. It was mid-afternoon and hot and here I learnt two very important things about life in Andalusia. Firstly everyone takes a siesta for up to four hours after lunch and, much more importantly, how to get the barman's attention. It's no good hovering at the back of the bar crowd trying to catch the barman's eye (in a typical polite English manner) - you'll die of thirst. No, the ERTC guys showed me the way - you shout loudly (almost bellow) "Oiga", to which the barman immediately responds 'Digame', whereupon in your rapidly improving Spanish you demand uno/dos/tres/quatro etc cervezas por favor. In fact even the "por favor" seems little used by the locals. To English ears the "Oiga", which is the imperative "listen", sounds incredibly rude, but Spaniards generally use please & thank you much less than Brits when ordering and/or receiving service. It's not rude, just a different custom. After a couple of beers we continued over the badly broken up road to Nerva and Minas de Rio Tinto.

Minas de Rio Tinto (coloured river) was a very ancient mining field. Archaeological work had disclosed mining/smelting artefacts from both Phoenician and Roman times. There were enormous dumps of waste material from thousands of years of mining, treatment and smelting, with many of these old dumps now being reworked by acid leaching. The local river is very aptly named the Rio Tinto. The desecration from mining has left a very unforgiving lunar landscape and this mining field was, of course, the birthplace of RTZ, when the original British Rio Tinto company merged with the Australian Zinc Corporation in the 1960s.

We were housed in the old British companies' management compound, surrounding a pair of tennis courts. ERT's senior management lived here as well, whilst the main labour force lived at the mining village of Nerva. The major mining activity was the giant Atalaya pyrites open-pit mine providing feed for the companies' sulphuric acid plants in Huelva, at the mouth of the Rio Tinto. In addition, a new open-pit copper mine, Cerro Colorado, was being developed and the new MSD underground copper project in the walls of the Atalaya pyrites open pit. ERT were and felt comfortable with open-pit technology, but had requested ERTC and thus RTZC to help them prepare a feasibility study of the underground MSD project. We had good accommodation in the single men's staff quarters. The single men's mess also provided excellent food assisted by the presence of unlimited bottles of Campo Viejo red wine available for everyone along with the more usual jugs of water.

Our initial work took place in ERT's engineering office where we examined the underground diamond drilling results, sampling and assaying procedures, ore reserve calculations and metallurgical testwork results. Next we spent several days underground. Access to the underground MSD copper project area was from some of the mid-level benches of the huge Atalaya open pit. The pit itself was virtually circular and steep sided in the strong (pyritic) ground. Unsurprisingly similar geotechnical conditions applied to the underground MSD copper project area. As usual we took check samples from several of the underground development crosscuts for later analysis at RTZ's UK laboratory. The massive, non-linear shape of the copper ore reserve together with the strong ground conditions indicated that the deposit could best be exploited by transverse blast-hole stoping combined with intermediate rib pillars. To avoid compromising pyrites production it was felt unwise to impose projected copper ore haulage on to existing Atalaya haul roads. The simplest solution appeared to be a vertical shaft (well away from the pit wall) developed by raising from the existing underground development followed by subsequent stripping and lining. An output of circa 4,000 tonnes/day copper ore was indicated and the feasibility study was developed on this basis. The new concentrator would comprise differential flotation to provide a 35% grade copper concentrate and a pyrite concentrate to augment Atalaya's production. The two ERTC consultants were invaluable in collecting local ERT operating consumable costs, labour rates and working practices. They also provided details/experience of Spanish engineer-constructor outfits who might undertake mine development, concentrator and mine infrastructure construction. In spite of a hectic work schedule we managed to get a Sunday break on the beach at Punta Umbria, just to the south-west of Huelva. The beach is on the Gulf of Cadiz about thirty miles east of the Portuguese border and at that time of the year the Atlantic ocean was pleasantly warm. Apart from us there were only local Spanish people (demurely clad) on the beach unlike the beaches of the Costa del Sol on the Mediterranean, which after the death of Franco in 1975, swarmed with northern Europeans, especially Brits seeking the sun.

A final week was spent at Minas de Riotinto checking out our facts and figures with ERT staff before heading out to Seville for the flight to Madrid's Barajas airport and onward flight to London. The two ERTC consultants came back with us to assist in the preparation of the MSD feasibility study, which took a further month or two to complete. The initial feed-back from ERT was that they were very happy with the feasibility study and that they would probably initiate the project early next year and would like further assistance from RTZC - good news indeed.

There were changes afoot at RTZC. Ken, the current MD, had just been elected to the main RTZ board and thus ceased to be involved in day-to-day RTZC business. Les was promoted to MD and Dick, the Australian from Bougainville Copper, was appointed Director of Mining and Dave, another Australian (transferred from Riofinex) was appointed Director of Metallurgy. Needless to say I and a number of other long-serving Brit consultants were somewhat unhappy at the takeover of RTZC by the johnny-come-lately Aussies. Nevertheless both of these Aussies were circa ten years older than most of the Brit consultants, so couldn't be faulted on lack of experience. In fact I got on well with Dick having got to know him on the Bougainville Copper Project in both San Francisco and Melbourne.

Our work load on the underground mining side seemed to be steadily growing and before I had gone down to Minas de Riotinto for the MSD job we had run an advertisement in the Mining Journal for experienced mining engineers, both open-pit and underground. A number of the applications had come from Africa, South America and Australasia. We had developed a short list and were contemplating bringing the most likely four or five applicants to London. However completely out of the blue RTZC were contacted by the Washington based World Bank (WB) with a request for assistance on the Bank's Mining mission to Zambia. Of course RTZC were registered with all the usual international, governmental and NGO agencies, but virtually all our clients had come from the private/commercial mining sector. Dick agreed I should front-up for the WB job in Zambia and on completion fly to Lilongwe in Malawi to interview applicants from Zambia, Zimbabwe and South Africa. The international hard rock mining industry was small and we felt it would be "politically" insensitive to interview people in Zambia where Roan Selection Trust (RST) and Anglo American Corp (AAC) were operating the extensive Copperbelt mines. I duly sent a telex to the WB mining/Africa division to confirm RTZC's agreement to join their mission to Zambia.

After numerous telex exchanges and phone calls with the WB it was agreed that I would meet the WB team at Gatwick for the British Caledonian flight to Lusaka, Zambia, where we were all booked in to the Pamodzi Hotel. I was somewhat discombobulated at Lusaka Airport where the six-member WB team swept through Immigration & Customs on Blue Laissez Passes passports whereas I, a simple WB subcontractor, had to struggle through the normal entry procedure. Needless to say the WB crew had long gone from the airport by the time I eventually managed to find a taxi to take me to the Pamodzi Hotel. (As you will have guessed the WB guys travelled first-class whilst the "engineering dumbo" slummed it in Economy on the flight from Gatwick!). It was quite definitely a two tier "mission", but the lesser engineering side was boosted by the presence of Dave a long time AAC employee, now retired, who had spent many years working in senior mining positions at AAC's Copperbelt mines. Dave was considerably older than me and had already done work for the WB, so knew the score as to what was required. Basically the WB mission was to assess the current status of RST and AAC operations and produce a ten year copper/cobalt production forecast and comment on both company's request for WB funds to purchase various mining and metallurgical plant & equipment. The WB had brought their own in-house metallurgical consultant, Dick, and thus Dave and I were the two "outside" mining consultants. Obviously the mining brief was split in two, Dave handling all AAC mining operations (which he knew well) whilst I examined RST's mines at Mufulira, Luanshya, Baluba & Chibuluma, starting from zero local knowledge. This was quite a daunting task as the WB had only scheduled two weeks (12 days) at the mines followed by another week for discussions with senior Copperbelt management.

Fortunately Dave showed me the type of information/format etc that he had prepared for the WB during a previous mining mission in 1969 - for me it was gold dust. The whole WB team, now 8, including Dave and me, flew up to Kitwe where we stayed at the AAC guest house. The guest house was still very colonial in style, set in beautifully maintained gardens with servants everywhere and "bed tea" came in on a silver tray at 7am! Here we split into the RST group and the AAC group. An RST driver and car took three WB guys and me to RST's head office at Mufulira. From there I went to Mufulira's geological and mine engineering offices, where their geological and mining staff gave me a briefing on current operations. At this time Mufuira was one of the world's largest underground copper mines using conventional blast-hole open stoping to produce about six million tonnes/year (NB there were larger underground copper mines in the USA, Chile & Philippines but all these mines employed the block-caving mining system). However apart from the sheer size of the mine it had been developed along conventional lines with access through vertical, circular shafts sunk in the footwall. Shaft crosscuts and main levels had been developed at 50m vertical intervals fully equipped with track haulage. Once again the old Stoakes 10% OE rule came into play and it was very apparent that the mine would struggle to maintain six million tonnes/year output in the future as ore expectancy in depth was rapidly reducing and overall development was way behind schedule. These two facts dominated everything and cast serious doubts on the veracity of Mufulira's tonnage and grade production schedule. I found similar problems at Luanshya, Baluba and Chibuluma and Dave also confirmed that most of the AAC underground mines were (tonnage) squeezed from lack of development and the Nchanga open pit was likewise squeezed through lack of waste stripping ahead of ore mining. This tonnage squeeze, of course, lead to a concomitant fall in rom grade as the mines, searching for tonnes, tended to put low grade and waste rock into the ore stream. As one can imagine we had some fierce discussions with both RST and AAC engineering and production scheduling staff, who were very unhappy to accept our reduction in contained copper output, particularly at Mufulira and the Nchanga open pit.

During our short stay on the Copperbelt I met a number of ex CSM students whom I knew from the 1950s, a number of whom were distinctly unimpressed with their own companies asking the WB for money - "what the hell did the WB know about mining and by implication what the hell did I know about Copperbelt mining!". Hey ho, as a consultant one certainly had to develop a thick skin and be confident in one's own assessment. However it was apparent that, in general, Copperbelt underground mining methods and machines were not at the forefront of modern mining technology.

We flew back to Lusaka and again stayed at the Pamodzi Hotel. Here I developed the RST copper & cobalt ten year production schedule whilst Dave did the same for the AAC underground mines and Nchanga open pit. We had a further couple of days with the WB guys to finalise production figures, with an undertaking to submit a written report on the mining operations to the WB in Washington within three weeks. The WB guys then flew back to Washington and I caught an Air Malawi plane for the 380 mile flight east to Lilongwe. I checked into a central hotel, where our potential RTZC applicants had been advised to present themselves for interview on such-and-such a date. The next day I contacted each applicant in turn for an hours' chat and to each suggested we meet up in the hotel bar at 7 pm. I was there early and introduced all the applicants to each other (there were 5) and after a few beers suggested we go for a bite to eat. I said I didn't know Lilongwe and waited to see who would take the initiative. John from Shabanie Asbestos in Zimbabwe duly obliged as the "go to/can do man" and unsurprisingly he got the job. I flew back to Lusaka then on to Gatwick. The next ten days or so were spent in the London office preparing a report on the Zambian mining operations of RST and spelling out in detail how the copper and cobalt ten year mining production schedules were derived. There were some telephone queries, but the WB seemed satisfied with the write-up & schedule.

RTZC received another request from ERTC to assist with yet another new copper project in Minas de Riotinto. This was known as the Masa San Antonio (MSA) project which was also under development. A new vertical shaft had just been completed by the Spanish contractor Obras Subterranean and friction winders had just been installed in the new concrete headframe. However there were, apparently, some difficulties with excessive vibration in the shaft steelwork. Dick and I agreed we needed additional geological, mining and mineral processing staff as soon as possible, since ERTC also had indicated that ERT intended to commission the MSD project shortly with RTZC selected as the Owner's Project Team on site. We immediately ran ads for Spanish speaking engineers in all three disciplines with at least ten years experience. However hiring new staff (generally from overseas) takes time and we needed to start work immediately on the new MSA project. Riofinex were unable to assist this time with a mining geologist so I approached McKay & Schnellman (M&S), London based geological consultants, for assistance. For a straight subcontract they proposed Don, a young Australian mining geologist, who turned out to be absolutely first class. With no one else available on the mining side it was back to Minas de Riotinto for me. Don & I flew via Madrid to Seville where we were met by two ERTC guys who were to assist on the MSA project. As before we stayed in the old British companies' staff compound. Don disappeared to the engineering offices to review the geological data and ore reserves whilst I went to the new MSA shaft complex. This was a 6m diameter concrete lined shaft equipped with twin skips and cage and counterweight running on steel guides supported on steel buntons. We rode the cage up and down several times. It was not a smooth run with noticeable vibrations, although the hoisting speed of circa 6m/sec was fairly slow. Later that day, after siesta, when they were not hoisting rock, we rode up and down several times on the skip bridle; again in certain parts of the shaft there were noticeable vibrations.

The following day with the ERT engineer we examined the shaft sinking design specifications, shaft furnishing (buntons and guides) specifications and tolerances and detailed drawings of the skip, cage and counterweight. Everything seemed reasonable, but the shaft conveyances were equipped with simple steel rubbing slippers for contact with the guides rather than the more usual spring-loaded trio of rubber wheels. The following weekend we took over the shaft, stopped the ventilation fan, and ran two plumb lines down. Then working from putlogs on the top of the cage we took key measurements at each set of buntons down the shaft. Plotting these results showed good overall shaft verticality, but in one section of the shaft 8 bunton sets were progressively out of position by 3mm rising to 8mm and back to 3mm. Not a big deviation but enough to cause problems. It would be a major undertaking to reset these misaligned buntons (and take the shaft out of commission for a considerable time) and the simplest solution appeared to be to remove the steel rubbing slippers from all conveyances and counterweight and retrofit each with conventional spring-loaded rubber wheels. Although this would not be an ideal solution the spring-loaded wheels should "iron out" the slight alignment discrepancy. ERT contacted the conveyance manufacturer for a meeting to discuss the problem. They came to Minas de Riotinto promptly, were very helpful and agreed to proceed with the required modification of the conveyance running slippers.

I then joined Don on several MSA underground visits to assess geotechnical conditions and the nature of the ore zone as well as collecting several channel samples for check analysis in RTZ's UK laboratory. We worked with the ERT and ERTC engineers reviewing the development schedule to ensure that it would meet the desired production build-up. Finally we spent several days working through the details of their proposed sub-level mining system before heading back to Seville and on to London. Here I talked to Dick and said how impressed I had been with Don, why don't we offer him a job? Not unreasonably Dick said we would have to square that with M&S. I phoned Ian, mining director at M&S, and invited him out to lunch. He said he knew exactly what was coming! He would be very sorry to lose Don, but could see that RTZC, the consulting arm of a large international mining company, would be very attractive for Don. Apart from paying M&S's consulting fees for Don's services in Spain we agreed a one-off compensation lump sum for "stealing their staff". It was all amicable and we often worked with M&S again. Don thus joined RTZC as senior mining geologist, but often returned to the M&S Friday lunch in the Red Lion pub when he was in London between assignments.

Back at home in Woodchurch we acquired another dog, from near neighbours. It, sorry he, was a Lhasa Apso cross puppy, apparently the runt of the litter. We called him Anjon to go with Matt and he had the most amazing red eyes and curly tail over his back. No one knew who or what the father was. Matt treated him with a certain amount of disinterest, but as far as Anjon was concerned Matt was God and he followed him everywhere. Over the next ten years or so the two were inseparable except when there was a bitch on heat within about three miles of the house, when Anjon was off like a rocket. He was a randy so and so whilst Matt was completely uninterested in bitches. By the time Anjon was twelve weeks old he was game for a reasonable length walk tagging along beside Matt.

I had hoped to have a quiet spell in the UK but Lepanto requested a visit to sort out some queries on ventilation and the detailed design of the new conical grit and sludge settlers ahead of the 700 Level pump station. We had also been in touch with Hutchinson Whampoa (HW) in Hong Kong, as to the possibility of them acting as our agents in the Far East. There had also been an interesting job application from the GM of Emperor Gold Mines in Fiji and finally we were discussing a possible tie-up with CRA's engineering subsidiary, Minenco, based in Melbourne. Dick suggested I go to Lepanto first, then down to Melbourne to see Minenco followed by a stop in Sydney to interview Barrie, the Emperor GM and finally Hong Kong for talks with HW. I warned Gillian that I expected to be away for three to four weeks, but by now that was no surprise.

This time I tried a new direct flight to the Philippines operated by SAS from London via Stockholm. Unfortunately all did not go smoothly. The plane (if I remember correctly a long range DC8) had engine trouble over the USSR and made an emergency landing at Tashkent in Uzbekistan. This was my first experience of the USSR and the dour apartment blocks visible from the coach as we were escorted into an equally dour town-centre hotel did not leave a good impression. All SAS passengers were confined to the hotel for about 36 hours until a relief DC8 arrived and we continued on our way to Manila. Not a great trial run; I never used that flight route again preferring to travel to the Philippines via Hong Kong with either Cathay Pacific or Thai International and later BA after it was de-nationalised. As usual Ponciano picked me up at MIA for an overnight stay at the Intercontinental Hotel in Makati. Early the following morning he drove me back to the MIA private terminal where Vic was waiting with the turbo Beech Baron. We had an uneventful flight up to the Lepanto strip, which as always seemed much too short. Nevertheless it was a little like coming home, as I joined Roger, Chief Geologist, Thomas, Chief Mining Engineer and Oscar project engineer for the new Tubo Shaft complex in Lepanto's mine engineering offices. Unfortunately CM's shaft sinking progress was well behind schedule, not through any technical problems, but due to changes with their shaft sinking staff. On the plus side this gave the mine more time to evaluate the additional hydrological data collected over the past two years. This in turn enabled the sizing of the conical grit/sludge settlers and 700 Level pump station to be slightly re-sized. Additional VRT measurements within the mine had confirmed the geothermic gradient, which indicated a VRT on the 700 Level of circa 97 F (36 C) This, combined with high relative humidity, confirmed the desirability of circulating 425,000 CFM below the 900 Level at the desired production rate of 3,000 tonnes/day. On the Lepanto social side it was more bridge playing, ten-pin bowling, drinking in the club and an attempt at golf. The small Lepanto golf course comprised oiled sand greens, which for me was a definite first.

After a couple of weeks it was back down to Manila for a Philippine Airlines (PAL) flight to Melbourne via Sydney. I stayed in the very pleasant Southern Cross hotel, which was not too far from CRA's offices at 95 Collins Street. Here I went to Minenco's offices where I met Brian, who had worked with me on the Bougainville Owner's team in San Francisco three years ago. Minenco had a couple of guys they would like to transfer to RTZC for additional experience - Martin, an open-pit mining engineer from Bougainville and Roger a financial analyst. This was a RTZ/CRA company interchange, already agreed, so my visit to Minenco was merely PR and getting to know these guys who would be joining us in London in a month or so. RTZC consultants had already been working at the MKU mine in the Northern Territory and, of course, the Bougainville mine in PNG undertaking open-pit planning and design. We each did a "selling job" to the other, Brian stressing Minenco's engineering, project and cost control whilst I extolled RTZC strengths in geology, underground mine design and open-pit planning. After all the bull we repaired to a local pub and put the world right! The following morning I flew up to Sydney.

I like Sydney, one of the world's great cities, beautifully situated around Macquarie harbour. I stayed in the Wentworth Hotel, almost nine years since I last stayed there with Mum & Dad who were then about to return to the UK after visiting us in Rosebery, Tasmania. I contacted the front desk to ascertain Barrie's room number, phoned him and agreed to meet him in my room in half an hour. Barrie was physically a big man, born in Yorkshire, where he'd worked in the pits. After that he'd moved to western Canada where he worked for an underground development contractor. He followed this with several years in Peru working for Cerro de Pasco and thus spoke reasonable Spanish. He was currently General Manager of Emperor Gold Mines in Fiji. From the outset we just clicked and I felt he would be a first-class, practical underground mining engineer for RTZC. We agreed to meet in the bar at 6 pm and after a few beers headed down towards the harbour bridge where we spotted the Ox on the Rocks fish restaurant. The Ox was really lively with excellent food and good ambience. Each of us had the next day free before flying respectively to Fiji & Hong Kong. We spent the "free" day at the Sydney (Agricultural) Show and really enjoyed the stockman sheep trials and the wood chopping events. Barrie had accepted our job offer and expected to be in London in about three months. I had explained that his likely first assignment would be in Minas de Riotinto on the MSD underground copper project, where his Spanish would be very useful. We agreed to keep in touch.

The next morning I flew to Hong Kong, staying in the Regent Hotel, Kowloon side. It was a quick trip across the bay by the Star Ferries to Victoria island. HW occupied their own large skyscraper building in the main downtown area. I was somewhat daunted by this grand building, but the HW man I met was very open and friendly. However I felt that initially he thought I was representing RTZ (!) rather than a small geological and mining consultancy, albeit wholly owned by RTZ. Once we'd sorted that out, he felt that RTZC, would be better advised to set up an Agent in the Philippines, where there was a long established mining industry mainly managed by expatriate American staff. He explained that HW had no expertise in Chinese mining (hence no contacts at present) and that, in the early '70s mainland China was virtually a closed shop. He also suggested that there were technical consulting opportunities in Taiwan. After a pleasant lunch at HW I made my way back to Kowloon and the Regent Hotel before catching the night Cathay Pacific flight back to London.

A week or so at home was spent on the never ending DIY required by a 15Ce old farmhouse. To be fair none of this was major as all the hard building and plumbing work had been completed by Humphry's team three years ago. However, whilst there were only small jobs in the house a major effort was required in the garden, putting in new field drains to prevent flooding around the garage. The soil was really stodgy Gault clay, almost unworkable when it was wet and sticky and equally unworkable when dry as it set hard like a grey-yellow brick. I bought a Westwood mini rotovator, but this also struggled in the unforgiving Gault clay. It seemed there were no more than a dozen days a year when the moisture content of the clay was "just so" and easy to work. We developed a potato patch on the eastern side of the front garden - somebody told me that potatoes were good for breaking up "difficult" soil. In fact the spuds did a pretty good job, then it became a problem finding a suitable day in the autumn to harvest the crop. Obviously this was made difficult by my frequent absence due to incessant travelling for RTZC.

Back at work the next job was an unusual, legalistic one. It was for Mogul Mines, at Silvermines in Ireland. Basically Mogul were suing the local Guarda for failing to prevent the IRA from blowing up the main mine transformer, thus stopping the whole Mogul operation. Our remit for Mogul was to independently ascertain their loss of profits over the period that the operation was stopped together with all other costs associated with the purchase of a new transformer and additional costs incurred by the unexpected shut down and later start up. The mine had had to hire additional emergency generators to power the main cage hoist as well, of course, as running mine pumps and main ventilation fan. Fundamentally it was an accounting job, although I had to ascertain the labour and power costs of running the main hoist, pumps and ventilation fans from emergency diesel generators. With regard to the loss of profits aspect we had to determine the average tonnage and grade of rom ore, mill recovery, and net smelter returns on the shipped concentrate together with the average lead/zinc prices pertaining to the lost production period. We also had to examine the details of the mine operating cost data. It was in no way an engineering job, but it certainly gave great insight into the breakdown of operating costs into fixed and variable elements. We spent a lot of time with Mogul's legal advisers explaining the fixed/variable split of mining costs. The legal eagles were very suspicious of the fairly large fixed cost element necessary for an underground mine irrespective of the tonnage broken and/or hoisted. To convince them we took them underground to the main pump station, main haulage and underground fans. Of course we also took them to the main hoist and main surface exhaust fan. In the end they seemed satisfied and we were not required to support them with personal appearances at the subsequent court hearings. I was very happy about that as "expert witnesses" were given a hard time by lawyers, who tend to be more articulate and devious than engineers!

11

Les, and Dick had been busy interviewing job applicants as a response to our earlier advertisements in World Mining. They hired two mining engineers, Brian, an underground-computer specialist from South Africa and Leo, an open-pit guy from Holland. They had also hired Keith, a Spanish speaking mineral processor ex Cerro de Pasco in Peru. I had already hired two engineers, John, underground and Barrie, Spanish speaking underground. In addition we were joined by the two guys from Minenco, Melbourne. So fairly rapidly we had built up the number of practical mining industry people. At the same time a number of management consultants had left the company (seeing which way the wind was blowing?) by transferring to a computer/management services subsidiary of RTZC, which had just been set up in Bristol.

There was then a totally unexpected event which impacted on RTZC. In early March, 1974, Les, the MD had gone to Paris to watch a five Nations rugby match - England/France. Over the weekend there was a snap BA engineers strike. About sixty returning England rugby supporters were transferred to the next available Paris - London flight. This was a Turkish Airlines DC-10. On the 3rd March 1974 this DC-10 crashed shortly after take-off from Orly Airport, killing all passengers and crew (346) after an incorrectly closed rear baggage door blew out. Les, a Royal School of Mines (RSM) mining engineer would be sadly missed at RTZC, not least by me. He gave me a lot of managerial support in my early years at RTZC. Later, most of us attended his funeral held near Didcot and afterwards for a wake at his nearby house.

The RTZC board quickly appointed Dick as MD and brought in a new David as Commercial Director to work alongside metallurgical Dave as the other Director. Both Brian and I were upgraded to Managing Consultants, which (apart from a salary increase!) meant that we tended to work as project leaders on major assignments. It was just as well we had taken on quite a few new staff as the demand for our geological, mining and metallurgical consulting services escalated rapidly, no doubt helped by the fact that our parent, RTZ, was seldom out of the mining press as they developed new operations in South Africa, Canada and Australia.

My next project saw a return to Ireland, this time to the old Avoca Mines in Wicklow. A Canadian company required an assessment of the potential for expanding this copper mine. Don and I flew to Dublin, hired a car and drove 65 miles due south through Bray and Wicklow to the small town of Avoca. The mine had been active in the 19Ce and had been worked through a series of adits. During the 1950s the Irish government had financed the building of a new concentrator as well as considerable underground development. In 1974 the mine was well mechanised with trackless LHDs and 15t dumpers working a pillar & stall mining system. However the mine was unable to fill the available mill capacity. It was the perennial problem of too little developed ground ahead of stoping. Examination of the geological plans, ore reserves and ore potential indicated that, although a sizeable deposit, it was not of a suitable disposition to sustain the hoped for production rate at the required rom grade of 1.6% Cu. We duly advised the Canadians not to attempt a mine expansion.

Back in London again we heard from ERTC that ERT wished to proceed with the implementation of the MSD copper project. The timing was great for us as we now had some Spanish speakers available. Barrie had joined from Emperor Gold Mines in Fiji and Umit, our Turkish metallurgical engineer, had been on a crash Spanish course with RTZ's language department, after finishing his graphite work for Ever Ready. Don was also available on the geological side and Brian would be the on-site project manager as well as handling project planning, scheduling and costing. We had also recruited a lady English teacher to look after the consultant's children whilst in Minas de Riotinto. As I was the link from our original feasibility study I accompanied the "team" to Madrid and on to Seville. There, as before, an ERTC mining engineer met us with two cars for the drive to Minas de Riotinto. We settled into the old staff quarters and I introduced the team to the ERT project engineering staff as well as the head ERT honcho for all Minas de Riotinto operations. Thereafter the team began to get up to speed with the current state of planning for the MSD copper project. Came the weekend and those consultants with family made the necessary arrangements (through ERTC & RTZC) for wives, children and personal effects to come out to Minas de Riotinto the following week. ERT had provided fully furnished/serviced houses for all our married consultants whilst single status guys, in this case Don & me, were accommodated in the single mens mess. It was obviously a little disruptive as wives and children settled it, but in fact, it went much better than I had expected - ERT bent over backwards to ensure smooth integration with their own staff. About a month after we arrived on site I heard from Dick that he and his wife Mary intended to accompany the new English teacher from the UK to Minas de Riotinto. He suggested that Gillian might join them, as he had arranged for the RTZ executive jet to fly them all down to Seville. He suggested I meet them in Seville with two cars for the drive up to the mine. We duly stopped at El Castillo de las Guardas for liquid refreshment where Dick was singularly unimpressed by my poor Andalusian Spanish, but did at least concede that I managed to obtain some beers! At the mine I introduced Dick to all the important "jeffes" and that night we had a MSD project team dinner with ERT, ERTC and RTZC staff their wives and children - it was a great fun evening.

Dick and I stayed at the mine for a further three days, visiting underground and going through the project in detail. We made sure all the families were well settled and undertook to sort out any remaining problems from the move. Then an ERT driver drove the four of us back to Seville where we stayed in the marvelously ornate Alfonso XIII hotel for a few days holiday. Of course we visited the great Giralda cathedral; took a horse and carriage ride around the city centre; visited the Plaza del Torres alongside the Guadalquiver river and went to a late night flamenco dancing school. We enjoyed the hot sunshine and dining alfresco with great Andalusian Spanish and/or Moorish cuisine. The four of us then flew up to Barajas for another three days holiday in Madrid. I forget the name of the hotel in central Madrid where we stayed, but what I do remember was that it was a very noisy city indeed. It was primarily traffic noise. Most of the major streets were one-way, some six or eight lanes wide and it appeared to be a mini grand prix from one set of lights to the next! Although there were some fine plazas, the Plaza Mayor was magnificent, the city was unfortunately dominated by the motor car epitomised by the La Puerta del Sol "a roundabout, or confluence of about six mini grand prix tracks". For us the highlight was a visit to the Prado Museum and Art Gallery. It was here that I first discovered the paintings of Hieronymus Bosch where there was a full gallery of his works - I found them fascinating, not beautiful, but an insight into the depiction of the options available in heaven and hell from a 15Ce religious, specifically Catholic, perspective.

Work enquiries were still coming in thick and fast. We were approached by Seltrust Engineering Ltd (SEL) to go into a joint venture (jv) with them to bid for a full feasibility study for the Tintaya Copper project of Centromin in Peru. SEL's idea was that we (RTZC) would look after the geology, ore reserves and mining aspects, including "sizing" of this huge open-pit project whilst they looked after the concentrator, all other project infrastructure, project scheduling and cost control. We had never undertaken a jv and Dick and I went across to SEL's offices in the city to discuss the Tintaya Project and the details of a jv. The project discussions were pretty straight forward, based on a good Invitation to Bid (ITB) document from Centromin. We agreed that a pre-bid visit to the site in Peru was necessary to ascertain local conditions and to briefly appraise the quantity and quality of the geological exploration data available. We agreed that two RTZC people (a geologist & mining engineer) would join the much larger SEL team next week for the pre-bid trip. We then moved on to the structure and details of the jv. To us greenhorns this seemed a very involved and protracted discussion but we kept up to pace until SEL's contracts manager asked us for details of a recourse agreement. Dick, leading our side as RTZC MD, kicked me under the table and said "Martin handles that side", thus pleasantly dropping me into it. However his kick, before his comment, gave me about five seconds to get my brain in gear and come up with something along the lines of "yes, yes, of course, I'll finalise the details with our legal department". At any rate this reply seemed to do the trick and we moved on to less arcane topics where Dick & I felt more at home. In the taxi back to RTZC we had a good laugh about our lack of knowledge on recourse agreements. The next morning I went down to see Patrick in RTZ's legal department and he explained that in effect it meant RTZ underwriting RTZC's financial/legal position in the jv. When I explained our proposed jv involvement with SEL and indicated the likely size (in cash terms) of the whole bid and RTZC's share of that he felt that RTZ would, in fact, provide a recourse agreement, albeit reluctantly. Basically it would say that if RTZC should fail to produce "the goods" or be late or go bust, then their 100% owner, RTZ, would "pick up the pieces" to fulfill the jv agreement. Dick and I both agreed that in future we would not do jv's as one wasted so much time/effort on the jv agreement rather then on the all important bid document. We agreed that either RTZC would lead a bid with other specialists as subcontractors or conversely that we would subcontract to others as lead bidder.

Don was available to go on the pre-bid trip as geologist and I had to go as mining engineer since both Dick and Roy were already scheduled to go on a bauxite open-pit mining project in Yugoslavia. Leo & Martin, the other two open-pit mining engineers, were also currently involved with RTZ group projects. Although it was not ideal I did have some open-pit experience from quarries at Penlee and Dunbar and, of course, Bougainville Copper. Thus a few days later Don and I joined a six-man SEL team at Heathrow for the long flight down to Lima. We spent the next day in Lima in discussion with Centromin's Tintaya project team. The following day we drove in two multi-cab ute's up the spectacular road east to Morococha in the Andes. Lima, although with some striking medieval Spanish architecture, was a rather dour, dreary place. The sun never shone, it never rained and everything was covered with a layer of dust. Often there was a thick sea fog, but ten miles inland as the Morococha road climbs out of the coastal plain one burst into glorious sunshine and one's heart lifted. Not for nothing is the siting of Lima city known as the Incas Revenge!

At the Tintaya Project site there was a well developed exploration camp. There were excellent and extensive geological, sampling and assaying data files together with ore reserve calculations undertaken by Centromins's central exploration division. The mine area was in typical Andean mountain topography, at circa 11,000ft elevation and a new open-pit mine would be, essentially, an initial side-cut operation before developing into a conventional open-pit. It appeared to be a fairly straightforward mining proposition. The SEL guys had a more difficult time assimilating data on power and water sources, areas suitable for tailings disposal, concentrator construction, housing and general services. However after three days we headed back down to Lima happy that we had collected all the relevant site data necessary to compile a "good bid". We were staying at the Crillon Hotel and as an end of visit relaxation/jv bonding session we repaired to the nearby El Gato Negro nightclub, which in fact was anything but relaxing! Nevertheless we fell out of the club by 2am as we were scheduled to catch an early flight back to the UK.

Don & I had done a little geographical research and when the KLM plane had an intermediate stop at Caracas, Venezuela, we deplaned leaving the SEL guys on board. At Caracas we caught a local Avianca flight down to Aruba, Bonaire and Curacao (the ABCs of the southern Caribbean). In Curacao we stayed in a smallish beach front hotel. The town's architecture was distinctly Dutch, reminding us that it was part of the Netherlands Antilles. Although pleasantly relaxed and Caribbean in style the town was dominated by a giant Shell Oil refinery which rather destroyed the overall ambience. Nevertheless two days bumming around the town and on the beach in the hot sun was a very pleasant change from the cool, thin air and stark mountainous surroundings of Tintaya. Sunday afternoon we flew up to Miami to catch a night flight to London. We were back into the RTZC offices by lunchtime.

For the next few days Don and I respectively wrote up the geological and mining sections for the jv bid for the Tintaya Project. We went across to SEL's office for final discussions on incorporating our sections into the final bid document. This was being prepared by SEL as they had by far the larger portion of engineering work to be undertaken. As it was a fixed price bid both SEL and ourselves had included a margin of 15% over and above our estimated number of man-days to cater for any unexpected problems or absence of fundamental data. I also took along a recourse agreement prepared by RTZ's legal department. As a consequence I felt more than happy to discuss this with SEL's contracts people following my crash course on such agreements from Patrick. SEL undertook to despatch the bid package by courier company by the end of the following week, in time to meet the ITB closing date. After that it was merely a case of waiting for a response from Centromin.

At home Gillian had been selected as Nurse of the Year (NOTY) at Benenden Chest Hospital, in acknowledgement of her caring professionalism whilst working on the Male TB Ward nursing patients from the Post office Union. The award was made by the Prime Minister, Edward Heath and I was sorry I had missed the occasion. Gillian commented that she was surprised that Mr Heath was so short in stature, much shorter than she was. It was apparent that all the media photographers had been instructed to photo the PM upwards from a low camera position; thus he never appeared short in most newspaper shots - and they used to say the camera never lies!

We next received a firm request from an American entrepreneur, based in Guatemala City, to carry out an engineering evaluation of a complex sulphide deposit he had been exploring for the past two years. Three of us, geologist, miner & metallurgist, not currently on fee paying work, immediately flew out to Guatemala City. This was my first visit to Central America and I was really looking forward to it. As it happened it did not disappoint, but not quite in the manner I anticipated. We had all squeezed into a single, large old yankee taxi at the airport for the drive to the city hotel. Just as we pulled up on the hotel forecourt there was a short, sharp burst of machine gun fire across the front of the hotel. I guess it was the quickest I'd ever moved; from the RH front passenger seat, opening the door and flinging myself over a low wall alongside the forecourt took all of three seconds. I was joined seconds later by the other two guys from the rear seat. The driver, on the other hand, just stayed put at the wheel. There was no more firing, but a lot of shouting as a car, further around the forecourt, accelerated rapidly away. Our driver shouted out to us "Hey gringos, no hay problema es finito". Well that's alright then. It transpired that there was, literally, a running battle between the hotel's owner and the hotel's building contractor who (apparently) claimed not to have been fully paid. Welcome to Guatemala City! Having prized ourselves out of the dirt we collected our bags and moved rapidly through the bullet scarred front entrance. Certainly our survival antics provoked a great deal of merriment from the driver. Needless to say we all rapidly repaired to the bar for a drink before setting off to meet Bill, the American owner of the San Jose poly-metallic sulphide prospect.

Bill was a very amiable, middle aged American who had lived in Guatemala for years, dabbling in the local metal mining scene. A couple of years ago he had followed up on some local geological scuttlebutt with a limited diamond drilling campaign on the San Jose prospect, which was located about 6000ft up in a very inaccessible area. He showed us maps of the area together with diamond drill logs and sample/assay results. It sounded quite promising. He suggested we go up to the prospect the next day, but said that he and his "buddy" would come round to the hotel that evening to "have a few beers and some chow". Bill duly turned up around 7 pm and a little while later his buddy, Chuck, an American Peace Corps guy arrived on a large Harley motorbike (Chuck was a fully paid up HOG member - Harley Owners Group). It looked like being quite an evening and so it turned out. Boy those americans liked to party! Feeling somewhat the worse for wear the next morning we fell into a couple of jeeps for the two hours drive up to the finca. This was an isolated hacienda buried up in the pine clad mountains. It reminded me of the northern Luzon mountains around Lepanto in the Philippines. There was no jeepable access from the finca to the San Jose prospect and this was to be undertaken on horseback. My heart fell, I am a very poor rider and the last time I had ridden was six years ago in northern Kashmir and I was sore for days afterwards. By contrast our metallurgist Keith, recently arrived from Peru, was an expert horseman and rapidly galloped off into the distance on a beautiful thoroughbred. I requested the slowest/quietest hack available and duly turned up at the San Jose site about fifteen minutes after the others. It wasn't a problem the horse knew where we were going and one of the finca lads rode with me to pick up the pieces if I fell off.

The prospect was situated on the side of a spur running down from higher mountains to the west, it was a spectacular setting. The light diamond drill rig had been flown in by helicopter along with the other exploration gear. Drilling water had been obtained from a dammed nearby stream. Apart from the boxes of completed diamond drill core there was not a lot else to examine. Obviously the drill core provided actual fresh samples of the host rocks as well as the nature of the mineralised zone, which commenced at a shallow depth of a few metres. It was apparent that, from a mining point of view, a side-cut open-pit would be the logical initial approach, followed at depth by extraction through adits into the steep hillside. However the two major engineering problems would be access and above all metallurgy. From the remaining split diamond drill core we took a number of samples for check analysis and an even larger number of samples for metallurgical testing; both the check analysis and the metallurgical testing to be carried out at RTZ's UK laboratory. On the trip back from the San Jose prospect to the finca the horses came into their own for carrying the weighty samples in custom made saddle packs. Unsurprisingly I offered to walk, feeling sorry for my old hack already weighed down with samples, but in truth preferring to walk than suffer another uncomfortable ride. Back in Guatemala City we went to Cia Minera San Jose Ltda's offices for further discussions. I told Bill that although the prospect was "easily mineable", the main difficulty, possibly a stumbling block, was the apparent complex nature of the poly-metallic mineralisation. We needed to undertake detailed mineralogical studies (eg thin sections, grinding/liberation tests, flotation tests etc) before we would be in a position to say whether it was feasible to produce separate, clean concentrates for sale. Only then would it be possible to size and cost any such operation. Thus we agreed to stop all other preliminary investigations until the mineralogical/metallurgical test work was completed. We agreed to provide him with a firm quotation for this work once Keith had finalised the programme with RTZ's laboratory. After wrapping up the discussion Bill suggested we all meet up in the hotel bar before going on to "a little place he knew". Yes, you guessed it. The little place turned out to be a very lively, raunchy nightclub, where both Bill and Chuck appeared to be very well know regulars. We crawled back to the hotel about 3am, thus achieving some four hours sleep before catching a flight back to the UK early next morning. Certainly one of the most interesting and entertaining projects I'd been on.

Keith spent a couple of days down at the RTZ laboratory working up the details of the mineralogical/metallurgical test work programme for the San Jose samples. These were expected to arrive at Heathrow by air freight in a couple of days. Back at the office we worked up a quotation for San Jose using the RTZ laboratory as our nominated subcontractor. We telexed the quote to Bill and received the go-ahead a day later. That meant Keith would be busy for the next few weeks. I had a message from SEL that said we had not been short-listed for the Tintaya job, which was very disappointing as both SEL and ourselves had put a lot of effort and time into that bid. Through the grapevine we heard that all three short-listed bidders were from the USA. That was food for thought. South America was obviously a USA stamping ground as far as the local mining industry was concerned. The Peruvian mining industry knew little of SEL since the Selection Trust group worked in Africa, nor of RTZC, since our parent, RTZ, was active in South Africa, Australia and Canada. The knock-back certainly got Dick and me thinking that we needed to have a more focussed approach to marketing mining/metallurgical consultancy than the one-off/opportunistic Tintaya bid. Hence over the next few weeks to Christmas

1974 I studied World Mining's Annual Review to ascertain which countries had sizeable metalliferous mining operations, divided into open-pit and/or underground. We also set an annual marketing budget and further agreed that each target country should be visited at least three times/year. As expected the old commonwealth countries Australia, Canada, India and South Africa appeared prime targets. In addition the Philippines, Spain, Bolivia, and Argentina each had a well developed metalliferous mining industry. Closer to home the main target appeared to be Eire. Continental Europe, like the UK, was dominated by the coal industry, which we felt was not our forte.

12

The new year brought some significant changes. Gillian left her nursing job at Benenden Chest Hospital and became surgery Sister/Dispenser at the Woodchurch surgery. Apart from being much closer to home she really enjoyed the "hands-on" work required at a busy village GP's surgery. In January 1975 I was appointed Director of Mining at RTZC, which was a great boost for my career. In fact very little changed, although I did even more overseas travelling as I took on a supervisory role for some projects in addition to my own specific project involvement. Early in the new year I had another trip down to Minas de Riotinto to review our team's work on the MSD underground copper project and introduce John, as a geotechnical specialist, to work with Barrie on the detailed design of the stoping method. At the same time Roy, an open-pit mining engineer who had joined us from Canada was to start work, with engineers from ERTC, on updating the final pit design of the Atalaya pyrites open-pit using RTZC's OPD computer program developed by Peter and his team in our London offices. Both Roy and John anticipated spending three weeks in Minas de Riotinto. I left after a few days and flew from Seville to Madrid where I had a meeting with ERTC's MD, Alberto. He was very enthusiastic about the cooperation between ERTC and RTZC and mentioned that ERT had some minority holdings in a couple of underground potash mines in Catalonia. He explained that ERT was anxious to obtain an independent review of the output potential and operational cost/tonne of potash from both of these mines before committing further funds to their development. I said that we (RTZC) would be able to handle these assignments in March with an integrated technical/financial team, including Keith our Spanish speaking metallurgist, who would have completed the San Jose testwork by then.

I next had a short trip to Ireland to examine mining methods at the new underground mine at Tara. The mine was in Co Meath about 25 miles north-west of Dublin, but an even shorter drive from Dublin Airport. This significant lead-zinc deposit had been originally located by someone who noticed anomalous lead values in analyses of milk produced from farms in the Tara area. A programme of detailed soil analysis and later diamond drilling located one of the largest lead-zinc deposits in Europe. As follow-up to the original discovery there had been a staking rush and an open-pit was developed very close to the Tara Mine by the Bula organisation. There was also a lot of legal goings-on concerning claim jumping and unclear claim boundaries - shades of the Californian Gold Rush! The Tara mine was a fully trackless operation accessed by a ramp-decline. Due to the relatively shallow mine workings and the difficulties for concentrator tailings disposal on the surface it seemed eminently sensible to use a cut-and-fill mining system whereby all de-slimed mill tailings could be pumped back underground as stope backfill. In addition the cut-and-fill mining system, although cyclical by nature, minimised waste dilution and ensured good, fairly rapid ground support to eliminate surface disturbance. I felt that the Tara operation had followed the right approach and, in fact, had done an excellent job in minimising the impact of a large mine on an essentially rural community.

With the arrival of John back from Minas de Riotinto we assembled a five man team to look at the Catalonia potash mines of Cardona and Llobregat. We flew from Heathrow to Barcelona and stayed in a city centre hotel. That afternoon we had a meeting with the Potash Miners group and a general introduction to the potash mining industry located around the town of Suria. That evening we went out in Barcelona to discover the delights of the Ramblas. An absolutely fascinating area, full of street performers, musicians, jugglers, numerous tapas bars and restaurants all absorbing the dense, lively crowd. As usual in Spain only foreigners eat before 9 pm and certainly eating in Ramblas's restaurants didn't get into its stride until 10 pm and kept going until 2am. The next day we hired two cars and drove NW for forty miles or so to the major town of Manresa. Cardona was a further fifteen miles NW passing through the town of Suria, where the other potash mines were located. Cardona was an old, well established potash mine, but quite different from the more usual flat bedded potash deposits. The Cardona potash deposit surrounded a large salt dome and the workable, very thick "bed" was near vertical. Thus the mine was much more akin to a typical steep dipping metal mine and consequently had been developed from a series of crosscuts driven from a main vertical shaft. This shaft handled ore hoisting in balanced skips and men and materials were handled in a large cage and counterweight. The mining method used was sub-level open stoping. Long-hole ring drilling was undertaken by conventional compressed air drifters mounted on simple skid or wheeled wagon rigs. The blasted ore was recovered from a grizzly scram drift below the undercut. Here the rom ore was loaded into Granby cars for haulage to the main ore pass ahead of the skip pocket. Conventional drill/blast methods were used for all mine development. Our most difficult task was trying to get a handle on the ore reserve position. It was essential to think in three dimensions since the reserves comprised an inverted bowl surrounding the salt dome. The footwall of the deposit was thus the salt/potash contact. Further down dip, away from the nose of the salt dome, the potash "bed" true thickness rapidly diminished as the dip flattened out to 15 degrees. The remaining ore reserves supporting this type of sub-level open stoping seemed fairly limited - the best had already gone. The Cardona mine, as presently configured, could thus sustain production for only a few more years. It was not a mine on which to contemplate further major expenditure.

The Llobregat mine, closer to the town of Suria, was an entirely different proposition. This was a relatively new mine and appeared to be a typical flat bedded potash deposit. The mine was accessed by a large decline containing a road alongside a main production conveyor. This conveyor led directly into the surface screening plant. We travelled down the decline in a diesel Land-Rover equipped with catalytic scrubber. The decline slope was 1 in 8, or about 7 degrees, with a length of about half a mile before it levelled off in the potash bed. This confirmed the plans which showed the potash bed as between 300 to 400 feet below surface. Because of the relatively shallow depth and the low inclination of the potash bed (from flat to +/- 10 degrees) the mine was worked on a typical pillar-and-stall system. Actual mining of the stalls was carried out with a Dosco Roadheader continuous miner type of machines, which were frequently seen in coal mines. These were ideal machines for mining soft bedded ground such as coal, salt, gypsum or potash. Behind the Roadheader a gathering-arm loader fed the broken potash on to stall conveyors which in turn fed onto the main trunk conveyor leading to the main decline. The mining layout and operation was exactly like a pillar-and-stall coal mine apart from the absence of black coal dust! All development including the original stall drives were also driven with Roadheaders. The mine was totally electric, well illuminated, clean and organised. In complete contrast to Cardona determining the potash ore reserve was very simple. The plan area of the lease was determined by planimeter and the relevant volume calculated by using the average bed thickness. This had been obtained from vertical diamond drill intercepts laid out on a regular surface grid. This volume was then discounted by a low grade/washout factor and an extraction percentage. The mine had extensive reserves and could easily expand production by introducing more Roadheaders, gathering-arm loaders and speeding up the main conveyors. It was a very efficient, well run mine (the Shift Bosses got around underground on small motorbikes!) with low operating costs. We obviously advised ERTC/ERT that production expansion was entirely feasible, provided, of course, that there was a ready market for the potash.

On the way back to Barcelona we drove up the zigzag road to the Benedictine Monastery at Monserrat, set over 4000 feet above the Cardoner river valley. The views across the Catalan coastal plain towards Barcelona were spectacular. Today there was easy access to the Monastery by zigzag road, cog railway and cable car, but before these modern methods of ascent were built the Monastery was virtually inaccessible - a veritable retreat. During the Spanish civil war, many Republicans escaped the clutches of Franco's execution squads by taking refuge in the Monastery. Back in Barcelona we had further meetings with the Spanish Potash group and then spent the afternoon visiting the Sagada Familia cathedral (still unfinished), Gaudi's museum/house and the nearby beach. That night, unsurprisingly, we went back to the Ramblas to sample again both the vibrant atmosphere and the numerous tapas bars. Everyone agreed that Barcelona had terrific ambience, in spite of the oppressive Franco dictatorship. Little did we know then that Franco would die in November of that year (1975) and all Spain would be liberalised with a new democratic government under the old royal family.

Back at RTZC we had a new Chairman as Ken had decided to take a sabbatical from all RTZ work and attempt to sail from the UK to the Caribbean. Since Ken had been the founding MD of RTZC back in the mid '60s, the current executive directors (Dick, metallurgical Dave, marketing Dave and I) decided to give him a "Farewell and Bon Voyage Party". So on a glorious early spring day a red London double-decker bus turned up outside 6 St James's Square, whence all RTZC employees & spouses em-bussed for the short drive to Westminster pier. Here we boarded a Thames river boat for the half hour trip downstream to the Royal Naval College Greenwich.

Wren's twin dome masterpiece was in a marvelous setting overlooking the lawns that sweep down to the river. After a brief look around the college we all had lunch in a private room. After the meal Dick made a short speech and presented Ken with a pair of oars for his Atlantic adventure. In fact I had made these oars when assembling the kit-dinghy for Beals ponds - at least they raised a few laughs. Ken, of course, was planning to sail, but all agreed the oars would provide back-up power in the doldrums. After that it was a pleasant, beery cruise back to Westminster pier and onwards to No 6 St James's Square. Not a lot of work was achieved that afternoon!

At home we decided to celebrate Gillian's new job at the Woodchurch surgery and my appointment as Director of Mining at RTZC by finally ditching Gillian's old blue Ford van for a brand new front wheel drive white Simca 1100 van. There were three reasons for sticking with a van, firstly it attracted no purchase tax, secondly it was very handy for lumping all sorts of DIY materials around as well as the Allen Scythe and thirdly it was essential for taking Matt out for walks; he really was too big to squash into the back of the GT6. We also purchased a custom made rear seat and grill which provided both extra seating capacity and kept Matt out of the driver's lap! It was a very well made, robust van with reasonable performance. The one drawback was it was very heavy on petrol for an 1100cc engine. Gillian really liked it and appreciated the short, direct gear stick after the incredibly long, wobbly one in the old Ford.

My next work at RTZC entailed two promotion/selling jobs in eastern Europe. I first flew to Ljubljana in the Slovenia province of Yugoslavia. Here I hired a car and drove north up in to the Julian Alps close to the Austrian border. In this area diamond drilling had located a potentially large uranium deposit and the Yugoslav exploration outfit had invited tenders for the evaluation of this discovery. My visit was to assess the local services available (if any in this fairly remote, but beautiful region) as well as, of course, the topographical and geological situation of the find. I spent two days in the exploration area and, to be frank, felt very uneasy about the prospects of a huge open-pit mine in this beautiful, wild, pristine area. Back in Ljubljana I had time to look around the town and found it was extremely attractive and laid-back with friendly Slovenians and gorgeous medieval architecture. The main square with masses of outdoor cafes and bars was the focus of this very agreeable town.

However I had to press on and flew from there down to Belgrade. The airport was on the north side and the short drive into the centre disclosed a rather drab, grey city dominated by large, soulless apartment blocks. My hotel was an enormous slab of a building (800 plus rooms I guess) on the south side of the wide grey/brown Danube - blue it wasnt! The next day I took a taxi back in to the centre, across the Danube for a meeting with the state copper mining company RTB. The Serbs were very hospitable and before the meeting we all sampled thick, Turkish style coffee and at least a couple of slivovitz, all before 10am! The meeting was to discuss the possible purchase by RTB of RTZC's suite of OPD computer programs developed by Peter and his cohorts in London. Peter had briefed me on all the general aspects of these programs, but, of course, I could not expound all the detailed "bells & whistles". Fortunately the Belgrade RTB people were managerial types more interested in the financial aspects of buying/leasing our programs rather than the nitty gritty niceties of programming - large (concealed) sigh of relief from me! We continued imbibing Turkish coffee & slivovitz throughout the morning and then repaired to a city centre restaurant, where, of course, the drinking continued. It reminded me, alcohol wise, of the time in Helsinki with the Rauturruukki shaft engineers. These miners certainly can drink. They said they would pick me up from the hotel at 7.30am next morning for the 150 mile drive SE to the Bor mines close to the Romanian and Bulgarian border. I declined their offer to "show me around the city", fibbing that I had to sort out documentation for the mine visit. In fact I caught a taxi back to my hotel and crashed out, but I'm sure they guessed the "Englander" was pissed as a parrot. Later that night I made a mental note to beware of slivovitz - it's strong stuff.

Good as their word the RTB guys picked me up from the hotel next morning in a large twin cab 4 x 4. The road was OK for the first seventy miles or so but then became fairly rough and quite tortuous as we headed into more hilly, wooded country. The big open-pit copper mines (probably the largest in Europe) were sited at around the 3000ft elevation close to the town of Bor, population about 25,000. The town itself lies just off the Borska Reka (BR) river, a tributary of the Timak river, which in turn flows into the Danube. I noted that a railway was located in the BR valley, which explained how RTB got products out and supplies in. We went first to the engineering offices to look at the geological plans and sampling data and then moved on to the open-pit bench plans. I was pleased we had an interpreter as everything was in either Serbian or Russian cyrillic script. We then drove around the large open pit(s). These were being worked in a conventional manner with fairly ancient Russian rotary blast-hole drills, rope shovels and rear dump trucks. Bench heights were about 12m and the waste stripping and ore mining sequence appeared a little haphazard. When we got back to the engineering offices I explained (through the interpreter) that our OPD programs would require the basic exploration/sampling data to be digitised into a three dimensional block model, which also needed to incorporate operating cost data. I said that if RTB purchased our OPD programs we would also send a computer specialist to assist in setting up the programs. I then requested full details of RTB's existing computer facilities, which they reluctantly provided.

From the mine we went to RTB's guest facility in the dour, grey town of Bor. The facilities comprised a small flat in a soulless apartment block that shouted its Russian heritage. In fact the whole place had a very Russian feel similar to that I had experienced when the SAS plane made an emergency landing at Tashkent in Uzbekistan. We had dinner in a joyless RTB owned cafeteria style restaurant in the town centre. However the RTB engineers were very friendly and, of course, very hospitable with ubiquitous slivovitz. Once bitten, twice shy, this time I restricted myself to no more than four and moved on to the safer beverage of beer! The following day we had another session in the mine engineering offices and left after an early lunch for the four to five hour drive back to Belgrade. I had a debrief meeting in the RTB head office the following morning followed by another long, liquid lunch (again, slivovitz restraint) after which two of their mine planning engineers gave me a tour of the city. There were many fine buildings from the middle ages, but also signs of aerial bomb damage from WW2 and bleak apartment blocks in the city suburbs. Back in the vast hotel again after my tour of the city it was easy to recognise the strategic importance of Belgrade at the confluence of two major rivers, the Danube and the Sava. I spent a quiet night in the hotel to be ready for an early morning flight back to the UK.

Back in London I learnt from Dick that we had had another enquiry from India. I expected this to be from HZL requesting us to assist with the implementation of the Rajpura Dariba project, but I was wrong. It transpired to be a brand new request from the Gujarat Minerals Development Corporation (GMDC) for a full feasibility study for their Ambaji multi-metal deposit situated about 120 miles due north of the city of Ahmadabad in the northern part of Gujarat State. In fact Ambaji was only ninety miles due west of the Rajasthan city of Udaipur and it seemed fairly certain that GMDC had learnt of our work for HZL on the Rajpura Dariba project. We rapidly assembled a team comprising a mining geologist, underground mining engineer, mineral processor, civil engineer, cost and financial analyst with me as overall supervisor and old India hand! We flew with Air India (AI) - "Your palace in the sky" (known by air buffs as Allah Informed) - to Bombay, where we stayed overnight before flying the next day with Indian Airlines Corporation (IAC) (known by 'said air buffs as I Aint Coming on account of its poor timekeeping) - to Ahmadabad. We then took two taxis' from the airport to a city centre hotel before going on to GMDC's head office. I was very surprised at the sheer size and bustle of Ahmadabad after the relatively relaxed pace of Udaipur. However it all made sense when they told us that Ahmadabad was the centre of the Indian cotton industry - it was the modern day Indian version of the Lancashire mill town, but on a huge scale. The Indian cotton industry had settled in Ahmadabad because of the warm, humid climate experienced in this area immediately to the east of the Rann of Kutch. The Ambaji project engineer gave us a brief run-down on the state of the project followed by a detailed description of the exploration work undertaken by the GSI and the associated sampling and analytical results. It all looked fairly straightforward and we agreed to drive up to the site next morning.

Two GMDC Land Rovers and an Ambassador car picked us up from the hotel for the four hour drive north. At the project site GMDC had expanded the original GSI exploration camp into a large project camp with permanent buildings. It was a very pleasant location with a lot of mature trees surrounding the camp. The topography was fairly gentle with slowly rising ground to the NE. Local streams drained into the Banas river which flowed WSW towards the Kutch. Examination of the GSI drill core and sample data confirmed a blind (ie non-outcropping) multi-metal sulphide ore zone extending from 150ft below surface to at least 1200ft and still open at that depth. It was thus immediately apparent that the ore zone disposition and local topography precluded the use of open-pitting or adit mining. The access options appeared to be a footwall vertical shaft in conjunction with a ramp-decline. The drill cores indicated a steeply dipping ore zone with reasonable strength footwall rocks but weak hanging wall rocks. Over the next few days we worked on determining the form and shape of a mineable ore reserve which enabled us to calculate the ore expectancy - t/vm. We then used the old Stoakes rule of 10% the ore expectancy to arrive at a sustainable mining rate of 1,500 tonnes/day and this was used as the basis for the feasibility study.

The camp accommodation was good and included a well run kitchen. Close by the camp were some enormous banyan trees and as dusk fell dozens of giant fruit bats used to come in to feast on the figs. In fact there were probably thousands of bats as the sky distinctly darkened as they descended on the trees with an eerie screeching - it was an amazing sight. As we sat out on the verandah for this early evening spectacle there was one real drawback - no booze. Gujarat, being the birth state of the Mahatma, was a dry state. Illegal rice wine was available from the local village, but after trying it (yuk) I determined to get a foreigners "booze pass" from the local authorities. I went to the local police station with our six passports to get six foreigners' liquor permits. Obviously liquor was not for sale anywhere in Gujarat State and one of the GMDC project guys said the best, closest source was the hill station of Mount Abu, just over the border in Rajasthan, a drive of some 35 miles from Ambaji. In fact Mount Abu sounded a fascinating place in itself, apart from the attraction of liquor stores. Four of us (but with six passports!) crammed into the Ambassador plus driver for the trip. The town was spread out along the southern upper slopes of Mount Abu at about 4000ft elevation. The highest point, a short distance north of the town, rose to 5,600ft The air was markedly cooler than the plains of northern Gujarat and it was obvious why a hill station had been established here. The driver took us to the best (he said) liquor store and we stocked up with local Indian whisky and gin as well as a couple of crates of Kingfisher beer - this mining malarky is thirsty work! I said we'd like a little tour of Mount Abu and he took us to the marvelous Dilwara Jain temples built of beautiful white marble in the 12th Ce. They were stunning in a glorious setting, cut into a steep cliff, looking SE over the Rajasthan/Gujarat border. A real bonus was the complete absence of camera toting tourists! Apart from several Jain temple attendants we had the place to ourselves. On the human front yes, but there was a large troop of monkeys bouncing around all over the place which added to the exotic atmosphere.

After cool Mount Abu Ambaji seemed hot and humid. However the Kingfisher beers greatly enhanced our verandah dusk watch of the fruit bats in the Banyan trees. Back at the project our data collection and investigations were going well. I undertook to complete the main shaft and ramp-decline designs back in the UK and left John to continue with the underground mining layout. Keith was busy with metallurgical testwork and Tony was following up on power and water supply. I went back to GMDC head office in Ahmadabad with Ron where he would stay to obtain local cost data, labour pay rates and financial details such as local taxes, import duties etc. After a progress meeting with GMDC management I caught the narrow gauge train to Udaipur, a six hour journey for the 190 mile trip. Here I went to HZL's Udaipur head office for a briefing and update on the Rajpura Dariba (RD) project. I stayed overnight in the Lakshmi Palace Hotel, overlooking Lake Pichola, yet another glorious Indian location. The next day the RD project manager collected me from the hotel in a Mahindra jeep for the fifty mile drive NE to the project site. It was great to see how far the project had developed. Shaft sinking was well underway, the main crushing/screening plant was under construction and a start had been made on the concentrator building. Many houses had been completed in the new Dariba village and, most importantly (for Indian projects), the wall encircling the whole industrial area had been finished. It was all very encouraging. The RD project manager felt that they might need further assistance from RTZC on detailed mine design once the shaft sinking was complete. I (of course!) agreed and said that we now had an underground mining engineer who specialised in geotechnics (John) and he was currently just over the border at Ambaji in Gujarat. It was agreed that the timing for RD's need for more detailed mine design was dependent on completion of the main shaft sinking work, still about twelve months away. In turn I said that RTZC planned to appoint a local Indian agent who would keep in contact with our present clients (HZL & GMDC) and attempt to locate further business in the Indian metalliferous mining industry. We returned to Udaipur that evening.

The following morning I flew from Udaipur in an IAC Vickers Viscount to Delhi via an intermediate stop at the pink city of Jaipur. I stayed in a city centre hotel and from there made an appointment (took ages on the local phone system) to see the (CS) at the British Embassy (BE). My meeting was for the next day so I took one of the ubiquitous tuk-tuk taxis for a tour of old Delhi including a visit to the huge Jama Masjid mosque. The following day I took a taxi to the BE in New Delhi where the (CS) was very helpful. He had a number of suggestions as to whom we might appoint as local agents for selling/marketing RTZC's geological, mining and minerals industry consulting service. I asked him about bribery and he said well..........it's not really necessary! He suggested we pay a fixed sum to retain the agent (exclusive basis) to cover his direct costs (travel, post, telephone etc) and a fixed percentage of any business/contract obtained. He said that many foreign consulting companies in other industries often worked in this manner. Pressed further he said that "maybe" some local agents paid a "sweetener" to the sought-after client, financed out of their own percentage, but..........? It all seemed entirely reasonable and pragmatic. I was extremely grateful for his practical advice and undertook to keep him appraised of any appointment of a local agent. I also told him of our current involvement with both HZL and GMDC.

After the meeting I took a taxi to look around the Lutyens designed New Delhi, ending up in Connaught Place. Here I located an excellent restaurant, recommended by the (CS), and enjoyed an authentic chicken tikka Madras. Over the next few days I contacted four or five possible agency firms and eventually decided on a small outfit run by a mining engineer called Shad. He had worked in the Indian metal mining industry and was well acquainted with the Geological Survey, Ministry of Mines, and several of the major State mining groups. His small offices were also based in Delhi, a prime requirement. I discussed the potential of Shad as agent with Dick over the (intermittent) phone and we agreed to offer him an incentive of 10% of any future contracts we secured plus a fixed annual sum for "agency expenses", based on my appraisal of his last years books. I spent the following day in Shad's offices (actually a room in his house!) running my calculator red hot converting rupees to £sterling. We agreed figures/amounts that evening and I undertook to send him a UK based Agency Agreement. He said that as soon as that was signed and the fixed sum paid he would visit both HZL and GMDC to appraise them of his new role. All in all it seemed to go well, but obviously future Indian consulting work for RTZC would be the true measure of the use of local agents. At the very least I had learnt a basis for setting up an Agency Agreement for consulting services. The next day I talked to GMDC in Ahmadabad to learn that all was progressing well with the investigations at Ambaji and that the RTZC team plus three engineers from GMDC expected to fly to London the following week to continue with the feasibility work. I left Delhi that evening on the overnight flight to London.

I had a couple of days at home to reacquaint myself (!) with Gillian, Matt and Anjon; it was good to be home after being away so much over the past two months. As well as the pair of Khaki Campbell ducks we now had families of moorhens on both ponds. To even up the "flocks" we decided to get a couple more Khaki Campbells - they really are very pleasant, sociable birds to have around. They kept a wary eye on the two dogs, but Matt was much more interested in human company and Anjon hated getting his feet wet! When I returned to the office to recommence working on the Ambaji shaft and ramp-decline designs, Dick told me that our parent company, RTZ, was prepared to finance the purchase of a new EU built car of under 1500cc, for directors of subsidiary companies such as RTZC. I cannot recall what sparked this largess but it seemed too good an opportunity to miss, especially so as the old Triumph GT6 was beginning to show its age. In truth I was sorry to see the GT6 go, it had a marvelous performance powered by the old six cylinder, twin carb, two litre engine married to a very slick four speed gearbox. Its one serious drawback was very dodgy road holding with the new fangled independent rear suspension (IRS). I had ended up facing the wrong way when braking hard coming into a roundabout in icy conditions - definitely discombobulating! In addition I had been having a lot of trouble with my lower back. The osteopath in Tenterden was firmly of the opinion that the low, legs almost straight out driving position of the GT6 was a major contributing cause of my back pain. I advertised in Motor Magazine and it sold very quickly. (I guess the old GT6 had a certain cachet as the poor man's E-type). I made a disastrous decision and opted for a front wheel drive Renault 5 TS. It had (as suggested by the osteopath) straight backed, upright seats, about as different from the GT6 as you could imagine. I went for the TS model, as this was the sports version (oh really?) and had, supposedly, a bit of oomph. After the GT6 it was like driving an ice cream van and worst of all it had a really sick-making body roll. Definitely one of my worst cars, but at least it was paid for by RTZ. Both Gillian and I preferred to drive our Simca van.

In the office I completed the Ambaji main shaft design and had extensive discussions with GEC's Erith office concerning friction winder specifications and budget costs for both balanced skip hoist and cage and counterweight. I had worked extensively with GEC on both the Rosebery, Tasmania shaft winders and more recently with the Lepanto Tubo Shaft winders in the Philippines and the Rajpura Dariba shaft winders in India. They (GEC) seemed more than happy to provide general arrangement drawings and layouts plus budget costs based on the outline duty specifications prepared by us. They were extremely helpful to RTZC as we prepared these engineering and feasibility studies. GEC never charged us for this work, but on reflection I realised that by being fully appraised of the requirements for these various winders they (GEC) were in the box seat to be included in a winder supply bidders list. Thus by the time the Ambaji project team arrived back from Gujarat I was well advanced with shaft designs and winder costs. In addition my contacts at Cementation Mining, Doncaster were also extremely helpful in providing budget costs/timings for both shaft sinking and the development of a ramp-decline at Ambaji. We had a full discussion on the detailed scope of the feasibility study with the Ambaji project engineers and I left John to put the whole thing together.

Dick had had some recent talks with BP Minerals and had arranged for me to join a small BP Minerals team to carry out an evaluation of the Touissit lead mine project near Oujda in Morocco. The London based BP guy and I flew from Heathrow to Marseille where we were joined by a senior Belgian BP geologist. This gentleman was very affable and apart from being an excellent mining geologist spoke fluent French and had previously worked in North Africa. In Marseille we transferred to an Air Inter-flight for the short hop across the Mediterranean to Oujda airport close to the Algerian border. BP maintained an oil exploration office in Oujda and their local staff had arranged for a four wheel drive vehicle to take us to a hotel in the centre of the city. The next day the three of us were joined by the resident BP Exploration Manager, who drove us about 45 miles south into the Jerada district. The area was quite undulating with sharp hills rising 200m above stoney desert intersected by several streams flowing north in semi-fertile valleys. The small Touissit deposit was located on the flank of one of these hills. This lead-silver occurrence had been known for a number of years, but systematic exploration only commenced in 1974. That comprised some diamond drilling together with a small exploration shaft and limited underground development. The very high grade lead veins were contained within a competent dolomite host. The geological interpretation showed steeply dipping veins of moderate true width but carrying very high lead-silver values. However the strike extent appeared limited and the depth extent, down dip and down plunge, unknown. After an inspection of the underground development and further perusal of the geological data my thoughts were that the deposits output potential was unlikely to be of sufficient size to interest BP. My old 10% ore expectancy rule indicated a possible extraction rate of circa 300 tonnes/day, utilising overhand cut-and-fill stoping to maximise recovery of the high grade ore whilst minimising waste dilution. We all agreed that the deposit was "small tonnage, high grade" mine territory.

That evening the resident BP exploration guy arranged for a typical Bedouin style meal. This comprised a young goat roasted whole over a log fire. I'm not sure why I drew the short straw (although I was later assured it was a great honour) but I was presented with one of the goat's eyes, to eat on it's own to get the feast underway. No, I did not enjoy it, nor thankfully did I gag, but concentrated my mind on "other things". In fact the eye had quite a pleasant taste, but the thought of what I was eating rather ruined the enjoyment. At any rate the other BP guys had a good laugh at my facial contortions! Oh the joys of travelling in the boondocks. The next day we headed back to Oujda. In the BP exploration office we sorted out how the Belgian mining geologist and I would complete our write-ups on the project and submit them to BP Minerals London office within ten days. We further agreed to cost a notional underground mining project on the basis of a 300 tonnes/day rom production with a 300 days/year concentrator operation. The London BP guy had collected all the relevant data on power and water supply as well as the small quantity of mineralogical data (for conceptual concentrator design). The local BP Exploration Manager also provided him with local labour and mining/milling consumable costs. I also took a copy of all the local labour and mining consumable costs. The next day we flew back to Marseille where we split up with the BP mining geologist, he back to Belgium and the two of us back to London. Altogether we had only been away for five days.

The next two weeks were very busy writing up and costing the 300 tonnes/day Touissit mine project as well as catching up with the Ambaji feasibility project. NC, the GMDC project manager, who was working closely with John and the team was also a mining engineer who liked both a beer (or two) and a game of three card brag. Whilst at Ambaji he had shown what a shrewd card player he was by successfully relieving most of the RTZC team (especially me) of considerable quantities of rupees. In London none of us were into the expensive casino/gambling scene so instead we used to get NC and his GMDC team mates mildly intoxicated on special (ie strong) English beers. It was all harmless but led to excellent team bonding between RTZC and GMDC. It was a very happy project and led to a long lasting involvement of RTZC in the construction phase at Ambaji.

Back at home I had really got fed up with the sick-making Renault 5, such a contrast to the splendid Triumph GT6. On my daily run from Woodchurch to Ashford station I passed a motor cycle shop which had caught my eye. Thus one Saturday I took Gillian into Ashford shopping. We went for a coffee and agreed to meet back at the parked Simca van in an hour or so after we each went our separate ways. I immediately went to the motor cycle shop and in a moment of mid-life madness/crisis (?) bought a beautiful, second-hand 1975 Honda 400/4 bike. I had read about this new(ish) Japanese transverse four cylinder bike in the motor cycling press - they all gave it the thumbs up. The Honda still had three months valid road licence, the shop arranged temporary insurance cover and my driving licence included motorcycles. I bought a crash helmet, some heavy gauntlets and some plastic (!) biker boots. I paid and rode gingerly back to the car park, parking alongside the Simca van. I had, of course, told Gillian what I might do so she was not surprised (nor enthusiastic it must be said) to see the bike. I followed her in the Simca van back to Beals trying hard not to fall off. Matt was most unimpressed, actually a little frightened, and barked his head off at the bike whilst Anjon was totally uninterested (bitches on heat were his forte). After getting used to the bike over the weekend I decided to use it for my daily commute to Ashford station unless it was tipping down with rain. They always say once a biker always a biker and the Honda 400/4 certainly gave me a new lease of life in the motor biking field. It was 22 years since my last bike, the 1935 OK Supreme, and boy had Japanese motorbike technology moved on with time (40 years). The little Honda's 408cc four cylinder engine revved to 10,000 rpm, pulled a six speed foot-change box, had hydraulic forks at the front, swinging arm hydraulic rear suspension, electric start and front disc brake. Top speed was quoted as 110 mph (I never did more than 90 mph) but acceleration was definitely quick at 7.4 seconds to 60 mph. I fitted a rear rack, behind the pillion seat, so that I could carry my briefcase on the Ashford commute; Renault 5 usage slumped!

13

I had a meeting with BP Minerals in the city to finalise the initial appraisal of the Touissit Project in Morocco. It was agreed that although high grade the current "reserve" was small and the tonnage potential limited. The project was considered too small to be of interest to BP. So that was that, a fascinating jaunt, but nothing more. However it did introduce RTZC to BP Minerals and I guess they must have been happy with my input since they asked if I could go to Canada and have a look at their Les Mines, Selabie copper-zinc project in northern Quebec. They said that the brief would comprise reviewing the exploration, geological and geotechnical data in BP Minerals Toronto office and possibly visiting the site. They wanted a start asap. I checked with Dick and he agreed I could be available for up to a couple of weeks before heading back to India where Shad, our new local agent, had drummed up some new business. I checked with BP Minerals and they agreed I should front-up to their Toronto offices on the following Monday. This meant taking a Sunday morning flight from Heathrow to enable me to have an overnight sleep to get over jet-lag. It was a bit of a scrum around at home and in the rush I somehow managed to leave my suit jacket hanging up behind the bedroom door. It was warm and I always travel casual (a suit gets ruined on a plane) so I didn't realise its absence until I unpacked in the hotel in downtown Toronto. Sunday, no shops open so......what the hell, no jacket, surely it wasn't a hanging offence? As it happened it was no problem at all since BP Minerals Chief Geologist in Toronto was none other than Victor, who I'd last seen at the Kiabakari mine in Tanganyika 14 years ago in 1962. He'd changed very little physically and was still the cheerful, optimistic person I remembered. We had a good laugh about my "no jacket" appearance and Victor said at least I didn't need to roll up my sleeves to get down to work! In fact we had a bullshit session on what we'd each been doing since leaving Kiabakari. Victor and wife, Peggy, had been in Canada for over ten years and were now settled in Toronto since joining BP Minerals. We spent the next few days in the office going over all the exploration data, which included geophysical, geochemical and magnetometer surveys as well as the follow-up diamond drilling and subsequent assay results. There was also detailed mineralogical analysis but very little geotechnical information. It was apparent that a fairly large copper/zinc anomaly had been located. Victor and I agreed that we needed to put "boots on the ground" to fully appreciate the topographic and geological setting. I had already said that I really needed to have a look at split diamond drill cores covering the hangingwall and footwall rocks as well, of course, as the potential ore zone.

They arranged for us to fly up to the site on Thursday by BP charter light aircraft. The project site was about 450 miles due north of Toronto close to the Quebec/Ontario border. The BP guys picked me up at the hotel at 6.30 and we left Toronto airport at 7.30 for the 2.5 hour flight putting us on the project airstrip by around 10 am. As one might suspect it was a very well organised and equipped project camp with all the usual facilities. It was a typical Canadian fly-in fly-out camp with good single mens bunkhouses and messing facilities. We had the customary briefing by the on-site project manager before a quick lunch. The afternoon was spent gumshoeing around the surface, looking at all available rock exposures. We stayed overnight in a visitors bunkhouse and the following day spent the morning looking a numerous drill cores. In the afternoon BP's project geologist and Victor explained their thoughts on the deposit's genesis and, for me, more importantly the likely sub-surface disposition of the mineralised zones. It was made abundantly clear that the deposit was still open at depth and their current deep drilling programme aimed to substantiate this. I asked Victor if we could stay over till Saturday so that I had the evening to work over some ideas for possible mine development for discussion with the project guys in the morning before flying back to Toronto in the afternoon. That was OK so next morning I outlined a possible mining plan. The site topography was fairly flat and the deposit outcropped beneath fairly shallow overburden, which could easily be stripped off. Thereafter a conventional open-pit could mine the deposit down to a depth of about 100m with an overall strip ratio of circa 5 to 1. The old 10% ore expectancy rule indicated a sustainable underground mining rate of 4,000 tonnes/day. The open-pit would contain about four million tonnes of ore down to a depth of 100m and this could provide mill feed for a little over three years whilst an underground mine was developed through a footwall vertical shaft for ore hoisting and ramp-decline for heavy trackless mining units. It appeared that the most pressing problem for Les Mines was to sort out the mineralogy/metallurgy so that construction of a copper/zinc concentrator could be started as soon as possible. Obviously an open-pit operation could commence rapidly subject only to the availability of blast-hole drills, shovels and trucks. During these initial open-pit years shaft sinking and underground mine development could proceed. The BP guys thought this was a reasonable mining concept, although there were reservations about ore losses and safety issues with the pillar required beneath the worked out open-pit. Victor picked up on the necessity to finalise mineralogy and metallurgical testwork quickly to enable concentrator design and construction to commence and this in turn put more emphasis on deep diamond drilling to determine any changes in ore mineralogy at depth. Victor and the site geologist then discussed bringing in additional diamond drill rigs to speed up this deep drilling work. We flew back to Toronto later in the afternoon and Victor dropped me off at the hotel saying that he would pick me up on Sunday morning for some Toronto tourism.

Good as his word he drove me all around the Toronto financial district and the main retail shopping and theatre district. We also had a good run along the Lake Ontario frontage and of course had a trip up the very impressive CN Tower, which I guess was the tallest free standing structure in Canada. The view from the observation deck was spectacular and only then did I appreciate that Toronto was a very large city indeed. Toronto, of course was only about 70 miles as the crow flies from Niagara Falls, which was on the southern side of Lake Ontario. That was when I realised it was nineteen years since I'd visited the Falls on my way from Elliot Lake to New York in 1957, as a second year CSM student no less. I caught the "Red Eye Shuttle", Canadian style on Sunday evening and was back in the RTZC office by late Monday morning.

There was good news on the Indian front as Shad (our new Indian agent) had made contact with Hindustan Copper Ltd (HCL) who wanted to know if we could assist them with the development and planning of their Malanjkhand open-pit copper project in Madhya Pradesh (MP) state. He had also been approached by Manganese Ore India Ltd (MOIL) who wanted an engineering evaluation of their underground Bharveli mine also in MP state. Dick and I looked at our Indian map and found that both of these projects/mines were located close to Balaghat which was 100 miles ENE of Nagpur. It was agreed that I should visit both sites making all arrangements through Shad's office in Delhi. I had yet another session with Peter who brought me up to speed on all the latest updates of our OPD computer programs, which appeared to be relevant for the Malanjkhand open-pit copper project. We assumed this would be a "selling exercise" similar to that I had used at RTB Bor Copper in Serbia. (Incidentally RTB Bor had, in fact, purchased some of our OPD programs and one of Peter's computer guys was out there now). Dick felt it would also be a good time to visit both HZL and GMDC with Shad to ascertain what further assistance both companies required on their respective underground projects. All in all it looked as if I would be away in India for quite a few weeks.

Since the Canadian trip had only lasted just over a week neither the short grass around the house nor the long grass in the orchard had got out of hand. Gillian managed to keep the lawns under control but the Allen Scythe, required for the orchard, was a little too much of a brute for her to handle. Besides, the 149cc Villiers two-stroke engine was very temperamental and a pig to re-start once it had got warm. Webbs, the marvelous hardware shop in Tenterden had found a cache of rivets for use in refitting the saw-toothed cutter blade to the Allen's reciprocating arm (technical stuff!) so the long grass now looked "cut" rather than "strangled". In addition I had purchased a smallish Westwood rotovator for helping develop a new potato patch in the glutinous clay soil as well as a new vegetable patch, also wired against the rapacious rabbits - oh the joys of country living! In fact with all my travelling it was quite a problem to keep on top of the 1.5 acre "garden" and the three acre orchard. How Gillian managed the estate during my frequent absence, as well as working full-time at the Woodchurch surgery, feeding the ducks and exercising the dogs I'll never know. All I do know was that whenever I was home the weekend seemed dominated by back breaking gardening work, but at least one didn't waste money on gym membership!

A week later I flew to Delhi. At Shad's office we plotted a preliminary schedule subsequently modified after Shad's interminable telephone calls to

HCL, MOIL, HZL and GMDC. Shad was certainly earning his money. I very soon realised just how important a local agent was and that was before Shad sorted out local flights, railway trips and hotel accommodation. Also the Indian telephone system was remarkably flakey and I had yet to regain my "India-speak" English from Chasnalla days, which was essential to at least give one a 50% chance of being understood on the dog-and-bone. Dick didn't (couldn't?) change his Oz accent at all and consequently no one on an Indian telephone could understand a word he said. He used to pass the phone to me for "favour of further needful" (to quote the Indians) for interpretation!

Shad and I took an IAC flight from Delhi direct to Nagpur in Maharashtra state, a major city of about two million people. Nagpur was considered to be the geographical centre of India. From here we took a local Indian Railways (IR) train for the 100 mile trip ENE to Balaghat in MP state. Shortly after leaving Nagpur station I spotted a lengthy coal train hauled by three huge steam locomotives (a triple-header no less) putting out an immense amount of black smoke as they struggled up a fairly steep incline. It was a magnificent sight and in a way highlighted the importance of both railways and coal to the Indian nation. In Balaghat we made our way to the HCL offices. The local HCL manager gave us a rapid run-down on the copper project and it became apparent that the project had only just cleared the exploration stage. It was agreed that we would need no more than two days to appraise the Malanjkhand site. Shad had booked us into a town-centre hotel and the HCL manager suggested he pick us up at 9am the following day. Shad also contacted MOIL by phone and said we would be with them in three days time if that was suitable - it was. The next morning the Manager turned up in a four wheel drive jeep (with driver, of course) for the 55 mile drive to Malanjkhand. To my surprise we soon entered heavily forested country, apparently passing into the Kanha National Park, although no road signs announced this. The Manager said we should keep our eyes skinned as tigers had been seen close to the road. Sure enough he spotted one in dense under-thicket about fifty yards from the road. We stopped and I tried to convince myself that I could see this tiger, but he (or she?) was not evident on the photo I took. However it is true that the Kanha National Park was, in fact, a major habitat for the endangered Indian tiger.

At Malanjkhand we were briefed by the project manager and Chief Geologist. There was a mass of exploration data covering geochemical and geophysical surveys, surface trenching and a large quantity of diamond drilling. The initial exploration work had been carried out by the GSI before the prospect was handed over to HCL when it became apparent that it was basically a copper anomaly. In turn HCL had done infill diamond drilling as well as putting down an exploration decline to confirm diamond drill sample results to provide a bulk sample for mineralogical and metallurgical testing. Looking at the geological vertical cross sections it was quite clear that this was an open-pit mining option - ideal for the application of RTZC's OPD and block modeling programs. I did some low key "selling" of our open-pit computer programs, saying that they had been used on major RTZ open pits such as Bougainville Copper, Rossing Uranium, Mary Kathleen Uranium and Lornex Copper in Canada. The Malanjkhand guys seemed keen and I agreed that we would send out an experienced open-pit mining engineer (Roy) and one of Peter's computer programmers subject to a LoI from HCL. This they duly provided when we got back to Balaghat the next day. We had another night in the Balaghat town-centre hotel and then headed for MOIL's manganese mine at Bharveli.

It was only a short drive (4 miles) by taxi to the mine offices. Here they welcomed us and immediately directed us to the Mine guest house where the Mine Manager joined us for tea and a general run-down on the operations at Bharveli. By Indian manganese mine standards it was a relatively deep mine as opposed to the more usual shallow lateritic deposits. The Bharveli deposit appeared to be a buried, shallow dipping lenticular body formed by earlier weathering or alteration of surrounding manganese rich sediments. The mine was accessed through a conventional short rectangular vertical shaft. Ore was hoisted by truck-in-cage and the operation sounded similar to a small conventional pillar-and-stall coal mine. We had a leisurely walk around all the surface facilities that afternoon. The Mine guest house was very comfortable and reeked of the bygone Raj era when the mine was British owned. In fact, against nearly all anti-Raj comment, the old Indian bearer who looked after us at the guest house said "that he wished the British were back, since you knew exactly where you were then". He didn't add that that probably meant "they" (the Brits) treated him like a dog, but at least things worked like clockwork. En passant I never experienced any anti-British feeling in all my times of working/consulting in India. Indians are unfailingly courteous, curious as to who, what, why you are here and genuinely seemed to want to talk about "things" and "how you are liking India?". I very much like India, as a place, and Indians as people, but it can be a very frustrating place to "do business" when time is of the essence and you are on contract (as with Cementation shaft sinking at Chasnalla).

Next day we went underground. As I half expected not much seemed to have changed in the thirty years or so since independence - the mine was crying out for investment in new plant and technology. It was a rail bound pillar-and-stall mining operation. The method was correct but could obviously be expanded to larger (and more productive) rooms by the use of rock bolts for roof support. However major productive advances could be made with the introduction of trackless equipment, such as wheeled jumbos, LHDs and articulated haul trucks. The introduction of diesel trackless equipment would, obviously require an increase in ventilation capacity, but this could relatively easily be obtained by raising two new shafts, one downcast near the main production shaft and another upcast near the extremity of the mining area. It was also apparent that the existing production shaft would need major modifications to handle a significant increase in mine output. However there was the possibility of increasing shaft hoisting capacity by nearly 50% by changing to skip hoisting from the current truck-in-cage method. We discussed all this with the Mine Manager who was generally in agreement but was certain that the biggest hurdle would be lack of finance for the investment required. He implored us to lobby the local General Manager and Directors in Balaghat. The following morning we spent with the Concentrator Superintendent looking at the surface ore handling facilities from the headframe bin through to the crushing and screening plant and fine ore storage. We also had a tour of the concentrator (as tourists!) and offered the services of a mineral dressing engineer to undertake a plant review if MOIL so wished. After lunch the mine kindly provided transport for Shad and me to our Balaghat hotel. Shad arranged for us to meet the GM at their offices the following morning.

The MOIL Balaghat offices could be classified as "run-down grand". By contrast there was quite a buzz about the place and Shad and I were made to feel "honoured guests". The GM was very enthusiastic and totally receptive to the idea of underground modernisation by changing from a tracked to trackless (diesel) operation. In fact with the Mine Manager he had been advocating this very change for the past year and MOIL's senior management had insisted on getting in outside specialists (RTZC as it happened) to, in effect, check out their own in-house suggestions. I guess we would not have been so popular if we had come up with a totally different suggestion! Shad undertook to keep in close contact with MOIL to see if they required any further engineering assistance from RTZC in detailed mine planning and implementing the mine re-equipping. A review of mineral processing was also mentioned. Afterwards we had a very pleasant lunch in the executive dining room (!) and later that afternoon headed for Balaghat station and the near three hour rail trip back to Nagpur. We spent the night in a city centre hotel.

The following morning Shad and I flew direct to Ahmadabad for a meeting with GMDC and the Ambaji project team. NC, their Project manager, who had only recently returned from our London offices, felt that he and his team would benefit from RTZC's continuing assistance with detailed mine planning and, in particular, helping to finalise shaft sinking and ramp-decline specifications prior to issuing ITBs to short-listed mine construction contractors. I said we would be happy (unsurprisingly!) to do this and intimated that RTZC intended to establish an Indian presence with at least two experienced underground mining engineers probably based at Udaipur. This would enable us (RTZC) to provide mining consultancy to both HZL's Rajpura Dariba project some fifty miles north of that city and GMDC's Ambaji project about eighty miles to the west. I added that we could also supplement these "local" mining engineers with geologists, mineral processors, civil, electrical and mechanical engineers as and when required. Shad and NC seemed to get along well, there was a lot of banter which augered well for our future involvement with GMDC. We did not visit the Ambaji project site as, apart from further deep diamond drilling, nothing much had changed. Thus later that afternoon Shad and I caught the narrow gauge train north to Udaipur in Rajasthan.

This time I introduced Shad to the delights of the Laxmi Villas Hotel, high on a steep bluff overlooking Lake Pichola. Later, sitting on the balustraded balcony supping a beer, a regular box-wallah appeared touting local crafts and paintings. I bought a batik/pastel painting in predominantly browns & yellow. The box-wallah seemed very happy with my purchase (I probably paid 100% over the going rate!) and urged me to come over to his display area. Here, in much secrecy, he produced some remarkable prints of pornographic "goings-on" depicted on the walls of the Khajuraho temples in central India. In fact I didn't buy any, not sure why, but was intrigued that the box-wallah did not want Shad (an Indian) to know what he was up to - bad form, what?

In the morning we went in to see the HZL GM and the RD Project manager, Hari. They insisted on taking us up to the project site to observe progress and Hari, in particular, seemed very keen for Shad to go down the exploration incline shaft and associated underground development. The exploration shaft had been driven at an angle of about 30 degrees and had rough concrete steps cast onto the footwall alongside a 2ft gauge rail track. On the way out Shad, who was a little overweight, was really slow coming up the incline steps. This really pleased Hari, as he knew Shad from mining school and had been teasing him about how he had become "a Delhi city office fat cat". It wasn't a problem, just the reverse since Shad and Hari were old mates, all of which helped cement RTZC's professional relationship with HZL. We had a brief tour of all the new construction activities and shaft sinking and then headed back to Udaipur. Here the main topic of conversation was our proposal to establish an RTZC Udaipur office. I said our senior engineer would be John (who'd worked on both HZL's RD project and GMDC's Ambaji project) assisted by Dave, an experienced Australian underground mining engineer, who had recently joined us from Minenco. For their part, to reduce foreign exchange costs, HZL undertook to provide a modern house, basically furnished, situated in a residential area alongside Lake Pichola. They would also obtain an Ambassador car for use by our engineers around Udaipur and, of course, jeep transport to and from the RD project site. With respect to GMDC Ambaji project work, it was agreed that John would keep detailed time sheets for both HZL and GMDC work and sort out scheduling with the two project managers - Hari and NC. HZL's GM said he would be in London within a couple of weeks and looked forward to signing a new Technical-Assistance Agreement with Dick. All in all very satisfactory and Shad and I entertained the GM and Hari to dinner at the Lakshmi Villas. The next morning Shad and I flew to Delhi via Jaipur.

At his office Shad made an appointment to see the BE CS in the afternoon and later we contacted Dick in London to bring him up to date with new business at HCL Malanjkhand, MOIL Balaghat and further work at GMDC Ambaji and HZL RD. Dick said he would set the ball rolling with Roy to go to Malanjkhand asap and also John and Dave for deployment to our nascent Indian office in Udaipur in the next month or so. He also said that Lepanto had requested me to visit in January (1977). I also said that Shad and I would be seeing the BE CS that afternoon to keep him appraised of our current and projected consulting work, as well as, of course, introducing Shad as RTZC's Indian agent. In response to Dick's query I said I expected to be back in London the following day, subject to getting a seat on the overnight flight and would really appreciate a few days off to renew acquaintance with Gillian! Over the past few weeks Shad had really proved his worth as our local agent. He had the Indian telephone system (in particular) knocked into shape and had an uncanny knack of not accepting "no" for an answer when booking flights on IAC or train travel with Indian Railways. Of course I could have managed, indeed had managed, on my own but Shad took all the stress out of internal Indian travel. Apart from that he was a fund of local knowledge and, very importantly, knew many senior figures in the Indian mining scene. We went to see the CS at the BE where I was able to introduce Shad as RTZC's man in Indian. We also told him of our work at HZL & GMDC and told him that we would be opening an RTZC office in Udaipur in the next month. As before he was very helpful and asked Shad to update him on any new RTZC business and to let him have names and passport details of all RTZC staff when they were in India. We took a taxi back to my hotel whence Shad went on to his office whilst I grabbed my case and caught another taxi out to the airport. Yes, good old Shad had got me on the overnight flight to London!

Back home Gillian seemed to have kept everything ticking over. Now December the grass had stopped growing which meant there was some "free time" at the weekend rather than struggling with mowers and the Allen Scythe. The Eight Bells pub in Tenterden was a fairly regular pit stop on Saturday morning followed, perhaps, by lunch with my parents who lived at High Halden, just three miles from Woodchurch. I still had some trouble with my back, but the sit-up-and-beg Renault 5 was a lot easier to get in and out of than the old GT6, so I really shouldn't be so critical of it. However if it wasn't raining the old Honda 400/4 was good for the Woodchurch-Ashford commute.

In the office Dick had got Roy and one of Peter's computer guys ready to go to Malanjkhand Copper in early January. John and Dave were away sorting out personal affairs prior to leaving for our new "RTZ House" in Udaipur later in January. There was a cable in from Lepanto requesting me to visit in January to ascertain why stoping outputs were falling. They also wanted a review of the new blast-hole stoping area. All in all things did not sound very good at Lepanto. The copper price had fallen sharply and Lepanto were over a barrel as far as ASARCO smelter terms were concerned on account of the high arsenic content of their concentrates. Lepanto were in talks with the Philippine government about the construction of a local roaster plant which would make Lepanto's copper concentrates suitable for the open smelter market.

There were also some new enquiries from South America. Yet another open-pit feasibility study for a potential uranium mine near Mendoza in Argentina and a request from COMSUR SA for an evaluation of the production potential of the famous Milluni tin mine, close to La Paz, Bolivia. (In fact I had visited this mine with Nick & Keith when we were looking for tin concentrates to feed Capper Pass's Humberside tin smelter). I agreed with Dick that it looked like a South American visit in mid to late February taking Don as the mining geologist. First up though it was the Philippines.

14

The direct SAS flight to Manila had been discontinued so it was Cathay Pacific (CP) to Hong Kong, then PAL to Manila. I still marvelled at the way the CP jumbo side slipped, skimming over the roofs of Kowloon as it settled into a final approach of Kai Tak airport. The approach to Manila International (MIA) was much more serene, the mayhem only commenced as one fought ones way out of the arrivals hall into the swirling mass of greeters and meeters. Ponciano, the Lepanto driver, was a welcome figure amidst the throng. He drove me to the Intercon hotel in Makati and said he would wait for me to check in and then drive me down to Lepanto's offices on Roxas Boulevard alongside Manila Bay. On the drive from Makati to downtown Manila I noticed a heavy army presence on the streets. Ponciano said there had been an "insurrection" in the Tarlac district north of Manila. President Marcos had suspended the constitution and introduced martial law some three years ago, but recently there had been an upsurge in civil unrest; a 9 pm curfew was in place. When I got to the Lepanto offices they explained that I would have to go up to the mine by road, with an army escort jeep (!), since all private flights over the city were banned. The road from Manila north to Baguio passed through the Tarlac region. It all sounded quite interesting.

The Lepanto and army escort jeeps arrived at the Intercon hotel at 8 next morning. Besides the driver there were two other Lepanto mine staff in the jeep with me. The army jeep contained four soldiers armed to the teeth with automatic weapons as well as a driver (lightly armed!) It all had a slightly surrealistic feel as we drove out of the northern Manila suburbs. However about thirty miles north of Manila we encountered our first heavily armed army road block. There was no problem as we had an authorised travel permit, but one could feel the tension. Thereafter we passed through several road blocks, at one of which there had been a shooting altercation the day before. About 120 miles from Manila as we climbed into Mountain Province the army soldiers all relaxed. They accompanied us for a further 35 miles into Baguio City, where they disappeared into the main army barracks. We continued on the Halsema Mountain Trail to Mankayan village on the flanks of Mt Pulog and turned west onto the access road to the Lepanto mine camp. There were additional (armed) guards on the access gate.

At the mine everything seemed normal, apart from the absence of any aerial traffic onto and off the Lepanto airstrip. For the first few days I was in the mine engineering office going over the recent mine and mill production statistics. It was apparent that both mined tonnage and grade had declined over the past year with a concomitant decline in mill recovery and thus overall copper concentrate output. With tonnage, grade and mill recovery each down about 6% overall copper output was only 83% of the previous year's production. However the mining stats disclosed a large fall in the quantity of development completed, a sure sign that the mine had become squeezed for lack of access to developed ground ready for stoping. Although it was obvious that the quantity of annual main level and stope development needed to be increased, this would take time to achieve. The immediate solution seemed to be to increase existing stoping output. The Lepanto mine employed two basic stoping methods, flat-back cut-and-fill in virgin ground and square-setting for remnant and pillar recovery - both entirely correct for the conditions. It was virtually impossible to increase productivity in the square-set stopes. It was by nature a slow, careful, "little by little" method suitable for heavy, dangerous ground conditions. That left the cut-and-fill stopes, which, anyway, comprised 67% of the total. These were currently mined flat-back using jacklegs to drill 2.2m deep horizontal holes across the width of the stope, blasting a 2m vertical slice. It was a daily repetitive cycle of drill, blast, scrape of a relatively small tonnage (dependent on stope width). However if we switched to up-hole drilling using stopers we could drill off the whole stope in one go, followed by sequential blasting and scraping. We all agreed that reducing the repetitive cycles would definitely increase the flat-back stopes productivity. With the engineering staff we immediately prepared plans for those stopes which had just been, or were about to be, filled with de-slimed tailings to commence the new cut over with 75 degree up-hole drilling. There were sufficient stopers available (ex raising work) for about eight stopes. More stopers would be required and an order was thus placed with Toyo Rock Drill Company in Manila for another 35 TY-280 JS stopers.

The next "problem" was the new blast-hole stoping area. Apparently the Toyo wagon drill had not performed well and was really struggling on the down-holes. The wagon drill carried a TY-150B drifter with independent rotation. It was a hefty 5in diam machine which guzzled air and having watched it operating it appeared and sounded laboured.. We checked the air pressure close to the drill - it was down to 60 psi, much too low! The wagon unit was being fed with compressed air from the old mine reticulation system and had not yet been connected to the brand new compressed air main just installed in the new Tubo Shaft. A swift change to the new compressed air range would hopefully ginger up the wagon unit's drilling performance!

We inspected the 970 Level rock winder. Because of shaft sinking delays during 1973, 1974 and Lepanto's current squeezed cash position the originally planned new GHH winder had not been installed. This was now a second-hand 780hp AC MB Wild 10ft diameter double-drum winder, ex-Cementation. It was far from ideal and would restrict production from below the 900 Level. Sinking was virtually complete with excavation work continuing on the main pump station and cone grit and sludge settlers. Shaft furnishing, loading station and pump station commissioning would be completed later this year. All in all it was very disappointing to see a half-arsed/compromised Tubo Shaft project approaching completion nearly eighteen months late. I did not enjoy this shaft visit one little bit. However there was much worse to come.

The general mine office said that they had had a message from Manila requesting me to be available for an urgent overseas call at 6 pm that night. It was bad, completely unexpected news. Gillian told me that Lofty, her father, had died of a heart attack. She was now in Cornwall at Glen View in St Mawgan and the funeral would be the day after tomorrow. I explained the position here in the Philippines with martial law and 9pm curfew as well as no private flying and that I would not be able to be back in time for the funeral. She said she was OK with her mother and sisters there at Glen View and would stay in Cornwall for the next week or so. She'd put the dogs in kennels, squared the Woodchurch surgery and shut up Beals. There was no point me rushing back (impossible to do anyway) so I should finish my Philippines work as planned, by the end of which she would be back at Beals again. That was that, Lofty had just made 70, a great character and now sorely missed by all of us.

The next day I sent a telegram of condolences from the mine office first thing in the morning. We had a wrap-up meeting with the Mine Manager on the changes to up-hole drilling in the flat-back stopes and the necessity of more air to the Toyo wagon drill. He also told me of the request from Black

Mountain Mines (BMM), near Baguio, for me to visit their underground copper project. I cleared that this was OK with Lepanto (it was) and they booked me into The Pines Hotel, Baguio for that night. We then arranged for a Lepanto jeep to pick me up from The Pines Hotel at 9am the day after tomorrow for the drive back to Manila complete with army escort! Later that afternoon I hitched a lift in a Lepanto truck travelling to Baguio City for stores. The Pines Hotel was quite luxurious, a little like a mountain chalet type place. I phoned the Black Mountain company and they said a jeep would pick me up at the hotel at 8am the next day. I had a short wander around Baguio. It was a busy place situated at around 5,000ft elevation and was pleasantly cool after the heat and humidity of Manila. There were plenty of offices here as it was the seat of RP government during the summer months.

The BMM project was a short distance to the east of Baguio in the rugged Kennon area. BMMs owner, The Benguet Corp, had undertaken some preliminary diamond drilling and located an interesting copper-gold anomaly. An adit had been driven into the surface exposure followed by a limited amount of underground development on the vein. The mineralisation appeared very similar to that at Lepanto. Benguet's own mineralogical studies confirmed the presence of enargite. Ground conditions did not appear very strong, although, of course, the existing development was still close to the surface. Diamond drill cores also showed heavily fractured ground around the mineralisation. On the very limited information available a cut-and-fill mining method might be applicable. However it seemed to me that the biggest problem (apart from the lack of a viable ore reserve at present!) was the nature of the mineralisation. The presence of arsenic. This already made Lepanto's copper concentrate virtually unsaleable other than to ASARCO's Puget Sound smelter in Seattle, USA. I suggested that they sound out Lepanto on the possibility of tolling any BMM Cu/Au ore through the Lepanto concentrator and also ascertain the position of the government vis-a-vis the chances of an arsenic roaster plant being built in the Philippines. There was little else I could contribute as their BMM project was at a very early stage.

The Lepanto jeep picked me up at The Pines Hotel the following morning for the drive back down to Manila. We collected our army escort from the Baguio army barracks. The drive down was as uneventful as the drive up, but I don't think I was complaining! I checked into the Intercon and the jeep, which had waited, then took me down to Lepanto's office on Roxas Boulevard. Here I had a meeting with Chito, an Executive Vice President (EVP), on the action to be taken to increase stoping productivity - he approved. I mentioned the possibility of BMM tolling their rom ore (similar mineralogy) through the Lepanto concentrator. We also discussed the practicality of BMM shifting their rom ore in Lepanto's own 15-tonne Peterbilt concentrate trucks on their return journey, empty, from Poro Point as they passed through Baguio to Lepanto. It was agreed Lepanto would wait for an approach from Black Mountain. Chito then joked that we (RTZC) should pay them an agent's fee for locating additional business for us and then told me of a recent request from Zambales Base Metals (ZBM). He gave me the telephone number of a ZBM contact in Manila. I called and agreed to meet at their office later in the day. At the meeting they explained that ZBM was exploring/developing a multi-metal deposit in Zamboanga province in southern Mindanao. They wanted me to make an initial appraisal of their prospect - basically, was there a viable mine and if so what potential size? They said they would pay the cost of air travel to and from Zamboanga City, hotel expenses in the city and would arrange for a geologist and driver to take me up to the project site for a two/three day visit. I said OK, told them I was staying at the Intercon and could go down the next day. They agreed to deliver air tickets to the hotel that evening, so that was that - sorted.

It was an early morning flight by a PAL BAC 1-11 twin jet pocket rocket. The flight was about two hours for the near 600 mile trip, virtually due south of Manila. The plane was crammed with returning locals toting just about anything you could think of including a crate of chickens, who didn't seem to enjoy the flight. Zamboanga was a port town right on the southern tip of Mindanao Island. As we came in to land in the early morning the surrounding sea and numerous islands appeared to be a tropical paradise. This image was somewhat ruined by the very heavy landing as the BAC 1-11 thumped into the runway. Nevertheless Zamboanga was an enchanting place with hibiscus and bougainvillea flowers everywhere adding to the exotic Pacific paradise feel - it did not disappoint. ZBM had booked me in to the Lantaka Hotel, right on the sea front overlooking a beautiful corral island. Getting enthused over an up-country exploration/mining project was going to be quite difficult. I took breakfast out on the terrace overlooking the bay. Outrigger canoes came right alongside selling all sorts of goodies (fish, of course!) even at that early hour. I made a mental note to bring Gillian here one day as it really was like paradise. The locals were friendly but curious since other "whiteys" seemed few and far between.

The geologist from ZBM arrived about mid-morning and, with driver and jeep we headed north-west out of the city. Almost immediately we entered thick, tropical jungle as the jeep climbed steadily on a poor dirt track for about half an hour. I guessed we were at an altitude of around 1500ft still in thick jungle, still very hot and sticky, when we came into a cleared area; the exploration camp. This appeared to be sited on a relatively flat part of a ridge which rose to higher ground on the east. Nearby the ground had been cleared by a Cat dozer and a nascent mini open-pit developed. Other jeep tracks led off to diamond drill sites hacked out of the heavy jungle. We gumshoed around the mini open pit where there were obvious signs of copper mineralisation, both oxides and suphides. We then visited three different diamond drill sites in turn and examined the adjacent core boxes. All showed some mineralisation, the deeper intersections, unsurprisingly, indicating the presence of primary sulphides. With the intervening thick jungle I found it very difficult to form a three dimensional picture of the anomaly as disclosed by the mini open-pit and diamond drill intersections. Back at the exploration camp we examined the surface plan and some preliminary vertical cross sections together with an idealised (ie speculative?) long section along the spine of the ridge. The data was too widely spaced to realistically determine a possible ore resource. With the geologist we agreed where infill drilling was required to intersect the "zone" about 100m below the interpolated surface. If these new holes confirmed the presence of mineralisation and hence its dip and plunge directions then further, deeper drill intercepts could be planned. However a major problem was the lack of a comprehensive surface plan showing elevations - ie a contour map. This could only be slowly achieved by cutting survey sight lines through the jungle along the spine of the ridge followed by other lines at, say, 50m interval, cut at right angles to this primary survey line. I appreciated that this was both difficult and time consuming, but felt that the absence of a robust survey datum made it impossible to gauge the size/worth of the anomaly.

We left the camp about 6pm as dusk was beginning to fall. On the journey down the geologist told me not to worry about the road block we would probably encounter further down the track. He said there had been a lot of trouble in Zamboanga Province with the Moro National Liberation Front (MNLF) Islamic terrorists from Jolo Island, which was ninety miles south-west of Zamboanga. I said how would we know whether it was a RP army road block or an MNLF road block? He laughed (nervously I thought) and said "don't worry just get out of the jeep very slowly with your arms in the air!" He added, by way of encouragement, "if it's the MNLF they won't shoot a whitey, their jihad is with the RP government". Not entirely reassured I awaited the possible road block with more than a little interest. Sure enough there was a road block. We got out slowly and all (driver included) raised our arms in the air, really quite a scary moment. Thank the lord it was an RP army road block, so normal breathing resumed - eventually. The ZBM geologist was given a bollocking by the senior RP army guy who said we should have been back into Zamboanga City before it got dark. I guess the geologist used the presence of a whitey (me) for his failure to do so. These RP army guys really were quite twitchy as there had been a shoot out with some MNLF terrorists in the city area only a few days before. As we drove back to the Lantaka Hotel I asked the geologist why he didn't use an army escort going up and back to the prospect. He laughed and said army escorts would be bound to attract the attention of the MNLF terrorists; he felt much safer on his own! He came into the hotel for a beer or two, but didn't stay to eat, as he had to be back home before the 8 pm curfew in Zamboanga. I thanked him for his time (and advice re MNLF) and said I would talk to ZBM management in Manila concerning the prospect's need for a detailed surface survey before any further drilling.

I left the following morning on the 9 o'clock BAC 1-11 flight back to Manila. It was nearly 1 pm by the time I checked into the Intercon after the interminable scrum and fight for a taxi at MIA's domestic terminal. I went into the ZBM offices in the afternoon and explained the position at the Zamboanga project. In fact it was really still a prospect rather than a defined project. This did not go down well and, in truth, I felt they rather wished they hadn't asked for my opinion - hey ho, such is life. I rather doubted they'd pay our invoice for two days consulting time. I left and dropped into the Lepanto offices to make an appointment to see Chito the following morning and ask them to book me on the PAL Manila - Hong Kong flight to connect with the CP 10 pm flight to London that night. Chito asked how it went with ZBM and I told him the "project" was still at a prospect stage, so no guesses as to size of any possible operation. He had no further queries for the Lepanto mine at present and expected to be in London next month for some contract talks with Cementation Mining vis-a-vis Tubo Shaft furnishing. I duly caught the PAL flight for the 750 mile trip from Manila to Hong Kong and then onto the CP jumbo night flight to London. I was into RTZC office by late morning the next day, feeling knackered.

I phoned home and Gillian answered, she had arrived back from Cornwall the previous day and from the sounds of barking collected the dogs from the kennels that morning. I said I'd be in to Ashford station at 3 pm and would be grateful if she could collect me. I had a quick chat with Dick about my Philippines trip and he told me that a Bolivia/Argentina visit was on for next week. I said I'd like a few days at home to see how things were, but a South American trip later next week should be OK. With a mad rush I just made the 2 pm fast service from Charing Cross to Ashford. Gillian came to the station in the Simca van, with two excited (and smelly!) dogs in the back; thank goodness for the grille. We all had a wander around the orchard when we got back to firstly get the energy out of Matt and Anjon and secondly for Gillian to tell me about Lofty's death and the funeral in St Mawgan's church. She had been very upset as she had been very close to Lofty, who always called her Snooks. Now back at Beals she was looking forward to getting back to work at the Woodchurch surgery. I also thought this was the right thing to do (back to normality?) as Dr Tommo was a kind, supportive, no nonsense, avuncular figure. Gillian called the surgery and said she would be back to work on Monday, four days hence. We did our "usual" things such as a drink at the 8 Bells in Tenterden on Saturday, and then taking the dogs down to Romney Marsh for a good walk. For me it was easy to unwind after the travelling as there was no grass to cut it being late February. However the normal sticky period on "reacquainting" after one of my overseas trips seemed even more difficult this time. Gillian said she'd be OK once she'd started nursing work again and didn't seem to mind that I expected to be off to South America with Don, the geologist, later next week. In fact she said it would probably be preferable as my absence would ensure that she had masses to do with dog walks and the ever present, house repairs!

15

Don and I flew from Heathrow to Frankfurt to catch the new Lufthansa service direct to La Paz via New York. It seemed an odd routing, but, of course, removed the need to change planes in Miami, Lima or Rio depending on airline. However what I had failed to realise was that the Lufthansa flight would be in a Boeing 747 Combi (half freight) rather than the normal comfortable Jumbo. The flight worked OK, but with the shortened seat pitch I vowed never to use it again, since my long legs were either wedged against the back of the seat in front or sprawled askew in the aisle much to the annoyance of other passengers. We stayed at the Hotel Sucre on the main drag only a few doors away from the COMSUR offices. Don, as I did, really enjoyed the spectacular drive down from El Alto airport into the centre of La Paz. We went into the COMSUR offices in the afternoon and I introduced Stan, their American Office manager, to Don. I had met Stan on my previous visit to Bolivia four years ago. In turn we met their Chief Geologist (CG), Carlos and Mining Manager (MM), Mario. We had a look at the geological, ore reserves and mining plans for the Milluni mine. It was agreed they would pick us up at the hotel at 8am the following day for the 1.5 hour trip up to the mine.

The COMSUR jeep turned out to be an early version of the V8 Range Rover. The big engine proved very handy when operating above 4500m. Milluni was located about 25 miles north of La Paz situated on the flanks of Chacaltaya mountain (5420m) close by the more spectacular Huayana Potosi mountain (6090m). This latter mountain was very popular with climbers as it was so easily accessible from the El Alto international airport, itself already at 4060m elevation. There was also a ski run complete with chair-lift on Chacaltaya. The mine was located on the side of a high level valley approached past a glacial lake, which supplied fresh water to the city of La Paz. As expected in this terrain the mine had been developed initially through a series of adits. An internal short rectangular vertical shaft had been sunk about 150m below the lowest adit level. The tin orebody occupied a steep dipping fracture zone which carried quite a lot of water. Typical narrow vein stoping used both shrinkage and inclined cut-and-fill methods. Waste fill was obtained from surface glory holes. Our (RTZC) brief was to determine the productive potential of the mine. Milluni was currently mining around 250 tonnes/day but COMSUR was contemplating a major investment in a new, expanded concentrator. Don was obviously the key man here. On the upper levels the ore zone had been cut off in the NE by a steep dipping normal fault, striking E-W. Efforts had been made to locate the ore zone on the other side of the fault by short diamond drill holes and limited development, but with no success.

Back in the mine engineering offices in the afternoon Don and Carlos spent a lot of time looking at the geological level plans of the NE part of the mine. They both felt that there had been a considerable horizontal movement across this E-W fault and that earlier efforts to find any displaced portions of the ore zone had not gone far enough. However Carlos pointed out that the lowest drainage adit had, in fact, been driven through this fault and moreover extended nearly a mile beyond it. So, yes you guessed it, that was where we were going the next day, equipped with boots and thigh waders!

It was the mine's old main drainage adit, about 2m high by 1.5m wide, sloping at about 1 in 150 inclination down. At this time of year, late February/early March (ie southern autumn) there was about 60cm depth of water flowing. With four of us in the adit (Mario had decided to join the fun!) the thigh waders only kept us dry for a while. Mario and I were kept busy cleaning the adit sides and back with stiff brushes so that the geologists could do their mapping. They spent a long time examining the fault and southern ore zone intersection in the adit. We worked our way NE along the adit and sure enough the ore zone reappeared in the eastern wall nearly 200m from the intersection of the fault with the adit - the geologists interpretation was confirmed. Well this put an entirely different picture on the ore potential at Milluni.

Back in the engineering offices we went over the geological plans of the lower levels which had been developed off the internal vertical shaft. At the NE end of these levels hardly any development had been driven on the north side of the supposed cut-off fault. These areas now became the focus for a new exploration programme. This would obviously take time to complete, but, utilising what we now knew of the original ore zone outcrop and the new ore zone exposure in the drainage adit it was feasible to predict an ore expectancy of around 7500 t/vm. This was based on a strike length of 2.4Km, an average vein width of 1.5m, a bulk density of 3.6 and an ore payability of 58%. We were all 100% sure that the same ore zone existed north of the fault (we'd seen it in the adit), but the biggest unknown was payability. The current mine operations had shown an ore zone payability of 65%, but to be on the conservative side I suggested we cut this to 58% or 90% of the historical figure. The geologists were happy with this. They suggested that it would be reasonable to expect an ore zone depth extent of 25% the strike extent, ie 600m. However existing Milluni operations had mined down to a depth of 250m which left 350m, which at 7500 t/vm indicated an ore reserve of 2.6Mt. This was our best guesstimate. Using the old 10% ore expectancy rule for a sustainable mining rate from a steep dipping tabular orebody indicated 750 tonnes/day. We cut this to 600 tonnes/day to take account of the fairly heavy ground-water problem. This implied an annual mining rate of 180,000t (based on 300 days). An overall orebody extraction of 85% of our guesstimated reserve would provide a twelve-year mining life - sufficient to invest in a 600 tonnes/day tin concentrator.

We worked over the concept and numbers with the COMSUR guys and it was agreed that this it what we'd present to Gonzalo, the boss of COMSUR. It was my first meeting with Goni, as everyone called him, and I was rapidly impressed by his practical knowledge of tin vein geology and mining. No bullshit, no faffing about, straight to the point. A few searching questions and decision made. Fantastic. What you can do when you own the company! He then asked me if RTZC could help his metallurgical people draw up the technical specifications for building a new 600 tonnes/day tin concentrator. Of course I said yes and added that Keith, one of our metallurgist, spoke South American Spanish having worked previously for Cerro de Pasco in Peru. I undertook to contact Dick in London and ask him to send a Technical-Assistance Agreement (T-AA) direct to Goni. Well that was that and wrapped up work at Milluni. We'd answered our brief and come up with a productive potential of the Milluni mine of 600 tonnes/day from an estimated 2.6Mt orebody. The icing on the cake was the request for RTZC to put in a (T-AA) for metallurgical assistance.

The next day Don and I went to see the CS at the British Embassy (BE) in La Paz. As I had done before in Delhi I explained who and what RTZC were and that we were looking to appoint a Bolivian firm to act as our local agents - had he got any suggestions as to whom we might approach? Indeed he had and as with the BE in Delhi was most helpful and supportive of British companies trying to drum up business in Bolivia. He pointed out that there were very few British or indeed European companies in Bolivia, apart, of course, for the Germans (said with a wry smile). Generally South America was seen as the USA's stamping ground. I later telephoned two or three of his suggested contacts and arranged a meeting with Carlos at Hein Ltda for the following morning. In fact Carlos, who already represented a number of German firms, seemed to be an ideal person speaking fluent Spanish, English and German and had many contacts in the Bolivian mining scene. Armed with our Agency Agreement format from India we "signed up" then and there, subject to Dick sending out a formal RTZC agency contract for Carlos's signature. We told Carlos of our current work for COMSUR and the hope that we might enter into a Technical-Assistance programme with them for metallurgical testwork and concentrator design. On the basis of a successful Bolivian trip Don and I went out for a celebratory dinner. Alas Bolivian wine and food was not great. Forget the wine, settle for a Pisco Sour (very good) and the food? Definitely not great - the well-known Bolivian Racing Chicken (or goat, difficult to tell!) which mainly comprised elasticated gristle. Next morning we caught a LAB 727 flight from El Alto down to Sao Paulo, and there waited for a Varig flight to Buenos Aires, Argentina.

The international airport, Ezeiza, was situated nearly twenty miles from the city centre. It was connected by a good modern freeway and the ride by taxi took barely thirty minutes. We checked into a downtown hotel and from there I phoned Lockwood y Cia who were the contact company for potential bidders for the uranium project feasibility study. We took a taxi to their offices, in fact, only a short distance from the bustling city centre. The Lockwood guy handling the uranium bid explained that the cost of the feasibility study would be underwritten by the World Bank or one of its associates. He hoped RTZC were a registered mining consultancy with the World Bank; I reassured him we were and said that I had already undertaken World Bank sponsored mining work in Zambia. Suitably reassured he gave us the follow-up detail to the ITB package. The uranium project site was in the Mendoza - St Juan region, on the lower slopes of the eastern Andes, about 650 miles due west of Buenos Aires. I asked if we could visit the site over the next couple of days and he agreed to alert the site manager of our impending visit. I said I would telephone Lockwoods with details of our flight number and ETA in Mendoza after checking with the domestic carrier, Austral. That wrapped up the meeting.

We booked an early morning flight with Austral from the city centre Aeroparque airport sited alongside the broad Rio de la Plata. I duly let Lockwoods know and they said a project pick-up would meet us at Mendoza airport. Everything sorted, Don and I did some tourism in downtown Buenos Aires. It was a huge, bustling city with a southern, European feel - think Marseille. Plenty of medieval Spanish architecture with some glorious plazas in which to take good coffee and pleasant vino. Although early March (ie souther autumn) it was warm enough to sit outside. Evening dining got under way by 8 o'clock and, of course, we opted for a churrasqueria, or Argentine steak house. In fact they serve huge wooden platters covered with nothing but char grilled meat of all types, not just steak. Not a sign of any vegetables but the finest steaks I've ever tasted. My poor Spanish eventually managed to secure some green salad and sweet potatoes. The portions of meat were huge but Don and I did our best, helped in no small measure buy a couple of bottles of Malbec vino from no other than the Mendoza/St Juan region. The trip the next day looked promising.

The Aeroparque airport was very busy in the early morning and our flight to Mendoza by an Austral 727 was almost full. After one and half hours we began our descent into Mendoza. Away in the distance, some 70 miles ahead, one could see the eastern Andes lit by the early morning sun, the highest peak Aconcagua (6960m) dominating the vista. We soon located the project pick-up amongst the usual airport scrum. He drove us the short distance to a downtown office. We were both surprised at the size and bustle of the city which had a definite desert town feel with 4 x 4 pick-up trucks everywhere. There were some nice looking buildings and plazas with fountains, but a really striking feature were the huge, open storm drains (shades of Manila?) alongside all the main avenues. These, apparently, were part of an extensive irrigation system fed from the Andean snow melt to water the local desert and, of course, nurture the surrounding vineyards. Everyone, it seemed, had some connection with growing Malbec grapes and producing wine. Unsurprisingly nobody wanted to hear about a nascent uranium mining project! In fact the uranium project was at a very early stage. A perusal of their exploration data showed some wide spaced radioactive surveys that had been flown a couple of years ago together with an initial diamond drilling campaign to test the anomalous area. We arranged to visit the site, about 25 miles NW of Mendoza the next day. Later that afternoon and evening we had a wander around the central part of the city. It had the appearance of a city built on a grid pattern (a la USA cities) and, in fact, this was so since the original city had been heavily damaged by a strong earthquake in the late 19Ce. However the rebuilding had incorporated many tree lined squares/plazas with lovely fountains.

In the morning the pick-up truck only took about fifty minutes to get to the project site. The proximity of the site to Mendoza made one appreciate why the wine industry was less than sanguine about a mining operation on their doorstep. Examination of the preliminary vertical cross sections interpreted from both the aerial survey and diamond drilling confirmed that any mining would be by open-pit methods in the gently undulating terrain. Don and I felt it was an ideal deposit for the application of RTZC's OPD computer programmes. Apart from observing the local topography and examining the drill cores and vertical cross sections there was little else to do at site. We thus returned to the project offices in Mendoza. Here we told them our initial impression, "an open-pit project", and that we had the necessary skills, manpower and technology to undertake the pit design. The Project manager wanted to know how we would handle the Argentine side of the feasibility study. I said we intended to use an Argentine engineering company to provide input on labour rates, cost of supplies and consumables, power and water supplies and costs as well as import duties and taxes. In fact everything pertaining to a major Argentine mining operation. I had to admit that RTZC had no experience of working in Argentina, but that we were currently engaged in mining work in Bolivia. That went down like a lead balloon. I belatedly realised that the Argentines are very machismo and totally dismissive of Bolivians as "coca-chewing mountain men". Major faux pas on my part. I tried to recover by saying that RTZC's OPD mining programmes were being successfully used at MKU in Australia and Rossing in Namibia both uranium operations. In addition they were being used at Lornex in Canada; Hammersley in Australia; RTB Bor, in Serbia and Malanjkhand in India. Of course we left him all the usual RTZC bumph, but it was apparent that our lack of direct Argentine mining experience was a serious drawback. I said we did not need to go back to the site again but would rather return to Buenos Aires for further talks with Lockwoods concerning local engineering input into our bid. Don and I agreed that our visit had not gone down well. We caught the early evening flight back to Buenos Aires via an intermediate stop at Cordoba.

Back in Buenos Aires we both suffered a sleepless night. No, not too much vino, although that can't have helped. Downtown Buenos Aires was incredibly noisy, even more so than Madrid. There seemed to be only a one hour window between 2.30 - 3.30am when the interminable traffic stops and the crash and crump of garbage collection ceases. For me this was the only black mark for Buenos Aires. Otherwise the climate, people, location, food, wine and general ambience were great, in marked contrast to the rather severe and enervating ambience in La Paz. We briefed the Lockwood guy on our site visit and then got on to the thorny question of where to obtain Argentine engineering input. No problem - Lockwoods could provide all that. I was more than a little taken aback as Lockwoods had indicated that they acted as an agency for foreign companies. Yes he said, but also we have an associated project engineering company who could handle all the local elements of the uranium project. He took us to an adjacent building where this associated company was based. Here they did a great selling job on us (role reversal!) to the extent that I signed an exclusive Agency Agreement for Lockwoods to represent RTZC in Argentina and they in turn undertook to provide RTZC with a subcontract lump-sum quote for the provision of local engineering services to be included in our bid for the uranium project feasibility study. Obviously it would have been preferable for us to have sorted this out before we went on the trip to Mendoza and the site. C'est la guerre. Hopeful I'd now learnt the lesson to get all ones' ducks in a row before one fronts up to the actual client! Somewhat chastened by the turn of events we took a taxi out to Ezeiza airport and boarded an Aerolineas Argentinas (AA) flight to London via Montevideo and Rio de Janeiro.

Don and I checked into RTZC's office in St James's and had a debrief meeting with Dick on Bolivia covering COMSUR, metallurgical Technical-Assistance and Carlos Agency Agreement all of which went down well (the good news first?) Then the bad news and the negative reaction on the uranium project. The only bright spot in the Argentine visit was establishing an Agency Agreement with Lockwoods and their agreement to provide us with a subcontract quote for local engineering to be included in our bid.

Dick agreed that both Don and I could take a couple of days off before we would be required for an evaluation of the Wheal Jane tin mine in Cornwall. Apparently prompted by the government (for political, vote-winning in the Camborne-Falmouth constituency?) our owner, RTZ, had been persuaded to take a significant equity stake in the Wheal Jane operation. As I commented to Dick "cart before the horse"? Surely it would have been logical to ask RTZC to carry out an evaluation of the tin operations at Wheal Jane before RTZ put money in rather than after. He replied that one or two senior RTZ board members, with strong political affiliations, felt that such an investment would "be a good thing". Not exactly rigorous engineering. Hey ho, it was more work for RTZC.

At home again I told Gillian of Don and my Bolivian and Argentine travels. She had settled down again into the routine of nurse/dispenser at the Woodchurch surgery, although still obviously unsettled by Lofty's death. I told her that my next assignment would be down in Cornwall at Wheal Jane. This would give me the opportunity to look in on her mother in St Mawgan as we would fly from Heathrow to Newquay airport, which, in fact, was the eastern part of RAF St Mawgan close by the village. I would then be able to recount how her mother was faring on her own.

However before that Don and I had to complete the write-up and costing for the Argentine uranium project feasibility study bid. Fortunately Lockwoods were very good and a complete subcontract quote plus back ground information on their engineering services arrived by air courier at the beginning of the following week. With the priceless help of Diane and Mandy (our report preparation wizards) we amended/rewrote the Lockwoods stuff and incorporated it into our final presentation. I spent some more time with our own civil and electrical engineers reworking Lockwoods' engineering man-hours into discrete packages. We then included an overall RTZC fee for managing the subcontract and hey presto the bid document was complete. We mailed this by air courier to Lockwoods for them to make the formal submission to the client by the deadline at the end of the following week. I was not at all hopeful of winning the contract in spite of submitting what I believed to be a good competitive bid. There was no doubt in my mind that RTZC could do a good job, after all, we had hands-on open-pit design experience from many major mining projects. However, as marketing director Dave correctly pointed out, we had only limited experience in completing a full feasibility study or "bankable document" in the modern argot. He was right. A month later we were informed that we were unsuccessful, but thank you for your interest etc. Lockwoods informed us that we were not even on the short list of bidders for negotiation, which was very disheartening. As I said to Dick later, RTZC and, more importantly, RTZ were virtually unknown in South America. Their only mining presence was the Paragominas bauxite deposit in the Brazilian Amazon and a Borax subsidiary in Argentina. We noted that all the short-listed bidders were from north America.

Don was not available for the Wheal Jane evaluation as he disappeared almost immediately to RTZ's Rossing Uranium mine in Namibia where there was a grade control problem. In fact this worked out well as we had recently hired Phil, previously CG at the Wheal Jane tin mine in Cornwall. His recent local knowledge of the mine and its geology would be extremely useful. The third member of our team was Alex a metallurgist. The flight from Heathrow to Newquay by SW Airlines (a BA subsidiary) took around one hour. We hired a car at the airport and I drove down into St Mawgan to see Gillian's mother. She was expecting us and put on late morning coffee. She told me that Pat, living at Mawgan Porth, three miles away, popped in to see her most days, so she was alright for company and anyway she'd lived in the village for years and knew plenty of people. We only stayed half an hour before driving on to Truro to check into an hotel. After lunch we drove out to the Wheal Jane mine situated between Baldhu and Bissoe. We had a general chat with the Mine Manager who then introduced us to the CG, Underground Manager and Mill Superintendent. Phil and I then went to the engineering offices with the CG for a run through the mine geology and ore reserves. He gave us a copy of the ore reserves. We also had a quick meeting with the Underground Manager to sort out an underground visit for next day. Alex, of course, had disappeared to the mill (concentrator). I then went back to see the Mine Manager to obtain copies of recent operations monthly reports as well as operations cost reports. As RTZ had become a major stakeholder there was no difficulty in us (RTZC) obtaining full operational facts and figures. That just about wrapped up our first afternoon.

Back in Truro I took the guys up to the Daniel Arms, an old CSM/RCI Nurses stamping ground. Interesting for me, probably dead boring for the other two, but at least they enjoyed the beer. Next morning we were at the mine by 8 o'clock. Alex went back to the mill and Phil and I went underground. There were two relatively small short rectangular timber shafts, the No 1 shaft served by a double-drum winder hauling twin 2.5 tonne skips and the Service shaft by another double-drum winder hauling a cage and counterweight. We went to the lower, developing levels. For me the first overriding impression was just how much water was flowing in the main level ditches. Typical steep dipping, narrow vein overhand stoping was in use. It was immediately obvious that the orebody was a major aquifer. This was confirmed when we visited the underground pump station, which, for a mine of this modest output (circa 220,000 tonnes/year), was large and obviously a major item of mine infrastructure. The mine was regularly pumping 8,000 gpm which meant that for each tonne of ore hoisted the mine pumped about 70 tonnes of water. On this yardstick - tonnes water per tonne ore - the average value of 70 placed Wheal Jane as one of the world's wet mines. In itself a fascinating fact, but with obvious major operating cost implications. In addition it was noted that all the pumps were of stainless steel construction to combat the low, acidic pH of less than 3. I made a note to check with Alex as to the quantity/cost of lime added to raise the mine water pH to 7 before discharge to Restronguet Creek. Ground conditions in the four stopes we visited were less good than those seen at the nearby recently closed Mount Wellington mine. The Underground Manager confirmed that Wheal Jane's pumping load had significantly increased since the cessation of pumping at Mount Wellington. In the afternoon Phil and I worked through the ore reserve statement and calculated a total ore expectancy of between 7000 and 8,000 t/vm. However this was contained in three or four distinct ore zones. The current mining rate of just under 750 tonnes/day seemed close to the maximum sustainable. However the overriding problem was high operating costs with a big fixed cost element (power for pumping, ventilation, hoisting and, of course, crushing, grinding, concentrating and thickening). On top of this the mill head grade was not great (so metallurgical recovery was down), labour costs were high and above all the tin price was low. The operating cost margin per tonne treated was heavily negative. We checked all our figures with the Mine Manager, thanked him and his staff for their help and stayed shtum.

Back to Truro, we stayed overnight then drove to Newquay Airport for the 10.30 flight back to Heathrow. We were in the office by lunchtime. We had a meeting with Dick that afternoon and told him, bluntly, that RTZ had bought "a bummer" and there was no way that Wheal Jane could make an operating profit without a huge hike in tin prices and a decrease in the cost of power. He asked us to produce a concise summary of the critical points for submission to the RTZ board. I believe our report saying, in essence, that Wheal Jane was a "dog" got quietly filed. The political decision had been made and Wheal Jane limped on into the eighties with both RTZ and their partner Consolidated Goldfields steadily losing money on the operation. In 1985 the International Tin Agreement fell apart and the tin price collapsed spelling doom for Wheal Jane. The government put in money to keep the pumps running for a while and South Crofty trucked ore for treatment through the Wheal Jane concentrator. The mine flooded in 1992 causing huge acidic pollution in Restronguet Creek and Falmouth estuary.

It transpired that the government had changed the rules on certain company perks, in particular cars. The engine size limit had been increased from 1.5 to 2.0 litres. Along with the other RTZC directors I was allowed to avail myself of this enhanced perk. The only other restriction was that the new vehicle must be manufactured in the EU. Gillian and I spent a few nights peering at motor magazines before plumping for a Lancia Beta saloon. Needless to say we were more than happy to see the Renault 5 go. To be fair it had proved a very reliable little buzz box, but its real no-no was the awful, sick-making body roll. By contrast the Lancia was very comfortable and sure footed with no body roll at all. However, over the years, it proved incredibly unreliable with major difficulties with the electrics (frequently just would not start) and a poor, baulky gearbox, but it was Italian, looked good and had a certain cachet. Finally, after only three years the Lancia duly earned the epithet of "rust bucket" and boy did those early Betas deserve that moniker. Again not a great choice of motor.

However troubles with cars was the least of our worries. Gillian had been feeling down for quite a while. I had assumed that this was a reaction to the death of her father, Lofty, to whom she had been very close. In fact it was on account of a serious internal problem and our local Tenterden doctor said that she would have to go into hospital for an operation. Fortunately he was able to arrange for her to go to Hythe, down on the Kent coast. It all went well, and, of course, I stayed at home for the convalescence period. In honesty it was great to spend some time at home, everyone, dog's in particular seemed pleased to have me around the place. I used to use the reliable, robust Simca van to take Matt and Anjon for a walk alongside the numerous dykes on Romney Marsh. It also gave me a chance to have a couple of sessions with the local osteopath to try and sort out my lower back problem. He approved of the Lancia driver's seat (phew, we got that right) and especially the fact that I wasn't shuttling around in aeroplanes at the moment. He felt strongly that the combination of squashed airline seats and the inevitable tension of flying here and there were major contributory causes of my back problem. Gillian picked up strength pretty quickly and was all for getting back to her surgery work. The doc agreed so it was back to work for me as well.

16

That December we had an RTZC board meeting and our new Chairman, Sir Alistair, dropped a bombshell - he proposed to wind RTZC up and merely retain a few senior technical personnel for internal RTZ work. If that happened then it was a wake up time for me, since, obviously, the senior mining person in RTZC was Dick. Sir Alistair was not a mining industry person and his appointment as Chairman of RTZ (and, en passant RTZC) was something of a surprise. He was not interested in the history and development of RTZC since its formation by Ken in 1965, and felt that outside (non-RTZ work) was a waste of time and effort. Oh dear, director in charge of non-RTZ work was me! After the board meeting Dick, metallurgical David (for RTZ work), marketing Dave and me - the executive directors - had our own meeting. Both Dick and I were in favour of trying to change Sir Alistair's mind, metallurgical David was ambivalent and marketing Dave said "he was off, he needed a change".

Dick told me to develop a short paper detailing all non-RTZ mining projects we had undertaken during the 1970s and the consequent international experience gained by RTZC staff and the revenue (admittedly modest) contributed to Head office. We presented this to Sir Alistair at a special board meeting in January 1978. In short it had no effect whatsoever and as far as he was concerned RTZC would be wound up by mid year and that was that! Marketing Dave had already resigned, and metallurgical David was quite happy to re-merge into RTZ's bosom. He had, after all, been forced out of Riofinex into RTZC. So Dick and I considered the possibility of buying out RTZC as a going concern - yes really. After we worked through the financial numbers we realised that we would need an external backer. At this time Dick was doing some consultancy work on a British Columbian open-pit coal property as a subcontract to Golder Associates (GA) of Toronto, Canada. He had previously done work for Golders and got on well with their Chairman, Vic. In Toronto Dick broached the possibility of GA buying out RTZC as a going concern. Vic said "maybe, but... early days, lots of things to look at etc", but he'd be in London next month, by which time he hoped Dick would have sounded out the staff.

Firstly the three directors, Dick, David and I plus wives Mary, Margaret and Gillian had a weekend lunch at the High Rocks Hotel (near Eridge, Kent) to discuss the buyout possibility. David & Margaret were clearly against such a move as David saw his future with RTZ. Dick and I felt it was well worth trying to keep the technical group together, but both agreed we needed an outside backer. I had reservations about GA, since they were a geotechnical consultancy rather than mining. We agreed to sound out some other UK based engineering outfits who might be interested, specifically W S Atkins, Seltrust Engineering & Davy McKee before we put any buyout option to the staff. Thus over the next few weeks Dick and I had meetings with these companies to see if there was any interest. Both W S Atkins and Davy showed some interest, but with a marked lack of urgency. In late February Vic from GA arrived in London full of enthusiasm for a buyout of RTZC as a going concern by GA. He proposed that both Dick and I put up US$ 30,000 each to demonstrate our commitment and he would appoint each of us as Principals of the parent GA. Other technical staff would become Associates of GA and all employees of a new company to be called Golder Moffit & Associates (GMA) would participate in GA shares. The buyout option by GA was put to Sir Alistair at a meeting by Vic with Dick and me in attendance. Initially Sir Alistair was quite dismissive, but Vic was very persuasive and assured him that GA would pay the market price for RTZC plus the going rate for any intellectual property rights, including all RTZC's computer programs. Having backed him in to a corner Sir Alistair insisted that he talk to RTZC staff and assure them that it was a "free vote" to join GMA or stay with RTZ. He added that if more than two thirds of the staff voted to go to GMA then RTZ would agree to sell RTZC to GA.

Dick and I set about canvassing all the staff. This immediately involved me flying to Madrid then on to Seville and finally driving up to Minas de Riotinto. Here I talked first to Brian, our local MSD project manager and then to all the rest of the guys. Much to my surprise they all wanted to know what everyone else was doing. I told them marketing Dave had resigned forthwith and metallurgical David had opted to stay with RTZ. Both Dick and I would opt for GA whence Dick would become the MD of GMA and I would become both a director and company secretary of GMA. All RTZC technical staff who opted to join GMA would become

Associates of GA and would thus participate with GA shares. GMA's new offices would be located in central London and their current salary & terms of employment (fringe benefits, pension rights etc) would be the same at GMA as those at RTZC. We talked long and hard over many glasses of vino over a couple of days. I asked them to let Dick know their position by the end of the week.

I then flew back to Heathrow and transferred to an AI flight to Bombay from where I took the train to Ahmadabad. Then a GMDC jeep up to Ambaji. I went through the same stuff as I had done with the guys in Spain. I stressed that these existing projects would continue as before but under a GMA label if that was the two thirds majority wish. Please let Dick know asap of their vote. Then I took a jeep eastwards to Udaipur for a talk with our two resident mining engineers. Same story, same request. I then flew up to Delhi for a quick meeting with Shad our local Indian agent. He was not at all happy about the possible change. He felt that everyone now knew of RTZC in the mining/metallurgical field in India, but no one knew anything about the GA group. I agreed but said GMA would trade as legal successors to RTZC and all terms of employment, agency agreements and existing contracts would be honoured. He was unconvinced. Finally I telephoned Roy and Peter's computer guy in Malanjkhand giving them the same story and same request for a rapid response to Dick in London. At this time I obviously did not mention any of this to our existing clients. Somewhat knackered, I flew back to London.

By the end of the following week the "overseas votes" were in and the upshot was that all, yes all geological, mining and support/secretarial staff opted for GMA and all the metallurgical staff opted to stay with RTZ. Must tell one something, but not sure what? Thus we had a +80% majority in favour of forming GMA. That was the easy bit. The next few months involved complex negotiations on pension transfers from RTZ to GA schemes and independent valuation of RTZC computer programs. There was also the task of inspecting numerous possible new office premises in central London. With the help of RTZ's legal department I went through a crash course in the duties and requirements of a company secretary. GA's legal guys came over from Toronto to sort out the new GMA company and structure. We worked closely with their existing geotechnical consultancy company, Golder Hoek & Associates (GHA) based in Maidenhead.

On a personal basis I signed up for a US$ 30,000 loan (from the GA group) as my "buy in" to GA shares. Big John, from the parent GA in Toronto, was appointed as Chairman of GMA and Brian the boss of GHA at Maidenhead was appointed as our third director. One really good aspect of GMA's articles of association was that a quorum of only two directors was required to enact business. This would enable Dick and me to run GMA's day-to-day business without recourse to Toronto all the time. Of course there was much behind the scenes activity sorting out financial matters between GA & RTZ lawyers which seemed to go on for ever.

As I was not required for all the detailed legal/financial stuff Dick agreed I could take a couple of weeks holiday. So we packed small and light, gunned up the Honda 400/4, installed Gillian on the pillion and set off from Woodchurch for the Dartmouth tunnel and points north. We stopped at Durham and thought it was lovely city - vowed to come back. At Newcastle-on-Tyne, we boarded the mv Venus ferry for Norway. We had a nice, small, outside cabin and got chatting to another couple who were motorbike touring as well, but on the new Honda Dream twin. I still much preferred the old 400/4!. The ferry first docked at Stavanger but we stayed on board until the final destination Bergen. It was 24 years since I'd last been in Bergen, about to join the Coastal Steamer for Kirkenes in the far north. We parked the bike and had a good look around. It was a lovely old Hanseatic city, with the harbour and bustling sea front at the centre. At about 150,000 population it was the second largest city in Norway. The quay was lined with lovely old wooden medieval merchant's houses. The town was surrounded by mountains and thus the weather was often wet. We were very fortunate it was sunny and warm. We took the Floibanen cable railway up to a beautiful flower strewn meadow about 1200ft above the town. Hard to believe but we lay in the meadow and sun bathed for a while. Back down in Bergen again, via the cable railway, we collected the Honda and headed east a short distance to Fantoft.

Fantoft was just outside Bergen and here we stayed in student type accommodation. Our very small all wooden room contained two bunks with a minimum of furnishing, but it was lovely and warm. The next morning we headed east up the north side of Hardanger fjord. I was glad it had been dry in Bergen as the numerous cobbled streets looked as if they would be tricky with a heavily loaded motorbike. The road inside the numerous tunnels were dirt and heavily rutted which skewed the bike all over the place. The 400/4 bike created a lot of interest whenever we stopped. I feel sure we boosted Honda's 400/4 sales potential in the Hardanger fjord area!

Twenty or so miles further east and Gillian said why don't we stop and go for a swim in the fjord. True it was a glorious sunny day and the water looked clear and enticing. So, skinny dipping, alongside the main road, in we went. My God, it was freezing (unsurprising really as there was a glacier at the head of the fjord) and blasted all one's breath out. I did about six strokes and fled back to the warmth of a large sun-baked rock. Gillian was much braver and did a good two dozen strokes before retreating to the same large rock. It has to be said there was hardly any traffic to be interested in two blue, naked bodies lying like stranded fish on a rock slab. We dried off, kitted up and set off east and then north to the town of Voss.

Here we spent the night in the very pleasant Fleischer's hotel with the ubiquitous cold plate for dinner. From Voss we headed north for Sognefjord, but after 35 miles disaster struck. The road had been good, sealed, but at Stalheim we reached the top of the notorious (I later learnt), zigzag dirt road dropping over a 1000 feet down to the Naerodal inlet. Of course I immediately noted the dirt road and steep, 1 in 4 descent and changed down into second but on the first zig, forgetting the additional pillion weight, lost the bike in the gravel and we slid (gracefully?) into the ditch on our side. Fortunately the rear panniers protected Gillian's leg underneath the bike. Apart from my pride, little damage was done. A bent front indicator stalk and bulb - that's all. Gillian wouldn't get back on the bike and walked the rest of the way down the vertiginous zigzag. I came down in bottom gear, very, very slowly. It was fortunate that we fell on that first corner, into the hill's highwall, as at the next corner we would have slid (acrobatically?) into the sheer drop into the inlet. We just caught the last ferry of the day across Sognfjord for the short trip to the little village of Kaupanger.

In Kaupanger we stayed in a lovely old farmhouse overlooking the fjord. Our bedroom fire escape comprised a thick, stout coiled rope attached to a large hook set in the room timbers. We really appreciated an excellent, hearty breakfast next morning prepared by the owner's friendly wife. The farmhouse was surrounded by fields of wild flowers. We rode into Sogndal and the local garage easily sorted out the indicator stalk and replacement bulb. As usual the Honda 400/4 created a lot of interest with the mechanics. We rode north for forty miles on a minor sealed road climbing steadily towards the Josterdal snowfield. The mountain scenery was spectacular, with hanging waterfalls plunging into the glacial U-shaped valley. The road became increasingly covered with old rutted ice and snow as we climbed above 3000ft and as the Honda became somewhat skittish I deemed it prudent to stop, since neither of us were keen to fall off again. We returned to Kaupanger for another night.

The following day we headed west along the north side of Sognfjord to Leikanger and Hermansverk where we found a grand old wooden hotel right alongside the fjord. I felt too embarrassed to clomp in to reception in my biker gear, so we parked the bike round the back and I stripped down to civvies before checking in. We had a downstairs room with a wooden verandah outside looking straight out across the fjord. We really enjoyed a good early dinner and treated ourselves to some wine. Alcohol of any description was very very expensive in Norway. As I had found on my previous visit Norweigans were both very patriotic and friendly to the English.

That was as far west down Sognfjord as we went. We headed back east passing through Sogndal and Kaupanger again before catching the ferry back across the fjord. I reckoned that we would be OK on the Honda climbing the Stalheim zigzag and so it proved to be; a very different proposition to the descent! At the top we stopped and took some photos of the dirt zigzag road, but it never looked as alarming as it had felt on the bike. Anyway we had mastered the Stalheim road and continued on to Voss, which was an important administrative town for the surrounding region and also boasted a station on the main Bergen to Oslo railway line.

Next day we only had a short ride on to our penultimate stop at the Strand Hotel in Ulvik. This was a lovely, relaxed place situated on a side branch of Hardanger fjord. By good chance we had booked there for two nights. Mid-afternoon we took one of the hotel's boats out onto the adjacent Osafjord. Out on the clear blue water of the fjord the reflections of the towering 5480ft high Orien mountain on the other side sparkled in the late afternoon sun - yes amazingly it was still warm and sunny. The hotel's restaurant served the best and most varied smorgasbord we had yet encountered. Afterwards we sat out on the balcony until late enjoying the tranquility of the fjord. It really was so quiet and un hassled. A far cry from overcrowded England.

Towards the end of the ninety mile ride in to Bergen we experienced our first Norweigan drizzle/light rain. I took things very steadily on the bike as we encountered the very slick looking Bergen cobblestones. We had booked a hotel close to the water front in old Bergen. I left Gillian with the bike and went to investigate. It was a real low-life, waterfront doss house. Not really what we had in mind. I'd parked the bike close to an information kiosk and the helpful lady there soon found us a B & B on the outskirts of town. It was a pleasant suburban house, very clean and comfortable. The owner looked slightly apprehensive when we turned up on the bike, but visibly relaxed when she realised we were not a couple of punks with steel bolts through our eyebrows. Marvelous breakfast, full English fry up that set us up for the day. We boarded the mv Venus at 10 am. Again we had an outside cabin and enjoyed the morning run down the coast to Haugesund. Here the boat stayed for less than an hour before heading south-west into the North Sea for Newcastle-on-Tyne, 22 hours away.

The mv Venus came up the Tyne estuary at mid-morning in light rain - welcome to England! After disembarking we headed south on the the old A1 as the rain got heavier and the side wash from trucks became distinctly hazardous to poorly protected motorcyclists. By the time we got to York I was absolutely soaked through. Gillian was a little less wet on the pillion but no less cold and unhappy. We repaired to the respective toilets on York station in an attempt to thaw out and mop up. Inspirational flash by me - put the bike on the train - and relax in a warm British Railways carriage.

So to my shame, as a biker, I pushed the 400/4 up the ramp and secured it to the side of the goods van with the aid of a helpful guard. Never had a good old BR third class carriage felt so warm and comfortable. We detrained at Euston and then biked gingerly through the central London traffic to the Elephant & Castle and finally onto the A21 Hastings road. It was a great relief to finally make Woodchurch. We both felt cold, wet, stiff and bandy-legged bike sore! Sad to say that proved to be the last time Gillian ever rode pillion on the Honda. Certainly the old Simca van seemed remarkably secure and comfortable after the bike, when I took it to collect two very smelly and excitable dogs from kennels.

On Monday Gillian went back to work at the surgery and I rode the bike to Ashford station for the train commute to RTZC on St James's Square. At RTZC Dick told me that the financial affairs between GA and RTZ had been finalised including intellectual property rights connected with the OPD programs. RTZ had retained copies but were prevented from marketing them outside majority owned RTZ group companies for at least two years. Both Dick and I had felt this to be of paramount importance in keeping our present clients happy. Our office agent had located a good fourth floor space, serviced by lift and stairs, above the Oasis Sports Centre at the west end of High Holborn near Drury Lane. That afternoon we went to check out the office taking Diane as de facto office manager in the absence of Roy in India. It all seemed OK, fully serviced and ready to go. Dick felt we should redecorate the whole floor, highlighting the GA green colour scheme. Diane then organised the supply of suitable office furniture and the provision of letterhead paper and business cards for all our transferring consultants - geologists and miners! We had noted a pub on the corner of Drury Lane and decided to give it a try to see if it would be a suitable local - it was! The walking time from Charing Cross station to the new GMA office would be a shade longer at fifteen minutes, still very good for London's West End.

I had some paperwork to sign for the US$ 30,000 loan from GA for me to buy my GA shares, which seemed a little incestuous. The repayment terms were quite onerous, certainly not charitable. I really needed the worldwide GA business to grow rapidly in the short term to prevent getting my fingers burnt. Our Holborn office tenancy would commence at the beginning of November. The painter/decorator expected to finish by mid October and the new office furnishings would be in the following week. This gave us the final week of October to move out of RTZC's St James's office and set up shop in High Holborn. It all went amazingly smoothly, thanks in no small measure to Diane's organisational skills ably assisted by Mandy, Bronwyn and Barbara. They did a great job making sure that all our extensive filing systems survived the move. Dick produced an announcement for the international Mining Journal of the formation of GMA and I prepared adverts for three experienced mineral processors to "join this exciting new company within the worldwide GA group". Not sure we believed all the hyperbole but - what the hell, better to let every one know we existed. After work that first day in High Holborn we all repaired to the local pub for a drink or two to toast our new venture.

During the last month at RTZC I had been up to Stockton-on-Tees for talks with Davy McKee (DM) about the possibility of me joining a large DM mission to China for discussions with the Chinese authorities about modernising a number of copper mining/processing operations. DM had warned me that as this was virtually "a first" for a western engineer-contractor to be invited into what was still a "closed China" they were not too sure how things would pan out, but felt it would largely be a talking shop in Peking, rather than any hands-on engineering at various mine sites. However one had to be in it to win it! There would be ten managers/engineers from DM and two outsiders - Mike, a specialist on tin and tungsten processing/marketing and me the "expert on geology and mining"! I should add that the ten strong DM team were basically process plant design/contractors for copper projects, and Mike and I were roped in to round out the "front and tail". Anyway, DM agreed to pay my normal RTZC daily fee rate, so I had said yes, count me in. With all the move hassle I had forgotten about the China job, but towards the end of November I had a call from Martyn, a DM mineral dresser to say that the visit was on, leaving next Monday. He reassured me that the fact that I would now be traveling under a GMA flag was immaterial since they (DM) had printed business cards for both Mike and me as if we were DM staff - thus no problem.

We flew from Heathrow, stopped somewhere in the Middle East then Hong Kong before flying on to Peking. At the airport we were rounded up by officials from the Chinese Mining & Minerals Corp (CMMC), shepherded onto a coach which took us to a city centre hotel. My initial impression of Peking was - where was all the traffic? No cars, no vans or lorries just tens of thousands of bicycles. I had not seen so many bicycles since I was in Calcutta. The hotel was fine, somewhat austere but clean and warm. Outside it was distinctly cold.

Nothing was arranged for that afternoon so Mike, Martyn and I decided to go out for a brisk walkabout and tourism. No it didn't work like that. We were not allowed out of the hotel without our individual official "minder". When the three minders were ready off we went the three of us followed a short distance behind by the three minders, very spooky. A short distance from the hotel we found a street market where we all bought Chinese army style fur hats - it was that cold. We rapidly beat a retreat to the warmth of the hotel. At dinner in the hotel that evening the DM team leader told us that our formal programme would begin tomorrow with various meetings with the CMMC. He also said there would be a number (!) of formal dinners and numerous tours around the sights of Peking. He reiterated what we had already learnt that we were not allowed to wander around outside the hotel on our own.

The interminable meetings were huge, comprising the twelve-strong DM team, a similar number from CMMC, four or five interpreters and various unknown others besides an army of stenographers, in all around 40. In the main the CMMC guys really wanted to know what DM knew about mineral process plant design and construction. They were particularly interested in DM's track record in this field and wanted details of each of DM's completed projects. The DM guys were very well prepared and put on a really good show. However it was very apparent that the Chinese were not used to dealing with western engineer-constructor companies and certainly not at all familiar with the differing methods of project management. The costs/fees for project management caused great consternation and the CMMC team was beefed up with several accountants and economists from their central finance office. The DM team leader was at great pains to point out that the type of project management deal was entirely project specific and largely depended upon the wishes of the client - CMMC. No one was interested in geology or mining so I was a bemused bystander. They were, however, interested in marketing either/both concentrates or metal and here Mike was kept busy explaining typical sales contract terms and how these were often based on London Metals Exchange (LME) prices. I also found this very interesting as concentrate sales terms had always been something of a mystery to me.

We had three days of these meetings and my only contribution to the talks was explaining the methodology of collecting representative ore samples for detailed analyses, microscopic examination and metallurgical testwork. For 95% of the time I felt a real spare part. The DM team leader told me not too worry as I would be much more in demand when we visited some open-pit and underground copper mines. Over the weekend some of the CMMC guys, who spoke English, organised several tourist trips for us. They took us to the Forbidden City (Ming Dynasty imperial palace), tomb of The Terracotta Army in Shaanxi Province and, of course The Great Wall of China. As a westerner I felt very privileged to visit all of these places in December 1978, when China was still a closed society. One of the side benefits of being a mining engineer.

Our big wrap-up meeting before heading off to the mines took place on the following Tuesday followed by a huge banquet in the evening. The really difficult task with Chinese banquets was determining how many courses there were. One was expected to participate in each course (it was the hight of rudeness not to) and for our big banquet there were nine or ten. All were fine, some a little strange, bar one and that was disgusting - sea slugs. They were real meaty jobs about 3in length and 3/4in diameter with the slippery consistency of very chewy rubber. Considered a great delicacy I had great difficulty to avoid gagging as one attempted to swallow them. Fortunately we could wash them down with beer.

After the meal there was the expected round of toasts between CMMC and DM to mutual cooperation, health, world peace, happiness you name it. As part of the "toasting process" the toaster and recipient had to be upstanding and empty their glasses in one swig, then hold the glass upside down to demonstrate that it had been emptied. We had, of course had drinks throughout the lengthy banquet, maotai (fermented sorghum), wine and beer. So by the time the toasts came around many of the Chinese were a little the worse for wear. The DM team leader pushed off with maotai (God bless him, it's vile), then somebody did the wine and then, after a quick DM huddle, I was selected to do the "beer toast" for the miners. The maotai was not only vile it was strong. Both the Chinese wine and beer (actually lager) were fairly innocuous brews. Although not a huge beer drinker I had no trouble downing the glass of beer in one, holding my upturned glass in triumph whilst my poor CMMC recipient had barely gulped/spilt a third of his. Diplomatically I think both teams ended up all-square, but at least I hadn't let the DM team down.

The following day we set off by train for the southern city of Wuhan. It was a long, overnight journey in a very long train hauled by an enormous steam locomotive. I was in a four berth compartment with Martyn (DM mineral dresser) and two CMMC engineers, one of whom had studied mineral processing at the Royal School of Mines (his English was excellent). The CMMC guys were very keen to play bridge against us. Both Martyn and I had played a little bridge before, but my goodness, the CMMC guys walloped us in three straight rubbers. I commented that the train ride was very comfortable (if not the bridge lesson!) and the CMMC guy explained that that was because (being important foreigners!) we were in a "soft coach". He suggested we walk along the corridor to a "hard coach" being used by the proletariat. Yes, one certainly felt the thump of the rail joints together with a much more twitchy movement. Apparently it was all to do with springing on the "soft" bogies and no springing on the "hard" bogies. About 11 pm we crossed the mighty Yellow River glinting in the moonlight. After that I climbed into my bunk and mused that it all felt quite surreal to be on an overnight train in China having just been playing bridge with two of them whilst heading for Wuhan on the mighty Yangtze river.

We pulled into Wuhan's large railway station sited on the north side of the Yangtze in late morning after the 800 mile run. I had no prior knowledge of Wuhan and was taken aback by its sheer size. The population must have run into millions. However, as in Peking, there was very little motor traffic, but thousands upon thousands of bicycles. It was obviously an industrial city based on iron and steel making as well as an important transport hub with the railway network and heavy boat traffic on the Yangtze. A coach took us about 35 miles NW to a copper mining/processing centre where we would stay for three days. On the trip out of Wuhan we passed extensive new road construction being carried out entirely by an army of coolie labour; no power shovels, front-end loaders or haul trucks. All the excavation and removal of the muck was by hand. It was an awe inspiring sight.

The copper complex combined both an old open-pit and an underground mine. A nearby flotation concentrator accepted rom ore from both. The first afternoon was spent in the general offices where senior managers outlined the activities of the copper complex. We stayed the night in the complexes' guest house, which was comfortable but very cold. When we enquired about the lack of heat in the house we were told that the heating was not turned on until the end of the month, as decreed by the local Hubei province. The joys of centralised planning perhaps?

The following morning Hank (a DM team American) and I went to the mine engineering offices for a perusal of the open-pit and underground mine geology. We then had a look at the operational plans for both the pit and mine and arranged for a visit to the open-pit that afternoon. Well, what an eye opener. It was a conventional shovel/truck benched pit but had the appearance of a pit from the 1930s. The benches were shallow, about 7.5m only. The primary drills were old-fashioned jerk-cable churn drills putting down 7in diameter holes. No slurry explosives were in use, only gelignite cartridges. The rope face shovels were small, three to four cubic metres units and the haul trucks about twenty tonne capacity. There was a rudimentary road grader and that was it. The mining concept of the pit was OK, but on a tiny scale dictated by the small size of the extraction equipment. To modernise it needed new rotary blast-hole drills, larger face shovels and haul trucks, all of which could be supplied from the west, chiefly from the USA. They could also benefit from GMA's OPD computer programs for optimising both tonnage and grade recovery. Hank and I left brochures and plenty of DM business cards.

The next day we (Hank and I) had arranged to go underground. Having seen the old-fashioned pit the previous day this trip was undertaken not without a degree of trepidation. My worries were not assuaged by a visit to the ancient surface double-drum winder, which looked as if it could do with a little TLC. Taking a deep breath we descended the shaft in a battered old cage, which, surprisingly, rode very smoothly. But that was the high point. The underground workings were absolutely shambolic. Main levels were semi-flooded with no proper drains, appalling trackwork, virtually no mine illumination (thank goodness we had electric cap lamps, one might have expected carbide ones!) and once inby from the shaft precious little through ventilation. We clambered up some rudimentary ladders into an overhand rill stope. The fill used was waste rock mined in a number of surface glory holes. Medium weight jacklegs were used in conjunction with small pneumatic powered twin drum scrapers. The broken ore was scraped over a grizzley atop a timber lined pass carried up through the waste fill. Simple Chinaman chutes (yes that is what they're called!) delivered the broken ore to two tonne side tip mine cars hauled by six tonne battery locomotives. Incidentally they must have experienced numerous derailments on the poor track. As we anticipated ventilation up in the stopes was non-existent - not a good place to work. However, looking on the bright side it was pleasantly warm underground in contrast to the freezing temperatures on surface.

I'm pretty certain Hank was as glad as me to survive the underground visit in one piece. There was, however, one final twist to our underground visit. As we emerged from the cage at the surface we were surrounded by a large, excited crowd. Our guide (the Underground Manager) explained, a little apologetically, that word had gone around that two gweilos or round eyes had gone underground and the locals, never having seen westerners before, wanted to have a look. Well Hank and I made a contrasting pair - Hank short, chubby and thick set, me tall, thin and lanky. Anyway it was a very weird experience to be in the middle of this gawping crowd of Chinese. No animosity, just sheer curiosity. It got even weirder when some youngster pressed up really close and seemed fascinated by the hair on our arms, so much so, that amidst huge giggles, they stroked Hank and my arms. Otherwise their chief interest seemed to be Hank's girth, my height and of course the (round) eyes. After this experience I've had a somewhat more sympathetic approach to animals in a zoo. All in a day's march in China, which certainly lived up to one of it's western epithets of mysterious.

We had a wrap-up meeting with the Underground Manager and his team. The CMMC guys stressed that their main requirement was to double or treble mine output. I explained that their copper ore expectancy could, in fact, sustain such an expanded output, but the mine would require converting from a tracked to a trackless operation. A move to trackless operations could be introduced into one section of the mine first and then slowly be expanded into the remainder of the mine. We felt that DM could assist with an overall mine redesign and provide hands-on assistance procuring modern underground mining machinery. The introduction of underground diesel equipment would, of course, greatly increase productivity, since at present it was a very labour intensive operation.

As the mine was relatively shallow, 6 to 700ft we suggested that a 1 in 8 ramp-decline should be developed for ingress/egress of wheeled equipment and a new ventilation shaft should be excavated by raising from the mine's furthest limits. The bulk of this new trackless development could be completed without directly impinging on the existing tracked operation. We left a pile of brochures of American, German, Swedish and Finnish trackless machinery covering drilling jumbos (hydraulic and pneumatic), LHD units, low profile articulated trucks, road graders and roof bolters. These brochures went down a storm in spite of the lack of Chinese script. Thus on this cheerful note we headed back to Wuhan where we were scheduled to stay the night. Here we joined up with the mineral processing guys and girded our loins for the inevitable "farewell banquet", as we were scheduled to fly south to Guangzhou tomorrow followed by the short flight to Hong Kong.

The 560 mile flight to Guangzhou took a little over two hours in a CAAC scheduled service operated by an ancient Tupolev turboprop aircraft. The Chinese cabin staff were very attentive and presented all passengers with a tiny porcelain reclining panda. The stop at Guangzhou was only two hours so we only had a chance to see briefly the newish terminal before going through the lengthy Emigration procedures required for leaving China. As we took off we noted a lot of construction activity around the periphery of Guangzhou but this was in stark contrast to the huge skyscrapers of Hong Kong island as we landed at Kai Tak airport on the Kowloon side of the harbour. The two cities are only eighty miles apart, twenty minutes flying time, but several decades apart in urban development. We had about five hours to look around Hong Kong before catching the overnight CP flight back to London. We all agreed it had been a fantastic experience, but no one was holding their breath that DM would sign up any Chinese minerals projects in the near future. The DM team leader felt that western involvement in developing China's mining/minerals industry was still five to ten years away. No matter, at least CMMC were now aware of DM and the type of services they could offer.

We arrived back in London, three days before Christmas. I had to remember to tell the Heathrow taxi to take me to GMA's offices in High Holborn rather than the old 6 St James's Square address of RTZC. Dick told me that GMA's formation as the old RTZC organisation had caused quite a bit of interest in the international mining press. The good news was that the enquiries were still coming in. In some respects the break from RTZ ownership would surely improve our independent label. On that independent theme Dick said GMA had been approached by Wardell Armstrong (WA) to assist them with a feasibility study for HZL's Rampura Agucha project in Rajasthan. The study was being bankrolled by UK government aid to India. Simon from WA had specifically requested my involvement on the mining side and John, from Imperial Smelting Processes (ISP), an RTZ subsidiary at Avonmouth, would also join the WA team. I asked Dick the obvious question "when?", and he said WA had agreed mid January (1979) with HZL. Phew - at least I would get Christmas and the New

Year at home. I gave him a quick run-down on the China visit and said that I didn't believe it would lead to any consulting work in China, but at least it had helped cement our relationship with DM. He also said that in early January we had two or three applicants to our mineral processing engineer ads coming in for interview. The news from India was OK; Roy had finished the Malanjkhand open-pit work and John and Dave had organised the GMA house/office in Udaipur; the RD job for HZL was progressing and the Ambaji deep drilling for metallurgical testwork was on target. Meanwhile Brian, another mining engineer (ex South Africa) was working on the recent Salidapura project for PPCL. Shad, our Indian agent still seemed unhappy about the change from RTZC to GMA, but Dick suggested I try and see him in Delhi after the Rampura Agucha work for WA. All in all 1979 looked as if it would be as busy as usual.

It was good to be back in one's own home again. Sure all this jetting around sounds very glamorous and one saw and experienced many different places and customs, but when push came to shove you couldn't beat home and your own little patch. Gillian and the two dogs were well and the list of "jobs to do" seemed remarkably light. In the depths of winter Beals garden was a complete no-no with the heavy, glutinous, unyielding Gault clay "soil". My parent's came from High Halden for Christmas day lunch and we went to Duxbury (their place) on Boxing day. Then on the 28th we headed off for Cornwall with Matt and Anjon in the Simca van. To make life easier on the long journey (the Simca wasn't a flyer) we had an intermediate stop at the Coker Motel in Somerset. Travelling with the dogs the Simca van came into its own as a mobile kennel just outside our motel room - sorted. We spent New Year with Pat and Tony in Mawgan Porth and collected Gillian's mother from St Mawgan for the day. We left on the 2nd, stopping at the Coker Motel again. Both of us went back to work on the 4th January.

After a couple of days clearing the desk I caught an early train up to Newcastle-under-Lyme for a meeting with WA on the scope of work and our site work programme for the HZL Rampura Agucha (RA) job. John from ISP, Avonmouth also attended. Although HZL were not contemplating building a new smelter at RA itself, but rather at Vishakhapatnam, they felt it essential that John had direct knowledge of the RA ore and the probable mineralogy of future concentrates from the project. Would an ISP furnace be suitable to treat the RA concentrates combined with the RD concentrates? From my point of view as a mere subcontractor it was a very relaxing get-together. Simon, the WA team leader, had all the worry of coordinating everyone's input. It went well apart from a Prof of Mining from the RSM, who was rather opinionated. WA were using him as an external sounding board and he seemed to disagree with just about everything I said. Not to worry, he talked a lot of nonsense and, importantly, had never worked in India, which was where I had the jump on him. Good old Simon had the job of keeping us apart! John from ISP, who also knew India, nearly split his sides laughing at us arguing. The really good news for me was that the RSM Prof of Mining was not coming on the Indian site visit. We caught a 6 pm train south, John leaving at Birmingham to travel to Bristol, whilst I continued to London and (eventually) very late home to Woodchurch.

In fact it was towards the end of January when I joined up with the six strong WA team and John at Heathrow for the flight to Delhi. Here we stayed in a central hotel in New Delhi. The following day we had meetings with officials of the Indian Ministry of Mines and the GSI. As a consequence of RTZC's and now GMA's work in India I knew several of these officials which, I think, proved helpful. Obviously Simon as WA team leader had to do most of the talking, so I could revert to cruise mode. Next day we flew down to Udaipur to meet the HZL management. Hari, the HZL Mining Manager, seemed pleased to see me again, albeit a little surprised that I was working for WA, but quite relaxed when I explained that it was a simple subcontract basis. He also wanted me to tell him the details of the change from RTZC to GMA. The HZL RA project team gave us an overview of the current status of the project. Both John and I were specifically interested in the original GSI exploration data, later infill diamond drilling and initial mineralogical and metallurgical testwork. Nothing really changed with any of these new mining projects. First one got to know the deposit - where was it; what was it's disposition; how big was it; what did it contain and how could one treat it. The basic nature of the deposit was absolutely fundamental. Everything else followed on and really entailed the application of suitable engineering and the concomitant expenditure, all secondary to "knowing" the deposit. It transpired that HZL had decided to house the WA team whilst in Udapur in the old "RTZ House", close to their Head office. For me a deja vu moment.

In the morning we set off for RA, which was situated in Bhilwara District about ninety miles to the north-east of Udaipur, towards Ajmer. HZL had extended and modernised the original GSI exploration camp. This was really helpful as it meant we could stay on site and not waste five hours/day commuting Udaipur to RA and return in the bone shaking Mahindra jeeps. At the site we split up into our various disciplines. John and I had a walk around the extensive site with HZL's senior site geologists. Our earlier discussion in Udaipur and perusal of the outline geological surface plan prepared by Rajasthan State geologists aided by the GSI seemed to indicate a very significant lead-zinc deposit. The site topography was gentle and the few vertical cross sections indicated little waste overburden. It was apparent that the RA prospect was still in the basic exploration stage. My initial feeling was that the deposit appeared likely to support a large open-pit mine. However the paucity of deeper diamond drilling data and the lack of any underground development made even this a dubious prognosis. Certainly there was insufficient exploration data to estimate the size of a future mine.

I had an early talk with Simon and we agreed that the current HZL geological data base was insufficient to determine a definitive project scope. He felt the best approach for WA was to draw up a detailed further exploration programme for the deposit to cover firstly both shallow infill and deeper (down-dip) diamond drilling. Secondly a full microscopic mineralogical analysis of the outlined ore zone and thirdly a preliminary geotechnical analysis of various drilling cores. We would also indicate where and how some underground development should be carried out as soon as possible to provide a bulk sample for metallurgical testwork. The underground development would also be used for geotechnical rock mass classification. As I was fairly certain that the disposition of the ore zone would be suitable for open-pit mining HZL requested WA to prepare a preliminary RA project based on a notional open-pit output of circa 6,000 tonnes/day with an overall stripping ratio of 2.5 to 1. This would, in effect, be an initial sizing exercise. Average projected rom grades were obtained from the geometrical mean of all 1m length drill core samples from within the defined ore zone. These were then discounted by 7.5% to cater for internal and external open-pit waste dilution. Of course at this point in the project's development these were only considered guesstimates, but they gave us a basis on which to prepare a preliminary engineering study with costs. Other WA team members had collected local labour costs, work routines, import duties as well as basic costs such as steel, concrete, explosives, power, reagents etc. Most of this information was readily available from HZL's existing operation at Zawar and the new RD project.

After three weeks and many meetings with HZL Simon felt further work on site was yielding diminishing returns and we should return to the UK to work up a draft notional project document for discussion with HZL by the second week of March. I entirely agreed with him since we had an agreed scope and all the basic cost data. Further cost data for capital equipment for the notional mine and concentrator could be much more readily obtained in the UK. We flew back to Delhi and I managed to have a brief meeting with our Indian agent, Shad, and reassure him, face to face, that his relationship with GMA was a continuation of that with RTZC. That same night the whole WA team flew back to London.

My job was relatively easy as there was no detailed pit design to undertake it was all notional - 6000 tonnes/day and 2.5 to 1 strip ratio. In house we had files of open-pit capital equipment costs, such as rotary drills, haul trucks, explosive trucks, dozers, graders etc plus designs and costs of open-pit maintenance facilities. I arbitrarily selected a 15m bench hight and operated the pit two shifts/day, six days/week. From this it was simple to determine size and number of drills, plus the same for rope shovels and haul trucks, since WA/HZL had determined where the notional primary crushing plant and concentrator would be sited. One of Peter's computer guys ran up this notional pit and produced some pretty snazzy print out. I was impressed, hoped WA would be and ultimately HZL. I bounced all this notional RA open-pit stuff off Dick, who generally gave it his blessing. I took all my write-up, costs and drawings up to WA in Newcastle-under-Lyme before the end of February. I stayed up in Newcastle for a couple of nights whilst Simon and his team went through my (GMA) stuff. Then back down to London where the next job was already banging on the door.

This next job concerned a limestone quarrying project in County Meath, Eire. All our open-pit engineers were gainfully employed, so Dick suggested I go on the grounds that I had undertaken the Swanworth Quarries evaluation a few years earlier. Fine by me since it only involved a short flight to Dublin and then a hire car for the thirty mile drive NW from the airport. The Premier quarry project, as it was called, was situated close to the Tara Mines complex, so I had first hand knowledge of the area. In fact the scope of work for the evaluation of the Premier limestone quarry was nearly identical to that for Swanworth. The current owner had been approached by a major Irish aggregates operator to see if he was willing to sell. The owner wanted to know what price he should ask. Obviously my advice was that he should sell the quarry as a "going concern". At their current rate of output their known (drilled off) limestone reserves would sustain production for slightly over thirty years - a long life.

My approach was to carry out a DCF at the present rate of output and determine a NPV over this thirty year span. Of course I made use of the quarries actual operating costs and sales revenue. Then we analysed and split the direct operating costs into their fixed and variable elements and hey presto we were in business. Using the fixed/variable cost split we doubled the rate of production and (obviously) halved the quarry life to fifteen years. Again, running a DCF at this doubled production rate enabled us to determine a new NPV over the fifteen-year span. Unsurprisingly this latter NPV was vastly greater than the first one. I suggested to the owner that this should be his (starting) asking price. Of course any potential purchaser would argue that this price was too high because he (the potential purchaser) would have to invest in new plant and machinery to double production. The owner's counter argument should then be, yes, but with economies of scale by doubling production, the gross operating margin would increase. The owner's approach obviously depended on whether it was a sellers or buyers market. However his "ace in the hole" was that he not only had the limestone reserves but also the planning permission to expand production, for both of which he had documentary and engineering proof. Also the proximity of the quarry to Dublin was surely a great selling point. I spent four days working through all the numbers with his accountant and the Quarry Foreman to derive a realistic fixed/variable split. The owner and I wrapped things up in the pub. He was delighted that my suggested asking price for the quarry as a going concern was about 70% higher than he'd anticipated. I said that if the aggregate company was really keen (and short of stone reserves) he could hold out for an even higher price. All it took was a willing buyer and willing seller!

Back at GMA's office I went through all my Premier quarry numbers with one of our financial analysts to make sure I hadn't made a gross mistake. Thank goodness I hadn't but he greatly improved the financial presentation. In addition I added a section on the existing plant and equipment together with a detailed statement of the limestone reserves. An appendix showed the extraction planning permission. Finally Diane turned it into a neat, presentable, green covered GMA report and we despatched five copies to Meath by air courier.

We had received a request from Lepanto for me to carry out a technical review of operations at their Mankayan mine in June. I thus arranged to take three weeks holiday over the April, May period to coincide with a visit to the UK by Rod, Kate, Geoff and Marg, old friends from Rosebery, Tasmania. It would be eleven years since we had last seen them. On the due day Gillian and I met them at Heathrow with both the Lancia and the Simca van. It was their first time in Europe, so great excitement. Also great consternation for Gillian and me driving from Heathrow, across London (we had to go over Westminster bridge, past the Houses of Parliament!) down to the Elephant & Castle to the relative safety of the A21 before we could relax. Ahead of their visit we had booked hotel accommodation all over southern and central England to give them a flavour of ye old English history. In most hotels we had specified four-poster beds for them. They spent two or three days at Beals, visiting Tenterden and the old Cinque Port town of Rye as well as Bodiam Castle before the "English Tour" started in earnest. I lead the way driving the Simca with Rod as passenger and Geoff followed driving the Lancia carrying the three girls. We first had a day trip to Canterbury, where the cathedral was of interest to the Tasmanians as they were all practicing RC's. Then we set off for a look around Winchester and then stayed the night at Salisbury. Next day it was a whizz around Stonehenge and on to Wells in Somerset for the night. This was followed by a day looking around Bath then on to Warwick for the night. They all really enjoyed Warwick Castle.

We then drove west crossing the Severn at Bridgenorth before spending the night at the Feathers Hotel in Ludlow. The following day it was north, close to the Welsh border to the lovely medieval town of Chester. Next day through the Birkenhead tunnel to Liverpool (twice for me as I left my jacket in Chester!), which Geoff, in particular wanted to see, because of his interest in the international freight business. Of course everyone wanted to visit the Cavern of Beatles fame. The Liverpool Atlantic Hotel was modern, no four-poster beds. One of the Tasmanians remarked that they thought that all English people must use four-poster beds, since all the previous hotels had had them! They wanted to see Birmingham as they imagined it to be nothing but houses. Thus after leaving Liverpool we picked up the M6 which took us across the Black Country and through north Birmingham to cross the M1 just NE of Rugby and onto the A14 for Cambridge. Here we had a slight problem as the Lancia got held up at traffic lights on the outskirts and I had forgotten to tell Gillian which hotel we were staying in (complete with four-posters again!). Rod and I had parked and were wandering around the central city streets when we fortunately saw the Lancia prowling - saved. All of us were very impressed by King's College chapel and amazed at the vast number of bicycles as a consequence of the undergraduate population. We completed our "round England whizz" next day heading south down to London where we left the Tasmanians at the Trafalgar Hotel just off Leicester Square.

Back at Woodchurch we recovered the dogs from kennels, fed them as well as some hungry Khaki Campbell ducks and attacked a somewhat overgrown garden and orchard. However over the weekend order was restored, the dogs and ducks happy and Gillian and I relaxed in The Eight Bells in Tenterden before both of us returned to work on Monday.

Simon from WA asked me to attend a meeting with the Professor of Mining at the RSM to "optimise" (his word apparently) all the mining details for the RA project. I had a bad feeling about this and so it proved to be. Basically he didn't seem to like the notional open pit - why 6,000 tonnes/day, why 2.5 to 1 strip ratio, why such-and-such a head grade etc? Simon was obviously in a bit of a quandry. I explained that the present exploration/geological data base was insufficient to optimise anything. This had been agreed with the Rajasthan State Geologist, the GSI and, most importantly the client, HZL. On the basis of the current geological knowledge of the (extensive) deposit we had selected the mining rate, the strip ratio, the head grade, the bench height etc as a reasonable basis for a notional project on which a financial analysis could be attempted. The Prof was still not happy! Fortunately it was not ultimately my problem, it was Simon's as he was WA team leader. They, WA, had decided to use the Prof as an external, overviewing consultant, so Simon was really in a cleft stick. I stuck to my guns and said to Simon it was his call, but if he and the Prof decided to use other notional basic parameters, then we GMA, would require a contract extension to redo all the mining capital and operating costs. It was not a happy meeting at all and completely strengthened my distrust of academics who are far removed from actual operations. My comment to Simon, in private, about a GMA contract extension seemed to do the trick as we heard no more about changing the basic parameters. Just as well as I had already committed to carry out the Lepanto annual operations review next week and would thus be unavailable to do further WA work for a while.

17

As usual I flew CP to Hong Kong and there transferred to PAL for the short flight to Manila. On that flight I changed passports and entered the Philippines on a different passport. I needed to do this as after the Lepanto work I planned to visit Taiwan to follow up on an enquiry GMA had received. I could not use my regular passport as this now had mainland China (PRC) entry/exit stamps in it from the late 1978 visit and those would obviously foul up my entry into Taiwan. It was basically the same problem that people had doing business in both Israel and Arab countries. All of which was great news for the UK Passport Office! Ponciano met me as usual and took me to the Intercon in Makati. He gave me a message from Chito that said he (Ponciano) would be at the hotel at 7.30 tomorrow to take me to MIA domestic terminal from where Vic would fly me up to the mine. Although martial law was still in place private flights were now permitted provided they had been logged the day before with the military authorities. The 45 minute flight with Vic in the Beech Baron was a lot easier than the three quarter day jeep drive up to Baguio and on to Lepanto.

My scope of work was quite specific, namely "An independent assessment of the capability of the Lepanto mine to sustain a monthly production of 5,000 dry short tons of concentrate grading 31.5% copper". Although quite specific this meant I had to work through the entire operation from geology and ore reserves to all aspects of mining - development, stoping, haulage, hoisting, mine services and organisation; milling - crushing, grinding, flotation, product handling, fill plant, tailings disposal, research and organisation; engineering services - power supply, compressed air supply, water supply, concentrate transport and camp facilities.

Of course I knew the mining operation well from previous visits but the mill and engineering services were only known to me in general terms. It was quite a daunting task and I only had three weeks to get a grip on it. However Lepanto lent me two full-time assistants in the mine and one each for the mill and engineering services, otherwise I would never have completed the task in time. In a nutshell the Lepanto operation could meet its desired monthly copper concentrate target, but, the inevitable but! The mine had fallen, was still falling, behind on development and their in-house diamond drill contractor, DDCP, was way behind schedule. The main hurdle to achieving the concentrate production desired was low stope productivity. This meant that the mine struggled to deliver the 3085 tonnes/day required. In turn this was exacerbated by delays to the completion of the new Tubo Shaft and its equipping with unsuitable second-hand Cementation double-drum sinking winders. In particular the Tubo cage winder was restricted to a maximum load of only 2.8 tonnes. This winder/cage combination would definitely have to be uprated within five years. The mine engineering department needed beefing up to undertake essential medium and long-term planning. Stope productivity could be improved with closer supervision and the application of R&D and O&M.

The mill was not a problem area, it had spare capacity and could handle all the tonnage the mine could deliver. However new Peterbilt trucks were necessary to sustain concentrate haulage from Lepanto to Poro Point. There was one major constraint with engineering services - power supply. Unless Benguet Electric Company could guarantee delivery of at least 5MVA by mid 1980, Lepanto would require an additional Worthington SW-12, 2.6MW generating unit to increase the actual generating capacity from 12.4MW to 15MW. The compressor plant was OK, but much of the mine's old compressed air pipe network needed replacing as well as increasing the stope lines to 50mm diameter.

These findings were discussed in detail with the respective department heads and where necessary modified, extended or restated. Time and again the point was made that Lepanto had suffered a low copper price over the last few years and onerous smelter terms from ASARCO in Seattle. All of which meant that the company was squeezed for cash and had had to follow an economy drive, hence the use of the second-hand Cementation winders rather than designed GHH winders, skips and cage. Nevertheless I felt this a very false economy for such key pieces of mine infrastructure.

After three weeks non-stop work Vic flew me back to Manila in the Beech Baron accompanied by Artemio, the Mine Manager. From the MIA private terminal Ponciano drove us to the Lepanto offices on Roxas Boulevard in downtown Manila. The office had a telex for me from Dick (currently in Australia) requesting that I meet him at the Hong Kong Mandarin Hotel in four days time. That afternoon we had extended meetings with Artemio, Chito and Adelina, the Finance Director. In the evening we all joined the owner, Carlos, for a formal dinner at the Manila Peninsular Hotel of which Carlos also happened to be Chairman. It was a grand evening, the Filipinos certainly know how to do things in style. For me, of course, a huge bonus was that the chatter was all in English, well American-English actually, and one could dress formally in an open neck shirt - the famed Barong Tagalog. We had more discussions the following morning at Lepanto's offices and I had the afternoon free before catching an early evening PAL flight to Taipei.

The weather at MIA was stormy, heavy rain and fairly gusty and there was some doubt whether the flight would leave. It did and turned into one of the bumpiest, most scary flights I had ever been on. Apparently there was a major weather system not strong enough to be classified as a typhoon - too early in the year - just north of the Philippines in the South China Sea. Well the PAL pilot must have been as worried as the rest of the passengers were. He had a couple of overshoots trying to land and finally, and thankfully, thumped the plane onto the runway at Taipei in blinding rain. Phew, welcome to Taiwan. However that was only the "softening up" shock. Once outside the terminal there were no signs in English at all, only Chinese script, it really did feel very very foreign. Fortunately our UK travel agent had given me a note of my hotel's name in English and Chinese script, which I showed to the taxi driver. The centrally located hotel was fairly modern if a little stark, but my room, although on the small side, was comfortable and I slept like a log. After breakfast I asked reception to phone my contact company's number and tell them that I was in this hotel and could meet them at their convenience. With some pidgin English she explained that the company would be happy to see me that morning. I asked her to write down the name of the hotel in Chinese so that I could (eventually) return!

The taxi wended its way through light traffic for no more than ten minutes to an address in central Taipei. The company was a general engineering construction outfit who had heard of our work in the Philippines. They were also doing road building and bridge construction in the Philippines and wanted to extend their activities into mining. So it all turned out to be a sort of Chinese Whispers game. They were selling to me rather than vice versa as I had imagined from their original inquiry through Lepanto. As usual when these situations occur we each spent an hour explaining how good we were. It was slow going with no Chinese from me and only fairly rudimentary American-English, picked up in the Philippines, from their Overseas Construction Director. They were very correct and polite and insisted on taking me out to lunch. Fortunately my experience of banquets in PRC came to my rescue over the meal and I paced myself over the innumerable courses and drank the minimum of their version of maotai. Back in their office we exchanged brochures, a taxi was called and I headed back to my hotel. Conclusion - a complete waste of time, but an interesting first look at Taiwan. PRC appeared to offer some opportunities for GMA, Taiwan none. Put it all down to experience.

Next morning I caught a PAL flight to Hong Kong and booked into the very mush Mandarin Hotel to await Dick's arrival from Australia. He duly arrived later that day in a very ebullient mood. His trip to Australia had been very productive as he had sold GMA's OPD programs to Griffin Coal. That company operated a large open-pit coal mine situated SW of Perth. He had then been to Melbourne to meet the directors of an associate GA company, Golder Moss Pty (GMP), to tell them about the geological, mining and processing services GMA could offer. Apparently they were enthusiastic about having these mining related services in-house as there was a lot of activity in the local mining scene. Naturally they appreciated the fact that Dick was an Australian. Anyway Dick felt we should celebrate his success and commiserate my wasted effort in Taiwan with a slap up meal in the Mandarin's top restaurant. All went well until the wine. Dick had ordered a bottle of Coonawarra claret. When invited to sample it he sniffed, sipped a little and said, politely, no good it's corked. The wine waiter took it back with bad grace and returned with another bottle. Same result. Dick asked me try it. It was vile, definitely "off". Dick said no, it's off. The wine waiter then got very huffy and up himself "oh no sir the Mandarin does not etc etc". Something snapped with Dick (usually a very level headed person) and he grasped the wine waiter's arm forcing him to sit down and calmly poured a glass of wine and said simply, but forcefully "then drink it". Dick, keeping a firm grip on his arm, quietly insisted that the wine waiter drink the wine. Reluctantly he did and spluttered all over the place, unsurprisingly, because it was disgusting. The restaurant had miraculously gone quiet and by now all eyes of the other diners' were focussed on our table as the Maitre d' appeared to see what the hiatus was about. Dick explained, the Maitre d' apologised, shooed the wine waiter away and said he would bring a "good" bottle. He returned a few minutes later and said that the whole crate of Coonawarra claret was off. He offered an alternative with the hotel's compliments. In truth the event made the dining experience memorable.

I am sure the Mandarin was happy that we checked out the next day for Singapore. Dick had previously worked in Malaya at Rompin Iron Mines and we followed up on some of his old contacts to see if we could sell GMA's OPD programs. In the evening after a few Tiger beers at Raffles we hired a rickshaw to take us down to the waterfront to sample some of the numerous girlie bars. After a few more Tiger beers we emerged in a mildly inebriated state to see that our old rickshaw wallah had waited for us sensing, perhaps, a good tip. Anyway Dick felt the old rickshaw guy had had a hard day, whilst I had done nothing useful - so change over. Thus Dick and a mildly flustered rickshaw guy reclined in the buggy whilst I struggled between the shafts to reach a slow trotting pace along the Singapore waterfront. Fortunately for me, before a heart attack, we were stopped by a policeman, who was not amused, but actually was. We did, in fact, give the rickshaw guy a big tip for the use of his rickshaw.

The following morning, not too early on account of hangovers we flew up to Bangkok where we had a meeting in the afternoon with a fluorspar mining company. They were interested in commissioning a feasibility study for an extension to their existing mine. We went through the usual selling spiel and left plenty of brochures. We did not visit the existing fluorspar operation as we had a late night flight on Lufthansa to Delhi for a meeting with Shad, our agent, HZL and GMDC. However things got rapidly out of our control. Around 6 pm there was a coup and we were advised to get out to the airport post haste before a curfew was imposed and the road was closed. In the event there was an army road block just short of the airport. We had to get out of the taxi (including the driver) and show our passports and air tickets for a flight that evening. It was all very civilised and it became apparent that the army, instigators of the coup, had been told to detain any government members attempting to flee the country. All very dramatic and a little bit worrying.

The airport was busy, but then Don Muang always was slightly frenetic. We checked in at the Lufthansa desk where they assured us the flight was operating normally. We each checked one bag for the hold. We then repaired to a bar for a beer and watched TV pictures of the army surrounding the palace and the government building. There were also shots of various road blocks around the city and an 8 pm curfew had been set. We were glad to have made the sanctuary of the airport. Our flight was scheduled for midnight and the first hint of trouble came around 10.30 pm when Lufthansa announced "wait for further announcements". An ominous sign, since the plane should already have been on the tarmac for a midnight take-off. Lufthansa's next announcement was very specific. Their Delhi flight was overflying Bangkok on account of the recent coup. So that was that. Their ground staff were most unhelpful and whilst Dick went and berated their local manager I went to the departures board and noted that an Air France flight to Bombay was scheduled to leave at 3am. That was the easy bit. The difficult bit was getting Lufthansa to transfer our tickets to Air France for their 3am flight and even more difficult to extract our checked bags from their clutches. I eventually achieved this with the help of an airport security chief who accompanied a Lufthansa baggage handler and me to their baggage storage facility. The Lufthansa airport manager complained bitterly that this was most irregular. We made him understand that GMA would blacklist Lufthansa if they didn't release our tickets and bags and also send a cable to Shad, our agent in Delhi. He was not a happy bunny. Anyway it was done and we eventually arrived at Bombay at around 6.30am local time after a five hour flight on Air France.

Having cleared Immigration and Customs we took a day room at the airport Centaur hotel, operated by Air India. After a clean up and early breakfast I went to IAC to book us on an afternoon flight to Delhi and then, eventually, managed to phone Shad and let him know when we expected to arrive. He said he would meet the IAC flight. In spite of all the Bangkok/Lufthansa hassle we finally arrived in Delhi only 14 hours later than planned. We had a quiet dinner in the hotel with Shad, where Dick did a great job reassuring him that everything would be OK with GMA. Shad had already cancelled that afternoon's meeting with HZL due to our non-arrival. We agreed to try for an afternoon meeting with HZL tomorrow followed the next day by a meeting with GMDC. I was thankful that it was Shad who would be battling with the Indian telephone system. Later that evening we both had an in-house massage, quite strenuous and not in the least bit sexy.

The following morning Shad picked us up at the hotel, with driver, of course. to do a quick tourist run around first New Delhi and the government buildings and then old Delhi and the Jama Masjid. This was Dick's first visit to Delhi although he had met both Chairmen of HZL and GMDC when they were in London to sign the RD and Ambaji contracts respectively. We had lunch in Connaught Place. The meetings with HZL that afternoon and GMDC a day later went well. Both Chairmen were obviously relieved to see that the person they had signed contracts with at RTZC was the very same at GMA. Shad I am sure was also greatly reassured by the reaction from HZL and GMDC. It clearly demonstrated that this type of work depends upon a certain empathy between client and consultancy. it was all down to individuals and trust therein. We sorted out all Shad's local expenses and confirmed all the percentage payments for the HCL Malanjkhand and PPCL Saladipura contracts. I am sure this really convinced Shad that GMA was a decent company to work for. The next day we flew back to London.

The GMA office in High Holborn was, at long last, starting to feel like our true home base. Two new mineral dressing guys, Alex and David had joined the staff and everyone seemed to be gainfully employed. Over the next couple of weeks I spent quite a bit of time at the Maidenhead offices of GHA, where their MD, Brian showed me exactly how the GA group liked to present their individual management reports. As company secretary of GMA I also spent time with GHA's accountant who was now also doing GMA's accounts. It sounded boring, but I found it something new to learn and therefore interesting. At RTZC we had led a sheltered life since the parent, RTZ, provided secretarial, accountancy, personnel, legal and travel services from in-house departments. Also GMA was employee owned as opposed to a limited liability company. While I was in Maidenhead, Peter, a mining engineer specialising in geotechnics, said that they, GHA, had been approached to undertake a review of operating costs in the Canadian nickel mining industry could we (GMA) assist? Of course I said yes, but added that it would probably be me since everyone else was busy! So that was how, a few days later, I found myself on a flight to Toronto, Canada.

Peter had booked us into an airport hotel for convenient access to the GA head office in Mississauga about fifteen miles SW of downtown Toronto. Here we made contact with the GA boss, Vic and his deputy John, who was also GMA Chairman. It was really a courtesy call to let them known that

GHA/GMA were undertaking some mining related work in Canada. They seemed genuinely pleased that both UK GA companies were cooperating on mining projects. Later that day we took the train from Toronto about 250 miles NW to Sudbury, Ontario. Here we hired a car and had a drive around the lunar landscape of Copper Cliff, home of INCO's copper/nickel mining and smelting business. It reminded me of the landscape at Queenstown, Tasmania where virtually all vegetation had been killed by pyritic smelting. A pretty site it was not. Just the reverse; it showed the enormous environmental damage caused by uncontrolled resource extraction. Thankfully things were now slowly improving.

We then drove twenty miles NE to Falconbridge where we stayed in the companys guest house. The next three days were spent underground at the main mine visiting numerous stopes, development headings, pump stations, underground maintenance shops, loco diesel shops and battery charging stations. On surface we tramped around winder houses, headframes, storage bins, conveyors, ventilation units, changing rooms/showers and power substations. In fact all industrial facilities that directly affected underground mining costs. Another two days were spent with accountants and cost clerks who gave us the detailed breakdown of direct operating costs. Our cost study had been sponsored by both Falconbridge and INCO to see if Canadian miners could learn off each other how to lower costs to compete with the new low-cost open-pit nickel mines in Australia. We left Falconbridge and went to Copper Cliff where we had a similar programme of underground visits at INCO mines before hoovering up cost data from their accountants and cost clerks. Everyone was very open and helpful.

We dropped the car off at Sudbury airport and flew 800 miles west to Winnipeg in Manitoba. Here we transferred to a smaller aircraft for the 400 mile flight due north to Thompson, a relatively new nickel mining camp. Again we stayed in a very comfortable company guest house. Although there was an open-pit mine here we did not visit it as our remit was to look at and analyse underground mining costs. Our routine was the same as that at Falconbridge and INCO, namely two days underground visiting a number of stopes followed by inspection of all major underground mine infrastructure. Then visits to all mine surface installations followed by sessions with accountants and cost clerks. By this time both Peter and I had become bombed out with the vast quantity of bumph we had accumulated.

So far it had been solely observation of mining operations and cost data collection, we had not attempted to evaluate any of it. We agreed that this would best be left until we returned to the UK. So after five days at Thompson we flew back to Winnipeg, where we changed planes for a direct flight to Toronto. Here we had a few hours before catching the "Red Eye Shuttle" for London landing at Heathrow around mid-morning the following day. Peter and I split at the airport he went to Maidenhead and I to High Holborn. We had agreed that I would work on our Canadian material for a week and then compare notes with him out at Maidenhead.

It took a day or two to sort out all the reams of notes and figures. Pretty soon it became apparent that direct underground mining costs per tonne hoisted at the three centres, Falconbridge, INCO and Thompson were not that different - plus or minus 20% would cover it. All these mines were using variations of the blast-hole open stoping method. However even the lowest underground cost/tonne was way higher than typical open-pit cost/tonne in Canada, USA, Chile, Australia, Europe or Africa. Crudely underground hard rock mining costs per tonne, using conventional blast-hole stoping were approximately eight to ten times open-pit mining costs per tonne moved (ore and waste). It was difficult for these Canadian mines to reduce their direct mining cost per tonne to compete with typical open-pit costs per tonne moved, unless the pit's waste stripping ratio was greater than 7 to 1.

The key, of course, was grade of the hoisted tonne. Comparing cost per pound of contained metal in the hoisted tonne then the underground Canadian mines were competitive. Typical underground ore reserve grades at these mines were circa 2.2% Ni whereas Australian open-pit mines were closer to 0.8% Ni. Then parity between the two would be reached if the open-pits had a waste stripping ratio of 2.5 to 1. In fact Canadian underground mining costs were only seven times greater than typical Australian open-pit costs (per tonne moved) and their waste stripping ratios were often above 3 to 1.

The Canadian mines were thus competitive on a cost per pound of hoisted metal. Obviously to improve their competitive edge they should minimise waste dilution as well as direct mining costs. I summarised all my underground cost data per tonne hoisted and converted this to cost per pound of metal hoisted. I then listed insitu grades of Australian Ni open-pits together with waste strip ratios from published reports. The next day

I caught the early train over to Maidenhead and spent the rest of the day going over the figures with Peter. He was happy that we were able to advise the Canadians that they were, in fact, competitive, but, of course could do better at reducing both costs and mining waste dilution. Peter confirmed that GHA would put our report to bed.

Back at the GMA office my next immediate job was to organise a team to undertake a full feasibility study for the development of the Sohar Copper Project in northern Oman for the Oman Mining Company (OMC). By good fortune most of the GMA project team were now back from Minas de Riotinto so it was sensible to assign them to the Sohar job. Barrie, ex GM of Emperor Gold Mines, Fiji had performed very well for us in Spain and was the natural project leader for this job. The Sohar project was up in the north of Oman on the Gulf, due south of the Straits of Hormuz, so it was obviously going to be very hot. For this reason, in agreement with the OMC, we planned the site work for January (1980).

Thus a team of seven of us flew direct with BA to Muscat. OMC had booked us into a town-centre hotel for two days to both acclimatise and meet their own project team. What a delightful place. Situated on the southern end of the Arabian Peninsular, Muscat was very obviously arabic but also easily embraced some western influence. For us, Gulf area greenhorns, the presence of a well stocked hotel bar with excellent local beer was the first port of call to combat the near 40 C temperature - it was hot. We spent the next two days in OMC's offices in Muscat going through their project report, in particular the geology and ore reserve calculations. It was definitely going to be an underground mine.

Two 4WD jeeps took us 150 miles NW, paralleling the coast up to Sohar, where we turned inland in the Al Batinah district. At the project site OMC had established an extensive Portakabin site with their own portable diesel-generator unit. All the Portakabins were fully air-conditioned and boy did they need to be. In the five days I spent on site before turning the job over to Barrie the maximum temperature hit 50 C! It was so hot we organised our field work from 5 to 8am then 4 to 7 pm. It proved essential to be inside and air-conditioned for four hours either side of midday. After breakfast finished at 9am we would work inside looking at drill core logs and mineralogical & metallurgical testwork data. We carried out check ore reserve calculations and prepared vertical cross sections based on diamond drill information as a pre-requisite to starting mine planning. There was little geotechnical data, but a ramp-decline had been developed into the ore zone and could thus provide large scale access for both grade-distribution studies and rock mass classification work. All meals were prepared by on-site caterers and after lunch around 1 pm we all took a Spanish style siesta until recommencing fieldwork at 4 pm. Our Minas de Riotinto guys had no trouble falling in with that routine. Just over a week after leaving London I headed back down to Muscat for a progress meeting with the OMC top brass. Their local on-site "spies" had informed them of our work routines and everyone seemed impressed by how many hours/day the team were putting in. So on a pretty happy note I caught a regular BA flight back to a more than chilly London.

We had a board meeting with John, our Chairman from GA's Toronto office, Brian MD of GHA from Maidenhead, Dick and me to review GMA's first years results from November 1978. Considering it was our first full year as part of the GA group it had gone well and GMA had made a positive contribution to the group's profitability. In spite of a number of one-off costs, such as new office set-up and recruitment of mineral processing engineers, we were still well in the black. Nevertheless John seemed less than happy.

It must be said that he was never much in favour of the GA group buying out RTZC anyway. That deal was put together by Dick and the GA Chairman, Vic. John felt that, to use an old Polish expression, we would be pissing in the soup, as far as full mining project feasibility studies were concerned. His worry was that GA was fundamentally a geotechnical consultancy and as such would offer these services direct to mining companies or engineer-constructor companies such as Bechtel, Fluor, Simon Engineering, Davy McKee etc and could then end up in competition with GMA who were either bidding alone or with an engineer-constructor company for the full feasibility study. He then went on to criticise the recent GHA/GMA nickel costing study in Canada carried out by Peter (from GHA) and me. I was somewhat taken aback by this as he had seemed perfectly OK when Peter and I had visited him before we started the work. He felt that this work should have been handled by or through a Canadian GA company. Dick was as diplomatic as usual and pointed out that that particular Canadian work had been done by the best qualified GA companies, who had the skills, and anyway the income earned came into the GA group. John seemed less than mollified and both Dick and I failed to see the danger signs.

18

I had a couple of weeks doing company-secretarial type work with our accountants sorting out PAYE, NI and continuing pension problems (transfers from the RTZ scheme to GA's scheme run by Sun Life of Canada) for our ex-RTZC staff as well as enrolling our new consultants. Actually quite interesting but obviously desk-bound with a large amount of figure checking. Anyway help was at hand (for me) as we had a call from COMSUR SA requesting my presence in Bolivia. I spoke to Stan on the phone and he said it was to do with development at Milluni and visiting another mine that Goni was considering buying. Stan felt it would require two to three weeks work. For whatever reason, probably feeling guilty for being away so much, when I got home that day I suggested to Gillian that she might like to have a South American holiday. What we discussed was that she arrive in La Paz during that third week whilst I finished off my COMSUR work. We'd have seven days or so in Bolivia, then wend our way through South America before returning to the UK. Gillian asked the surgery if she could have her three weeks holiday starting in three weeks time and that was OK. At the office Dick cleared my holiday extension after the Bolivian job and that was that.

Sheldon Travel had thought that the easiest way for Gillian to travel out to Bolivia was Heathrow to Miami by BA then Braniff down to Lima and finally LAB to La Paz. I thus chose the same routing to suss out any snags. It was, in fact, straightforward, apart from restrictions in Miami, unless one held a USA visa. Thus in Miami, with no USA visa one was held in a not too friendly transit lounge, where one was viewed with great suspicion by the US Customs and Immigration people. However the airport's lingo was a vaguely recognisable form of English, which would help Gillian. The American airline, Braniff, was quite delightful and zany with their stewardesses dressed in aluminium foil mini skirts. More importantly the planes were excellent, clean, tidy and ran on time. At Lima airport, between twenty and thirty passengers from Miami were transiting to La Paz by a connecting LAB flight. It was well signed for a Bolivian transit lounge. All in all nice and straightforward.

COMSUR's driver met me at El Alto airport in the old Range Rover for the descent into La Paz. I stayed at the Sucre Hotel just a short distance from their offices. The following day I caught up with Carlos, COMSUR's CG for a briefing on the Bolivar mine, which was situated in the Oruro district, about 150 miles south of La Paz. We set off the next day in a company Landcruiser complete with driver. The main road, La Paz to Oruro was sealed, but thereafter I was thankful we had a driver experienced in negotiating pretty awful dirt roads and tracks to the mine. The local Mine Manager and CG gave us a comprehensive overview on the operation that afternoon before a fairly heavy beer and pisco sour drinking session preceded dinner in the mine's very basic hostel accommodation. Normally I try to steer clear of alcohol for the first two or three days in Bolivia, so as not to aggravate an aggressive siroche headache. Not this time, I had a "thumper" before the night was out. What a fool, I really should learn from past experience.

The mine itself was a typical steep dipping, fissure vein, carrying high copper values in the upper levels, moving through a copper/tin zone and ultimately a tin only zone at depth. Both the NW and SE extremities of the vein had been terminated by steep dipping normal cross faults. No vein extensions had been disclosed by exploration beyond these faults. The main mining method was shrinkage although where the ground conditions were less good a variety of rill cut-and-fill was used. It was a tracked mine using jacklegs and two drum air scrapers with small battery loco haulage of 1 tonne side tip wagons. A small rectangular shaft, equipped with a 125hp double-drum winder, hoisted the broken ore to the lowest adit level for haulage to the 150 tonnes/day concentrator. We only needed to spend one day underground. The mine's ore expectancy was low at a little over 1,000 t/vm and appeared to be decreasing at depth. Carlos and I agreed that there was absolutely no possibility of increasing the production rate for this mine. With zero upside potential the mine was of no interest to COMSUR. In the morning we headed back for Oruro and then La Paz. That afternoon we wrote up a very brief summary of the salient points for presentation to Jaime and Goni the owner. The meeting with Goni took place in the early evening and a decision was taken not to proceed further with the Bolivar project.

The following day it was up to Milluni.

This would be my third or fourth visit to the Milluni mine - it was becoming personal! It was one of Bolivia's best known tin mines with a colourful history. It's most famous visitor had been the Duke of Edinburgh, who sometime in the 1960s opined that the local mine accommodation "wasn't fit for pigs". But that was then. Now under COMSUR ownership new bunk houses and mess facilities had been built. Nevertheless conditions were harsh at the mine, whose elevation was over 4,500m situated on the flanks of Chacaltaya mountain. I found it very difficult to sleep at that altitude (severe siroche) and consequently wasn't very effective the next day. I stuck it for three days and then opted for the 1.5 hour jeep trip from La Paz to the mine and return. Although this obviously involved three hours/day travelling I obtained a good nights sleep at lower altitude and was thus able to put in a full days work at the mine.

The expanded 600 tonnes/day gravity concentrator was now under construction and my scope of work was to finalise the location and specifications of a new internal shaft to serve mining operations below the main haulage level. A new shaft location was relatively easy to determine with the help of Carlos. We looked at the orebodies centre of gravity at successively deeper levels below the main haulage level. We also preferred the stronger footwall rocks. This had the added advantage of not tying up ore in a shaft pillar had we opted for a hangingwall location. Once the shaft location was selected the next task was to fix the size and shape. As this new shaft would be the main ventilation fresh air downcast below the main haulage level it was soon apparent that, in fact, this would be the key to determining shaft size. I also had to establish shaft pipe sizes for compressed air, water and de-slimed mill tailings (for stope fill) supply as well as a rising main for pumped mine drainage. Here, of course, I had numerous discussions with both Jaime and Mario before the shaft duty specifications were finalised.

For Gillian's arrival COMSUR provided the Range Rover and a driver for me to meet the LAB 727 flight at El Alto. There was quite a kerfuffle at the airport as Dr. Jonathan Miller, the polymath deplaned with a small retinue. Eventually Gillian appeared looking remarkably relaxed after the long flight from London. I was very pleased to see her and told her to take things quietly until she acclimatised to the altitude. However she did not suffer from a siroche at all. To avoid personal expense confusion I had moved from the Hotel Sucre to a corner room in the new Hyatt Hotel just past the bullet scared university building. We had a lovely view of the distant snow capped Illimani mountain across the lower parts of La Paz.

Gillian was full of get up and go and wanted to "attack the city sights". She told me that on the train from Ashford to Charing Cross a young man had helped her with her suitcase with the words "going anywhere interesting"? When she replied "Bolivia", he responded with "now that is interesting"! Of course at this time (1980) South America had yet to become a mainstream tourist destination. Anyway we headed out to stroll along the main drag, to the huge street market alongside the Catholic cathedral at the upper end of the city. We also wandered around the Plaza Murillo, complete with its famous hanging lamppost, where several presidents had met their end in one or another of Bolivia's endless coups.

Gillian still had no sign of siroche, but when we went for lunch it rapidly became apparent that she had no appetite. The sight and smell of food made her feel sick. A local told me that this was quite normal for visitors to the altitude, one or the other - siroche or sickness, generally not both, so thankful for small mercies! She decided to take it easy in our room for the rest of the day whilst I went back to COMSUR's office to check over the Milluni shaft duty specifications write-up. There was a message to phone Carlos, our Bolivian agent. He invited us to join them the following day for a visit to the Tiahuanaco ruins and a short boat trip on Lago Titicaca. Carlos said he would pick us up from the Hyatt Hotel at 10am. Gillian took it easy that evening, just a room service snack and hoped to feel less nauseous in the morning.

Not exactly bright eyed and bushy tailed, but Gillian was ready for some altiplano tourism next day. Carlos and his wife arrived spot on time (perhaps a reflection of his German background)? He drove a large, comfortable Willys jeep. We climbed out of the La Paz bowl and turned west, off the Oruro road, towards Guaqui and the Peruvian border. After forty miles or so we reached the pre-Inca ruins at Tiahuanaco. The ruins cover a huge area and Carlos explained that the major large standing stones were oriented towards the midday sun at the spring and autumn solstices. Many of these standing stones had intricate carvings on them. We then drove into the border town of Guaqui situated on the southern tip of Lago Titicaca. Here we stopped for a light lunch. A further twelve miles west we stopped at Desaguadero, the southern outlet of the lake, where the bridge provides the border crossing from Peru. To Gillian's and my amazement dozens of mountain men were carrying huge loads of toilet rolls on their back from

Peru into Bolivia. Carlos, a long-term resident of La Paz, was not in the least surprised. Apparently toilet rolls were as rare as hen's teeth in Bolivia and these cross-border smugglers knew which product would give them an excellent return. Not exactly the "small volume, high value" product one would expect to see smuggled.

After lunch we boarded a small ancient steamer for a trip around some islands at the southern end of the lake. It was very peaceful with a strong, clear light and one had to remind oneself that we were on the world's highest lake, 12,505ft (3812m) above sea level. In the late afternoon Carlos drove us back to La Paz; it had been a marvellous days sight seeing.

Next day I thought Gillian ought to see some of the mines I worked at otherwise she might have the impression that I swanned around La Paz all the time. COMSUR duly produced the Range Rover and driver to take us up to Milluni. Obviously Gillian had seen mining camps before (Kiabakari, Rosebery, Lepanto etc) but even she was amazed at how primitive and run down Milluni was. However we went one better. The driver took us up past the snout of the Chacaltaya glacier to the small COMSUR owned Huaatani adit mine situated at over 5200m (17,000ft) elevation. Unsurprisingly a little voice said "can we go down now". I was more than happy to agree, but at least Gillian had seen that it was not all beer and skittles. Nevertheless Gillian survived the high altitude very well. Her major problem was an almost complete lack of appetite. Back in the Hyatt Hotel we had a quiet late afternoon. At 8 pm Goni and his wife Ximena collected us from the hotel to take us out to dinner. We were both very appreciative of this Bolivian hospitality which seemed to cement my long-term involvement with COMSUR.

We had one more day looking around La Paz, doing a little souvenir shopping for typical Bolivian alpaca sweaters as well as locally crafted silverware. We had an early LAB flight back down to Lima the following day. Gillian was also intrigued by how long it took for the Boeing 727 to get airborne from El Alto airport. In Lima we stayed in a town-centre hotel known locally as The Jail, since it closely resembled the internal layout of many prisons. That afternoon we headed for the popular centre of the city, the Plaza San Martin. Here the hotel of the same name served the world renowned "Cathedral" pisco sours. It was a very large pisco sour, in fact it was a triple! Extremely good, but two just about blotted out the rest of the evening. The Plaza, complete with fountains, was surrounded by lovely medieval Spanish architecture. An incongruous feature was the presence of 1930s huge, flashy, battered American automobiles used as taxis lined up outside the San Martin Hotel. The following morning we went down to have a look at the Presidential palace with the bizarre strutting guards outside. We also had to visit Lima Cathedral where Pizarro's mortal remains were on display. We found it dark and forbidding - putting the fear of God into one, but I suppose that was the idea. In the afternoon we took a taxi out to the SE suburbs of the city to visit the Gold Museum. Heavy security, of course, but what an amazing place. For me the most memorable object was not made of gold but a full skull with large emeralds for eyes and teeth - very disturbing. We took an early supper as both of us felt very drowsy, the normal effect of becoming super oxygenated at sea level after spending time on the altiplano.

A little more sight seeing on the following morning then it was out to Jorge Chavaz airport to catch the Air France flight for Quito, Ecuador. The plane was absolutely filthy, rubbish everywhere. We complained and the crew were very apologetic and promptly upgraded us to First Class - much better. Other than the squalor in the Economy cabin it was an uneventful flight. Quito was set in a broad open valley at around 9,000ft elevation, high but no trouble whatsoever with siroche. As we came in from the SW we had a marvelous view of the Cotopaxi volcano south of the city. We stayed in a colonial style hotel in the centre of this beautiful, if a little run down, medieval Spanish city. We seemed to do a lot of walking around markets, museums and art galleries. Three days later we caught another Air France flight to Paris.

Very unimaginatively we stayed in the same Hotel Litre in Montparnasse that we had stayed in with Pat twelve years ago on our way back from India. It did not disappoint, it was still the same if a little more careworn. We did all the usual tourist haunts - a trip up the Eiffel Tower; visit to the Louvre gallery to get a glimpse of the Mona Lisa painting. Huge crowds, but my biggest surprise was how small the painting was; trip on the Bateaux Mouche on the Seine; walk around Montmartre; walk through the Luxembourg gardens and, of course numerous cafes on the Champs Elysées. I'm sure there were many more places/things we "did", but we felt touristed out by the time we caught a flight back to Heathrow. It might be grey old England, but it was home for both of us. Certainly back in Woodchurch the next day, two very excited dogs, released from kennels, really did make it feel like home. We both agreed that this type of rolling holiday, covering four countries and a considerable amount of flying, was anything but relaxing.

The next week, back at work, there was more travelling for me, but only to Cornwall. It was the CSM annual dinner and I had asked Dick to be my guest at the Tregenna Castle Hotel in St Ives. There was a little method in this madness as we had landed a consulting job for Holman Brothers in Camborne. I drove the Lancia across to Dick's place in Surrey where I transferred to his company Rover for the long drive to Cornwall. We said hello to Gillian's sister Pat in Mawgan Porth before continuing down to St Ives. The CSM dinner was fine and it was interesting to catch up with some of my old contemporaries. However the current crop of students all seemed incredibly young and brash, but then it was 22 years since I'd left the CSM - quite a shock. At least we had enough brains not to get too hammered at dinner so that we were able to front-up at Holman's office in Camborne with relatively clear heads. We had a simple remit from Holmans, "what areas could/should they diversify into"?

About eighteen months previously Holmans had bought out the BroomWade company who specialised in portable diesel compressors and paving breakers. From our consulting work with both RTZC and GMA it was apparent that mining machinery manufacturers were switching from pneumatic to hydraulic underground rock drills and jumbos. Surface drilling wagons (both drifter and DTH rigs) were likewise shifting to hydraulic power. That was definitely the way the industry was going. We also suggested Holmans beef up their after-sales service, which had declined sharply over the past few years. I mentioned how Lepanto had changed from Holman jackhammers to Toyo machines simply because Holmans' local Philippine agent could not supply essential spares. Our recommendations seemed well received and we motored back to the south-east.

Unbelievably only a week or so later there was a note in the mining press to say that the Finnish mining machinery company Tamrock had bought out the Holman/BroomWade group. That deal had obviously been done before our meeting, but for some reason Holmans never told Dick or me that their group was being taken over by Tamrock, specialist in underground hydraulic mining machinery! Strange.

During July Dick and Roy were back out at the Muja open-pit coal operations of Griffin Coal south of Perth, Western Australia. It was an upgrade on the pit planning program and an evaluation of equipment requirements for the expanded operation. For a change I was UK based. Unfortunately disaster struck in late July when Gillian and I were driving the Simca van back from Rye along the Old Military Road. A car coming the other way failed to take one of the sharp bends and slammed into our right hand front side. Nobody killed, but we both suffered serious whiplash and rib damage from the seat belts. The van was a write off. We were taken by ambulance to A&E at Ashford hospital, but allowed home, bruised & battered after several hours. Neither Gillian nor I enjoyed driving over the next month or so. In a funny way I felt safer on the Honda motorcycle for the Woodchurch - Ashford commute than in the car. Gillian continued using the Lancia for the run to the village surgery.

19

Dick returned from Australia in early August and the following week we had a visit from John (GMA Chairman) and CEO of the GA group. The three of us had a board meeting and immediately John began to rant and rave about GMA doing work in Australia. He said it had got to stop and all/any Australian work, be it geotechnical or mining oriented had to be handled through GA's Australian company GMP. John, of course, was referring to Dick and Roy's work for Griffin Coal. Dick in his calm, diplomatic way said that this was unacceptable since GMA had spent a lot of time and effort developing both business and contacts with several major Australian mining companies. Well John went absolutely berserk, said that Australia was henceforth "off limits to GMA". Dick and I again tried to argue whereupon John leapt up and proceeded to smash his office chair to pieces - really. Absolutely unbelievable!

Dick and I looked at each other, stood up and said we were going to the pub until John had cooled down. We left a very quiet, shell shocked office. The chair smashing had made considerable noise. After a couple of beers we both agreed it was impossible to work harmoniously with a maniac Chairman, like John. We went back into the office after an hour and both of us resigned forthwith - Dick as MD and me as Director and Company Secretary. I gave the required six months notice as an employee of the GA group, thus terminating my employment at the end of February 1981. I do not recall the details of Dick's resignation, but by the end of next week he had left. Brian, MD of GHA, Maidenhead also became MD of GMA and another GHA director took over my company-secretarial role. Yes, bloody, but quick and final. John then decided to shut the High Holborn office at the end of the lease period, also February 1981 and all GMA staff were offered continuing employment at the GHA, Maidenhead office. That put the cat amongst the pigeons.

At home Gillian and I talked about "what next"? We both felt we wanted to stay in England rather than try another overseas posting. My only expertise was underground hard rock mining. Opportunities in that field were very limited in the UK. I felt I might be able to survive as an independent mining engineer specialising in shaft design and mining projects. Next thought, as an independent I didn't have to live within commutable distance of London.

Thus choose somewhere nice to live, for example the Welsh Marches within fifty miles of an international airport - Birmingham. Therefore sell Beals and buy somewhere in the country for cash and use cash balance to tide us over the first year or so, whilst I saw if I could make a go of being self-employed. We put Beals on the market straight away and completed the sale by the end of September. A family in Woodchurch snapped it up at the asking price as they wanted the land for their horses. We then rented a local "cowman's cottage" for three months through until the end of the year.

There was one additional complication in that we had two Tasmanian visitors, John and Anne, arriving in the last week of September. They were very good and joined in the confusion of clearing Beals and moving some essential stuff into the cottage. On completion day there were four removals vans outside; our two taking the bulk of our belongings into storage and the purchasers two vans waiting to move in! As instructed by our solicitor I wouldn't release Beals keys until I heard from him that the purchase money had been cleared into the firms account. That took place around 1 pm and our circus comprising John and Anne, Matt and Anjon and Gillian and I decamped for the rented cottage. How we all fitted in I can't imagine, but we did. John and Anne were marvellous and said the moving house experience made their UK holiday much more interesting! A week later we took John and Anne up to London for a days tourism and left them to continue a more ordered holiday.

After my GA resignation and the decision to sell Beals were made I contacted a number of Herefordshire estate agents asking them to send me details of old places that required modernisation. Although the small rented cowmans cottage was nicely situated for the Woodchurch surgery the future looked a little worrying with no home and no job secured. Daily we'd scan the post for estate agent flyers of possible places. By late October we had our short list. We put the dogs in kennels and set off for the Welsh borders. We first stayed at The Red Lion in Weobley. This was a lovely cruck framed old inn owned by Bulmers the cider maker. We had specified a quiet location, lying in the area west of the A49 to the Welsh border. Well, quiet in Herefordshire and quiet in overpopulated Kent are somewhat different. A couple of places in the Golden Valley towards the Brecon Beacons were so remote we couldn't even find them! After a couple of days we moved to the Feathers Hotel in Ludlow, South Shropshire and continued looking at (generally) unsuitable places. On Saturday we had gone down to the agents RB&B in Leominster to pick up a key for a property near Pembridge. Whilst waiting for the key Gillian noticed a flyer on the table for a place called Ghorsty Hill. We asked the RB&B lady where this was and she said about four miles out of Leominster, but it was way above our price range. So it was but we picked up the flyer anyway.

    The Pembridge place was a disaster, a back and white shell. We decided to go and have a look at Ghorsty Hill the next day - Sunday. It was a glorious sunny autumn day. We parked the Lancia alongside a cattle grid. A 120 yard farm track led to the house, standing alone in a field. No smoke from the chimneys so nothing venture, nothing win we walked along to the house. There was a fantastic view west over the North Herefordshire plain to Radnor Forest. I can remember saying to Gillian "it's got possibilities". No one at home. We spent an hour going around the outside, pacing distances and taking compass bearings. Super location and orientation and only four miles from Leominster. Back to the Feathers Hotel to talk it over - yes go for it. First thing Monday morning phoned RB&B for an appointment to look at Ghorsty Hill. OK 11 o'clock. Not so sunny but still looked good and importantly had a nice, warm feel inside. Back to RB&B made an offer, £4,000 below asking price. Left contact telephone number of Feathers Hotel. In afternoon call from RB&B, our offer not accepted, but would split difference. I said yes and we went back to RB&B to complete offer and personal details. Confirmed that ours was a cash offer, no house to sell. We headed back to Kent feeling a lot, lot happier.

    There was a slight hitch when I received a call (in GMA's office) from the Leominster surveyor we'd engaged, who told me he had been approached by someone else to do a survey on Ghorsty Hill. Sounded like gazumping. I talked to my solicitor (who swore!) and said he would attack vendor's solicitor whilst I should attack vendor's agent RB&B. In a nutshell we said two can play that game and our (cash) offer would be withdrawn by the end of the week unless they gave us three clear weeks to finish our searches. Gillian was terrified we'd lose Ghorsty, but I was damned if we'd be gazumped after we had made a deal. The vendor backed down, we had all the searches completed and we exchanged and completed by mid December. I think cash in the hand was very persuasive. At least we now had a home and some cash to sustain us for a year or so.

Back at GMA again and my main activity seemed to be going through our accounts with Brian and the GHA accountant. I was also involved in some supervisory/advisory work on a number of our ongoing jobs. Roy had finished the Griffin Coal job and was now working at the Mamut open-pit mine in Sabah, Malaysia. Don had finished the Rossing project in Namibia and was now in Australia (job came through GMP!) working for the Avocado Holdings group and John and Dave were still in Udaipur looking after HZL in Rajasthan and GMDC in Gujarat.

Fortunately for me it was one of my longest periods in the UK uninterrupted by overseas travel. Thus a few days before Christmas I gunned up the Honda and set off for North Herefordshire. We went back to the original spelling - Gorsty - was pretty cold (and empty) as I awaited the arrival of our Kentish storage company with our personal bits and pieces. Unfortunately they arrived in an artic, which was too big to turn off the Gorsty lane over the cattle grid. Thus a day was wasted whilst they went back to Leominster to arrange for a Transit van to shuttle our stuff from the artic to the house. Of course on that second day we had light snow so much of our stuff got damp, but at least it was finally in the house. I left the Honda at Gorsty, walked into Leominster and caught a train to Hereford, then London and eventually Ashford. Gillian picked me up in the Lancia for the final leg to the cowman's cottage.

It was a busy Christmas saying goodbye to local friends we had got to know during our ten years in Woodchurch. Gillian's last day at the surgery was the 31st December and she was back at the cottage by 1 pm. The surgery had given her a leaving present of some lovely, but bulky china, which seriously disturbed the carefully packed Lancia. Anjon was perched on the rear window shelf and Matt, the huge sheepdog, was somehow stashed on part of the rear seat. Gillian, in the front passenger seat, had our little black and white TV stowed under her legs. We finally arrived at Gorsty about 8.30 pm on New Year's Eve, feeling tired but elated. Anjon then became the star turn as he went into every room in the house and christened all the door jambs with a short spurt. Well he'd certainly made his mark. The Aga, which I'd lit before Christmas had gone out, so we made friends with an electric fire. The next day our neighbouring farmer, Rowley, turned up with a load of logs, which was a really nice welcoming gesture. We had the next few days to sort out the house before I had to go back to work again.

It was not practical to commute from Gorsty to London so on Monday Gillian drove me to Worcester where I caught the early train to Paddington. I had already sussed out some cheap hotels (£10/night) in the Bloomsbury area, close to the British Museum. From there it was a short walk to the GMA office on High Holborn. So I stayed in these hotels four nights, Monday to Thursday inclusive, and caught the train back to Worcester on Friday evening. It wasn't ideal but as they say doable. With Roy, our de facto Office manager, away in Sabah, I took over this administrative job which kept me occupied. I also had to sort out transferring my old RTZ/Sun Life of Canada pension fund into a new "portable" fund as I moved towards a self-employed basis. I had to sell my GA shares back to GA. Fortunately GA's global business had thrived over the past two years so that their current value enabled me to pay off the original $30,000 loan plus interest and still leave a little cash over - phew! In quiet periods I organised new letterheads for myself and prepared my "Consulting Mining Engineer" ads for inclusion in the Professional Directory in the Mining Journal and Mining Magazine. I also sent a short clip to the Institute of Mining & Metallurgy (IMM) for inclusion in "News of Members" and finally updated my CV.

The last week of February was busy collecting and crating up the GMA files and library for transfer to GHA's office in Maidenhead. It was a sad task as we all felt GMA had developed a good team ethos over the past two years, but we were never masters of our own destiny. As an about to be self-employed person I should at least be in control of that. We had a final beer/wine wake in our local pub at the top of Drury Lane, and that was that. The final GA task for me was to deliver the company Lancia back to Maidenhead from Gorsty. This I did the following week, returning from Maidenhead by slow train to Reading and fast(er) Cotswold Line train to Great Malvern. Here Gillian picked me up in our brand new little VW Golf 1100, complete with tow bar. I had already bought a small trailer for the car.

During my time in January and February in the Bloomsbury doss-house hotels Gillian had been busy organising the Gorsty household. The first thing was warmth. She found a local Aga engineer in Tenbury Wells who came and serviced the brute (to get it going) and also explained that it needed a new water heater fitted, whereupon Gillian ordered one. Again great decision. However her pièce de résistance was locating an enormous

Franklin Stove in Burgess Heat in Leominster. They came and installed the stove in the living room as well as inserting a new stainless steel flue liner. Once it got going it threw out a great amount of heat. Rowley's logs were very, very welcome. Finally we agreed to install a number of off-peak Economy 7-night storage heaters, scattered around the house. At that time Economy-7 electric power was cheaper than heating oil and, of course, there was no town gas available. Midlands Electricity installed them and did a very good, neat job. Both dogs really appreciated the warmth of the Aga, especially Matt who was now eleven years old, a good age for the big Old English sheepdog.

Now no longer putting in an appearance at GHA offices in Maidenhead I started to give some serious thought as to how I could generate some mining consulting work. The Professional Directory ads were out in the weekly Mining Journal and the monthly Mining Magazine, but still the phone didn't ring. I soon realised that selling individual mining consultancy was not easy - well what a surprise! I had the great "thought", must make it more personal, and that meant specific letters and visits until my availability for such work became known. Hence a rapid trip to Hereford to buy an electric typewriter to replace the ancient manual portable. I also made an arrangement with a commercial secretarial business in Hereford who had cable and telex facilities. Over the next few weeks I ran off dozens of electrically typed personal letters to many of the international mining industries' executives, managers and project engineers that I had encountered over the past 23 years since graduating from CSM in 1958. My idea was that these letters, themselves, would not generate any jobs, but my letter and accompanying CV would be on the recipients file and if in the future they had a requirement......? Well that was the thought. Not exactly pushing the boundaries of original marketing, but a start.

However as March turned into April with no takers, I went down to the Friday Market in Leominster to see if there was any scope for a stall selling mineral specimens and polished stones. Yes, possibilities, but obviously I would need some kit. So off to a specialist minerals shop in Evesham, Worcestershire. The owner was very helpful and realised that I knew very little about mineral specimens and absolutely nothing about stone polishing, cabochards etc. Rather than trying to sell me some expensive polishing equipment he suggested some practical books on the "mineral specimens business". With unbelievable timing the next day I received a call from Barrie, now at GHA, asking if I could come up to Maidenhead to discuss a possible job for Ken (ex Bougainville Copper) now head honcho with Australian Amax. I said yes I thought I could fit in a visit!

I went up by train the next day. It was a funny feeling seeing a lot of the old RTZC and GMA guys again who were now working under the Golder Associates (UK) Ltd banner. It was my luck that GA(UK) did not have a specialist underground mining engineer who was available at short notice and the Amax job required one immediately to meet their schedule. That was that. I was hired forthwith and welcomed my first job, No. 001.

20

Of course it was a little more complicated than that, sorting out fee rates, expenses, terms of subcontract, liability etc, but by the end of the day Sheldon Travel had tickets for me booked on a flight to Perth, Western Australia five days hence. For me it was a great job, about six weeks duration in Western Australia, Tasmania, New Zealand and finally Amax headquarters in Sydney. I couldn't wait to get home to tell Gillian the good news. I'm pretty sure she was pleased for us both, albeit a little apprehensive about the responsibility of keeping Gorsty ticking over on her own. This was particularly true with regard to the garden, which was beginning to burst into life. However we had decided to leave everything as it was to see what came up when and where over the full calendar year. Basically it was a wildlife garden with some ancient cider apple trees interspersed with old damson trees. I'd purchased a medium size hover mower, which was light enough for Gillian to manage. We wouldn't worry about the rough grass under the fruit trees until late June when the trusty Allen Scythe would come into its own. In fact the rough grass area had produced a patch of snowdrops (in late January) and then a lovely mixed crop of spring flowers - primroses, daffodils, cowslips, milk maids forget-me-knots, wild arum etc. I was really glad we hadn't rushed in and cut the rough grass.

I flew through the Middle East to Singapore and then down to Perth, Western Australia. I'd never been to Perth before and was quite surprised at its isolated feel; a long way from anywhere. In fact Bali in Indonesia was closer to Perth than Melbourne or Sydney. I stayed a couple of days at an hotel overlooking Kings Park, close to the Western Australia offices of Amax. Then with an Amax engineer we few 350 miles NNE to Cue followed by a twenty mile dusty trip by ute to the Big Bell mine site. This was an old gold mining area where the underground Big Bell mine had been a significant gold producer fifty years ago. The old underground operation had mined right through to the bottom of the initial open pit. Ground conditions were strong and the mining method had been blast-hole open stoping. Amax were resampling the readily accessible underground workings as well as undertaking some deep diamond drilling to ascertain the extent of the main gold orebody at depth. Perusal of the old underground plans and sampling records did not look very encouraging, but the current high gold price certainly warranted the re-evaluation that Amax were carrying out. I collected enough prime data to enable me to estimate likely ore reserves and the all important ore expectancy. With the Amax engineer we had to make an assessment of power and water availability as well as that key resource - skilled mining and metallurgical labour. The definite trend in Australia for operating these relatively isolated mine sites was the same as that in Canada, man the operation on a "fly-in fly-out" basis with a mine camp run by a professional catering company. As we were on a tight schedule we flew back to Perth after seven days. We then had a one day debrief with the Perth Amax guys on my initial impressions and then it was a flight eastwards to Melbourne.

Here we stayed overnight before taking the short flight south to Launceston in northern Tasmania. This was relatively familiar ground for me after my four and a half years spent at Rosebery in the west of the island. Beaconsfield, another old underground gold mine, was about 25 miles north of Launceston close to the west bank of the Tamar river. At present Amax crews were attempting to dewater the main Beaconsfield shaft. That was proving exceptionally difficult since that short rectangular wooden shaft contained the old wooden pumping rods from a Cornish Beam Engine pumping unit. From the size of the rods and the massive cast iron pump column, Beaconsfield had been (still was?) a very wet mine. That was confirmed by the Amax crews who had suspended two large Sulzer submersible pumps to keep the shaft water level below their sinking scaffold as they attempted to cut out the old pump rods and the cast iron pump column. It was an extremely tricky, hazardous and very slow operation. The scaffold was only 300ft from the shaft collar and it had taken nearly a year to achieve that depth. What was certain was that the complexity of the shaft recovery would only increase as one (eventually) neared the shaft sump and the lower-end pump-works of the beam engine. My immediate advice was to stop this old shaft recovery work and await the results of the deep diamond drilling campaign and if it was encouraging on width and grade sink a new footwall prospect shaft. I had already witnessed several failed old shaft recovery projects on Cornish tin mines. It was always better to start with a clean slate, which one designs and controls.

Needless to say my advice to stop the shaft recovery work immediately put the cat amongst the pigeons and a flurry of cables and telexes went off to Amax, Sydney. There was little else for us to do on site, since neither diamond drill rig had intersected the ore zone. We were scheduled to fly from Melbourne to New Zealand next Monday afternoon. I phoned Ken and discussed the shaft de-watering and why it should stop forthwith (staunch the money flow!). As it was Friday I asked Ken if it would be OK for me, obviously at my own expense, to drive down to Hobart to meet up with my old mates from Rosebery. I would catch the Monday morning Hobart - Melbourne flight in plenty of time for the afternoon Auckland flight. Ken said that would be good - he wouldn't have to pay my hotel bills over that weekend!

The Amax engineer drove me back to Launceston airport where I hired a car for return on Monday morning to Hobart airport. I phoned Rod in Howrah and said I was looking for a bed for the night and would be in Hobart in a little over two hours after the 120 mile drive from Launceston. Good old Rod just said "you beauty, see you". It was great to catch up with Rod and Kate and later Geoff and Marg, who had all been close friends with us over our four and half years in Rosebery. Of course it was only two years since all four of them had visited us in England on their big European tour. Now it was my turn to see how they had all settled into Hobart. In fact very well indeed. Rod after a brief dalliance with a retail shop had gone back to running a Howrah garage and enjoyed utilising his motor mechanics skill again. Geoff was involved with a freight company and both the girls were involved in just about everything. They made me very welcome and we painted Hobart red over the next two days. All too soon it was Monday morning and I dropped the hire car off at Hobart airport. The 400 mile flight to Melbourne took an hour and a half and by midday I was in Collins Street. On the spur of the moment I went into Minenco's office to see if Brian (from Bougainville Project days) was there. He was and we went out for a typical "Counter Lunch" to sample a "Floater" (meat pie upside down in gravy!) and a drop of VB (Victoria Bitter), all very typical Oz fare. Then it was a gallop out to Essendon Airport for the mid-afternoon flight to Auckland.

The 1700 mile flight took about three and half hours and with the time difference it was 9 pm before I was signing for a hire car. I called the hotel in Waihi to say I would be late, but please keep my room. The map showed Waihi about 100 miles SE of Auckland on the southern end of the Coromandel Peninsular. It was not easy driving an unfamiliar Holden car out of an unknown city in the dark. In the event the drive took me close to three hours and I turned up at the Waihi hotel around midnight, somewhat bushed in the local parlance. Too tired to eat I crashed.

The following morning showed Waihi as a fascinating country town with a very, very wide main street, said to have arisen from the need to turn a four horse dray around in one movement. A good story at any rate. The Amax project geologist found me at the hotel and we piled in to the inevitable ute for the short ride to the project site, which, in fact was only just outside the town. The old underground Martha mine had been in existence for nearly 100 years working a system of gold rich quartz veins. The mine ceased production a decade or so ago at the time of low gold and silver prices, but the recent surge in the gold price had sparked Amax's interest in reopening the property. They were currently resampling the extensive underground workings as well as carrying out deep diamond drilling below the orebody as well as surface trenching/sampling looking for lower grade disseminated mineralisation which might be a target for future open-pit extraction.

My work thus naturally split up in to assessing the production potential of a typical steep dipping, tabular, hard rock orebody where the upper sections had already been mined-out and a potential grass-roots low grade open-pit operation. Mining conditions underground were good with strong host rocks. It was also a relatively dry mine. Thus as usual it all came down to ore expectancy - t/vm. This was obviously derived from strike length, average true vein thickness, average vein dip, average bulk density and the all important percent payability. In turn 10% of this ore expectancy would indicate a likely daily production rate that the underground mine could sustain. So far so simple. The main mining question was how to access this ore and bring it to surface for treatment? The vein dip was steep. The upper sections all mined-out, so that the "sub-outcrop" of the remaining ore was deep. This seemed to preclude a new ramp-decline (too long) thus QED access via a new vertical shaft. The strong ground conditions allowed either a footwall or hangingwall location, which could be decided on purely economic grounds, cost of crosscutting against loss of ore in a shaft pillar. I would develop a notional underground mine with the Amax guys back in Sydney. The Waihi site visit was basically geological and geotechnical data collection plus, of course, physical observation.

As far as a potential open-pit operation was concerned there was only preliminary exploration data available, since Amax's primary focus had been on the old underground Martha mine. However they had completed a fair amount of surface trenching and limited sampling of numerous quartz stringers and veins exposed. Their next stage considered relatively shallow flatly inclined diamond drill (DD) holes to test continuity and depth extension to about 100m of these surface stringers and veins. It was apparent that stringer/vein correlation surface to underground DD intersection would be fairly tricky, but an essential element in attempting to calculate possible open-pit ore reserves. I felt that this limited surface exploration data was insufficient to develop a notional open pit, but definitely warranted further, deeper exploration.

The Amax guys were a great bunch and we drank much too much beer in several Waihi pubs. The town had quite a frontier feel to it, much like Rosebery in western Tasmania, although the Waihi main street was definitely a lot lot wider! On my drive back to Auckland, now in daylight, I observed what I thought were fields of miniature wire frames for low growing grapes. Wrong. They were, in fact, frames for the cultivation of Kiwi fruit. Apparently this part of the Coromandel Peninsular was considered the centre of worldwide Kiwi fruit production. So another useless fact accumulated and I don't even like the fruit - tasteless. The late afternoon flight to Sydney gave me time to have a quick look around the city. Plenty of new shiny mini skyscrapers but markedly less frenetic and aggressively antipodean than the Aussie counterparts. Unsurprisingly, the countryside around Auckland had a softer, more compact feel than big, bold, brash Oz.

Sydney, NSW was certainly that, but what a magnificent setting with the iconic coat hanger Bridge and Opera House in full view as the plane swept in from the North Shore across the harbour to land at the airport jutting out into Botany Bay. I stayed in a downtown hotel not far from Amax's office on Circular Quay. Spoke to Ken and said I'd be in their offices just after 8am tomorrow. Many Oz offices start their day at 8, knocking off at

4 pm - more time on the beach or firing up the barbie? The Amax offices had a lovely view out across the harbour. Ken hadn't changed much, still the straight-talking, optimistic, go-getting exploration geologist now promoted into an Exploration Manager for an international mining company. He was obviously not so keen on the head office scenario but came alight when we got onto their "projects". He wanted to talk about Beaconsfield first, since halting the main shaft de-watering had rather upset the apple cart. Fortunately my hands-on experience of shaft work in the UK, Philippines, Tasmania and especially India assisted in making the case. If he was still unconvinced I suggested he contact a specialist shaft sinking firm such as, yes you guessed it, Cementation, who had offices in Melbourne. It was, after all, very specialist work and the Amax Beaconsfield crew were really beginners. It was agreed he'd contact Cementation and ask them to send an experienced engineer down to Tassie for a second opinion. That was the nub of the Beaconsfield discussion.

We moved on to the Big Bell project, where I said I needed two or three days in their office to run through all the data we had collected on the site visit. My objective was to come up with a potential ore reserve, determine the ore expectancy and from this suggest a notional sustainable mining rate. Then use this to "construct" a notional mine with related costs. Amax's own field work had included mineralogical testing which would provide input into a notional metallurgical flowsheet. Their own in-house guys provided input on capital plant and operating consumable costs such as power and explosives. Provided I got cracking on estimating a sustainable mining rate we felt we could produce a very preliminary feasibility study in a little over a week. Ken felt that that was OK and we would discuss the Waihi project after we'd completed the Big Bell "study".

After I had crunched all the exploration data I ended up with an ore expectancy of about 12,000 tonnes/vm, implying an underground mining output of 1,200 tonnes/day with a head grade of circa 4g/t. The Amax guys and Ken in particular were quite disappointed at this, relatively, small sized mine. As we all anticipated at this modest rate of production the economics would not stand up - the project would not fly. In any case Amax senior management were really looking for a "large mine". We all agreed that the most sensible option for Amax was to sell their stake in the Big Bell project and cut their losses.

So on to the old underground Martha mine at Waihi. This looked much more encouraging with an ore expectancy of circa 30,000 t/vm with good diamond drill intersections 550m below surface. Over the next few days we worked up a notional 3,000 tonnes/day underground mine accessed through a main footwall vertical shaft with a second vertical shaft on the hangingwall side for ventilation and secondary access. The project economics looked OK, but it was never going to be a large money spinner. It soon became clear that what Amax was really looking for was a large open-pit gold project. On reflection this was unsurprising since their American parent operated the huge Climax molybdenum open-pit mine in Colorado. Amax's forte was open-pit mining, moving vast daily tonnages of ore and waste (agricultural mining!) rather than the more technically involved underground operations. Although we felt there was insufficient surface exploration data currently available at Waihi we all agreed that this project had to be the number-one target for Amax to develop a sizeable open-pit gold mine. It was here on the surface around the old Martha mine that Amax should concentrate their exploration dollar. En passant, Ken got a call from Cementation whose engineer confirmed that de-watering the old Beaconsfield shaft was a lost cause. They recommended sinking a new shaft, but then they would say that wouldn't they?

That wrapped up my work for Amax. Off the record Ken was interested to know what had happened to RTZC & GMA. He had heard on the grapevine that Dick had turned up in Western Australia working for Ricky, who controlled Griffin Coal. Ken knew Dick well from Bougainville Copper days when he was Exploration boss up on the island and Dick was Project Mining Engineer in Melbourne. He wished me the best as a nascent independent mining engineer and hoped that Golder Associates (UK) paid my bill! After yet more beers I caught the evening flight back to London. I took the RailAir coach out to Reading station and then a Cotswold Line train to Hereford where Gillian picked me up in the little Golf. She was full of all the "goings-on" at Gorsty and seemed full of energy. By contrast after the 28 hour flight back and three hour rail journey I felt knackered. Nothing a good sleep in the peace and quiet of Gorsty couldn't fix; it was good to be home.

It was now nearly mid July and I had to attack an overgrown "wild patch" under the fruit trees with the old Allen Scythe. Most of the spring wild flowers had died down apart from some trailing vetch. We raked up the grass cuttings into rows and so began a regular, annual battle with the weather as we attempted to produce hay. I'm sure I would have been a grouchy farmer as the unpredictable weather would have driven me nuts. Anjon enjoyed stalking rabbits between the grass/hay rows. Old Matt had slowed right down and now only came for short walks, but as always he was Anjon's hero. This bucolic life was interrupted by a telephone call from Mary at the World Bank in Washington. Could I join a Bank mission (!) to Zambia next month? Yes I could, job No. 002. Prepaid air tickets could be picked up at the American Express offices in Haymarket as well as a bundle of travellers cheques for expenses - clients like this I needed.

A week or so later a World Bank (WB) consultants' agreement form arrived together with a broad scope of work and an itinerary. I was asked to meet Mary and four other WB guys at Brown's Hotel in London in the first week of August leaving for Zambia that same evening. I caught the early Cotswold Line train to Paddington, then to the Haymarket to collect my air ticket and travellers cheques from Amex. From there it was a short walk along Piccadilly to Browns Hotel in Mayfair. One of the objectives of the meeting was for the WB guys to get to know me and vice versa. Mary was an excellent team leader and explained exactly what we had to do. My remit covered a technical audit of the RCM Copperbelt mining operations of Mufulira, Luanshya, Baluba and Chibuluma. Dick, one of the WB guys, was a metallurgical engineer who would be looking at the concentrators so my responsibility ended at the headframe coarse ore bins. Mary explained that an ex Anglo American consulting engineer, still living in Zambia, would join the team and carry out a similar technical audit on the NCCM Copperbelt mines. We would spend one night in Lusaka and then fly up to Kitwe.

After a very fine Browns Hotel tea we piled into two taxis for the short run to Victoria Station to catch the Gatwick Express. That was the last I saw of the WB team until downtown Lusaka as they disappeared to the First-Class check-in and lounge whilst I joined the hoi polloi battling at the Economy check-in. The joys of being an "independent". In fact, the British Caledonian (BCal) flight and service to Lusaka was excellent. The flight left around 10 pm and arrived at Lusaka early morning local time. By the time I'd struggled through Immigration and Customs the WB team had long gone. I grabbed a taxi for the 25 minute run to the Pamodzi Hotel and later caught up with them plus Dave, the Anglo American consulting engineer, on the terrace in time for lunch. Mary and the senior WB economist then paid courtesy visits to both the RCM and NCCM head offices. The rest of us spent the afternoon around the pool in the plus 27 C temperature - great life, but it wasn't to last as it was definitely busy, busy, busy once we got to the Copperbelt.

The small RoanAir plane left early the next morning for the 200 mile flight north to Kitwe's Southdown airstrip. Here we split into two groups. One WB economist and I went to the GM's office of RCM's Mufulira mine, whilst the others went to NCCM's Nchanga offices. Mufulira was still one of the world's great underground copper mines hoisting around six million tonnes/year. The larger underground copper mines in the USA, Chile & Philippines all used block-caving as their primary mining method whilst Mufulira used conventional blast-hole sub-level open stoping with subsequent hydraulic fill. After a brief chat with the GM I left him a list of the type of recent operating reports we would like and then went off to see the Chief Geologist for a run through on the ore reserve position. This had been steadily declining over the past five years. What immediately stood out was the shortfall in diamond drilling and development. In the afternoon the Underground Manager confirmed that the mine was indeed seriously "squeezed" for lack of developed ground ahead of stoping. He arranged to take me underground the next day. Before we left the office a secretary brought me a bunch of Mufulira operating reports for 1980 and said that the other RCM mines would provide similar documentation. That was great, nay essential data collection.

Other than the Philex mine in the Philippines, Mufulira was the largest mine I'd been down. Certainly the major mine infrastructure was very impressive, headframe(s), winders, shafts, pump stations, main haulages etc. Ground conditions were strong and the practice of using hydraulic fill in the hangingwall stopes had ceased after the 1970 disaster. However one was aware that stoping activity was, indeed, very close behind primary development - the mine was "squeezed" for tonnage and as a direct consequence the rom grade was declining. This of course meant a depressed mill head grade, which in turn meant a lower recovery since the concentrators were run to a constant tails grade. The mine had obviously been starved of fresh capital, presumably because both RCM and NCCM could see that the Zambian copper industry was heading for nationalisation.

The disturbing picture seen at Mufulira was repeated at all the other RCM mines. After ten days visiting all four RCM mines we joined up with the NCCM technical/economical team. Their impressions were similar to ours but not quite so bleak. Our review of each of the mines' 1980 operating statistics confirmed our worst fears. The RCM Copperbelt mining operations were some of the most inefficient, low productivity and high cost operations in the world. The mines only survived because of their high in situ ore grade. We flew back to the Pamodzi Hotel in Lusaka where I spent the next five days preparing a draft report on "the mining picture" and a five year production forecast for both copper and cobalt. Dick supplied me with the relevant metallurgical data. Mary seemed satisfied with my draft, but said she would like a final version, after checking and subject to WB queries sent by air courier to Washington within ten days of my return to the UK. We had a final wrap-up dinner and then after three and a half weeks went our separate ways back to Gatwick, courtesy of BCal, WB guys in First, yours truly in Economy. So what, the trip would certainly help pay the bills.

21

Back home, now early September, the garden was beginning to slow down, but rough grass cutting and hedge cutting loomed large. However first I had to attack my WB report. This involved tidying up my English but, more importantly, checking and rechecking my five year production forecast for the RCM group. I sent the completed report plus time sheets and expenses form to Washington via DHL Couriers the following week. A few days later the phone rang - "Hi Martin it's Goni can you get yourself to New York by next Tuesday, the Waldorf-Astoria, we're taking a look at the Friedensville Mine in Pennsylvania". Answer, "of course Goni see you Tuesday", job No. 003. I drove down to Hereford to book air tickets and set up an account with Thomas Cook, a little more convenient than Tony Sheldon Travel in Maidenhead.

What was finally becoming clear to me was that as an independent you had no back-up services (secretarial, accounts, legal, travel etc) that were readily available at RTZC or Golders. So whilst in Hereford I went to see the accountants, Kidson Impey, who recommended "their man" in Leominster, Tim. Without doubt that was one of the best decisions I made. Tim was marvellous, knowledgeable, totally practical and pragmatic and a really great guy. We used to meet at Gorsty every now and then, do the books, finance, expenses, VAT, pensions, employing Gillian, everything other than mining and then relax with a couple of beers. I soon realised Tim was my one-man back-up office, fantastic.

So on Tuesday it was the early train to Reading, coach to Heathrow and plane to New York. Asking the cabbie to take me to the Waldorf was a little like a clip from a Bogart film. In fact it all went smoothly and I caught up with Goni and the other COMSUR guys, manager Jaime, legal guy Stan, geologist Carlos and Bobby, the Manager of South American Placers Inc (SAPI). For COMSUR corporate reasons we were all representatives of SAPI, COMSUR's Peruvian subsidiary. The team were studying the "sales package" for the New Jersey Zinc (NJZ) Friedensville Mine. The next day Bobby hired a large car for the ninety mile drive down to Philadelphia joined by the three engineers, Jaime, Carlos and me. We checked into an enormous downtown hotel, where Bobby made contact with the Friedensville Mine

Manager. The following morning they picked us up in a twin cab ute for the thirty mile drive to the mine.

It was a 3,000 tonnes/day underground lead-zinc mine feeding a differential flotation concentrator producing separate lead and zinc concentrates. We started, of course, with the Chief Geologist, who was very helpful explaining the geological setting of the orebody as a large replacement in limestone. The orebody was shallow dipping at a depth of between 100 to 200m and mine access was by a large, spiral ramp-decline. The mine was trackless and the mining method was a variation of pillar-and-stall, the stall mined by an overcut and subsequent bench. Later, old stalls were filled with de-slimed tailings. The operation seemed very well run, but the over riding impression was of water everywhere. It was an extremely wet mine, probably the wettest I'd seen. Their Underground Manager said they were pumping around fifty million gallons/day - that was around 345,000 gallons/min, a huge quantity. Put another way that was 75 tonnes of water for each tonne of ore hoisted, a shade wetter than even Wheal Jane in Cornwall on a tonne water/tonne ore basis.

Unsurprisingly the underground pumping installation was immense, the major piece of mine infrastructure together with huge rising mains up a pump shaft and numerous water tight doors. A look through the mine's operating statistics confirmed that power for pumping was a very large fixed cost, independent of the actual mining rate. From a straight forward engineering viewpoint I felt that the "water problem" was not something that a relatively small Bolivian mining company wanted to take on. Of more importance to Goni and Bobby was the fact that the gross operating margin per tonne mined and treated would not provide the return they were looking for. So we returned to Philadelphia and then New York with a consensual "thumbs down". Goni was disappointed but felt that COMSUR had to look at these opportunities if they wanted to grow. We all went our separate ways the following day.

I was back at Gorsty by Sunday having been away just five days. The rest of the month was quiet on the work front so we made sure we had plenty of logs in for winter. I then appreciated that I needed a splitting, rather than a chopping, axe. To corral these logs we decided to build a block wall along the eastern side of the terrace. It looked pretty ghastly but we hoped it would soon get covered by the ivy we had planted on either side. Into November and there was a call from Dick, now with Jacia Consulting Services in Perth, Western Australia. Could I take a look at a tin/wolfram prospect at Brampton, Devon? Yes, job No. 004. Brampton was on the eastern side of the river Exe valley close to the Somerset/Devon border. I had noted some comments about Brampton in the Mining Journal so gave my mate on the Journal a call. He said it was a junior Canadian explorer, particularly interested in wolfram, he thought they now had a drill on site. I thanked him and said I'd go to the IMM library to do some background research.

Next day I took the train to Paddington, tube to Oxford Circus and short walk to 44 Portland Place. There was virtually no information on potential mineralisation in that eastern part of Devon. Dick had given me a site telephone number, which I duly called. When I explained who I was and that I would like to visit the site I was told politely and firmly that that was not possible. So short of going down to Brampton and skulking around hedgerows with a pair of binoculars that was that - a non-starter. When I got home I phoned Dick with this information. He seemed unperturbed by the lack of progress I'd made and said just mail him a single page summary of what little I had dug up. That's it. Definitely a very unrewarding "job". Still three out of four wasn't a bad strike rate.

A week or so later there was a call from Stan, COMSUR's legal guy. Hard to believe but he said could I meet the SAPI team in Spokane, northern Idaho in three days time? Apparently Gulf Resources had just put the Bunker Hill Mine in Kellog, Idaho up for sale. He said I should check in to the Radisson hotel in Spokane, where they would book me a room. He also said call Nick at Capper Pass as he would be coming to assess the smelter. Again, yes I could, job No. 005.

I phoned Nick and we agreed on suitable flights Heathrow to Detroit, Minneapolis and on to Spokane. Thank God for Thomas Cook, I said I'd pick the tickets up that afternoon. I met Nick the next day and was glad we'd agreed to fly business class on the long haul to Spokane. We duly met up with Goni and the other SAPI guys in the Radisson hotel. Spokane is actually just over the border in Washington State. The Gulf Resources sales documents indicated that it was an integrated sale - mine, concentrators, lead and zinc smelters - quite a mouthful for a small company like COMSUR/SAPI to swallow.

From Spokane it was only a forty-mile drive to Coeur d'Alene in Idaho and a further fifty miles east to Kellog and the Bunker Hill complex. The size and complexity of the operations were in a different league to anything COMSUR or SAPI were operating. I am not sure if the Gulf Resources people took us seriously - a Bolivian/Peruvian medium miner looking to take over the famous Bunker Hill company. Still they were the ones who had put the complex up for sale and we were merely assessing the merchandise. To be fair they were extremely helpful to our "due diligence" work. Carlos, the COMSUR geologist and I spent the day with their Chief Geologist and later their Underground Manager.

The mine was working an extensive, steep dipping, silver rich, narrow vein system. Unusually, the down-dip extent of the vein appeared to be similar to the surface strike extent, which meant that the mine had reached a depth of over 5000ft The main mining method in use was cut-and-fill with some square-set mining on pillar recovery. En passant this was the first time I had encountered women jackhammer miners working in the stopes. (I had seen women underground before but generally driving locomotives or underground sub-shaft winders, never rock breakers). Indications were that the payable strike length of the vein system was reducing with depth. Not a good sign. Also the extreme depth meant that both ore transport, particularly hoisting, and ventilation were becoming major engineering constraints. Neither Carlos nor I felt that the basic resource, the orebody, was a suitable target for COMSUR/SAPI.

Nick was also unenthusiastic about the smelter (old technology), Stan was unhappy about some of the operating permits (carbon dioxide & sulphur limits etc) and Bobby noted that unit operating costs were high on account of high labour costs due to a militant union. Thus all in all a thumbs down all round. Goni was quite cheerful though as he felt it showed that many of his smaller COMSUR/SAPI operations were competitive in the world market. The next day we had a bit of a "jolly" with a visit to the famous Sunshine mine which was a little further east of Kellog towards Wallace. After that we headed back west for Spokane, on the way stopping for lunch at an American Diner in Coeur d'Alene. Well, the meal portions were enormous. However the steaks were absolutely delicious (as good as those in Buenos Aires) and the baked Idaho potatoes (also delicious) the largest I'd ever seen. No wonder they develop big burly miners, both male and female. At Spokane the group split up going their separate ways. I ended up with Bobby on an afternoon flight to Minneapolis where we checked into an airport hotel for half a day waiting for a connection to New York, Bobby's target destination and my transfer for a Heathrow flight. Unsurprisingly we ended up in the bar and then one of the hotel's restaurants. I had not had much contact with Bobby and was interested to learn about SAPI's business. Although based in Lima, Peru they had a major dredging operation for gold on the Beni river in Bolivia. The Beni is one of the Amazon's main southern tributaries draining the eastern cordillera. Bobby gave me a standing invitation to visit their Beni dredging operation.

Our two hour flight from Minneapolis put us in to New York around 10pm, where I had a couple of hours before catching a "red-eye shuttle" to Heathrow landing around midday. Then it was coach to Reading and the Cotswold Line train to Worcester where Gillian picked me up (almost literally, as I was completely knackered) for the forty min drive back to Gorsty. It seemed lovely and peaceful after the razzmatazz of America and Heathrow. Inside Gillian had got a good pile of logs and kindling ready for the Franklin Stove and Matt and Anjon seemed pleased to see me, but reluctant to leave the warmth of the Aga. It was, of course, quite dark by the time we got back.

Next morning, bright eyed and bushy tailed, I had a huge shock when I realised that old Matt was just about on his last legs. Gillian purposely hadn't said anything knowing I'd be really upset at the old fellow's condition. I tried taking both the dogs for a walk, but Matt only managed a few yards along the track. So, inevitably I called the vet, took him down to Leominster and after an examination agreed to have Matt put to sleep. It was a sad day, he'd been a faithful friend for nearly twelve years. Poor old Anjon was devastated, he spent days searching every room and the garden looking for the "big fella" who was his hero.

Both Gillian and I agreed Gorsty needed a big dog and so on New Year's day (1982) we headed north on deserted roads for Halsall in Lancashire. Matt's Kennel Club name had been Halsall Jolly Roger. We had already phoned the Halsall kennels and they produced a pedigree Old English sheepdog pup aged nine weeks. We immediately named him Luke, to slot in with the old testaments of Matthew, Mark, Luke, Anjon. Anjon was very circumspect with the new arrival, but after a few weeks seemed to accept Luke as a fully paid up member of the Gorsty Gang.

In mid January I had a call from Alan at Babcock Woodhall-Duckham (BW-D) asking me to assist them with a new mining project in Bihar, India. I went by train to Reading and then on to Crawley, near Gatwick where BW-D had their offices. My scope of work, fees and contract were all sorted out and the project was scheduled to start the following week, thus job No. 006. Well no. Five days or so later Alan rang to say their bid had been aborted, sorry, that's it. I was really glad we didn't have a Gorsty mortgage hanging on that work. BW-D didn't even offer to pay my travel expenses. That was a good lesson for me - the bigger the company the tighter they were with expenses and definitely slower paying one's invoice.

A couple of weeks later, much to my surprise, I had another call from the World Bank, actually the International Bank for Reconstruction & Development (IBRD) in Washington this time from Philippe, a very cultured Frenchman. As anticipated during last years' August visit NCCM and RCM were now effectively nationalised forming a giant new state mining corporation, Zambia Consolidated Copper Mines (ZCCM). Philippe asked me to join an IBRD mission to Zambia to comment on ZCCM's recent submission to the Bank for "rehabilitation funds" for the Zambian copper sector. Of course I said yes and Gillian and I celebrated job No. 007, which more than made up for the disappointment of the non-job 006. Philippe said a terms of employment contract would be mailed to me together with an authorisation to pick up air tickets and travellers cheques. Departure date was set for the middle of February by a BCal flight from Gatwick as before.

There was no sign of any WB guys at Gatwick, but then I guessed they were either inter-lining from the USA through a transit lounge or already imbibing in the First-Class lounge! No matter, I expected to finally catch up with them in the Pamodzi Hotel in Lusaka and so it proved to be. In their team I only knew Dick, the metallurgical engineer, from the previous visit. Philippe was very pleasant and welcoming and told me that Mary, the previous WB mission's team leader, had been promoted to a different section in the Bank. This time I was the only mining engineer on the team. Off the record Dick told me that the Bank had decided that they wanted completely independent advice/comment from people who had never been associated with the Zambian copper industry and that, obviously, precluded Dave from Anglo American. I was happy about that as it gave me the opportunity to now look at the NCCM operations as well as revisit the RCM ones. As ZCCM was a state (political) organisation we inevitably spent longer in Lusaka meeting the new ZCCM board and the Zambian Ministers of Finance and Trade. This took up two full days before we flew with RoanAir up to Kitwe.

The key objective of the WB mission was to comment on ZCCM's 15-year copper and cobalt metal production forecast. Over recent years both NCCM and RCM's production forecasts had been overly optimistic. I thus spent two days with the consulting geologists of both NCCM and RCM going over the respective companies latest ore reserve statements. Both companies now used the same reserve classification system which incorporated a 2% Cu cut-off grade with a 3 metres minimum mining width. Detailed discussions with all Mine Managers identified the squeezed position of all mining operations indicated by less than six months Fully Developed reserves ahead at three of the old RCM mines and less than twelve months in the old NCCM mines. Apart from the paucity of Fully Developed reserves there were severe delays with the expansion project at Baluba and the sinking of Mufulira's new sub-vertical shaft by Mowlem-Fry which was already six months behind schedule after only twelve months on site.

All of these observations lead to the inevitable conclusion that copper and cobalt production forecasts would not be achieved in the short term, say the next five years. The importance of the NCCM Chingola unit was also apparent representing 65.5% of NCCM's total copper production. Overall total tonnage mined by the two previous companies was virtually identical at around 15 million tonnes/year, but NCCM's average head grade of 2.64% Cu was appreciably higher than the 1.87% Cu of RCM. This was primarily due to the very low grade factor of 67.5% at RCM compared to 84.6% at NCCM. Taking all these items in to account I estimated that ZCCM's total annual copper production would be 579,000 tonnes against ZCCM's forecast of 635,000 tonnes, a fall of 56,000 tonnes or 9%. This tonnage shortfall would directly affect ZCCM's short term cash flow.

In the second part of the WB brief Dick and I had to technically and financially review the numerous "rehabilitation projects" put up by each of the operating divisions. These "projects" included new mining machinery (surface and underground), new concentrating equipment and various electrical infrastructure upgrades. Of course Dick and I were assisted by the WB financial gurus. After three weeks on the Copperbelt we headed back to Lusaka for a further two days of heated discussions with the ZCCM board on our copper and cobalt production forecasts. As our shortfall stemmed almost entirely from problems in the mines I had a very, very busy couple of days at the sharp end! Philippe was very supportive and said that he felt we (the WB) might even still be a little too optimistic. In the end ZCCM and the WB agreed to disagree, but whether or not the WB lent money to ZCCM for their "rehabilitation projects" would be based on our own, lower forecast. That was that and we all boarded the BCal flight to Gatwick. I caught the train link to Reading and the Cotswold Line service to Worcester Shrub Hill station. I spent the next six days checking figures and doing a small write-up before despatching the completed report to Washington by DHL Couriers. It was now early March and the end of my first independent year - seven distinct jobs, one non-payer and one non-job. Overall conclusion, not too bad, could do better, but we survived.

22

On reflection I realised that just two clients, Goni at COMSUR and the World Bank had provided the bulk of my work, whilst Golders engaged me merely because they were bereft of underground engineers at the closure of GMA. I had previously worked for all three organisations and thus had not been able to generate any new clients over the past twelve months. That was worrying and I repeated my letter onslaught to anyone in the hard rock mining industry who might need an additional pair of mining hands. The current economic downturn had seen a fair number of major mining projects either scaled down, postponed or cancelled.

Anyway time to attack the Gorsty garden, accompanied by a very enthusiastic five months old sheepdog, Luke, who thought everything was for his personal enjoyment. I had forgotten the energy a young dog had and daily tramps across Bache Camp did little to curb his enthusiasm. Anjon, now aged 6, was not so mad, except when a local bitch was on heat, when he wouldn't eat and howled most of the time. When not troubled by the "ladies" Anjon battled with rabbits and numerous mole tumps in the Gorsty garden.

In early April I had a call from Malcolm, a Riofinex geologist I had previously worked with at Minas de Riotinto. He was still with Riofinex, but now based in Jeddah, Saudi Arabia where Riofinex had an exploration contract with the Saudi government. He wanted to know if I was available to undertake a preliminary project appraisal of a bauxite deposit. I said yes (of course!) and he asked me to come up to London and discuss the scope of work etc with Keith at their office in St James's Square. So this time I drove myself to Worcester station and left the VW Golf in the day park. The train to Paddington took about two and a quarter hours.

Keith and Malcolm greeted me like a long lost friend, it was very reassuring. They told me the broad outline of Riofinex's exploration work in Saudi. They had established a Riofinex compound a few miles outside Jeddah itself, as had other exploration contractors such as the United States Bureau of Mines (USBM) and the French BRGM. The bauxite project in question was called Az Zabirah, discovered by Riofinex in December 1979, and since investigated by surface geological mapping, sampling and extensive diamond drilling by the Arabian Drilling Company (ADC).

Keith, unsurprisingly, wanted to know if I had had any direct experience of bauxite deposits or mines. I told him it was limited to a ten day site visit to Paragominas (an RTZ project) in Para State, Brazil during the mid 1970s when I was with RTZC. That seemed to help things a bit. After discussing fee rates and contract terms (basis: Association of Consulting Engineers) he asked if I could visit the project before the end of April. I said yes and we signed a Retainer Agreement to cover the next two years for "various Saudi projects", job No. 008 was thus agreed.

Thus in the third week of April Gillian drove me to Worcester station for the subsequent rail/coach journey to Heathrow. Then a six hour flight by Saudia airlines to Jeddah on the east coast of the Red Sea. As the Riofinex exploration work was a government contract we were obliged to travel on the State airline, Saudia. Not my favourite airline. It was dry (no alcohol on board) for a start. But that was just a warm-up to the Saudi welcome. Immigration was slow for all non-Saudis, but with the requisite visa no problems. However Jeddah Customs was another story. Without doubt the rudest, most aggressive petty officials I ever came across in nearly forty years of international travelling. Having recovered my case from the carousel, after an interminable wait, I eventually reached a Customs "officer". Instructed to open my case, I did, whereupon he upended my case onto the floor (yes, really) and then proceeded to turn everything over with a baton-like stick and his boot! Apparently they were looking for pornography or alcohol. He became very interested in a Boots Beer making kit (Malcolm had asked me to take some so the lads in the Jeddah compound could brew up) which I eventually convinced him was a special yeast for babies. After that I was on my hands and knees scrabbling around to collect my possessions and repack. Thankfully a Riofinex Land Rover met me and drove me to a downtown hotel.

It seemed a normal hotel with a nice looking bar just off the foyer, but soft drinks only were dispensed. I could have murdered some beer as it was hot, close to 30 C and humid. My room was OK and there was a message saying Malcolm and Ross would be around to see me at 6pm. So with some time to spare I thought I'd cool off in the pool I had spotted out of my room window. Nice thought but a non-starter, today was "ladies only", so no mixed swimming, sun bathing or co-mingling with the opposite sex. I thought I'm really going to like this place - not.

Malcolm and Ross duly arrived and we repaired to the bar for a stiff orange juice or two. They said relax, we'll move you out to the Riofinex compound tomorrow where you can sample the home brewed hooch. The Saudis know what goes on in these "foreign" compounds (yes, walled with gate staff) but choose to turn a blind eye so long as the drinking stays inside the compound. They said we'd spend a couple of days there going over the exploration data before Ross and I headed up to the Az Zabirah site, about 550 miles NE of Jeddah towards the Iraq border. After our bracing orange juices we set off for a local restaurant in the main shopping area of town. I was amazed to see the place seething with Filipinos and Filipinas, the former various construction workers and the latter nurses and nannies. It seemed evident to me that the indigenous Saudis only undertook office or driving work. The religious police were much in evidence making sure there were no overt signs of interest between the sexes! What an awful repressive place.

The following morning Ross picked me up from the hotel and we drove north, towards the airport, and then east to the Riofinex compound. One thing I did like about Jeddah, their roundabouts. They had the most amazing collection of very large, modern, metallic "sculptures" on them - bicycles, planes, boats, rockets and who knows what. The Riofinex compound was very comfortable. A collection of about twelve air-conditioned bedrooms with a communal dining room run by a catering contractor. An excellent drawing/draughting room, several offices, stores and a motor pool and garage completed the compound. It felt quite relaxed after the strictures of Jeddah itself. We studied the surface geological plans, sampling and assaying data as well as the drilling logs from ADC but I definitely needed a site visit to get the feel of the place. Malcolm was the Manager of the Riofinex Saudi operation and spent most of his time in their Jeddah compound dealing with the various Ministries along with numerous administrative duties not least of which was keeping Riofinex's boss in London, Barry, happy. Ross was the Az Zabirah Project manager and although he had a rented house in Jeddah, where his wife Sheelagh stayed, he spent most of his time up on site. I stayed in the compound that night and enjoyed some really quite good home brewed beer. They all had a good laugh at my scrabbling around on the airport floor trying to repack my case and all reckoned the Customs officer fancied me and wanted to see what I looked like on all fours!

Early next morning Ross and I plus another couple of Riofinex guys headed out to the airport, where a Short SC7 Skyvan was waiting to take us the 550 miles north-east to Az Zabirah. The Skyvan was a high winged, twin engined monoplane, known by everyone whose flown in one as The Shed. Plus points are short take-off and landing (STOL), and a cargo body suitable for large bulky items, like vehicles. From a passenger perspective it is incredibly noisy and uncomfortable. The flight to the Az Zabirah strip took three hours and in spite of ear defenders one staggered out like a deaf, dumb mute. Hey ho welcome to the Saudi stony desert. A short distance from the strip Riofinex had set up a PortaKabin camp. All the cabins were new and fully air-conditioned. There also were several offices a communal mess and lounge. Close by was a smaller ADC drillers camp.

The first thing that struck me was that the immediate area was a stony desert with but a light covering of sand and not a tree in sight. Ross commented that about thirty miles NE towards Iraq there were the extensive Ad Dahna sand dunes running NW-SE for nearly 200 miles. We first drove around the preliminary delineated bauxite occurrence stopping at both ADC diamond drill rigs. Ross reiterated his comments from the Jeddah compound about the very low core recovery achieved by ADC where half the holes had recoveries of less than 90% and a third less than 75%. The present 33.7 million tonnes of indicated ore and 109.9 million tonnes of inferred ore (58.5% alumina & 6.6% silica) was based on only 26 holes.

I felt that the emphasis of Riofinex's planning should shift from geological evaluation to outlining in situ geological reserves and the provision of suitable data for preliminary mine planning. Ross agreed. We also felt it necessary to do some close space drilling to get a feeling for variability and the presence of kaolinisation displacing economic bauxite. In addition these core samples could be used for bulk density measurements. The sample preparation facilities were good but I felt the initial weight reduction of the sample by riffling was carried out at too coarse a size.

No preliminary mine planning had been undertaken other than using an arbitrary core drilling cut-off of 10 to 1 for overburden to bauxite thickness. Since the bauxite outcroped this implied an average 5 to 1 overburden ratio. Although high by world bauxite deposit standards it was a suitable starting point to develop tonnage/grade curves and tonnage/overburden curves. Overburden stripping could be handled by bucket wheel excavator (BWE) or scrapers and bauxite mining by wheeled front-end loader (FEL) and haul trucks for selective mining. Beneficiation testwork was being carried out by AMDEL. What soon became apparent was that a Bauxite Mining Project was in economic terms really a Bulk Mineral Transport Project.

Az Zabirah was an isolated location. It was very evident that transport of supplies in and bauxite product out would dominate the viability of any mining project. I undertook a preliminary project evaluation on the basis of a geological resource of 160 million tonnes producing eighty million tonnes of recoverable beneficiated bauxite which with a mine life of twenty years would indicate an output of four million tonnes/year. The need for a deep water port to export the product suggested Al Jubail near the head of the Gulf.

To investigate potential rail routes Riofinex arranged for a helicopter to take Ross and me over, and around the Ad Dahna sand dunes to the oil pipeline (TAPline) some 140km NE of Az Zabirah. It was quite a buttock clenching flight. Firstly the pilot was an American, ex Vietnam war chopper flyer. Ross asked him to fly at about 150ft up so we could eyeball the stony terrain. Brad, the pilot, had the distinctly unsettling habit of continually leaning his head right back over his seat and sweeping his eyes steadily around from rear right, through centre back to rear left every couple of minutes or so. Spooky. He commented laconically "gotta keep a sharp eye on the bogeys creeping up on ya". Well, that's alright then. He just couldn't get out of his old 'Nam habit. As we approached the Ad Dahna sand dunes he put the chopper down at the foot of the dunes. We got out and struggled up the dune slope. It was not easy, free running sand and obviously difficult country to put a rail track through and keep open at times of high wind. Well that answered one question - have to go around the Ad Dahna dunes. We reboarded the chopper and flew SE, paralleling the dunes before rounding the southern dunes "nose" and heading NE towards Hafar al Batin. We were still flying at about 150ft slightly higher than the dunes (c.100ft height), now on our left hand side. Brad felt that was a little too low so we went up to about 250ft above the stony desert or 150ft above the adjacent dunes. As we levelled off at this higher altitude a huge complex came in to view about 30 degrees left of dead ahead. Nothing showed on our topographical maps, only the delineated Neutral Zone on the Saudi/Iraq border NE of the TAPline. A sharp "shit" from Brad, then, "that's the secret King Khalid Military City we better get the hell out of here". Whereupon he immediately put the chopper down on to the stony desert at the foot of the dunes. He explained that it was, apparently, a restricted military zone, where the Saudis kept a large fleet of fighter jets to look after any troubles along the

Iraq border. He felt an unidentified chopper in this area would be extremely foolhardy. We scuttled back SW at 50ft height in the shelter of the dunes then turned WNW for Az Zabirah.

After further four wheel drive exploration of the adjacent Aruma scarp we located an easily graded wadi that headed NE on the limestone plateau. This seemed a possible route through to the TAPline and on to Al Jubail, a distance of 650 Km. At an estimated construction cost of US$0.6 million/Km the complete rail link to Al Jubail would cost US$390 million. Railway operating costs would be 1.2 US cents/tonne-Km equivalent to US$ 7.8 per tonne hauled with an additional US$0.5 for loading, stockpiling and reclaim. Without doubt transport capital and operating costs would be critical. Another key aspect would be water supply in an area with an annual rainfall of about 100mm. The major aquifer in this part of Saudi was the Tabuk formation but that was believed to be at a depth of 1100m in the Az Zabirah area. Water requirements were mainly determined by the beneficiation plant and were estimated at one tonne water per tonne washed bauxite plus an additional 0.75 tonne water for other industrial and domestic use. Thus a daily water demand of 20,000 tonnes or 4.5 million gallons would be indicated. This would require the development of an extensive well field. Power would be derived from an on-site diesel plant. An installed capacity in the range of 10 to 15MW was indicated, say six 2.5MW units total with four on load and two on standby/maintenance. On the basis of these broad brush assumptions, namely a four million tonnes/year beneficiated bauxite product railed to Al Jubail on the Gulf I derived the following capital & operating cost estimates as at first quarter 1982.

Capital Cost	**US $ (million)**
Mine & Plant	100
Infrastructure & General Services	80
Railway (650 Km)	390
Owner's Cost (10%)	60
Engineering & Construction Management (20%)	115
Construction Overhead	30
Working Capital	20
Contingency (13%)	105
TOTAL	**900**

Operating Cost	**US$/tonne bauxite**
Strip & Mine	5.5
Beneficiation	1.5
Transport & Handling	8.5
General Services	3.5
Infrastructure	2.0
TOTAL	**21.0**

The estimated capital cost of US$ 900 million was assumed to cover a three year construction period. On the basis of a desired 15% DCF return (gross) on the total project cost with a twenty year operating life the annual cash margin required would be US$ 166 million, on top of an annual operating cost of US$ 84 million (ie 4 million x $21) a total of US$ 250 million. This would require a bauxite price of US$ 62.5 CIF Al Jubail.

We agreed all the basic assumptions with Ross and his team on site. Without exception everyone was stunned by the huge transport cost. Instead of flying back to Jeddah, Ross suggested he drive us back in his Range Rover. I was all in favour as this would give me a chance to observe (any) Saudi infrastructure. The Range Rover was very comfortable and quite at home in the poor road conditions. Ross was a very experienced off-road driver. We left Az Zabirah at 6am and drove SE for about 100 miles before turning SW, heading for the Red Sea. The track improved to a reasonable road and Ross made good progress to the outskirts of Medina, where we stopped at around 3pm. It was a stark scene, the road dropping down through a bare, black basalt scarp. We attacked our "picnic" with relish, sitting in the shade of the Range Rover, accompanied by the sounds of Sibelius pouring out of the car's door speakers - very surrealistic. Only a short stop as Ross wanted to make the Jeddah compound before dark.

This we did arriving around 8.30pm, a Herculean piece of driving by Ross for, I guess, not much short of 700 miles over desert roads, albeit with minimal traffic. The following day we went through our notional bauxite project with Malcolm. As with those at site he was shocked, nay incredulous, at the cost impact of transport on the overall viability of the project. My reverse economic exercise had indicated that a bauxite price of US$ 62.5/tonne CIF Al Jubail was required. This was felt to be too high and Malcolm suggested I rework the numbers with the project carrying only the rail cost for the 170km section from Az Zabirah to the TAPline, the remaining 480 Km, alongside the TAPline, being paid for by "others". Unsurprisingly this demonstrated the importance of transport, dropping the required price of bauxite to US$ 44/tonne CIF Al Jubail to achieve a 15% DCF return (gross) on the total capital outlay. Although a very preliminary economic analysis it showed the desirability to move the project from exploration to outlining mineable reserves, undertaking hydrological studies and above all obtaining specialist advice on transport, both rail and pipeline.

That basically was that. So after twelve days in Saudi I headed to Jeddah airport and an early morning (dry) Saudia flight back to Heathrow followed by the usual express bus to Reading, Cotswold Line to Worcester and personal pick-up by Gillian in the VW to Gorsty. An interesting experience Saudi Arabia, but I really did not like the oppressive Muslim regime nor the treeless country itself. Definitely not my cup of tea. I would not like to be on the three year contract that Ross was on, even less Malcolm who was on his second tour - good money, tax free but....I spent the next few days preparing a brief Az Zabirah Project Appraisal report as well as checking my cost estimates for strip mining equipment, bauxite beneficiation plant, water well drilling, diesel power generation and, of course, capital and operating costs for standard gauge railways. I then tumbled all the numbers and derived my bauxite prices for CIF Al Jubail. I took the train from Worcester to London and spent a further day at Riofinex's St James's Square office going through my report with Keith and Barry. They were not really happy on the outcome, but seemed unable (or unwilling) to dispute my numbers and conclusion. They said my report, suitably edited/amended, would form the basis of Riofinex's submission to the Saudi Department of Mining & Mineral Resources (DMMR) as a preliminary economic assessment of the Az Zabirah project. Keith commented that, depending on the DMMR's response, there might be similar work for me on their Turayf phosphate project next year. Obviously further paid work would be good, but Saudi? I guess independent contractors couldn't be picky.

The next month was quiet and I enjoyed working in the Gorsty garden. We put up a new stock fence around the top side of the orchard to keep

Rowley's sheep out. We also de-stoned the rough patch of ground in the western corner, where I noticed the ground was somewhat squelchy. Digging down I found the end of the French Drain, or soakaway was unplugged and the septic tank effluent was pooling there. I perused Peele's Mining Engineers Handbook and decided to lengthen the soakaway several yards in both the eastern and western direction, making sure the trenches sloped at 1 in 200 down from the septic tank overflow entry point. Conventional field tiles were then laid in the trench and surrounded by 0.5in crusher run gravel. Both end tiles were plugged. The whole was covered with soil and then grass seeded. After those "adjustments" the septic tank/soakaway never gave us any trouble whatsoever.

23

Towards the end of June I received a call from John, geologist at GA(UK) - could I help with an evaluation of a barytes mine in Mexico for an oil service company, KCA Minerals in Houston, USA? Be delighted, job No 009 was all set to go. John anticipated a two to three week exercise, but said all details would be sorted out at KCA's offices in Houston. Thus five days on I met John and Peter at Heathrow for the long flight to Houston. As expected a big, brash, modern skyscraper oil boom town. Lots of guys in big stetsons and cowboy boots, straight out of a John Wayne movie. What did surprise me though was that the first lingo on room cards in the downtown hotel was Spanish and then (American) English. As anticipated everything was larger than life, especially the food portions and one sunk under a hail of "have a nice day" or "enjoy". On the positive side everyone was cheery and helpful. KCA Minerals produced some fairly rudimentary geological plans and sections of the barytes deposit in the Sierra Madre mountains near Matehuala. The following day we took an Aeromexico plane for the 600 mile flight SSW to Tampico on the Gulf of Mexico. This was a bustling port city full of crazy drivers. We stayed overnight and a local KCA Mexican geologist picked us up in a big twin cab ute for the 230 odd mile drive NW to Matehuala. At a height of around 1500m above sea level it was somewhat cooler than the sticky heat of Tampico. We checked into a small lively hotel in the town.

The barytes prospect, an old mining area about twenty miles north of the town, occupied two north striking en echelon ridges separated by a shallow valley. It was essentially desert country with plenty of cactus and thorny scrub. The Mexican geologist was a very cheery fellow who had a large pistol stuck in his waistband. As we traversed the surface looking at both old and new trenches he explained which cactus fruit was both edible and quite refreshing. The cactus fruit were also, I recall, an hallucinogenic known locally as peyote or the medical drug mescaline. I can remember very little of the barytes deposit itself other than it appeared to be present as a major gangue mineral in what had originally been an old underground lead mining operation, now long since abandoned. KCA Minerals' interest, of course, was in a source of cheap, bulk barytes as the main ingredient in oil well drilling mud. The 4.5 bulk density and inertness of barytes being the desired properties.

Their surface exploration effort had thus been directed towards attempting to locate parallel lead vein structures carrying gangue barytes in the limestone country rock. This made sense since the local ridge topography and mining economics indicated an open-pit operation as the most likely option. Tramping out to yet another surface trench the Mexican geologist suddenly held up his hand and said "oiga" (listen). Sure enough we could hear a faint, but distinct rattling noise. Yes, it was a rattlesnake! The geologist moved cautiously forward and the three of us, John, Peter and I, levitated a couple of feet at the sharp crack of a pistol at close quarters. He had shot the rattler just behind the head. Although the Mexican geologist was quite blase about the rattler, I felt he was happy to demonstrate his bush craft to los gringos ingleses. We were certainly glad he was wide awake. He cut off the rattle, about 1.5in in length and presented it to me.

We spent two or three days in KCA's project office in Matehuala going through the surface exploration data and drawing up a series of preliminary vertical cross sections incorporating the scant information from the old underground workings. The old mine had been developed by three strike adits driven in from the side of the ridge. Unfortunately there was no underground data on possible parallel vein structures since no exploratory crosscuts had been driven. Although surface trenching had, in fact, disclosed some parallel vein structures carrying lead and barytes we and KCA had no information on their downward, vertical extent. A series of shallow inclined crosscut DD holes would be required to confirm or otherwise a possible barytes resource. I spent time in Matehuala with the Mexican geologist visiting the local power company whose response was - "senor we have no spare power to give you". That meant an on-site diesel plant. Also the local authority concerning water supply - similar response "no hay agua. senor". The geologist took us to a small river in a deep valley about five miles NW. Water supply would definitely be a major problem in this dry limestone country. That was really all we could hoover up on-site and in Matehuala so we headed back down to Tampico. Here I spent half a day with the Port Authorities discussing the likely requirements for storage, loading and shipping bulk barytes. Better response this time - "no hay problema, senor"! With that we said cheerio to our Mexican geologist and flew back to Houston.

At KCA's offices we discussed the barytes project and in the end, I think, convinced them that it was not yet at an evaluation stage. Fundamentally the "project" was still at an exploration stage and was really a "prospect". However they asked us to prepare a notional project evaluation based on producing 1500 tonnes/day of crushed and screened barytes from an open pit, transporting the bulk product to the port of Tampico for export to the USA. KCA provided a barytes price CIF Tampico. We had collected basic service, labour and consumable costs in Mexico and thus had all we needed to develop this notional Matehuala barytes operation. It was agreed that a draft evaluation report would be despatched to Houston by courier inside two weeks. With that we left for the long flight back to Heathrow. We all caught the express bus to Reading where John and Peter caught the local train back to Maidenhead and I made friends, yet again, with the Cotswold Line train to Worcester and Gillian duly obliged with the car run to Gorsty.

Having only just completed a broad brush open-pit evaluation exercise for the Az Zabirah project in Saudi it was relatively simple for me to develop capital cost estimates by factoring daily outputs (4,000 to 1,500) and operating cost estimates by scrutinising fixed and variable costs. Obviously I had to consider local Mexican costs and productivities. Nevertheless I had a draft write-up complete with financial numbers ready by the end of the week. So a day trip by train to Maidenhead. John and Peter edited my draft write-up and by early afternoon we had agreed the basic economic numbers for the notional barytes project. It was now in GA(UK) hands and that was the end of my involvement, apart from submitting an invoice for my time and expenses - the easy bit.

We had a clear August and really enjoyed Gorsty garden with several projects on the go. I continued to extend the nascent vegetable garden over in the far western corner where masses of building rubble had been tipped and covered with soil and turf. We also continued to explore the Welsh Marches area with extended dog walks over Bircher Common and through the Lugg River gorge near Lingen. It was slightly to the west of Lingen that Gillian and I spotted our first buzzard. What a majestic bird. Towards the end of the month we collected masses of damsons and commenced the slow, messy process of attempting to make damson wine. Later in September I also collected sloes from the numerous blackthorn bushes to make sloe gin. The house was inundated with bubbling demijohns. In late September we drove down to Cornwall to stay with Pat and her lighthouse keeper husband, Tony for five days.

All had been quiet for a couple of months when I received a call from the Asian Development Bank (ADB) in Manila, Philippines. A certain gentleman, Hank, wanted to know if I was still available to undertake mining consultancy work. I reassured him that I was and he responded by saying he had spoken to the mining division of the IBRD (the World Bank) and they had confirmed that I had worked for them in Zambia. Hank then said that the ADB had a mining job in Sri Lanka and that the ADB management had said that they should employ a Britisher on that job! So, not recommended by the IBRD but merely buggins turn to keep the Brits happy (the UK was a major contributor to ADB funds). Hank said an ADB contract and Terms of Reference would be mailed straight away with an expected start around mid November. He anticipated an initial few days in Manila followed by two weeks in Sri Lanka and a final week or so in Manila. As promised the contract etc turned up ten days later with a firm start date of the 12th November for me to be in Manila. Gillian and I agreed that this would be a great chance to tack a Far Eastern/Australia holiday on to the end of this job, No. 010. With the help of Thomas Cook in Hereford we sorted out a Heathrow-Manila-Perth-Melbourne-Hobart-Sydney-Hong Kong-Heathrow ticket for Gillian.

I duly left Heathrow on the 10th November, flying CP to Hong Kong then PAL down to Manila. The ADB had booked me in to the Bayview Hotel on Roxas Boulevard alongside Manila Bay. It was OK, certainly close to Ermita and Malate, the centre of downtown night life. The ADB offices were only a short distance further west, away from the Bay, in Mandaluyong City. It was a large, modern building somewhat daunting after the small, compact head office of Lepanto in Ermita. However, the leader of the Sri Lankan project, Zaidi, a Pakistani, made me very welcome and ensured that I was suitably accredited with an ADB name badge so that I could come and go unhindered in the building. He introduced me to the other four members of his Sri Lankan project team, Fred an American economist living in Manila; a Sri Lankan management consultant; Oscar, a Filipino geologist and an Indian specialist in minerals marketing and the tax and tariffs regime of Sri Lanka.

Zaidi outlined the ADB's Terms of Reference which briefly was the rehabilitation and expansion of graphite production from the Bogala and K/K mines of the state mining corporation, SMMDC. So only two, purely technical people, the geologist and me. Fortunately for me the geologist, Oscar, had already visited both mines and had obtained the most recent ore reserve tabulations. I told him I had had some experience of graphite mining at Skaland in Norway. However, he said that that would not be relevant in Sri Lanka since those deposits were almost pure graphite veins in metamorphic rocks whereas the Norwegian deposit was a much lower grade dissemination. From my point of view it was really great that Oscar was au fait with the Sri Lankan deposits geology.

The next couple of days were spent working through the reserve data of both mines as well as the major mine infrastructure and recent production data. This initial data appraisal would enable us to hit the ground running. The next day we flew to Colombo. Here we were all booked in to a central downtown hotel, the Ramada. Our first full day in Colombo was spent in introductory meetings with SMMDC and other government Ministries. They all seemed to be courting the ADB quite openly, but then, of course, they were after a large loan. The following day we headed sixty miles NE by road from Colombo to Kurunegala on the western side of the central highlands. The trip was memorable for the incredible array of brightly flowering trees with attendant huge butterflies. Passing through forested areas we saw numerous elephants doing logging work and at a couple of river crossings more elephants were being washed down/cooled off. In fact I saw more Asian elephants in Sri Lanka than I ever saw African elephants in East Africa. We unloaded our personal gear at a small hotel in Kurunegala and then headed for the first mine at Bogala.

After the GM's welcome we split into two groups. Oscar and I joined the Chief Geologist and Underground Manager for an underground visit. We went down the small rectangular wooden Alfred Shaft to the 72 Level (132m depth) in a small single deck cage hauled by a single drum Wolfe hoist. This shaft handled men, materials, graphite and waste rock hoisting. At the 72 Level we transferred to the internal No 5 Shaft hoist for the trip to 205 Level, a depth of 243m. Again the hoist was only a single drum unit. At this depth, 375m or 1230ft below surface the ambient temperature must have been over 35 C with very little through ventilation and the local miner's attire was restricted to hard hat, shorts and working boots. It looked a deal more suitable than our overalls. The mine appeared very dry with no sign of a drain alongside the tracked development. Prior perusal of the mine plans and sections indicated a vein dip of about 55 degrees. Stoping took place straight off the level with simple Chinaman chutes set into the drive timbers. The stoping method was overhand, a combination of conventional shrinkage allied to open stoping on to random stulls. Fairly lightweight jacklegs were used for drilling.

I said I would like to climb up into an active stope and have a look at the exposed hangingwall. My request was answered by the Underground Manager who said "you must take off your boots and go barefoot". I replied "yeah, yeah pull the other one" or similar. He said "no I'm serious, in boots you will be unable to keep your feet on the unctuous graphite" Well, that made sense so we all removed our boots and socks. He was absolutely right, ones bare feet managed to get some traction on the extremely slippery, but soft graphite. It was one of the most weird experiences I've had clambering around a narrow vein stope in bare feet. I noticed that the local stope miners were also bare footed, in fact, apart from a hard hat and minute loin cloth they were virtually bare! It was extremely hot, humid and airless. I imagined UK Health and Safety would have gone berserk about the lack of safety boots and hot ambient conditions in the stope, but this was Sri Lanka and these were accepted working conditions.

The broken ore passed from the Chinaman chutes into small rail trolleys (0.7 tonne) for tramming to the No 5 Shaft where the trolley plus graphite cargo were hoisted from the 205m Level to the 72 Level where it was cross trammed to the Alfred Shaft for hoisting to surface. Here it passed through a screening/sorting plant to produce three final bagged products, Chip, Lump or Powder. There was, of course, no need for a beneficiation plant since the mined rom graphite was plus 99% pure. The main mine services (shafts, hoists, trackwork, trolleys etc) were old, inefficient and undersized when contemplating an expanded production. The ore reserve base could certainly sustain a higher rate of production. So too the actual stoping of graphite could be readily increased by opening up additional stopes on the new, lower levels. Of course this would require additional jackleg machines and an improvement in the underground compressed air reticulation system and an expansion of the surface compressor plant. No, the bottleneck, was hoisting in the No 5 and Alfredo Shafts. They were equipped with only small (100 to 150 Kw) single drum hoists pulling a single deck cage holding one small trolley. In particular the No 5 Shaft had a graphite hoisting limit of 5000 tonnes/year. SMMDC had some preliminary plans on how to increase hoisting capacity and we would examine these back in Colombo.

After three days at Bogola we transferred to the other SMMDC mine, Kahatagaha & Kolongaha, better known as the K/K mine. The mining conditions were similar to Bogala with shrinkage or open stoping onto stulls being undertaken with lightweight jacklegs. It was a tracked mine and the same 0.7 tonnes capacity trolleys were used for moving the graphite from the stope chutes to the surface via the 345m (1132ft deep Kahatagaha Shaft.) Again this old, small shaft equipped with a 75 Kw single drum hoist pulling a single deck cage was the constraint to expansion. Its current capacity was circa 4000 tonnes/year graphite. SMMDC also had preliminary plans for increasing hoisting capacity at K/K mine.

Over the weekend we drove the thirty or so miles SE to the hill city of Kandy for a little R & R. It was the second city of Sri Lanka and a sacred Buddhist site. The central highland hill slopes around the city were covered with very extensive tea plantations. We did the usual tourist sites including several temples but my lasting impression came at breakfast, the next day, before we headed back down to Colombo. This was eating a string-hopper! No it was not a variety of charcoal grilled jumping cockroach but a mesh, like a slim waffle, made of steamed rice flour. One could eat them "as is", but they were a little bland and I preferred them with some jam - interesting and quite pleasant.

Back in Colombo we checked into the Ramada hotel. We spent the next few days in the SMMDC offices working through their rehabilitation and expansion plans. I was also required to list international engineer-constructor firms as well as specialist shaft sinking firms and winder manufacturers. In the evenings the Asian team members tended to eat fairly early whilst Fred and I got into the habit of walking around the corner to the classical, old-fashioned, colonial style hotel, the Galle Face. Here we would sit out on the verandah drinking beer overlooking the gardens that ran down to the Indian ocean. The setting was pure Somerset Maughan, it was very relaxing. The food was also good, although the dining room, unlike the modern Ramada hotel, did not have air conditioning. Our Asian team members thought we were "peculiar" (hopefully not queer!).

On the following weekend I suggested to Fred that we take a taxi out to the Mount Lavinia Hotel a short distance south of Colombo. Gillian and I had visited this hotel on our way back from Australia by boat in 1965. It's location was marvellous set on a rocky prominence jutting out into the ocean. It had beautiful, lush gardens interspersed with a number of comfy outdoor bars. The service and food were excellent. To my mind one of the world's great hotel locations. All too soon it was a flight back to hot, sticky Manila.

As before the ADB had booked me in to the Bayview Hotel. At the ADB offices I had plenty of work running hoisting and power calculations for the various shafts at Bogala and K/K. There were also ventilation and compressed air requirements to be determined and costed. All of this data had to be integrated into the ADB financial model. Finally I had to draft Terms of Reference for nine additional engineering staff for the Bogola and K/K mines.

With Gillian arriving on the 8th December I had booked us in to the Regent Hotel, a little further down Roxas Boulevard, to avoid any confusion with my hotel expenses on the ADB account. I collected Gillian from MIA by taxi. She remembered the heaving scrum of greeters and meeters outside the arrivals gate and was glad I had a captive taxi at the ready. I explained we were staying in the Regent Hotel, rather than our preferred hotel, the Intercon in Makati, since I was still working at the ADB which was close to the Regent. She was happy to have a quiet day to recover from the long flight whilst I went back to work. The following evening we went round to Fred's place for a drink with his Filipina wife and admired their new baby. Then the four of us went to the American Club for dinner.

I completed my work at the ADB next day and in the evening we decided to try out Imelda Marcos's new project, the Philippine Plaza Hotel on Roxas Boulevard. Very mush and smooth. We went to their huge disco and danced (gyrated a better description) to the BG's music - Saturday Night Fever. The noise was stupendous and the crowd enormous. Great fun, but a relief to get some air and space. The Filipinos certainly know how to enjoy themselves.

Early next morning we took a taxi to MIA to catch a PAL DC9 plane for the 570 mile flight to Zamboanga at the southern tip of Mindanao island. The flight took a little over an hour and the clear blue sea and offshore coral islands looked stunning as we swept in over the city just after sunrise. We took a taxi to the Lantaka Hotel which was situated right on the sea front. We put our bags in the room and went straight down to the terrace, alongside the sea wall, for breakfast. At that time of day, 8.30am, the temperature was very pleasant. Already there were outrigger canoes and bum boats hawking various wares right beside the hotel's terrace wall. After breakfast we hired a local taxi for a look around the city. Zamboanga was known as the city of flowers and true to its moniker there were colourful bougainvilleas and hibiscuses everywhere - very memorable. A little way out of the city we visited the traditional cottage weaving industry of the Yakan natives who produced very striking, banded cloth. Our driver then insisted he took us up to the very new, very posh, Garden Orchid Hotel up in the forested hills above the city. It certainly looked as if all the VIPs would have stayed there. There was a large spectacular aquarium alongside the entrance atrium. However, we restricted our activity to cooling off with a Singapore Sling in the air-conditioned grandeur of a piano bar overlooking the terrace and forest.

We then visited the huge market by the port, where we appeared to be the only Europeans there. The Philippines, especially southern Mindanao and Zamboanga Province in particular, had a bad international press on account of the terrorist activities of the Moro National Liberation Front (MNLF), Islamic fundamentalists based on Jolo Island to the south-west. Our driver assured us the Philippine Army had things under control and to prove his point took us to Zamboanga Prison on the sea front further to the west. He said I should go in to the prison and see the numerous captured MNLF prisoners for myself! Unsurprisingly I declined fearing I'd never get out again. Filipino prisons are reputedly extremely tough. Right outside the main prison gate a six man traditional jazz band atop a flatbed truck were playing their hearts out. There were several prison warders on the back of the truck as well. I quizzed our taxi driver and he told us that, yes the band members were all prisoners, but classified as "trustys". It could only happen in the mildly anarchic Philippines.

Glad to escape the clutches of the Philippine penal system I asked our driver to take us out to a nice peaceful beach where we might find a simple light snack lunch. He drove us back through the city and out to the eastern side to Bolong Beach a magnificent curve of fine white sand backed by palm trees. It was almost deserted apart from a group of local fishermen beaching a boat and taking their catch up to a small nipa thatched hut. Our driver lived just off the beach and was very happy to provide soft drinks and fruit - well he asked his wife to do so! After a long day he drove us back to the Lantaka Hotel.

We had a memorable dinner on the Lantaka terrace that evening with shielded candles on the tables, excellent sea food followed by juicy mangos whilst a small combo played quietly - very romantic. We even managed a dance or two, which created something of a record for us since it was only a couple of nights since pounding the disco floor at the Philippine Plaza. Next morning we took a motorised canoe from the hotel out to the coral islands about a mile offshore. Completely unexpectedly a heavily armed Filipino army guy accompanied us in the boat "for our protection from MNLF terrorists". He made himself comfortable in the shade of some palms whilst Gillian and I hobbled over the really sharp coral sand. If there was one thing that would arouse the interest of the MNLF it was the presence of a RP army guy. It was, of course, the RP army they were fighting, not European tourists.. Hey ho, again could only happen in the Philippines, a crazy, cheerful, country, but nevertheless governed by a ruthless dictator, Ferdinand Marcos.

Next day we caught the early morning PAL DC9 flight back to Manila which was much more humid than Zamboanga. Here we transferred from the domestic to the international side of MIA for a Qantas flight to Perth, Western Australia. There we stayed a couple of nights with Dick and Mary. It was just over three years since I had last seen Dick at the chair smashing event at GMA's office in High Holborn. They had packed up after an eight year spell in the UK and settled into Perth where Dick was MD of Jacia Consulting Services, a sister company of Griffin Coal. They had a lovely house not far from the beach, although we seemed to spend more time in and around their pool clutching a tinny. The second night we all went out for a meal with Barrie and Hazel who had also moved from the UK to Oz. Barrie had been working with Jacia but shortly planned to join another engineering consultancy in Perth. We shot the breeze about Ken, Bougainville Copper and Amax Australia and they both wanted an update on GA and RTZ.

On the move again we flew from Perth to Melbourne with ANA and transferred to TAA for the short flight down to Hobart, Tasmania. Here we stayed for three nights with Rod and Kate in Howrah. Of course we caught up with Geoff and Marge and the next couple of days passed in a blur as the six of us enjoyed the ambience of Hobart. Then another TAA flight to Melbourne and a transfer to BA for a flight to Hong Kong via Sydney. However the BA plane had a "technical problem" and we made an unscheduled stop at Manila of all places, where we were stuck in the MIA transit lounge for a number of hours. Better late than never we eventually put down into Hong Kong's Kai Tak airport.

As a surprise for Gillian we were staying at the Peninsular Hotel in Kowloon so a superb grey-blue Rolls Royce limo picked us up from the airport for the short drive to the hotel. One was almost tempted to wave at the passing crowds so regal did the Rolls feel. Without doubt the Hong Kong Peninsular was one of the world's great hotels. The peace and quiet efficiency inside was in stark contrast to the organised (?) chaos of Kowloon. I did have a slight shock when the porter, who brought our bags up to the room, asked if he should unpack the bags and perhaps run a bath for sir or madam? I declined the offer and we did our own unpacking! No, neither of us took a bath (then) but we quickly went down to the grand foyer, found seats on the upper level and ordered two ice cold Singapore Slings whilst we watched the stream of people coming and going. After a couple of drinks we then went to explore the hotel. It was certainly grand but the over riding impression was the sheer efficiency of the army of staff who seemed to second guess what one might wish to know, order or desire.

We decided to go out for a gentle stroll to sample the flavour of Kowloon. We turned east, onto Salisbury Road, which seemed reasonably relaxed. However in a couple of hundred yards we turned north onto Nathan Road where mayhem broke out - busy, busy, busy. Fantastic array of sounds, sights and smells. We continued north past Tsim Sha Tsui Metro station to the large Kowloon Park on the western side of Nathan Road. This was definitely a green and quiet oasis. Masses of youngsters (and not so young people) flying beautiful, steerable kites. We cut through to Kowloon Park Road and continued our circuit back round to the Peninsular. Rounded off the day with more cocktails and a great meal in one of the hotel's restaurants.

The following morning we took the Star Ferry to Hong Kong Island. The ferry operation was very slick, amazingly quick turn around with masses of commuters to get on and off. We spent the rest of the day going around the main tourist sights such as Victoria Market, Happy Valley, Aberdeen and the outlying islands. In the evening we took the famous tram up the Peak to the restaurant with a panoramic view across the island, Victoria harbour, Kowloon and mainland China beyond. We settled for the return by Star Ferry again rather than the Metro.

Our final day at the Peninsular was quiet as we had both collected heavy colds. Early evening saw us take a taxi back to Kai Tak airport to check in for the late evening BA flight to the UK. Although long it was an uneventful flight and we arrived at Heathrow two days before Christmas 1982. It felt very cold and grey after the heat and colour of Australia and the Far East, but it was definitely home for me after six weeks of living in hotels. We had arranged for a taxi to pick us up from the airport not fancying the coach/train/taxi routine back to Gorsty with our heavy colds. The first job was to relight the Aga and get a good fire going in the Franklin Stove as the house felt distinctly cool inspite of the night storage heaters. Next I collected Anjon and Luke from their boarding kennels near Pembridge. They seemed fine, slight kennel coughs, but apparently Anjon had had a small safari when one of the adjacent farmer's bitches was on heat. Plus ca change. Although there was a light covering of snow it was less than the previous year.

24

In late February I received a call from James (ex-RTZC) now with a small RTZ subsidiary, Mineral Search Limited. He wanted to know if I could carry out a market survey for coal from the old Hunthouse colliery near Clows Top in Worcestershire. Unsurprisingly I said yes and welcomed job No. 011. This was an ideal job for me since the old mine site was only eighteen miles from Gorsty just south of the A456 road from Tenbury Wells to Kidderminster. Time to fire up my research assistant - Gillian! We spent an hour or so at the old Hunthouse colliery site, now occupied by the M & M timber company, merely to familarise ourselves with the location. I had to tell myself it was not a mine engineering job but a coal selling market job.

Then we made our way to Bewdley. The local museum provided plenty of background data on past mining activity on the small Mamble coalfield. We then went to the library and used the Yellow Pages to ascertain how many coal merchants there were in each of the towns within a twenty mile radius of Hunthouse. Thereafter we wandered around Bewdley trying to make an educated guess as to the percentage of homes which had smoke emanating from their chimneys! It was early March and still very cold. We then repaired to a High Street pub for a drink in front of a blazing coal fire. After that we visited the local coal merchant where Gillian obtained delivered prices whilst I attempted to determine the tonnage of coal stocks in the yard. That completed our rudimentary data gathering.

Back at Gorsty I got out the local Ordnance Survey maps in order to estimate road distances from Hunthouse to all major towns and villages within a twenty mile radius. I also noticed that the old colliery was 11.5 miles east of the Marches railway line (South Wales to Crewe) and nine miles west of the Worcester to Kidderminster line. Almost a perfect location close to the centre of a "no railways" district.

Of course most of the major towns such as Kidderminster, Worcester, Droitwich, Leominster and Ludlow obtained their coal supplies from their local railway goods yards. I went down to Leominster station to assess coal stocks at the local coal merchant and also obtain delivered coal prices. Meanwhile Gillian was using a local gazetteer to ascertain populations of the twelve towns we had identified. That completed our basic data collection from which we calculated some basic parameters. The average "town" population per coal merchant was circa 8000 or about 1850 households, 50% of which burnt solid fuel, ie 925 and of these we assumed 500 to burn coal. The others, particularly in village/country districts burn anthracite in the ubiquitous Aga or Rayburn stoves. An average coal burn of 25 pounds/day for 180 days/year indicated a consumption of about two tonnes/year or 1000 tonnes/year per coal merchant, equivalent to twenty tonnes/week. This checked with coal merchant's yard stocks of 40 to 80 tonnes household coal restocked fortnightly or monthly from railway deliveries.

After making allowances for smokeless zones in Worcester and Kidderminster we derived the following estimates for household coal demand:-

Local village merchants (8 miles)	120 tonnes/week
Bewdley/Kidderminster/Stourport (11 miles)	140 tonnes/week
Droitwich/Worcester (17 miles)	200 tonnes/week

A grand total of 460 tonnes/week. Mineral Search's proposed output of 150 tonnes/week from Hunthouse represented 33% of the estimated local consumption. A household coal market existed and could be penetrated by either selling to the existing coal merchants or by undercutting on price and selling direct to customers. Delivered prices ranged from £80.00/tonne in Leominster to £89.00/tonne in Worcester with COD discounts of zero in Leominster to £4.50 in Worcester.

However there appeared to be some technical drawbacks. The Hunthouse colliery had worked the Upper Coal Measures or Highley Beds of the Forest of Wyre coalfield and these had a high sulphur content. Incidentally the high sulphur content was much desired for hop drying in the nearby Frome Valley area, but was likely to be less welcome in the towns household open fires. Finally the literature stated that Hunthouse was the last colliery to close on the Mamble field in 1973 on account of water problems underground. On our visit to the Hunthouse site we had observed that the M & M timber company was obtaining water from a submersible pump hung in one of the old Hunthouse shafts. So our caveat to Mineral Search was beware sulphur in the coal and water underground!

A few days after completing the report for Mineral Search I received a call from Philippe of the World Bank requesting me to join his team on a visit to Zambia in a couple of week time to review ZCCM's progress since our February 1982 visit. This would be job No. 012. Thus by mid March I was once again on the BCal flight from Gatwick to Lusaka. As before we stayed initially at the Pamodzi Hotel for a couple of days whilst Philippe lead discussions with ZCCM senior management and government officials. Then it was a RoanAir flight to Kitwe for detailed data collection at each of the eight operating divisions.

My first task was to examine the insitu copper and cobalt reserves as at 31st March 1982 (the latest available figures) for each division. Next the Fully Developed reserves were compared with projected mine production estimates for FY 1983/84. The mines had become even more "squeezed" than they were last year strongly suggesting that production forecasts would not be met. The two biggest copper producers, Nchanga and Mufulira were both down to nine months cover only. In fact Mufulira's Fully Developed reserves were only 57% of those in 1982 whilst their production target had increased by 15% over 1982. A completely untenable scenario. In addition the contractor, Mowlem-Fry, sinking the new Mufulira sub-vertical shaft was only achieving 7.5 metres/week, less than 50% of that originally scheduled.

To compound the falling tonnage the grade factor (millhead %Cu to ore reserve %Cu) had also fallen, indicating more waste dilution. To combat these problems ZCCM had set up a Stoping Team. At Mufulira they planned to phase out sub-level caving in favour of sub-level blast-hole open stoping in an attempt to raise the rom grade by reducing waste dilution; a decision I fully endorsed. With input from the WB metallurgist, Dick, on metallurgical recoveries I recalculated a five year production forecast for ZCCM of 580,000 tonnes/year copper through until 1986/87 when there should be an increase on account of the Tailings Leach 3 project coming on stream.

With the other WB team members we then had to comment on ZCCM's rehabilitation projects for each operating division. For Nchanga this involved looking at the cost/benefit of, for example, the "South Face Trolley Assist" project. This was combined with the purchase of twelve new 170 tonne electric wheel Haulpak trucks and Bucyrus Erie 55R rotary blast-hole drills to cater for single pass drilling for the new increased bench height of 13.5 m. For Mufulira it was replacing the underground LHD fleet. For Nkana it was replacing front-end loaders and similar for the other divisions. Incidentally a new list of projects was introduced by ZCCM on the 22nd March which bore little resemblance to the original list submitted to the WB in January this year and had no technical or economic back-up. This caused considerable friction between Philippe and ZCCM's senior management. I was also asked to comment on a June 1982 proposal from Stamford Research Institute (SRI) to ZCCM for Research Assistance. It was almost completely irrelevant to ZCCM's crying need for technical assistance at the sharp end of production - underground. It was full of "management-speak", typical of a research organisation.

On account of the new list of rehabilitation projects Philippe basically cut short our discussions with ZCCM and told them we would have to "go away and study them" to see if they were suitable for WB financial support. He told them the WB thought the SRI Proposal did not address ZCCM's current requirements and that they, the WB, would draw up some Terms of Reference and ITB for a "Critical Review of ZCCM Mining Operations". Back at the Pamodzi Hotel in Lusaka Philippe vented his frustration at ZCCM continually changing their requirements in a haphazard way in a blatant attempt to "bounce" the WB into providing finance to keep ZCCM afloat. Before heading for the airport he asked me to provide technical/financial comments on ZCCM's new project list and prepare a draft Terms of Reference for a technical assistance package and courier both of these asap to Washington. So, courtesy of BCal back to Gatwick where the WB guys headed for Heathrow and then Washington whilst I returned to Gorsty.

It was now well into April and there was plenty to do in the Gorsty garden. I had to be strong willed and spend full days, including weekends, working on the ZCCM new project details and preparing the draft Terms of Reference. Philippe also sent me an IBRD staff pre-appraisal report and requested both comments and corrections, again to be returned asap. In the end I managed to send all three separate write-ups back to Philippe via DHL Couriers at the end of April. Nevertheless I was very pleased that after just two years as an independent consulting engineer I had managed, somehow, to obtain sufficient fee paying work to keep us financially afloat. Early days, of course, but in depressed economic times I had averaged about six jobs per year which involved 100 to 120 fee paying days. This was manageable and allowed sufficient slack time to undertake some promotional work. Gillian found the uncertainty of where the next job might come from disconcerting and if truth be told so did I!

With nothing in sight for May we really enjoyed the garden and began a major project to excavate the area off the SE end of the house. The presence of an ancient pollarded willow indicated that there must be a source of water nearby. So it proved to be. We dug down into builder's rubble which had been dumped into an old pond then covered by rough turf. We moved the rubble by wheelbarrow to form a large tump near the nascent vegetable patch. The pond excavation took weeks by hand, whereas I reckon a day with a JCB back-hoe would have fixed it! No problem, it kept us busy, was physically rewarding and the dogs joined in the digging - a full family activity.

Around the second week of June I received a call from Bobby, President of SAPI, last seen at La Guardia, New York after the Bunker Hill visit in November 1981. He wanted me to join Bernie, a consulting geologist, to carry out a review of mining operations at three separate mines in Bolivia, namely Milluni, Porco and Huari Huari. I was surprised to hear from Bobby. No matter it was job No. 013 and unlike the World Bank work it would be a real, hands-on job. Apart from anything I enjoyed the ambience in South America and a few weeks at altitude in Bolivia guaranteed I would lose at least half a stone in weight!

I flew BA to Miami, then Braniff to Lima and finally LAB to La Paz. COMSUR had booked me into the Hotel Sucre on the main drag, some 300 yards from their office. Fanny, COMSUR's faithful office secretary greeted me like a long lost friend and Stan, the office manager, explained that Goni was away, but still pulling the strings. Bobby up from his Lima haunt was temporarily in charge. Now, the unexpected call from Bobby was clear. I met Bernie, an American exploration geologist-cum-promoter, whose consultancy was based in Santiago de Chile. He was well known in South America and had been involved with some of the major Chilean copper discoveries. His forte was large open pits rather than small, narrow vein underground mines.

As usual I suffered from siroche on our first trip up to Milluni and consequently took things steadily. Mario was still Mine Manager and remembered me for my earlier visit. It helped break the ice and he teased me that my Spanish was no better, "we have verbs in Spanish" he said with a grin. As we were scheduled to be at Milluni for four days only Bernie and I quickly reviewed the ore reserve position. Over the past four years this had improved markedly to 739,007 tonnes at 1.06% Sn by December 1982. This had been achieved by development on the lower levels of the Rotschild vein enabling the attitude of the post mineral faults to be reliably determined. The Rotschild vein and extensions had an indicated ore expectancy of 8,500 t/vm. There were additional reserves in the Cuadro and Campana sections. I was confident that the Milluni mine could sustain a mining rate of 750 tonnes/day, a considerable increase from the current 400 tonnes/day production rate.

Ground conditions were generally weak and cut-and-fill stoping was the correct narrow vein stoping method. However I felt the existing back-stoping (up-hole drilling with stopers) should be changed to breast-stoping, utilising horizontal drilling with jackleg machines. This would definitely minimise shattering the hangingwall and thus reduce waste dilution. It would also produce a more level fill surface for subsequent stope scraping. There were no grizzlys on the stope chutes, but a 6in one on the main ore pass. This was much too small and required increasing to 9in (derived from 50% of the primary crusher's open side setting). It was much cheaper to crush rock than drill and blast it. I explained the rationale of these suggestions to Bernie and Mario and was greeted with much scepticism - the mining industry was incredibly conservative. I also suggested expanding the stope drilling layout to 0.5 square metres of face area per drill hole, whilst increasing the hole depth to 2.2 m. Then blasting with a half stick of 60% gelignite and loaded with ANFO at a density of 0.5 Kg/m to within 20 cm of the collar. All of these modifications were suggested to reduce over-blasting and costs whilst increasing productivity. I predicted a drilling factor of 1.41 tonnes/m drilled and a powder factor of 2.70 tonnes/Kg explosive.

We then looked at the -197 Level main haulage and determined that its capacity could be improved by adding two more mine cars to the haulage rake. The main ore hoisting took place on the vertical Cuadro Dorn shaft. Hoisting from a depth of 225m, indicated a maximum daily hoisting capacity of only 455 tonnes/day. However the tare weight of the existing skip was excessive for the 1.3 tonnes capacity. With a correctly designed skip its net capacity could increase to two tonnes and daily output to 700 tonnes. The Cuadro Dorn Ramke Blane winder had sufficient rope capacity to hoist eventually from a depth of 340m. Shaft deepening, by raising, would be required in three to four years. Power, compressed air and water supplies were adequate. The main constraint on stoping output was a shortage of fill material from the Sink & Float plant, the shortfall being met by surface glory-hole waste quarrying.

All of our recommendations were discussed in detail with Mario and Bobby who requested a detailed write-up and, in particular sketches of the proposed flat-back breast hole stoping method. Then, with Bernie and Mario, it was off to the Porco zinc mine. This involved a 350 mile drive south on sealed roads through Oruro to the old silver mining town of Potosi, home of the famous Cerro Rico, then a 45 mile drive SW on a tortuous dirt road to the small pueblo of Porco. The mine itself was about two miles further away on the flank of Apo Porco mountain at around 4000m elevation. The mine had been developed through a series of adits. Levels below the lowest haulage/drainage adit had been driven off an internal vertical shaft.

As usual we started off working through the ore reserve data. The December 1982 reserves indicated 583,966 tonnes at 13.5% Zn, after considering a 0.9m minimum mining width and a bulk density of 3.0. However we noted that the original block grades had arbitrarily been reduced by a "dilution factor" of 20%. We felt this was an unhelpful approach and that original block grades should be used. Then an actual Mine Call Factor (MCF) of reserve grade/mill head grade could be used as a basic management parameter. A major difficulty was the complete absence of vertical cross sections which were required for grade control and stope planning.

The total ore expectancy (OE) of the Porco mine was circa 11,000 t/vm, however much of this tonnage was contained in many small veins with OEs of only 300 t/vm. The mine used shrinkage stoping. This was undoubtedly the correct method on account of the steep dip, narrow average vein width and the strong, competent dacite wall rocks. Taking all these factors into account I felt that Porco's sustainable production potential was 600 to 700 tonnes/day.

The current level interval varied from 45 to 80 metres. As it was impossible to drive open raises much higher than 35m this ensured that most of the shrink stopes were operated "blind" with no raise connection to the level above. As a consequence there was no through stope ventilation and no alternative safety access to the upper level. New levels should be driven at a 30m vertical interval. All shrink stopes should work off a sub-level driven 5m above the rail height of the lower level thus ensuring that this level was protected by solid ground. A raise from the centre of this sub-level should be driven through to the upper level for each stope. A balanced stope break and draw operation would be as follows:-

Activity	Tonnes/month	%
Draw from breaking stopes:		
40%(32 x 364)	4660	45
Development ore	1660	16
Required from Shrinks (balance)	4080	39
Monthly Mill Feed Tonnage	10400	100

Development advances at Porco had been notoriously slow. These could be markedly improved by installing better track; installing 50mm diam compressed air lines for each heading; using compressed air venturi blowers for ventilation and using a three man crew with two jackleg machines for drilling. Main haulage on the San Cayetano level could sustain 500 tonnes/day. However there were concerns about the capacity of the Yaskawa hoist on the Central Shaft which had an output of only 168 tonnes/day from the - 105 level. The existing skip has been limited to a 1 tonne net load, although it should be closer to 1.75 tonnes capacity. The mechanical specifications of the hoist had to be checked.

Power supply came from the Porco Pelton Wheel (hydro), the COMSUR Arofilla hydro plant which fed power into the COMIBOL grid and the COMIBOL distribution system itself. There was adequate power for an expanded operation of 600 tonnes/day. There was also sufficient compressed air capacity but underground air reticulation was poor and needed up-grading. There were no problems with drainage, it was a dry mine. The limited ventilation was purely natural, there was no mechanical assistance. This would be greatly improved by ensuring each stope had a raise connection to the upper level. We had spent four hectic days at Porco and it was now on to the other zinc mine at Huari Huari.

From Porco we drove back to Potosi and continued east and then north-east on the road to Sucre, the old capital. The 500 tonnes/day zinc concentrator was situated at Don Diego close to the road and railway. This plant was constructed by the American company New Jersey Zinc and had been operated by Caballo Blanco Ltda until COMSUR assumed ownership of the operation a few years ago. The Huari Huari mine was situated a couple of miles further up the side of the valley. It was an adit mine with no internal workings below the lowest adit level. Total accessible reserves were quoted as 122,835 tonnes at 9.26% Zn and 0.43% Sn. It was essentially a remnant vein mining operation in quite difficult ground conditions comprising weak greywackes and altered shales. The main Anton Bravo vein was near vertical with an average width of 1.2m and an indicated ore expectancy of 2880 t/vm implying a potential mining rate of 300 tonnes/day. However this would have applied to the original Anton Bravo vein before subsequent mining by Caballo Blanco. COMSUR was now faced with mining old remnants at both the north and south ends of the main vein. Under these conditions a "clean up" mining rate of about 160 tonnes/day only would be achievable.

Unfortunately the previous operator had attempted to use shrinkage stoping which was quite the wrong method for the weak ground conditions. This method should be phased out and replaced by overhand, flat-back cut-and-fill stoping as soon as practical. The wisdom of attempting to mine the old fill (taqueos) was questioned as apart from the extensive hangingwall sloughing causing dilution, there was a major safety issue. It was also noted that the eucalyptus drive timbers were of very poor quality appearing to dry rot in less than six months. Natural ventilation in the mine was quite good as all stopes had through raise connections to their upper level. There were no problems with power or compressed air supply, apart from poor reticulation underground. The major difficulty was remnant mining in weak ground. There was no way the Huari Huari mine alone could fill the 500 tonnes/day concentrator at Don Diego. Exploration of the surrounding area should be pursued with vigour in an attempt to locate similar structures to the Anton Bravo vein. On reflection it was not, perhaps, a suitable mine for COMSUR as it had a very limited life (4 years max) with almost zero potential and a high production cost.

After three days at the mine we drove back to La Paz. It was good to get back to the Hotel Sucre and have a good shower to wash off all the grime and dust from the altiplano. We had a couple of days in COMSUR's office with Bobby discussing our major findings at each of the three mines. Basically, bullish about Milluni and Porco and definitely bearish about Huari Huari. Bobby asked me to complete brief engineering reports on each of the mines. I said I planned to complete these as soon as I got back to the UK and certainly no later than mid July and that was that. Mario went back to the day job at Milluni whilst Bernie and I headed for El Alto airport for the LAB flight to Lima. Here Bernie headed south to Santiago de Chile and I caught the Braniff flight to Miami where I transferred to a BA flight for Heathrow. As usual after a Bolivian trip I had lost more than half a stone in weight and slept like a log for hours, super oxygenated in the Herefordshire countryside.

Over the next couple of weeks I completed my engineering calculations for both the Milluni and Porco mines. There was no such work required for Huari Huari. It was then a case of writing up the separate reports. Gillian was very good at helping with both the typing and subsequent proof reading. In the middle of this I received a call from Keith at Riofinex, London asking if I could go to my favourite place, Saudi Arabia (!), next week for an initial evaluation of the Turayf Phosphate project. I said yes to job No. 014.

25

On Thursday of that week we noticed an ad in the local paper, the Hereford Times, showing a picture of a young lad with a bicycle, with the caption "can you give this lad a home", or words to that effect. It was all about fostering. We talked it over, felt we could now survive on my independent earnings, so why not? Gillian phoned the Worcester County Council (WCC) number and so set in train a tortuous evaluation/selection process to become prospective foster parents that was to take the best part of eighteen months. Neither of us appreciated just how involved and intrusive this selection process would be.

Earlier that year we had experienced problems with the VW Golf's clutch, to the extent that the cable mechanism had broken yet again. We had both found the car somewhat cramped and lacking in oomph on the long journey to Cornwall. I traded it in at Steels in Hereford for a very smooth Honda 1.6 Accord hatchback complete with tow bar. It was quite a bit more lively and had a superb gear change, which was a pleasant change from the VW.

Thus Gillian could enjoy the drive to (and from) Worcester station for my regular drop-off for the Cotswold Line train to Reading and the coach to Heathrow. Then it was my favourite airline Saudia (joke) to Jeddah. At least this time Customs didn't empty my suitcase contents on the floor but neither were they wreathed in welcoming smiles. Malcolm was at the airport exit to meet me and drove me straight out to the Riofinex compound where he had arranged single room accommodation. In reality it was preferable to a downtown Jeddah hotel since illicit hooch was available within the bounds of the compound. Anyway I gathered I was flying straight up to Turayf early next morning with Gordon, the Project manager of the phosphate exploration programme.

The dreaded Short Skyvan was waiting at Jeddah airport to fly us the 730 miles to Turayf in the extreme north of Saudi Arabia only twenty miles south of the Jordan border. As before the extremely uncomfortable and noisy three hour flight left me completely brain dead on arrival at Turayf. However the jeep drive out to the Riofinex camp near Um Wu'al made me realise I was still alive. Gordon then gave me a run-down on their programme. The exploration area was absolutely vast, about 95,000 square Km. The objective of their work was to obtain a general geological picture of the area with specific reference to phosphate rocks. They had first established a 20km survey grid so that subsequent drill crews could establish their location in the field. The region was flat with very little outcrop, especially in the Al Hamid area. They decided the only way to obtain stratigraphical information was by vertical drilling on a wide spaced grid. A trial of both percussion and rotary (core) drilling was undertaken and the former chosen, utilising DTH machines. The initial exploratory drilling was done on a 5Km grid with infill holes at the centre, which meant that holes were approximately 3.5km apart. This implied an area of influence of about 12.5 square Km/hole - definitely exploratory!

My Terms of Reference were to review present exploration/evaluation procedures and prepare preliminary capital and operating cost estimates for a 3.5 million tonnes/year phosphate rock mine. Finally to undertake a reverse economics exercise to estimate the revenue per tonne of phosphate rock to give a specified gross rate of return on total project expenditure. The first bit was relatively easy. Examination of the sample preparation plant showed that the first weight reduction was carried out at much too coarse a size (25mm) rather than 2 to 3mm to ensure sample size and grade repeatability. Numerous correlation tests were also required of grade against phosphate rock type (friable, siliceous or calcareous) against hole volume to determine % recovery and of prime importance for mine planning studies tonnage-grade curves, isopachs and isograde plans.

Some basic mine design data had been obtained such as depth of overburden; sub-surface contours of top and bottom of phosphate rock horizon; bulk density values and volumetric stripping ratios. A short trench had been dug by an 807 JCB and from this I could see that it was unable to dig through the phosphate rock bed. We developed the following mining parameters: average grade 21%; average thickness of phosphate bed 2.5 m; average overburden thickness 13.5 m; average stripping ratio 5.4:1; in situ bulk density 2.0; tonnage 5.0 million/square Km. The overburden could be removed by a combination of heavy dozer and ripper plus some light drilling and blasting followed by excavation with an electric walking dragline. Mining of the phosphate rock itself would be by FELs or hydraulic excavators loading dump trucks. Allowance for moisture, dusting and selective mining losses indicated a phosphate rock mining requirement of

3.85 million tonnes/year and 10.4 million m³/year of overburden. From these quantities I estimated a capital cost of US$ 70 million for stripping and mining equipment and an operating cost of US$ 6.5/tonne of phosphate rock at the 3.5 million tonnes/year production rate.

A crushing/screening plant was needed to produce a 200mm product ahead of a stockpile for blending and subsequent load-out to standard gauge railway wagons. Power would have to come from an on-site diesel plant to meet the average demand of 11MW with a peak of over 15MW. Water would come from deep (1500m) wells into the Saq sandstone horizon which were believed to be free flowing at this location. These minesite infrastructure and service costs were estimated to be another US$ 70 million capital and US$ 3.0/tonne operating (at 3.5 million tonnes/year).

The isolated location and the need for large quantities of water for beneficiation and a deep water port to export the product inexorably led to Al Jubail on the Gulf. An earlier Granges Mining company study had suggested such a railway, 1180km in length alongside the TAPline. Railway construction costs were estimated at US$ 0.75 million/km and operating costs as US 0.72 cents/tonne-Km, or US$ 8.5/t phosphate rock transported. The beneficiation plant at Al Jubail would use a calcination and slaking process to treat the calcareous phosphate rock. This would cost US$ 118 million with an operating cost of US$ 11/tonne treated (3.5 million tonnes/year at 21% grade = 46% BPL). Overall plant recovery would be 77% when producing 1.7 million tonnes/year of phosphate rock product at a grade of 72.5% BPL. This grade would be required to compete on the world market.

As expected from my previous visit to Saudi the Turayf's project capital cost was dominated by the cost of a lengthy standard gauge railway to get the mined product to a deepwater port. The railway element, construction, locomotives and rolling stock comprised 58% of a total project capital cost of US$ 1525 million and an operating cost of US$ 29.0 tonne/mined, hauled and treated or US$ 59.7/tonne product at Al Jubail. The reverse economics exercise based on a 15% DCF return on total capital required a price of US$ 286/tonne phosphate rock, CIF Al Jubail. This was an extremely high price and totally uncompetitive. Removing the construction cost of the railway on the assumption that this might be built by the state, the price would reduce to US$ 118/tonne CIF Al Jubail, which was still very uncompetitive, since top grade Moroccan phosphate rock landed at Al Jubail costs just US$

50/tonne. Everyone on site was aware of the enormous cost of building a railway, but were taken aback at how uncompetitive the project was even without the railway cost. In a nutshell it all came down to the low insitu grade of the Turayf deposit.

Gordon and I flew back to Jeddah and then to the Riofinex compound to discuss my proposed alterations to the sample preparation plant with Malcolm and his team. We got involved in basic sampling theory, size and grade-distribution and eventually agreed on the sampling procedures developed by Pierre Gy. Malcolm asked me to go over all my capital and operating cost estimates to ensure that I had not made any gross mistakes. He felt that the disastrous reverse economic phosphate rock prices at Al Jubail would not go down well with Riofinex management in London (surprise, surprise). After three days of working through all the basic engineering estimates Malcolm accepted that, so far, they, Riofinex, had not identified a viable phosphate rock resource in the Turayf area. We agreed that the next phase of their exploration programme should be step-out drilling from their highest grade hole in an attempt to locate an area with a markedly higher insitu grade. Then it was the night Saudia flight to Heathrow.

Whilst I had been away in Saudi Gillian had received a reply from WCC inviting us to an open-day forum on fostering at the County Hall on Spetchley Road on the eastern side of the city. The Forum was later next week, which gave me time to tart up and type my Turayf report. I despatched it to Keith who called back two days later and asked me to come up to Riofinex's London office for a meeting with Barry. I drove to Worcester and caught the early Cotswold Line train to Paddington. As well as Keith and Barry, Gordon was present, but unfortunately not Malcolm. It turned into quite a grilling for me. Keith and in particular Barry were most unhappy with the results of the reverse economics exercise. They felt that the huge estimated price/value of Turayf phosphate rock at Al Jubail would be entirely unacceptable to the Saudis and could very well jeopardise Riofinex's Saudi exploration contract with the DMMR. They wanted me to change the numbers!

Unsurprisingly I said no and that I was confident my estimates were in the plus/minus 20% range. I also pointed out that the basis of the huge railway costs were derived from a very recent Granges study and it was the railway cost that dominated the project. I again reiterated that even without the Turayf project having to carry the huge railway costs beneficiated Turayf phosphate rock was just not competitive with imported high grade Moroccan rock. Why? The Turayf deposit as currently identified was too low grade. My suggestion was to use this critical aspect as a reason for the DMMR to continue the Riofinex contract, whilst they, Riofinex, attempted to locate higher grade areas within the existing wide spaced exploration holes.

Barry agreed that this was a reasonable scenario, but said my report would have to be rewritten in a "more delicate fashion to lessen the disastrous economics". Of course I said that that was their prerogative, I was, after all, only a subcontractor, but I stood by my estimates. It was also agreed that the poor economics could be put to good use in planting the idea that the State should take over the huge cost of building a TAPline railway from the Jordan border to Al Jubail. Notwithstanding all this I had the feeling that I was not flavour of the month.

On Thursday Gillian and I headed for WCC's County Hall for the Fostering open-day forum. There were around 70 of us, mostly couples, but also some singles. The Social Services (SS) staff made a general presentation followed by a film. They pointed out that the vetting process for potential foster parents was both involved and intrusive. The SS would need to know all about our backgrounds, jobs, housing, habits, health, finances etc. If we were not prepared for this we should depart now. After a break for lunch at a nearby pub, it was good to chat with other potential fosterers and find out what their worries were. In the afternoon the SS identified some WCC run care homes, which they felt it would be helpful to visit to learn first hand of fostering difficulties. They also noted that there was always a bigger demand to foster babies than hard to place children (as the SS called them - not great marketing!), six to sixteen years old. For us that was good news as we did not wish to foster a baby. Back at Gorsty, feeling a little daunted, we decided we definitely wanted to visit a WCC run care home and learn first hand all about fostering problems.

However that afternoon I had a call from Peter of Davy McKee asking if I could come up to their offices in Stockton-on-Tees to help them with the mining section of a bid they were preparing for a feasibility study of a Moroccan phosphate rock mining project. Hard to believe phosphate rock again. Obviously this was flavour of the month unlike me! Peter thought two days maximum input from me. I said yes to job No. 015 and Peter said he would book me hotel accommodation for next Sunday and Monday night.

So around midday Sunday I set off for the 4.5 hour drive to Stockton. It was the first long drive I had had in the Honda Accord and I really enjoyed it. So much more comfortable than the VW Golf with a lot more zip. Stockton looked pretty depressed but the hotel staff were very friendly and my room adequate. Monday morning I fronted up at Davy's offices which were modern and functional.

I knew a number of the Davy "Moroccan team" guys from my visit to China with them back in the late seventies. Martyn and I recalled our appalling bridge playing on the overnight train from Peking. Like me he said he had given up playing bridge after our mauling by the Chinese. Following my very recent phosphate rock experience at Turayf in Saudi it was a doddle coming up with a proposed mining method after a swift appraisal of the Moroccan deposit features. I had, of course, brought my Turayf working notes with me and so was very quickly able to come up with relevant budget estimates and time schedules. Just after lunch on Tuesday I was done and heading back to Gorsty.

During the last week of August we visited the WCC care home in nearby Bromyard. The Manager of the home was absolutely brilliant in describing all the wrinkles he and his staff experienced in looking after fifteen "hard to place" kids who were just waiting for a foster home. Gillian and I had mutually agreed that, if feasible, we would prefer to foster a boy rather than a girl. The Manager had no fixed take on that other than saying it was entirely up to us. What he did say though was try to find a boy no older than eight or nine, since after ten or so they had become so set in their own ways it was that much harder to get them to blend in with ones own life style/pattern, hence "hard to place". He said it was difficult to generalise and in the end everything came down to "chemistry". He also said that the SS would want to know everything about you both. Make sure they, the SS, tell you everything about the boy and his home background. Finally he said if you've got this far thinking about it - go for it.

We also visited a married couple in Ledbury who were fostering a young lad. Again they confirmed so many of the points made by the Bromyard care home Manager, but added that they had both found it very disruptive for the first few months having another person in the house continually demanding attention. They also made the point that you must start the way you meant to carry on. Set out limits or boundaries as to what was or was not acceptable. Overall they felt it had been very rewarding but, as expected, tended to take over ones life unless one rigorously continued with ones own hobbies/interests. Nothing daunted Gillian phoned the WCC SS back and said we would like to be considered as potential foster parents. The SS said they would contact us soon to start our personal assessment for suitability.

In early September I had a call from Richard (ex Mineral Search) now with Castle Mines Ltd (CML) who asked me to carry out a market survey for coal from their Acres Nook drift mine situated at Ravenscliffe just north of the Stoke-on-Trent/Newcastle conurbation. My remit from CML was to consider a production of 500 tonnes/week comprising 175 tonnes of house coal and 325 tonnes of industrial coal. Welcome to job No. 016. This was obviously another job suitable for my trusty research assistant - Gillian. We popped the dogs into their spacious barn-kennels at Bearwood, near Pembridge and set off for the Potteries, location of our honeymoon 25 years ago!

We booked into a commercial hotel in Hanley to be within walking distance of the public library. First I went with Gillian to the reference section of the Hanley library and located the Coal Mines Directory and asked her to note down the NCB and private colliery names together with their coal output in 1982. I had already located an Ordnance Survey map of the area and noted all major towns within a twenty mile radius of Ravenscliffe and identified and named 16. I also asked Gillian to note down the population of these towns from the last census. With this I hopped into the car and drove to Acres Nook for a meeting with Roy, the mine owner and Stan a director of CML and local coal industry insider.

Firstly I explained our approach to establishing a relationship between population and the number of coal merchants to estimate household coal consumption. Stan liked the idea but warned me to reduce these estimates on account of extensive smokeless zones in both Stoke and Newcastle as well as the free coal delivered to NCB workers. That was good information as Gillian would be able to find NCB employment numbers from the library. I said we could obtain actual coal output figures in the North Staffs coalfield (NCB and private mines), again from the library, but our biggest difficulty was trying to estimate industrial coal consumption from firms such as the CEGB, Twyfords, Michelin & Blue Circle cement. I asked Stan if, through his industry contacts with coal factors/wholesalers etc he could have a punt at this.

Roy told me that Acres Nook coal had a high sulphur content of 3.5%, but a low ash content of 7.5%. The average calorific value was good at over 12,500 BTU/tonne. We drove down to Kidsgrove station, a mere 1.2 miles from the mine, to look at the local coal merchant W J Smithson. We estimated his yard contained about 70 tonnes of coal. Roy also commented that the Harecastle Tunnel of the Trent & Mersey canal was only 52m below the mine portal and 200m further to the east. After a beer in the local pub I said we (my assistant and I) would work on the figures we obtained from the library and come back tomorrow afternoon for a final discussion on supply/demand and price. With that I headed back to Hanley library.

Gillian had done a fantastic job in obtaining, town populations, coal merchants, NCB workforce, NCB and private mines coal production. With this basic data we set to work extracting some numbers. Total population within a twenty mile radius was 670,000. The NCB operated five deep mines, Wolstanton, Silverdale, Holditch, Hem Heath and Florence, where I had worked with Cementation in the late fifties.

Sector	Output (1000 t/yr)	House Coal	Industrial
NCB Deep Mines	3800	266	3534
NCB Opencast	250	25	225
Private Mines	75	26	49
Total	4125	317	3808

After making an allowance for the rural population of south Cheshire the average population per coal merchant was estimated to be 5500. The library provided details of smokeless zones and from this we estimated that 200,000 people would not be burning house coal. Average solid fuel sales per coal merchant were estimated to be 40 tonnes/week of which 27 tonnes/week would be house coal. Thus the house coal demand:-

(670000 - 200000)/ 5500 x 27 or approximately 2300 tonnes/week

The NCB employed 6800 men in the north Staffordshire area and we assumed 50% of these men lived in unrestricted areas and received free coal then,

3400 households x 0.05 tonnes/week or 170 tonnes/week

Thus an estimated 106,000 tonnes/year of free market demand after allowing for NCB free deliveries. However this was expected to drop drastically as both Stoke and Newcastle planned to introduce complete smoke control. Although the proposed Acres Nook household coal output of 175 tonnes/week represented only 8.5% of this market the total demand of about 106,000 tonnes/year was dwarfed by the supply of 317,000 tonnes/year. In fact the Stoke/Newcastle area was an "exporter" to elsewhere in the UK. Thus the outlook for marketing Acres Nook household coal must be bleak and could only be achieved by undercutting existing suppliers on price. The position with industrial coal was believed to be similar with a surplus of supply over demand, approximately 3.8 million tonnes/year supply against 2.5 million tonnes/year demand.

Telephone enquires were made of coal merchants throughout the region from Congelton in the north, Leek in the east, Nantwich in the west and Stoke/Newcastle in the south. The quotations were remarkably consistent, £77/tonne, indicating a virtual retail cartel. I went back to discuss our findings with Roy and Stan, who were unsurprised by the conclusion. On both household and industrial coal the local market was heavily over supplied. They agreed the only possibility was to tie up with W J Smithson at Kidsgrove station and undercut the market by £10 to £15/tonne. Stan said he would recommend that CML should open talks with Smithson. That wrapped up my work at the mine. I drove back to Hanley, collected Gillian and we said goodbye to a much cleaner Potteries than we had known in the fifties.

Back at Gorsty it took me a day and half to type up the Acres Nook report, which worked out well as a couple of days later we had a telephone call from WCC SS asking if they could visit to start their assessment of us as potential foster parents. Unsurprisingly this sparked a blitzkrieg on house cleaning and tidying up the garden. Well it was as good a stimulant as any since late September was the time for final grass and hedge cutting.

Two people from Malvern Hills (MH) SS arrived, an administrator and a younger field worker called Jane from near Bromyard. Jane was to be our main contact with MH SS over the next year and half. Basically they (the SS, perhaps well abbreviated?) wanted to know everything about us both. Our own life history and full details of both our parents history or at least what we could remember. Then it was on to our married life and where and what we had done. The crunch stuff seemed to revolve around "why now for fostering"? I'm not too sure they fully accepted that we had now, finally, put down roots and stopped travelling. Why no children of our own? Anyway I tried to convince them that my independent consulting business of nearly three years was going OK, we felt settled and now, at age 47 felt the time was right. Well that was our selling bit. The SS also required both of us to have a full health check with our local doctor. They looked around the house and wanted to know where a foster child would sleep. I also explained that we planned to convert our downstairs junk/storage room into a playroom. They seemed pleased that we had dogs and bicycles and went swimming at the Leominster pool. After the SS had gone we looked at each other and agreed we really did need to clear out the junk room and develop a playroom, whatever that meant.

There was an old Rayburn in the junk room and when we inspected it we found that the body was cracked right through so that was the end of the Rayburn. It was too heavy to move en masse so I swung into action with a sledge hammer and slowly produced chunks of cast iron of a size that we could manhandle. After that we decided that a wood or solid fuel type stove was what our nascent play room needed. We also had a blitzkrieg on stripping off old paint and plaster ahead of polyfilling the walls and removing a tacky green linoleum off the floor. However help was at hand for me in the shape of a telephone call from Paul.

26

Paul, from Mackay & Schnellmann (M&S) in London wanted to know if I fancied a spell in Portugal. I metaphorically bit his hand off, especially when he asked if I could manage the beginning of October. Job No. 017 sounded very interesting, particularly so since I had never been to Portugal. Thus a few days later I took the train to London to visit M&S's offices in High Holborn. Here Paul explained that their remit was to review the French company, SOMINCOR's preliminary study of the Neves Corvo copper deposit near Castro Verde in south-central Portugal. Paul said M&S's client was a bank who were considering providing funds for the development of this project so the bank was particularly interested in the likelihood of the mine reaching its stated output (copper concentrate) within the proposed timetable at the indicated costs, capital and operating. Gavin, an M&S geologist, would concentrate on the mineable ore reserves whilst I was to look at all the mining plans and mining infrastructure and Keith, a subcontract metallurgist, would comment on the processing plant flowsheet design, construction and operating costs.

We left that same evening flying TAP from Heathrow to Lisbon. From the airport we took a taxi to an hotel in the Palma de Baixo area of NW Lisbon. It was about a 150m walk to the Jardim Zoologico Metro station. From there it was a six station Metro ride to Rossio in the centre of downtown Lisbon, then a short walk to the SOMINCOR offices. They had provided us with an office, several copies of their report and a complete set of geological plans and assay data. It soon became apparent why Paul was M&S team leader - he spoke very good, if accented, French, which neither Keith, Gavin nor I did. On the first day I worked with Gavin getting a feel for the geology and in particular the disposition of the ore zone and the nature of the hangingwall and footwall rocks.

The initial mining operations were planned for the copper rich portion of the Corvo deposit. SOMINCOR estimated these to be 12.11 million tonnes at 8.68% Cu. These reserves had considered a minimum mining width of 2 metres and an insitu bulk density of 4.5. The top of these reserves were 300m below surface and the bottom of the reserves 650m below surface. The dip ranged from 10 to 30 degrees, averaging 24 and the true thickness from 2 to 42 metres. The average ore expectancy was 27,000 t/vm. Deep diamond drilling had indicated additional potential both laterally and down-dip. Greywacke and schists formed the hangingwall and acid tuffs the footwall.

The combination of very high insitu copper grades and dubious ground conditions indicated that a flexible high recovery mining method would be required and I fully endorsed SOMINCOR's selection of transverse cut-and-fill as appropriate. Both Gavin and I said we would like to look at some retained split DD core at the mine site to confirm ore and host rock conditions. Preliminary geotechnical work indicated that 40m wide rib pillars oriented down-dip would separate 100m wide stoping panels on strike. Thus a mining ore recovery of 71% was implied which seemed reasonable. However SOMINCOR had indicated 25% waste dilution which seemed excessive. I suggested a more reasonable waste dilution figure would be 10%, derived from 1m overbreak on the footwall and 1.5m on the hangingwall, which, assuming zero grade for the waste dilution gave a grade factor of 91% compared to only 80% in the SOMINCOR plan. Obviously this higher grade factor would increase the projected mill head grades.

The SOMINCOR plan was based on a mining rate of 4,000 tonnes/day, or 15% of the ore expectancy. This I felt was right on the upper limit representing an average deepening rate of 37m/year - very difficult to sustain. The present shape, form and size of the reserve did not justify nor would they sustain this rate of production. A more realistic production rate would be 3,000 tonnes/day. The transverse cut-and-fill stoping method was conceptual at this stage since no underground development had taken place in the ore zone nor within the immediate hangingwall or footwall rocks, yet another reason to physically examine some split core from the ore zone and adjacent host rocks. This essential underground development would also provide ore material for bulk sampling and a test bed for basic geotechnical work. The mining plan envisaged a full trackless operation with electro-hydraulic drilling and diesel LHD units. The stoped ore would pass to an underground crusher for hoisting in a footwall vertical shaft.

This vertical shaft was well sited for both mining the Corvo ore body and exploring the nearby Neves, Zambujal and Graca mineralised zones.. The shaft diameter of 5m only was apparently sized solely by the criteria to hoist three million/tonnes year and the spatial requirements of a single large skip and counterweight. All men and materials would be handled by a 1 in 5.5 ramp-decline, also located in the footwall. This seemed an expensive solution to developing an orebody which was 300m below surface. A single vertical shaft of about 7.3m diam could handle all requirements, ore, men and materials. The development equipment was larger than one would expect for a 4,000 tonnes/day mine. Much of the main mine infrastructure was considerably oversized in relation to the known ore reserves. However in fairness to SOMINCOR this was determined by the Portuguese government's insistence that the mine's facilities be capable of handling three million tonnes/year. Of course the current reserves warranted nowhere near this annual output.

Their plan utilised two complete crushing/loading stations off the shaft at the -300m and -450m levels, hence the need for a single large skip and counterweight when employing a friction winder. Boliden, the Swedish engineering firm, had suggested using an inclined conveyor for ore handling below -300m level and this had considerable merit. The SOMINCOR plan incorporated an immense 3500 kW low voltage hoist pulling a large single 30-tonne skip. For a more realistic output of 825,000 tonnes/year (3,300 tonnes/day for 250days/year basis) from the -357m loading station a 2500 kW twin motor drive friction winder fitted initially with one 1250 kW motor pulling balanced six tonne capacity skips would be adequate, as well as considerably cheaper. However to meet the government requirements the hoist mechanicals, rope grooving etc would be designed to handle twelve tonne capacity skips with the addition of the second 1250 kW motor.

The whole question of underground ore handling, crushing and hoisting needed a complete rethink. The current proposals were unsuitable, heavily over designed and expensive in both capital and operating costs. This aspect of the project (underground ore handling, crushing and hoisting) caused heated discussion between the SOMINCOR engineers and me with Paul doing stalwart service as interpreter. It ended as a "no score draw", but they agreed to reconsider the Boliden conveyor suggestion, which naturally lead on to only one loading station which in turn lead to considering balanced skip hoisting. Later we came back to the main shaft diameter which I felt was undersized to provide sufficient ventilation capacity for the diesel LHDs. The internationally accepted figure for estimating ventilation requirements for underground mines using diesel equipment was 0.05m^3/s/HP for all operating machines. The use of the small 5m diameter shaft ensured high air velocities at very high water gauge, 250mm rising to 400mm, which would absorb a lot of power.

At the time of our visit both the ramp-decline and main shaft sinking were stopped and these delays would obviously affect the overall project development schedule. This was obviously a negative factor for M&S's banking client as was our estimate of a reduced, sustainable mining output, albeit at a likely higher mill head grade. A major positive aspect was our belief that total capital would be about US$75 million rather than the US$92 million estimated by SOMINCOR. Our reduction was brought about by replacing much grossly oversized items of fixed plant and a less conservative approach to equipment utilisation and availabilities.

On one day we made the 120 mile road trip down to the mine site near Castro Verde. That first involved crossing the Tagus river by the magnificent 25th April suspension bridge from Lisbon to Almada on the southern bank before heading SE to Setubal and Ferreia. We were unable to go down the shaft (sinking stopped, why?) but walked down the steep ramp-decline which at least exposed the footwall acid tuffs, although not close to the orebody. For me the boxes of split half DD cores were essential in providing a "feel" for ground conditions within and adjacent to the orebody. These confirmed that the hangingwall greywacke and shales would be weak; the ore zone reasonable and the footwall tuffs strong. Sigh of relief - transverse cut-and-fill was definitely the correct stoping method! You have to see and feel the rocks to appreciate mining conditions. Better still would have been an examination of underground development, but unfortunately this was not yet available.

Over a couple of Sundays we had a chance to have a look around Lisbon. It had a distinctly Victorian aura to it after the hustle and bustle of Madrid and no bad thing for all that. The Rossio area seemed to be the heart of the city but the area immediately south-east towards the river had a different feel having been completely rebuilt after the huge earthquake in 1755. The city, like Rome was built on seven hills. We had time to examine two. The Barrio Alto area with its famous fado bars and for me much more interesting the impressive Castelo Sao Jorge. From the ramparts there were great views across the city and the river Tagus. The castle, which pre-dated the 18th Century earthquake, suffered only minor damage, which spoke volumes for the castle's strength. Finally the cool relaxing Botanical Gardens, the Estufa Fria, situated under glass at the NW end of the central Eduardo VII park. Then it was a TAP flight back to Heathrow. At the airport I promised Paul that I would check and rework all my shaft and winder calculations and complete a write-up by the first week in November.

Gillian had done a grand job in completing the stripping out of the nascent playroom. We fairly rapidly finished the painting and set out to look for a suitable wood/multi-fuel stove, eventually locating one at Ironworks in Ludlow. They duly installed the stove and fitted a ceramic flue liner surrounded by a coarse pumice like filler in the surrounding annulus. Proof of the pudding was it worked a treat and transformed this previously neglected room. Our next project was to build a block wall across the end of the terrace to corral the ash and oak logs.

In late November Gillian and I went to another fostering session at WCC County Hall in Worcester. In effect this turned out to be more of the same from the SS to fewer of us potential fosterers, as it appeared that a number, maybe 15% or so, of the original attendees had had second thoughts. Again I found that the most useful time was chatting with other (hopeful?) fosterers. So much of the SS guff seemed self evident, but perhaps my over confidence was derived from ignorance of just how difficult "hard to place" children might prove to be. No time to ponder on this for too long as in early December a call came from Richard, an economist with Riofinex, who asked me to come up to London to discuss their mining project in Yemen - job No. 018.

In fact as part of my Riofinex two year retainer the Yemen job was simply a single days work reviewing a preliminary mining report on a small gold prospect. Basically this involved reading a brief geological report to understand the nature of the mineralisation and adjacent wall rocks. Then ascertain the disposition of the ore zone and calculate its all important ore expectancy, t/vm to determine a feasible rate of mining.

As expected the report's estimate was too high. The steep dip, narrow vein width and strong wall rocks confirmed that the selected stoping method, shrinkage, was correct. The deposit was near surface and mine access would obviously be via a footwall ramp-decline. Shrinkage stoping details were bog standard for this type of small deposit and my only serious reservation was that the proposed mining rate was too optimistic and unsustainable after a couple of years. Richard seemed happy with my overall conclusion, so I headed back to rural Herefordshire, glad to leave the London crowds behind.

Just into the new year and Mike from RTZ Technical Services (RTZTS) in Bristol called asking me to come down to Castlemeads to discuss assisting them with a review of Ghana State Gold Mines (SGMC) operations at their Prestea and Tarkwa mines. I drove down the next day using the M5 and the M32 spur to Bond Street and Temple Way turning in to Castlemeads. It was a curious feeling going in to RTZTS's offices as, in effect, they were the reincarnation of RTZC, after an agreed two year "no competition" agreement, following the formation of the now defunct GMA. As they say, what goes around comes around. I knew many of the old RTZC metallurgical staff and even some geologists and mining engineers who had completed the full circuit from RTZC to GMA/GHA and back to RTZTS.

It was slightly embarrassing meeting Mike again whom I had last seen in Blantyre, Malawi when I was recruiting for RTZC six or seven years ago. After I had a quick run around saying "hi" to old acquaintances Mike explained their scope of work for SGMC. Basically it was a rehabilitation project to boost combined mine production from Prestea and Tarkwa from the current 215,000 tonnes/year to 720,000 tonnes/year over a four year period. Mike then said that one of the major mining constraints were problems with the main production shafts, which explained my involvement. He gave me a SGMC document which set out their expansion plans, asked me to get familiar with the operation and we agreed a start date. We agreed my daily fee rate and I duly signed the RTZTS contract and that signified job No. 019.

The BCal plane from Gatwick to Accra took just over six hours for the plus 3000 mile flight. No problems with jet-lag though as the flight virtually followed the Greenwich meridian all the way. Accra airport was busy but both Immigration and Customs worked smoothly in marked contrast to the lengthy delays at Lusaka. Mike team leader, John geologist, Dave metallurgist, Ron costs/finance and I checked into a downtown hotel. This also worked well and my initial impressions of West Africa were favourable. Certainly it was very warm and humid, but no more so than Manila. Mike arranged a meeting with SGMC senior management in Accra and our progamme was duly arranged starting with the Prestea operation.

The following morning two SGMC twin cab utes picked us up from the hotel for the 130 mile drive due west. Not long out of the outskirts of Accra we saw numerous locals at the roadside holding up enormous dead bush rats for sale. We asked the driver to stop to take a closer look at them. They were huge, maybe 12 to 15in from nose to tail base - quite gruesome. At Prestea we debouched into a senior staff bunkhouse. As with most West African commercial undertakings European staff usually were hired on a twelve-month contract followed by three months home leave. Unsurprisingly many of these European staff came out on a single basis since it was not a popular spot with the ladies. This was on account of the debilitating climate. Consequently the bunkhouses were well fitted out with the ubiquitous, noisy individual air con units and with plenty of mosquito netting in evidence. It was a timely reminder to take the chloroquine tablets. After a general chit chat by the General Manager we split into respective spheres, geology, mining, processing and costs/finance.

The Mine Manager gave us a rapid run-down on the reserves which totaled 1.578 million tonnes at 4 dwt/t contained in two separate reefs. These dip steeply at 70 to 85 degrees with true widths of 1 up to 2.3m - narrow veins. The veins (or lodes) lie within a fault zone with incompetent host rocks of graphitic schist - weak ground. There were three distinct underground operations, Ariston, Bondaye & Tuappim, each served by a separate rock hoisting shaft. Because of the poor ground conditions the mine was developed from footwall drives with crosscuts to the lode developed at about 50m strike interval. Stoping was by rill cut-and-fill using development waste as fill. Prestea was a very old mine and much of the remaining reserves were scattered remnants or pillars.

However the main constraint on increasing production was lack of rock hoisting capacity. The main rectangular vertical shafts had, unfortunately, been collared on the hangingwall side of the reef and thus at some depth had to pass through the weak reef shear zone. There were, of course, shaft pillars, but it was unsurprising that in these areas there were serious ground control difficulties. To assess the problem at the Ariston Shaft I persuaded the Mine Manager to allow us to travel down (on slow!) riding on top of the cage. The long rectangular shaft was furnished with steel (RSJ) buntons and wooden guides to accommodate twin skips and a cage and counterweight. All was OK until we entered the shaft pillar region. Here in a heart stopping moment the cage became wedged between the guides! The Shift Boss riding with us immediately rapped stop on the bell line but not before the now slack hoist rope began coiling alongside us onto the cage top. In a trice the three of us (Mine Manager, Shift Boss and I) were off the cage top and perched on the top of the surrounding shaft steel buntons, all breathing deeply.

It certainly provided an excellent demonstration of the Ariston Shaft ground problems. The Shift Boss rapped "slow up" on the bell line and the hoist rope pulled the cage out of the constriction like a slow motion cork from a bottle. We traversed carefully round on top of the buntons to the ladderway compartment and climbed down to the level below. The cage was then "run through" the constriction at higher speed to pick us up at the lower level. It was apparent that over a shaft length of about 30 m, intermediate buntons at 2.3m vertical interval with the I beam placed horizontally (rather than vertically as now) would be required to reestablish the structural stability of the shaft's guidance system. This incident certainly saved a lot of time clambering around the shaft taking detailed measurements across guide faces and comparing them with both skip, cage, counterweight and shaft steelwork dimensions.

The ground squeeze in the shaft pillar area was also evident in the Bondaye Main and Tuappim Shafts as well, though not yet as serious as Ariston. The Mine Manager confirmed that both skip and cage hoisting speeds had been reduced at all these shafts and that this was the major factor constricting ore production. He also confirmed that the Ariston Shaft was scheduled to be out of commission for nine to twelve months, starting from March. Shaft repairs would be undertaken by a specialist contractor. Well that was a relief, otherwise I could see a serious accident occurring.

The heavy ground conditions where the shafts passed through the pillar region was the most immediate problem to rectify. Next the narrow, tabular, steep dipping veins had strike/width ratios of 400:1, which, taken with the need for footwall drives and crosscuts on account of weak ground meant that development advance was paramount. SGMC estimated that annual footage at Prestea would need to rise from 12,400ft to 34,000ft to meet the proposed production increase. It seemed essential to introduce an additional jackleg machine into the development crews to decrease drilling time and to work development ends on a two shifts/day basis. However a detailed ventilation survey would be required to reduce smoke clearance times and keep the wet bulb temperature below 90 degrees F. On surface we examined the three shaft's double-drum winders which all appeared in need of some immediate TLC and the establishment of a rigorous planned maintenance programme. There was no doubt that overall rock hoisting capacity was the bottleneck to increasing production.

We then moved on to the old Tarkwa mine. The conglomerate reefs have a flatter dip than the Prestea veins and are hosted by a strong, competent quartzite. The proposed production schedule increased tonnage from 123,000 tonnes/year to 360,000 tonnes/year both at 3.5 dwt/t grade over the next five years. This would also require mine development to increase from 9,000 ft/year to 23,500 ft/year over the same period. Here the constraint on production was entirely different - the mine was using the wrong mining method! For some inexplicable reason they were using underhand cut-and-fill. The strong quartzite host rocks, narrow reef width and medium to steep dip strongly suggested that a combination of conventional (dynamic) shrink and assisted shrink stoping be employed. The existing underhand stoping method had many disadvantages and nothing to recommend it. In particular it had very poor face availability on account of previously blasted material lying on the drilling face, poor access and service facilities and poor stope face ventilation, all leading to very low stope productivity. In three words no, no and no! Overhand shrinkage stoping overcame all these problems and, of course, was entirely compatible with the strong quartzite host rocks. I also felt that the level interval of 150ft and a strike interval between raises of 400ft were both too large. To increase output it would be necessary to get more stope breaking faces per unit volume of reef. All these recommendations referred to the AVS Syncline area of the mine.

In the Apinto area the average reef thickness was around 2m and the dip from 10 to 20 degrees. Here a room-and-pillar method of mining was used with rooms 50ft by 50ft and pillars 20ft by 20ft Thus there was the flexibility of easily opening up new rooms to meet the desired increased output. However all ore (and waste) from both the AVS Syncline area and the Apinto area were handled by a single vertical shaft - the AVS Shaft. The AVS Shaft double-drum winder had a rated full speed of 1250 ft/min with acceleration and retardation rates of 2.1 ft/sec/sec and the load/dump time for the 4.2 tonnes capacity skips was 30 seconds. Hoisting from a depth of 2015ft indicated an annual hoisting output of 429,000 tonnes. This output would exceed the 1988 rehabilitation target by a mere 5%.

However the present capacity of the AVS Shaft rock winder was appreciably lower than this. The Mine Manager confirmed that the full speed was reduced to 1000 ft/min and that skip load/dump times were a painfully long two minutes. He agreed that his mine engineering guys should have a close look at the underground loading station and surface headframe dump arrangements. He also needed his engineering crews to determine if the speed constraint was due to poor shaft steelwork/guide alignment or the electrical and mechanical conditions of the winder itself. So here we were back on to shaft rock hoisting restrictions being a major impediment to increasing production.

After fifteen days we headed back to Accra for a wrap-up meeting with SGMC senior management. Although somewhat unhappy at our overall reservations on their achieving their desired production schedule I felt they appreciated our specific recommendations to overcome various bottlenecks and improve both development and stoping activities. With that it was the six hour BCal flight back to Gatwick. It was good to be back into a cold crisp February after the heat and humidity of West Africa. I needed four or five days to check calculations and type up a brief report before driving back down to Bristol to finalise things with Mike and agree my input into RTZTS's final submission to SGMC. Sorted.

Back at Gorsty Gillian had taken a message from Keith of Riofinex, London asking me to call him. He asked me to contact a pipeline specialist and prepare a brief note on the feasibility of pumping phosphate and/or bauxite slurry from Turayf and Az Zabirah to Al Jubail on the Gulf. Not too urgent, could I produce something inside six weeks or so? I said yes, somewhat hesitantly, as I knew next to nothing about long distance slurry pipelines, but fairly certain I could locate someone who did. So this was job No. 020.

I first contacted Weir Pumps in Glasgow and an old Australian contact from Warman Pumps who I had met when working for TAZI Pty, beach sand dredging on Stradbroke Island in Queensland. They both said that for long distance work you required high pressure piston-diaphragm pumps rather than their own centrifugal units. Out of these discussions the name of a German company Pipeline Services International or PSI GmbH came up. I duly telephoned PSI in West Germany and eventually spoke to a Dr G, who seemed to be exactly the expert I was looking for. He was somewhat taken aback at the distances involved, plus 1100km for rock phosphate and 550km for bauxite. I agreed to send him full size distribution details of both products ex their respective crushing and screening plants. I also told him that if they (PSI) were interested in pursuing this preliminary enquiry I could obtain clearance for him to visit RTZ's Chessington laboratory to examine samples from both Turayf and Az Zabirah. A week or so later Dr G phoned to say that PSI would be happy to undertake some basic rheological studies on the two minerals. On that basis I told Dr G that it would be simpler if he dealt directly with my principal, Riofinex, as I had merely been a "head hunter" for a slurry pipeline expert and that was him!

27

A few days later I received a call from Bernie at COMSUR in Bolivia asking me to come out as soon as possible to physically introduce breast-stoping at a trial cut-and-fill stope at the Milluni mine, along the lines I had suggested in June last year - job No 021. I arrived in La Paz on my birthday, 19th February, having travelled out the usual way, BA to Miami, now Eastern to Lima since Braniff had gone bust and LAB to La Paz. I spent the first day in COMSUR's offices going over the breast-stoping plan with Bernie, Mario and Carlos. It was going to be a difficult job since Mario, ever the conservative Bolivian Mine Manager, clearly thought it was a "mad gringo inglese scheme", no doubt willing it to fail. Carlos had picked a typical stope at the southern end of the -167 level on the main Rotschild vein. The trial stope was in its first cut above the sub-level, itself 5m above -167 rail level. That was very good since the stope back would still be relatively flat. Mario said they had accommodation for me up at the mine, so the next day we headed up to Milluni. For the next few days I spent most of the shift showing the stope miner how to drill and blast a closely controlled breast stope face.

Milluni's vertical level interval was 30m and the typical stope block was 60m on strike split into two 30m length stopes either side of the central chute/manway raise. Combined ventilation/fill raises were driven at the stope block extremities (ie. 60m strike interval). The true vein width was 1.83m and the average dip was 75 degrees. The % dilution was defined as (Stope Width - Vein Width)/ Vein Width x 100. With the current back-stoping method, using stopers for up-hole drilling, dilution in this section of the Rotschild vein was around 25%. With controlled breast-stoping I anticipated reducing this to 10%, with a consequent increase in stope rom grade. The jackleg was an Atlas Copco BBD 90 machine drilling 2m length 38mm diameter holes. Over the next week after four blasts we achieved good drilling yields of 1.5 tonnes/m drilled, but explosive yields were only 2.1 tonnes/Kg explosive. This over-blasting was caused by the ANFO loader giving too high a loading density, which, of course, would exacerbate waste dilution. We adjusted the ANFO loader to provide a less dense loading rate of about 0.55 Kg/m of drill hole length to within 20 cm of the hole collar. Holes were initiated by a bottom located primer comprising a No 6 plain detonator in half a stick of 60% dynamite. With the ANFO loader duly adjusted the next two blasts produced a satisfactory explosive yield of 2.5 tonnes/Kg explosive. Measuring both stope width and vein width over the six blasts indicated that dilution had come down to 15%, better, but could and should be lower still.

An associated problem with stoping at Milluni was the very low air pressure, 70 psi static and only 40 to 60 psi dynamic in the stope. This was much too low for the BBD 90 drill to work efficiently. A supply of 70 to 80 psi dynamic would make a vast difference to penetration rates. Although there was plenty of compressor capacity on surface the problem was underground reticulation where the -167 level compressed air line of 50mm diameter should be increased to 100mm diameter. This was true for all underground levels. With better compressed air in the stopes penetration rates would increase and overall drilling time would decrease. It was also noticed that the stope filling cycle was frequently delayed through lack of fill. Every effort had to be made to increase the recovery of fill material from the Sink & Float plant. It would also be necessary to develop a new surface waste pass to service the Rotschild central section.

Mario was still unconvinced that the breast hole stoping system would both increase productivity and reduce waste dilution. I reiterated that it was cheaper to crush rock than drill and blast it and provided all stopes were fitted with 9in grizzlys (half the crusher's smallest open side setting) then one did not need to over-drill and over-blast to produce material smaller than a 9in cube in the stope! On the positive side the miner seemed happy as he was on contract - breaking more tonnage at a better grade. More importantly Bernie could see the improvement in tonnage and grade over the past twelve days.

To be honest I was glad to get back to the lower altitude at La Paz. The Milluni camp was sited at over 4600m elevation and I had had difficulty sleeping with a persistent siroche headache. Then it was back up to El Alto airport for the LAB flight to Lima then to Eastern for Miami and finally BA to Heathrow. This time I had really lost weight due to the physical work underground in hot, humid conditions plus poor food at the camp allied with little sleep. But at least with a permanent siroche whilst at Milluni I hadn't drunk much beer let alone pisco sour!

Although now early March it was still wintery at Gorsty and Gillian was happy to have me home again to do some log splitting and giving the dogs a good long walk. There had also been some sporadic communication with the WCC SS who seemed to have a never ending stream of questions. Of course neither Gillian nor I had any first hand knowledge of how fostering "worked", but to us it appeared an interminable process with as many obstacles as possible placed in our way to hinder likely acceptance. We appreciated that the SS had to do rigorous checks on our backgrounds (no hidden child abusers?) but the SS did not appear to apply common sense in physically observing us and our way of life as a guide to the sort of people we were. It seemed to be largely a "tick box" exercise, very unspecific to the subjects - us!. All very frustrating.

About this time I heard from my parents who indicated that they wanted to move out of the South-East and come and live closer to us. As they were in their mid seventies to early eighties I did my best to try and dissuade them. I felt it would be extremely difficult for them to uproot from the Kent/Sussex area where they had spent all their lives. They would leave all their long-term friends behind and Herefordshire was a very different place to the environs of Tunbridge Wells. Not to be discouraged my father sent us a general specification of the type of place and local facilities they were looking for. So for the next couple of months we were never short of something to do - browsing local estate agent's windows and inspecting a few likely properties. We originally thought that the Great Malvern area might be suitable being a Spa town like Tunbridge Wells. However we soon realised that the steep hills around the town centre, close to the shops, were quite unsuitable for people in their eighties. It did, though, introduce us to a local Malvern estate agent, Andrew Grant, with whom we left my parents house specs.

Towards the end of March COMSUR's Goni called me from London. He had just had a meeting with the Dominion International Group who had a controlling interest in Southwest Minerals Ltd (SWL) who were investigating a multi-metal occurrence near Callington in Cornwall. He asked me to join Nick, from RTZ's Capper Pass tin smelter to make a brief on-site appraisal of the SWL project. I duly drove down to Cornwall and checked into The Bull at Callington, job No. 022 was underway. The project was all very hush-hush and I was asked to sign a confidentiality agreement as was Nick on behalf of COMSUR. SML's exploration licence took in the old Redmoor Mine and Haye South a mile or so south of the Kit Hill granite outcrop. No underground work had been undertaken but an extensive surface diamond drilling campaign had located a low grade "sheeted vein mineralisation" (SVM, so called). During 1981 outline planning permission for a 1,200 tonnes/day underground mine and surface treatment plant had been obtained. However SWL's present order-of-magnitude study envisaged a 2,000 tonnes/day trackless mine accessed through a 1 in 8 ramp-decline. Based purely on DD core a blast-hole system of open stoping had been selected and costed as a suitable mining method.

The old Redmoor Mine had worked typical steep dipping, narrow hydrothermal tin/copper veins, but the SWL's surface DD work had shown a large (up to 80m width) low grade SVM and it was this structure that the project was based on. The SVM dipped NW at 60 degrees and would intersect the Kit Hill granite at depth. DD core recovery was excellent at plus 95% and a poly-metallic ore resource of 4.6 million tonnes had been outlined. The size and grade of this type of resource would be totally dependent on the cut-off grade selected. SWL had recognised this and had produced tonnage-grade curves, ranging from 45.41 million tonnes at 0.25% tin & wolfram (0.1% cut-off) to 3.00 million tonnes at 1.0% tin & wolfram (0.6% cut-off).

SWL's mining proposals were obviously conceptual but compatible with the rock types disclosed in the DD cores. Preliminary metallurgical testwork had indicated that acceptable concentrates could be obtained by dense media separation and jigging to recover tin and wolfram whilst sulphides could be recovered by subsequent flotation. Initial capital cost had been estimated at £20 million. Tin concentrates could be sold to Capper Pass and copper concentrate to Boliden in Sweden. SWL was a small company and was looking for a joint venture partner with money. With no current access underground the SVM ore resource was the key to the project. Recent Cornish mining projects had not been successful and thus I said to Nick that if Goni was at all interested then his geological consultant/ director, Bernie, should visit the project before COMSUR made any further commitment. So after a couple of days at the project site I drove back to Gorsty to complete a brief write-up for Goni. It was very pleasant to have a UK based hard rock mining project even if it didn't look very encouraging

Andrew Grant, the Malvern estate agent, sent us particulars of a bungalow in the village of Alfrick, about eight miles west of the city of Worcester. We went to have a look. It met my parents specs and there was a village shop, a butchers and two pubs. It had about a third of an acre flat garden alongside the village hall. We took some photos and sent them plus the bungalow details to my parents. They reacted positively as they wished to leave their present house in Tunbridge Wells having recently moved back there from High Halden. They arranged to come up to Gorsty to stay whilst they looked at the Alfrick bungalow as well as a couple of other places. I took them to Alfrick where they had a good look around the bungalow and we went to the local pub for a drink and lunch. Then I took Dad along to the nearby river Teme, so he could see the possibilities for fishing, which was one of his retirement pursuits. We then drove to Malvern to see Andrew Grant, where Dad made an opening offer (house buying/selling was, after all, his business) after gleaning more background information. We then had a look around Malvern, which they liked, but agreed it was too hilly. Back to Gorsty and from there my parents headed back to Kent the following day.

I was busy overhauling the mower and Allen Scythe as the garden suddenly shook off its winter slumber. This should have been done back in January, but I had been away in Ghana most of that month. The phone rang it was Keith at RTZTS in Bristol asking if I could assist them with a review of the Portuguese Neves Corvo project. I told him I would have to check first with M&S to see if there was any conflict with their banking client. I phoned Paul at M&S, who said he'd check and let me know. Clearance came the next day and in turn I phoned Keith at RTZTS and said yes - job No. 023. I agreed to meet the RTZTS team at Heathrow the following Monday for the flight to Lisbon.

On the flight out I asked Keith who was their client, if it wasn't confidential. He laughed and said it was an in-house assignment for them - RTZ was the client! I was surprised and said so. Keith said that the rumour was that the Neves Corvo shaft sinking had abruptly stopped when it hit water and that SOMINCOR's majority owner, the French company Pennaroya had immediately put "the project" up for sale. Apparently RTZ was one of the first mining majors to show interest. It appeared, once again, that my involvement with the RTZTS team was to do with possible shaft problems. In essence it was a due diligence exercise.

In Lisbon we stayed in an hotel in the central Rossio district, just around the corner from SOMINCOR's offices. There was a notably different atmosphere with the SOMINCOR guys from that in evidence six months ago on my visit with M&S. They were far less forthcoming. On the M&S visit they bent over backwards to help presumably hoping that M&S would present a favourable report to their banker client, a potential source of finance for their project. Now it was quite different. Pennaroya were selling off "their project" to outside mining outfits, in this case RTZ, the dreaded rosbifs. In fact, not a great deal had changed. The mining reserves (massive ore) had increased at Corvo to 13.5 million tonnes at 7.7% Cu. The ore expectancy had increased to 38,000 t/vm. At Graca the mining reserve was 3.6 million tonnes at 11.1% Cu. Here the average dip was 40 degrees and average thickness was 9.5m with an ore expectancy of 21,000 t/vm.

The high insitu grades suggested that a high recovery/low dilution mining method should be employed, whilst the irregular orebody outlines and structural discontinuities would require a flexible method. The proposed transverse flat-back room (15m) and pillar (7.5m) system oriented along the strike at 20m vertical intervals worked in an underhand mode on account of the strong hangingwall and weak footwall followed by post-filling and extraction of the rib pillars appeared to be a practical approach. A mining rate of 4,000 tonnes/day for Corvo and 2,000 tonnes/day for Graca were also deemed reasonable at around 10% of their respective ore expectancies.

Main mine infrastructure would comprise a 17 sq m section 1 in 8 ramp-decline sunk in the footwall close to a vertical circular shaft. All mine development and stoping would use electro-hydraulic twin boom jumbos and 5 to 8m^3 diesel LHDs for mucking. Broken ore would pass to a DC trackbound trolley haulage system delivering to a shaft loading station just below -300 level. An inclined conveyor ramp from the -450 level (the

Boliden solution) would also deliver ore to the -300 level. Ventilation would be by a continuous exhaust system through bored raises. Main sumps and pumps would also be sited close to the shaft at -300 level and at -450 level at the base of the incline conveyor.

The size and layout of these sumps/pumps could await our site visit to inspect the shaft ground-water problem. The proposed schedule considered a three year construction period followed by a production of 300,000 tonnes in 1987 building up to 1 million tonnes in 1989 all from Corvo with 200,000 tonnes coming from Graca in 1990 rising to 400,000 tonnes in 1991 to maintain the annual throughput at 1 million tonnes until 2003. The head grade would steadily decline from 11.7% Cu to 6.7% Cu over the seventeen year period. This was RTZ's preferred production schedule to maximise Cu grade in the early years to maximise the DCF rate of return on the project. It was agreed we would visit Pennaroya in Paris to discuss cost estimates, the construction and operating schedules.

Peter, the geotechnical engineer, examined the split DD core and ground conditions in the ramp-decline, whilst I investigated the "water problem" in the shaft. It was, in fact, no great problem. Unfortunately the shaft sinking contractor expected the shaft to be dry and had omitted to carry a central pilot hole ahead of the sink. Had they done so this would have warned them of the water fissure before they broke into it. The water inflow was not huge, about 150 gal/min, but enough to cause sinking difficulties. A suspended submersible pump was keeping the sump clear. Now it was necessary to go back 7m or so above the fissure and put in a grouted curb ring followed by backsheets behind freshly poured concrete down to 5m below the fissure and install another grouted curb ring. Then a process of backwall injection of cement grout behind the backsheets from the bottom upwards over this 12m section of shaft. Thereafter resume sinking behind a central pilot hole and carry out pre-cementation injection if more water bearing fissures were encountered. It was felt this would delay the sinking programme by four to six weeks, but was now unavoidable.

After three days at site we returned to Lisbon for a final discussion with the SOMINCOR guys before heading to the airport and flying to Paris. Here we fronted up to the Pennaroya offices for further talks on the project. As expected these talks focussed much more on financial matters and the proposed construction schedule and build-up in copper production. I had little technical input apart from overcoming the shaft "water problem" and my disagreement with the project's very conservative utilisation and availability figures for mining equipment. These had led to overstated mine capital costs and unit operating cost. We only spent three days with Pennaroya so there was little time for any Paris tourism apart from one evening in Montmartre. Then it was the Paris shuttle flight back to Heathrow.

During the short time I'd been away Gillian heard from my parents that their offer for the Alfrick bungalow had been accepted and their solicitor was now engaged on the necessary local searches. They hoped to exchange contracts by mid June with completion expected in August. This would enable my parents to be established in their new home before the weather turned colder. After contract exchange they planned to come up and stay with us for a few days so that they could visit Alfrick to measure up for curtains etc and see exactly what they wanted to bring up from Kent and what they needed to get rid of. I was worried about their impending move, but they seemed set on it. They said they would be able to manage the Kent end of things with their local removal firm and besides there wasn't that much "stuff" as the bulk of their possessions had gone when they left High Halden eighteen months ago.

In June I had a call from John, a mining engineer with Fluor (GB) Ltd in London. I knew John well as he had previously worked at GMA. He told me that he had been with the UK subsidiary of the USA engineer-contractor firm, Fluor Mining & Metals, for a couple of years. Now they had been invited by the Chinese to bid for the design and construction of two pairs of very large shafts for two new coal mine developments. He wanted me to come up to their London offices and assist with the preparation of their bid. I thought it was strange that Fluor hadn't gone to established shaft sinking contractors, such as Cementation or Thyssen, but perhaps they didn't want to advertise the paucity of their in-house shaft design expertise. No matter, I said yes and welcomed job No. 024.

As John wanted me to work in their offices I had to collect all my own shaft design and sinking data files to take up to London with me. My faithful driver, Gillian, duly deposited me at Worcester station for the two and half hour rail journey to London. Then a taxi ride to a small hotel in Hammersmith close to Fluor's offices.

The Fluor offices were located in an unremarkable modern building close to the M4 Hammersmith Flyover. John came down to the reception desk to ensure I was issued with a Visitor's badge. Upstairs it was a typical open plan floor with plenty of drafting tables surrounded by individual offices and a large conference room. I was settled into an office with a complete set of the Chinese ITB document. It was set out in an unusual format and my first job was to ensure that I correctly understood the duty specifications for each pair of shafts. They were all large shafts, 8.5m in diameter, each equipped with a pair of twin large bottom dump skips, a cage and counterweight and the usual services compartment. There was to be only one underground loading station at each mine, just below the coal seam horizon, so that it would be feasible to use multi-rope friction winders. The ITB also specified a fixed steel guidance system on account of the high ventilation air velocities in both pairs of downcast and upcast shafts. It was on this particular aspect that I felt I could earn my keep by suggesting that in their bid Fluor would use SHS buntons and guides. Their use would reduce the overall weight of steel in the shaft and, very importantly, would significantly reduce the aerodynamic resistance of the shaft furnishings. I also suggested that Fluor could enclose a copy of the British Steel (Tubes Division) brochure on "SHS in Deep Mine Shafts" that I had prepared when I was at RTZC. This was the key element of the design apart from stressing the importance of orientation of the friction winder ropes to ensure that the tail ropes do not twist on account of the coriolis effect (earth's rotation).

On the shaft construction (ie sinking) side I unashamedly used my personal knowledge of Cementation's layout and methodology for the Rosebery, Lepanto and Chasnalla shafts. It all looked very different when drawn up by the Fluor guys and to be fair the Chinese shafts were of much larger size and complexity. I checked through the draft drawings as well as the accompanying blurb and that was me done. At a final meeting with John and their team leader I said I thought that Fluor should tie up with a shaft sinking firm as it was a specialised activity especially if the sinkings proved to be wet. They firmly agreed with this and said my involvement now was to "get them up to speed" before their discussions with shaft sinking contractors. I felt it might have been simpler all round if this had been made clear to me from the start, but hey ho, no damage done, rather the opposite, as the bank balance prospered. On Friday, after five days, I headed back to Gorsty

We heard from my parents that they had exchanged contracts on the Alfrick bungalow. So with no mining work in sight we suggested they come and stay at Gorsty for a few days and we would show them around the Marches, to get the flavour of the area before they moved. We visited the two cathedral cities of Hereford and Worcester, but they seemed to prefer the smaller towns like Ludlow and Weobley. A week or so after they had returned to Kent, Jane, our WCC SS contact came to visit. She was very cheerful having just completed the purchase of a cottage just outside Bromyard. She showed us photos and said that a farmer friend said it "looked like a pig with two 'yers (ears!) since it had huge stone chimneys at each gable end. On the fostering front she was also positive and thought we would finally be accepted as suitable by WCC before the end of the year. She said that would be our Gold Seal of Approval! Then the difficult bit would begin (oh really?) to find a lad suitable for us and us for him. I wondered if it would ever happen, as it was already fifteen months since our first enquiry. In early August my parents duly moved in to the Alfrick bungalow and we were kept busy moving furniture, putting up pictures and curtains and generally helping them establish a new home. At least we were only thirty minutes away if there were any problems.

Towards the middle of the month I had a call from an independent quantity surveyor in Shropshire who had seen my professional ad in the local Yellow Pages. Yes sir it pays to advertise! He had a client in the Hope valley who was attempting to get planning permission to convert an old Engine House into a private dwelling. The planning glitch was the presence of an open vertical shaft. The planners required this to be made safe by quote "a competent person" unquote, could I help? I said I thought I might be able to and we agreed to meet at the Six Bells pub in Worthen, Shropshire, a drive of 45 miles from Gorsty. The shaft in question was the Wood Engine

Shaft of the East Roman Gravels mine in the old Shropshire lead mining district on the western side of the Stiperstones some twelve miles south of Shrewsbury. After our meeting I said I would drive on up to Shrewsbury and go to the reference library to try and find out a little more about the Wood Engine Shaft and then give him a call saying yes or no. The library was very helpful and old records indicated that the shaft was of a short rectangular size, sunk in Mytton Flagstones and was used as a main pumping shaft. Of particular interest was the fact that it intersected the Wood Level drainage tunnel about 100ft below the shaft collar. I phoned the surveyor and said yes and we agreed to meet at the East Roman Gravels site the following morning.

At the site the owner had done an excellent job of excavating the extensive backfill and exposing the solid bedrock around the shaft. The bedrock comprising the shaft collar was sound and relatively unweathered. Its solidity was confirmed by the presence of the foundations of the Engine House a mere 6ft from the shaft. The shaft dimensions were 11ft x 7ft. I explained that we had to cap the shaft, so that we did not impede water flow in the drainage tunnel, since the Wood Level drained several other old mines further up the Hope valley.

The shaft was vertical, intersecting the Wood Level at approximately 100ft below collar, whilst the original shaft sump was a further 400ft below that Level. With the aid of a back-hoe the owner cleared more backfill to give a 2ft clear footing around the shaft. I then provided a sketch showing three 11ft long 4in x 3in RSJs placed at 2.75ft centres parallel to the short axis of the shaft. A 12in diameter open slotted pipe was sited to take surface water through the cap into the existing shaft. We then poured a 6in concrete slab reinforced with weldmesh top and bottom, which required about 3.5m^3 of OPC Readymix at a water/cement ratio of not more than 0.55 to give a compressive strength of 4000 psi at 28 days.

After seven days the owner could backfill the area to a desired surface level making sure surface water could reach the slotted pipe. I then had to prepare a Completion Certificate on my professional letterhead for the owner to present to the South Shropshire planning department. In due course this was accepted and the owner went ahead with his building conversion. For me it was a little sad sealing off an old shaft but at least it enabled the lovely old Engine House to be brought back into use and we didn't disturb the drainage work of the old Wood Level. That was job No 025 signed off.

The first part of September was a busy time cutting all the Gorsty hedges, digging out ditches and the final Allen Scythe cut of the rough grass in the old orchard. We also got in some more ash and oak logs for the winter, waiting for splitting when I had the time and energy. Both Gillian and I went over to Alfrick to help my parents get the garden under control. This was mainly hedge cutting and grass mowing as well as clearing the overgrown vegetable patch. Dad had decided to have a small greenhouse delivered and erected but now felt it needed some heating, which is where I came in to do some wall drilling and the installation of a power cable via a safety breaker - all good DIY fun.

Harlesford Farm at Tetsworth in Oxfordshire in the 1940s

My 1932 6 cylinder OHC L Type MG Magna 2-seater

Peter, Underground Manager at Kiabakari in the Club Bar (1961)

"Titania" dredge at North Stradbroke Island, Queensland (1963)

Aerial ropeway on North Stradboke Island, Queensland

"Clyde" pulling empty rake of trucks into EZ's Hercules Mine, Tasmania (1964)

"Clyde" waits underground for trucks to be filled from chute (1964)
(The full trucks go out by gravity, controlled by a brake car. Clyde walks out on his own to await empty truck rake to pull back into the Hercules Mine, Tasmania)

EZ's No 2 Main Shaft steelwork at Rosebery, Tasmania (1971)

Cementation Mining shaft sinking plant at Chasnalla East Mine, Bihar, India (1967)

Chasnalla East Mine shaft sinking Supervisors relaxing (1968)

Diamond Drilling at Rajpura Dariba, Rajasthan, India (1971)

Old lead workings outcrop along hill top, Rajpura Dariba, India (1971)

Exploration decline at Rajpura Dariba (1971)

Erecting headframe for sinking Tubo Shaft, Lepanto, Luzon, Philippines (1972)

Beyer-Garratt steam loco at SOB Shaft, Nkana, Zambia (1991)

Shaft sealing at old Wotherton baytes mine, Shropshire, UK (1985)

Cooks Kitchen headframe South Crofty Mine, Cornwall, UK (1991)

With my geologist mate, Arthur at Andaychagua Mine, Peru (1995)

Gillian's XJS Jag in pole position at Taylors Hotel, Portugal with the Rolls Royces from their Tour of the Douro valley (2000)

28

Later in September I had a call from Dave of Zambia Engineering Services (ZES) in Ashford, Kent asking me to come to their offices to discuss the design for the new sub-vertical shaft at the Mufulira mine of ZCCM. I caught the London train from Worcester.

I crossed by tube, Paddington to Charing Cross, and caught the fast train to Ashford arriving at ZES office by 11am. Dave wanted me to review a bunch of reports, memos and letters concerning the new sub-vertical shaft (SV2) at the Mufulira mine and come up with a definitive design based on the mine's basic duty specification. Well talk about the sublime to the ridiculous in terms of shafts. I had just finished looking at the East Roman Gravels 18th Ce rectangular shaft in Shropshire and now to a brand new circular shaft at Mufulira, one of the world's great underground copper mines! This had got to be a really interesting assignment.

Dave was aware that I knew Mufulira from my work with the World Bank and felt I could undertake this review at my Leominster base without the need to visit Zambia. He said if I had any queries for the mine I should pass them through ZES. So job No. 026 was on the go. After a cheery pub lunch I collected a stack of reports, memos and letters and, weighed down with paper, made my way to Ashford station for the homeward trip.

The next day I steadily worked through all the bumph. This would be the heaviest duty shaft I had worked on, namely 4.32 million tonnes/year of rom crusher run ore hoisted vertically 1051.5m. Ore hoisting was to be carried out for sixteen hours/day for 28 days/month equivalent to 804 tonnes/hour. It was a sub-vertical (ie underground) circular shaft of 6.7m diameter required to downcast 409m^3/s of ventilation air. So first things first (for a change maybe?) the ground conditions. Basement rocks comprised massive micaceous and chloritic quartzite with intact rock strengths of 120 to 150 Mpa. On the CSIR Rock Mass Quality Index these rocks would appear to lie in the middle of Class 2, good rock. There was little fracturing and less than 25 litres/s ground-water. As this would be Mufulira's main production shaft in the future and considering the huge ventilation air quantity to be downcast the SV2 shaft required lining. I suggested a nominal 305mm thick lining of 30 N/mm^2 strength of unreinforced concrete. The very high indicated air velocity of 11.6m/s precluded the use of rope guides and a fixed guidance system of buntons and guides would thus be necessary.

I next tackled winder selection. A hoisting duty of 845,400 tonne-m/hour indicated a large winder by any standards. To minimise power and capital cost I considered a multi-rope friction winder as most suitable. Maximum rope tension ratio of T1/T2 of 1.5 static was selected with a coefficient of friction assumed as 0.2. With these values the maximum acceleration (a) of ascending load or retardation (r) of descending load that could be used without risking rope slip was about 1.1 m/s/s. For hoist depths over 1000m a & r rates of 0.8 m/s/s were usual practice. Full speed of hoist was usually selected as 0.4 to 0.5 of Vmax. In the case of the SV2 shaft I selected a full speed of 12.5 m/s. Allowing six seconds for creep time and twenty seconds for loading/dumping skips which gave a cycle time for balanced skips of circa 130 seconds or 27 cycles/hour. For balanced hoisting this implied 30 tonnes capacity skips, which would have a tare weight of 22.5 tonnes. To meet a static Factor of Safety of plus 6 and a D/d bending ratio of 100 on the friction wheel (3300mm diameter) I selected six number 33mm diameter locked coil head ropes and two number 70mm diameter multi-flat strand tail ropes.

With this configuration the maximum suspended load would be 158 tonnes and the rope tread pressure would be 0.24 Kg/mm^2. Motor ratings (twin motor drive) would be 2 x 2000 kW RMS, 2 x 3000 kW peak indicating, unsurprisingly, a very large winder. The winder friction drum axis should be N - S so that the orientation of the tail ropes between skips would be E - W and thus the coriolis effect would open and close the tail rope loop rather than attempting to twist it. After sizing the 30-tonne capacity bottom dump skips I was able to finalise a shaft steelwork layout using aerodynamic RHS steel. Finally I produced preliminary sketches of loading station, ore storage bins, transfer conveyors, skip changing, spillage handling, rope changing and winder chamber layout. All the calculations and writing took me three weeks before I headed back to ZES in Ashford in mid October. We spent the rest of the day working through my report with their Chief Engineer (CE). As I had shown all my assumptions and calculations in detail in the report they could dissect it as they wished. Overall the CE was fairly happy although he felt that the Mufulira mining guys might have some reservations about installing a huge 4000 kW 6-rope friction winder and associated electricals underground. He said he expected some robust observations back from the mine and he would pass these on to me for comment.

Back home again it was good to realise that that was another job wrapped up - well until the queries started arriving - and I could have a break with the inevitable DIY required for maintaining a 250 year old farmhouse. In fact, I found general house maintenance quite therapeutic in the winter when the garden had gone into hibernation. I also enjoyed good long walks with the dogs over Bircher Common followed by a pint in the Bell pub at Yarpole. Around this time Jane, our WCC SS contact dropped in for a coffee to give us the news that we finally had our "Gold Seal of Approval" from the WCC as potential foster parents. To celebrate we had something slightly stronger than coffee. Jane said that as soon as they, the WCC, had identified a suitable boy they would send us his details for our perusal and reaction. Jane felt we would be unlikely to hear until the new year, but at least we had finally been approved.

A week later I had a call from my quantity surveyor friend in Worthen to say that he had had a call from a Shrewsbury firm of solicitors asking him about another planning application which involved making an old shaft safe. I couldn't believe it, this would be the third 'shaft job' in a row, now job No 027. I duly arranged a date with the surveyor to visit the old Wotherton barytes mine in Shropshire. It was a forty mile trip from Gorsty.

The shaft in question was the new engine shaft, two miles from Chirbury, just a short distance east of the B4386 road, alongside the byroad to Rorrington. The area was low lying in the Rea Brook valley close to the river Camlad. The area round the old Engine House was covered with unconsolidated backfill with no sign of any rock outcrop. Fortunately on the south side of the byroad to Rorrington there were old outcrop workings (circa 1000ft SE of the new engine shaft). These workings showed that the host rocks of the barytes vein were composed of competent andesitic tuffs. It also confirmed that the shaft was sunk in the hangingwall and would intersect the vein about 550ft below the collar. The Engine House was constructed from dressed andesite and I was thus confident that the actual shaft would have been collared in these competent tuffs.

We had no means of knowing the actual shaft size but on the basis of other shafts in this Shropshire mining district I estimated it would be 12ft x 8ft In discussion with the surveyor we agreed that it would be necessary to use a long reach back-hoe to ramp down from the eastern side to reach bedrock and the shaft collar. From previous experience he recommended Dave Bishop from nearby Chirbury. I asked the surveyor to contact Dave and then phone me when the ramping was complete. Once he'd exposed the shaft collar I could design a suitable shaft cap. After the regulation pub lunch I drove back to Gorsty.

On a recent visit to us my parents had said they would like to buy me one of those new fangled computers to say thanks for finding the bungalow and helping to settle them in. We said it was absolutely not necessary but they insisted. Thus we had a day out in Worcester where we looked at an IBM and an Amstrad, but found the input directions to these early PCs incomprehensible. Someone said why don't you try an Apple Mac? The local Apple distributor was Celtip Computers in Kidderminster so that's where we went. They gave us a quick demo on this funny little elongated box with a tiny screen and it answered to a point and click with a gadget called a mouse. None of this input gibberish that the PCs required. The key selling point was that Celtip said "take it home for a day, play with it and see how you get on". We did this and inspite of being terrified we'd blow it up, within an hour or so we could set out a letter and generally produce some typescript on the screen. That clinched it - Apple Mac for me. Next day we went back to Kidderminster, bought the little Mac and a cumbersome dot matrix printer, which was so big we had to go to Hereford and buy a special office stand for it! Welcome to the eighties.

Just after the new year Don from GA(UK) called and asked me to come up to their office to discuss pillar recovery at the Mochia Mine of Hindustan Zinc Ltd (HZL) in Rajasthan, India. GA(UK) were already providing HZL with geotechnical advice and thus had a full set of underground stope plans of the Mochia mine. There were three separate pillars to be recovered. A 4th level sill/5th level crown of 105m strike length of width varying from 17 to 41m and a height of 11.8m. A Main Shaft pillar of 20m strike extent with widths from 19 to 46m and a vertical height of 112.8m. Finally a Rib pillar of 9m strike, width 13 to 40m and similar vertical height of 112.8m.

I suggested that a trough drilled undercut with north side drawpoint crosscuts would need to be developed on sub-level 15 for broken pillar ore recovery. This could be undertaken by the Atlas Copco BBC 120F drifter. Then both the Main Shaft and Rib pillars could be recovered by parallel down-hole benching from the 5th level using the Atlas Copco 4 DTH rig drilling 115mm diam holes blasting into the adjacent mined-out stopes. The ore was quite brittle so a high density, high velocity explosive (good brisance) such as semi-gelatine, SG 80% should be used on a 3.5m burden by 4m spacing pattern to give a yield of about 4 tonnes/Kg explosive. The sill/crown pillar, to be mined last, should be ring drilled from three vertical raises (Horodiam stoping) using the Atlas Copco BBC 120F drifter drilling 57mm diameter holes up to 35m length. Ring toe hole spacing 2m and a burden of 1.5m between horizontal rings to give a yield of 3.5 tonnes/Kg SG 80% explosive. For me the whole exercise put the clock back 24 years to when I was preparing ring drilling layouts for stoping at the Kiabakari gold mine in Tanganyika. At the end of the day I told Don that I needed one more day at my Leominster base to draw up the respective drilling layouts and type up a brief report (ho ho on my new Apple Mac) and that would complete job No. 028.

I had no sooner finished and mailed this report to Don at GA(UK) when Keith of Riofinex asked me to come up to their offices to discuss doing some desk studies on mining operations in Saudi Arabia. It was just a single days briefing in London so I drove to Worcester and caught the train up to and back from Paddington. This was job No. 029 and in essence he asked me to prepare reverse economic studies of four notional mines. These were underground gold, silver and tin mines and an open-pit tin mine. Riofinex provided me with the basic orebody parameters. For the underground mines this included - strike length, dip angle, average true thickness, payability, bulk density, depth of vein, total ore resource, nature and competence of wall rocks, ore mineralogy and metallurgical testwork results, operational details etc. From this basic data Riofinex wanted me to develop and cost a suitable mine, process plant, services and infrastructure in order to determine the required in situ grade to give a specified DCF rate of return on the total "notional project" expenditure. Armed with the basic mines data I headed back to Gorsty.

In fact it was a straight forward, though extensive, exercise. For example the notional underground tin mine had similar characteristics to South Crofty in Cornwall. With all mines the first thing was to calculate the ore expectancy in terms of t/vm. Then consider the vein dip and competence of the wall rocks. These three factors enabled one to select a suitable mining method and daily mining output based on 10% ore expectancy. The rom ore would be crushed underground before hoisting to surface headframe bins. The ore then passed through a two-stage crushing and screening plant, the coarse, plus 2mm material, passing to an Heavy Media Separation (HMS) cone, where floats were rejected and sinks passed to a fine ore bin. The minus 2mm fines would be cycloned whence the minus 10 micron material would be discarded as slimes and the plus 75 micron material would pass to the fine ore bin. From there the balance of the rom ore would pass to rod milling with subsequent treatment by spirals and sand/slimes tables. An overall recovery of 70% into a 45% Sn concentrate, bagged for despatch by road to Jeddah (distance given as 800 Km).

It was then necessary to calculate the power demand for the mine, beneficiation plant and mine site services. A reliable source of water was stated to be available 50km distant. Planning for high water recovery at the beneficiation plant with conventional thickeners, to minimise raw water make-up. With all the project's "hardware" defined I then had to estimate their capital costs, feasibility study and owners costs, engineering and construction management costs, contingency and working capital cost. This would give a total notional mine capital cost. A total minesite operating cost was then calculated. For the underground tin mine the financial numbers indicated that an ore reserve grade of 3.53% Sn was required to give a 15% DCF return This grade referred to total project costs. Finance, interest, royalties and tax liabilities were excluded. Although the capital cost for this notional project was high at US$ 220 million, I noted that the 400 tonnes/day Mahd adh Dhabab underground gold mine in Saudi was reported to have a capital cost in excess of US$ 200 million.

The other notional mines followed a similar process, the open-pit mine obviously considering aspects such as stripping ratio. Each one of these mines took me three to four days to complete and write up. Boy, was I pleased to have the old Apple Mac for all the typing and laying out all the tables of figures. In fact Keith commented that "You seem to have dragged yourself into the computer age". I didn't respond "yes and not with those daft PCs you use at Riofinex", but it was tempting.

Right at the end of January Jane, our SS contact, came to see us. She brought with her details of a young lad who the WCC wished to see settled with foster parents. He sounded a good lad who had been in care for a long time. It was not easy to be purely objective, but both Gillian and I felt that at his age, 12, he would be too set in his ways and would find it difficult to adjust to our way of life and, of course us to him. If truth be told Jane felt the same, but thought we should have a look at his details. We reiterated our earlier thoughts on ages and Jane said they would try and locate a suitable "candidate" no older than 8.

The next day I had a call from the quantity surveyor telling me that Dave Bishop, the back-hoe contractor, had completed ramping down at the new engine shaft at Wotherton and could I come and inspect the site? Of course I could and duly drove up the following morning. It was not as I expected.

The excavation was approximately 30ft in diameter at surface reducing to about 18ft diameter at depth. The water table had been reached 28ft below the base of the old Engine House. Interestingly down at the water table the excavation was heaving with rats, again not what I'd expected. It was apparent that the top 12ft of the excavation had been dug through backfill whilst the lower 16ft had been dug through geologically recent gravels and alluvium. It had thus not proved feasible to reach bedrock nor the throat of the shaft. A bridge cap could not be placed. The solution was to place a reinforced mass concrete plug in the excavation as soon as possible.

The procedure was to first lay old GI sheets across the bottom of the excavation and cover with old steel pipes or rails followed by 3/8" weldmesh. Then place five 14ft long 6in by 3in RSJs horizontally at 2ft centres (web vertical) oriented at right angles to the centre line of the winder house, 2 to 3ft above water table. Then place bulk ordinary portland cement Readmix (C20P spec) into the excavation working well in and around RSJs until covered by 1ft of concrete. Place second mat of weldmesh on top of the poured concrete. Continue pouring concrete to a depth of about 6ft. Total volume of concrete 30 to 35m³. Leave for seven days then backfill to desired surface level. I suggested that the quantity surveyor took a series of photographs to make a permanent record of the work undertaken. I told him I would be away for the next few weeks, but would issue a Completion Certificate on return after viewing the construction photos and a final site inspection.

There was another call from Keith of RTZTS asking me to join his team down in Portugal. It was all very hush-hush, called Project Juno, but every man and his dog knew it was RTZ's continuing due diligence on the Neves Corvo project of SOMINCOR. As before we flew TAP to Lisbon airport where a SOMINCOR vehicle drove us down to their camp at Castro Verde. This was my third trip to Neves Corvo in the last six months and this job was No. 030. My first task was to prepare a draft write-up of the mining section for the due diligence report. I won't go over all the details of the Neves Corvo project again since these were largely covered in my previous jobs, numbers 017 and 023. The salient points were that it was now a one-million-tonnes/year underground copper mine accessed through a vertical shaft and a ramp-decline, both sited in the footwall. It was a trackless mine using electro-hydraulic drilling jumbos and diesel LHDs for muck handling. The mining method was transverse underhand room and pillar with second pass pillar recovery. Lateral haulage on the -300 level was by DC trolley haulage to an underground jaw crusher at -325 level. Ore mined below the -300 level at Corvo would reach the same crusher by an inclined conveyor.

The small 5m diameter, concrete lined shaft was currently being sunk by the Spanish contractor Obras Subterraneum. They would deepen the shaft to the -393 level and cut the -355 loading station. All rock hoisting would be handled in this shaft. Preliminary estimates had indicated that a four-rope tower mounted friction winder, rated at 1100 kW, pulling 9 tonnes capacity balanced skips could hoist up to 1.3 million tonnes/year from the -355 loading station. Ventilation was a problem area with the combination of a small shaft for downcast air and a large underground diesel fleet. The shaft was to downcast 150m³/s and the ramp-decline 70m³/s. Preliminary hydrological studies had indicated a base load pumping duty of 500m³/hour.

My next task was a complete reappraisal of the main shaft duties, albeit stuck with the existing small 5m diameter size. The hoisting distance from -355 loading station to a new headframe dump bin would be 602 m. Ore tonnage to be hoisted would be two million tonnes/year (dry) plus waste 220,000 tonnes (11%), moisture 88,800 tonnes (4%) and an overall design margin of 230,900 tonnes (10%) giving a total of 2,539,700 tonnes, say 2,540,000 tonnes/year. The hoisting routine was to be 16hrs/day for 300 days or 4,800 hours indicating a design hoisting output of 529.17, say 530 tonnes/hour. On the basis of precedent practice I selected a & r rates of 0.8 m/s/s and a full speed of 10 m/s. I further selected a winder creep time of five seconds and a skip loading/unloading time of 15 seconds.

	Distance (m)	Time (s)	Rate
Acceleration	62.5	12.5	0.8 m/s/s
Full Speed	477.0	47.7	10.0 m/s/s
Retardation	62.5	12.5	0.8 m/s/s
Creep	-	5.0	-
Load/dump	-	15.0	-
Full Cycle	602	92.7 allow 93 seconds	

Using a 55 minute hour the winder cycle would be (55 x 60)/93 = 35.48 cycles/hour. The desired skip capacity would thus be 530/35.48 = 14.94, say 15 tonnes. Modern bottom dump, fabricated skips hung from a top pivot within a fixed bridle had tare weights of 65% to 75% of the net skip load. Thus a gross rope end load of 25 tonnes was indicated. My initial rope selection was restricted by the need to maintain reasonable friction drum/rope diameter (D/d ratio) whilst keeping the friction drum diameter to around 2400mm or less to ensure a suitable shaft layout without recourse to deflection sheaves. British Ropes "Mine Shaft Ropes" catalogue suggested using 4 off 24mm diameter locked coil (LC) ropes and 2 off 40mm diameter MFS tail ropes.

The static Factor of Safety on the head ropes was 6.0, right on the limit. The total loading on each head ropes (including dynamic and bending stresses) was about 13.5 tonnes indicating a fatigue stress of 27% which would be satisfactory. The total suspended load on the winder would be 52.0 tonnes and the rope tread pressure on the friction drum groove linings would be 52,000/(4 x 2400 x 24) = 0.226 Kg/mm² (2227 kPa) well below the upper limit of 0.28 Kg/mm² which could be tolerated by modern LC hoisting ropes. The total motor rating would be about 2050 kW. Obviously friction winder manufacturers should be consulted to finalise the installation.

With careful design it would be feasible to incorporate a 1500mm by 3300mm cage and counterweight in conjunction with the two balanced 15-tonnes skips. This single deck cage would carry 35 men and the whole day shift complement could be handled in less than thirty minutes. This would be half the time taken to transport the men by vehicles in the ramp-decline, as proposed by SOMINCOR.

Because of the small shaft diameter rigid guides and buntons had to be used to enable a minimum running clearance of 75mm to be maintained, thus making maximum use of the space available. The correct design approach was for rigid guides and flexible buntons to minimise the horizontal loads applied to the shaft guidance system by reducing the rate of change of direction of the shaft conveyances. In addition guide butt joint gap < 3mm; individual guide verticality 3mm per 300m guide length and the tolerance between pairs of guide faces plus/minus 2mm. The mining requirement to downcast 150m³/s of ventilation air in the shaft suggested the use of flattened pipe buntons to reduce the aerodynamic resistance. A 350mm x 100mm x 10mm wall thickness buntons and 200mm x 200mm RHS guides met the design criteria and available space. This shaft steelwork reduced the total shaft area by only 7.2% so that the downcast air velocity would be 9 m/s.

That completed the shaft redesign. My final task was to comment on RTZTS's Development & Drilling tender documents. Their approach had been to draft a "screw the contractor" document. As I had worked for mining contractors (Cementation), I suggested they make it more equitable, especially as it was to be a Schedule of Rates contract which was quite normal for this type of sub-surface works. When I told Keith that concluded my work at Neves he said he had a message from George, GM at Minas de Riotinto, (also a non-executive director of RTZTS) asking if I could go and have a look at the main shaft at Masa San Antonio. Rio Tinto was only eighty miles due east of Neves Corvo so I said yes, why not? In fact it was around a 160 mile drive north through Beja in Portugal then east to Aracena in Spain. There was no frontier post and it was impossible to tell when you crossed the border. It was definitely deja vu turning up at the Rio Tinto mines again after nine or ten years. I went to see George, who I had not met before, and he sent me to see the Underground Manager at the San Antonio Mine.

The main shaft was a concrete lined circular shaft of 5.5m diameter. It had been sunk in the early seventies. Tower mounted multi-rope friction winders handled twin balanced skips and a cage and counterweight with RHS structural steel for buntons and guides. At present both winders were operating at 75% their rated full speed on account of excessive vibration in the shaft steelwork. Of course this was seriously restricting ore production and men and materials handling.

I had to wait until the next night shift to first ride the shaft at about 90% full speed to observe/feel these vibrations (and they were quite heavy) and then ride both the top of the cage and then on the skip bridle at slow speed to observe the buntons and bolted shaft wall attachments. Although the mine ground-water was acid the steelwork did not appear unduly corroded. Initially I could not see anything obviously amiss. It was apparent from the shaft inspection and perusal of the shaft steelwork drawings that the bunton layout included some short stub buntons which led to the undesirable rigid format. In turn this ensured that dynamic horizontal hoisting loads were directly transferred, via the buntons, to their attachment to the shaft concrete lining.

I suggested that we should now run two vertical laser beams down the shaft to check each individual bunton set for correct positioning. Back to night shift, on top of the cage, now fitted with hinged putlogs which could extended into the skip compartments we slowly descended the shaft gauging each bunton set. About 150m down the shaft we found that the skip guides were slowly deviating from their correct location. This took place over 26m (6 bunton sets at 4.5m vertical interval) the discrepancy rising from 3mm to 9mm and back again. Close inspection of the the two mid buntons showed that the bunton attachment plates had loosened their grouted wall anchors. This was not evident from a normal shaft inspection made from inside the cage. Phew, a sigh of relief all round. Not a huge job to rectify. Of course the shaft would be out of commission for a week or two, but with hydraulic jacks and quick setting cement that should be the size of it.

With the Underground Manager we broke the news to the GM, George. To my surprise he seemed more worried about the two week shaft shutdown, rather than happy that the "vibration problem" might have been solved. He gave the impression that we (the Underground Manager and me) were the cause of the problem! Time to go.

At least George arranged for a Riotinto car to drive me to Seville airport. From there an Iberia flight to Barajas, Madrid, then another to Heathrow. Well that was job No. 031 finished. I wondered if I'd get paid for the three days I had spent in Riotinto, since the client (George) had seemed so unhappy. C'est la guerre.

Gillian had taken a message from the quantity surveyor that the mass concrete plug at the new engine shaft at Wotherton had been completed and could I come up and inspect it? She said I would be back in a couple of days and would phone. This I did and told him I would bring a Completion Certificate with me that afternoon. I drove the forty miles to Wotherton where the surveyor gave me fifteen photos recording the different stages of constructing the shaft plug. The finished job looked fine and I had no qualms about giving him the Certificate. All of us seemed happy with the job and we had a celebration drink in the Worthen pub. Not too many, I had to drive back to Gorsty!

At last we had a call from Jane who said that Pauline from Malvern Hills SS would like to bring Michael over to see us on Sunday afternoon, Mothering Sunday. She had met him, seen all the background notes and felt we would be suitable foster parents. He was seven years old coming up eight in April. At present he was living in a professional care home in Worcester with three other children. We said yes, great, looked forward to seeing them both. In truth both Gillian and I felt very nervous as, of course, we had no parenting experience whatsoever. We need not have worried. Pauline, Michael's SS minder, was a mature lady who had her own children and was a very experienced SS worker with "hard to place children". She was obviously quite attached to Michael and we felt that she, as much as us, would ensure that the three of us were compatible.

Michael really liked the dogs, especially Luke, the big English sheepdog, who on his best behaviour was allowed into the living room. The two of them eyeballed each other and had a good roll around the floor. At teatime Gillian organised some hand washing, which was rather superfluous, as Michael wasn't too keen on the cakes on offer. Good old Pauline saved the day and ate some. Out of Michael's earshot she explained that he, whilst not exactly a fussy eater, was unused to home baked produce, surviving on a diet of chips and snacks. No matter this first meeting went as well as we had hoped. We agreed with Pauline to phone her after a couple of weeks to see if it was alright for us to collect Michael from his care home to come and spend a half day at Gorsty again. Well it was a start and he seemed a really good kid.

29

In early April I had a call from Dave at ZES, Ashford asking me to go to Zambia to have a look at the No 1 Rock Shaft at the Baluba Mine of the Luanshya Division of ZCCM. I could not believe that it was yet another shaft assignment. Baluba would make it the ninth in the past fifteen months. No matter, they were all interesting and helped to pay the bills, but I certainly seemed to be getting a "shaft guru" reputation. This time it was Zambia Airways (ZA) from Heathrow rather than BCal from Gatwick since ZES was a wholly owned subsidiary of ZCCM, which in turn was a Zambian state owned company. ZA was fine but the in-flight service was definitely inferior to BCal, Notwithstanding that, the much more important thing was that the ZA flight arrived on time with no technical hitches.

This time I stayed overnight at ZCCM's Kwacha Lodge in Lusaka and caught the early morning RoanAir flight to Ndola airport. A Luanshya Division car picked me up at Ndola for the short drive to their Director's Lodge cum guest house, very comfortable indeed! Baluba was the newest, cobalt rich mine on the Copperbelt and unlike the other major mines had primary access via a ramp-decline. The No 1 Rock Shaft was, as it's name suggested, the main ore hoisting shaft of the mine. However it was not currently achieving the rock output desired on account of hoisting speed restrictions in the shaft. I was given a 1984 report from the Shaft Sinkers Group and an internal ZCCM memo on the problem. First off, go underground and ride the cage normal speed then on top of the cage running through on shaft examination slow speed.

It was immediately apparent that the vertical interval between bunton sets was huge, 6.1 m, and the bunton layout was very rigid. The existing steelwork configuration was completely wrong with very flexible guides, due mainly to the large vertical bunton span. The present Jeto bottom dump skips had a capacity of 15.5 tonnes and a skip tare weight of 10 tonnes - a total rope end load of 25.5 tonnes. Precedent design practice had considered horizontal loads ranging from 6.25% (very good guide alignment) to 17% (bad alignment) on the shaft steelwork. The latter obviously applicable for Baluba. Applying such a horizontal load of 4.34 tonnes to the bunton midpoint would produce a deflection of just over 2mm only indicating a very rigid bunton. Using the same horizontal loading to the midpoint of the guides would produce an alarmingly high deflection of over 70mm. Normal shaft steelwork design practice limits midpoint deflections to no more than 25mm. This extreme flexure of the guides was imposing huge shock loads on the buntons and their shaft wall attachments. An obvious solution was to halve the bunton set vertical interval to 3.05m which would reduce midpoint guide deflection to 6.6mm, very satisfactory, but, of course expensive and time consuming to implement.

The existing guides were the old-fashioned South African style "top-hat" guides weighing 59.3 Kg/m. Interestingly if SHS guides of a slightly lighter weight of 56.6 Kg/m had been used the midpoint guide deflection would reduce from 70mm to 16mm on account of their higher section modulus. This seemed a better, quicker and cheaper solution than installing intermediate buntons and was my main recommendation. However as a "bodge-up" Shaft Sinkers had suggested stiffening the existing top-hat guides by battening the two central guides together and strapping the outside guides back to the shaft lining with channel. I was not in favour of this compromise bodge-up, but agreed that it would greatly stiffen the existing guides at little cost and time delay.

Winder full speed had been restricted to 13.1 m/s with a & r rates of 0.98 m/s/s. With a six-second creep time and 15 second load/dump time the full cycle from a hoisting depth of 722.5m was 90 seconds, indicating 36.67 cycles/hour (55 min hour basis). A daily rock output (wet ore & waste) of 10,120 tonnes was required from Baluba, which over sixteen hours/day rock hoisting meant 632.5 tonnes/hour. Hence net skip capacity had to be 632.5/36.67 = 17.25 tonnes. To maintain the gross rope end load at 25.5 tonnes would inevitably require a skip tare of no more than 8.25 tonnes a tare/payload ratio of 0.478, quite impossible with steel skips. The only solution was to replace the steel skips with lightweight aluminium skips designed to suit the physical shaft space available whilst maintaining a minimum running clearance of 75mm. I also suggested that these new aluminium skips should be dumped by headframe mounted skip hydraulic ramming gear rather than the on-board dump gear (Sala type) skips suggested by Shaft Sinkers. Locating the dumping gear off the skips keeps the skip tare weight to a minimum. That was the job, No. 032 complete and I headed back to Lusaka by RoanAir and onwards to Heathrow by ZA again, the whole round trip taking only eight days.

Mid April Gillian and I arranged with Pauline to collect Michael from his present care home in Worcester for a day out at Gorsty so that we might all get to know each other a little better. It was good to see the professional carer's home and to note that everything of value, for example the television in the children's room, was kept out of reach on a high wall shelf. There was also a 4ft gate on their playroom to ensure that no one slipped off unnoticed. It seemed a bit draconian, but on reflection was entirely sensible. The carers, a married couple, were both kind to their four "care children", but were entirely practical. As they noted, we also have a life of our own and can't physically watch over them the whole time so it was essential to have a safe, secure playroom for them to be on their own. We noted this, but felt it should be slightly easier for us with only one to look after.

Michael seemed to enjoy the car trip to Gorsty and was very pleased to see the sheepdog, Luke again. It looked as if our first major problem area was going to be food. Neither Gillian nor I knew anything about what eight-year-olds liked eating, but it certainly didn't seem to include our usual diet! Hey ho, something we asked the carers about when we took Michael back to Worcester in the late afternoon.

The next time we took Michael back to Gorsty both my parents were there. They had been very supportive of our efforts to become foster parents and also wanted to meet Michael to "see what the lad's like". They both found him a little "wild and unruly" but were 100% in favour of him joining the Gorsty household. So that was it, I phoned Pauline to say yes from our side, could she determine if Michael was happy to have us as foster parents and if so could we get on and do it? A week or so later she said yes and that she would bring Michael over plus his "things" and, of course, the inevitable paper work. Finally after eighteen months of vetting we had become foster parents. It was life changing.

In the absence of the SS we quickly established that he preferred to be called Mike and almost as quickly this morphed into Sproggs, the services' moniker for young 'uns. My first, urgent job was to take Sproggs to see the Kimbolton School headmaster, Mr Watson. I hoped this village primary school (C of E) would be able to take Mike for the forthcoming summer term. Once Mr Watson appreciated that Mike was a new (for us!) foster child he was very helpful and accommodating. I asked if it would be possible for the school to see Mike safely across the A4112 Tenbury road and onto the Mennals footpath where either Gillian or I would meet him for the one mile walk back to Gorsty. No problem. Everything about living in the countryside was a brand new experience for Sproggs as he had lived in a town, well city, Worcester, all his eight years. I'd take Sproggs with me when walking the dogs every day. He would discover mole tumps, rabbit holes, sheep droppings, brambles, dandelions or trees. He had never climbed a tree, didn't know that that was what young boys did, but he soon learnt along with telling the time from dandelion clocks and trying to create a screech from blowing a blade of grass. In turn for me it was reliving ones own youth spent on a farm in Oxfordshire during the war.

All too soon work reared its (essential) head again. Late May and a call from John at Davy McKee in Stockton-on-Tees. Could I come up to discuss a new mining project in the UK? Of course I said yes to job No. 033 especially when John said it could involve me in quite a lot of work. I decided to go by train, Gillian dropping me off at Worcester before driving on to Alfrick with Sproggs to see my parents. From Worcester I took the train to Birmingham New Street to catch the cross country service to Darlington and local shuttle to Stockton.

John explained that Davy had been commissioned by Imperial Metals Co (IMC) of Canada to prepare a costing study for developing the old Parys Mountain multi-metal mine on the Isle of Anglesey, North Wales. They required me to prepare the mining section of the study. Apparently IMC had completed an outline study based on only 14 surface diamond drill holes. That was little data to design a mine on, but then Davy had precious little mineralogy or testwork information to design a beneficiation plant so we were in the same boat. Davy's plan was to visit the project site the following week and asked me to join them.

After lunch on Sunday I drove north on the A49 to Shrewsbury then turned north-west onto the A5 for Oswestry, Llangollen, Betws y Coed and the Menai Strait bridge on to Anglesey. Finally the A5025 to Benllech where we were all booked in to a pleasant pub. The next day we walked around the project site with the IMC Project manager and thereafter I peeled off with the project geologist into the DD core shed. The geological interpretation of the complex mineralisation (Cu, Pb, Zn, Ag & Au) was of an overturned syncline in host rocks of rhyolite. The top of the mineralisation was 160m below surface extending down to 550m below surface. The DD split cores showed that the acid volcanic host rocks would provide mainly good, Class 2 Ground (CSIR Classification). The ore lens thicknesses ranged from 1.4 to 10 m. The ore expectancy of the two major lenses was about 8,500 t/vm.

IMC had already decided that a production rate of 250,000 short tons/year should be used for project costing. A working year of 250 days had also been decided giving a daily mining rate of 1000 short tons equivalent to 907.4 tonnes/day. That was higher than I would have selected on the current data base but IMC felt that further drilling would increase the reserves. I discussed likely mining methods with IMC's project mining guy over a few beers in the pub that evening and we agreed that a system of sub-level open stoping with parallel down-hole drilling from a top overcut with ore removal via flank drawpoint crosscuts by diesel LHDs was the way to go. The method would, of course, require good ore continuity on both strike and dip and this had yet to be proved. It also seemed logical to access the ore lenses via a vertical shaft rather than a lengthy ramp-decline since the top of the ore was 160m below surface. I said I would work up a mine design on these basic parameters and come back to discuss it with IMC before undertaking a costing and a development schedule.

I spent another day with the IMC and Davy guys collecting basic information on local power and water supplies as well as local labour rates and various bulk supplies such as Readymix concrete and structural steel. Davy, as a major UK engineer-contractor, had a huge data bank of construction consumable costs and these would be readily available to me for this job. Well that would certainly make my life easier, relieving me of the necessity to phone umpteen suppliers for quotes.

After three days with nothing more to be gained on site I headed back to Gorsty. I decided to take the scenic route back and headed for Caernarfon after crossing the Menai bridge, then turned south on the A4085 for Beddgelert and on to the A470 past the closed Trawsfynydd nuclear power plant to Dolgellau and Newtown. From there I took the back road down the upper Teme valley to Knighton and thence to Leominster. The mountainous countryside around Snowdonia and central Wales was magnificent and with little traffic it proved a glorious, relaxing drive.

On the home front Sproggs was settling in at Kimbolton School, but finding it difficult to adjust to both the discipline and natural hierarchy of the children themselves. Packed school lunches hadn't yet managed to hit the spot, but Gillian was picking up tips from other Mums. In reality everyone seemed to give their children crisps and snacks, good old-fashioned sandwiches and apples were definitely not de rigeur. No matter, Sproggs enjoyed the walk back from school. In the field just past the derelict "Hole" cottage there was a large oak tree that we sat under to wait for him. It seemed quiet and peaceful but was often enlivened by the furious activity of grey squirrels overhead producing a veritable snowstorm of oak tree "bits".

I certainly found it more difficult to work at home with an eight-year-old around who wanted attention. My working day now split into two parts, 9 till 3 (school time) and 9 till 10 or 11 after Sproggs had gone to bed.

As IMC had fixed both the production rate and number of annual work days my first task was to locate a main vertical shaft. This was easy since the ore lenses were compact with strike lengths of 155m only. A minimum distance of 50m from the shaft centreline to stoping activities was maintained to prevent the necessity of sterilising ore in a shaft pillar. The chosen location also ensured crosscutting distances to the ore zones would be less than 100m. I selected a circular shaft of 5m diameter mainly on account of ventilation needs for underground diesel units and to provide space for a cage large enough to handle major items of trackless equipment. Final shaft depth would be 540m with levels established at 50m intervals from the 140m level to the lowest level at 490 m.

All mine development would be of $14m^2$ section drilled off by twin boom electro-hydraulic jumbos with mucking by $2m^3$ diesel LHDs. Initial stope development would open up the Engine Zone on the 140, 190, 240 and 290m levels to enable three stoping lifts to be prepared ahead of production. At the SW extremity of the 140m level a 2.4m diameter raise borer hole would be driven through to surface to form the Engine Zone ventilation upcast. Drawpoint crosscuts would be developed at 15m strike interval on the 190, 240 and 290m levels. Stope drilling overcuts and draw undercuts would be developed across the full width and strike of the lenses. An access ramp of 1 in 6 grade would be driven between the 140m and 490m levels to provide trackless access throughout the mine.

Trackless, longitudinal sub-level blast-hole stoping would be the basic mining method. A central slot raise would be developed at the mid-strike position and then an electro-hydraulic drifter rig would put down 64mm diameter holes on a 2m burden by 2.2m spacing pattern to give a drilling yield of 8.5 tonnes/m drilled and a blasting yield of 3.1 tonnes/Kg explosive. The blasted ore would be recovered from the flank drawpoints by diesel LHDs. These LHDs would either dump directly into bored ore passes where the haul distance was less than 250m or load 12-tonnes capacity haul trucks. Broken ore would collect on a main grizzly on the 490m level, equipped with hydraulic pick breaker ahead of the primary jaw crusher (rated 75 kW). The crushed ore would pass to a crushed ore bin feeding the loading station conveyor. Rock hoisting output would be 71.3 tonnes/hour over a lift of 540m by a single 4.5 tonnes capacity bottom dump skip and counterweight hauled by a DC friction winder rated at 460 kW. The large cage (4000mm by 1850mm) with a net payload capacity of eight tonnes would be hauled by a 500 kW DC friction winder. Both winders would be tower mounted. Power would be taken underground at 6.6 kV to the main load centre alongside the main pump station close to the main shaft on the 500m level. Cone type grit settlers and clear water sumps would provide eight hour storage ahead of the pumps. There would 3 pumps each rated at 125m^3/hour drawing 300 kW at full output. There would be no need for a compressed air line. Ventilation requirements would be based on 0.05m^3/s/HP of all operating diesel units indicating a fan duty of 65m^3/s at a pressure of 2.5kPa.

I phoned John at Davy and said I was ready to discuss my notional mine with the IMC guys. We arranged to meet up on Anglesey in a couple of days time. I opted to drive up the scenic way again as it was much more relaxing and picturesque than the A49, A5 route. We stayed at the same pub in Benllech and had a cheerful, beery get-together the first night. The following day we worked through the "notional mine" which IMC were generally happy with. However they wanted me (well Davy actually, since I was merely a subbie) to nominate specific mining machinery. After much argument we decided on Tamrock twin boom Minimatic jumbos for development. GHH LF-4.1 2m³ LHDs for mucking and GHH MK-A 12.1 diesel dump trucks for lateral haulage. For blast-hole stope drilling the Tamrock SOLO H 405 RR unit was preferred. Both Tamrock drilling rigs were, of course, electro-hydraulic units.

There was also a preference for GEC friction winders and Robbins raise borers which I totally endorsed. IMC had no firm thoughts on pump or fan suppliers so I could use my own selection. We also confirmed the hourly ore hoisting rate, moisture content and that this material would be minus 150mm from the underground crusher to the Davy guys designing materials handling ahead of the beneficiation plant. With all the loose ends and interface details between the mine and surface works tied up I headed back to Gorsty on the scenic route, but after Dolgellau I headed east on the A458 for Welshpool, then south-east through Churchstoke, Lydham and Craven Arms. If anything the central Wales countryside on this route was even more attractive than the more southerly route through Newtown.

Back at Gorsty I now had to work up the development schedule, capital and operating cost details as well as a final written up report for submission to Davy. The schedule was fairly straightforward. If the current DD campaign produced acceptable ore lens intersections and grades then the decision would be made to go underground in order to access the ore zones and carry out development and evaluation "on-lens". To achieve this the main exploration/production shaft would be sunk at full size to a depth of 300 m. Crosscutting and development on the 290m level would then be undertaken. To establish ore dip continuity it might also be necessary to carry out development on higher levels such as 240m and 190 m. If this development confirmed ore lens grades and disposition then shaft sinking would resume from the initial 300m level sump to the proposed final shaft sump at 540m level. The initial sink to the 300m level would take 27 months to complete and subsequent development to put the mine into production a further 24 months.

All preproduction development, undertaken by contractor, would cost £15.1 million. Fixed plant (winders, transformers, fans, pumps, crusher etc) £3.8 million; mobile mining plant £3.5 million and capitalised spares £0.7 million. Thus total mine capital was estimated at £23.1 million (mid 1985 basis). On the operating side a total manpower of 118 would be required, comprising ten supervisors and 108 workers (including an allowance of 9% for non-attendance). Mining manpower costs did not include 14 technical staff who would be considered as part of the operations general administrative overhead. In fact manpower costs represented 37% of the total mining cost of £16.8/tonne ore mined.. I slotted all these numbers, together with back-up and derivation into a draft report and duly mailed this to Davy a couple of days before the end of June for incorporation in their report to IMC.

In early July I had a call from John at RTZTS asking me to come down to Bristol to discuss a new mining project in Botswana. As it happened job No. 034 was a very simple desk study of a proposed underground nickel mine. I abstracted all the relevant geological, geotechnical and topographical data from a promoter's report and said it would take me two days at home to produce a hypothetical mine with some very crude costs factored largely from my recent Zambian experience. I completed the work at Gorsty and three days later went back to Bristol for a discussion on my notional mine and crude cost estimates and that was that.

In the third week of July I had a call from John at Davy asking me to attend another meeting with IMC on Anglesey to chew over, yet again, the subject of mine access. Again I took the scenic drive through Welshpool, Dolgellau and up through Snowdonia to the island and the pub at Benllech, where by now they welcomed me in English rather than Welsh. I had finally become an accepted "foreigner" who only spoke English. In fact almost all the local shops, garages etc on the island spoke Welsh rather than English.

The IMC mining guys still felt that a ramp-decline on its own was the way to open up the mine rather than a vertical shaft. I countered by saying that there was no general rule governing whether a shaft or ramp-decline was the correct approach. Ramp-declines were, unsurprisingly, limited to relatively shallow deposits, since for greater depths they required between five and ten times the linear distance of a shaft. Of course ramps were considerably cheaper than shafts per linear metre but where continuous up-ramp ore haulage would be required, as at Parys Mountain, the ramp grade should not exceed 1 in 8. The bottom of the Engine ore lens was 500m below surface thus a ramp-decline would be over 4Km in length. Firstly this would take a long time to develop (much longer than the shaft alternative) and secondly it would be a very onerous up-ramp haulage duty.

I pointed out that most production ramps, as opposed to purely exploration ramps, were of no greater length than 2.5 to 3Km. I estimated that a 4Km ramp would take 36 months to complete and cost £5.8 million whereas a 5m diameter circular shaft would take 24 months to complete and cost £4.05 million. A 5m diameter circular shaft equipped with a 4.5 tonne capacity skip/counterweight and a large cage/counterweight would be able to handle all major mining units with minimal dismantling. A key point in favour of the shaft would be its ability to easily handle the downcast ventilation quantities required, which a 14m^2 section decline could not. In fact the use of a ramp-decline for ore haulage would require eight no 135 HP 12 tonnes diesel haul trucks to transport 907 tonnes/day on a two shift basis. This additional 1080 HP would require circulating 85% more ventilation air, the requirement rising from 65m^3/s to 120cu m/s.

Of course there were additional shaft option costs such as the headframe and winders (£2.4 million) and the internal ramp (£2.5 million) this was offset by additional haul trucks (£1.15 million), additional ventilation fan (£0.15 million), additional bored vent raises (£1.0 million), additional workshop excavation and equipment (£0.15 million) and additional power reticulation (£0.2 million). Overall the ramp-decline option would show a reduction in capital expenditure of about £0.5 million. However the ramp option delayed the project by a year; had difficulty in handling ventilation quantities; required fifteen additional truck drivers and eight maintenance men but no longer needed four hoistmen a net increase of 19. The ramp option would increase total mining costs by 12% or £2.0/tonne. Thus on technical, timing and overall cost grounds the shaft/hoisting scheme would be the better approach for developing the Parys Mountain project. Needless to say I had to produce detailed technical and cost back-up as well as some articles on worldwide precedent practice on ramp-decline haulage. All in all the calculations and arguments together with several beery evening discussions kept me in Anglesey for a week before I headed back to Gorsty to write up a four or five page report to mail to Davy.

In August I had a call from Jaime, the new General Manager (GM) of COMSUR who asked me to come out to Bolivia and provide further help with the breast-stoping at the Milluni mine. He told me that Lufthansa (LH) had started a new direct service to La Paz using a modified Boeing

747 providing half passenger and half freight, why didn't I try it out? So I asked my faithful travel agent at Thomas Cook in Hereford to book me on a BA flight from Heathrow to Frankfurt transferring to the LH flight to La Paz via New York - yes, really, weird way to fly to South America from Europe!

I have never found Frankfurt an easy airport to find ones way around. Of course, flying in from Heathrow I appreciated I would need to transfer by bus to another terminal for the La Paz flight. However no one seemed to know where this (very new) flight departed from. Eventually I located a small check-in desk and mini lounge tucked away behind an escalator. There were only fifty or so passengers for the flight which did not auger well for it's long-term sustainability. From a passenger viewpoint this was marvelous as one could stretch out over three adjacent seats and put in some serious sleeping across the Atlantic. We had a ninety minute stop in New York, where a further forty passengers boarded. With less than 100 passengers the 747 cabin looked distinctly empty not withstanding that it was of reduced size on account of the commercial cargo compartment. However the real fun began as this giant plane (in comparison to LAB's 737) began its approach to El Alto airport. Whatever the reason, the pilot decided not to land, but merely had a "look-see" at the immense strip from about 300 feet up, before powering over La Paz city, turning south-east towards Illimani. Those of us who knew the El Alto airport well were more than a little discombobulated. The LH jumbo completed a fly around, landed and finally came to a stop after some serious braking.. A number of us did wonder how au fait the LH pilots were with landing at very high altitude strips. Without doubt the 747 looked quite out of place alongside the fairly modest El Alto terminal building. I made a mental note to stick with South American trained pilots for future flights in to La Paz on the smaller sized Boeing 737.

As usual I was booked in to the Hotel Sucre on Avenida Arce not far from the COMSUR office. The next morning I fronted up to their offices to see Jaime, the new GM. Jaime was a Bolivian, an electrical engineer by training who spoke perfect English. I really felt bad about my very poor spanglish, but, hey ho they were still using me. He explained that they wished to extend the breast-stoping system I had introduced in a trial stope on the Rotschild vein eighteen months before to other veins in the mine.

However Mario, the Milluni Mine Manager (MM), was not keen on the method. An old miner himself, Mario was a solid back-stoping afficionado and not at all keen on the idea. I explained to Jaime that I first needed to look back through the operating records of the original trial stope to convince myself that, in fact, breast-stoping with jacklegs had increased productivity, tonnes/manshift (TMS), increased drilling output (tonnes/m drilled) and blasting output (tonnes/Kg explosive). There was also the very important aspect of improvements to the Mine Call Factor (MCF).

I spent the next couple of days working through the last eighteen months stoping statistics. In the original trial stope and half a dozen other stopes the mine had converted the TMS and drilling factor had both improved, but the explosive yield was still below 2.5 tonnes/Kg explosive and, very disappointingly, the average stope grade was only marginally higher. Nothing for it but some "face time" (doh!) in the stopes was required, so we set off in the faithful Range Rover for the eighty minute grind up to the mine. Underground it was immediately apparent that the mine had installed new 4in compressed air lines on the main levels, greatly increasing the dynamic air pressure in the stopes producing, unsurprisingly, much higher drill penetration rates. There were two reasons for low explosive yield and poor grade improvement, both interlinked. Examination of a number of stopes showed many drill hole barrels outside vein limits into waste wall rock and a complete absence of 9in stope grizzlys. The lack of stope grizzlys encouraged the stope miners to over-blast (increasing explosive consumption) to ensure that their broken ore would pass easily through the level chutes. In turn the over-blasting damaged the vein contacts and exacerbated waste dilution consequently pushing the mined grade down.

Back in La Paz I had a session with Carlos, Mario and Jaime. First the good news. Drilling performance had improved due to new machines and better dynamic air pressure in the stopes as a direct consequence of the new 4in air mains on levels. Bad news. Poor hole direction in stopes (thus breaking waste) presumably caused by poor, lax control by Shift Bosses. Stopes must be fitted with 9in grizzly to curtail desire by miners to over-blast. The ANFO loaders should be adjusted to produce a loading rate of no more than 0.5 Kg/m drilled in a 38mm drill hole. None of these improvements were rocket science. With the exception of adjusting the ANFO loaders which was an engineering matter, everything else came down to hands-on mine management, thus over to Mario to implement. Carlos noted that the flat-back breast hole stopes were simpler for his geologist/samplers to mark up vein wall contacts, thus no excuse for over breaking.

After that I spent a further week accompanying Mario and his Shift Bosses around all the existing and planned breast stopes. The final conclusion was that I really, really must improve my South American Spanish. Then it was up to El Alto to board the giant LH 747 combi for the flight back to Europe. Thankfully the much more relaxed take-off procedure of the LH jumbo compared well with the frantic scramble and scrabble of the LAB 737, but the 747 was still alarmingly close to the ground several minutes after apparently becoming airborne. New York passed in a blur and then it was the organised Germanic mayhem at Frankfurt before the disorganised mayhem at Heathrow. No one of a sane disposition can truly enjoy being confined to an aluminium tube, pressurised to 8,000 feet, breathing recycled air for close on eighteen hours with a guaranteed hassle boarding and de-planing. I never could take the Air Canada ad seriously - "It's so comfortable you won't want to get off" - oh really?

Sproggs, still at home for the long summer school holidays had proved more than a little trying for Gillian to manage on her own whilst I was away in Bolivia. Fortunately Pauline, his Malvern Hills SS minder had come to the rescue and taken him off for a day to Kidderminster, where the public swimming pool, complete with water slide had proved a winner. In fact I had taken him to the Leominster pool every week in a concerted effort to channel some of his bottled up resentment/energy into learning to swim. After two or three false starts he had begun to develop into a useful swimmer and had joined the local Kingfisher swimming club.

With no immediate work on the horizon we decided to hire a narrow boat from Maestermyn Cruisers at Whittington on the Llongollen Canal. Both of us were a little apprehensive of how Sproggs would react but he was great fun and thoroughly enjoyed feeding the ducks and swans from the boat's rear deck. We only took the boat for a week but it was long enough to experience cruising over both the Chirk and Pontcysyllte aqueducts, the latter very spectacular as it crossed the River Dee 120 feet below. I really liked the relaxed, hassle free life on a narrow boat where one could escape from most external irritations, such as the telephone! As a consequence of the Llangollen trip I took out a subscription to Waterways World monthly magazine to learn more about the UK's canal system and its history

In October Dick from RTZTS called asking me to go down to Bristol to review underground mining methods at the Cardona potash mine in Catalonia, Spain and thus job No. 036 came into being. It was purely a desk study, but Dick felt my experience of visiting the Cardona mine in the seventies might be useful. As usual I drove down to Bristol via the A417, the M5 and the M32. It was an easy run taking about two hours. At Castlemeads, home of RTZTS, a group of us had a brain storming session on how to improve underground productivity and reduce operating costs. Unlike conventional, generally flat bedded potash deposits which are mined in a similar manner to coal mines, the Cardona mine was a sub-level blast-hole open stoping operation. This was because the potash deposit had been intruded by a volcanic plug which forced the potash into a near vertical cylinder surrounding the plug itself.

Electro-hydraulic trackless rotary rigs were employed for stope drilling and appeared entirely suitable and efficient. However blasted ore withdrawal from flank drawpoints into the undercut was by (coal type) gathering-arm loaders feeding short stub conveyors, which in turn fed a trunk conveyor. These loaders were inflexible and slow when trying to handle the inevitable chunks of oversize. To me it seemed the wrong application for this type of loader. We obviously were not going to visit the mine so the only clue we had to probable size of primary blasted stope ore was details of the drilling burden/spacing pattern. Bingo! A $5m^3$ diesel LHD seemed to be the ideal unit for this stope load-out duty, provided the mine's ventilation system could handle the increased operating diesel HP. We did some very crude simulation and reckoned that a LHD of this size would increase production per drawpoint by 150% and, of course, it had the flexibility to service three or four more drawpoints to ensure a steady draw. Agreement reached, Dick said he'd contact the mine to ascertain ventilation details and that was that. I headed off back up the M32 and M5 for Leominster and home.

John from Davy phoned me to say that their client, IMC, had now submitted a planning application for their Parys Mountain project to Gwynedd County Council (GCC). Surprise, surprise GCC had a number of technical queries on the application and IMC required their engineering consultant, Davy, to front-up to the council offices in Caernarfon. In turn Davy asked me to attend to provide mining back-up. We were all booked in to a town-centre hotel in Caernarfon, which was a pleasant town with a magnificent castle on the banks of the Menai Strait. The GCC offices had to be seen to be believed. Very modern, steeply banked wooden seats forming a half circle around a central platform, each seat equipped with full audio facilities for both Welsh and English transmission. In fact all questions and answers were made in first Welsh and then English which seemed unbelievable, since no one from IMC, Davy or their specialist subcontractors (including me) spoke nor understood Welsh. This certainly slowed down proceedings, but at least it gave one "thinking time" before answering the GCC Chief Planning Officer's questions.

On the mining front the first question related to mine ventilation and was easily answered by quoting the international standard of providing $0.05m^3/s/HP$ of all operating diesel units underground. I had to stress that this was operating units and not the total number of diesel units underground. This lead on to the selection of a circular vertical shaft rather than a ramp-decline as better equipped to handle these ventilation volumes. It transpired that the GCC favoured a ramp-decline for mine access as "it was less intrusive on the environment than a headframe and associated winder house". Davy said they would submit a detailed technical note justifying the selection of the vertical shaft option. In fact, of course, I had already done this, but IMC had not submitted all the detailed back-up calculations in their planning application.

The next query concerned the underground crusher. GCC felt that this should be on the surface for health (ie dust pollution) grounds. I first pointed out that the 915mm by 610mm jaw crusher produced a 150mm rom product which could easily be handled by the 4.5 tonnes capacity skip. The crusher and feeder would be equipped with a dust extraction hood connected to a scrubber unit. Dust was not expected to be a problem since the rom ore would contain 3% moisture.

So far so good but we now moved on to a major GCC worry - ground vibration from underground blasting affecting nearby properties. Firstly I confirmed that mining operations would take place on a two shifts/day, five days/week and 250days/year basis. Annual development of 1600m would require a single 3.5m round/shift, pulling 3.2m. The 14m^2 cross section would require 42 holes (38mm diameter) and would be charged with 60% AN gelignite at a loading density of 1.5 Kg/m giving a total charge of 200 Kg. The velocity of detonation of this type of explosive would be circa 2500m/s and the round would be initiated by millisecond electric delays. These development blasts would take place twice per day at approximately 1330 and 2130 hours. Long-hole stope blasting would use a powder explosive with a loading density of 2.7 Kg/m in 45m deep 64mm diameter holes. To assist fragmentation four typical rows (12 holes in total) would be blasted with millisecond electric delays breaking 4,700 tonnes using 1500 Kg explosive. A single blast of this size would be required each week and would be scheduled for 2130 on Fridays to ensure good smoke clearance over the weekend.

For an accurate assessment of ground vibrations produced by blasting at Parys Mountain I said a controlled vibrograph survey would be required. However this would not be practical until the mine had been developed. GCC were not at all happy with this reply. I attempted to dig us out of a hole (no pun intended) by saying that likely vibrations could be estimated from the following formula: A = k x sq root of E/d where A was the ground movement in thousands of an inch; k was a constant (100 for Parys Mountain volcanics); E was the weight of explosives (lbs) and d was the distance (ft) between blast and observer. The average depth of mining below surface would be about 350m and applying this depth to the formula indicated the following amplitudes at surface immediately over the blasts: development 0.0018in & stoping 0.005in. The maximum amplitude for prevention of structural damage was usually quoted as 0.008in. At shallower mining depths (185m) the weekly stope blast would produce a surface amplitude of 0.0095in, which would exceed the usual guideline limit. Worried faces all round, ours as well as the GCC.

In later discussion with John of Davy, I said I was not an expert on ground vibration and would go up to the IMM library in London to obtain some additional data on peak particle velocities (ppv) and a USBM publication by Nichols, Johnson & Duvall titled "Blasting vibrations and their effects on structures". He agreed for me to do some further investigation into the vibration problem. This aspect concluded GCC's queries on the mining side of IMC's project so after lunch I packed up and headed back to Leominster.

Three days later I headed for the IMM library at 44 Portland Place, London. The more I read about ground vibrations the more I felt we (the IMC + Davy team) needed a real expert in this field to assuage GCC's genuine concern. I phoned John and voiced my fears and he agreed that I could subcontract a "vibration expert" (no smutty jokes please). I then phoned Simon at Wardell Armstrong in Newcastle-under-Lyme and he said yes they had a vibration guru. We agreed that I'd visit Newcastle the next day and supply their guru with all the pertinent blasting and geotechnical data relating to a Parys Mountain mining operation. Thus the following day I drove to their offices and spent half a day with Mike going through the blasting aspects of the proposed mine. Mike said he would send me a brief report in three days. This he did, I added a covering note and sent it up to John at Davy who decided, correctly, to send the complete Wardell report to GCC as an integral part of the IMC planning application. We all hoped that that would put the subject to bed.

Fortunately I had no mining work over the Christmas period so we could decorate Gorsty, put up lights and, of course a Christmas tree. Gillian and I both wanted to make it thoroughly enjoyable for Sproggs. Gillian's Mum was staying with us and she and Sproggs seemed to get on well playing various board games and attacking the chocolates with relish. On Christmas eve we finally got Sproggs off to bed by about 10 o'clock and close to midnight we put the turkey in the Aga slow oven to cook overnight. Then I crept into Sproggs bedroom and positioned a couple of pillowcases stuffed with toys in his bedroom. I went down to baste the turkey around 7am and on the way up was amazed to find Sproggs wide awake, but still in bed, staring at the pillowcases, not daring to look. He couldn't believe they were his presents. The next half hour he charged to and fro from his room to ours to show off his latest find from the pillowcase. It really made all the trauma of fostering worthwhile. My parents drove over from Alfrick to join us for a traditional Christmas lunch. Gillian and I relaxed as the grandparents took over amusing Sproggs.

30

The start of 1986 was quiet on the mining work front, which was good, since I could provide Gillian with some support with Sproggs. We often went over to Alfrick to see my parents and help out in the garden and around the bungalow. Their central heating gas boiler was playing up and I thought I could fix the ignition problem. Gillian overheard my father saying to my mother in a loud stage whisper "do you think the boy knows what he's doing"? Nothing changes, but he was right on the money. I didn't and they had to get a new boiler. No, not because of me it was very old and kaput. Browsing through Waterways World March issue I noticed that Maestermyn Cruisers were advertising a 38ft second-hand narrow boat for sale. It had a traditional slow speed Petter PH2W engine and had been in Maestermyn's hire fleet for a number of years. I was very tempted and we all drove up to have a look at it. That was it, I made an offer and after the usual haggling we agreed a price. The yard undertook to repaint the boat in traditional green and red and do a maintenance check on the electrics, gas and water supply. Meanwhile I had to find a home mooring. Not so easy. Stourport on the Staffs & Worcester canal was the obvious place being only 35 minutes drive from Gorsty, but no available berths. Eventually I located one at Norbury Junction on the Shropshire Union Canal (SUC), more than an hour away. I drove up to take a look. The mooring was linear on the eastern bank of the SUC and seemed reasonably secure. I duly paid the mooring fee and sent off these and the boat's details to British Waterways (BW) for the necessary licence. With the requisite bumph in hand we took the train up to Oswestry and from there a taxi through to the Maestermyn yard.

The newly painted boat looked great. We had decided to rename her Toadflax, mainly on account of her two round portholes in the front bulkhead, but also the oft noted presence of the flower on the canal banks during last August/September. The yard gave us a run through of everything, we filled up with red diesel, collected food and drink from their own provision shop and with some trepidation set off at a stately three miles per hour down the Welsh branch of the SUC. It was thirty miles to Hurleston Junction where we would join the SUC main line. There were a few isolated locks but at

Grindley Brook there was a three lock staircase. We were pleased to see a BW lock keeper to help us. It took us over two days to reach Hurleston and we then had 25 miles on the SUC main line to reach our mooring at Norbury. However first we had to work up the five Tyrley locks and then the huge 15-lock flight at Audlem. Gillian was steerer whilst I operated the locks pretending to know what I was doing. It was quite hard work and the Audlem flight took us nearly seven hours to navigate. All in all it took us two and half days from Hurleston Junction before we finally tied up at Norbury, but very happy that nothing had broken on the boat and we hadn't hit anything other than various lock walls. For security reasons the linear moorings were on the private, or opposite, side from the towpath. We had a 150 yards walk to the padlocked gate close by the Norbury Junction boatyard. One of the resident boaters kept a tethered goat on this private bank side and for some unaccountable reason the goat took an instant dislike to Sproggs, attempting to butt him as we tried to walk by. The goat, thereafter, was known as Billy Goat Gruff and Sproggs gave him a very wide berth whenever we came up to go for a cruise on Toadflax.

At the beginning of April John from Davy phoned and said that the GCC Planning people had come round to the technical superiority of a vertical shaft over a ramp-decline for the Parys Mountain project. However, they now required a detailed description of the surface buildings required for shaft sinking and an exposition on the actual sinking process. Could I write up a technical note on this and be prepared to visit GCC in Caernarfon around mid April for the usual question and answer session? I duly mailed him a five page note plus outline drawings within six days. This was a simple task for me based on my time with Cementation and a variety of other shaft projects. I prepared a number of sketch plans and vertical cross sections at a scale of 1 in 500. The sinking headframe was 26m from surface to sheave wheel platform with raker legs at 60 degrees, the whole fabricated from SHS steel with a 9m high portal frame fabricated from RHS and platework. The shaft sinking Winder House containing a 30 kW scaffold hoist and a 450 kW AC geared double-drum sinking hoist and associated electricals. The Compressor House containing three Atlas ER6-Pack water cooled two stage reciprocating compressors each with FAD of 492l/s @ 7 bar with a 180 kW motor drive. There were Site Offices and Change Rooms. A Concrete Batching Plant comprising ground storage for both sand and coarse aggregates (60m^3 each) with a cylindrical concrete silo. Stores, Maintenance Area and Plant Yard. Shaft Muck Removal would be by 12 tonnes tipper trucks to dump or sale as LQF and finally a car-park area.

The actual sinking method would follow conventional practice, namely drill/blast/muck and subsequent pouring of a monolithic concrete lining of nominal 350mm thickness. The shaft would be vertical with an ultimate depth of 540m. Straight shaft sinking would advance 40 m/month. On the basis of 10% overbreak the volume of waste rock would be 28m^3/m of shaft sunk or about 77 tonnes/m sunk. The concrete lining would require 8.4m^3/m of shaft sunk. In addition eight shaft stations would be cut as the shaft was sunk.

A shaft collar and foreshaft to a depth of 16m would be developed first utilising a mobile crane and the foreshaft then lined with concrete. On completion of the foreshaft the main three deck sinking scaffold would be installed followed by erection of the sinking headframe. The three deck scaffold would then be roped up to the scaffold hoist and and twin sinking kibbles would be roped up to the sinking hoist. Conventional sinking would then commence with a six machine drill jumbo drilling about 60 no 38mm holes to a depth of 4m. After hoisting the drill jumbo to surface the sump holes would be loaded with about 330 Kg of 60% special gelatine explosives fired electrically from surface using millisecond delays. The 3.5m advance would break 270 tonnes. After a period of smoke clearance by forced ventilation the scaffold would be lowered to about 7m from the shaft bottom and braced against the shaft lining by side jacks. A pneumatically operated cactus grab suspended from the underside of the scaffold would be used to load the blasted rock into the 2m^3 capacity kibbles for hoisting to surface and dumping by lazy chain into the 12 tonne tipper trucks.

As sinking progressed the rough shaft side walls would be supported by rock bolts and mesh. When the exposed shaft wall reached 6m this section would then be lined with unreinforced concrete poured down a pipeline from the surface batching plan to the annulus behind heavy metal falsework. Verticality would be maintained by laser beam. On completion of sinking, the shaft would be furnished with permanent steelwork, pipes and cables.

Following furnishing all sinking gear would be removed and the permanent headframe and winders would be installed. The shaft conveyances would then be roped up and a period of exhaustive testing/running would complete shaft commissioning.

No sooner had I despatched the shaft sinking note to Davy than I had another call from John who said that GCC also required additional back-up on the mine ventilation system; details of the permanent headframe; explosive storage and distribution and, of course an update on ground vibration from underground blasting. Another crash job required by mid April. I said this would take me a further three or four days and I planned to send him a copy of the technical note a couple of days before our scheduled meeting with the GCC Planning guys in Caernarfon on the 17th April. In any event I would bring the technical note with me.

On the ventilation front I had calculated a total flow of 65m^3/s at a pressure of 2.5kPa for an rom ore output of 226,860 tonnes/year. This total air volume would downcast the main shaft with an average velocity of 4.4 m/s. There would be two 2.4m diameter bored raise upcasts, the SW handling 40m^3/s and the E handling 25m^3/s. To minimise the surface visual and noise impact both exhaust fans would be installed underground on the - 140m level.

The main production shaft headframe would house the tower mounted friction winders and would incorporate a 285 tonnes capacity rom coarse ore bin. The outside dimensions would be 9.5m by 7.5m with an overall height above shaft collar of 43m. This assumed ore recovery from the headframe bin by conveyor. I also prepared layouts for the alternative of ground mounted winders in conjunction with a conventional skyshaft. An explosive magazine with a storage capacity of fifteen tonnes (equivalent to four weeks production) would require an inside floor area of 35m^2. I obtained a leaflet from HM Mines Inspectorate which gave full details of construction; safe distances and operation thereof.

Then on to the continuing problem area - ground vibration. The WA report noted that a safe blasting limit of 2.0 in/s peak particle velocity (ppv) in the ground adjacent to a structure should not be exceeded if the probability of damage was to be less than 5%. Stope blasting in the early years between the 190m and 140m level (average depth 163 m) would produce the most onerous conditions. With a stope blast of 375 Kg from three long-holes with millisecond delays, the 2.0 in/s ppv trace would describe a circle of 406m radius on the surface around the blast epicentre. Reducing stope blasting to a single hole or 125 Kg blast would reduce the 2.0 in/s ppv trace to a 193m radius circle around the epicentre. Again we, the IMC-Davy team, must stress that stope blasting of this nature would only take place once a week. I despatched these notes to John and had a couple of days to mug up on all the other contentious areas of the planning application before once again heading for Caernarfon.

In fact the meeting went better than we all expected. There seemed to be, finally, a realisation by the GCC Planning guys that an underground hard rock mining project was never going to enhance the natural environment, but would definitely produce a considerable number of local jobs. Notwithstanding that their main areas of concern continued to be noise and ground vibration from blasting.

I managed two weekends back at Gorsty when we all went up to Norbury to take Toadflax out for a short run and do some internal furnishing to make the boat feel more homely. Then it was business as usual with a call from the World Bank to join a "Supervision of Loan" visit to ZCCM in Zambia from the 10th to the 23rd May. This would be job No. 037. At Heathrow I joined the WB team, led by Jim, in the Zambia Airways departure lounge. The old Pamodzi Hotel in Lusaka was our home for three days whilst we had discussions with ZCCM senior management, Ministry of Finance & Ministry of Mines in Lusaka before flying to the Copperbelt by RoanAir on the 14th May. The next eight days our new home was the old, but very comfortable Anglo Directors Lodge in Kitwe. As the only underground mining guy on the WB team I had a very busy time visiting various operations at the four divisions of Nkana, Mufulira, Luanshya and Nchanga as well as Central Services in Kitwe.

At Nkana I made underground visits to the SOB and Mindola sections. As elsewhere on the Copperbelt mining output was drastically down from previous years. There was a chronic lack of fully developed ore available for stoping as a direct consequence of a serious shortfall in development. However there was now no shortage of new mining equipment thanks to the loans from the World Bank, Sysmin and the ADB, but their application was abysmal. Output of new Eimco 922 & 925 LHDs was less than 50% of what the rest of the world achieved. I saw a new US$ 200,000 twin boom Tamrock rig which was specifically designed for deep parallel hole drilling for development work (utilising a burn cut) and noted that the operators were using it to drill an old-fashioned drag round! One despaired. I pointed this out to the Shift Boss and Underground Manager (both Zambian) who were accompanying me and really they had no idea what I was talking about. The mine's engineering department should train the Shift Bosses and Supervisors how to use these expensive machines correctly and in turn they should instruct the operators.

The "Tamrock" incident was symptomatic of what was now wrong on the Copperbelt. When AA and RST were nationalised a short while back to form the state mining company, ZCCM, a huge number of experienced expatriate miners, Supervisors, Shift Boss' and Mine Captains upped sticks and left for private mining companies in South Africa, West Africa and Australia. This had proved catastrophic for ZCCM. I witnessed the same poor front-line supervision in further underground visits to Chibuluma, Mufulira and Baluba. I also visited the Mufulira concentrator and the Nchanga new Tailings Leach Plant (TLP). It was patently obvious that both these plants were drastically short of ore feed and in the case of the TLP also short of sulphuric acid from the Nkana smelter. The problem was in the mines - lack of development, leading to shortage of fully developed ore blocks, thus shortage of stoping areas. In addition to this long standing problem was now the shortage of experienced mining supervision. There was no longer a shortage of mining equipment

The dire state of ZCCMs current mining production was exemplified by the Copperbelt's largest underground mine, Mufulira, where annual ore production had fallen from 6.930 million tonnes in 1975 to 3.596 million tonnes in FY 1985/86. This was almost one million tonnes less than the forecast, which was made only fifteen months ago! The mine's own forecast for production to rise to 5.760 million tonnes in three years time would definitely not be achieved. The orebody strike length and average width, hence ore expectancy, was drastically decreasing with depth and based on a sustainable mining rate of no more than 10% of the ore expectancy, Mufulira would become a 3.0 million tonnes/year mine in a few years time.

With the exception of Chibuluma all the other mines had less than six months Fully Developed reserves. This was a real hand-to-mouth position and confirmed the "squeezed" nature of ZCCMs Copperbelt mines. The host rocks at Mufulira were quartzites with very high strengths in the 150 to 250 Mpa range permitting open stoping. However this had not been possible due to the past use of caving methods and the disastrous tailings inrush of 1970. These factors lead to the introduction of safety pillars, remnants and a haphazard mining programme which had had an adverse effect on ground conditions. Thus today mining induced stress was another major constraint on productivity.

We had wrap-up meetings with the GMs, Underground Managers and CGs of each of the four divisions, as well as ZCCMs Consulting Mining and Metallurgical Engineers. Without exception everyone recognised the mining problem - lack of adequate development ahead of stoping and a severe shortage of experienced front-line supervisors. Unlike the WB team they felt things could rapidly be turned around with all the new mining equipment. However, each of the four divisions production forecasts were, in my view, unrealistically optimistic. We pointed out that all the major mine capital projects, namely Mindola Deepening; Mufulira's Mining at Depth (MAD project!); Baluba Stage 2 Expansion and Nchanga Mine Deepening were all seriously behind schedule. All these delays on underground mining projects would adversely effect future production. The GMs optimism was great, but sadly misplaced.

We flew back to Lusaka on the 21st evening and spent the next two days in fairly stormy meetings with ZCCM senior management, the Ministry's of Mines and Finance. Since the problem area was in the mines I took the lead in explaining the WB view that ZCCM's short term (next five years) copper production forecast would not be achieved. I presented the WB production forecasts, down 60,000 tonnes/year finished copper, to howls of dismay from ZCCM. However Jim, the WB team leader, capped it all by saying that the WB was also very unhappy with the way that ZCCM were utilising the new equipment, financed largely by a WB loan.

In fact, he intimated, in diplomatic language, that ZCCM needed to rapidly pull it's socks up if it wanted any more cheap loans from the WB. That certainly put the cat amongst the pigeons and our final days discussion was, unsurprisingly, focussed on financial matters. We flew out of Lusaka on the 23rd evening with Zambia Airways for Heathrow. Here Jim put the squeeze on me to complete my technical report and copper production forecast by the end of the month. Apparently there was to be a Zambian loan meeting at the WB in Washington in mid June and he needed all the technical back-up.

The last week of May was thus very busy indeed bashing the computer keyboard and tumbling numbers on the calculator. DHL came on the 31st to pick up the report for immediate overnight despatch to Washington. I phoned Jim and apologised for being one day behind his schedule. He was quite relaxed, jovial in fact, since he had reckoned he wouldn't get my report until the following week!

With that out of the way I now had time for Gillian, Sproggs, the dogs and garden, so no time for the feet up! At the weekends we went up to Norbury and spent a couple of nights on Toadflax, going for a leisurely ten mile, lock-free, run down the SUC to Brewood, where we moored overnight. It was a nice, quiet mooring in a cutting a short walk from the village. It was very peaceful and hard to believe Brewood was only five miles from Autherley Junction where the SUC met the Staffs & Worcester canal in Wolverhampton. One disadvantage of canal cruising after the 10th June was that the coarse fishing season opened and there appeared to be no love lost between the fishermen and boaters.

In the third week of June I had a call from the MD of Manitowoc (UK) Ltd. He requested me to visit the West Linton open cast coal site where one of their draglines was being operated by Taylor Woodrow (TW) on behalf on the NCB Opencast Executive. Apparently TW claimed that the Manitowoc 4600 crawler dragline was not achieving the outputs claimed, or indeed, expected. I was to be an independent arbiter as to what was or was not being achieved. It was not really my forte, but seemed fairly straight forward to observe and measure what the 4600 dragline was actually shifting. Thus I agreed to undertake the work which became job No. 038. It was a long drive. I headed north on the A49 for Shrewsbury then the A53 towards Stoke where I joined the M6 north for Carlisle and there turned east onto the A69 eventually spending the night in the market town of Hexham.

The West Linton site was about eleven miles due north of Newcastle-on-Tyne or about 32 miles from Hexham. I had an early breakfast and made my way to TW's West Linton site office by 8.30. Here I met Geoff, the

Project manager and Alan the planning engineer. There were four 0.7m thick coal seams and the upper seam outcroped at the western edge of the site close to the embankment of the main BR rail line from Newcastle to Scotland. The seams dipped east at 1 in 10. The overburden comprised a few metres of drift overlying conventional coal measures of shales and sandstone. The initial overburden and the Top Main coal were removed by a Ruston Bucyrus (RB) face shovel ahead of the Manitowoc dragline operation. The dragline was digging 5.3m of Upper Overburden (UO), 4.3m of Middle Overburden (MO) and 8.2m of Lower Overburden (LO), a total of 17.8m. The UO was generally shaley and would be classified as easy to medium digging. The MO had more sandstone and would be classified as medium digging, whilst the LO had appreciably more compact, cemented sandstone and would be classified as medium to hard digging.

From their experience at the nearby huge Butterwell open cast site TW were using a Swell Factor of 1.25 when converting bank cubic metres (BCM or in situ) to loose or swelled volume. In fact TW had not made any Swell Factor measurements at this West Linton site and observation of the blasted overburden shales and sandstones indicated (subjectively) a higher Swell Factor of 1.30 to 1.35. The pit operated up-dip in 20m wide strips. The RB face shovel kept at least a bench and half ahead of the dragline. A Reed SK25 drill rig put down 130mm diameter holes on a square burden/spacing pattern of 3.65m by 3.65m to 4.25m by 4.25m. Thus four or five holes were drilled across the bench width. Blasting used conventional ANFO with a SG80 primer and electric mili-second delays. The drilling yield was about 17m^3/m drilled and the explosive yield 8m^3/Kg explosive.

It was immediately apparent that these high yields plus the large hole diameter of 130mm meant that the low density ANFO was concentrated in the bottom of the hole. No decking was applied. The loading density of ANFO in a 130mm hole was about 11.2 Kg/m which meant that only 0.75m to 2.0m of each hole would be loaded - a very poor vertical distribution of explosive. The basting engineer confirmed my interpretation by stating that the average stemming was 3.7 m/hole. Thus over the full overburden drilling depth of 16m, since each hole stopped 0.6m short of the coal seam, there would be 11m of stemming leaving a mere 5m or 1.7 m/hole to be filled with explosive. To me this poor vertical distribution of the explosive was the prime reason for the poor fragmentation of the LO.

The consequent large slabs were adversely affecting the fillability of the relatively small bucket on the dragline. To overcome the poor fragmentation I suggested they reduce the burden/spacing pattern and use an Airtrac drifter rig to put down 83mm diameter holes. This would give better vertical explosive distribution and thus better fragmentation compatible with the 7 cu yard bucket on the Manitowoc dragline.

I then spent two hours or so watching and timing the dragline operation. With the 43m boom at a 35 degree inclination the dumping radius was 37m, meaning that most of the inter-seam overburden could be moved by a simple dig and cast. There appeared to be some re-handling on the LO, about 15%, but TW converted this to equivalent BCM. The scheduled operating routine for the dragline was eight hours/shift, three shifts/day and six days/week. The 7th day was for scheduled maintenance. Operators changed on the dragline and had a thirty minute meal break. The management, maintenance and operation of the dragline was good. My main reservation was the unsuitability of this (relatively) small machine trying to dig poorly fragmented competent sandstone within the confines of a tight pit configuration. Fundamentally the fragmentation of the MO and LO should be improved to be compatible with the draglines 7 cubic yard bucket size. I physically measured the internal bucket capacity to the back of the digging teeth; 5.15m^3 which was within 4% of the theoretical 7 cubic yard or 5.35m^3. The cycles per hour for 90 degree swing was 50 to 60 seconds on hard digging falling to 40 to 50 seconds on easy digging. I selected an average swing time of 50 seconds indicating 72 cycles/hour. The tight pit layout caused the average swing angle to rise from 90 to 120 degrees and the corresponding swing factor was thus 0.91 implying an average cycle time of 55 seconds.

TW quoted an overall dragline availability of 90% of scheduled hours, somewhat on the low side but the machine was still available for over twenty hours/day. Operational scheduling considered a 50 minute hour, ie 83%. The bucket factor depends on fillability, itself dependent on blasting fragmentation, and the Swell Factor (ie bank to loose). I estimated fillability to be no better than 0.85 and accepting TWs Swell Factor of 1.25 the bucket factor becomes 0.85/1.25 = 0.68. The final consideration was propel time for moving and repositioning the dragline, estimated to be 6%, thus factor 0.94. Thus BCM/scheduled hour = Bc x C x S x A x O x Bf xP, where Bc was bucket capacity; C was theoretical cycles/hour for 90 degree swing; S was swing factor; A was availability within scheduled hours; O was job operational factor; Bf was bucket factor and P was propel factor. Thus estimated output was 5.35 x 72 x 0.91 x 0.90 x 0.83 x 0.68 x 0.94 = 167 BCM/ scheduled hr.

My conclusion was that the Manitowoc 4600 dragline was performing as well as could be expected under the present operating environment. Changes in drilling and blasting procedure would improve the fillability and reduce the Swell Factor. This should increase the dragline's output to nearly 200 BCM/scheduled hour. It was also apparent that there had been some confusion between TW and Manitowoc concerning the units of measurement for productivity comparisons. Manitowoc quoted an output of 385 cubic yards/hour which was a loose, or swelled figure since that was the material actually being dug. On the other hand TW the earth moving contractor worked and planned in BCM/hour. The Manitowoc figure of 385 cubic yards/hour equated to 235 BCM/hour using the TW Swell Factor of 1.25 and, of course, a cubic yard was only $0.76m^3$. I talked this over with Geoff and Alan and they somewhat reluctantly agreed that the Manitowoc was doing OK for the conditions. They both agreed that the drilling/blasting layouts needed re-jigging. We went for a couple of beers in the local pub before I drove back to Hexham for the night before setting off for Gorsty early the following morning.

After a rapid unwind I spent one day writing up a brief report for the Manitowoc MD. I spoke to him on the phone and he was really pleased to learn that the 4600 dragline was delivering the output they had indicated to TW. He had a good laugh at the confusion over the bank (in situ) and loose (swelled) units further complicated by imperial and metric volumes. We agreed that it was hard to believe but accepted that as a manufacturer he was looking at the loose ground to be shifted whilst TW were looking at the bank ground to be dug.

31

I was free of (mining) work most of July and really enjoyed walking the dogs over Bircher Common with Sproggs. The bracken was now very tall and we had good games of hide and seek, albeit somewhat spoilt by the dogs who didn't seem to understand the core point of the game. Sproggs also learnt how to pull up a bracken and use it as a throwing arrow, but the highlight was his first attempt at tree climbing, very carefully! Out of the blue we had a telephone call from Oliver, an old school friend of mine from Tonbridge. He had spent ten years in the marines, including the Suez landings in 1956 and had now taken early retirement from the Foreign Office (FO). He was currently living in Hay-on-Wye in the holiday house of a FO friend. The first time he came over to see us at Gorsty Sproggs, in all innocence, asked him what he did and Oliver replied, straight faced, "I kill people". Well that certainly wiped the enquiring smile off Sproggs face. Typical Oliver, I had to explain to the lad that he was an ex-marine, a sort of water borne soldier, who kept our country safe. Thereafter Sproggs was somewhat wary of Oliver and years later he said "he was weird".

Right at the end of July I had a call from Simon of WA asking me to join a WA team who were about to start an ODA funded review of the Rampura Agucha (RA) project in Rajasthan, India of Hindustan Zinc Ltd (HZL). This would be job No. 039 The objective of the WA review was to identify items of plant and equipment which could be supplied by British companies financed by the ODA. In fact I had joined a WA team visiting the RA project site a few years ago when the British ODA were looking for suitable engineering consultants. I joined up with Simon and his team in the BA departure lounge. The 747 flew direct to Delhi after an intermediate stop in the Middle East. We stayed in Delhi overnight and caught an early morning IAC Viscount flight to Udaipur. Here we were picked up by two HZL cars for the drive north to Bhilwara and the RA project camp site. My goodness how the previous stark exploration camp had expanded into a small village. We stayed in the new site guest house, which was well furnished with western style facilities.

That afternoon the RA Project manager outlined the salient points. The geological reserves for the proposed open pit were 42.5 million tonnes grading 13.27% Zn and 1.94% Pb, whilst the mining reserves were 45.8 million tonnes at 12.06% Zn & 1.76% Pb on account of operational waste dilution. The size of the operation had been set by HZL at 70,000 tonnes/year of zinc metal output from their smelter. In turn this required an open-pit mining output of 750,000 tonnes/year of ore. With a twenty year average waste stripping ratio of nearly 3.5 this would require the removal of 2.6 million tonnes/year of waste. Pit operations were scheduled for three shifts/day, 280days/year. Daily output was thus 2670 tonnes ore and 9290 tonnes waste. A 10m bench height had been selected. Primary drilling would be by electric rotary rigs drilling 225mm diameter holes and blasted with ANFO. Electric 4.6m^3 rope shovels would load the blasted ore into 50-tonnes capacity diesel dump trucks. All the usual ancillary pit equipment such as dozers, front-end loaders, graders, powder trucks, water bowsers and drainage pumps were specified. The major inputs for the operation were stated as power 22,500 kWh/day, maximum demand 1.6MW; diesel fuel 17,500 litres/day; ANFO explosives 4.2 tonnes/day; water 1,000m^3/day and a labour force of 32 supervisors and 273 workers.

The first point in our review was that the RA project's mining reserves could support a much larger operation. In fact the ore expectancy was over 100,000 t/vm and Taylor's Law indicated a mine life of seventeen years, implying a mining rate of nearly 10,000 tonnes/day. The selected mining rate of 2670 tonnes/day would be seriously under-mining the deposit, but HZL's selection of a 70,000 tonnes/year zinc metal output had determined this mining rate. The open-pit design had been generated by a computer block model utilising blocks each containing about 3750 tonnes. There was no need for tonnage-grade curves since the orebody was defined by the presence of massive sulphides. From a geotechnical standpoint the host rocks were competent, good Class 2 ground (CSIR classification). Ultimate pit slopes were designed at 48 degrees on the hangingwall and 38 degrees on the footwall. It would be a conventional shovel/truck pit. Drilling and blasting patterns would be finalised after trial mining. The proposed use of 4.6m^3 capacity rope shovels meant there would only be one such shovel on ore and two on waste. This was by no means a large shovel but the lowly output of 2670 tonnes/day would be moved by this size shovel in only six hours! Obviously this one shovel arrangement gave no flexibility and no chance for ore blending within the pit. Bluntly it was not matched to the proposed output. The design was based on a 10m bench height with in-pit haul roads restricted to 6.25% gradient. All of this basic pit design work had been done by SNC of Canada.

Now HZL planned to let a tender for trial mining. This would involve the pre-stripping of 280,000m^3 of waste and about 10,000 tonnes of ore which would be sent by road for treatment by the Sala Caravan mill based at Rajpura Dariba. HZL, of course, was an experienced underground miner and operator of sulphide flotation concentrators and electrolytic smelters, but had virtually no experience of open-pit mining. We, WA, felt strongly that HZL must insist that the final development contractor for the main pre-stripping must include a strong training element for HZL operators. The list of mining equipment for the RA project was originally drawn up by SNC in 1982 and later modified by HZL. It included three - 4.5m^3 electric rope shovels; 9 - 50 tonnes haul trucks; one - Cat 992 FEL; three - electric rotary drills; one - DTH truck drill; three RT dozers and one lube truck. The estimated forex cost for this was just under £8 million. The forex cost for metallurgical equipment was £8.2 million with a further £1.0 million for computer software and training. There was an involved discussion with HZL and Rajasthan State Electricity Board (RSEB) covering not only the RA project but the associated Chanderia smelter project. The upshot was that the RA project would require an additional 3.5MW diesel-generator set in the early years with a forex cost of £1.7 million. A total of £18.9 million's worth of equipment could potentially be financed by an ODA loan.

After two and half weeks at the RA site and a wrap-up meeting with HZL management in Udaipur the WA team caught the IAC plane for Delhi and onward connection with the BA flight for Heathrow. I confirmed with Simon that I would send him a write-up/review of the project together with details of all possible UK financed mining and metallurgical equipment within five days. At Heathrow we went our separate ways. Back at Gorsty it was head down to complete the review and equipment costing. In fact it only took me just over three days which was very pleasing.

I mailed my report to Simon at Leominster Post Office and set off to Alfrick to see my parents. Well what a shock! My father told me that he had sold the bungalow and that they were moving back south, to Chichester, "to be near Judy (my sister) and Bob". I was gobsmacked, I had no idea they had even put the bungalow on the market. He said their move to Worcestershire just hadn't worked out, they'd given it two years, but felt they hadn't "fitted in to the rural scene" and would be more at home in the south. I recalled that I had done my best to put them off the move up from Tunbridge Wells, but that was of little use now. They had already arranged to move into a private, sheltered housing unit not far from Chichester and expected to complete the sale and move by the second week of September - the speed of light, but, of course, I had no idea when they had put the bungalow on the market (we were not reading the property pages). Everything seemed arranged, cleaners, packers etc, typical of Dad once he'd made up his mind to do something. In a bit of a daze I drove back to Gorsty to break the news to Gillian, who seemed far less surprised than me - female intuition?

I attacked the garden, long grass, hedges and ditches with great gusto (morbid anger?) and wondered what else I could or should have done to make my parents feel more at home in Worcestershire and Herefordshire. Unlike Gillian and me who had been nomads for a great part of our life my parents had always lived in the south-east, Kent or East Sussex, which, with close proximity to London was very different to the shire counties of the West Midlands and Welsh borders. Thinking it through I thought it really would be the best for them, although I was not at all sure about the private (nursing?) sheltered home. They didn't even need us to help clear their bungalow as they had decided to take everything with them and put it into store until they had finalised accommodation. Their packers would clear the house. Fortunately for me, rather than feeling surplus to requirements over my parents impending move, I had a call from Brian of Davy McKee in Stockton-on-Tees. Could I come up their offices for a day or two to look at a mining venture in Panama? Yes I could and that would be job No. 040.

I travelled to Stockton by train. The Panamanian mining venture of interest to Davy McKee was in the Cerro Chorcha region. It was very early days in the exploration of the area but there were indications of a nascent porphyry copper deposit. Of course Davy were interested in designing and building a copper concentrator, but felt it would be beneficial to have a view on the mining potential (if any) of this venture before committing too much time and money chasing shadows. In fact, it really was too early to start talking about engineering a metallurgical plant. At present it was a grass-roots exploration project with limited surface trenching and stream sampling. Photographs revealed that the area was mountainous and covered with tropical forest and apart from some preliminary assay results and mineralogical notes - that was it! All I could say was that the terrain and type of mineralogy was similar to the copper porphyry that I had seen on Bougainville Island, but that was as far as I was prepared to go. It was impossible, nay foolish, to suggest the size of an operation or even if a deposit, viable or not, existed. Davy were relaxed and said they'd merely keep their eye on it. We adjourned to the pub and attempted to put the world straight. I stayed overnight in Stockton and next day headed back to Gorsty.

A couple of days later I had a call from Noel of Technical Audit Ltd (TAL) in Guildford asking me to come to their offices to discuss an underground coal mining project in Nigeria. I somewhat reluctantly said yes as the combination of underground coal and Nigeria did not auger well for a straight forward job, which would be No. 041. Thus the next day I set out on the three hour drive to Guildford. TAL were a fairly new technical management consultancy who were keen to break into mining work. It soon became apparent that TAL merely required me to provide some underground mining input into a bid they were preparing for management services. Actually I breathed a sigh of relief that my job was restricted to a Guildford office rather than groveling around a grotty, underground Nigerian coal mine. Apart from explaining the difference between longwall and pillar-and-stall coal mining methods and shaft versus inclined drift access, I felt I had very little to contribute. Although I had had a little experience of West African gold mining conditions in Ghana this was of little relevance to coal mining in Nigeria. In fact, the most useful piece of advice I was able to give Noel was to suggest that he contacted British Mining Consultants (BMC), who were specialist coal mining consultants set up originally by the NCB. It was all very amicable but both Noel and I realised that there were better horses for courses.

There was a note from Simon of WA confirming all the mining and metallurgical equipment required for the Indian RA project which could be financed by a British ODA loan. As an extension of my earlier work on this WA review he asked me to approach relevant manufacturers to obtain budget quotations for this equipment. Of course I agreed and job No. 042 came into being. Thus over the next couple of weeks I was almost continually on the phone to British manufacturers of mining and metallurgical plant and equipment. For the drills I contacted Ingersoll Rand and Compair-Holman. For the electric rope shovels Bucyrus Europe. Aveling-Barford and Volvo BM for 50-tonnes dump trucks. Caterpillar and Volvo BM for $5m^3$ wheel loaders, RT and track dozers. Grove Coles for 15 and 35 tonne cranes. Water, lube & powder trucks from Aveling-Barford, Volvo BM and Howard Trucks. The bulk of the concentrator equipment involved contacting Rexnord, NEI Int Combustion, GEC Mechanical Handling, Joy Process Equipment and Dorr-Oliver. For the Chanderia smelter plant most of my calls were to ISP/Lurgi, Worthington-Simpson, Demag, Metpro, Clayton and Howden-Carter. For the 3.5MW D-G sets I contacted Mirrlees Blackstone.

The manufacturers in the main were very co-operative and provided budget sterling prices on a FOB UK port basis within three weeks. The RA site equipment for mine and concentrator totaled £21.6 million including initial spares and £23.4 million for the smelter equipment at Chanderia. In addition a total of £16.9 million was estimated for licence fees, know-how, training, basic engineering by Lurgi and detailed engineering by Davy McKee for the Chanderia smelter. I compiled all these budget quotations into a comprehensive list and despatched them to Simon as a key part of WA's formal presentation to the ODA.

I had only just finished this job for WA when John from Davy called with a request for me to come up to Caernarfon for further discussions with IMC and GCC Planning officers. So yet again it was the central Wales drive through Welshpool and Snowdonia. Following earlier discussions with the Principal District Inspector of Mines & Quarries it had been established that two entirely separate exits from the mine would be required. The first major and normal means of ingress and egress would be through the large cage in the main vertical shaft. We proposed to erect a 17m fabricated steel headframe over the collar of the East Bored Ventilation Raise. A single drum 150 kW winder would haul a single deck cage running on fixed steel guides attached directly to the walls of the raise. The cage capacity would handle thirteen men over a 2.5 minute full cycle. The maximum number of men underground would be 65 on day shift so that five trips would be needed to hoist all these men to surface in under 14 minutes. Under normal mine operating conditions this emergency second exit cage would rest on top of air lock doors on the collar of the East Bored Ventilation Raise. The second exit headframe would also be clad and air locked.

The Mines Inspector also stated that Health & Safety would not allow the main exhaust ventilation fans to be sited underground on the -140 level. Both fan manufacturers, Novenco Aerex and Davidson Sirocco, indicated that horizontally mounted axial flow fans would be suitable for the desired ventilation duties whilst producing the minimum noise and visual impact. The raises would be capped at ground level and the fans would be located in a 45 degree inclined fan drift just below ground level. These changes meant that I had to rework the mine capital cost and update them to an end-1986 basis. Mine development by contractor was estimated to be £12 million and fixed plant £2.3 million with a further £3.2 million for mobile mining equipment for a total mine capital cost of £17.5 million (excluding contingency). This was a reduction of £5.6 million from the mid 1985 estimate, due mainly to scrapping the tower mounted friction winders and using second-hand drum winders and a fabricated steel headframe. One final task was to rework the direct operating cost, again on an end-1986 cost basis. The final direct mine operating cost at the same production rate of 226,860 tonnes/year was £17.4/tonne mined. I worked up both the capital and operating cost estimates at Gorsty and mailed the detailed cost back-up sheets to John at Davy by the end of November. I did not know at the time, but that would be my last involvement with the Parys Mountain project, as early in 1987 IMC put their planning application on hold.

Things were quiet on the mining front during the first part of December apart from a call from Jean Luis of the World Bank asking me to join his team in mid January to undertake a review of ZCCM's "Export Rehabilitation Project" in Zambia. Basically to comment how the State mining company was utilising the recent WB loan. As usual I said yes and job No. 044 awaited the new year.

However all thoughts of that job disappeared a few days later. We were having supper when the phone rang, I answered, it was Bob, my sister Judy's husband. He said simply I have bad news, both your parents are dead, you must come immediately to Chichester to carry out a formal identification of their bodies. He said the police were investigating and he, Bob, had told them that I was named as family Executor in my father's latest Will. I was totally shocked by what Bob had told me and said, of course, I would come down early tomorrow. Bob said go straight to Chichester Police Station, where they would take me to the mortuary for the identification. After that, he said Judy and he would meet me at my parents apartment at the Residential Home. He said they would be there from 3pm onwards and rang off.

Gillian realised that something was seriously wrong, but we waited until Sproggs had had his bath and gone to bed before we talked. Like me she was astounded and even more so when I said that the police were investigating. I said I did not know what had occurred but doubtless I would by tomorrow evening. In the morning I phoned Chichester Police Station and, having identified myself, said I expected to be there by lunch time. I left immediately taking the A417, M4 to jcn 13 for Newbury and the A34 for Winchester, then the M3, M27 and finally the old A272 into Chichester. It was after 1pm by the time I reached the police station close to Canal Wharf. They said I should leave the car there and they would drive me to the mortuary at St Richards Hospital. One officer came in with me whilst I confirmed that it was, indeed, my Mum and Dad. Outside a second lady officer brought me a cup of tea and generally provided support. They drove me back to the police station, where I signed something. Having got over the grisly identification business I asked what had happened. The police said they were both found dead in their own car on the edge of Goodwood racecourse. Their joint demise appeared to have been self inflicted by a combination of alcohol and barbiturates. There was no note or message. The police told me there would be an inquest, probably in the early new year, and I must attend. I gave them my Gorsty address and telephone number.

I drove slowly out to the nearby Residential Home where Judy and Bob were waiting. I confirmed the identification and also said that no notes or messages had been found. In a bit of a daze I said I did not know Dad had made me Executor in his last Will. I read through a copy of the Will they had found in the filing cabinet and noted that I was joint Executor with

Michael of Thomson, Snell & Passmore (TSP) in Tunbridge Wells. I phoned TSP and made an appointment to see Michael the following day. As we were all a bit edgy I decided to set off that afternoon spending the night at a Travelodge near Lewes from where I phoned Gillian to say I would be home late tomorrow afternoon having seen Michael in the morning.

TSP's offices were very close to Dad's old office alongside Tunbridge Wells Central station. Michael had been my Dad's solicitor for many years and he had helped us on the sale of Beals and purchase of Gorsty. Like me he was stunned at what had happened. He confirmed that he had a copy of Dad's latest Will and that we were both named as Executors. I repeated what the police had told me of the circumstances of their death and that an inquest was to be held in early January to which I had to attend. We agreed that he, Michael, would handle everything but clear things with me first. He also confirmed that we could do nothing until the inquest had been held. After coffee I made the long drive back to Gorsty. Unsurprisingly we had a quiet Christmas and New Year.

I attended the fairly short inquest, answering several personal questions about the family. In due course the Recorder registered a double suicide with my dad pre-deceasing my mother. A funeral director took the released bodies and I arranged with him for an early cremation at Chichester crematorium. This was done and we had a wake at a nearby hotel. It was an altogether gloomy few days compounded by the falling out of my sister and me. I collected the necessary death certificates and drove home via Tunbridge Wells dropping off the certificates at TSP. Fortunately for me there was an immediate distraction with a call from Jean Louis about the ZCCM Zambian job for the World Bank. He asked me to join his team at Heathrow next week. This meant Gillian had to hold the fort over any early queries from Michael at TSP, but I did not expect to be away for more than three weeks.

It was the usual Zambian visit. ZA flight from Heathrow to Lusaka, where we stayed in the Pamodzi Hotel over night before flying RoanAir to Kitwe. Jean Louis and two WB economist stayed in Lusaka for talks with ZCCM Finance Director and the Mininstry of Finance people. The technical guys, including an open-pit engineer and a mineral processing engineer plus yet another WB economist and I stayed at Anglo's old Director's Lodge and guest house. After that we did the rounds of the main mining and processing centres of Konkola, Nchanga, Nkana, Baluba, Mufulira, Chibuluma and Luanshya. As in previous WB visits the emphasis was in obtaining the back-up to ZCCM's main asset - the in situ geological reserves. For each mine it was then necessary to derive a MCF for predicting mill head grades and finally a metallurgical recovery factor covering the respective concentrators and smelters. That was the relatively easy bit. For the underground mines (my area of analysis) we had to take a view on how squeezed each mine was with a shortage of fully developed ground ahead of stoping. In the giant Nchanga open pit mine it was a case of how little ore was exposed on the mining benches behind a seriously delayed waste stripping programme. We also had to take cognizance of how delays in each mine's major capital projects (eg Mindola shaft re-deepening) would impinge on near future ore production.

The omens for ZCCM copper production were not propitious. Over the last eleven years total copper production had fallen from 712,900 tonnes in 1976 to 460,000 tonnes in 1986. The shortfall in underground development and waste stripping in the open pit was now worse than ever. Since the copper industry had a key role in Zambia's economy a US$ 148 million loan, co-financed by the IBRD (World Bank), the EEC and the ADB, had been made to the government. However the Zambian government needed finance for many other areas (eg agriculture & infrastructure) besides the mining industry. However it was this industry, represented now by ZCCM, which generated most of Zambia's foreign exchange. Thus in addition to the technical mining problems brought about by poor operational and project management only a portion of this "Export Rehabilitation and Diversification Project Finance" was, in fact, being passed on to ZCCM.

With the cessation of mining at Kansanshi, Chambishi and Konkola No. 3, the combined annual mining capacity of ZCCM was estimated to be 25 million tonnes/year plus or minus 5%. This tonnage came from a reserve of about 413 million tonnes grading 3.08% Cu, with an overall grade factor of 69.5% indicated a mill head grade of 2.14% Cu, which with an overall metallurgical recovery of 86% would yield 460,225 tonnes finished copper plus a further 35,300 tonnes/year finished copper from reclaimed tailings - a total ZCCM output of 495,525 tonnes/year. A 5% variation on this implied a likely production range of 470,000 to 520,000 tonnes/year.

It would be these basic output figures which would determine ZCCM's likely cash inflow.

Back in Lusaka we had some extended discussions with ZCCM senior management, who, as always, were more optimistic than we were regarding the next five years copper production. We argued our position strongly backed up by sound technical analysis and again as always agreed to disagree. However ZCCM were well aware that the World Bank would use their own production estimates for ascertaining possible further loans. Back at the Pamodzi Hotel Jean Louis, ZCCM's MD and Finance Director, plus the Zambian Minister of Finance had a meeting with an International Monetary Fund (IMF) group in one of the hotel's conference rooms. Jean Louis asked me to attend as, he said "they might ask a technical question or two". Well they asked one and I could easily answer it. On the way in one of the IMF guys asked me if I knew where the toilet was and yes, surprise, surprise I knew exactly where it was! Nevertheless a career high point I attended an IMF meeting!

Later that evening Jean Louis asked me if I could come back to Washington with his guys to finalise the five year copper production estimates and meet the WB director of his Industry & Mining Department. They had already booked me a seat on their return flight to Washington. He thought I would be in Washington for about five days.

At Heathrow I phoned Gillian and said I was off to Washington for a week or so and hoped she was coping with Sproggs and Michael, the TSP solicitor in Tunbridge Wells. All right for some she replied! The WB had booked me into a self-catering apartment at the Guest Quarters on K Street midway between Georgetown and the World Bank on H Street. Everything in the apartment was very automated and strange for a Brit from the Herefordshire boondocks, but a cheery janitor helped me sort things out. He pointed out a nearby mini mart where I was able to get some essentials, bread, coffee, milk etc.

One thing immediately struck me about Washington DC, it was so multi-ethnic. This was particularly noticeable within the huge World Bank building which was a veritable United Nations of nationalities. Jean Louis had arranged for my visitor's badge and had found me an empty office near Dick, the WB metallurgist who, of course, was providing input on the overall metallurgical recovery figures. We had worked up all the basic numbers whilst on the Copperbelt thus our main activity now was double checking the arithmetic. After three days Jean Louis called his Zambian team together to make a short presentation to the WB director of the Industry & Mining Department. Although an obvious go-go MBA type I'm not too sure that he had a great grip on central African copper mining. By contrast Jean Louis was an exceptionally sharp guy, eminently suitable for the ZCCM job being a French mining engineer. He always maintained that he'd forgotten all his engineering and had become an economist, although I took that with a pinch of salt. He was definitely one of the sharpest guys I met connected with the international mining scene. It was all wrapped up on the fourth day so that evening I caught the "red eye" night flight back to Heathrow, eventually arriving at Gorsty by mid-afternoon the following day.

We had been having a bit of a battle with the SS who kept interfering with our efforts to settle Sproggs down into family life with us. Things came to a head when we had a "review visit" which involved a weasel-bearded know everything (but actually knew nothing) in accordance with the latest fostering theory. Well he got right up my nose and fortunately Frank, head of Malvern Hills SS, could see our antipathy and suggested that Gillian and I have a session with their tame shrink to discuss Sproggs' progress. It was arranged that we met this psychologist at our local doctor's surgery. Well it very soon became apparent that he was analysing Gillian and me not Sproggs! It all came neatly to a head when in reply to a cod-scientific question Gillian succinctly replied "common sense". "Oh well" the shrink harrumphed "there's not much point continuing" to which we totally agreed, stood up and took our leave. Back home Gillian and I felt that the only way to get the SS off our back was to adopt Sproggs. We contacted the SS, filled out all the necessary forms and submitted a formal request to adopt. We understood that that process would take about six months.

As follow-up on that we looked around for a local school to take Sproggs education on from Kimbolton primary. We settled on St Richards at Bredenbury a Catholic Services co-ed establishment set in glorious countryside about nine miles east of Gorsty. The head was not keen to take Sproggs, after all we were not Catholics nor from the Services, but agreed when we explained his foster/adoption background. We planned to enroll him as a day boy for the new term beginning in September.

In March I had a call from Ken of WA asking me to assist them with an open cast coal operation at Ashby-de-la-Zouch - job No. 045. The site was known as Coalfield North and Shand Mining (SM) was the contractor for the NCB Opencast Coal Executive. I drove to Tenbury Wells and east on the A443 to Droitwich then around Solihull to new sections of the M42 and on to the A42 and Ashby-de-la Zouch, where I checked into a local hotel. The Coalfield North site was now in a difficult, tight position. The site was bisected by the small River Sence which crossed the site from the NE to SW. Two major faults also crossed the site striking NW - SE dipping 50 degrees SW with the downthrown block to the SW and throws of 5m to nearly 30m. Previous spoil tips were also present.

The current unsatisfactory position with the pit had been caused by two fundamental errors. Firstly the River Sence should have been diverted off the centre of the site to the periphery to provide a clear uninterrupted area for working. Secondly the site should have been worked from the the SW to the NE, commencing with the initial box cut in the deepest, downthrown portion of the lowest coal seam, the Kilburn. This would have enabled full 700 to 800m length blocks of 40m wide strips oriented NW - SE (ie paralleling the faults) to proceed up-dip to the NE. With this layout it would have been feasible to use the large Rapier 1260 dragline in a conventional strike cut and up-dip advance. At present the pit was virtually snowed in with short, 300m block lengths, caused by the presence of the River Sence. These short blocks were quite unsuitable for the big dragline and it had virtually become a tight shovel and truck operation. Overburden and inter-burden ranged from 64m to 117m for a total coal seam thickness of 9.91m contained in eight seams ranging from 0.6m to 2.28m thickness.

With the River Sence diverted off the site to the SE it would be possible to extend the blocks to the SE boundary providing a more reasonable (but still short) block length for the 1260 dragline. In essence this would change the site from a tight "pit" into a strip operation to maximise output from the excavating machinery and provide room for the large dragline.

SM's contract required 20,000 tonnes/week of coal and that required the removal of 140,800 BCM/week of overburden. The current output of the 1260 dragline at 310 BCM/scheduled hour was woefully low. A machine of that type pulling a 24m^3 bucket in those coal measures should dig and cast, including 30% chopping, nearly 700 BCM/scheduled hour. The basic problem was that the current pit was too small and compact for a dragline of that size. To meet their coal production targets SM had had to introduce face shovels and a large truck fleet. Even the BE 195 and BE 150 rope face shovels outputs were only 70% of what one would expect, because their outputs were reduced by the short strip length and the consequent high proportion of time spent moving.

Ken, from WA, and I discussed our concerns with the SM site manager. He was entirely in agreement and commented that his senior management had foisted the 1260 dragline on him as it had finished work at another site and management wanted to use it. He said our comments would help him in persuading the NCB Opencast Executive, the planning authority and Environment Agency that the River Sence should, nay must, be diverted off the site to provide sensible and safe working conditions. He felt his own management would react favourably when they appreciated the reduction in overburden removal costs when the 1260 dragline had more reasonable working conditions. With that Ken headed back to Newcastle-under-Lyme and I drove back to Gorsty.

It was good to get back home in time for Sproggs tenth birthday on the 3rd April. We had invited a number of his friends from Kimbolton School. I had assumed the kids would amuse themselves but we found that they needed an organiser and that turned out to be me. Gillian and I had laid out a treasure hunt in the garden and along the track as far as the cattle grid on the lane. However my lack of parental experience showed in that most of our clues seemed too obscure for the youngsters to work out. That inevitably meant that I had to race around, to and fro along the track with "suggestions" to help them unravel the clues. After that I decided a less frenetic game was in order, not least for me. The good old wire coat hangers came to the rescue. Each of the children were given a tangled mass of eight hangers. first one to untangle won a prize. In truth most of the children were really waiting for teatime, jelly, cake and lemonade to the fore. I think Sproggs enjoyed being the birthday boy and it was certainly good training for Gillian and me as green parents.

Two days later I had a call from Edwin, ZCCM's Finance Director asking me to meet him in London for a trip to the EEC in Brussels the next day. That would be job No. 046. Gillian dropped me off at Worcester, as usual. and from Reading I took the RailAir coach to Heathrow to join Edwin at one of the airport hotels close by Terminal 4. Edwin had flown in from Lusaka that morning. The following morning we flew to Brussels and a taxi ride from the airport delivered us to the vast EEC building. It was daunting for me but Edwin knew his way around the huge, bureaucratic complex and we located the African Loans (Zambia) area after tramping through miles of corridors. Edwin was at great pains to make sure that the EEC guys knew that I was not a ZCCM employee and therefore biased, but a mining expert retained by the World Bank. He asked me to outline what had happened to Zambian copper production over the past decade and our view (well the World Bank's) of what copper production would be over the next five years. That was all straightforward since that was precisely the ground we had covered with Jean Louis' WB visit to ZCCM three months before. There was an EEC mining specialist who wanted to know the derivation of our estimates, but generally his queries were simple to answer.

In fact I had very little to do, merely being present as back-up for Edwin's prediction of the financial squeeze on ZCCM, and hence the need for additional finance from the EEC Sysmin loan. For their part the EEC guys wanted to know how much of their loan (and those from the WB and ADB) were being released to ZCCM from the Zambian government, rather than disappearing into agriculture or infrastructure projects. The actions of the Zambian government, rather than ZCCM itself, seemed to be of much greater interest for the EEC. I stayed in Brussels overnight for further talks the next day and finally caught an afternoon flight back to Heathrow, leaving Edwin to continue his battle with the EEC bureaucrats. I did not envy him.

No sooner had I got home than Gillian gave me a note to call George at Griffin Coal's London office. Griffin Coal from West Australia I knew and, of course, Dick was MD of Jacia Consulting, an associated company, but George

I did not know. It transpired he was a Canadian who was helping Griffin with possible coal industry acquisitions in the UK. He wanted me to accompany him to an opencast coal site near Mansfield and to the Grimethorpe coke plant near Barnsley in Yorkshire. We agreed that the most convenient way to tackle the visits was by hire car and since George was in London and I was in Leominster I suggested we meet at BR Derby station. George would have a fast direct rail service there from London and Gillian could drop me off at Worcester for a train to Birmingham and then mainline service to Derby. We met "under the station clock" so no need for recourse to folded newspapers of the Toronto News or Hereford Times for identification.

George had arranged for a hire car at Derby and wanted me named as an additional driver. He suggested I drive since I was a local, well, a native at least! It was a short drive of 25 miles NE up the A608. That was the first time I'd visited the coal mining town of Mansfield and there were two surprises. The town was much larger than I expected and the twisted spire on the parish church was very spectacular. We found the opencast site a few miles to the NW not far from the M1. George had already spoken to the NCB Opencast Executive local manager to arrange our visit. We first discussed the remaining coal reserves within the site, but it was apparent that there was a misunderstanding in that Griffin believed the site was for sale and the NCB thought Griffin was interested in bidding as an opencast contractor to take over the existing operator who was in financial difficulties. No real harm done, it was an interesting visit and we set off in mid-afternoon up the M1 to junction 37 for Barnsley. We stayed overnight in a town-centre hotel and we were both surprised that so many local pits were still operating after the disastrous miners' strike of 1984 to 1986. Certainly the town had a depressed, sullen feel, which, given what had happened was to be expected.

The next morning we drove six miles east to Grimethorpe colliery and the associated coke plant. Here we had to use a little subterfuge to get a look around the coke plant as Griffin had learnt on the qt that the owner might be interested in selling. I used my Consulting Mining Engineers business card to establish our professional identity and said my Canadian friend had never seen a coke plant and would very much like to. Well that, at least, was true. To my amazement they said yes and we spent about three hours on a guided tour of this huge complex. I'm not too sure how useful it was for George, but for me it was fascinating to learn how smokeless fuel, coke and briquettes, were manufactured from a soft coking coal obtained from the adjacent colliery. The soft coking coal was very different from the South Wales anthracite steam coals. That more or less wrapped up job No. 047 and since George had said he'd like to see a bit of central England I set out to drive cross country to Leominster.

We picked up the A628 trans Pennine road heading for Manchester, but turned south through Glossop, Hayfield and Chapel-en-le-Frith joining the A6 for Buxton. Then past the Staffordshire Roaches outcrop to Leek and the A520 around the southern side of Stoke to Stone. Again cross country through Newport and Shifnal, crossing the river Severn at Bridgenorth. Finally the B4364 around Brown Clee and up onto the flank of Titterstone Clee where we stopped at the pub on Wheathill at just over 1000ft elevation. I phoned Gillian to let her know George would be staying the night, but no supper required as we would shortly be hoeing in to bangers and mash. We arrived back at Gorsty around 9pm and being May it was still light. George thoroughly enjoyed our old farmhouse (actually not that old - 1723) which confirmed his vision of English country houses. He was a very erudite and entertaining Canadian visitor and I really enjoyed the opportunity to drive him around central England.

I sorted out his route back to London, A417 to Cirencester, then A419 to Swindon and onto the M4 for London. After the Hammersmith flyover I said he was on his own. He left at 10.30 next morning. We had another visit from the Malvern Hills SS people that afternoon who seemed incredibly worried about our impending adoption of Sproggs. In conversation with Pauline the SS worker who looked after him we leant that this would be Malvern Hills SS very first adoption. No wonder they were as nervous as we were. The powers that be had set a date for the adoption "hearing", before a judge, for the 10th June at the imposing Shire Hall in Hereford.

In mid May I had a call from Dave, MD of ZES in Ashford, Kent asking me to come down to their offices to discuss marketing ZES engineering services to the mining and metallurgical industry at large. That would be job No. 048 and it would only take one day so I caught the early train from Worcester to Paddington, tube to Charing Cross and fast service to Ashford. ZES's offices were in a modern office block right by the station. Dave I knew quite well from CSM days, then Lepanto in the Philippines and more recently in his role as Consulting Mining Engineer to Anglo on the Copperbelt. It was all very convivial with half a dozen of ZES's senior engineers and project managers all putting in their ten cents worth of ideas.

It was fortunate that Dave knew me well and was sure that I would not gild the lily. I said that the first problem was the name. It was inextricably (and correctly) linked to Zambia and their owner ZCCM, a state mining company. It was also an undeniable fact that ZCCM was no longer at the forefront of mining and metallurgical innovation. I agreed with their proposed name change to Techpro, or anything that didn't have Zambia or ZCCM in it. However that would just be cosmetic as anyone could ask a few pertinent questions and the Zambian link would be disclosed.

I then described the engineering and consulting competition in the mining and metallurgical fields. It was very extensive and over the past few years many of the major engineer-contractor organisations had swallowed up front-end consulting companies. Davy had bought Lingren Associates; SNC bought into Robertson Research; Mitchell Cotts bought out Mackay & Schnellmann; Matthew Hall took over PAH and NRC took over Behr Dolbear. Also many of the operating mining companies had entered the consulting field such as LKAB, Boliden, Granges, US Steel, Cominco, Outokumpu and Mitsui. Most of these contractor outfits had made swingeing cuts to their permanent staff and now "project hired" people as shown by Fluor at ZCCM's Nchanga division. My strong view was that this was not an industry that ZES or Techpro should be attempting to penetrate.

I noted that the FT reckoned that leisure and waste disposal were both growth areas. On this front perhaps Techpro could join the Canterbury based quarrying company Bretts in utilising their quarry "holes" for leisure (flooding & subsequent boating) or as waste landfill reclamation. There might be some opportunities in the UK coal industry with possible privatisation and the Opencast Executive looked a prime candidate. I was sorry to be so negative but from my view, within a very conservative industry, felt they needed to get a market/management consultant to look at Techpro's core skills. In spite of my gloomy comments we still had time for a couple of pints before I caught the train back to London, finally arriving at Worcester after 10pm for a dark drive back to Gorsty.

32

The big adoption day, 10th June, drew nigh and all three of us were carefully polished and powdered. It was quite daunting at the Hereford Shire Hall. The adoption hearing was held by a circuit judge. Although the judge did not wear a wig and gown he sat on a dais well above us and was a rather testy, unsympathetic character. Both Gillian and I had minor disagreements with him. When questioning where Gillian was born - Cranwell - he opined that that was not a bomber station, having previously learnt that Lofty Lawson, Gillian's father, had been a bomber (and fighter) pilot throughout WW2. Of course it wasn't it was the RAF officers training establishment. When the judge asked me how long we had been married I replied 29 years, to which he replied "no, no that can't be right it must be nineteen years" (we obviously looked so young!). I corrected him, but he wouldn't have it - maths was definitely not his strong subject. However he was the judge and it was his hearing so like good adopters we said nothing..

He then leant over and addressed Sproggs saying "do you want to be adopted?" To which Sproggs replied "yes sir" in a quiet voice and that was that, done and dusted. Spoggs had decided to stick with his forename, Michael, and had elected to change his middle name to James. Thus as of this day he became Michael James Stoakes. We all signed some forms, said our thanks and repaired to a nearby cafe where Sproggs tackled a number of very sticky meringues. I'm pretty sure Gillian and I had some as well. It was a huge relief to have finally completed our family. I was now aged 51 and we had been afraid that the adoption panel might consider me too old. Although not stated explicitly we were certain that Malvern Hills SS gave us a good recommendation.

Fortunately I was free of mining work throughout the remainder of June, July and much of August so that we could concentrate on family activities. I set up a Swing-Ball post in the garden as well as a football goal net to keep Sproggs (and me) active during the summer holidays. We also went swimming regularly at the Leominster pool and Sproggs continued swimming with the Kingfisher Club.

In the early part of August I had a call from Jim, Exploration Manager of COMSUR asking me to join their evaluation team who were contemplating buying the Aguilar lead - zinc mine in northern Argentina. They planned to be at the mine on the 26th August. Of course I said yes to job No. 049. I had to go to the Brazilean Embassy in London to obtain an Argentine visa since there was no consular representation as a consequence of the Falklands war. Also there were no direct flights between Argentina and the UK, but that was not a problem as I planned to fly Varig from London to Rio, then Aerolineas Argentina (AA) down to Buenos Aires. The AA flight was due in to Buenos Aires by mid-morning of the 25th. The plan was for me to join the COMSUR team at Aguilar's Buenos Aires office before flying up to Jujuy in the north. From there two Aguilar mine 4 x 4's would drive the team up to the mine, close to the Bolivian border.

However things did not go to plan. The Varig flight was fine but there was a technical glitch with the AA flight and it left Rio six hours late. As a consequence I not only missed the COMSUR team at Aguilar's office but also failed to catch the afternoon Jujuy flight from the domestic Aeroparc terminal alongside the Rio Plata. The Aguilar Buenos Aires office phoned their office in Jujuy and said el Senor Ingles would be on the last flight into Jujuy, that night, please book him in to a local hotel. That all worked OK, but I had to be up very early the next morning to catch the long distance bus heading for La Quiaca on the Bolivian border, but to make sure I got off at Tres Cruces. The bus terminal was busy but the one for Bolivia was easily identified. Unsurprisingly, I was the only gringo on the bus. The bus stopped several times around Jujuy, which occupied a broad fertile valley, before it began to climb steadily up the Quebrada Humahuaca accompanied by the railway. By the 3000m elevation all trees had vanished to be replaced by a dry, dusty and rocky outlook. At one of the stops I used hand gestures (!) to indicate that I needed to take a pee. No problem, only it was a problem. Very difficult to start with a bus load of Andean mountain people, noses to the windows, watching a tall gringo trying to have a pee at the roadside. Hey ho, a full bladder plus gravity finally overcame my embarrassment.

The bus pulled into Tres Cruces about 1pm. It had the appearance of one of the dirt poor, dusty towns in a Wild West movie. The bus driver was very good and made sure that el gringo Ingles realised that this was his destination. I felt more than a little conspicuous toting my suitcase and briefcase in the centre of that godforsaken place. However after a few minutes the inevitable big Ford ute turned up with the welcoming sign writing of Cia Minera Aguilar SA (CMASA) on the door panels. The driver had no doubt that I was his target and the luggage and I were swept up into the ute.

We turned SW out of Tres Cruces and headed up, continually climbing, into the Sierra Aguilar (Eagle mountain). It was a forty minute drive on a tortuous dirt road before the main Aguilar camp came into view at an elevation of 4500 m. It was a very barren spot. The mine was owned and operated by the American St Joe Lead Co, who had now decided to put the mine up for sale. The bulk of the mine's facilities, such as diesel power plant, sawmill, metallurgical concentrator and accommodation, both workers bunkhouses and staff houses were situated on that 4500m level shelf. That was also the main haulage level of the adit mine which extended further up the mountain. Although fully self contained the mine had a very isolated feel in that harsh, high altitude location.

I settled into one of the very pleasant staff houses and lay down having succumbed to a fairly savage siroche. The COMSUR team emerged from the mine offices around 5pm, comprising, three geologists, Bernie, Jim and Carlos plus Mario, mining and Carlos, processing. Apparently Stan had remained in Buenos Aires to go over all Aguilar's financial documents. I knew all of them from previous work for COMSUR in Bolivia. They gave me a hard time for being late and absolutely no sympathy for the siroche. I said I'd stay off the beer tonight (hollow laughter from Jim, Bernie and Mario) and said I'd be OK in the morning. So it proved to be on both counts.

We only had two days at site and I'd already missed half a day. Fortunately I didn't have to worry about the geology, the three guys had hoovered up all that data. My focus was an extensive underground visit to see ground conditions (geotechnics), mining methods, mining equipment, fixed mine plant (winders, ventilation fans, pumps etc). I also had to collect basic data on the diesel power plant; the sawmill; surface detritus (for underground fill) as well as full details of recent operating costs.

The underground visits were pretty strenuous considering the high altitude. As an adit mine of a steep dipping tabular deposit that involved interminable climbing of ladderways. Who says underground mining doesn't keep you fit? We also took a jeep run around the side of the Sierra Aguilar up to just under 5000m elevation to look at a big surface diamond drill rig that was putting down deep holes looking for parallel ore structures. From there it was an awe inspiring, barren view. Away to the north the southern part of Bolivia running up towards Tupiza and away to the west the 6050m peak of Acamarachi in Antogafasta province of Chile. There was scarcely a sign of any human impact on the vista, a sobering thought.

The lowest adit level was 18, at 4500m elevation, and handled all mine drainage and tracked ore haulage to the surface concentrator. Below 18 level a trackless mine was under development via a ramp-decline. I had a quick trip down the decline and was able to visit some new development into the ore zone. The ground conditions were much improved from that exhibited in the existing mine above 18 level. I felt that the central portion of the main orebody might be mined by a variety of top overcut-and-bench open stoping. That was all the time we were allowed as another potential buyer of the mine was due on site that afternoon.

We packed in to two 4 x 4's for the twisty dirt road run down to Tres Cruces and continued south down to Jujuy. Here we had a short visit to Aguilar's office to pick up a copy of last months operating costs before being driven to the airport. For me there was a pleasant surprise. COMSUR's own Aero Commander twin turboprop plane was waiting on the Jujuy airstrip. The 550 mile flight north to La Paz's El Alto airport took just over two hours. It was a fascinating flight along the spine of the Andes with marvelous views of both the eastern and western cordillera. Then the always awe inspiring drive from the airport down into La Paz itself.

As usual I was booked in to the Hotel Sucre, where Bernie from Santiago was also staying. We spent the next three days in COMSUR's office preparing an evaluation of the Aguilar mine based on our two day site visit. The geologists concluded that there were 5.6 million tonnes of ore grading 5.6% Pb and 7.4% Zn above 18 level and 2.9 million tonnes grading 5.0% Pb and 9.6% Zn below 18 level. For the tracked mine above 18 level historical records indicated an ore expectancy of 30,000 t/vm. In that section of the mine production had been derived from square-set (72%); cut-and-fill (18%); open-cut (6%) and development (4%). With that mix of mining methods the current daily mining rate was 1950 tonnes/day about 6.5% of the ore expectancy. Over 300 days annual output would be 585,000 tonnes.

The ground conditions indicated that the mine could use open stoping or at least cut-and-fill. Aguilar had, belatedly, realised that they did not require slow and costly square-set mining below 18 level, where the ore expectancy was 14,000 t/vm. Overall I suggested a production of 575,000 tonnes/year steadily rising to 750,000 tonnes/year over a six year period. Aguilar's long-term MCF of 85% implied mill head grades of 4.8% Pb, 6.2% Zn and 103g/t.

Mining above 18 level was haphazard, scattered over several levels and many of the square-set stopes were mining both rib and sill pillars. The mine consumed huge amounts of timber, about 14bd ft/tonne mined. Stoping explosive yield was 4.7 tonnes/Kg and the drilling yield was 1.1 tonnes/m. Below 18 level development used a twin boom jumbo and 5 cu yd LHD with 18 tonnes capacity articulated haul trucks. The new ramp-decline was of a suitable size and gradient for continuous up-ramp haulage of the 1200 tonnes/day production forecast.

Being an adit mine the average power demand was small. Main consumers were two underground hoists, crusher, stope scrapers and main haulage trolley system. There was adequate compressed air from the plant located at the 8 level portal. Ventilation was reasonable provided by three surface exhaust fans. Generally the mine was well run with good engineering support services such as geological mapping, sampling, surveying, drilling and explosive supply. I estimated that an immediate expenditure of US$ 2 million would be required for another electro-hydraulic drill jumbo; two new LHD's; three new 18 tonne haul trucks; pumps, fans and jeeps and a 360m extension to the ramp-decline.

Current mining direct operating cost was US$ 14.2/tonne. Labour comprised 47% of that, due mainly to the use of labour intensive square-set mining. That was reflected in the low productivity of 5.25 tonnes/manshift (TMS) in timber stopes and 10.8 TMS in cut-and-fill stopes. As the tonnage from trackless mining increased, direct mining costs were predicted to fall to US$ 11.7/tonne. All of these estimates/predictions/costs were handed over to Stan to undertake the financial analysis to provide a NPV of the Aguilar operation for Goni to decide whether to buy the mine.

The next day Jaime, GM of COMSUR asked me to visit the Todos Santos silver prospect situated in Atahualla province close to the Chilean border. One of their geologists, Saloman, picked me up at the Hotel Sucre at 6.30

for the 180 mile drive. We first drove south on the main sealed road towards Oruro then turned west on to a dirt road through Umala, skirting around the Nev Sajama peak (6542 m) to a remote spot near the village of Sajama on the Chilean border. Close by the Todos Santos prospect a dirt "trucking" road from the coastal town of Arica in Chile tortuously climbed the scarp of the western cordillera. Saloman told me that a lot of contraband goods from Chile (and Peru) were trucked into Bolivia by this route. That was unsurprising since it was a remote region with no frontier post.

The prospect lay on the north-western bank of the small Rio Todos Santos. That bank, in reality a small cliff, had been penetrated by several ancient Spanish crosscut adits and old workings. Those workings appeared to follow very narrow steep dipping NW striking veins into the hillside and then chased the silver mineralisation into flat lying banded tuffs. The net result was a typical erratic "gopher" type of mine working. COMSUR's exploration programme had comprised driving several crosscut adits into the hillside (at about 30m strike interval), followed by drifting within the favourable tuff horizon. They had also put up 65 degree raises on the full dip of the stringers and veins. Samples had been taken of each round in crosscuts, drifts and raises. A number of vertical sections, along the line of the crosscuts had been drawn. From these sections COMSUR had calculated a reserve of 895,000 tonnes of material with a grade of 4.9g/t Ag suitable for open-pitting at a 2 to 1 stripping ratio and underground 568,000 tonnes at 4.6g/t of sulphides and 327,000 tonnes at 5.4g/t of oxides. Using Taylor's formula for mine life indicated a possible open-pit production rate of 400 tonnes/day and a sustainable underground rate of about 135 tonnes/day.

The assay data indicated a log-normal distribution of silver values and combined with a 12.5% mining dilution would reduce the mined grade to 3.95g/t. I prepared a capital cost estimate for a 400 tonnes/day ore and 800 tonnes/day waste open-pit operation. In fact an open pit was a misnomer, it was in effect a side-cut. The capital cost was US$ 1.8 million and the direct mining cost was US$ 2.51/tonne mined or US$ 7.53/tonne ore with a 2 to 1 stripping ratio. Processing cost was US$ 8.5/tonne and overheads US$ 2.4/tonne for a total operating cost of US$ 18.4/tonne. The gross value of the ore was estimated to be US$ 20.5/tonne leaving a gross operating margin of only US$ 2.1. The gross annual revenue would be US$ 0.25 million. That would be before payment of any taxes or royalties. An operating margin of US$ 6.8/tonne would be needed to give a gross return of 25% on capital. That could not be achieved. Underground mining on a random room-and-pillar system would be unlikely to cost less than US$ 16/tonne, more than twice the open-pitting cost. The Todos Santos silver prospect was not a financially viable project.

Before we left we went to Sajama village. Salamon had told me that it was famous in Bolivia for growing garlic. Alongside the Rio Todos Santos there were numerous beds of garlic. It was quite a sight and smell! We set off for La Paz arriving in darkness about 9.30pm. Over the next two days I worked in the COMSUR offices preparing a brief technical report on the Todos Santos project. Jim, the exploration geologist was delighted with my conclusion as, he said, he'd been telling Goni for the past year that the Todos Santos project was a bummer!

I had expected to be on my way back to the UK now, but Jaime asked me to accompany Jim and Carlos to the Quioma mine situated in the province of Misque, in the department of Cochabamba. Thus mid-morning the next day three of us, plus driver, set off by jeep on the Pan American Highway (main drag La Paz to Argentinian border) turning off east at Caracollo for Cochabamba. The 230 mile trip took around six hours. The city was set at a lower altitude of 2600m in an open valley. It had a sub-tropical feel, with flowering trees and shrubs in the wide streets, quite unlike the harsh, dry and dusty altiplano. Nevertheless it had been dusty on the drive down from Caracollo so as soon as we'd checked into a small hotel we repaired to a local bar, well known to Jim, to slake our thirst with beer.

We were up early to catch a fascinating, small, diesel hauled, ancient train running on a tortuous metre gauge track initially down the Misque river valley before looping north and then east towards the major city of Santa Cruz, situated at the much lower altitude of about 400 m. After a three hour run, nearly all down hill, at a rickety 20 to 25 mph we drew into an isolated halt at an elevation of circa 1500 m. Here there was a parallel track lined with mineral wagons alongside which was a loading ramp complete with FEL. I mistakenly thought we had arrived at the mine. Instead we de-trained and clambered into a large 4 x 4 pick-up truck, which headed in a general southerly direction whilst it climbed steadily back over 2300m before cresting a ridge at the head of a spectacular valley that lead down to Quioma. It was the expected barren, rocky, dusty vista of the Andes, but half way down this valley, at about 2000m elevation, there was a magnificent jacaranda tree in full blue/violet blossom. What a surprise (for me) as I had always assumed it was an African tree having marvelled at their stunning appearance lining roads in Kitwe and Ndola in Zambia. Carlos told me that it was a sub-tropical tree, a native of Brazil, but also quite common in Bolivia on the lower slopes of the eastern cordillera. We settled in to the Quioma mine bunkhouse had a quick snack and repaired to the engineering office to work through the geological, assay and mine development plans.

The total reserve at the end of 1986 was 447,273 tonnes at 13.8% Zn, 8.3% Pb and 1.5g/t Ag. Isolated high assay values had been reduced to the arithmetic average of the adjacent assays and these final assays were reduced to 80% of their value to account for sample, assay and grade-distribution bias. Ore reserve blocks were generally 40m on strike between levels ranging from 20m to 85m apart. A quick plot of assay values of the new -40m level development on the main Candelaria vein showed an approximate log normal distribution (typical of hydrothermal veins), whence the geometric mean would provide a better estimate of average grade than the arithmetic mean. More than 55% of the industrial reserve was contained in the Candelaria vein.

The mine neatly divided into two. The old mine, above the lowest -1867m level, comprised numerous small narrow veins and remnant rib and sill pillars and the new mine, below the -1867m adit level, comprised the Candelaria veins. The future of the Quioma mine obviously depended on the Candelaria vein with a 700m strike length, true width of 1.3m plus 80% payability indicated an ore expectancy of just over 3,000 t/vm. The suggested mining plan would be to maintain production from the remnant, upper veins at 250 tonnes/day for 2.5 years and thereafter stope the Candelaria vein at 300 tonnes/day for the next seven years. The high strike/width ratio of the steep dipping veins gave a lateral development yield of only 70 tonnes/m which emphasised the importance of development when mining narrow veins. In fact at Quioma development would provide 23% of the mill feed tonnage.

For operations below the -1867 level a new sub-vertical shaft would be required to handle production from a depth of 200m (5 levels). An annual production of 90,000 tonnes ore, 4,500 tonnes waste (5%), 3,780 tonnes moisture (4%) with a design margin of 9,830 tonnes (10%) gave a total of 108,110 tonnes. Scheduled hoisting 14 hours/day over 300 days/year indicated a hoisting duty of about 26 tonnes/hour over the full 260m lift. That could be handled by a two tonne skip inter-changeable with a cage for handling men and materials. The existing small development shaft would enable the new shaft to be raised from the -80m level and sunk below.

The main power intake along the -1867m level would require doubling to cater for the increased load from winders, pumps, fans and trolley haulage. The compressor plant would require up grading to three 750 CFM units, so that two units would cater for a demand of circa 1440 CFM whilst the third unit was on standby or maintenance. With two shifts/day working on ten stopes, two development ends and two raises the total ventilation requirement would be 60 to 65,000 CFM.

We spent four days at the mine and had a wrap-up meeting with the Mine Manager. Overall Quioma was in pretty good shape. It had a good, although small, ore reserve base which would sustain a high grade 300 tonnes/day operation for at least seven years. From my viewpoint the major problem area was the lack of any mine engineering input. The mine had merely continued doing what it always had done. However, now a new mine was being developed below the adit level on the Candelaria vein that required both planning and engineering. I suggested that would need a Chief Mining Engineer (CME) and two qualified engineering assistants.

We took the 4 x 4 pick-up truck back out of the Quioma valley to catch the return train from Santa Cruz, which finally struggled (up hill almost all the way!) in to Cochabamba around 7.30pm. We stayed overnight in the same hotel and drank (more!) beer in the same bar, leaving the following morning for the six hours drive back to La Paz.

I spent the next three days writing up a bullish report on the Quioma mine, based, obviously, on Jim and Carlos's geological report. From the point of view of both geology and mine engineering it was a simple, straight forward "good little, high grade mine". Jaime, the GM was very pleased with our conclusions, but he had yet another surprise for me. Apparently the lady Marketing Manager of Empressa Minera Bernal Hermanos Ltda (EMBHL) had approached Jaime to ask if I would undertake a review of their Mina Rosa de Oro. It was now apparent to me that everybody knew everybody in the Bolivian private mining sector. To be fair Jaime said he'd ask me, but felt it would be OK since, EMBHL knew I was already here in La Paz. Thus on the 13th September I set out on job No. 050 from La

Paz on the Villazon train for Tupiza passing through Oruro and Uyuni. That was certainly the way to travel on the altiplano. Definitely sedate, but pleasantly free of the ubiquitous Bolivian dust.

At Tupiza I was met by Mrs Aida Bernal Cruz of EMBHL. We set off in a four wheel drive jeep on reasonable dirt roads in a south-western direction for the 2.75 hour drive to Estarca canton in the Sud Chichas province close to the Volcan peak (5545 m) and the Argentine border. As with so much of the central Andes it was pretty desolate country. Mina Rosa de Oro was a small antimony mine. The mineralisation, mainly stibnite, antimony sulphide, occurred in steep dipping, low temperature hydrothermal veins hosted by conformable Ordovician shales. The veins had been traced for 2.5km on surface. At present the geological reserve was 26,446 tonnes at 5.81% Sb. Average vein width was 1.56m with dips from a low of 65 degrees through to vertical. Historical records indicated an ore expectancy of 1500 to 2200 t/vm. In the central section where mining was currently taking place over a 550m strike length, the ore expectancy was 500 t/vm sufficient to maintain a 50 tonnes/day mining rate. The mill capacity was four tonnes/hour or nearly 100 tonnes/day. The existing geological data would suggest that the full vein length was quite capable of supporting that rate of production.

Two other antimony mines of a similar disposition were operating in the same general area. The Candelaria mine of San Juan and the Chittcobin mine of EMUSA. Both these mines were understood to have worked their antimony veins to 400m below surface. At present the Rosa de Oro mine had only worked to a depth of 150m below surface, a mere 6% of the known strike length. There was thus good evidence to suggest that about 337,500 tonnes of, say, 5.5% Sb ore would be present to a depth of 300m below surface, still only 12% of the known strike length, sufficient to sustain a 100 tonnes/day mining rate for eleven years.

The flat topography, steep dip, large strike extent and very high strike/width ratio dictated that the mine was developed by trackbound equipment accessed by a vertical shaft. Because of the low % payability and erratic nature of the ore shoots a level interval of no more than 30m should be maintained. Under these conditions development ore would provide 28% of the total mill feed. Poor ground conditions dictated that cut-and-fill stoping was the correct method. However the big problem in the mine was the absence of any suitable hoisting plant. The existing shafts in the Filadelfia and Velasquez sections were quite unsuitable. In fact the Filadelfia shaft/hoist experience was one of the scariest I'd experienced in 29 years in the industry. I rode up and down in a cut-off 44 gallon oil drum! Braking on that ancient hoist was achieved by the driver applying his foot to the end of a timber baulk jammed under the winder drum. I'm glad I looked at that after I had come back up rather than before the descent!

To meet and sustain a 100 tonnes/day output both shafts should be stripped out to, say 2m x 2.5m size, and be equipped with hoists capable of hoisting 10 tonnes/hour over a 200m lift. Additional haulage side tip wagons and another 1.5 tonnes Little Trammer would be required. Compressed air consumption would rise to 560 CFM suggesting three 285 CFM units, two on load one on standby. Additional pumps and ventilation fans would be needed and once all the additional plant had been sized a reappraisal of total power demand could be made. There was a desperate need for the application of some basic mine engineering.

Crude ore from the mine was trucked the short distance to the mill, or concentrator. The plant was in a state of disrepair - cracked ball mill foundations, conveyors damaged, pipes leaking and spillage and sludge everywhere. Not a pretty sight. At present, due to shortage of ore from the mine (lack of hoisting capacity) the plant was "campaigned", only running fifteen days/month. Although the plant was stated to have a capacity of 100 tonnes/day that would be extremely unlikely without a major overhaul of the entire installation. Mill recovery was understood to be 65%. Average current monthly production was 44 tonnes of 64% grade concentrate. In addition approximately 50 tonnes/month of Lump Ore (Broza), also grading 64% Sb, was produced. Both Lump and flotation concentrate were then trucked to EMBHL's roasting/smelting operation on the outskirts of Tupiza where both antimony trioxide and metallic antimony were produced. These facilities we visited on completion of my visit to Mina Rosa de Oro. I thanked Mrs Bernal Cruz for all her assistance at the mine and boarded the ENFE train at Tupiza station for the relatively relaxing train journey back to La Paz.

I checked in at the COMSUR office where Jaime and Jim were interested to hear my views of the Mina Rosa de Oro. Of course, I could only make a general comment to the effect that there appeared to be plenty of ore to boost current production for more than ten years at least. Jaime confirmed that COMSUR would put in a bid to buy the Aguilar mine from its current owner St Joe Lead of the USA. With that I nipped off to pack at the Hotel Sucre before Jaime could think of another mine for me to look at! Next morning the COMSUR Range Rover ran me up to El Alto to catch the LAB flight to Lima where I transferred to Eastern for the flight to Miami and there transferred to a BA flight to Heathrow. Gillian said I appeared to have lost a lot of weight, maybe ten or twelve pounds and I guess she was right. Over four weeks at high altitude and the generally unappetising Andean food had certainly reduced one's calorie intake (beer and pisco sour not withstanding), whilst interminable climbing of ladders underground had burnt off what little calories I did have. It was great to be home again, although the long grass, hedges, ditches and log splitting kept me busy after a twelve hour sleep.

Gillian, of course, had been busy since the first week of September running Sproggs to and fro to St Richard's school in Bredenbury. Fortunately some of his Kimbolton School friends had also started at St Richards at the same time, which made his life a little easier. I took over some of the daily school-run driving duties and was pleased to see that he seemed to be enjoying the new school "buzz". His natural sporting ability served him in good stead and the older boys (and girls) ensured that he soon learnt his place in the children's hierarchy. In that winter term he learnt to play the team sports of hockey and rugby whilst continuing with individual activities such as swimming, running and squash. On the academic side he excelled at divinity, which left us somewhat non-plussed as non-believers in conventional religion. All in all the step up from the village school went well and Gillian and I were really happy about that.

In fact preparing the Gorsty garden for autumn/winter seemed to occupy the next couple of weeks through into October. Then it was time to move inside and tackle a few DIY jobs. I tried to redecorate at least one room per year, more if time was available plus the usual patching/repair/painting of some outside windows in the summer. Earlier in the year I had asked BT to run in an additional telephone line as I wished to have a dedicated line for a fax machine. Most of my work was overseas and this new communication system, suitable for drawings and plans as well as text was ideal for an independent such as me. The Hereford Staff Agency had provided me with a good telex service over the past five years but the home fax would improve my own service. I located a suitable Sharp's fax machine at an office in, of all places, Church Stretton and bore it home in triumph. Of course it took a while to set it up and work out how to use it and as with all new technological purchases - if all else fails, read the instructions. Yes, good advice, but some of the Japanese-English needed an interpreter. Once up and running the next thing was to get some new letter heading incorporating the new fax number alongside the phone number. It really looked as if I meant business! As before Orphans Press in Hereford Road, Leominster did a first-class printing job.

In early November I received a call from Terry of Brook Hunt & Associates (BHA) asking if I could assist them with an operational review of Falconbridge's copper and nickel operations in Canada. BHA produced independent technical and financial reports on various companies, metals or countries that were available (to purchase!) by, for example, stock brokers, industry analyst or individual investors. I knew Terry well from RTZC days and had no hesitation in accepting job No. 051. Thus on the 8th November I joined BHA's Graham at Heathrow and we flew Air Canada to Toronto. Then took a connecting flight to the mining district of Sudbury, just north of Georgian Bay on Lake Huron. I had been to this part of the world eight years previously when working for the Golder Associates group.

We hired a car in Sudbury so that we had our own transport to visit the operations of the Fraser mine, the Strathcona mill and the Falconbridge smelter. We only had two days so it was, of necessity, a data gathering exercise, with some physical assessment of the actual operation. The large underground mechanised Fraser mine made an interesting contrast to the small, narrow vein mining operations recently visited in Bolivia.

We then took the short flight north to Timmins to visit the Kidd Creek mine, mill and smelter over the next two days. Here the Kidd Creek management provided transport to take us around the different facilities. Again it was something of a touristic "bums rush" collecting data, with little time to absorb new mining equipment and different mining methods. I did pay particular attention to the Kidd Creek No. 1 shaft which was equipped with twin 27.5 tonnes capacity skips running on rope guides in conjunction with a large single cage and counterweight operating on fixed steel guides. The use of both rope and fixed steel guides in the same shaft was unusual, but the reason stated was that skip hoisting took place from a single loading station but that men and materials access was needed on multiple levels - so? I suspect that the main reason was cost of the shaft furnishing. The No. 1 shaft was hoisting over 13,000 tonnes/day from a depth of around 2600ft The ore expectancy in that area was 130,000 t/vm so that actual production neatly confirmed my 10% rule-of-thumb. It was much easier to work out than Taylor's Rule!

Blast-hole open stoping was practised using 2.25, 4.5 & 6in DTH percussion drill rigs and an 8in rotary drill rig. Drawpoint loading from the undercut was handled by Wagner ST8 and ST5 LHDs. The ST8s output was quoted as 500 tonnes/shift. The No. 2 shaft was hoisting 5,000 tonnes/day from a depth of 4600ft The total underground labour force was quoted as 600 which, with a combined output of 18,000 tonnes/day, indicated a productivity of 30 TMS. Although reasonable it was not as high as one might expect for a new(ish), highly mechanised Canadian underground mine.

I would have liked to have spent more time at the sharp end of the underground operations, but our remit of collecting company handouts did not permit that. In fact the total four day visit to both Falconbridge's Sudbury and Kidd Creek operations merely gave one a skimpy overview and I found it very unsatisfactory from an engineering standpoint. But hey, it was good to visit the famous Kidd Creek mine and the visit would certainly help pay the bills. We left loaded down with ore reserve statements, production records and, unusually, detailed operating costs of mining, smelting and refining along with various company promotional literature. On our flight from Timmins back to Toronto Graham explained to me that BHA would produce a Review of the Canadian Nickel Industry and that limited publication would be available for purchase. Needless to say a complimentary copy would be sent to Falconbridge! I felt a little uneasy about the whole exercise as, obviously, we had merely skimmed the surface of, for example, mining difficulties at both the Fraser and Kidd Creek mines. To me it was a little like producing a "sunny side up" promotional brochure for Falconbridge - Clean, Caring, Careful Nickel Miners!

From Toronto it was yet another "red-eye shuttle" night flight to Heathrow arriving late morning the next day. On going our separate ways from the airport I promised Graham that I would send him a write-up before the end of the month. That would be later than I had planned on account of the huge amount of company data I would have to work through and the non-engineering style of writing required. However I said I'd send my first draft through by fax (wah hey!) asap so that he could amend, chop and change as he saw fit. Thus it was head down for the next week or so, interrupted every now and then with a flurry of fax exchanges to BHA where Graham was doing a cut-and-paste on my notes. In spite of everything and much to my relief BHA produced an eminently plausible Canadian Nickel document packed full of hard facts and figures. I'm not sure I would have paid the price asked for the document, but then I had an insiders viewpoint.

33

The work front was quiet during December so I was able to improve my slim parenting skills running Sproggs to and fro to St Richards in Bredenbury. The School had a Wind Band and both Gillian and I felt it would be good if Sproggs could participate. With some helpful advice from the School's music teacher we all agreed to settle for a clarinet. Fortunately the small music shop in Leominster advised me on where and what to buy. At the same time Gillian decided to buy a flute - "pour encourage les autres" - though I'm not sure if she was referring to Sproggs and clarinet or me with the alto sax. Whatever, it seemed to work and Gorsty trembled with more huffing and puffing than usual, whilst poor Luke and Anjon hid in the store with very pained expressions. We went down to Pat and Tony's place, in Mawgan Porth for Christmas. Tony dressed up as Father Christmas complete with full white false beard and ladies red coat on back to front. He crept into Sproggs bedroom after midnight with much ho, ho, ho'ing and poorly stifled laughter. I was sure Sproggs would be terrified if he was still awake, but he slept on.

Jim from COMSUR called me early in January 1988. He asked me to run up some capital and operating costs for a notional open pit in the Cerro Rico area of Potosi. He said he was sending the crucial parameters for that notional open pit by fax and could I fax a reply back in the next couple of days? He also said that COMSUR expected to complete the purchase of the Aguilar mine from St Joe Lead in the next few weeks and for me to be prepared for an extended visit to that mine in March. This was an open-pit exercise, job No. 052, and yes I would keep March free for an Aguilar visit. The notional pit details duly came through on the fax and I rapidly drew up a crude pit design based on the stated topography, rock types and orebody (silver) size and disposition. I ended up with a 3.5 to 1 strip ratio for 3,000 tonnes/day ore production. That meant shifting 13,500 tonnes/day. Fortunately I had recent budget quotations for open-pit plant and equipment. Those prices were inflated to early 1988 FOB UK figures then guesstimated to CIF Bolivia values. I suggested that ex-pit ore grades should be reduced by 7.5% to account for waste dilution. Order-of-magnitude open-pit capital cost was US$ 12 million and direct operating cost US$ 9.9 tonne ore (3.5 to 1 strip ratio). I faxed those costs plus a diagram of the pit to Jim. He replied by fax three days later saying "no go at the present silver price" and that was that. Once again, good old fax!

A week later I had a call from Don of GA(UK) in Maidenhead. He asked me to accompany him to India to visit the HZL Mochia mine at Zawar, Udaipur, India. He told me that apparently HZL had carried out a large pillar blast at the mine and the surface crown pillar had collapsed down in to the mine's main undercut level. Don and I had advised HZL about recovering the 4th and 5th level crown pillar, along with the rib and main shaft pillar from the 5th level to 15th sub-level. I was immediately worried that this might reflect badly on Golders and we could end up in jail. Don said no, relax, our pillar blasts had been completed, successfully, over two years ago. This was HZL's attempt last week to take out the crown and rib pillar between the 4th & 3rd levels. I said OK, if he was sure. He reaffirmed that HZL had said "no problems with earlier pillar blast" but urgently wanted advice as to what to do as the mine was now shut. We arranged to meet at Heathrow in two days time.

As before we flew AI to Delhi and then transferred to an IAC Vickers Viscount flight to Udaipur. After settling in to HZL's guest house we went to see Hari, HZL's Chief Mining Engineer, in their Head office. He gave us a concise run-down on what had happened. The pillar blast, using SG 80% explosive and millisecond electric delays was successful, but approximately one hour later the surface safety crown pillar collapsed, en masse, into the mine producing a huge air blast throughout the underground workings. Foul air and dust billowed from the main shaft collar frightening the nearby surface workers. Of course there were no people underground and no one was hurt. However the Mines Inspector had visited and decreed that no one was allowed to enter the mine until HZL's geotechnical consultants, Golders, had examined the situation. That was it in a nutshell.

So welcome to job No. 053 which had every appearance of being challenging. With Hari we drove down to the Mochia mine and met the Chief Geologist in the engineering office. Examination of the surface and 3rd level plans indicated that perhaps more than 275,000 tonnes of crown safety pillar had collapsed into the existing mine's undercut level. Don was initially mystified as to why that large crown pillar had failed. After all the average width was no more than 28m, the vertical thickness was over 30m, the orebody dip was vertical and both hangingwall and footwall rocks were competent dolomite.

We were joined by the Mine Manager and Underground Manager and all six of us piled into two jeeps and drove up to the north, notional hangingwall side, of what was now an elongated, near vertical slot. We kept reasonably well back from the northern edge until it became apparent that the failed crown pillar had broken cleanly to the dolomite contact. Don had sensibly brought some binoculars with him and almost immediately noticed a plethora of ancient workings along the exposed southern face of "the slot". All of us were surprised at the extent of those old workings as current HZL plans had shown minimal disturbance of the orebody by ancient Roman workings. Moving around to the southern side we could also see extensive old workings along the northern face. Everything became clear. The believed solid crown pillar was anything but solid, since the near surface orebody contacts had been honeycombed by ancient workings, effectively severing the sides of the crown pillar arch. No wonder it had failed when a 90,000 tonnes blast had taken place immediately below it.

It was certainly a shock to all of us. In particular Hari was worried about how this lack of knowledge of ancient underground workings would play out with the Mine Inspector. Both Don and I felt that we, Golders and HZL, could only say mea culpa. In hindsight we, well HZL, should have driven several crosscuts through the crown pillar from the southern side probing for old workings. Easy to be wise after the event. Now that all dust in the mine had settled Hari and I agreed that we should explain the reason for the pillar failure to the Inspector and then get his permission to undertake a full shaft inspection. After that we could enter each level crosscut from the shaft to observe the ground conditions of "the slot" walls at successively deeper levels. We expected the main undercut level to be largely crushed and the main haulage level to be severely damaged.

The Inspector came the following day and was entirely reasonable. He would require an independent (Golders) report on the crown pillar failure and an overall plan of how the mine could be put back into production safely. The shaft inspection went smoothly until we reached the main haulage level where a five tonne trolley loco had almost been blown into the shaft. Obviously if it had it would have destroyed the shaft from that level, past the loading station and pump chamber into the sump. The programme to reopen the mine was fairly simple and in essence involved a new mine being developed below a 25m pillar from under the old haulage level. Of course this would be time consuming, involving immediate shaft deepening and subsequent driving of crosscuts, strike drifting, stope development and raising on each of these new, lower levels. I guesstimated that the mine would be out of production for around eighteen months.

That was bad news for HZL, but Hari felt that they could increase output from the new Rajpura Dariba underground mine and the new Rampura Agucha open-pit mine. There were also the nearby Zawarmala and Baroi mines where production could also be increased. Nevertheless the Zawar Debari smelter would be short of concentrate feed in the short to medium term. Don and I accompanied Hari and the Mine Manager to make a verbal report on the pillar failure. Don described the geotechnical position and that the presence of ancient workings was the underlying cause of the collapse. He had taken photographs of both walls of "the slot" at surface to show the ancient workings. Thereafter Hari described our inspection of the shaft and our proposal to leave a 25m safety pillar below the existing haulage level before recommencing mine development below that level. The Inspector was adamant that no one should enter the old stoping or undercut areas above that haulage level. He agreed that examination of the two ventilation exhaust raises could take place from either the surface or from the haulage level. We all agreed that air tight stoppings would need to be placed on all crosscut connections from the ventilation raises to all old levels above the proposed new safety pillar.

At our final meeting with Hari he again requested that Don submit Golder's report as quickly as possible since the HZL management would not undertake any work to reopen the mine until their report had been considered. For his part he would draw up a new mine plan for working at depth. He also asked me to send him any further thoughts I had on this reopening plan and schedule. With that Don and I headed for Udaipur airport for the early evening IAC flight back to Delhi. We caught a 10pm AI flight which delivered us to Heathrow at 1pm the following afternoon. Don said he would send me a draft of his report by fax. I had only been away seven days but there was plenty of update news from St Richards school and Gorsty.

At weekends we used to take Sproggs back to St Richards for rugby matches on Saturday afternoon. Of course we provided vociferous pitch side encouragement and Gillian was convinced she was yelling her head off shouting "come on St Richards" when in reality it was little more than an animated whisper. Nothing I said would convince her that she wasn't shouting like a Billingsgate fishwife until Sproggs blithely said he hadn't heard our supporting cheers. After the match we used to join other parents and some teachers for tea and buns and a match post-mortem. One of the teachers commented that Sproggs had the makings of a very good all round sportsman. He seemed to be able to turn his hand to any moving ball game (rugby, hockey, squash, ping pong) and had good stamina as exemplified by his cross country running. Naturally Gillian and I were pleased. His first, autumn, term report had also been quite encouraging and more importantly he had entered into school life with gusto.

I received a fax from COMSUR telling me that I would need an Argentine business visa to undertake consulting work at Aguilar. As before I had to go to the Brazilian Embassy in London to obtain one. It was all very bureaucratic and entailed interminable waiting. I let COMSUR know that I now had this business visa and they asked me to make myself known to the GM of CMASA, Miguel, in Buenos Aires on my way up to the mine in the first week of March. This time the flights were perfect by Varig from Heathrow to Rio then AA from Rio to Buenos Aires. We landed at Ezeiza International Airport virtually on time, but then the trouble began.

At Immigration I was pulled out of the line and taken to a small interview room for heavy interrogation in Spanish and Spanglish. No, my visa was incorrect/not valid/not recognised/a forgery whatever, but I could not enter Argentina. My passport was removed and I spent the next two hours or so in solitary. My interrogator returned and said I would be put on the first plane out of Argentina. He reluctantly allowed me to make one telephone call to CMASA, whence I advised Miguel's secretary that I had been declined entry, in spite of a valid, business visa.

To be fair the Immigration and Customs people had recovered my bag and told me I would be put on an AA flight (back) to Rio. In due course I was marched out to the plane, the last one to board and my passport was handed to me at the door. I was seated alone, up front in First-Class (so that's how you do it!) and generally treated as if I had a contagious pox. So back to Rio where I had a bit of a hassle to recover my bag. Then into the departures area to suss out flights to La Paz. There was an early morning Cruzeiro flight going to Sao Paulo, Santa Cruz and finally La Paz. I phoned the COMSUR office, told them what had happened, asked them to book me on the next La Paz to Juyjuy flight and ask CMASA there to contact Aguilar to pick me up from the airport.

I slept in the airport overnight - what a waste in Rio, of all places. It was impossible to get transport into the city as there was some carnival wing-ding going on. At 5 in the morning I unfurled myself from a seat, staggered along to the public loo and buried my head in a basin of cold water. Suitably awakened I checked in at the Cruzeiro desk for the La Paz flight. We eventually landed at El Alto, La Paz at around 8.00 am, where much to my surprise the COMSUR Range Rover was waiting to take me to their office. Here I was greeted by Fanny, who thought it was very amusing that el gringo ingles was not allowed into Argentina at Ezeiza Airport. Stan, the office manager, checked my Argentine business visa and said it was perfectly valid. Presumably I had encountered a stroppy Immigration guy who was still fighting the Malvinas war. Stan said I definitely shouldn't have a problem at Jujuy. I had around two hours in the office before the Range Rover ran me back up to El Alto for the midday AA flight to Jujuy. The plane was only half full and, as Stan predicted, there was no trouble at Jujuy. In fact both Immigration and Customs were very cursory, apart from dogs, presumably sniffing for drugs? A CMASA ute was waiting for the final four hour drive up to the Aguilar mine.

It was nearly dark as we pulled in to the Aguilar camp. This time I didn't suffer from a siroche. The driver took me to one of the staff bungalows. They were very comfortable, pleasantly warm, heated by radiators utilising cooling water from the power station diesel plant. A little later Mike, the English Aguilar GM, dropped in to say "Hi" and ask what my programme would be. I told him that COMSUR had asked me to look at "everything" relevant to sustaining and improving production and profitability. That caused Mike to raise an eyebrow. I said I expected to be here two or three weeks and would like to start, with geology tomorrow. In spite of Aguilar's 4500m elevation I managed to sleep well, no doubt catching up on a wasted day and night in Buenos Aires, Rio and La Paz.

Pablo, the Chief Geologist, joined me for breakfast at the Bunkhouse Mess. I had met him last year on our "appraisal visit" and been impressed with his knowledge of Aguilar's geology and his organisation of the Geology Department. First we went through the ore reserve position. Proven and Probable reserves were 4.7 million tonnes at 5.3% Pb, 7.0% Zn and 118g/t Ag with a further Possible reserve of 3.6 million tonnes at 5.2% Pb, 9.2% Zn and 110g/t Ag. The calculation considered a minimum horizontal mining width of 2.0m and a "combined metal" cut-off grade of 8.2 in accordance with the following formula:- (0.55% Pb + % Zn + g/t Ag/42) = 8.2. Basic input data was from diamond drill intersections and conventional underground development. The orebodies strike north-south, dipped west at 65 to 70 degrees and plunged south. Apart from a variable DD sample length, which should be standardized at 1m, the reserves above 18 Level, the lowest adit, were well calculated. However below 18 level where DD intersections had increased to 50m on strike with a reduced level interval of 20m the methodology was incorrect and those reserves required recalculating.

Examination of ore exposure underground indicated that there would be a range of reserves depending on the cut-off selected within the quartzite host rocks. That was because the "inter-bed waste" was, in fact, mineralised. As a matter of urgency CMASA should prepare a range of tonnage-grade curves. Until those were prepared it was not feasible to plan a mining strategy. As expected with that type of mineralisation the grade-frequency distribution for all three metals was approximately log-normal. Thus the use of an arithmetic average for a group of samples would consistently over value ore reserve blocks. CMASA included the grade-frequency distribution error in their calculation of the MCF relationship between delivered rom ore grade to average mill head grade. Nevertheless the MCF did give a rough guide to the efficiency (or otherwise!) of the mining activity. The sample preparation plant was good and in accordance with the sampling theory developed by Pierre Gy. With regard to DD core (AX size) samples a quarter core should be sent to an independent laboratory to check the half core assay value obtained by the Aguilar lab.

The total reserves were spread over a large vertical (several levels) and lateral extent. Main mine access and services were via 8 level and 18 level was the lowest adit level carrying the rail haulage system from mine to mill. Although nearly 66% of the total reserve was above 18 level the ore expectancy was only 12,500 t/vm. This low figure confirmed that the tonnage was scattered in remnants and pillars over a large vertical height of about 450 m. Below 18 level, the trackless mine, the remaining 34% of the reserve had an ore expectancy of 20,500 t/vm. What became clear as I struggled up and down numerous ladders, between 18 level (4500m elevation) and, unbelievably, 2 level (4950m elevation). The mine should make a concerted effort to rapidly mine out the old upper levels and concentrate mining between, say, levels 12 to 18. At the same time development of the trackless mine below 18 level should continue apace. All in all I felt the Aguilar mine could sustain an output of 2,500 tonnes/day.

The mine did not have any geomechanics rock mass classification. In fact there was a complete absence of any basic geotechnical data. I suggested that the CSIR rock mass classification system should be instigated as a priority. The Geology Department could undertake many aspects of the CSIR system, for example, measuring drill core quality (RQD), joint spacing, joint quality (rough to soft gouge) and ground-water (none to > 125 l/min). Core samples should be sent to a materials testing lab in Buenos Aires to ascertain uniaxial compressive strength. That information would be fundamental to planning stoping methods and layouts in the trackless mine. In the absence of any data I made a subjective assessment of the mine's rock quality. I recommended that a geotechnical consultant be retained by the mine as soon as possible.

In the upper levels of the mine the present stopes were scattered randomly throughout the area. It was, in fact, a remnant mining operation with all its attendant problems of induced bad ground conditions, stretched services, difficult supervision, low productivity and high mining costs. The fundamental point was that the ground was not inherently bad, it was the past random mining operations which had caused the present poor ground problems for mining those remnants. Localised support was using split set rockbolts and chicken wire. They were definitely not suitable for that type of ground, where their effect was mainly cosmetic. They should be changed to grouted rebar and weldmesh to provide effective support. Subject to detailed stope by stope cost analysis many of the old remnants could only be mined by square-set or restricted cut-and-fill methods.

However that was certainly not true for virgin ground areas where mechanised bulk mining could be implemented. On 15 level CMASA had been developing 30m long 4 to 6m wide transverse stopes with 3m intermediate pillars. It need hardly be pointed out that a 3m wide pillar 40m high (the level interval), a plus 13 aspect ratio, had virtually no strength. In fact subsequent pillar recovery between two cement fill walls (from the primary stopes) was a complete shambles. The sill pillar cut started as a cut-and-fill stope but before the hangingwall contact was reached it was necessary to convert to a fully timbered square-set stope. Why? Of course, because of "bad ground" produced by a totally unsuitable mining method! Outcome? Very low productivity and high stoping cost from a virgin, competent ground part of the mine. That was absolute madness and I had a long session with the Underground Manager pointing out the unsuitability of their stope layouts for the trackless mine. He agreed that CMASA definitely needed basic geotechnical input.

In the 15A Lower footwall area the basic stope/pillar panel size should be increased to circa 10 m. With reasonable ground conditions it would be feasible to mine these 10m wide stopes by transverse open stoping. Briefly that would comprise the development of a fan-drilled trough-undercut; the development of a vertical slot raise against the strong quartzite hangingwall followed by production down-hole drilling from a top overcut. The blasted ore would be recovered by 2 cu yd LHDs operating in flank drawpoints accessing the trough-undercut. The mine should make a concerted effort to reduce the amount of slow and costly square-set mining. First obtain basic geotechnical data followed by detailed mine planning.

The general mine housekeeping was good. The existing mine engineering department handled reticulation of power, compressed air, trackwork, drainage, trolley lines and ventilation, but no mine planning, per se, was undertaken. CMASA urgently need to fill that yawning gap in Aguilar's mining operation. Apart from redesigning stoping systems and layouts in the old, above 18 level mine, there was now an urgent need to plan and design the new trackless mine, below 18 level.

Surface ore handing from the 18 level haulage to the mill required alteration to remove the unnecessary trucking link. Discussion with the

Mill Superintendent confirmed that the plant could handle 2,500 tonnes/day with some minor modifications to the secondary crushers. At present the mill was operated only six days per week. It should be placed on a seven days/week basis provided the mine could deliver an average 2,920 tonnes/day for six days.

The power plant was clean and tidy but contained four ancient MAN-5 diesels from the 1930s. Nos 1, 2 & 3 were rated at 265 kVA each and No 4 656 kVA. There were later MAN-8 A2 fuel oil units from the 1950s, 1960s & 1985. No 6 was 700 kVA, No 7 was 640 kVA and Nos 8 & 9 both 1680 kVA. There was also a modern MAN-12 A2 fuel oil unit of 1990 kVA. A 1930s Nordberg-6 diesel of 572 kVA had not run for four years awaiting spares. The effective total rated capacity of the power plant was 8.141MVA. That was a sea-level rating and the actual generation capacity at Aguilar was quoted as 7.805MVA.

The plant's bus voltage was 2.3 kV at 60 Hz. Although the plant used capacitor banks and there were synchronous motors on the main mine compressor, operational data implied a 0.8 Power Factor (PF). Hence with all units on stream the actual plant output was 6.24MW. Records showed that the average load on the plant was 4.6MW with a peak load of 5.3MW. Load swings of up to 0.7MW were not unreasonable considering the size of the main underground hoist (350hp) and the 18 level trolley loco (150hp). The power plant thus had to have a spinning reserve of about 5.4MW on-line leaving a paltry 0.8MW in reserve. That was much too close for comfort and if either of engines 8, 9 or 10 were down for maintenance or repair certain sections of the operation would have to practice load shedding. In fact there had been a number of occasions where demand had exceeded spinning reserve and the whole plant had shut down! It would appear that an additional unit, such as the MAN-12, should be purchased. I recommended that CMASA urgently contact a power generation specialist to look at the power demand/supply position.

The mine compressor plant, situated by the 8 level portal comprised eleven Ingersoll Rand units, four diesel and seven electric with outputs ranging from 450 to 2400 CFM. Total capacity at sea level was 14,050 CFM which at the 4750m elevation was effectively reduced to around 9,000 CFM. That appeared adequate for a 2,500 tonnes/day mining rate. Compressed air demand would fall when mining below 18 level began due to the use of electro-hydraulic and diesel equipment.

The mine accounts only gave one overall cost irrespective of the mining method. That was obviously inadequate since rational mine planning would require separate costs for open-cut, square-set, cut-and-fill (with or without cement), trackless cut-and-fill and open stoping. Those cost centres should be refined further by level and finally by individual stope. As noted previously Aguilar was a very isolated location. In fact communications with the outside world were almost non-existent. There were only poor, non-confidential, radio links with the Jujuy and BA offices. The mine needed telephone, telex and fax facilities. Too ensure a good, confidential, telephone call it was necessary to travel 3.5 hours to Jujuy and, of course, 3.5 hours back. A whole day wasted. Now with COMSUR as owner there would be increasing travel between La Paz and Aguilar. Thus it would appear sensible to construct an airstrip on the flat area beyond the mill. Negotiations should be opened with the Argentinian authorities.

On the 25th March I returned to the Jujuy office to collect further costing data and then on to the airport to catch the afternoon AA flight from Jujuy back to La Paz. There I checked into the Hotel Sucre. The next three days were spent in COMSUR's office writing up a draft report and going through the main points with Goni, Stan, Jim, Jaime and Carlos. Goni's first reaction was "jeez wasn't anything good?" I countered by saying, perhaps not a great deal, but all the "problems" could be fixed and that meant plenty of upside potential on both production and reduced costs. He laughed and lit another large cigar and said "so we haven't bought a bummer?" I agreed, he had not, as long as the Pb and Zn prices held up. The following day I flew LAB down to Lima then Eastern to Miami and finally BA to Heathrow. I was totally knackered after all the strenuous ladder climbing at high altitude in northern Argentina and felt as if I could sleep for a week

However as April Fools Day arrived I had a call from a Professor Henry who wanted me to come down to Brockenhurst to discuss a gold project in Sierra Leone. He said "bring your wife", there will be other wives, girlfriends present at this lovely hotel in the middle of the New Forest. Well, what's not to like? Job No. 055 had arrived.

With Sproggs birthday only two days away Gillian arranged with Eddy for him to stay with their son, Matty, out at Hatfield. The two lads had been together at Kimbolton School and were both now at St Richards. Henry had indicated that the discussions at Brockenhurst would only take two days. Thus four days in all, one driving down, two days there and one driving back. Eddy and husband John said they could manage Sproggs for those four days. I hoped they knew what they were taking on. So we dropped him off at their old farmhouse in Hatfield early in the morning before setting off on the three to four hour drive down to Brockenhurst. We arrived mid-afternoon at the pleasant looking Careys Manor Hotel. Our double room had been booked by Henry and there was a little note saying rendezvous in the bar at 6.30 - 7.00 for a "get-together dinner at 8.00". It all sounded very civilised.

We soon located Professor Henry and his wife in the bar and were introduced to Dr Leslie and his wife, Dr John & his wife, all from Southampton University and a really nice guy, Mike from Zimbabwe. Over drinks Henry, who was a geologist, explained that the well-known diamond dealer, Harry Winston, had acquired a gold prospect in eastern Sierra Leone. In order to facilitate his purchase of diamonds in that country he had made an undertaking to the government to explore and develop the Baomahun Gold Prospect. To that end he had contracted Southampton University to carry out geological mapping and sampling. He had also retained Mike of Geomet Services in Zimbabwe to carry out sample analysis and metallurgical testwork. Apparently it was an old gold mining area that had been explored and mined before WW2, but had returned to the bush over the last few decades. He felt that the project now needed some practical mining input hence my presence. With the intro and preamble complete we all settled down to some steady boozing and a very agreeable dinner. Henry wrapped up dinner by saying that the guys would have a full day technical session in the hotel's conference room the following day, whilst the four ladies sorted out their own day.

Henry ran through the background to the Baomahun prospect. In the 1930s Maroc Ltd commenced mining alluvials in the west flowing streams draining the Kangari Hills. The best gold grades were at the base of the hills around the western and southern edges. Maroc traced those alluvial values eastward and located a north-south striking gold bearing schist zone dipping steeply east into the western flank of the hills. Those structures had been opened up by a series of crosscut adits and was known as the Pujehun mine. Maroc carried out underground mining from 1934 to 1938, when all work ceased. Interpretation of old records indicated two lenses, one assaying 14.8g/t Au over 5.2ft and another 12.5g/t Au over 30ft (?). The cessation of mining was stated to be high operating cost, poor ground conditions and low gold price.

Other concession holders since WW2 had undertaken some diamond drilling but the collar locations, elevations and drill azimuths were poorly documented. Drs Leslie and John then described the university work in bush clearance, surface and dump sampling. Mike confirmed that preliminary metallurgical testwork indicated a gold recovery of 60% on oxidised dump samples, but there was no unoxidised underground samples. Dr Leslie confirmed that no underground sampling had been carried out. He also confirmed, as I had suspected, that there was zero services or infrastructure at the prospect.

So, apart from the location, almost a clean sheet! I told Henry that it appeared that we first needed a topographical survey to tie all the adits, top of hill, base of hill, stream location-direction, dump location etc together with x/y/z coordinates. The adits needed to be blown out with compressed air venturi blowers and then all the underground workings should be geologically mapped and where mineralisation was indicated systematically sampled. After that we might be able to guesstimate an ore reserve and ore expectancy. Underground examination would enable me to select a suitable mining method. The ore expectancy would determine output and once that was decided a "project concept" would emerge which could then be costed, both capital and operating. I said that with zero services and infrastructure at the prospect that would greatly increase "project" costs. However I could only make rational comments following a site visit. Henry agreed that that was necessary and after discussion with Drs Leslie and John asked if I could make a short visit next week, flying to Freetown on the 9th April. I agreedand that more or less wrapped up the meeting. Dr Leslie suggested that we (Gillian and I) come down to the university tomorrow and he would show us around the Geology Department where the Baomahun plans and sample data could be perused.

Gillian was back in our room having had an interesting day with Dr Leslie's wife wandering around southern Hampshire. They had had a pub lunch near Calshot overlooking the western part of Southampton Water. That was quite emotional for Gillian as her father, Lofty, had been stationed at Calshot, before WW2, whilst flying RAF seaplanes. The two ladies had got on well having found a common interest in each having an adopted son. Their experience with SS and the adoption process sounded no less frustrating than our experience.

I broke the news of a visit to Sierra Leone next week (went down like a lead balloon). Then we drove down to the Southampton University campus. I spent a couple of hours in the Geology Department looking at the Baomahun "stuff", in truth not a great deal, and then we clambered into Dr Leslie's ramshackle Land-Rover. We collected the ladies from the Uni coffee shop and then drove to their house in the suburbs. It was here that I gathered from Dr Leslie that conditions at the Baomahun prospect were very primitive and in fact our accommodation would be in the local Chief's hut! Yeah, yeah I thought, pull the other one, just how naive did he think I was. After a convivial pub lunch we went back to the university and collected the car for the long drive back to Gorsty, a day ahead of the expected schedule.

We collected Luke and Anjon from the kennels and had a day to ourselves, in spite of the attention of two excited and smelly dogs! I collected Sproggs from Hatfield the next morning. Apparently there had been no major mishaps and, in fact Eddy said Sproggs could come and stay during the summer holidays. I packed some light clothes for the West African trip and two days later Gillian dropped me off at Leominster station for the trip to Bristol where I caught a cross country service to Southampton. There Dr Leslie picked me up for a stay at their house overnight. The following afternoon we joined Dr John on the south coast train through Chichester and up to Crawley and Gatwick airport. The overnight BCal flight to Freetown was now operated by British Airways, which had recently taken over BCal. I was sorry to see the demise of BCal as it had provided an excellent service to Africa. However that seven hour flight by Boeing 707 went without a hitch, landing at Lungi International airport in the early morning. There, much to my surprise, we had to transfer to an ancient Russian helicopter for the short flight across the Sierra Leone river to Freetown. It was hot and humid and had the distinctive smell of coastal West Africa.

My first set back was no luggage. Hard to believe on a direct fight, with no inter-lining, but there it was - el zippo pour Monsieur Estowackes. I filled out the missing baggage form and we grabbed a taxi for our downtown hotel,

The Mammy Yoko. It was quite a reasonable place with a very acceptable bar. Dr Leslie then contacted Dick, GM of MAGS, an export-import company who provided logistical services for the Southampton University team. Dick was very useful as he knew the local scene and soon took me to a clothes store to purchase some jocks, socks, bush shirt and safari pants. I was wearing safari boots and had my cap with me in my carry-on briefcase. Dick was very doubtful that I would ever see my hold luggage again.

Later that morning we took off in a short wheel base Land Rover for the 160 mile trip SE towards the country's second town, Bo. But first we had to negotiate an army roadblock just outside Freetown's limits. It was manned by very young, aggressive youths armed, of course, with AK47 assault rifles. Our local driver was very patient and explained that his three whitey passengers were not mercenaries from Liberia, but were geologists (for once I was quite happy to be called a geologist) working on the Baomahun prospect. Naturally the army lads had never heard of the place but, fortunately the driver mentioned that it was past Mongeri further east of Bo and that seemed to keep them happy. I noted that the two Drs also kept very quiet.

The Freetown - Bo road was sealed and in quite good repair. Thereafter the 25 mile road from Bo to Mongeri was passable dirt crossing the Teye river on a Bailey and 9-span concrete deck bridge. The final ten mile stretch of dirt track, Mongeri to Baomahun, was very poor, heavily rutted with several palm-log "bridges" crossing water courses. Whoever said there was little or no infrastructure was spot on. Facilities on site were virtually non-existent. There was a small corrugated iron shack containing a small sample preparation area adjacent to an "office" of a couple of chairs, small table and a battered plan cabinet. There was no power supply, so everything stopped when the sun went down. It had an enthusiastic amateurs feel about it, but the best was yet to come. You guessed it, our accommodation and victualing was in the local Chief's palm thatched hut! As a visiting "fireman" I was given pride of place to a portion of beaten earth in the Chief's section of the hut. Ablutions were OK in the nearby stream and there was unlimited surrounding bush for calls of nature. Of necessity it was totally working to the sun's hours. At least there wasn't interminable chatter after the Chief's supper, really quite good, cooked by one of his tribe on a wood fire. It was like being back at school with early "lights out". I had a strong feeling that I could wrap up my work in three days flat.

The following morning, nursing a very sore hip, after a sunrise breakfast we clambered into the jeep and headed for the eastern area of interest. Here there was approximately 200,000 tonnes of superficial material completely masking the sub-outcrop. It was being worked and reworked by illegal miners. Previous grab sampling by the Drs indicated a grade of 1.0g/t Au. Although some diamond drilling had been done by previous concession holders it was difficult, nay impossible, to correlate anything on the ground in the absence of any topographical survey grid. The Drs had postulated two underground resources of 540,000 tonnes at 8.0g/t Au comprising a strike of 150 m, width of 12m and vertical extent of 100 m, plus a smaller lens of 120,000 tonnes also at an 8.0g/t Au grade with an average width of 4m only. Of course we wanted to go into the old crosscut adits and examine the mineralised zones. We had brought shielded candles with us to test for bad air. So it proved, after ingress of only 40m the candles started guttering so we beat a hasty retreat. We then went to the western or Pujehun area and tried to examine those adits, but again, no go on account of foul air.

The old Geological Survey records indicated an annual ore development of 1300m. If we assumed a level interval of 15m (small because of poor schist ground), an average width of 5m, a bulk density of 3.0 and a payability of 25% then the ore developed per metre would be: 15 x 5 x 3 x 0.25 = 56 tonnes. Thus an annual development rate of 1300m would develop nearly 73,000 tonnes. Development rates were usually set to match extraction rates. If we further assumed operations took place over 300days/year, then the indicated mining rate would be 73,000/300 = 243 tonnes/day, call it 250 tonnes/day. With an insitu grade of 13.0g/t Au, a 30% waste dilution and a 60% metallurgical recovery an annual throughput of 75,000 tonnes would yield 14,150 oz Au.

Although that was a very crude analysis for potential output from the western area it was in line with the Geological Survey gold production records. In the eastern area there was insufficient basic data to do a similar exercise. The only clue in the higher, or Bolia area, was the presence of a 1m by 1m scoop ball mill and a 45 HP single cylinder Ruston diesel engine. That suggested an output of circa 150 tonnes/day at 8.0g/t Au. It was all a guess but hopefully a realistic guess. We took the jeep around some small bush tracks to investigate local valley streams from the Kangari Hills, searching for a suitable project water supply. The main source of water appeared to be the Kimboye stream, approximately 500m east of the village. In mid April the flow was estimated as 15m^3/min, which would, presumably, reduce to 5m^3/min by February, the end of the dry season. Obviously those visual estimates needed checking by basic stream gauging data. There was no IDF data available. The best local information was from Bo airport, thirty miles SSW of the site, which recorded 2153 mm/year (c. 86 inches) with a maximum of 489mm in August. At 9am average annual humidity registered 88.6% and average temperature 32.4 C. It was definitely typical West Africa - hot and humid.

We selected a low elevation area between the eastern and western ore deposits as a suitable site for a central processing plant. That would minimise the water pumping head and enable ore from both deposits to be trucked downhill to the plant. The project would be based on a throughput of 400 tonnes/day with 250 tonnes/day from the western and 150 tonnes/day from the eastern providing 120,000 tonnes/year. In the absence of any metallurgical test work we assumed a conventional crushing/grinding/gravity/cyanidation process followed by a Merrill-Crowe gold recovery plant. Heap leaching appeared impractical because of excess fines from the schistose ore and heavy tropical rainfall, whilst the carbon-in-pulp (CIP) technology would be too sophisticated for that "bush" location. A full 400 tonnes/day underground mining and gold concentrating plant plus ancillary support facilities would require an installed power supply of 1.6 to 1.7MW.

Power supply would have to be on-site diesel generated or there was a slight chance of running in a power line from the old Bo power station. Dr Leslie sent a message to the Bo power station Superintendent asking if we could have a brief visit/discussion with him the day after next on our way back to Freetown. Initially power demand would be low for water supply pumps, compressors, sample preparation, pilot plant, workshop and lighting. That could best be met by medium speed (1500 rpm) skid mounted diesel generators such as Cat 3208 units delivering 105 kW or the larger Cat 3408 delivering 205 kW. For a full scale project then 3 by 550 kW heavy fuel oil (HFO) engines of a basic rugged design, eg Mirrlees Blackstone, would be required.

We prepared a project plan for Dr John, the site manager, to implement. First up 1) topographical survey of whole prospect area - surveyor required.

2) Upgrading the Bo to Mongeri and Mongeri to Baomahun roads such that a low loader with a 15-tonne load (Cat D6) could pass. That would entail installing some Hume/Armco culverts in place of palm-log "bridges". 3) Bring in Cat diesel generators, fuel tankage and two-stage reciprocating compressor of 170 CFM capacity. 4) Blow out and open up all old adits. 5) Underground geological mapping and sampling. 6) strip overburden from eastern area. 7) Excavate surface trenches across exposed eastern area, geologically map and sample. 8) Engineering appraisal of western area. 9) Engineering appraisal of eastern area. 10) Develop central area stockpile and (if warranted by earlier work) erect pilot plant. 11) Develop workshop facilities and campsite (no Chief's hut and illumination with candles!).

On the fourth day we headed back for Freetown stopping at the Bo power station. This was a new "state-of-the-art" plant of 5.0MW comprising three HFO MAN engines, one of 1.2MW and two of 1.9MW each, financed by the EU. In my opinion totally unsuitable for this isolated location. The Bo town day load was only 0.5MW rising to 1.2MW at night and thus handled by the small engine. The bus voltage was 11 kV and that was stepped up to 33 kV for transmission to the town of Kenema, where the load was stated to be 1.8MW. If that was correct then the station would be operating at 60% installed capacity and there would thus be no power available for the Baohamun project. On top of that there were technical problems commissioning the two 1.9MW alternators. We could forget that as a possible source of power - shame. There were also two old 1.0MW Mirrlees Blackstone units awaiting spares, but the MAN alternators were not synchronised to those units. Really one despairs of aid projects to the boondocks of Africa. Thus, again no go.

We continued back to Freetown and the bosom of the Mammy Yoko hotel where the good news was that my delayed/lost luggage had turned up. Hooray. I noted that the contents of my case had been rifled (I have a particular way of packing my working boots with certain things eg Swiss Army Knife, torch, compass etc), although nothing was missing as far as I could tell. The remainder of the day was spent with Dick of MAGS in his Freetown offices discussing costs of various consumables - cement, steel rebar, GI etc and hire rates for D6 dozers, Cat 3408 diesel generators, low loaders, Hume/Armco culvert etc. He was absolutely brilliant and knew the price of everything including the mandatory bribes. He was au fait with local taxes, import duties, levies etc and for anything imported from the UK said we must add 11% to convert FOB UK to CIF Freetown. What price a local agent who knew his onions - priceless! I was really happy to buy him a beer or two in the Mammy Yoko bar.

I got to bed at a reasonable time for the 8am check-in at the downtown helipad for the short chopper flight across the river to Lungi International Airport and the erstwhile BCal now BA flight back to Gatwick where we arrived around 5pm. I caught the next rail link to Reading and eventually arrived at Worcester Shrub Hill by 10.45pm. Now into the second half of April I was quite discombobulated to find that it was not fully dark, but even more pleased to see that spring was definitely here.

I caught up on all the home news the next day, in particular how Sproggs was getting on at St Richards. No major alarms, though treading water on the academic front unlike sporting activities where he seemed to excel at everything he tried. As the games master commented - great eye/hand coordination, a natural with a moving ball. Well that was great since St Richards had excellent sporting facilities.

Over the next few days I worked up a short report on the Baomahun gold prospect in Sierra Leone. I estimated that the next, exploration phase, would take nearly two years and cost US$ 2.2 million. Most of the cost would be earth moving plant, diesel generators and compressors. If that exploration phase confirmed the underground reserves then a 400 tonnes/day underground operation could be considered. The capital cost for developing an underground mine and conventional gravity/cyanide process plant for treating 120,000 tonnes/year plus all services and infrastructure was estimated to be US$ 26 million. The direct operating cost was estimated to be US$ 72/tonne treated. Assuming a net US$ 385/oz gold price an insitu geological gold grade of 9.1g/t would be required to breakeven on direct operating costs. The insitu geological gold grade would need to rise to 14.5g/t to give a gross 15% DCF return on total project capital expenditure. I sent fax copies of my conclusions to Professor Henry and also Dr Leslie at Southampton University. Finally I sent my full report by DHL Couriers to Harry Winston at the exotic address of Sunset Boulevard, Los Angeles, California. That certainly felt a far cry from the beaten earth of the Chief's Hut in Baomahun!

34

At half term, in early May, we put the dogs in kennels and went off on Toadflax for a weeks canal boating. James, one of Sproggs friends from Kimbolton, came as well. There was a rear cabin with two bunk beds for the boys whilst Gillian and I had the front cabin dinette converted into a very friendly double bed. We decided on the lock-free southern end of the Shropshire Union canal as a suitably safe section for the boys to get used to the boat. We spent the first night at Brewood and all went well. The next day we continued to Wolverhampton, where disaster, James fell overboard. The two boys had been racing along the side gunnels - my fault, I should have stopped them. I shut down immediately and put the drive into neutral and fortunately James, who had disappeared (!) came straight up again clutching his wallet minus the wellingtons. We shouted at him to make for the towpath bank, which he did. Having moored Toadflax we collected James, coughing and spluttering, got him on board, stripped off, into the shower, reclothed and warmed up. Usually the canal was only three to four feet deep, but here close by the Wolverhampton sewage works the canal was over six feet deep. By luck James had been wearing Gillian's gum boots which were a little large so they had come straight off and didn't hinder his rapid rise to the surface. Gillian was worried that the pretty foul canal water might really upset his stomach, but not so and we all agreed he would be an accountant when he grew up since he had never let go of his wallet. After that the boys both wore life jackets when on deck.

At Autherley Junction we turned south onto the Staffs & Worcester canal to Compton Wharf lock and Wightwick Mill lock where we moored for the night. In fact the boys were very useful in helping with the lock operations and mooring the boat. We had a short walk up to the Mermaid Inn on the Wolverhampton - Bridgnorth road, where we all tucked in to some typical pub grub. It sure beat knocking up a meal on Toadflax's small stove. The boys really enjoyed some "puds" as we only had fruit on the boat. Next morning we turned the boat in the nearby winding hole and started our two day return trip to Toadflax's base at Norbury Junction, free of any further disasters. On arrival the boys engaged in an energetic game of tag with Billy Goat Gruff.

More work arrived in mid May, which, much to my relief was local, as I was heartily sick of cramped aircraft seats. A Mr David of Hanwood, near Shrewsbury, wanted me to undertake a shaft sealing job at the New Central Snailbeach (NCS) Mine and that would be job No. 056. I phoned Dave, the back-hoe contractor, in Chirbury and arranged to meet him and Mr David at the NCS mine in two days time. It was about 45 minutes drive from Gorsty. Mr David had bought the property at Crow's Nest, just south of the old mining village of Snailbeach. However the planners required him to make safe the old Engine Shaft, which was still open to surface. The Engine House, which would have housed a Cornish Beam Engine, had an unusual square stone and brick chimney truncated at about 55ft height. It was a well know local architectural feature close to the Snailbeach - Pennerley minor road. To cap it all Mr David showed Dave and me the circular ends of two Lancashire boilers which intruded into his new living room.

To work. The area surrounding the shaft was completely covered with unconsolidated backfill. I used a rope to lower myself down the backfill slope into the mouth of the shaft. The natural slope of the ground affected the backfill depth; about 20 to 25ft deep on the eastern and southern sides and only 12 to 15ft to the north and west. The shaft dimensions were about 7ft by 11ft and the bedrock was Mytton Flags. Unsurprisingly I selected the northern side for Dave to use his long reach back-hoe to ramp down to the underlying bedrock and develop a 7 to 8ft cleared ledge around the shaft. This excavation work took Dave five to six days. We then placed some old corrugated iron sheets directly across the shaft collar followed by some 3/8 in weldmesh. Then five No 15ft long 6in x 3in RSJs, spaced at 2ft centres, at right angles to the long axis of the shaft. A second mat of 3/8 in weldmesh was tied to the top of the RSJs. Finally C20P Readymix was poured into the sump to provide at least a 12in cover over the top of the upper weldmesh. That was left for three days before Dave backfilled the area with the previously pre-stripped material. We all repaired to the nearby Stiperstones Inn for a couple of beers. I then had to produce a professional Completion Certificate suitable for presentation to the South Shropshire Council.

I'd no sooner wiped the froth off my lips from the Stiperstones beer when the phone rang. It was Colin from Davy McKee in Stockton-on-Tees. Could I undertake a review of the reserves and open-pit operations at Nsuta of Ghana National Manganese Corporation (GNMC) next week? I said maybe, but....I needed to know a little more of what was required. He said that Davy were retained by GNMC as engineer-contractor for upgrading the materials handling, crushing, screening and kiln plant. However they, Davy, required assurance that the mine could deliver the quantities required. They also needed capital costs for pit equipment and new operating costs. I said yes, welcome job No. 057, but I would need a subcontract geologist to check out the ore reserves. Colin said OK and I told him I would immediately contact Ross, an independent geologist living in Scotland. I phoned Ross, yes from him, and then phoned Colin back to say that both Ross and I would front-up at Gatwick on Monday for the overnight flight to Accra. I gave him full details of our names and passport numbers for Davy to purchase our air tickets and then phoned Ross back to confirm everything was "go". In turn he said he would fly Edinburgh to Gatwick and meet me at the BA check-in for the Accra flight.

As usual I took the train from Worcester to Reading and then the "airport special" to Gatwick. I soon found Ross and together we located Dave, the Davy Project manager, and his four team members at the Accra check-in desk. It was an overnight 707 flight arriving at Accra at 7.30. What a contrast to the shambles at Lungi Airport in Sierra Leone. Here everything was well organised and both Immigration and Customs worked like clockwork. GNMC had sent a brace of 4 x 4s to take us through to their Accra Head office. After the formal glad-handing, Dave agreed that Ross and I should take straight off to the Nsuta mine with their Chief Geologist (CG) whilst the main Davy team stayed in Accra to sort out their own programme. Ross had previously worked on tin exploration in northern Nigeria so was not in the least surprised to see the giant bush rats held up for sale alongside the road as we travelled SW to Sekondi & the port of Takoradi. There we turned NW for Nsuta, which was only twenty miles or so south of the Tarkwa gold mining area. The 180 mile journey took under four hours as Ghanaian driving was definitely a "push on" variety. At the mine we dropped our luggage in to an unoccupied, furnished Supervisor's house and headed for the Mine Engineering Offices close by the open pit.

The CG gave us a brief run-down on the nature of the deposit which included both oxide and carbonate ore types. Ore reserves had been calculated by the prismoidal method from numerous vertical cross sections, which in turn had been prepared from surface trench sampling and diamond drill hole data. It all appeared well prepared. We then took a drive around the open pit, or pits, as there were several. The CG explained that "the problem" was a severe shortfall on production that year. Last year production had been 190,000 tonnes of oxide and the same quantity of carbonate. That combined output of 380,000 tonnes had been achieved with a stripping ratio of 3.42 to 1 implying 1.3 million tonnes of waste; total material moved 1.7 million tonnes. The 1988 budget, driven by market demands, was for 250,000 tonnes each of both oxide and carbonate with an overall stripping ratio of 5 to 1. However after four months combined ore production was 61% of budget and waste stripping only 51% of budget. A large shortfall in production was the crux of the problem.

The GNMC budget of 3.0 million tonnes (ore & waste) for 1988 represented a huge 76% increase over that achieved in 1987. Hardly surprising that the mine was struggling since no specific mining expansion plan was in place. Provided the ore reserves were there (Ross's problem!) we would have to do a radical pit redesign plus, quite probably, re-equip the operation. The bench height was only 6m and the primary drilling rigs were small Holtrac rigs mounting a Silver 115R drifter putting down 2.5 in. diameter blastholes. The burden/spacing pattern was 1.2m by 1.2m with 10% sub-grade drilling. Blasting was using site mixed ANFO with SG80 primers initiated with Cordtex. Loading was carried out by five old diesel Ruston 38RB rope face shovels and two new diesel 61RB rope face shovels. It was immediately apparent that the 6m bench height was too small for the 61RB shovels. It should be increased to 10m.

The small Holtracs should be replaced by a self contained high pressure (12 bar) DTH rig such as an Ingersoll Rand DM25 Drillmaster which could drill 4in. diameter blastholes 11m deep with just two tubes. The burden/spacing pattern should be expanded to 3.5m by 3.5 m. With a 10m bench height, 4in. holes and a 3.5m square drilling pattern the drilling yield would be 38 tonnes/m in ore and 29.5 tonnes/m in waste. Indicated blasting yields would be 10.1 tonnes/Kg explosive for carbonate ore and 8.0 tonnes/Kg for greenstone waste. It was not feasible to progress pit designs any further until Ross had reworked the ore reserve data.

On this we agreed to request a full suite of reserve vertical cross sections from GNMC for us to take back to the UK. However further examination of the in-pit geology and geotechnics enabled me to select ultimate pit slopes of 45 degrees for both hangingwall and footwall. On consideration of the high ambient temperatures and humidity a maximum gradient of 8% was selected for continuous up-ramp haulage. Certainly the old 38RB shovels should be retired since their output was only 19 BCM/scheduled hr. The new(ish) 61RB shovels were producing 85 BCM/scheduled hr. Those estimates considered a job operational factor of 0.75; a bucket fillability factor of 0.85; a swell factor of 1.40 and a propel factor of 0.85. Outputs for truck haulage, hence fleet size would have to await our pit redesign as would requirements for pit ancillary equipment.

The existing Pegson 36in. by 46in. primary jaw crusher would be too small to handle the maximum kiln production rate. Davy were suggesting that a new 44in. by 48in. Pegson crusher should be installed along with an expanded 60-tonnes capacity dump hopper. Obviously the rom ore dump hopper location was fixed but the location of the new waste dump had to await our pit redesign. Only then could I calculate haul truck cycle times for waste disposal and thus total number of trucks required. Apart from collecting GNMC operating cost data (labour rates; company add-ons; major consumables - diesel fuel, ANFO, SG80 etc) there was little more Ross and I could do. I told Dave, the Davy Project manager, that we had collected all the site data we needed for Ross to produce a geological/ore reserve report and me an open-pit redesign with full capital and operating costs. He seemed surprised as the Davy team expected to remain in Nsuta for another day and half. We agreed to meet up at the GNMC offices in Accra the day after next. So with nothing more to do in Nsuta Ross and I arranged with our company driver to do some tourism on the old Slave Coast and went to visit Elmina Castle on the coast not far from Takoradi.

It was a massive, white painted fort overlooking the fabled Gold Coast. It had, apparently, been built by the Portuguese in the 1480s, initially as a heavily fortified trading post for the exploitation of gold from the inland Ashanti region. In the late 1630s it fell into Dutch hands during colonial African wars. The Dutch concentrated on the export of slaves to Brazil and the Caribbean. Our guide said that 30,000 slaves per year passed through the "door of no return" on the seaward side of the fort. The upper levels of the fort had quite large rooms for the European governor and his staff. The lower level dungeons split into male and female cells, by contrast were tiny. They were reputed to hold up to 600 males and 300 female slaves at any one time awaiting the next ship for transportation. It really was a fearsome place. The British ousted the Dutch in the 1800s and did not indulge in slavery from Elmina since the Abolition of Slavery Bill was passed in 1837. Now the Elmina Castle or Fort was an UNESCO World Heritage site administered by the Ghanaian government. What was the British Gold Coast colony finally became the nation state of Ghana in 1957.

We spent half a day looking around Elmina Castle and then went on to have a look at the Takoradi docks, in particular the GNMC load-out facilities for its sintered manganese products. In the afternoon we drove back the 130 miles to Accra. The hotel's swimming pool was very welcome after the heat and humidity. We had a short look around Accra city the following morning before fronting up at GNMC's offices in the afternoon with Dave and the rest of the Davy guys. There wasn't a lot I could say at that final meeting since we had not yet completed the geological report and ore reserves and hence no open pit had been designed. I said we expected to complete the geology/reserves report within a week and the open-pit design(s) and costing in a further week to ten days. That slotted in with Davy's timetable and seemed acceptable to GNMC. We repaired to the hotel and got "scrubbed up" for a formal dinner with GNMC senior staff. It all seemed very civilised in a smart restaurant in downtown Accra a far, far cry from the dirt and horrors of the Elmina slave trade.

Next day it was the early morning BA flight back to Gatwick. The Davy guys were taking an internal flight up to Newcastle and Ross, of course, was flying direct to Edinburgh. I trudged off to catch the train to Reading and onward connection to Worcester. Ross and I agreed to keep in regular contact. Two days later Ross phoned. He said he really needed a planimeter to calculate all the odd shaped areas on the geological vertical cross sections. He said it would reduce the time he took to recalculate the ore reserves by two to three days. He could obtain a digital Planix unit in Edinburgh for about £400. I said go ahead and buy it. When he'd finished the ore reserve calculation I asked him to let me know and I would drive up to Crieff to collect the cross sections and the planimeter. I could see how it would also help me working out ore and waste stripping areas for the new Nsuta pit.

So five days later I did a quick trip up to Scotland, stayed overnight, and drove back. Having completed the ore reserve calculation Ross could now proceed with writing his geological report, whilst I tackled the pit design.

My first task was to distribute the total ore reserve into 10m vertical "chunks" representing individual bench tonnages. Excluding the two upper benches where both erosion and previous mining had removed the carbonate ore, the ore expectancy was about 55,000 t/vm in the Hill D area. The old 10% ore expectancy rule as a sustainable mining rate for tabular deposits implied a 5,500 tonnes/day output, which over 300days/year indicated a mining rate of 1.65 million tonnes/year. That would exceed the kiln's desired input of 1.24 million tonnes/year of carbonate ore. In turn that indicated an annual deepening rate of 22 m, just over two full benches, which could easily be achieved. The Hill D reserve could sustain carbonate production for four years. There were five other Hill areas of carbonate, which GNMC should actively outline by diamond drilling during those four years. The overall geological/ore reserve picture was strong and quite capable of meeting the desired kiln output.

Within the confines of 45 degree ultimate pit wall slopes I planimetered ore and waste areas off the vertical cross sections, converted these to volumes by the horizontal distance between sections and finally to tonnes of ore and greenstone waste by bulk densities of 3.38 and 2.65 respectively. That gave an overall stripping ratio of 3 to 1 (t/t basis). GNMC had indicated that they would operate the pit on a two shifts/day, six days/week, 300days/year basis. However because of heavy tropical rain in the April - July period the total mining scheduled hours were reduced to 4,400/year. I then located a nearby area for waste dumping (on the plans) which would not sterilise any future reserves and thus had all the data I needed to determine pit equipment specifications and fleet size.

To meet the kiln's new maximum production schedule of 1.24 million tonnes/year of carbonate ore I estimated that the following open-pit equipment would be required:-

No	Unit	Cost US$ million CIF Takoradi
4	Ingersoll Rand DM25 drill rigs	1.56
1	RB61 Face Shovel	0.63
2	RB71 Face Shovels	1.47
8	Terex 33-058 27t dump trucks	1.74
1	Grader AB AS6021	0.22
lot	Ancillary pit equipment	0.44
lot	Drill/Dozer/Truck shops	0.25
	Capitalised initial spares (10%)	0.63
Total		**6.94**

I stressed that that equipment was in addition to the existing GNMC fleet. Direct operating costs were estimated to be US$ 1.31/t moved, which, with a 3 to 1 overall stripping ratio meant a cost of US$ 5.24/t carbonate ore delivered to the crushing plant dump hopper.

I took a further four days to complete an open-pit design report plus breakdown on capital and operating costs. Ross's geological and ore reserve report had already arrived so that I was able to send both our reports by courier to Davy in Stockton-on-Tees. Their Project manager, Dave, phoned back the next day and said our "stuff" was OK and would be incorporated verbatim in Davy's draft report to GNMC. He expected to go out to discuss the draft with GNMC in Accra next week. If there was any follow up needed on the geological or mining side he would let me know. He seemed genuinely pleased with our efforts. I guess the proof of the pudding would be if Davy paid our invoices! In fact they did, albeit rather tardily, but that's engineer-constructor clients for you.

It was great to catch up with "home going's on" after a fairly busy African work front. We managed to go over to St Richards to watch a cricket match on Saturday. Sproggs went well with the bat and excellent throwing when fielding in the deep. He had a go at bowling but somehow had not quite coordinated his leg strides with overarm movement. The Games Master, wary of parents perhaps (?) said "not a problem, little bit of coaching on the overarm action and he'll be a good cricketer". Hell, he was only eleven.

35

For me though, no peace for the wicked. Simon from Wardell Armstrong phoned saying they had been awarded an ODA contract to appraise certain aspects of the Zambian Ministry of Mines, could I assist? You bet I could, job No. 058 was up and running. Simon said that the objective of their ODA study was to review current exploration, mining and processing of gemstones and how the Zambian government might control and maximise the State's revenue from those operations. It sounded fascinating as I had zero experience of gemstone mining. Apparently we were to study three gemstone fields - Ndola emeralds; Kalomo amethysts and Lundasi aquamarines. I met Simon at Gatwick in late June for the overnight BA flight to Lusaka, Zambia. We checked into the Pamodzi Hotel (my recommendation!) and spent the rest of the day in tedious discussions with the Ministry of Mines in their downtown office. Next morning we took the early RoanAir flight to Kitwe and checked into the Kitwe Hotel. Well that was a shock, what a tip! Obviously I had been spoilt rotten by the various Director's Lodges of Anglo and RCM now under the ZCCM banner.

The Ndola emerald field lay about thirty miles south of the Copperbelt city of Kitwe. The Mines Development Department (MDD) had issued 134 Prospecting Licences and 36 Mining Licences. It was a restricted area with police guard posts on the main access roads, but, of course, unlimited access through the surrounding bush for emerald smugglers. The productive areas lay on either side of the Kufubu river. The largest operator was Kagem Mining Ltd a joint venture between the Reserved Minerals Corp (RMC) and Israeli-Indian interests. Kagem produced 80% of the recorded emeralds & beryl from this field. The presence of emeralds was associated with magnetite-chrome schists adjacent to pegmatites. Those pegmatites formed topographic highs and thus provided the key to basic exploration. The laterite and unconsolidated overburden was stripped by a conventional dozer, then loaded by a Cat 966 FEL into small dump trucks for haulage to waste disposal areas. Hard rock waste was drilled with light Airtrac units and blasted with ANFO. Diesel-hydraulic back hoes were then used for final clean up. The favourable beryl/emerald ground was then worked by hand - hammer and tap. Hand sorting took place at the pit face, the recovered material being placed in locked steel boxes which were taken to the processing compound. All pit activities took place under the scrutiny of a large security staff.

The stripping operation removed about 3000 tonnes/day and current production was about 135 kg/month, comprising 8.5% high grade emerald; 34% low grade emerald; 57.3% beryl and 0.2% specimen. Estimates for theft ranged from 15 to 30% of the declared production but could represent around 40% of the production value.

Processing involved crushing, trommel-washing, picking belts and grading. Again a heavy security presence at all stages. The plant treated fifty tonnes/day. Power was supplied by two Petbow 96 kVA diesel generators. The plant was run intermittently depending on the availability of feed. Apart from Kagem all other "mines" were small, shallow, hand worked operations that generally ceased at the water table in the absence of serviceable pumps and diesel generators. We had a chat to Kagem's Head of Security (HoS). He said it was impossible to prevent some theft due to the nature of the emerald workings and its location surrounded by unguarded bush, together with a large security force who were open to bribery. However he felt that Kagem's operation were more secure than all the other small mining operations, which he felt probably lost 50% of their production to theft.

On the next day we visited eight other small mining operations along the south side of the Kufubu river. Certainly these small, generally hand worked, mines had nowhere near the intense security system used at Kagem and their HoS's comment on 50% theft seemed entirely feasible. The Kitwe Hotel lived up to its deserved poor reputation as each night I amused (?) myself by quickly switching on the light (yes, the hotel had power) and hurling my working boots at the army of cockroaches I shared the bedroom with. Needless to say I made sure to empty my boots out in the morning to remove cockroaches and, possibly, scorpions. Fortunately none of the latter appeared.

All marketing of production (official, or recorded) was handled by the parastatal organisation RMC. It was also the major (51%) share holder in Kagem. Every Wednesday in Ndola City RMC valued, in US dollars any stones submitted to them and paid the owner 50% of the value in local Kwacha at the official exchange rate. The stones were finally auctioned in Lusaka or Geneva (Switzerland). Those international auctions took place once every six months. After the auction the seller received the balance of the sale price in Kwacha, less a hefty discount (up to 25%!) to cover RMC selling expenses and payment of an 11% Minerals Export Tax (MET). All in all the poor old producer (the miner) had a long delay before receiving a much reduced Kwacha payment for his production. No wonder theft, smuggling and the black market thrived.

The Ndola emerald field's Restricted Area was very large, 1200 sq Km. However there was only one active Police check point on the Kitwe - Kalulushi road. We made a jeep trip to the village of Tshombe, within the Restricted Area. There were many unauthorised vehicles about and plenty of Senegalese traders/smugglers and their Zambian cohorts dealing in US dollars at exchange rates considerably above the official rate. A disparity of plus 300% exists between the official and parallel rates! Naturally no commission was payable to RMC nor 11% MET to the government on those illicit sales. Once those "illegal traders" realised that we weren't police they continued their business activities quite openly. I began to feel that the official returns of emerald production from the Ndola field would be unlikely to represent 45% of the field's actual production.

We had meetings with RMC and the Mines Safety Department (MSD) in Kitwe covering operational aspects, particularly security, of the Ndola emerald field. The MSD had sensibly taken over MDD's role, since they were based in Kitwe rather than Lusaka. Everyone agreed that the Restricted Area was much too large and impossible to police. We flew back to Lusaka for several days discussions with the Ministry of Mines and MDD. Virtually everyone was aghast that we felt that about 50% of the Ndola emerald fields output was not passing through RMC, but was smuggled out of the country by Senegalese traders who paid "producers" (ie illegal miners, thieves, smugglers etc) in US dollars. We felt that the main difficulty for the government in attempting to control emerald mining and, of course, increase their tax take was the huge difference between the official and parallel (black market) exchange rates of the Kwacha to the US dollar. That was obviously a problem that only the Ministry of Finance and Bank of Zambia could address. In addition to the exchange problem there was the classic difficulty with gemstones, that of small volume and high value making them ideal material for theft and subsequent smuggling. Finally the location of the Ndola field relatively close to the porous international boundaries of Angola and Zaire (Democratic Republic of Congo) meant that Zambian emeralds ended up on the international market, provenance unknown.

Our next task was to look at the Kalomo amethyst fields down in the south of the country. The British Embassy, supporting the ODA work, had arranged for Simon to hire a reliable 4 x 4 Land Rover for our trip. We set off early for the 200 mile drive SW to Kalomo on the main road to Livingstone. At Kalomo we turned SE for about sixty miles towards the south-western end of Lake Kariba. The area was remote and hilly with moderate bush and poor dirt roads. From Kalomo it took three hours in the 4 x 4 to reach the amethyst mining area centred on the village of Simani in the Mwakambiko hills. The amethyst occured either as a stockwork (vein widths 10 to 150mm) within weathered biotite gneiss or as in the case of the No. 6 Mine, steep dipping veins up to 500mm wide in unaltered biotite gneiss. Exploration was simple. The hard amethyst occurred as float in several stream beds. These were followed upstream until the float disappeared whence the surrounding valley sides were trenched to expose the stockworks or veins. All the workings were simple side-cuts with the exception of the No. 6 Mine, which had been developed initially in 1960 by Northern Minerals (Lonrho) and later in 1970 and 1980 by International DGC (German interests).

Laterite overburden was removed by dilapidated dozers and contour side-cuts were developed on the hillsides. The exposed stockworks or veins were worked with hammer and tap followed by hand picking. A small (Hagomag) FEL cleaned up and dumped the material in a rough-stone stockpile. From here it was shovelled onto 10mm screens to remove the lateritic soil. That crude amethyst rom was then hauled by a tractor-trailer unit to the "plant", which comprised a petrol driven concrete mixer (!) to tumble and wash the material. That material was then spread onto white picking tables. The picked amethyst then went to "knocking", ie hammering, where the poor colour, low grade and waste was removed. The final "knocked" material, amounted to 1 to 3% of the crude rom. Four grades of amethyst were recognised; rom; Low; High and AEXP (amethyst export grade). The No. 6 Mine was now worked by Kariba Minerals and reported an annual production of 2500 Kg comprising 95% Low Grade and 5% High Grade/AEXP. It was a quintessential artisanal type mining operation extremely difficult to mechanise and control. Unsurprisingly theft of High Grade and AEXP stones was said to be high, perhaps 30%.

We headed down to the shore of Lake Kariba, where Simon, a keen bird watcher, was very excited to see a huge fish eagle majestically soaring above the lake. At Gatwick on our way out Simon had helped me buy a pair of compact binoculars, as he said bird watching in central Africa should be quite stimulating after his usual patch in Newcastle-under-Lyme and the nearby Roaches. He was right as I also saw a brilliant kingfisher diving alongside the lake shore. We agreed it was too late to head back to Kalomo and Lusaka and thus headed due west for Livingstone, the very rough seventy mile journey taking three hours. As Simon said, and I agreed, having looked at crude amethysts so close to Lake Kariba we had to have a look at the mighty Zambezi and Victoria Falls. It was dark as we finally drove into Livingstone and gratefully collapsed, dust covered and battered into the Ridgeway Hotel. My goodness those beers were life savers.

Next morning, up early, after breakfast on the stoop, we drove the short distance to the Vic Falls Bridge. It certainly lived up to its reputation, it was truly awe inspiring. The drop must be over 350ft and the thunderous noise and immense curtain of spray made one feel very small. Definitely worth a few hours bouncing around the bush in a short wheel base Land Rover. We didn't stop long (ODA work called!). Pity, as I had hoped to see a narrow gauge (3ft 6in) train crossing the bridge - maybe next time. The drive back to Lusaka took nearly six hours in the 4 x 4, albeit on a sealed road. The old Pamodzi Hotel felt like home. The following morning we met the Ministry of Mines and MDD guys to talk about the Kalomo amethyst field. In truth there wasn't much to discuss apart from the ever present problem of illegal activities associated with gemstone mining. We felt that, unsurprisingly, theft and illicit mining of amethyst were much less of a problem since amethyst was of much lower value than emerald and the Kalomo field was quite remote and inaccessible. So onto the next gemstone, aquamarine at Lundasi in eastern Zambia close to the Malawi border. Lundazi was, apparently, about thirteen hours drive NE from Lusaka and the aquamarine fields were 25 to 50 miles west-south-west of Lundazi. Rather than drive the MDD boss suggested contacting the state copper mining company, ZCCM, as they had a mining lease in the north of the aquamarine field. He said he often bummed a ride on the ZCCM plane, which took less than an hour and a half to the Lundazi gravel airstrip. He put through a call to ZCCM and bingo, we were fixed up for a sparrow's flight tomorrow.

Simon and I were out at the Lusaka domestic terminal by 7 for a 7.30 flight in ZCCM's turbo Beech Baron plane. A MDD guy accompanied us as well as providing a 4 x 4 jeep at Lundazi. Everything went like clockwork. The area was flat to slightly rolling with very light bush. Most of the northern area visited was under extensive cultivation. Aquamarine production from the area was first noted four years ago in 1984. Current production was around 40 Kg/month. The aquamarine was associated with swarms of pegmatites. The MDD guy told us that at least 500 pegmatites were actively being worked in that vast, 8000Km^2 field. No large scale, organised mining had commenced. Small pits were developed alongside the pegmatites. Two operators, ZCCM and Kuber Minerals used compressors and jackhammers for drilling then blasting the hard, resistant pegmatites. Primitive washing and tumbling plants (concrete mixers, as at Kalomo) were used to free the stones from the laterite before passing over riffles and screens to hand sorting tables.

A simple washing rocker would be an improvement over the current static, batch operation. Although official production was now thought to be close to 500 Kg/year the quality of stones, beryl and aquamarine was not good. Security, so close to the Malawi border, was a major problem, and official production was estimated to be only 30% of the fields total output of 1600 Kg/year. The aquamarine was likely to command a price of about US$ 5,000/Kg. As at Ndola, miners were supposed to sell to RMC and get paid 50% of the value in Kwacha at the official rate. Unsurprisingly most miners sold directly to Senegalese traders who paid, promptly, in US dollars. In truth it was the same, depressing picture as that at Ndola and Kalomo. The requirement to sell to the state company RMC did not attract business because of their poor, slow payment terms. But the real bugbear was the enormous spread between the official and parallel exchange rates Kwacha to US dollar.

Courtesy of ZCCM we flew back to Lusaka in late afternoon. We had a final meeting with the Ministry of Mines and MDD the following day and re-hashed, for the third time (!) the problems with the size of the mining leases; policing of the leases; RMC buying and payment system and, of course, the Kwacha/US dollar exchange rate problem. I felt they all knew what the problems were, but I'm also sure they really didn't want to hear about it from the British government sponsored ODA team.

We split up the next day. Simon flying to Lilongwe in Malawi chasing other business whilst I caught the BA flight back to the UK. I had received a fax at the Pamodzi Hotel from Gillian saying that COMSUR had phoned saying that Peter, a geotechnical consultant, would be in Aguilar at the end of July and wanted me to be there at the same time. I had recommended Peter, ex Golders, to COMSUR, as the right guy to set up the geotechnical monitoring system at Aguilar. It obviously made sense for me to be there with Peter so that we could set up a geotechnical monitoring programme applicable to the proposed open stoping method below 18 level.

As it was still school holiday time I felt it essential to spend a week at home before heading off for Argentina. Apparently Sproggs had been badgering Gillian to let him become a boarder at St Richards for the next school year beginning in September as "there was so much going on at weekends that he was missing"! Neither of us were very keen on the idea, but he also badgered me so that we went over to St Richards to see the Head to ask if he would take Sproggs as a boarder next term. Yes he would, he felt it would do Sproggs good to integrate (?) with his peers. Naturally it would take a load off Gillian, who had to do all the school running around whilst I was away. So that was that sorted and, on reflection, I felt quite happy about it both for Gillian and Sproggs. He had now been with us for three and half years and had got used to calling us Mum and Dad.

With job No. 059 on the go I phoned Thomas Cook. However, this time I asked them to book me from Birmingham. There was a regular British Midland (BM) service between Brum and Heathrow. The new M42 motorway was now open and this provided a simple easy seventy minute drive from Gorsty to Birmingham Airport.

On the 26th July Gillian and Sproggs drove me to Birmingham Airport. Parking was very convenient, about 200 yards from the terminal doors. Sproggs enjoyed the "buzz" of an airport and we had time for tea and buns before I ambled off to catch the BM flight to Heathrow. What a contrast. The Birmingham Airport experience was almost pleasant compared to the ever worsening Heathrow hassle. There I caught the overnight Varig flight to Rio and there transferred to the AA morning flight down to Buenos Aires. There was no problem at Ezeiza International Airport and after clearing both Immigration (phew!) and Customs I took a taxi to the Aeroparque domestic terminal alongside the Rio Plata. I phoned CMASA office and told them I would be on the afternoon flight for Jujuy. There a CMASA car met me and took me to the Jujuy offices.

To my surprise (and joy) they had booked me into a hotel for the night. I took the opportunity to have a wander around the city, which was much larger and more cosmopolitan than I had earlier thought. There was a splendid Spanish style cathedral with palm type trees planted around the courtyard. Although the snow covered Andes could be seen through some of the street vistas to the west, the city had an almost tropical feel to it. Some of the older buildings were of white painted stucco, but most were modern eight to ten storey edifices with no architectural merit. At around 1200 metres above sea level and only just south of the Tropic of Capricorn I guess it had every right to "feel almost tropical". Certainly there were plenty of bars with tables outside encouraging one to imbibe a few San Miguel beers.

Reality arrived with a bump at 7.30 next morning with the arrival of the Aguilar ute, followed by the long, dusty drive north towards Bolivia and the Sierra Aguilar. Again it was striking how virtually all trees abruptly disappeared as one passed through the 3,000m elevation. We arrived at the mine at 11.30pm. I was taken to a staff bungalow which I would be sharing with Carlos, COMSUR's Chief Geologist, who had arrived from Bolivia the day before. Peter, the geotechnical consultant, was in an adjacent bungalow. Thankfully I did not have any siroche. I caught up with the guys in the Mess for lunch and afterwards we repaired to the geological and engineering offices.

There was great excitement as Peter had brought out a Compaq 386 laptop (well if you were very large!) computer and it was going down a storm with the Argentinian geologists and engineers. Without a doubt it would greatly simplify ore reserve calculations. The current, end 1987, ore reserves had considered an 8.2% combined metals cut-off grade utilising NSR values for Pb, Zn and Ag FOB Tres Cruces. Changes in metal prices and operating cost meant that the 1988 recalculation of ore reserves should use a 6.2% combined metals cut-off grade. Since our last visit in March of this year Carlos had produced a preliminary tonnage-grade curve which demonstrated that the Aguilar deposit had no single reserve, it all depended on the cut-off grade selected. These ranged from 5.25 million tonnes grading 12.31% combined metals at 7.2% cut-off to 0.79 million tonnes grading

19.49% combined metals at 16.2% cut-off grade. At US$ 2.91/% metal grade the in situ reserve value fell from US$ 187.8 million to US$ 45.2 million.

That confirmed that Aguilar's ore reserves should be presented as a tonnage-grade curve since ore outlines were mainly determined by assay limits. The introduction of new, cheaper blast-hole open stoping below 18 level should reduce mining costs by US$ 4 to 5/tonne and that would enable a lower % combined metals cut-off grade to be used. Reserve information in that form would enable management to follow a specific strategy at any particular time. For example with high metal prices and a fixed mill throughput management could raise the cut-off grade to put more metal on to the market. Pablo had now changed the random sample length (dependent on lithology) into a standard 1m length. That would make handling the data by the Compaq computer much simpler. It would also enable the production of grade-distribution plots for both Zn and Pb values. The very skewness (approximate log-normal) of these distributions would indicate the extent of overvaluation bias caused by using the arithmetic mean, rather than the geometric mean. Certainly that grade-distribution bias was a major component of Aguilar's MCF ranging from 0.83 to 0.93.

Over the last four months the Geological Department had collected basic structural data from levels 18, 19 and 20 and that data was a prime input to Peter's geotechnical study in the last half of July. His report noted that the Aguilar stress field was low - Sz 12.5 Mpa; Sy 15.0 Mpa and Sx 25.0 Mpa. Intact rock compressive strengths were - Quartzite 140 Mpa; Mineral 110 Mpa and Hornfels 80 Mpa. Both quartzite and ore were Class 2 ground and hornfels Class 3 ground. General rock reinforcement was not required. Perhaps 10% of the ground might require support with grouted rebar, weldmesh and shotcrete. Square-set stoping should be phased out except where needed to mine old pillars and remnants. The incipient rock strength favoured transverse stoping. Stopes were planned for 50% primary extraction 50% secondary. Above 18 level the basic mining method would be cemented cut-and-fill. Where secondary (or pillar mining) was required it was essential that cemented fill was used in the primary stopes.

Below 18 level transverse, 12.5m wide (subject to geotechnical monitoring), blast-hole open stopes would be used. A slot raise would be developed on the hangingwall and subsequently slashed into a 12.5m width slot. A 12.5m width top overcut would then be developed over the full orebody width. For production long-hole and trough fan drilling of the undercut I suggested a Tamrock SOLO H 606 RA rig would be suitable, subject to detailed discussions with Tamrock. Flank draw points angled in to the undercut should be driven upgrade and of a size suitable for a 2 cu yd diesel LHD.

Examination of old reserve data showed an ore expectancy of 30,000 t/vm, which suggested a sustainable mining rate of 3,000 tonnes/day. In fact I believe that, with rational, sequential mine planning the old, tracked, above 18 level operation could sustain 2,000 tonnes/day whilst the new, trackless mine below 18 level could, within two years deliver 1,000 tonnes/day. Thus the mine should plan to expand milling capacity from the present 2,000 tonnes/day to 3,000 tonnes/day over the next two years. Obviously the Mine Department needed strengthening with a CME and a Mine Planning Engineer. There was much basic mine engineering work to be done - introduction of grouted rebar; changing cartridge ANFO to prilled bulk-blown ANFO; basic work study of stoping and blast-hole stope planning.

The two small jaw crushers at the 18 level portal were an unrealistic constraint on the size of primary blasted rom ore. The proposed new sub-level, blast-hole open stoping system would naturally produce material of up to 0.5m size. A cone crusher of 30in gape crushing to 4in should be installed. The mine urgently required specific unit costs for each and every stope to enable rational tonnage and grade scheduling. With a proposed increase in production to 3,000 tonnes/day the power station would require additional generating capacity.

After a busy and energetic (all those underground ladderways!) twelve days at the Aguilar mine. Carlos and I were driven down to Jujuy, where we caught the afternoon flight to Buenos Aires. Here we stayed in a central, downtown hotel. That was definitely the noisiest hotel I had ever stayed in. Even noisier than central Madrid hotels and that really took some doing. It was not the hotel, per se, but the fact that Buenos Aires residents party and play boy racers until 3am and then street cleaning/garbage collection starts at 4am. There was thus a single hour "sleep" period only. We spent the next four days days in CMASA offices in discussion with Miguel, CMASA's GM, and preparing our geological and mining reports. Out of the blue Miguel asked Carlos and me to make a swift technical appraisal of two small gold mines located in Neuquen province in northern Patagonia. He had, apparently, cleared this with Jaime, the GM of COMSUR, Carlos's boss and my client.

The 630 mile flight SW from Buenos Aires domestic terminal, Aero Parque, to Neuquen took just over an hour and half by 727. The owners of the Sofia and Erica gold properties, Cormine SE, had sent a ute and driver to meet Carlos and me at the airport. The city appeared very prosperous and bustling and our driver told us it was based on nearby oil and gas production, extensive orchards to the east and tourists heading SW to the resort of San Carlos de Bariloche on the Andean frontier with Chile. We headed west on good sealed roads to Zapala then north to Chos Malal and finally west again on a dirt road to the small town of Andacollo in the Rio Neuquen valley below the del Viento mountains. After the long six hour drive from the airport we were happy to check in to a well equipped small motel in the town. Although fairly remote, close to the Chilean border, Andacollo had all normal facilities including State power supply, telephone, TV and a local radio station.

The following morning we visited the Sofia mine which was only three miles north of Andacollo. The main vein strikes NE - SW with a steep dip NW. It had been traced on surface and by strike adits for 800 m. The known vertical extent was 200 to 300 m. Host rock was massive, competent andesite. The Cormine data indicated a "high grade core" of 30,000 tonnes grading 28g/t Au. This would almost certainly be an over valuation on account of the log-normal type distribution of gold grades. Underground examination showed that shrinkage stoping had been used with stope widths from 1.8m up to 4.5m. Shrinkage was definitely the correct mining method. An ore expectancy of circa 800 t/vm would indicate a possible mining rate of 50 to 100 tonnes/day largely dependent upon the vein's overall % payability. Immediately to the north of the Sofia lease was the abandoned Julia mine. Should CMASA contemplate developing a 100 tonnes/day operation of Sofia it would seem prudent to take over the Julia property as well, whence additional reserves might support, say, a 200 tonnes/day output. Carlos and I agreed that the likely rom grade would be about 10g/t Au after discounting for grade bias.

There was no metallurgical data whatsoever, but visual examination (by hand lens) of fresh ore samples from underground showed very little sulphides (<2 %) and the ore appeared easy milling with predominately "free" gold, suitable for cyanidation treatment. Both State power and water supplies were available near by. A check sampling/assaying programme plus preliminary metallurgical testwork should be undertaken before taking an option on the property. If these were satisfactory then a rapid evaluation on a 150 tonnes/day project to determine financial viability should be carried out before committing to buy out Cormine.

The Erika mine was six miles north of Andacollo near the village of Huinganco. There were extensive surface "scratchings" over a distance of 400 m. The steep dipping vein, outcroped along the side of a valley and appeared to occupy a very sheared zone. Underground the presence of graphitic gouge on the hangingwall contact was noted. Unsurprisingly that had lead to difficult mining conditions. In fact where a shrinkage stope (quite the wrong mining method) had been attempted, that had produced disastrous hangingwall sloughing. Cut-and-fill was the correct mining method and Cormine were currently developing a trial stope. However below the lowest level they were sinking an open winze with no support whatsoever. I rather foolishly allowed myself to be lowered down this 40m winze to look at the lowest ore exposure and was extremely glad to reach the winze bank (top) without any slabs peeling off the sidewalls. Health and Safety definitely would not have been amused! Between us, Carlos and I persuaded the Erika Mine manager to install supporting stulls throughout the winze.

Ore expectancy at Erika was less than Sofia and the rom grade likely to be much lower on account of 100% waste dilution due to poor ground conditions exacerbated by ground-water in the vein structure. We felt that an output of fifty tonnes/day with an rom grade of 7 to 8g/t Au was a realistic estimate of Erika's potential. As at Sofia underground check sampling & assaying should be undertaken before any further discussions between CMASA and Cormine took place. In a word, Erika looked a "bummer". We headed back to Andacollo, collected our gear and prepared for the long ride back to Neuquen. We settled in to a pleasant mid-range hotel followed by dinner with the inevitable huge Argentinian steaks (delicious) washed down with a couple of bottles of excellent Malbec wine from the Mendoza region. Carlos reckoned I definitely needed the wine as he said "you were a real pale-face when you came up the Erika winze". He, being a geologist and knowing the Argentinians, had more sense than to go down that dangerous hole!

Our plane back to Buenos Aires was not until midday so I asked Carlos if he thought the Cormine driver could take us out to have a look at the Patagonian pampas. He said yes and we headed south-east out of Neuquen first through orchards and then on to the plains. There were plenty of cattle to see and much to my surprise there were more Herefords (now I knew why the steaks were so good) than you see in Herefordshire. After that the other major breed was the hump-backed Brahmin. On our two to three hour drive these were the only two breeds we saw. Disappointingly the gauchos were in 4 x 4s or utes although we did see some horses alongside one hacienda we passed.

We were back in Buenos Aires by early afternoon and went straight to the CMASA offices. Here we had a brief session with Miguel about the two Cormine gold properties. He asked Carlos to set out a sampling scheme for CMASA's exploration crews to carry out at both Sofia and Erika. He would get that cleared with the Cormine owners. Carlos and I completed our respective reports on the gold properties and checked through the draft write-ups on the Aguilar mine, which the office staff had typed up during our visit to Andacollo. I telephoned Jaime in La Paz and told him that we (Carlos and I) had discussed everything with Miguel and he was clear what had to be done asap at Aguilar. He asked me to come up to La Paz with Carlos to go through our Aguilar reports with Goni. That meant one more night in the "noisiest hotel" so that Carlos could go through the sampling programme with CMASA's Exploration Manager next morning before we both caught the afternoon AA flight to La Paz. The COMSUR driver dropped me at the Hotel Sucre before taking Carlos to his home in the lower altitude part of the city.

The meeting with Goni went well. He was greatly encouraged that we felt the Aguilar ore reserves could sustain an expansion from 2000 to 3000 tonnes/day and that the new trackless mine below 18 level could be mined by blast-hole open stoping which would reduce mining costs by US$ 4 to 5/tonne. His main worry was the sloppy Argentinian work ethic. He was somewhat riled that the Argentinians dismissively referred to the Bolivians as "the mountain men". Well we'll show them how to run a mine was his response. I could see some fairly radical changes coming to CMASA's management at Aguilar, Jujuy and Buenos Aires. Later that day I took a LAB flight to Rio via Santa Cruz and Sao Paulo. In Rio I transferred to an overnight Air France flight arriving at Charles de Gaulle airport, Paris around lunch time the following day. I then went to the departures board and booked on the next flight to Birmingham, followed by a quick telephone call to Gorsty asking Gillian to meet me at Brum Airport. It was now the 20th August and I had been away for nearly four weeks. The pick-up at Brum worked like clockwork and Gillian had Sproggs for company since it was still school holidays. The M42 was still like ones own private motorway and in an hour and a quarter we were back at Gorsty. Birmingham airport condemned the "Heathrow experience" to the rubbish bin as far as I was concerned.

36

It was good to be back from the thin, dry, air of the high Andes and get ones breath back with some good old rain soaked Herefordshire air. Gillian was busy getting Sproggs clothes organised for the move to St Richards as a boarder. Apart from anything else this involved sewing name tabs on to everything. At least it confirmed to Sproggs that he was now a fully paid up (?) member of our family. Early in September we drove him and all his clobber over to the school at Bredenbury. One of the masters took us to his dorm where we helped stow his things, then after a very quick goodbye it was apparent that we were both surplus to requirements, at least as far as Sproggs was concerned. That evening Gorsty seemed very quiet and both Luke and Anjon wandered round the house looking for him.

The old Apple Mac computer needed an upgrade so Gillian and I had an outing to Kidderminster after I'd left the Mac with Celtip Computers. We went down to Stouport to see if there were any narrow boat berths available, but no such luck. Back at Gorsty I was busy doing the rough grass cut with the Allen Scythe as well as the final year cut on all the hedges. Oh yes, Sproggs bedroom needed an overhaul - patching, filling and painting. Just as I was beginning to feel like a break from garden and home maintenance the phone rang. It was Peter from Davy McKee. Could I help them with a beach sand mining job in Mozambique? I said yes, but for no more than two weeks, as I was scheduled to be back in Bolivia in early November. Peter laughed and said relax, the job would require no more than three days in Dublin. The job involved a review of the Irish company Kenmare Resources project, which was sited in Mozambique. Kenmare had appointed Davy McKee to carry out a preliminary feasibility study and in turn Davy wanted me to look at the ore reserve data and sand mining methods. So job No. 061 was on the blocks.

I took an Aer Lingus flight to Dublin on the 12th October. Davy had booked me in to the Gresham Hotel in the city centre. It was very comfortable. Unsurprisingly I found the four strong Davy team in the bar. After the usual shooting the breeze of what we had all been doing, Peter gave a quick run-down on Kenmare's heavy minerals project at Moma in northern Mozambique. For me it sounded very like a rerun of TAZI's operations on Stradbroke Island in Queensland, where I'd worked in the early 1960s.

Peter agreed and said that was the reason I was here! No secrets then, Big Brother knows. In fact the international mining scene was small, dominated by no more than a dozen large companies and a similar number of engineer-contractors. Everybody made it their business to know everybody else's.

We spent the next three days in Kenmare's downtown offices. I worked through their Banka Drill mineral sand reserves which identified ilmenite, rutile and zircon values. They were well done with grade-distribution data and the requisite tonnage-grade curves. All I could really play around with was looking at differing pond elevations and sustainable throughput rates. As at TAZI the obvious way to mine the sands would be by suction dredging to a floating gravity plant. Thereafter the gravity concentrate would be pumped ashore to a concentrator. Davy were specifying and costing all the materials handling plant including the dredge(s) so my input was restricted to confirming the total sand tonnage reserve, average heavy metal grades and feasible daily sand throughput. That was it, end of story on my side. On the afternoon of our third working day I flew back to Brum. The Davy guys stayed on in Dublin for the rest of the week.

I had a couple of weeks respite at Gorsty to finish decorating Sproggs bedroom and building up a decent stock of split logs for the woodburner and Franklin stove. A phone call from Jaime at COMSUR put paid to any further home improvements. Thus on Guy Fawkes Day Gillian drove me to Birmingham airport. Here I boarded an NLM City Hopper F27 Fokker for the short flight to Amsterdam's Schiphol airport, where I transferred to a DC8 KLM flight for Caracas, Venezuela. I had a three hour wait here for a connecting Avianca flight to Lima, Peru. That Venezuelan airline did not fill me with confidence after a hairy take-off at Caracas where the pilot immediately banked the plane at low altitude across the harbour and followed this up with a "controlled crash" on landing at Lima's Jorge Chavez airport. After that good old LAB to La Paz's El Alto airport seemed like a dream. I took a taxi down to the Hotel Sucre, which was fast becoming my second home! I went in to the COMSUR offices in the afternoon where I joined Jim, Carlos and Mario for a meeting with Jaime. It was going to be a busy few days. He wanted us to assess the production potential of three separate mines, Porco, Cerro Grande and Quioma. Porco and Quioma I knew having visited them a few years ago, but I knew nothing about the Cerro Grande tin mine.

The COMSUR Range Rover picked me up at the Hotel Sucre at 7.30 with Jim, Carlos and Mario already on board. I was really pleased to learn that we were flying down to Potosi in the company's Aero Commander rather than making the six hour road journey. A twin cab ute picked us up at the airport for the sixty mile twisty and dusty ride SW to the Porco mine.

The Industrial reserves were quoted as 1.19 million tonnes at 15.8% Zn, 1.66% Pb and 2.27g/t Ag. However that tonnage was spread over a large number of veins (+20) and only two, SAP & SR2 had ore expectancies greater than 1,000 t/vm. Nearly 40% of the reserves lay below the lowest adit level and could only be developed through internal hoisting facilities. Veins were steep dipping with competent dacite tuff wall rocks enabling shrinkage stoping to be practiced. A sustainable mining rate of 900 tonnes/day could be achieved. The mine had now standardized on a 45m level interval and the development yield was 60 tonnes/m. Since visiting the mine five years ago I noted that the average shrink stope output had increased from 14 to 22 tonnes/day, a huge improvement. Production would comprise 35% from breaking stopes; 15% from development and 50% from shrinks. That mix ensured that the underground broken ore reserve remained constant. Stope drilling yields should be increased to 1.5t/m and blasting yields to 2.5 t/Kg.

Underground lateral haulage was planned to be concentrated on the San Cayetano level. GE and Goodman four tonne trolley locos could each handle 12 no. 2 tonne Granby cars. With a round trip time of 35 minutes the output per rake would be about 170 tonnes/shift or over 500 tonnes/day on a three shift basis. Hence two haulage rakes would be needed to meet the 900 tonnes/day production rate.

The main SAP vein had a strike length of 950 m. It would be reasonable to expect a dip extent of 50% strike extent, say 500 m. The San Cayetano level was 250m below surface thus the SAP vein could be expected to extend 250m below that level. With an allowance for an ore pocket below and hoist dump above a total vertical hoisting distance of 300m was indicated. The 150hp double-drum winder from the Milluni mine would be able to hoist 500 tonnes/day in 2 tonne capacity skips over two shifts/day.

Examination of the mine's compressed air consumption indicated that an additional 600 CFM (sea-level rated) compressor was required. Because of the 4000m elevation of the Porco mine it was necessary to increase the air supply by 48% to compressed air driven plant for a similar mass air flow and compatible efficiency. Good engineering practice suggested that the estimated base load demand of 2550 CFM should be about two thirds of installed capacity of 3825 CFM. Incidentally that installed capacity checked well with the rule-of-thumb requirement of 4 CFM per daily tonne mined.

All four of us agreed that Porco looked a very good mine with the potential to become a 900 to 1,000 tonnes/day operation. With a relatively modest injection of capital plus the transfer of some redundant plant from Milluni (trolley locos and double-drum winder), Porco could become one of Bolivia's main producers of zinc. Definitely a plus for COMSUR's mining portfolio. Then, after three days at the mine, we set off for the dusty drive back to Potosi airport, where the Aero Commander was waiting to fly all four of us down to Cochabamba. The 150 mile flight only took fifty minutes.

Cochabamba airport was a real eye opener. I had never seen so many DC3 (Dakota) aircraft in one place since I had visited Lei in Papua New Guinea in 1969. It was amazing. The rest of the guys thought it was unremarkable, since everyone knew (except me) that they were all kept busy flying raw coca leaves up to Colombia. The DC3 was ideal for this job. It was a rugged, easily maintained piston engined plane with a short take-off and landing ability entirely suitable for the remote, dirt jungle strips in Colombia. Surely an unstoppable industry with the huge demand for drugs in North America and Europe. A DC3 pilot or engineer-mechanic would have a job for life provided he avoided the American DEA guys when up in Colombia. Most of the planes were 45 years old but with plenty of TLC on hand looked good for another 45 years. A couple of 4 x 4s were waiting to drive us forty or so miles north to the Cerro Grande mine in Arque province.

The mine's Industrial reserves were quoted as 469,000 tonnes grading 1.39% Sn. The mineralisation comprised a mass of small veins exhibiting typical pinch-and-swell characteristics. Strike lengths were short with poor payability and poor to very poor ground conditions. Although the five veins had a combined ore expectancy of 2560 t/vm the dips were flat, 30 to 50 degrees and all development was off-vein on account of difficult ground conditions. There a sustainable cut-and-fill mining rate was unlikely to exceed 5% of the ore expectancy. Total production potential of the Cerro Grande mine was estimated to be 200 tonnes/day only. In fact the plastic ground and plentiful ground-water in the southern shear zone had led to difficulties with both drilling and blasting. Both Mario and I believed that waste dilution in that type of weak ground would be plus 50%, leading to a low rom grade.

Operations at present were all above the adit haulage level, which was close to the valley bottom. The ore potential at depth could not realistically be probed by diamond drilling on account of the sheared, weak ground whence core recovery would be very low. The only option was to continue with the internal winze and develop a new level, 40m below the haulage level, and develop the vein structures on a "suck it and see basis". So far so negative. The good news was adequate power supply from the State and sufficient compressed air capacity.

We spent two days at the mine and all agreed that it was not an operation of interest to COMSUR. In short, small tonnage mine - maximum 200 tonnes/day; difficult ground conditions; high waste dilution leading to low rom grade; no obvious potential to expand output. With that we drove back to Cochabamba and the friendly town-centre hotel. The bar was well used as one could imagine with two thirsty geologists and two thirsty miners. At a rather fuzzy breakfast next morning Jim took off for the airport to fly back to La Paz whilst Carlos, Mario and I headed for the station. Here we caught the narrow gauge diesel rail car that headed generally eastwards down the Rio Misque valley. We arrived at the Quioma mine sidings after the 3 hour train trip. Here a twin cab ute was waiting to take us out of the valley, over the ridge and down into an adjacent valley where the Quioma mine was sited.

The Industrial reserves were 567,000 tonnes at 12.7% Zn, 10.5% Pb and 1.5g/t Ag. The production potential of Quioma was estimated to be 350 tonnes/day. Development and stoping practice had declined sharply since my last visit fourteen months ago. Stopes should have been developed off sub-levels driven 5m above main level rail, rather than straight off the level by "taking down backs" which inevitably required the placement of level drive timber. Ridiculous - Quioma management should be given a large kick up the backside for that appalling mining practice, which was compounded by the absence of ventilation stope raises driven through to the upper level. Mario, as COMSUR's Mining Manager, read the riot act to the Underground Manager and Mine Manager. The language was, unsurprisingly, beyond my primitive Spanish comprehension! Obviously I supported Mario on the technical side of what needed to be done. As we had done at the Milluni mine with Mario we proposed to convert Quioma's back-stoping to breast-stoping in both the shrinkage and cut-and-fill stopes.

Lateral haulage on the -1867 level was adequate with 3.5t battery locos hauling rakes of 10 x 2t Granby cars. The Candelaria Main Shaft required re-equipping with a double-drum winder pulling twin 2t skips. An additional 650 CFM compressor was required to maintain 350 tonnes/day output. With that, much to the relief of the local management, we set off back to Cochabamba by first twin cab ute and then narrow gauge railway. In Cochabamba Carlos phoned Jaime and was told we should all come back to La Paz for urgent discussions about the three mines. He would arrange for a suitable vehicle to pick us up at mid-morning the next day for the drive back to La Paz. The three of us thus had one final night in our "favourite bar" in Cochabamba putting the world right and giving the Quioma management a good verbal kicking.

We eventually arrived back at COMSUR's offices in La Paz at 2pm after the long dusty drive up from Cochabamba. Jaime said there would be a meeting with Goni between 5 and 6pm and we had better get our ducks in a row. Since my Spanish was poor the meeting took place in English. Goni, Jim and Jaime were all fluent in English. Goni looked directly at me and said "well, what have we got"? I replied Porco good. About 1000 tonnes/day Zn mine. Quioma reasonable 350 tonnes/day Zn mine. Cerro Grande poor, low grade Sn mine. Goni then asked Jim & Carlos to quickly go through the respective ore reserves. Putting the reserve tonnages and my throughput figures rapidly together Goni said "so we have four to five years known reserves at each of the zinc mines - what's the reserve potential"? Carlos said that we could confidently double the known reserves. That was it! OK we'll go for Porco and Quioma and not pursue Cerro Grande. Goni seemed happy about that since he was now very interested in the zinc market having just acquired the Aguilar mine in Argentina. Goni wanted an update on Aguilar but Jaime interrupted and said that Carlos and I would be going down to Aguilar in four days time (news to me!) and would be back in La Paz in early December to provide an update.

So whilst Jim went back to exploration matters, Mario went back to the Milluni mine, Carlos and I settled down to prepare geological and mining reports for the three mines over the next four days. I asked Fanny to send a fax to Gillian saying I was now going down to Aguilar and expected to be back in La Paz again during the first week of December. Jaime confirmed that Peter, the geotechnical consultant, had agreed to visit the Aguilar mine around the 20th November. Fanny and the other girls did a fantastic job in typing up Carlos and my reports in double quick time so that on the 19th November Carlos and I caught the morning AA flight to Jujuy. The CMASA ute picked us up at the airport so that by mid-afternoon we were ensconced in an Aguilar mine staff house.

The next morning Carlos and I went to the mine engineering office to hear an update on geological matters from Pablo. The reserves had been recalculated using a 6.2% combined metals cut-off grade and were now 5.55 million tonnes at 6.7% Zn, 4.7% Pb & 113g/t Ag. There was an additional 3.72 million tonnes of Possible reserves at similar grades. Use of the new cut-off grade had increased the tonnage by 17.3% and the contained metal by 10.4%. Using the latest cost data had yielded a break even grade of 8.5% combined metals compared to a new average reserve grade of 11.4% combined metals, which gave an average value of US$ 4.53 per 1% metal grade. That gave a gross operating margin of US$ 13.1 per tonne milled.

Pablo and his geological team had been very busy and produced tonnage grade curves for the total reserves ranging from cut-off grades of 6.2% combined metals to 11.2% combined metals. That had demonstrated that the selected cut-off grade of 6.2% combined metals was close to the optimum since, under the prevailing economics, the value of the in situ reserves reached a peak of US$ 285 million with a cut-off grade between 6 and 7% combined metals. They had also plotted grade-distributions for different reserve categories. That indicated that Probable reserves were overvalued by 6% and Possible by 11%. Without doubt that grade-distribution bias was a major component of the MCF.

A detailed tonnage/grade/metal content production schedule by stope and development heading was still urgently required. We noted that one particular stope was scheduled to produce only 32 t/day throughout the year and yet the stope face area was 60m^2. The ground conditions were good and that face area should be able to produce over 200 tonnes/day. To put things in perspective that one stope had a greater working face area than the total stope face area of the whole of the Quioma mine! Without doubt the Aguilar mine planning and production guys needed a really good shake up. The mine's fundamental objective must be to concentrate mining activity in high productivity stopes. Aguilar was a scattered mining operation with 53% of its production coming from slow, costly square-set stoping. At present 66 stopes delivered less than 14 tonnes/stope/shift, a very low output. Ground conditions were good above 18 level and most could be worked by cemented cut-and-fill, whilst below 18 level blast-hole open stoping should be instituted. Square-set mining in virgin ground should quickly be consigned to the dustbin.

Output from above 18 level should easily be sustained at 2,000 to 2,400 tonnes/day for at least three years whilst the new trackless mine utilising sub-level, blast-hole open stoping below 18 level was prepared for production. The multi-level adit access above 18 level provided great flexibility for planning and scheduling stope production. Peter, the geotechnical consultant, had indicated where extensometers should be placed in the top overcut of the trial stope on 18 level. As a matter of urgency the mine now needed to obtain a supply of 19mm diameter threaded rebar with head nut and plate as well as several Spedel type 5000 pneumatic grout pumps and matching B2100 mixer. The slot raise, stope down-holes and trough fan drilling must use the mine's Atlas Copco BBC 120F drifter rig. That would manage the 20m lift of the trial stope. If the trial stope confirmed that a 40m lift could be mined then the Tamrock SOLO rig would definitely be required.

At the weekend the geologists, Pablo and Carlos challenged "los gringos", Peter and me to a game of tennis. Well - il disastre!. Firstly at the high altitude, 4500 m, the tennis ball bounced high, like a thing possessed and secondly and definitely more important, los gringos had absolutely no puff for running around a tennis court. After just two or three games both Peter and I were on our knees. Discretion etc we conceded the game, set and match and repaired to the Mine Club for several life saving beers. In this endeavour I'm pleased to report the gringos more than held their own.

The last two days of our twelve day visit were spent in discussions with the Underground Manager and the new Mine Planning section. First we went over the detailed programme for the trial stope. Then the requirements for stope scheduling above 18 level and finally several engineering studies that needed to be carried out - fill distribution system; 18 level trolley haulage; replacement of small primary jaw crushers; testwork and design of backfill mixtures; ventilation survey of south end of mine and compressed air reticulation.

It was then arranged for Carlos and me to accompany the Mine Manager and Underground Manager to Buenos Aires for a debriefing with Miguel, the GM. We travelled in two utes down to Jujuy and after a couple of hours at the CMASA office collecting the latest cost data caught the afternoon flight to Salta and onwards to Buenos Aires Aero Parque. Carlos and I, yet again, ended up in the world's noisiest hotel, but even so sleep came easily at the lower altitude.

At the meeting with Miguel it seemed that we were not the flavour of the month. Apparently, before COMSUR came on the scene, the Aguilar Mine Manager had convinced Miguel that the way to mine below 18 level was by "ramp-in-stope" cut-and-fill. He was not at all happy about my selected method of sub-level open stoping. His objection was that Aguilar had "bad, weak ground" and was not suitable for large open stopes. I explained that the ground was, in fact, quite competent, and that the so called bad ground was the result of poor planning and incorrect stope pillar design. I said we should wait for the outcome of Peter's trial stope between 18 and 20 level when we would have factual geotechnical data available. Unconvinced, Miguel asked me to prepare a financial comparison of mining the 18 - 20 block of ground by ramp-in-stope cut-and-fill on one hand and sub-level transverse open stoping on the other. I agreed to do that. However it was very apparent that the GM, Miguel, was not putting pressure on the mine management to make the changes we (COMSUR) required.

After two days of scratchy discussions at the CMASA's offices Carlos and I were really happy to catch the AA flight back to La Paz, where the old Hotel Sucre looked a lot more welcoming than Buenos Aires "noisiest"! Over the next four days I worked up my mining report, whilst Carlos did likewise with his geological report. We had a wrap-up meeting with Jaime and Goni, who both seemed happy on the technical front, but distinctly unhappy on the Aguilar management front. Basically CMASA management had not accepted that they were now owned by COMSUR and were required to follow their instructions. It was agreed that COMSUR's management would visit both the mine and the Buenos Aires offices every month to "keep the pressure on". That more or less completed jobs No. 062 and 063 and I set off back to Blighty with LAB to Lima, then KLM to Amsterdam and finally NLM to Birmingham. Gillian picked me up for the M42/M6 drive to Droitwich and the back roads to Tenbury Wells and Gorsty. I was more than happy to reassure Gillian that I wasn't going anywhere (abroad) before the new year.

37

Now that Sproggs was boarding at St Richards, Gillian had begun working as a volunteer nurse at St Michael's Hospice, just outside Hereford. She found the work very rewarding and was happy to make use of her nursing skills. Obviously she used the car for the twenty mile run to and from the Hospice, but I still had the old Honda 400/4 motor bike for getting me around. After a couple of days relaxing and dog walking I got stuck in to working up the cost comparisons between ramp-in-stope and sub-level open stoping of the 18 to 20 level block as requested by Miguel, the CMASA GM. I had mentioned it to Jaime and he said "OK, do it, just to convince the old b....". To be fair Miguel had been greatly influenced by St Joe Lead, the previous owners of Aguilar, who seemed convinced of bad ground and thus used square-set mining. For them open stoping would have been a non-starter. I completed that work in a week or so and sent copies to CMASA and COMSUR by my friendly couriers, DHL. They provided an excellent service, picking up at Gorsty and guaranteeing delivery to South America inside 48 hours.

We had a good family Christmas and New Year, untroubled by work demands, but it was not to last. My best client, COMSUR, in the shape of Jaime, called a few days into the new year. Could I accompany Jim, their exploration geologist, on a visit to northern Peru to appraise the Quiruvilca multi-metal mine of Corporacion Minera Nor Peru SA (CMNP)? CMNP was a subsidiary of the American copper outfit ASARCO, who had put the mine up for sale and as I now realised COMSUR was in an expansion mode. Of course I said yes and job No. 064 was on a roll. Jaime asked me to come to La Paz first for a briefing before Jim and I headed for Peru. My neighbour, Clive, drove me to Birmingham airport as Gillian was working at the Hospice. Sproggs had gone back to St Richards for the spring term. As before, avoiding Heathrow, I flew with NLM to Schiphol Amsterdam, then KLM to Lima and finally LAB to La Paz. I seemed to have almost permanently set up shop in the Hotel Sucre over the last nine months. In fact, the hotel staff's English was improving faster than my Spanish - so no surprises there then!

Jim, a big Canadian exploration geologist, had lived and worked in South America for years. Most Saturday mornings you would find him seated outside the Copacabana Hotel on the La Paz main drag nursing a large beer. A shrinking violet he was not. After Jaime's briefing on the Quirulvilca mine Jim suggested we fly down to Lima for the weekend to be ready to front-up to CMNP's offices first thing Monday morning. Seemed a good idea to me so we duly caught the Saturday afternoon LAB flight to Lima. Jim knew Lima well and we booked in to his "tame" hotel out in Miraflores. After his regular two beers at the Copacabana in the morning he said he felt like a pisco sour or two so we took a taxi into the central Plaza San Martin and repaired to the Colonial Bar of the main Hotel. Their pisco sours were famous and Jim, of course, opted for a "Catedral". In fact, that was understandable, it was a triple! After two of these we decided food was essential and Jim suggested we go down to the Ouro Verde beach where there was a good fish restaurant. He was right, the food was great, but somehow he also convinced me that the pisco sours were OK as well. That was me done and I couldn't blame siroche troubles at sea level, although the next day he told me we ended up in some low club in San Isidro. My recall of that next morning was zilch. The pair of us made a sorry sight at a late breakfast next morning.

However we duly fronted up to the CMNP offices on Monday morning, the 16th January. Here we met the company's senior management. All conversation took place in Spanish so, of course, Jim was the one who had to be bright eyed and bushy tailed. It was a very general briefing on where and what the Quirulvilca mine was all about. They quoted Industrial reserves of 2.40 million tonnes at 5.0% Zn, 1.76%Pb, 0.64% Cu, plus 0.2 oz Au and 8.4 oz Ag, a genuine multi-metal deposit. It was, apparently, a multi-vein deposit (over 100 identified veins!) worked generally by cut-and-fill. Present production was 1500 tonnes/day. The Storey concentrator was upgraded eight years ago and produced separate zinc, lead and copper concentrates. Power was supplied from the Peruvian national grid at Trujillo via a 138 kV line owned by CMNP. That line was currently de-energised following the destruction of a pylon by the Sendero Luminoso (Shining Path) terrorist group. The company's own standby diesel plant was now supplying power to the operation. That was it in a nutshell. They suggested we catch the afternoon Fawcett flight to Trujillo, stay there overnight and travel up to the mine next morning.

We said we felt four days "due diligence" at the mine would be sufficient and agreed to meet at CMNP's offices in Lima next Saturday. We headed out to Jorge Chavez airport and boarded an ancient, dark yellow painted Vickers Viscount for the 330 mile flight NW to Trujillo. A company driver met us and took us to a small motel close to the beach. He said he would pick us up at 7.30 in the morning. We decided to only have a couple of beers that evening as the mine was over 4000m altitude and I, for one, did not want another siroche.

Good as his word we left the beach motel at 7.30 and headed east, whence the road began to climb steadily. It was fascinating to see the different climatic regions we passed through as we gained altitude. Trujillo itself was tropical, being only 8 degrees south of the Equator. By Simbal we were nearly through the temperate zone and at Otuzec, only sixty miles from Trujillo we were entering the alpine zone at 3000 m. At Samne, twenty miles further on the 138 kV line was stepped down to 33 kV through a 12MVA transformer. As noted earlier that line was currently out of action. Close by at Plaza Pampa the company's own 6MVA diesel power plant comprised a ten year old 1100 kVA Ruston, four twenty year old 870 kVA Nordbergs and three other fifty year old Norbergs each of 480 kVA output. At the time of our visit (17th January) the plant was on full load. Bus voltage of 2300 was stepped up to 33 kV for onward transmission to the mine. Power factor was 0.85 lagging. Although the plant was old it appeared very well maintained with excellent housekeeping. Armed security guards were in evidence, unsurprising after the recent (two weeks ago) attack by the Sendero Luminoso on the mine's main power line at Trujillo.

Journey time from Trujillo to Samne was about two hours over mainly sealed roads. That was the terminal of a bi-cable Riblet ropeway of thirty miles length from the mine's Storey concentrator. Here the concentrate was transferred to truck for haulage to Trujillo. Beyond Samne the dirt road was poorly maintained and the tortuous sixty mile road distance to Quirulvilca took over three hours. It was now the middle of the western cordillera rainy season and, boy did that last section of the "road" need the attention of a grader!

As we had been told in Lima the mine was a typical, steep dipping narrow multi-vein deposit (104 in all). Strike lengths were up 1000 m, but depth extent of individual veins seldom exceeded 350 m. Vein widths were only 0.3 to 0.4m with occasional swells to 2.5m. On account of the high strike/width ratio all development was track bound and carried out on-vein. With an overall mine payability of 40% the development yield was only 45 tonnes/m. With a mining rate of 1500 tonnes/day that would require a development advance of 33m/day to merely replenish reserves. However during 1988 the mine only achieved a development advance of 14m/day. That raised a large warning flag for me - the mine was becoming squeezed. With Jim and their Chief Geologist we examined the ore reserve vertical sections in detail. It was immediately apparent that most vein's ore expectancy was steadily declining with depth. That would require increased development to maintain present output, implying a yearly advance of 9 to 10 Km, a heck of a lot of tunneling.

Production was obtained from 76, yes 76 active stopes, indicating an output of less than 20 tonnes stope/day or only 10 tonnes stope/shift. They were cut-and-fill stopes using jacklegs (Ingersoll Rand & Atlas Copco machines) and Canadian IR two-drum electric or pneumatic scrapers. Approximately half the stopes used rough waste rock fill and the other half de-slimed mill tailings. There was a lot of sticky gouge plus water on the pyroclastic wall contacts leading to difficult broken ore handling (ie blocked passes and chutes, mud-runs etc). A Peruvian contractor was sinking a new 3-compartment shaft below the bottom level. That was planned to be sunk 160m to provide access to two new levels. Mine services such as trackwork, electric cabling and compressed air lines were well maintained. The surface compressor plant comprised Centric and Joy units with adequate capacity. Underground haulage on the numerous adits used 3.5 & 5t class AGEVE & Titan trolley locos with Greensburg 12t diesel units on the main, Alimirvilca level.

The Storey concentrator was located about one mile west of the Alimirvilca tunnel portal on the opposite (south) side of the valley. The plant was conventional. First producing a bulk Cu-Pb concentrate followed by Pb and Cu separation and a Zn concentrate. Concentrate grades were 39% Cu, 78% Pb and 85% Zn with recoveries in the 85% to 90% range. As noted before the concentrator had been upgraded in 1980 and was now capable of easily handling all that the mine could deliver.

Overall direct operating costs, mine, mill and services was US$ 46.3/tonne milled. In summary the mine's ore expectancy was falling with increasing depth and mine development was steadily falling behind. Although the concentrator was good and modern the operation would appear to be running at a loss or breakeven at best. Quirulvilca was an old mine entering its declining years with no upside potential. Jim and I agreed, definitely not a mine for COMSUR to purchase. At Friday midday we drove back down to Trujillo arriving in time to catch the evening Fawcett flight to Lima. We took a taxi to Jim's Miraflores hotel and spent a "quiet" night in one of the local bars. Saturday morning we fronted up at the CMNP offices, where Jim gave a tactful resume of our findings to their senior management. He said COMSUR would contact them by the end of next week.

We flew back to La Paz that afternoon as Jaime had called saying that Goni wanted a meeting tomorrow to discuss Quirulvilca. As usual it was a straightforward meeting. Goni was always aware that mines and mining projects were all about the basic resource - the ore reserves. Once Jim had outlined the decrease in ore expectancy with depth and no evidence of strike extensions or parallel structures that was it, no potential. I hardly said anything except to confirm Jim's comments and add that the most useful assets were a modern flotation concentrator, good compressor plant and useful 6MVA power plant all of which might be picked up on the cheap if no else was interested in buying CMNP from ASARCO. Jaime asked Jim and me to complete our respective reports in the next three days so that they were available for him to take down to Lima for discussions with CMNP next Friday.

As usual, Fanny et al, were marvellous at typing up my report and we had it finished by Wednesday evening. Jaime then asked me to review the December operating report from the Aguilar mine. Like me he was particularly interested to see if the mine had started to follow some of our recommendations. Not a lot seemed to have changed but at least the Accounts Department had started to allocate specific costs to individual stopes - progress indeed. I finally left La Paz on the 28th January following my (now) usual route LAB to Lima, then KLM to Amsterdam and finally NLM to Birmingham. I had sent a fax to Gillian telling her of my ETA at Brum and she asked our neighbour, Clive, to collect me.

I found things unusually quiet at Gorsty, apart from the enthusiasm of the dogs, which did not abate until they had had a decent walk. With Sproggs boarding at St Richards and Gillian working at St Michael's Hospice I had the place to myself. However boredom was not on the menu with logs to chop and the interminable demands of an old farmhouse for oodles of

TLC - mainly patching and water-proofing windows as well as internal wall repairs and painting. One weekend we went up to Norbury Junction to see how Toadflax was surviving the winter only to find that the boat had been gutted by burglars. They had even taken Gillian's hand-stitched lace curtains. They (the burglars) must obviously have been boaters, since only non-boat stuff (ie books) was left behind. We were somewhat miffed as we had only just completed our DIY rehab of the cabin. Well that decided it, the Norbury moorings were not secure. I found alternative moorings up at Whixall Marina on the Llangollen canal and planned to move there when the canal reopened after the winter lock maintenance closures at Audlem and Grindley Brook.

It got me thinking and after a little research on the Petter PH2W engine's power, I decided to ask Teddesley Boats at Penkridge to lengthen Toadflax by 8ft from 38 to 46ft. We decided to put an 8ft mild steel extension in the centre of the boat plus new steel forward bulkhead and a transverse sewage holding tank. The cabin to be lined with t & g boarding plus installation of a new gas cooker, electric fridge and pump-out loo. The cost estimate for that work would be similar to the original purchase price! To be fair the boss of Teddesley Boats said we would be lucky to get our money back on the refit if we wanted to sell the boat a few years later, but if that's what we wanted, why not? I arranged to bring Toadflax up to their yard in late April after the winter canal closure.

Towards the end of February Jaime from COMSUR called, requesting me to visit Aguilar yet again to undertake a review of operations. 'I flew from Brum to Amsterdam and on to Buenos Aires and finally Jujuy, where I stayed over night. A mine ute picked picked me next morning for the drive to Aguilar. Again no siroche so perhaps I was finally becoming accustomed to the high altitude. First I caught up with Pablo. The overall ore reserve position was the same. They had done some controlled sampling tests on a development heading. That showed good correlation between chip sampling of the drive walls and grab sampling from each blasted round, but very poor correlation with DD core samples taken from a predrilled hole along the drive access. That confirmed the lower level of confidence ascribed to the Possible ore classification whose data was mainly obtained from DD core. The controlled test showed that the DD assay values were 12 to 20% higher than bulk grab and chip sample assay values. The mine was now cutting DD sample values by 15% for use in ore reserve calculations.

The 1989 production schedule was still not "stope-specific" in that individual stope's output and grade were not combined to give a steady mill feed tonnage and grade. A proper tonnage/grade stope schedule was still urgently required. The Accounts Department had done their bit by allocating specific mining costs to each mining method and were now refining it to individual stopes. Hooray, progress was being made. The vertical distribution of reserves had now been re-compiled by level, which made the task of attempting to concentrate mining activity possible. As noted before the Aguilar ore expectancy was circa 30,000 t/vm. Current stope productivity was woefully low - cemented cut-and-fill stopes 10.1 TMS and square-set 5.4 TMS. The number of active stopes was 67 and the average output per stope-day was only 30 tonnes. However I noticed that one stope had broken the 2,000 tonnes/month barrier. However that had been achieved with a three man crew and a three shifts/day operation. Analysis of the January report showed an average output of 28.9 tonnes/stope-day only. That was very worrying as productivity had declined from my November visit.

I analysed those January stope results in detail and they showed many disturbing features. Why weren't the more productive stopes worked three shifts/day? Some only averaged 1.6 shifts/day over the month - why? The average stope drilling yield was a mere 1.04 tonnes/m drilled, again why so low? The problem appeared to be the use of "home-made" ANFO cartridges (poor hole contact) with inverted primers leading to numerous cut-offs and misfires. In that type of ground a drilling yield of 1.5 tonnes/m should be achieved with a burden/spacing pattern of 0.60m by 0.70 m, that was $0.42m^2$ /hole. Those outputs would require bulk-blown prilled ANFO not the ANFO cartridges and a straight (ie not inverted) primer of half a stick of 60 - 80% gelignite initiated by a No 8 detonator. I also noted that actual drilling output of the jackhammers (Ingersoll Rand JR300A, Atlas Copco 656-4W and Seco S250 machines) was also very low, yet again - why? A variety of reasons; low air pressure; poorly maintained jackhammers; incorrectly sharpened drill steel; absence of line oilers and poor miner's bonus system. Most of the Atlas machines had passed their useful life, many had drilled more than 70,000 m! The economics of pneumatic drilling machines (initial cost + spares cost versus machine performance) indicated a useful life of 20 to 25,000 m. The jackhammer was a precision "instrument" and yet it was one of the most abused machines in mining. The usual life of a rock drill in metal mining would be three years with a normal output of 7,500 m/year.

Aguilar's annual drilling requirement was about 700,000 m, requiring 100 operable jackhammers in the mine. Allowing for planned machine maintenance and repair would increase that to 110. The mine should immediately place an order for forty more Seco S250 jackhammers and budget for an annual replacement of twenty to thirty machines. I had banged on about the "drilling problem" since stope productivity was all about drilling holes. It was the key. If few holes were drilled little tonnage would be broken - QED.

Development of the trial open stoping method below 18 level was progressing well, apart from the BBC 120F drifter which became inoperable. A DD rig had to be used for long-hole drilling. Atlas Copco had so far been unable to supply the 120F spares required although this was brought to their attention months ago. The sooner the Tamrock SOLO rig was delivered, the better.

Although the surface compressor plant had sufficient capacity of 14388 CFM at sea level that reduced to 8761 CFM at Aguilar's altitude, only just adequate. A review of the underground distribution network showed a pressure loss of 38 psi due to inadequate pipe sizes. Thus the dynamic air pressure at a stope's jackhammer would only be 65 psi or 4.4 bar, much too low for efficient drilling (back to drilling again!). The Main shaft air line needed to be replaced with a 200mm line and all level pipes required increasing from 50mm to 100mm. Another project for the new Mine Planning section, which would need additional engineers to cope with ventilation, fill distribution and primary crusher studies, but hey, Rome wasn't built in a day. Finally, after a year of "rattling the cage" the Aguilar mine was beginning to take notice of the "Bolivian Mountain Men", which from an Argentinian perspective, included me. On the general admin side three shift working, six days/week had been introduced together with an incentive bonus scheme for miners and the concentrator now operated seven days/week. However the mine was still not connected to the Argentinian telephone system although talks had started.

After three busy weeks visiting and observing stoping operations all over the mine I departed for Jujuy with a stack of detailed information on the nitty gritty of mining at Aguilar. As usual I called in to the CMASA office in Jujuy to collect the latest cost data before catching the afternoon AA flight to Aero Parque. The following morning I had a long session with Miguel, the GM. I noticed a marked difference to my reception. It appeared that the COMSUR "heavies" had made their dissatisfaction known. With a large sigh of relief I took a taxi to Ezeiza International boarding the afternoon KLM flight to Montevideo, Rio and finally Schiphol, Amsterdam transferring to a NLM City Hopper for Birmingham. Here I picked up a hire car for the drive to Gorsty as Gillian was working at the Hospice and Clive was away, transporting horses rather than people.

Over the first week of April I was busy preparing my report on Aguilar. That included detailed long-hole drilling and blasting layouts for the slot raise of the new open stope on the 18 - 20 level as well as 60mm diameter production down-holes and the fan holes for the trough-undercut. I despatched the report to Jaime via DHL Couriers and that brought job No. 065 to an end.

The Department of Trade & Industry (DTI) had run an ad in the national press stating that they were looking for a "Mining Engineer" to assist them monitoring an underground UK metal mine that had recently received a large government loan. I suspected that would concern the Cornish tin mines of Wheal Jane and South Crofty. Of course I had registered my interest and sent off my "sales bumph". I was pleasantly surprised when I was asked to come up to London to make a presentation at the DTI offices. I travelled up to London by train on the 21st April, taking the tube to the DTI offices in Victoria. The interview process was obviously running late and whilst waiting for my "turn", who should appear but Ian and Bill from Mackay & Schnellmann. We glared at each other and then had a good laugh about all chasing the same job. Unsurprisingly there weren't many UK metal mining jobs around. We half expected to see Robertson Research, Golder Associates and Wardell Armstrong as well. In fact as I later found out all three of them had attended for interviews. My "turn" occupied no more than forty minutes. The DTI interviewers were particularly interested in my work with Bolivian narrow vein mines such as Milluni, Porco and Quioma. They said they would let me know by the end of the month and this they did saying I was successful (wah hey) and John of the DTI would be in contact for a visit to the Cornish mines around the middle of May. I was really chuffed as it would be great to have a UK based job for a change.

Gillian arranged for some time off from the Hospice and we decided early May would be a good time to move Toadflax to the Teddesley Boatyard. As the Shropshire Union canal was free of locks for several miles south-east of Norbury Junction we decided that Gillian could manage the boat on her own whilst I drove the car over to Penkridge, parked at the boatyard and cycled back on a small folding bike aiming to meet Gillian and Toadflax near Church Easton bridge. I asked her to go slowly, no more than 2.5 mph, as I was unsure how long it would take me to cycle on the small bike. As it worked out I just arrived at the bridge as Toadflax hove in to view; relief all round. With the bike on board we chugged on to Wolverhampton and then turned north on to the Staffs & Worcester canal. At Teddesley boatyard we removed the few personal bits, that the burglars had not wanted (!), and left Toadflax moored close by the yard's large crane.

A week or so later the yard boss phoned and said they'd lifted the Toad out and she (the boat) had got "hardly any bottom plate", what should he do? No choice really, no bottom plate, boat doesn't float! So, yes, please over-plate the entire bottom and yes I did understand that this would cost a bob or two. Toadflax had spent most of her earlier life on the Llangollen canal which was notoriously shallow and her seriously abraded bottom plate was probably a reflection of that. With some trepidation we left them to it.

Back at Gorsty there was a message from John of the DTI asking me to meet him at the St Michaels Hotel in Truro on the evening of the 14th for visits to Wheal Jane and South Crofty tin mines over the next three days. Gillian took some time off from the Hospice so she could come along on the trip to Cornwall. We drove south through Hereford and on down the beautiful Wye valley, past Chepstow and over the Severn Bridge to join the M5 south for Exeter and on to the A30. I dropped Gillian off at sister Pat's place in Mawgan Porth and continued on to Truro, where I found the St Michaels Hotel up Lemon Street and out on the Falmouth Road.

I had met John at the DTI interview in London. A long time civil servant, he was a convivial character. Over a beer he explained that the government had made Carnon Holdings (the holding company that operated both Wheal Jane and South Crofty mines) a multi-million £loan to keep the company afloat during the recent period of low international tin prices. The obvious question, why use government (ie tax payers) money to prop up an ailing commercial enterprise? The general public believed that that was a blatant attempt by a Conservative government to "buy" votes in the staunchly labour constituency of Falmouth-Camborne, where unemployment was high. Both the docks in Falmouth and the mining machinery companies, Holmans and Climax Rock Drill in Camborne, were operating on short-time.

Whatever the reason, and that loan certainly had the feel of the DeLorean car fiasco in Northern Ireland, I couldn't imagine Joe Public getting its money back. So looking on the bright side I realised that this job, No. 066, should at least return a smidgin of money back to a tax paying member of the public - me! The following morning I drove us over to the Wheal Jane (WJ) offices at Baldhu in the Bissoe valley, about six miles west of Truro. At our meeting with the Mine Manager we (John and I) were joined by Keith, the DTI's geologist who had driven down from his home in Devon. John went off to see the Chief Accountant to go through the books whilst Keith and I had a brief run through the geology and ore reserves before heading underground down Clemow's shaft.

Total reserves were 1.69 million tonnes at 0.97% Sn, 2.68% Zn and 0.5% Cu. Although generally well calculated both Keith and I felt that grades were likely to be overstated on account of the positive skew log-normal type grade-distribution associated with hydrothermal tin veins. The WJ geology guys should do more investigation into that likely over valuing grade bias. The main South Lode dipped N at 50 to 60 degrees within killas host rocks. Vein payability within the strike limits was remarkably high, plus 90%. The South Lode had an ore expectancy of 7,000 t/vm, which should support a daily mining rate of 10% or 700 tonnes/day. In fact Carnon had scheduled an annual output of 175,000 tonnes equivalent to 673 tonnes/day over 260 mining days/year, which appeared to be spot on.

However I had some reservations on the WJ schedule. They were following a retreat stoping sequence, which produced convergence on a central rib pillar of steadily diminishing dimensions. That naturally tended to stress the pillar as the adjacent stopes unsupported hangingwall spans increased. Those stopes had an hydraulic radius (area/perimeter) of 6 to 8, which was quite high for the killas country rock. Stoping sequence should be planned to converge onto the adjacent abutment for maximum ground stability. Notwithstanding that, the major mining problem at WJ was water and lots of it. The orebody itself, South Lode, appeared to be the main aquifer. During the winter months the mine pumped up to 19 million gallons/day, about 13,000 gals/min. Over a full year the average pumping rate was 80 tonnes of water for each tonne of ore hoisted and this water tonne to ore tonne ratio of 80 would make WJ one of the wettest mines in the world. The presence of up to 10% sulphides in the ore ensured that the mine water was very acidic, around 3.0 pH.

The main mining method was sub-level long-hole open stoping. On account of the flattish dip a 15m level interval was used with up-hole drilling only using both pneumatic and hydraulic drifter rigs. Mucking was by trackless diesel LHDs. Although an inflexible method it appeared suitable for the regular lode disposition. The main capital development at the mine was the sinking of a ramp-decline below 15 level. Until new sub-levels were developed below 15 level, off the decline, the mine would be squeezed for readily available Fully Developed reserves. There was thus no possibility of an increase in tonnage output and, as a reflection of that squeeze, the actual rom grade was well below that projected. There were standby diesel generators (V-16 English Electric units) available to supply power to the pumps, winders and ventilation fans in the event of a SWEB power failure. These EE generators could be synchronised with the SWEB supply and were frequently run for peak-lopping/load shedding reasons. At the time of our visit the mine was generating 1.5MW and SWEB was supplying 4.0MW.

The WJ concentrator (mill) was clean and well maintained. It was also treating South Crofty (SC) ore, which was delivered to the WJ coarse ore bin by road transport. That was a surprise to me as I had not appreciated that Carnon had recently closed the SC mill. Large quantities of lime were added to the mill water circuit as well as the mine's pump discharge to raise the pH of the very acidic water. In the afternoon we went back to the engineering offices to go over the ore reserve calculation details, mine scheduling/forecasting and the SURPAC computer modeling.

John joined us from the accounts office and we drove back to the Truro hotel, where Keith also checked in. As John said he felt like a walk before dinner I persuaded him and Keith to walk back down to the Daniel Arms at the top of Lemon Street for a pint. That was memory lane stuff for me, since it was here as a CSM student I was chasing student nurses at the RCI during the 1950s. Between the two of them and more beer they managed to stop me blathering on about the old days!

Next morning we drove over to the South Crofty mine, situated in Tuckingmill between Camborne and Redruth on the eastern side of the Red river valley. The river, well stream, rather than red was a deep ochre colour from the numerous mine's pump discharges further up the valley towards Carn Brea. Current ore reserves were quoted as 3.86 million tonnes at 1.50% Sn. Unlike WJ the SC reserves were contained in a number of discrete, steep dipping veins scattered over a large area (3km east-west and nearly 1km north-south). The seven largest veins had a combined ore expectancy of over 15,000 t/vm, more than double the WJ figure. Provided the main mine infrastructure was suitable, there should be no difficulty in meeting Carnon's production target of 180,000 tonnes/year from SC.

Ground conditions at SC were better than at WJ, since the vein's host rock was granite rather than killas. However the mine was getting quite deep at 470 fathoms, or over 2,800ft and there were visible signs of rock de-stress around some stopes and on the lower development headings. The VRT at the bottom of the mine was also quite high creating difficult conditions for the miners. Certainly mine ventilation required improving on the lower levels. The mine was relatively dry, currently pumping 1.5 million gals/day or a little over 1,000 gals/min.

Veins generally dipped at plus 70 degrees and a 45m level interval was used. In addition to sub-level long-hole open stoping some older stopes in the upper levels were worked by conventional shrinkage with hand held stopers. At SC the sub-level stopes were long-hole drilled both up and down (because of the larger 45m level interval) by either pneumatic or hydraulic drifter rigs. Tracked Atlas Copco LM-56 overshot loaders or Cavo 310 units were used for stope mucking.

Mine deepening via the second leg of the conveyor decline was continuing (boy it was hot and humid at the face). That would elevate ore from the new deeper levels up to the existing skip loading station on Cooks Kitchen shaft. It was good to see an attempt to arch the back of the decline and to learn that staff from the CSM were assisting with monitoring the geotechnical conditions. The Tuckingmill surface ramp-decline had been stopped once it was appreciated that it would be incapable of delivering unvitiated ventilation air to the bottom of the mine. Instead a new vent raise would be driven from the 470 to the 445m level. The rehabilitation of Cooks Kitchen shaft was being accelerated as the condition of the Robinson shaft rapidly worsened on account of ground movement caused by adjacent old workings. The new headframe coarse ore bin had very little storage capacity (only twenty tonnes!), but that was no longer a problem with the closure of the SC mill. SC ore was now trucked from the headframe bin to the WJ concentrator. However there were problems with the Markham 1250 HP double-drum rock winder. Apparently the hoisting system did not meet the NCB Markham regs and further improvements to the safety/monitoring controls of the hoisting cycle would have to be made.

The next morning we returned from Truro to Carnon's general offices for discussions with both Mine Superintendents and the General Manager. We expressed our reservations about WJ's ability to meet it's tonnage and grade targets, because of the squeezed development position at that mine. The GM concurred and said that they intended to drop WJ's tonnage to 160,000 tonnes/year and increase SC's output to 200,000 tonnes/year. We fully endorsed that move. On the cost side we felt that shrinkage stoping should be phased out and replaced by the cheaper, higher productivity of sub-level long-hole open stoping. Although SC mining costs at £39.6 were marginally higher than WJ at £37.8, they were appreciably lower per pound of contained tin on account of a much higher in situ grade and higher metallurgical recovery. Again that confirmed the economic wisdom of increasing SC's output. By world standards Carnon was a high cost operator with an overall direct operating cost of £54.3/tonne treated. John commented that the DTI would find it extremely helpful if those operating cost were split into fixed and semi-variable categories. That would enable the cost impact of various operating strategies to be more easily be assessed.

After an agreeable sandwich lunch we headed back to Truro where John caught the London train, Keith drove east to his Devon home and I drove across Cornwall to join Gillian and Pat in Mawgan Porth. The following morning we drove back to Gorsty, but this time I stayed on the M5 north of the Severn Bridge turn until Gloucester where we followed the A417 right through to just south of Leominster. Over the next two days I prepared a brief report on the Carnon visit and mailed it to John in London. We retrieved the dogs from kennels and since Gillian was not due back to work at the Hospice until next Monday we went over to St Richards to watch Sproggs playing in a school cricket match .

In mid June I received a fax from Jim (COMSUR's Exploration Chief) with details of the geology of the Cascabel mine in Bolivia. The fax said Jaime would call and ask me to send back my thoughts on how that orebody could (should?) be mined. He also said he had spoken to an Ing Arauco, the GM of Cia Minera Raura SA (CMRSA) in Lima, who was interested in engaging me to make an appraisal of their Raura multi-metal mine in Peru. Jim had known Ing Arauco for many years and had assisted him with exploration work around their mine. Apparently a recommendation from Jim was all I needed. His fax gave me the fax number of CMRSA in Lima and Jim said "get on to it!". So I did, pronto and sent a fax with my brief CV details plus daily fee rate. Almost by return fax they asked me to come to Lima at the start of July. I duly confirmed that that was OK.

In the meantime Jaime called and, as Jim had outlined, asked me to send him details of a notional mining method for use at the Cascabel mine. Of course I said that would be "site unseen" and wholly based on the geology and orebody description outlined in Jim's fax. That was understood, could I do it as soon as possible? In turn I said I would fax two or three pages by the third week of June. I also said I would be in Peru during July and would call him from Lima. So job No. 067 was a nice little desk study for a couple of days.

From Jim's description the orebodies were small, but regular with steep dip and plunge. The orebody was tough and competent and although the host rocks were steep dipping Ordovician slates and shales, crucially their strike was normal to the orebodies. The main characteristics were 70m strike, 7m average width, +85 degree dip and 70 degree plunge. The secondary vein was similar but the average width was only 2.5m. The two existing levels were 94m apart vertically. The first requirement was for an intermediate level to produce a 47m level interval. Thereafter mining could be by sub-level long-hole open stoping with up-hole and down-hole drilling by a bar mounted drifter rig. A 4in diam pneumatic drifter (ie BBC-120F) would drill 51mm diam holes using 1.2m length extension steel on a 1.35m burden and 1.5m toe hole spacing. Blasted ore recovery at the lower level by LHDs or tracked rockershovels operating in footwall drawpoints off stub crosscuts from a footwall drive. Under Bolivian conditions I estimated a direct mining cost of US$ 15/tonne mined.

I mentioned that this method was used in Cornish tin mines and, of course, variations on this method were currently being introduced at COMSUR's Aguilar mine in Argentina. If they wanted to stick with known Bolivian operations then shrinkage with jackleg drilling, as practised at Porco, could be used, but sub-level open stoping was the much preferred option. The brief notes and a typical transverse section sketch were despatched by fax. Phew, sorted. Yet again the fax demonstrated its usefulness in being able to transmit sketches and plans.

Later that week we drove up to Teddesley boatyard to see what had happened to Toadflax since we left her there in the early part of May to be lengthened. Well what a sorry sight! The fore and stern sections, 8ft apart, were sitting on a new mild steel base plate, itself sitting on wooden blocks. A welder had completed the bilge cross members in the new section and was now working on one of the new side panels. All of the original steelwork appeared to have been grit blasted. He said they would finish the side panels and new curved roof in the next day or so. After that it would be the construction and welding of a transverse pump-out storage tank just ahead of the engine bay, followed by a new mild steel forward bulkhead. Thereafter it was a few "odds and ends" of welding such as completing the cabin roof side rails. He felt that all steelwork would be completed by end June when internal fitting out in t & g pine could commence. After that the new gas cooker, Squirrel multi-fuel stove and flush loo would be installed. He estimated that if all went well they should be painting her traditional green and red by the end of July. For Gillian and me it was hard to envisage how the re-vamped Toadflax would emerge, let alone whether the old Petter PH2W would "do the business" and how she would handle.

38

July appeared and once more it was the South American run via Birmingham and Amsterdam through to Lima, where I arrived on the 2nd July and stayed in the downtown Crillon Hotel. Next morning after phoning Ing Arauco's secretary I set off by taxi for the CMRSA offices in the San Isidro quarter of the city. It was an old but impressive building. Ing Arauco, the GM, was very welcoming and said that I came with Jim's recommendation that I was a good, practical engineer who had assisted COMSUR on many projects over the past five years - praise indeed. The GM said there was a slight change in plan and he would like me first to visit the San Rafael tin mine of an associated company, MINSUR SA. Apparently the mine had the previous week been attacked by Sendero Luminoso guerrillas and three senior staff had been killed. He must have noticed my nervously raised eyebrows since he added that it was an entirely safe time to visit as a detachment of the Peruvian army was now billeted at the mine. After the MINSUR visit I could then go on to Raura. He said the San Rafael mine lay on the western flank of the Sierra Oriental at a height of 4500m in Estacion Tirapata in Puno Department. It was sixty miles NNE of the northern end of Lake Titicaca and about a four hour drive due north of Juliaca. After an informal lunch the GM arranged for a car to take me back to the Crillon Hotel to pick up my stuff and then drive me out to the airport.

I joined three other MINSUR staff for the just over two hours flight SE in a charter Beech aircraft landing at the San Rafael strip as the light was fading. Well, quite a welcome! The strip was lined on both sides by Peruvian army guys, fully armed, spaced every 50 yards or so. Quite spooky. As soon as we had deplaned the Beech, turned, taxied and took off for the return flight to Lima. We drove to the staff quarters with army escort jeeps in front and behind. Even in the Mess there were armed soldiers scattered around. I was quite discombobulated to find that my adjacent diner was a Peruvian army guy with an assault rifle resting on his lap. I soon got used to the army presence over the six days I was on the San Rafael site. Two to four soldiers accompanied me everywhere on surface, but not underground! Both the Mine and Mill superintendents had been killed in the recent surprise attack by the Sendero Luminoso guerrillas.

Next morning I started in the geological and mine engineering office. The main hydrothermal vein had a strike length of over two Km, an average width of 2m, a payability of over 90% and a flattish dip of 50 degrees. Total ore reserves were 2.50 million tonnes at 3.37% Sn and 1.1% Cu. Host rocks were strong comprising indurated slates and intrusive quartzites, both of which would be classified as good, competent mining ground. The present ore reserve had considered a 1.5% Sn cut-off grade (eat your heart out Wheal Jane and South Crofty) and the breakeven cost was quoted as US$ 57.8. Over the past eight years the ore reserve had increased from 1.47 million tonnes to the current 2.5 million tonnes a very healthy state of affairs. As expected with an hydrothermal deposit the frequency-distribution of Sn grades was highly skewed, approximately positive log-normal. Thus the use of the arithmetic mean would consistently overvalue the deposit by around 20%.

The main Veta San Rafael had an ore expectancy of 8,000 t/vm, the so-called Ore Shoot 5,000 t/vm and other veins 2,500 t/vm a total of 15,500 t/vm. My old 10% ore expectancy rule would indicate a production potential of up to 1,500 tonnes/day. The main Veta San Rafael was expected to continue for another 350m below the lowest level, reaching a depth from surface of 1000m or 50% of the 2Km strike extent. However the Ore Shoot was much more massive in form and was less likely to have such a dip extent, so perhaps a sustainable output of 1,200 tonnes/day was more realistic.

All development above the lowest adit level (533) was trackbound. The competent ground conditions had enabled conventional shrinkage stoping to commence off a sub-level driven 5m above rail level. Below the 533 Level the mine was a trackless operation with a 40m level interval. The main ramp-decline had been driven at 4m by 4.5m size and minus 10% gradient. The ramp was currently just below the 330 Level and planned to access the 270 level. That would then entail a continuous up-ramp haulage of nearly 2.7km to the primary crusher located on 533 Level. I suggested that that would be the absolute limit for trackless up-ramp haulage. Thereafter ore hoisting through a raised vertical shaft would prove a far more efficient and cheaper option. All trackless development was carried out with twin boom AC Boomer H115 or Jarvis Clark (JC) jumbos. Mucking was by Wagner ST-2D or JC 350 LHDs. Ramp haulage was by JC 26t low profile trucks or 12t Volvo box cars. With the exception of the Volvo trucks all underground trackless equipment was fitted with Deutz diesel engines. Much of the underground development was undertaken by contractors - INNESA or Minera Hill. Total development scheduled for that year, 1989, was 8188m lateral and 2204m vertical.

All stoping was by the shrinkage method. AC BBC-16W jacklegs drilling 35mm diam holes on a 0.9m by 0.9m burden/spacing pattern giving a drilling yield of 1.41t/m drilled and an explosive yield of 2.15t/Kg explosive (site mixed prilled ANFO & 65% Semexa 7 primer). Both yields were good as was the fragmentation. Present production was 264,000 tonnes/year over 300 days indicating a mining rate of 880 tonnes/day only. With 20% of the mill feed tonnage coming from development normal shrink stope planning should be based on a 40% draw (the Swell Factor) from active stopes supplying 32% of the mill feed (80% x 40% = 32%) and the balance, 48% derived from passive stopes (shrinks). At present MINSUR was breaking 47% more tonnage than it needed to meet the 880 tonnes/day mill feed. I was unable to understand why that was required. In effect the mine was producing enormous quantities of broken ore in the underground shrink piles. Of course that confirmed that the mine's production potential was closer to 1,200 tonnes/day than 880.

However the whole question of stoping in the trackless area of the mine required re-thinking. Basically we had a completely trackless mine infrastructure with modern drill jumbos, LHDs and diesel haul trucks supporting a stoping operation of hand held jackhammers! That did not appear logical. The ground conditions would permit the orebodies to be extracted by open stoping methods. I suggested that a basic sub-level open stoping method with long-hole drilling be introduced in those areas of the mine with reasonably constant dip between levels and little pinch-and-swell. A 120mm piston pneumatic or hydraulic drifter rig would be required for both up and down-hole drilling. With a burden of 1.5m the drilling yield would be 3.8 tonnes/m drilled and drifter output would be around 90 m/shift or an output of 340 tonnes/shift. Allowing for a drifter availability of 75% and a 67% utilisation, only four drifters would be needed to drill off 1,200 tonnes/day over two shifts.

Examination of existing shrinkage stoping practice showed that stopes of up to 250m continuous strike length were being mined with dip extents of circa 90 m. That gave huge unsupported hangingwall spans with an hydraulic radius (area/perimeter) of 33 m. I strongly recommended that stope strike extents should be limited to 100m with an 8m rib pillar (down-dip) separating stopes. That would reduce the hydraulic radius to circa 20 m. Still high, but probably acceptable for the ambient ground conditions.

Mine services were sited on the main 533 Level. The 5MW diesel power plant comprised three nine-year-old Sulzer 8ASL units each of 1062 kVA and two six year old Sulzer 12ASV units each of 1600 kVA. Power was generated at 440 volts, 60 Hertz with a 0.81 lagging power factor. The engines burnt Petrodiesel No 2 as it was too cold for Bunker C. The average load was 2.6MW and maximum demand 3.2MW. Specific generation performance was 12 kWHr/gal for the small units and 16 kWHr/gal for the large units.

The compressor plant was located alongside the power plant. It contained four electric Atlas Copco ER8 reciprocating two-stage compressors each rated at 2225 CFM at sea level, delivering 1625 CFM at San Rafael's plus 4500m elevation. There was also a Joy diesel unit rated at 750 CFM or 480 CFM at altitude, giving a total installed capacity at the mine of 6980 CFM. The rule-of-thumb compressed air consumption of 4 CFM/daily tonne mined implied a demand of 3200 CFM or about 46% of the installed capacity. Two of the ER8 compressors were nine years old and two were only three years old. Both the compressor plant and power plant were clean and well maintained.

The concentrator or mill was also close by the power plant. The upper levels of the mine produced a Cu rich ore and this was treated through a conventional crushing, ball milling, flotation, Atkins spiral classifying with overflow to the primary grind cyclones circuit. The larger tin circuit comprised primary jaw crushing by a COMESA 24in x 36in unit followed by both standard and shorthead Symons cone crushers. Primary grinding was by a Denver 10ft by 5ft rod mill and a COMESA 8ft by 8ft ball mill in close circuit with an Atkins spiral classifier. The overflow passed to a Stokes hydrosizer whilst the underflow passed to a regrind ball mill. Thereafter the different size products were treated on Holman sand and slimes shaking tables. An AMDEL on-stream analyser monitored feed rates and grades at various stages of the operation. Although the hillside plant appeared to have grown somewhat haphazardly it appeared clean and well maintained. Overall tin recovery had ranged from 67.7% to 71.6% over the past five years. Final tailings grade was around 1.07% Sn, higher than many underground tin mines head grade! That was an area of concern. MINSUR's own testwork had shown that the tin loss mainly occurred in the fine, minus 200 mesh fraction. A 5% increase in overall tin recovery would mean an extra 430 tonnes fine tin worth US$ 2 million/year.

The total San Rafael site workforce was believed to be 463 although there were many additional workers employed by the mining subcontractors INNESA and Minera Hill. I was unable to obtain details of those subcontract miners. The accounts department also declined to provide any operating cost data, which was very irritating, but hey it was their operation so bugger the gringo from head office! Thus after a full week at the mine I was ready to say goodbye and thanks to the Peruvian army guys, clambered aboard the Beech aircraft for a great flight over the western cordillera and finally luxuriate in the oxygen-rich, sea-level Lima air. I slept like a log that night in the Crillon.

Next morning I met Ing Arauco and gave him a brief verbal report on the MINSUR operation. Great mine with excellent potential. At present seriously under-mining the resource. Should increase output from 880 tonnes/day to 1,200 - 1,500 tonnes/day. Change from high cost/low productivity shrinkage stoping to sub-level long-hole open stoping. Reduce the strike extent of stopes between 8m wide rib pillars to circa 100m only. Start planning for a shaft hoisting system for operations below 270 level. In the concentrator investigate ways to increase tin recovery from minus 200 mesh fraction. I guess that was the good news he was pleased to hear after the killing of their Mine and Mill Superintendents.

However there was bad news for me as there was now a wildcat strike at the Raura mine. Obviously I could not visit the mine, but Ing Arauco felt the strike would be over in a few days. Thus I spent the next five days in their San Isidro offices working on grade-distribution and tonnage-grade curves as well as developing a sub-level open stoping system together with a report write-up. Over the following weekend the strike was called off so that on Monday, 17th July I headed NE out of Lima in a CMRSA ute.

It was a six hours drive up the valley of the Rio Huara to Huanuco Department where the Raura mine straddled the Andean watershed at elevations of 4300m to 4800 m. Similar to the trip up to the Quirulvilca mine, the climb passed through the full climatic range of a sub-tropical seashore to a montane one. The Raura camp was spectacular, with the old compressor plant being sited a short distance from the snout of a glacier. Yes I found it quite cold and was glad to get underground to warm up.

The local geology comprised Cretaceous sediments, mainly limestone, invaded by dacites and granodiorites. The main orebody was a massive skarn type replacement of 3.85 million tonnes at 0.4% Cu, 1.7% Pb, 7.1% Zn & 2.5 oz/t Ag. There was also 440,000 tonnes of hydrothermal veins at 1.37% Cu, 3.56% Pb, 4.38% Zn & 10.4 oz/t Ag and 315,000 tonnes of stockwork/breccia grading 0.19% Cu, 7.5% Pb, 6.2% Zn & 4.6 oz/t Ag. These were all sulphide reserves and totalled 4.6 million tonnes. There was an additional 381,000 tonnes of oxide reserves. The mine had prepared tonnage-grade curves for a range of combined metal COGs from US$ 35 to US$ 75 for the skarn section of the mine. Those showed that a natural $ value COG occurred at about US$ 50 when the net worth of the skarn reserve alone was about US$ 285 million.

During the previous year the company undertook geotechnical investigation as a consequence of glacial moraine material entering the mine workings in the skarn section. The Rock Mass Rating (RMR) for that orebody was three and Raura proposed longitudinal cut-and-fill stoping leaving 4m by 4m pillars. However the incipient rock structure in the skarn section favoured transverse stoping and I suggested that the sequence of attack should be from footwall towards hangingwall with continuous rib pillars of at least 8m width. That would ensure that the stope's hydraulic radius was kept in the 4 to 6m range rather than 10m with the small square pillars. Also those rib pillars could be recovered by second pass transverse stoping.

The massive skarn body had an ore expectancy of 54,000 t/vm based on a 420m strike length and 40m width. It was huge. On its own I felt that the skarn orebody could easily sustain a 5,000 tonnes/day mining rate. With the additional ore expectancy of just over 10,000 t/vm in the vein and stockwork bodies the Raura mine had the potential to sustain a 6,000 tonnes/day mining rate. I noted that the total ore expectancy was five times that of the Quirulvilca mine where current production was 1,500 tonnes/day and all from narrow veins!

Without doubt the Raura mine was seriously under-mining its considerable ore reserves. Current production was 245,000 tonnes/year or only 742 tonnes/day a truly pitiful output from such a marvellous deposit. Numerous visits underground over the next seven days clearly demonstrated why.

The mine was in a terrible state and obviously very badly managed. Mine housekeeping, per se, was completely absent. There was rubbish everywhere (including discarded explosives). Lateral development was ragged, poorly mined and the railtrack was often without sleepers, fishplates or bolts and generally under water. There were no drains whatsoever so that where hydraulic fill was being used in the stopes the overflow silt buried the track. Ladderways were downright dangerous with missing rungs and no overlap on raise stages. Ventilation was very poor and seemed to be provided from the myriad leaks in the compressed air lines. There was a complete absence of victaulic pipe couplings and Atlas snap couplings for air hose connections. Instead the dangerous "Raura" system of wire bands twitched together with baling wire were ubiquitous. One can only ask why? Yes, poor management and presumably lack of capital investment in plant and equipment. There appeared to be a complete absence of any mine engineering or planning. A good start would be the appointment of a new Underground Manager, CME, two or three mining engineers and at least two additional geologists.

An interesting feature of the mine was that the 380 level main adit drained water into Laguna Tinquicocha which overflowed north-eastwards into the River Amazon drainage basin, whereas the lower levels drained south-westwards into the Rio Hua and ultimately the Pacific ocean. That southern area, known as Sucshapa, alongside the road from Churin and Lima at an elevation of 4300m would provide an ideal site for a new concentrator. A new adit from this site would intersect the down-dip projection of the main skarn orebody at a distance of 3.5 Km. The power line from the company's Cashaucro hydro-power plant also passed through that area.

The massive skarn deposit was being developed by a contractor using trackless methods. That development work was also poorly executed. However the potential to develop a brand new high tonnage mine was apparent. The ground conditions would allow transverse sub-level open stoping to be practiced, rather than the cut-and-fill stoping in use at present. I suggested a top overcut from which parallel down-holes blasting sequentially into a vertical slot with ore recovery from a trough-undercut via flank drawpoints would be the ideal large tonnage method entirely suitable for trackless mining units. That would certainly be the way forward for Raura coupled with a new concentrator at Suschapa if the necessary funds could be found.

The main compressor plant comprised six old Ingersoll Rand XLE 2-stage piston units installed in 1965 to 1979 with a combined derated output of 5780 CFM plus a Sullair screw unit installed in 1980 of 675 CFM. The installation was cramped in an old GI building with no EOT or decent lay-down area. The installation was scruffy and uncared for. The plant was tucked out of the way close by the snout of a glacier. On the day I visited the plant was working flat-out with all units on full load. Of course with a daily mining rate of less than 750 tonnes, the rule-of-thumb of 4 CFM/daily tonne would indicate a demand of 3000 CFM only. The fact that it was delivering 6455 CFM more than double the expected amount merely demonstrated the appalling state of the underground compressed air reticulation. Yet again, poor or absent management.

The concentrator was a partial hillside type plant and space was obviously limited. However as with just about everything else at Raura it was scruffy, run-down and poorly maintained. Absolutely no sign of any TLC and a wonder that it managed to treat nearly 750 tonnes/day. Without a doubt for Raura to develop into a plus 5,000 tonnes/day operation (a realistic proposition) a new modern concentrator needed to be built at Sucshapa asap. The differential flotation plant produced three separate concentrates - copper 24% grade at 60% recovery; lead 60% grade at 80% recovery and zinc 56% grade at 84% recovery. The concentrates were trucked down to Lima.

Power supply was obtained from the Cashaurco hydro plant which comprised one AEG and four Siemens turbines designed for a maximum head of 132m and a maximum water intake of 0.945m^3/s. Bus voltage was 2300 at 60 Hz and a 5MVA transformer stepped it up to 33 kV for transmission by overhead line to the mine. The plant was about twenty years old, but unlike nearly everything else at Raura was very well maintained and operated. The operational problem was shortage of water supply restricting output to around 3MVA in summer. To make up this shortfall there was a small diesel power plant at Raura itself comprising two six-cylinder MAN units and two eight-cylinder MAN engines with a combined output of 4.74MVA. All generators were AEG. Since hydro-power was much cheaper the diesels were only run in the summer to make up the hydro shortfall, about 1.9MVA. There was thus sufficient hydro and diesel power available for the current operation, but nowhere near enough for a 5,000 tonnes/day operation.

Direct operating costs per tonne were quoted as mining US$ 33; concentrating US$ 9.2; power supply US$ 2.7 and administration US$ 20.4. Sales costs and Lima office expenses added another US$ 15. Taken at face value both the mining and administration costs were very high. Having seen the poor state of the mine I was not surprised. The best thing about the mine was its location, which was very dramatic amidst the glaciers and snow capped peaks of the Andean watershed. Apart from the visual aspect I was not sorry to leave the dilapidated Raura mine and return to Lima. I checked into the Crillon again.

The following morning I had a difficult meeting with Ing Arauco. The difficulty was on my side as I decided to give the bad news first - that the mine was in a totally run down state with no appearance of any management control. Ing Arauco was extremely upset and unhappy to hear this and asked me to put my comments on management failure in a separate letter to my technical report. His only immediate response was that the company had been starved of funds for investment in plant and equipment, and that the local miner's union was very belligerent and strike prone to any proposed changes to working methods. When I moved on to the good news - the marvellous skarn orebody and the huge potential to develop a plus 5,000 tonnes/day operation he seemed a little disbelieving that that could be achieved. Of course not straight away and certainly not with the current management I said, but the resource was there in the ground. To develop a new mine, concentrator, power plant etc would require a lot of money, but Raura owned a major resource which could attract investment capital from outside companies. I said that I thought COMSUR of Bolivia might be interested in taking an equity position in Raura. We agreed that I could mention my good impression of the potential of the mine to Jim whilst in La Paz on my way back to the UK, but nothing more.

Thus I found myself in the Hotel Sucre in La Paz once again during the last days of July. I first talked with Jim and Jaime about my notional mining method for the Cascabel mine, which I had sent over by fax in June. They felt the sub-level, blast-hole, open stoping method might be too big a change for Bolivian jackhammer miners, although help could perhaps come from the Aguilar mine at a later stage. They (COMSUR) would evaluate Cascabel on the basis of conventional shrinkage stoping. Both Jim and Jaime pricked up their ears at the mention of a possible

5,000 tonnes/day multi-metal operation at Raura. That was particularly relevant after the disappointment of the Quirulvilca mine, since Goni was still keen to diversify COMSUR's mining portfolio in to Peru. Jim said he would try and sound out Ing Arauco on his next visit to Lima. Jaime asked me to schedule yet another visit to Aguilar in about three months time after they had updated and recalculated the ore reserves in October. Then it was LAB flight back to Lima followed by KLM to Amsterdam and NLM to Birmingham, where Kevin, a Leominster taxi driver, picked me up for the run back to Gorsty.

It was early August, hence school holiday time. Sproggs was at home and now aged twelve full of energy. I pitched a small 2-man pup ridge tent in the garden so that Sproggs and a school mate could sleep out there, gorging themselves on "midnight snacks". The dogs thought it was great fun and more than once threatened to collapse the tent with their exuberance. Well, in reality following their noses to the boy's food. Luke seemed to be pre-programmed to stumble over the guy ropes at night in his enthusiasm to share the midnight snacks.

The news from Teddesley boatyard was that the fitting out work on Toadflax was complete and she had been craned back into the canal and the really good news was that she was still floating. We checked that our new mooring at Whixall Marina was ready to accept us, popped the dogs into kennels and prepared to head up to Penkridge to collect Toadflax and move her up to Whixall. I was amazed at how much bigger she seemed. They had made a very nice job of fitting her out and the cabin, complete with Squirrel stove seemed very luxurious, not to say anything of the posh flushing loo! Having settled the bill and feeling distinctly lighter in the pocket we set off south down the Staffs and Worcester canal. It was a run of eleven miles and six locks to Autherley Junction by Wolverhampton. In fact the new, lengthened Toadflax handled much more easily than the original, shorter version. She reacted more quickly to changes in direction and the old Petter PH2W engine seemed to have sufficient grunt to push her along at about 3.5 mph. Gillian was steerer as we steadily locked up to Wolverhampton. It was great to have Sproggs assistance on working the narrow gauge locks.

We reached Autherley Junction in under six hours and turned on to the Shropshire Union Canal (SUC) making for Brewood where we moored for the night. Next day, apart from a single lock at Wheaton Aston, we chugged steadily NW past our original mooring at Norbury and on through the five Tyrley locks to moor for the night at Market Drayton. That days distance was 21 miles and we seemed to take between 15 and 20 minutes to work through a lock. So about an 8.5 hour run for the day. We were now locking down towards the Cheshire plain. The next day was hard work for the lock crew (!) and boy was I glad of Sproggs help. Only three miles on from Market Drayton we encountered the five Adderley locks followed in two miles by the fifteen locks of the Audlem flight. Fairly knackered we moored just below the bottom lock and ambled into the town of Audlem for a slap up dinner.

The following day was a much easier run through the two Hack Green locks to the embankment above Nantwich, a distance of six miles. Here we stopped and walked in to that lovely town to do some tourism and collect food and drink supplies. From there it was only two miles to Hurleston Junction where we turned west onto the Llangollen canal. At Hurleston there was a four-lock staircase and fortunately I remembered how to work them without flooding or grounding Toadflax. It was then a twelve mile run with ten more locks and several lift bridges before we moored for the night just below Grindley bottom lock. Our final day of the trip was a short one up the five Grindley Brook locks to Whitchurch, where we again moored and went into the town. After that a further six miles until we turned onto the Prees branch and the final mile or so to Whixall Marina where we found our new mooring on one of the pontoons. It was not ideal, but we had to moor the boat somewhere. Anyway getting here had provided us with nearly a week of canal boating through very varied countryside.

Our final day of the holiday comprised a taxi to Whitchurch then train to Shrewsbury and on to Wolverhampton and another taxi to Penkridge to collect the car from Teddesley Boatyards car park. I popped in to say how pleased we were with the "extended" boat. The biggest drawback was obviously going to be the distance of Whixall Marina from Gorsty, which I imagined would take at least one-and-a-half to two hours to drive, involving passing through Shrewsbury.

With no immediate work commitments Sproggs and I set off for a short cycle and camping trip along the Welsh borders. First we headed up the back roads to Ludlow and then turned west climbing up through Mortimers Forest followed by a great run down to Burrington and on to Leintwardine on the river Teme. On the way we passed the huge pipe bridge over the Teme which carried Birmingham water supply from the Elan valley reservoirs. We cycled north to Hopton finally turning west through Clunton, Clun and Newcastle to finally camp alongside the Clun stream on the south side of Clun Forest. I guess we'd cycled nearly forty miles. Not too hard for me with a ten speed adult road bike but hard going for Sproggs with a three speed small fold-up bike. However he showed the energy of youth when we cycled back to the pub in Newcastle easily beating me by a couple of minutes over the half mile ride. We attacked steak and chips with gusto washed down with pints of bitter for me and coke for Sproggs. Later back at our tent I had forgotten just how hard the ground was on one's hip. Brought back memories of the Chief's hut.

The weather stayed fine and we cycled back to Gorsty by a different selection of byroads. We were not quite so trouble free that time as both of us collected punctures. That was from hawthorne spines from a recently flailed hedge. We were unlucky since most farmers around the borders don't cut (well, flail) their hedges till late September or early October. Hey ho the enforced stop to patch tyres allowed me to get my breath back, but even so I only just managed to cycle up Gorsty Hill (well it was about 1 in 4 past the farm). For Sproggs it was a case of getting organised for returning to St Richards for the winter term. I was busy in the garden doing the final year's cut on the long grass and attacking the hedges. After that it was digging out the drains and splitting and stacking logs. I had only just completed these jobs when I had a call from Nick, ex Capper Pass, who I had last seen on our visit to Bolivia in the 1970s when I was with RTZC. Nick was now with the Cookson Group and asked me to undertake a technical review of the Wadley antimony operation in Mexico. Sounded interesting, welcome to job No. 070.

39

In early October I took the British Midland (BM) flight from Birmingham down to Heathrow. Here I transferred to an Aeromexico flight to Mexico City, where I checked into an airport hotel, which Nick had booked for me. I was due to meet Wally, President of ANZON Inc, who would brief me on the operations of Cia Minera y Refinadora Mexicana SA (CMRMSA) near Estacion Wadley in San Luis Potosi State. We duly caught up with each other in the hotel's bar. Wally said the mine was ten miles east of Wadley at a height of 2400 to 2800m on the western flank of the Sierra Catorce. Wadley itself lay alongside the main rail line from Monterrey to San Luis Potosi (SLP). SLP itself was 220 miles NW of Mexico City. A new HMS plant had just been installed and ANZON, a major shareholder, was now concerned that the operation was losing money and unable to meet the HMS plant's capacity. So in a nutshell what production could the mine sustain and what services were needed to support it. That's all! There was another small problem - for me - no one at the mine spoke English. That should really test my Spanglish. Wally said he would contact the mine and arrange for someone to meet the early morning Mexicana flight from Mexico City to SLP. He was also staying overnight so after his "briefing" we settled down to telling stories and some steady drinking. He was a very likable chap.

In the morning I staggered over the connecting bridge, hotel to airport, trying to clear my head and locate the domestic terminal within the vast airport complex. Yet again, note to diary, I must, absolutely must, graduate from Spanglish to half decent South American Spanish. Well at least the Wadley camp threatened to give me plenty of practice. By hook or by crook I eventually located the check-in (Salidas!) for SLP. The flight by turboprop aircraft took just under the hour and good as Wally's word a CMRMSA ute was waiting for me at SLP arrivals area. Relief. I wasn't too keen on trying to persuade a taxi to take me out to the Wadley camp, Spanglish or no Spanglish. It was a three hour drive due north to Estacion Wadley (the CMRMSA camp) where I was taken to the single mens Mess. After dropping my bag I went to meet the GM. After the usual flim-flam I said I'd like to start on the mine's geology. The actual mine was a further ten miles east of the camp on the western edge of the Sierra and that was where the geological and mine engineering offices were. The drive from Wadley to the mine was flattish for the first five miles then climbed steeply, rising over 750m in the last five miles. We passed the HMS plant at the foot of the Sierra, some 3 km from the mine.

The local geology comprised Jurassic sediments, mainly strongly bedded limestone overlain by shales and interspersed with beds of gypsum and aragonite. The antimony mineralisation, chiefly oxides with the sulphide stibnite occurred in a series of mantos, or thin horizons conformable with the limestone bedding. Present mining operations were confined to five mantos in the Upper Series and four mantos in the Lower Series. The overall thickness of the Upper Series was 65m and of the Lower Series about 30 m. The two Series were separated by 200m of unmineralised limestone. The average manto thickness was 0.9 m, ranging from 0.5m to 3.0 m. They generally outcroped along the western flank of the Sierra Catorce. However the area had been extensively folded and over-folded so that dips ranged from horizontal to vertical. Considerable faulting had also occurred. The Upper Series had numerous old workings which extracted high grade areas leaving random "gophering" outlines. Total reserves for the San Jose mine were quoted as 732,000 tonnes at 3.07% Sb at a 1.5% Sb cut-off grade. The frequency-grade-distribution approximated a positive skew log-normal trace, suggesting an overvaluation bias of 10%. There was an additional resource of 100,000 tonnes at 2.00% Sb contained in old surface waste/tailings dumps. In fact it was this old surface material that was providing 85% of the current feed to the HMS plant. Apparently the underground mine was still under development!

The strong competent ground indicated that unsupported stoping methods could be used. Conventional shrinkage stoping where the manto dip was greater than 50 degrees and jackleg breast hole stoping with three drum scrapers where dips were less than 55 degrees. The narrow average stope width and presence of random old workings precluded the use of trackless long-hole stoping. Above the San Jose haulage level the ore expectancy was 4 to 5,000 t/vm indicating a sustainable mining rate of 500 tonnes/day. Examination of the various mantos physical dispositions suggested the following mining programme:-

Source of Ore	Tonnes/d	%
Shrinkage Stope Draw:		
40%(6 stopes x 44t/d)	104	20
Breast-stoping:		
(7 stopes x 42t/d)	294	60
Development:		
(4 headings x 1.6m/shift)	102	20
Total Mine Production	500	100

Of course, with only a 40% draw (the broken ore swell) the shrinkage stopes would build up a static shrink stockpile at the rate of 156 tonnes/day. Those production rates were based on two shifts/day working for six days/week.

That analysis demonstrated the impracticality of delivering 1,000 tonnes/day from the presently developed mine area. Why 1,000 tonnes/day? Well that was the stated capacity of the new HMS plant. One wondered who decided that. At the moment the HMS plant was virtually running at that rate, but the bulk of its feed (85%) came from the surface dumps and they would be depleted in the next four to six months. The underground mine was still delivering less than 150 tonnes/day. Without a doubt CMRMSA would have a grossly under utilised HMS plant in a few months time. The mine would physically be unable to achieve an output of 1,000 tonnes/day even when fully developed. There was, of course, the possibility of developing "another mine", further north on the large existing lease to supplement the inadequate San Jose production, but that could take years to develop. On top of the tonnage shortfall most of the underground mining equipment was old and second hand. Even worse there were absolutely no maintenance facilities whatsoever for the ancient diesel equipment, merely a rough graded stone area on surface - no building; no EOT crane; no inspection pit; no lube facility; no tyre change facility; nothing. Quite unbelievable.

The geological and mine engineering "offices" were sheds and, in fact there was no mine planning or engineering activity apart from survey and sampling. Underground compressed air reticulation was rudimentary (numerous leaks), whilst ventilation was insufficient to dilute the noxious diesel fumes from clapped out diesel engines. It was a disaster zone and the mine would have been shut by most Mines Inspectors.

On surface the one shining light was a newish compressor plant comprising two electric Joy Twistair rotary screw units and three Atlas Copco two-stage piston units. There were also three diesel rotary screw portable units and the total plant's derated capacity was 6700 CFM. That was more than adequate to meet the mine's estimated demand of 2500 CFM.

Both the recovered dump material and underground ore were picked up by an ancient Cat 977 Traxcavator and loaded into a very old Cat 769B truck (30t capacity) for the two mile downhill haul to the HMS plant bin. The mine's accounts showed that as costing 83 US cents/t-Km, more than double an acceptable figure and that was for downhill haulage! CMRMSA were planning to put that job out to contract. Couldn't come quickly enough.

Well I expected the new HMS plant built by Fives Cail Babcock (FCB) to be OK. Wrong. It had several serious design faults. It should have been a hillside type layout to make use of the natural ground slope close to the mine and water supply borehole. The truck dump bin was built "up in the air" to provide dump headroom to the flat plant. That was both crazy (use the ground slope) and dangerous for the reversing dump truck. There was no grizzly and no means for handling oversize or tramp material. The capacity was a tiny 40 tonnes, one truck load only. When the bin was full the dump truck had to drive back down the ramp to a ground dump area nearly 100m away. Didn't anyone think about re-handling? The primary jaw crusher was also "up in the air" (!!) making maintenance such as changing jaw liners virtually impossible. The secondary cone crushers also had no EOT crane or lay-down area. Chutes and the fine ore bin were constructed of MS with no liners or wearing strips and a ludicrously small capacity of sixty tonnes. I could not believe it. Finally the tailings disposal area was a shambles. It required a complete redesign by a firm of specialists, eg, Golder Associates.

ANZON wished to produce 5.5 million pounds of Sb/year. From a throughput of 1,000 tonnes/day for 292days/year and a head grade of 2.2% Sb this implied an HMS plant recovery of 38.85%. The plant had never achieved that. On commissioning the actual recovery was around 15%. The CMRMSA operating staff with help from Ian, a British metallurgical consultant, had finally increased the recovery to 32.5%. However in six months time with the exhaustion of dump material the plant would only receive 500 tonnes/day (at best) from the underground mine implying an annual output of under 2.5 million pounds of Sb, less than 45% of the production desired. Yes, both the mine and the plant were disaster areas.

Power supply from the State was not a constraint. The Mexican Power Corp had a 33kV 4MVA transformer close to the mine site. The final nail in the coffin was cost. The total CMRMSA operating cost was quoted as US$ 15.3/tonne treated. Antimony's current price was US$ 1800/t CIF, or 82 US cents/pound, whereas the recovered antimony per tonne treated cost around 91 US cents/pound to produce. In fact the future operating loss would be much higher since the current operating cost of US$ 15.3 embraced the cost of easily dug dump material. Underground hard rock mining would cost much more thus greatly increasing the operating loss. I could see no light at the end of the tunnel. In a Spanish nutshell - Il disastre.

After four days at the mine and HMS plant I thankfully returned to Estacion Wadley to take my leave of the GM. He said "esta bien?" In my best Spanish I replied "non, hay muchos problemas en la mina tambien el concentrador, lo siento". With that I scarpered in the CMRMSA ute for the three hour drive to SLP airport. There I caught the first Mexicana flight back to Mexico City where I transferred from domestic to the international terminal and managed to get a seat on the night Aeromexico flight to Heathrow. A quick phone call to the Leominster Taxi service to arrange for Kevin to meet me at Birmingham airport, where I would (eventually) arrive on a BMI flight. I finally reached Gorsty late in the afternoon shortly before Gillian returned from St Michael's. The two dogs went bananas and wouldn't quieten down until I'd taken them for a walk into the Long Field over the top of Gorsty Hill.

The next day I phoned Nick at Cooksons to let him know I was back and give him a brief run-down on the visit. He did not sound a happy bunny. Apparently the Cookson Group handled antimony marketing for ANZON and if CMRMSA wasn't producing much antimony then there wouldn't be much business. I said it would take me four or five days to write up my report. He then asked me to come up to London to discuss the Wadley operation with him and Ian, the metallurgical consultant. We arranged to meet in a St James's Club early next week. I rode the old 400/4 Honda over to Worcester Shrub Hill station and duly caught an early Cotswold Line train to Paddington. The club was just as one imagined, lots of leather and hushed tones. I was directed to a small private room to join Nick and Ian.

Nick was aghast that the mine might only deliver 500 tonnes/day with no foreseeable chance of delivering 1,000 tonnes/day, whilst Ian was equally upset by my criticism of the HMS plant. To be fair to Ian he had been working on the metallurgy (to raise the recovery of antimony) and not the physical operational side. In time they both agreed that the FCB plant layout/design was poor. However the big unanswered question was who had commissioned a 1,000 tonnes/day HMS plant in the first place when patently the mine was quite unable to deliver that tonnage of plus 2.2% Sb material? I confirmed the size of the direct operating loss and pointed out that that loss would soar in four to six months time when the surface dump material was exhausted. Nick thanked me for the report, said it was OK, though not what he wanted to hear, but, in fact, had suspected. He would now have to break the news to Wally of ANZON. With a grin he said he didn't think there would be any further work for me on CMRMSA's Wadley operation. So that was that and I headed back by train to Worcester followed by an enjoyable ride on the old 400/4 back to Gorsty.

Well no peace for the wicked as Jaime from COMSUR called asking me to visit Aguilar with Carlos in the first week of November. That would be job No. 069. There was some hiatus with KLM flights to South America so Thomas Cook booked me from Birmingham to Heathrow by BMI then BA to Miami transferring to LAB for La Paz. The BMI flight went like clockwork. At Heathrow I had cleared Immigration and Customs and checked into the BA Miami flight departure lounge. Here I was approached by a plain clothed man who demanded to see my ticket and passport. Unsurprisingly I said "no, who the hell are you"? He was quite stroppy and finally produced an ID card confirming he was a Customs Officer. I gave him both my ticket and passport. His next question was "why are you travelling to Santa Cruz"? I had two separate tickets, Heathrow-Miami and Miami-La Paz. I had only given him the Heathrow-Miami ticket as that was the flight I was about to board. Of course I replied "I am not, I am flying to Miami". He said "we know you are flying to Santa Cruz - why"? I denied that I was, telling him that after Miami I was flying on to La Paz. Anyway it transpired that the LAB flight from Miami stopped at Panama City, Rio, Sao Paulo, Santa Cruz and finally La Paz. Obviously I had not shown my Miami to La Paz ticket to Immigration or Customs, but they knew exactly where I was going. After a bit more hassling he went through my passport commenting on the number of times I had been in and out of Bolivia, Argentina and Peru. It slowly filtered into my skull that Customs had picked up my travel routes (including using Birmingham and Amsterdam) and suspected that I might be tied up with drug trafficking. He was an aggressive guy and interrogated me for about ten minutes.

On reflection I realised that Custom's computer must have flagged my flight patterns of fairly frequent visits to South America, hence their interest. It certainly got me thinking. On many occasions I inter-lined in Lima, Rio and Miami where ones hold luggage was accessible to numerous baggage handlers. That was an epiphany for me. In future I would only travel with a cabin bag, which stayed in my possession. Thinking back on several trips I was aware that my hold luggage had been searched. I knew that because I packed my mining boots with certain things and those had been disturbed. Nothing amiss at Miami where the USA Immigration guys were their usual charming self - not. The LAB flight took for ever and even stopped at Manaus on the Amazon. In fact Santa Cruz de la Sierra in eastern Bolivia appeared a modern bustling city unlike the altiplano feel of La Paz. The check-in staff at the Hotel Sucre greeted me like a long lost friend. Later that day I went to the COMSUR offices to see Jaime, the GM, and Carlos. Jaime wanted an update on activities at Aguilar. He felt that the mine was still reluctant to introduce the changes that COMSUR had requested.

Next morning Carlos and I flew with AA down to Jujuy. The CMASA ute was there to pick us up and we drove straight up to the mine arriving in mid-afternoon. We went straight to the Geological office to meet Pablo and discuss the latest (October 1989) ore reserves. The mine had done what we asked and excluded all "reserves" unavailable due to falls of ground or contained in mine infrastructure or uneconomic/marginal grade etc. That removed 183,000 tonnes from the reserves. During the past year exploration and development had added 501,000 tonnes or 80.7% of the tonnage mined from reserves. Overall the reserve had fallen by 511,000 tonnes, year on year, a very unwelcome trend. The mine had to make every effort to increase exploration and development. Nevertheless the current reserve of 5 million tonnes would sustain a 700,000 tonnes/year production rate for just over seven years. However Pablo confirmed that Buenos Aires management had told him to use the old 1988 COG of 6.2% combined metals, which obviously did not reflect current costs or metal prices. That was contrary to COMSUR's instruction - ho ho!

Pablo also pointed out that the mill head grades requested by Buenos Aires for 1989 could only be achieved by over-mining the average reserve grades, where the mine itself was applying an operational COG of 8.2% combined metals. Use of that policy by Buenos Aires management would effectively remove 630,000 tonnes, or 12% from the Industrial reserves. The whole aspect of reserve marginal COGs, operational COGs and consequent changes in available reserve tonnages seemed to have been given scant attention by the Buenos Aires management.

On the exploration front surface diamond drilling (DD) had identified a resource of about 700,000 tonnes close to the northern exhaust ventilation rise. The correct approach to developing that potential "open pit" area should be:- exploration, reserve definition, transverse cross sections, pit planning, sizing operation and equipment selection. A key part of that process was, of course, the use of a realistic "open pit" COG, probably circa 3.0% combined metals. Pablo had been unable to prevent the Mining Department from rushing ahead and commencing open-pit mining before a rational pit exploration and design had been completed.

Structural geological mapping and rock classification was still required in the upper levels of the mine, above 18 level. It was required to assist in selecting the correct stoping method, direction of attack, stope spans etc. Below 18 level all aspects of the new sub-level, open stoping system had been tested bar only the performance of cemented fill, which would shortly be completed on filling of the trial stope. Then all major design parameters for the new method would be known.

Expansion from the current 2,000 tonnes/day would involve considerable incremental expenditure on upgrading the concentrator and power plant. An Aguilar Expansion project should be assessed and ranked financially with other mining projects available to COMSUR. However to achieve that CMASA desperately needed to appoint a CME and at least two additional mine planning engineers. The mine still did not have a stope-specific production schedule, a glaring omission, which we had identified eighteen months ago. Things certainly moved very slowly (if at all) with Aguilar management.

The sub-level method had been proved viable. Since there was sufficient accessible tonnage above 18 level to maintain a 2,000 tonnes/day production rate all stoping below 18 level should stop, whilst the ramp-decline was deepened to the 22 level. Then the 22 level F/W drive should be driven to provide access for DD exploration of the orebody at 25m strike intervals. With up-ramp ore haulage restricted to 2.5km (250m vertical at 1 in 10 gradient) the present ramp-decline would be economically viable to the 26 level. A really encouraging feature of the trial stope was that the mined grade, determined by samples from the LHDs was 4% higher than that predicted by the reserve block grades.

The latest monthly operating statistics showed an encouraging reduction in the use of square-set mining, now down to 38% of the total underground tonnage delivered. Whereas square-set stoping output was 4.3 TMS, underhand 6.0 TMS, cut-and-fill 9.8 TMS the new, trial, sub-level stope was an encouraging 21.6 TMS with much better drilling and explosive yields. Although the number of stopes breaking over 1,000 tonnes/month had doubled the TMS of those larger stopes had actually fallen from 11.5 to 10.2. The increase in stope production had been achieved by working more shifts/day up from 2.13 to 2.38. In itself a good trend, but not supported by more efficient stoping activities. Again the front-line mine management appeared to have been interested in breaking more tonnes, but not by improvements in TMS and drilling and explosive yields - hence, ultimately cost/tonne.

It was good to see the Spedel grout pumps in action and the use of grouted 19mm rebar as the main means of rock reinforcement. Ing Werner had been of great help in designing high density backfill. He undertook to do testwork on the Aguilar mill tailings, but felt that the cemented common fill (from surface detritus) would be better as it was more akin to concrete! As Carlos and I agreed some good news, but also some bad. In the latter category it was apparent that cooperation between the Geology and Mining Departments had deteriorated. We both felt it was a personality clash between the two Heads of Department. Pablo the geology boss was more inclined to listen to COMSUR whereas the Mine Superintendent jumped to the Buenos Aires management's tune. Hey ho it was always about people. After a week at the mine, stirring the pot and rattling the cage Carlos and I returned to La Paz, flying AA from Jujuy, to give Jaime a run-down on our findings. He said that he and Goni would have a serious session with Miguel, the CMASA GM and the Mine Manager next week. I was quite sorry I couldn't be there, but I had heard from Gillian that the DTI had requested that I visit South Crofty before the end of November.

Back at Gorsty I got straight on to writing up the Aguilar visit, which involved checking the various COG calculations we had made at the mine and preparing tonnage-grade curves. The recent mine operating cost data and NSR values for Pb, Zn and Ag metal at Tres Cruces certainly indicated that the COG for ore reserves should be closer to 5% combined metals than the 6.2% combined metals used. No doubt Carlos would fight our corner in La Paz when the CMASA jeffes arrived for talks with Goni and Jaime.

I phoned John at the DTI, he was away, and I was put through to Mark. He asked if I could join him and their consulting geologist, Keith for a visit to South Crofty on the 30th November and the day after at Carnon's Technical Services offices. He said the objective of the visit was to update our findings from the earlier May visit. Welcome to job No. 071. This time they had booked into the Greenbank Hotel in Falmouth. With Sproggs safely boarding at St Richards, Gillian obtained a few days off from Hospice work. We drove on the A417 past Ledbury to join the M50 and on to the M5 south for Bristol and Exeter then the A30 to Goss Moor where we diverted to Pat's house in Mawgan Porth, where I dropped Gillian off. I continued SW through Truro to Falmouth. The Greenbank Hotel was very comfortable and I caught up with Keith in the bar, where he introduced me to Mark of the DTI.

The following morning Keith and I duly went underground at South Crofty. Mark, a lawyer, unsurprisingly was closeted with Carnon's senior management. What was immediately apparent was that SC was placing increasing emphasis on the geotechnical aspects of mining at depth. On the 420 level all the drawpoints in the footwall tramming drift had been pattern bolted with resin grouted 19mm rebar. On the new 470 fathom level 150mm x 150mm RSJs had been placed to support the back of that level station and a composite fill had been blown over the steel caps. Also, where the conveyor decline passed through the Great Crosscourse, a little above 470 level, full steel arch support had been placed. I was also pleased to learn that SC were introducing down-dip rib pillars in low grade zones to reduce the hydraulic radius of stope hangingwall spans. At a depth below surface of over 2800 feet geotechnical conditions were now influencing development layouts and stope design. With the ground stability problems at Robinson's Shaft a decision had been made to connect the bottom of the Tuckingmill decline with a vertical Alimak raise from the 380 level. That would be equipped with a simple hoisting gear and the Mines Inspectorate would certify it as a second exit. The primary exit, of course, being the new twin cages operating in Cooks Kitchen Shaft.

The new 400 level pump station construction was well advanced with the installation of new multi-stage Sulzer pumps, each rated at 1MW, which could pump to surface through the new 250mm rising main in Cooks Shaft. However the emergency diesel-generator sets still required to be synchronised with the SWEB supply.

With an ore expectancy of 1,500 t/vm, more than double Wheal Jane (WJ), it made sense to increase SC output to 210,000 tonnes/year whilst reducing WJ's output to 160,000 tonnes/year maintaining the WJ concentrator at its 370,000 tonnes/year capacity. Carnon proposed to increase SC production even further to 240,000 tonnes/year. That also made sense since the SC rom grade was appreciably higher than WJs and the metallurgical recovery on SC ore was almost 10% higher than WJ ore. Finally WJ was squeezed through lack of developed ore and would remain so until the next level off the ramp-decline had been developed, whilst SC developed ore position was strong. All in all a win, win, win management decision.

The following day Keith and I spent in the geological and engineering offices. SC ore reserves were strong at 3.86 million tonnes at 1.5% Sn, whereas WJ was markedly less so at 1.59 million tonnes at 0.97% Sn, with additional Zn, and Cu values. As expected reserves had risen at SC and fallen at WJ. Carnon's latest quarterly report showed that the total labour force had increased from 553 to 562. The actual SC and WJ operations did not appear to carry too many people but the Technical Services Department seemed hugely over-manned with 32 staff and 16 hourly paid. Mining costs at SC were £36.7/tonne mined and £34.8/tonne mined at WJ and the combined weighted overall cost for Carnon was £52.6/tonne mined and milled. By world standards it was still very high. As a result of the dramatic drop in world tin prices the direct operating loss was now £11.7/tonne mined and treated which would imply an annual loss on direct operations of £4.3 million - worrying times indeed for Cornish mining.

I drove back to Mawgan Porth to collect Gillian from Pats and we made our way back to Gorsty. Again I had to get my head down and finish my brief report for the DTI as soon as possible, since I had had a call from Jim at the World Bank (WB) who wished me to join their mission to Zambia at the end of next week. Phew, deep breath, welcome to job No. 072. Jim assured me that the job would not overrun as all his guys wanted to be home for Christmas. Well, that certainly was a relief!

40

The WB had arranged my flight tickets Heathrow to Lusaka return with the American Express office in Haymarket together with a quantity of Amex travellers cheques. They really were a good client in helping ones cash flow stay positive. I went up to London by train in the morning to collect tickets and cheques and then took a day room at one of the Heathrow hotels before going to Terminal 4 to catch the overnight BA flight to Harare (Salisbury) and then Lusaka. I didn't see a sign of the WB guys, but then they would have been in the First-Class lounge.

The flight was uneventful and I was interested to wander around Harare airport for a brief look-see at Zimbabwe. In fact the airport looked like any other in central Africa. One had a better look at the fertile surrounding countryside as we took off in the early morning for the short hop to Lusaka. Still no sign of the WB guys, but with Laissez Passes (Diplomatic Passports) they were obviously whisked through Immigration and Customs. I eventually ran them to earth on the Terrace of the Pamodzi Hotel, where I recognised Dick, the WB metallurgical engineer.

It was eighteen months since I'd last been to Zambia with Simon of Wardell Armstrong looking at the gemstone industry, but the old Pamodzi still felt quite homely. As usual that afternoon we had a "get-to-know-you" meeting with ZCCM senior management in Lusaka. Basically the WB mission was an update on ZCCM's Copperbelt operations. As the only mining engineer on the team I was expected to visit each of the four Divisions, Nchanga, Mufulira, Nkana and Luanshya. After that in conjunction with Dick we had to produce a five year copper production forecast and a Mining Capital Investment programme. All this to be undertaken in no more than eleven days, so quite a doddle really!

Early next morning we flew with RoanAir to Kitwe's Southdowns airport. I was pleased to be based at the comfortable Nchanga Directors Lodge. My first trip was to Nchanga's LOB underground mine. This was my first visit to that mine which operated a unique (for me) continuous down-dip "longwall" caving system. I had no previous experience of that type of mining so I had to be on a swift learning curve. What was immediately apparent was the large amount of development required. The system required experienced miners to control the cave draw such that the interface between broken ore and the caved waste remained horizontal in order to minimise ore loss and the "piping" of waste into the finger raises. The caved ore was recovered by two drum electric scrapers operating from herring-bone scram drifts. The in situ ore grade was very high, close to 10% Cu, but the ultimate draw grade (including waste dilution) was closer to 3.2% Cu. In spite of that and a large labour force the LOB underground mine was one of the cheapest ZCCM producers per Kg of copper.

A major problem at the LOB mine was the presence of a surface Tailings Dump (TD1) overlying the A Block reserve. The present ZCCM schedule showed that the LOB would mine the lower portion of A Block before the upper portion was mined from the Nchanga Open Pit (NOP). That was obviously incorrect and dangerous since the LOBs down-dip caving system would, in essence, undercut and cave the NOP's ultimate hangingwall slope. The upper, or shallower, A Block must be mined first through the NOP before the lower A Block was mined by the LOB. It was essential that surface hydraulicking remove the TD1 dump as soon as possible to permit NOP mining of A Block. However there were serious problems with the Tailings Leach 3 (TL3) plant because of shortages of sulphuric acid and lime as well as plant/process difficulties such that current production was removing 2.7 million tonnes/year only of dump material rather than the 9.0 million tonnes/year planned. Big problem for both LOB and NOP production - for sure ZCCM production forecasts would not be achieved.

The NOP was a very large open pit. It was scheduled to mine over six million tonnes/year of ore and 30 BCM/year of waste (about 84 million tonnes). It had a huge fleet of 101 units (100 & 120t class, mainly Unit Rig and WABCO trucks). However overall truck availabilities were low, under 50%. That had seriously delayed waste stripping so that fully developed ore within the pit was only 320,000 tonnes or just over three weeks production. At the risk of stating the obvious that was a frighteningly small quantity of ore available to be dug with an annual target of six million tonnes of ore. A new trolley assist line had been installed on the southern, footwall side, but like the original trolley line on the hangingwall waste ramp was not in use. Why not? Those trolley lines would greatly increase up-ramp haulage speed, as well as reduce costs since electric power from the Kariba dam was much cheaper than imported diesel fuel. The number of blast-hole drills and rope shovels appeared adequate for both ore and waste quantities. The constraint on production was insufficient waste stripping capacity due to low truck availabilities.

Both LOB and NOP ore passed to the Nchanga concentrator. It was presently treating just under 9.5 million tonnes/year. As noted earlier the Tailings Leach Plant was well below scheduled output on account of numerous operational difficulties and shortage of sulphuric acid. My final visit at the Nchanga Division was to the Konkola No. 1 shaft mine. Output was just over 1 million tonnes/year or about 3,500 tonnes/day from sub-level open stoping. The main production difficulty was a shortage of drifter spares. The mine was clean and well run with excellent engineering facilities to handle the huge water inflow of 350,000m^3/d or 77 million gals/day. Konkola was believed to be the wettest mine in the world pumping 100 tonnes of water for each tonne of ore hoisted. (NB compare Wheal Jane tin mine in Cornwall which pumped 80 tonnes of water for each tonne of ore hoisted). The power load on the pumps was a staggering 40MW. Thank goodness for cheap power from the Kariba dam hydro scheme! I also visited the project office of Mineral Resource Development Ltd (MRDL) of the USA. That natural resource consulting company was undertaking a feasibility study of reopening the No. 3 Shaft area with the goal of mining three million tonnes/year. It was an ambitious scheme taking nearly ten years and costing around US$ 500 million. In truth it was hard to believe such a project would be economically viable.

Mufulira was the largest underground mine on the Copperbelt. Current production was around 5 million tonnes/year but would almost certainly fall in the coming years on account of the mines "squeezed" position with less than seven months Fully Developed reserves ahead of stoping. In addition the Mining at Depth, or MAD project, was running over a year late on account of sinking delays on the SV1 and SV2 internal shafts.

The mine was scheduling a production of 4.2 million tonnes/year from below the 1040 level. I did not think that was feasible. Ore reserves between the 1040 and 1540 levels were 39.6 million tonnes indicating an ore expectancy of nearly 80,000 t/vm. Application of the 10% rule implied a sustainable production rate of 8,000 tonnes/day or only 2.65 million tonnes/year. If one applied Taylor's Rule annual production was calculated to be 2.45 million tonnes/year. Close agreement to my 10% OE rule and much, much less than the 4.2 million tonnes/year planned by Mufulira. ZCCM had to face the fact that the mine's orebody strike length was rapidly reducing at depth and the diminishing ore expectancy simply could not support the mining rate proposed. In the short term the mine must increase development advances by introducing electro-hydraulic jumbos for drilling headings rather than the inadequate jackleg machines. It was nothing short of farcical to see those hand held machines and wooden platform used to drill large 17m² headings. A total mismatch with a 5 cy diesel LHD.

At the Nkana Division I visited the underground Mindola section. Here it was encouraging to see that improvements in development advance had increased the fully developed reserve cover to thirteen months. That had produced a win, win with increased tonnage at a higher grade. As at Mufulira the mine was introducing electro-hydraulic Tamrock jumbos to replace the hand held jackleg machines for development drilling. The Mindola section was also embracing new bulk mining methods such as Vertical Crater Retreat, or VCR mining. That method had been developed in Canada by CIL and INCO during the 1970s. For the trial VCR stope the mine was using a mission DTH rig drilling vertical 165mm diameter holes sequentially advancing upwards, blasting down into a trough-undercut with ore recovery through flank drawpoints by diesel LHDs. Apart from the advantage of reduced stope development it was good to see a Copperbelt mine using modern mining methods. The Mindola sub-vertical re-deepening project was running about six months behind schedule. The CSV shaft had reached the 5220 level and cross cutting back under the main Mindola shaft had been completed. Thereafter it was planned to deepen the Mindola shaft by drilling a pilot hole from the current shaft sump through to the 5220 level and back reaming the pilot hole, with final slashing to full shaft size. Although behind schedule it was encouraging to note the good clean mining on this important shaft project.

My final underground visit was to the Baluba mine of the Luanshya Division. Because of basic design problems with the No. 1 shaft steelwork, hoisting output had been restricted to 9,000 tonnes/day or about 2.75 million tonnes/year (ref job No. 032). That would be 600,000 tonnes/year less than that envisaged in the expansion project. However since the mine was very "squeezed" with less than three months cover on Fully Developed reserves, the forced reduction in output would provide a little more breathing space. The Baluba orebody was rapidly flattening down-dip and a new mining method such as drift and fill or variations on room & pillar must replace the current sub-level blast-hole open stoping in use in the upper levels where the dip was steeper. It was good to see that the poor Eimco 915 and 925 LHDs (supplied by an earlier WB loan?) were being replaced with Toro 150D and 400D LHDs - the best on the market.

Dick and I had a meeting with the Divisional GMs and the ZCCM Operations Director at Kalulushi. A listing of ZCCM's latest (March 1989) ore reserves for each of the ten ore sources were presented. In addition a very illuminating summary of the fall in Fully Developed reserves over the past eight years perfectly demonstrated the "squeezed" state of all mines. With the exception of the small Chibuluma underground mine, Fully Developed reserves had halved. At Mufulira, the largest underground mine, reserves were now only 46% of what they were in 1981. That was, without doubt, the core problem affecting copper and cobalt production right across the Copperbelt. That lack of developed reserves blocks ahead of mining had a triple negative effect on metal outturn. Ore production declined and as a consequence of a tonnage shortfall, waste got put into the ore stream and thus rom grade declined. The reduced mill head grade inevitably meant a lower metallurgical recovery since the concentrators were operated to give a constant tailings grade. If the tonnage, grade and recovery were each down 10% the overall recovered metal would be down by 27% - a significant fall. At least all the GMs agreed that everything must be done to mechanise development.

If that wasn't enough we then considered the delays on all ZCCM's major Mining Capital Investment Programme. There were many other smaller capital projects all of which were behind their respective schedules. Why? Obviously part of the problem was the delay in receiving foreign exchange from the Bank of Zambia (BoZ). Another problem was the shortage of experienced front-line supervisors, especially underground. When Anglo and RCM were nationalised to form ZCCM, a significant number of the expat labour force took early retirement or left for South Africa, Australia or Canada. That perforce meant rapid Zambianisation with, perhaps, not suitably experienced people. On that cheerful note (!) we flew back to Lusaka and the Pamodzi Hotel, where Dick and I had to work our socks off to come up with the WB Five Year Production Forecast. Of course it was going to be quite a lot lower than ZCCM's forecast, and Jim, the WB leader, stressed that we (Dick and I) must be able to justify our estimates.

The wrap-up meeting with ZCCM senior management in Lusaka took place on the 18th December. Our forecast (well, the WB's, actually) for 89/90 was 451,000 tonnes of finished copper, declining over the next three years to 400,000 tonnes, then rising marginally to 404,000 tonnes in 94/95. In broad terms our finished copper outputs were 10% to 12% lower than ZCCMs. We justified that by referring to the development squeeze on all underground mines and the shortfall of waste stripping in the NOP. Delays on all major capital projects. In particular the new TL3 tailings plant was running at less than 30% of its design capacity, meaning a shortfall of 20,000 tonnes/year finished copper. I don't think the WB team made many friends with the GMs and senior management, but no one flatly refused to accept our estimates. In truth everyone knew that ZCCM was in dire straits. Of course they (ZCCM) weren't going to be too rude anyway - they wanted the WB's money to keep them afloat. In fact a grim production outlook should/could help them persuade the WB that they did need help. Their big problem was how to get the WB's money out of the BoZ, since the WB's loans were made to governments. Fortunately that was not one of our problems.

That was it. Nobody in the WB team wanted to hang around so we all made haste to catch the evening BA flight back to Heathrow. On arrival, the WB guys headed for the transit lounge for an onward flight to Washington and I made for the RailAir coach to take me to Reading station. Before I went Jim asked me to get my report over to the WB by mid January. I said no problem. That would leave Christmas and New Year clear. The old Cotswold Line train got me to Worcester by mid-afternoon, followed by a taxi home.

It was now the 20th December and we collected Sproggs from St Richards for the winter break. A couple of days later we loaded up the car and trundled off to Mawgan Porth for a five day holiday with Pat and Tony. It was great that Tony was on home leave from his lighthouse duties with Trinity House. He was very good at treating Sproggs like an adult and, in fact, I think Sproggs was just a little wary of him. It was a really good family Christmas and Sproggs found some local guys to muck around with. We headed back to Gorsty the day after Boxing Day as I had to get stuck in on my report for the WB. The write-up went well but checking and rechecking the tonnage and grade estimates for no less than thirteen separate ore sources (yes, really) including the Tailings Leach Plant (TLP), over the next five years was time consuming. In spite of New Year intervening I sent the report off by DHL Couriers on the 10th January, thus meeting Jim's deadline. I had no other jobs on the blocks which was just as well as there were several faxes and phone calls with both Dick and Jim over the next two weeks.

My old school mate Ollie had been living in Hay-on-Wye on the Welsh border for several years now. Like me he enjoyed a good walk with our dogs followed by a couple of pints in a local pub. One of our walks was over Hergst Ridge from Kington down to the Oak pub in Gladestry. On the way I could bore Ollie's socks off whilst pointing out the delights of the nearby limestone quarries at Nash Rocks. We even walked up Hanter Hill to get a better look at the quarry (for me!). We realised that that particular walk over Hergst Ridge was part of the Offas Dyke long distance trail. It got us thinking perhaps we could manage the 178 mile trek from Chepstow on the Severn estuary to Prestatyn in North Wales. So we did a little planning. I bought a copy of the OS book of Offa's Dyke and visited the Dyke's Visitor Centre in Knighton to get a listing of B & B places along the way. We were both in our mid fifties and perhaps felt it was now or never. Ollie had taken early retirement from the FO and could organise a two week break from his volunteer work. As I was self-employed with no outstanding jobs at the moment we decided to go towards the end of March.

I stayed overnight at Ollie's place in Hay and his son, Will, drove us down to the start of the walk where the river Wye joins the Severn estuary in the shadow of the magnificent Severn Bridge. The weather was perfect, cool, crisp and sunny. Ollie, ex-Marines, set of at a cracking pace, much more quickly than my more steady plod. We soon arrived at our usual "dog walking pace", well why wouldn't you? We were glad we'd decided on March before the leaves were out since the views of the lower Wye valley were spectacular including a splendid sight of Tintern Abbey from the cliffs on the eastern shore. We only walked about eight miles to our first B & B in St Brievals, but I wondered if I was up to tackling the remaining 170 miles through much more hilly country. No matter, I slept well after a couple of beers in the local pub.

The next day we continued north up the Wye valley to the Naval Monument on a high spur overlooking the compact town of Monmouth. We descended from the eastern bluff and crossed the Wye into the town, where we stopped for a pie and pint. Refreshed we turned west and in about four miles located a farmhouse for our second night stop on the edge of the Trothy river valley. The day's tally was about twelve miles and I was feeling distinctly knackered. Our third day continued westwards through rolling countryside towards Llantilio Crossenny then NW towards the White Castle where we stopped to have a wander around that isolated 12th century fortification. From there we passed NE of the Skirrid to cross the A456 and turn north for a short distance to the Rising Sun pub in Pandy where we spent our third night. Although tired after another twelve miles walk I had begun to get accustomed to steady walking. We had an early dinner for an early start next morning.

We were underway shortly after 7.30 on a glorious sunny day, everywhere white from the heavy overnight frost. After crossing the main Abergavenny - Hereford rail line we had a steep climb up Hatterall ridge onto the eastern edge of the Black Mountains. It was a marvelous day for walking and although peaty and sometimes boggy along the crest the view eastwards across the Midlands was fantastic. Ever gluttons for punishment (and food) we decided to drop off the crest westwards down into Llanthony Priory for lunch. That was the easy bit. The slog back up to the crest, nearly 1300ft, after a largely liquid lunch was made in low gear. Further north along the crest we passed the highest point on Offa's Dyke path at 2306ft. As the path followed the county boundary between Powys and Herefordshire, it was also the highest point in that English county. We stopped on Hay Bluff to watch several brightly coloured hang gliders launching themselves towards the Wye valley. It looked an easy way down. We eventually trudged into Hay-on-Wye around 6pm having covered twenty miles (including the diversion into Pandy) and climbed over 3,000ft Tired yes, but not knackered. We were definitely becoming walkers. Ollie's friends house was almost opposite the Blue Boar, so naturally we refuelled in that hostelry.

Our fifth day started with an easy walk alongside the Wye, but where the river swung east, then south-east we continued north into the border hill country. We stopped for a pint at our regular pub in Gladestry before climbing Hergst Ridge and dropping down into Kington to spend our fifth night in a small B & B. Our sixth days walk from Kington to Knighton, about sixteen miles, covered some glorious hill walking country lying to the east of Radnor Forest. Plenty of up and down, into and out of the east-west river valleys such as the Arrow, Lugg and Teme. In Knighton we arrived at a small guest house to be greeted by the Polish owner, Danuta, with a very welcoming "Velcom, veery travellers, I haf a sixteen year old daughter to revife you". Well that certainly got our attention, but sad to say we didn't meet the daughter (apparently at evening classes in Hereford, which rather begged the revival invitation). No matter, after a good soak in the bath to reinvigorate the legs we repaired to the George & Dragon pub where Gillian and Peter, Ollie's FO friend, joined us for dinner. In truth I think they both wanted to see how "the walkers" were faring.

Out of Knighton we immediately crossed the river Teme and struggled up the very steep Panpunton Hill. Thereafter it was glorious hill walking over Llanfair Hill. However everything came to a sudden stop as we were descending into the Clun river valley, as Ollie turned his ankle climbing through a stone stile. That was it - walk over! I continued down to the B4368 road and walked west the half mile to Newcastle-on-Clun where I phoned Gillian from a public call box (mobile phones were not yet a reality). I explained exactly where we were and Gillian said she would be there inside an hour. I returned to Offa's Dyke path and helped Ollie hobble down to the road. Duly picked up by the memsahib we returned to Gorsty somewhat deflated. Ollie stayed for a further three days with us (recuperation?) since he had lent his own place in Hay to friends. We said we'd finish the northern part of the Dyke walk at a later date.

At the start of April I had a call from Colin of Billiton International Metals to come to Leidschendam, The Netherlands to discuss their Zimbabwean Hartley Project. So for job No. 073 I headed for Birmingham airport and an NLM City Hopper flight to Schiphol airport. There I took a taxi for the 22 mile drive SW to Leidschendam. The Billiton offices were well known. Colin wanted another opinion as to whether the proposed herring-bone and scraper system was the correct approach for mining the flat dipping MSZ zone within the Great Dyke. There was a geotechnical report from SRK which showed that the hangingwall pyroxenites had a high intact rock strength of plus 200 Mpa. However the rock mass was extensively fractured (0.5 to 1.5m frequency) and those joints were weak, coated with chlorite or serpentinite. The net result was weak ground that would not permit large unsupported hangingwall spans. Thus why go to the trouble to fully hold the hangingwall as required by the herring-bone/scraper method? Subject to checking with SRK that there were no other engineering difficulties (eg; surface water; aquifers; property) then I suggested that an en echelon down-dip caving system could be used. That involved side slashing on strike, advancing in a down-dip direction. It would need low profile drills, loaders, trucks and shuttle cars. The working faces would be supported by grouted rebar and weldmesh and the cave would be maintained to follow about 6m behind the rill stope face. It was all wrapped up in a single day but Colin seemed happy to take up my proposal directly with both SRK and the Hartley Project mining guys. So back to Schiphol, Birmingham and finally Gorsty - an interesting trip, besides which I like the Dutch.

However I only had two weeks to cut the grass and prepare the vegetable patch, before Jaime from COMSUR called asking me to visit Aguilar again with Carlos, thus job No. 074. He asked me to come to La Paz first for discussions. So over the third weekend of April Gillian drove me to Birmingham for the NLM flight to Amsterdam where I inter-lined to KLM for the flight to Lima changing again to LAB for the final leg to La Paz. That time the COMSUR driver took me a little further downtown to a furnished company flat that they had recently bought. It didn't have the central position or ambience of the Hotel Sucre, but was quite comfortable, albeit self-catering. It was though a steady twenty minute walk uphill to the COMSUR office, so that I always arrived somewhat breathless, much to the amusement of the secretarial staff. There was a briefing session for Carlos and me with Jaime. His main concerns were that:- CMASA were not using the correct marginal COG for current operations; the mine planning section still required mining engineers; an open-pit design had not been completed; most stoping statistics were still declining; the Wright Engineers feasibility study for a 50% concentrator expansion had to be matched by a mining expansion programme, which required a capital budget. We said we'd follow up on all those queries and planned to spend eight days at Aguilar.

Carlos and I flew with AA to Jujuy the following morning and the CMASA ute duly transported us to the rarefied atmosphere of the mine by late afternoon, but, hey, no siroche again - thank goodness. As usual we first went to see Pablo in the geological office. Here we encountered our first big problem, Pablo had resigned after twelve years at Aguilar. For the mine that was a serious blow. Pablo was an excellent, practical mining geologist with a good grasp of statistics as well as the necessity for collecting geotechnical data. There had been a personality clash with Oscar, the Mine Superintendent and Miguel, the GM. He had accepted a position with a new mining outfit in Ecuador. He would be sadly missed by the Aguilar Geological Department. Both Carlos and I wished him well.

The underground ore reserve position was unchanged from our previous visit. However additional surface exploration work, both DD and trenching, had outlined three separate areas containing nearly 1.7 million tonnes with grades of 2.5% Pb, 3.0% Zn and 68g/t Ag at a 3.0% COG. Pablo reckoned that this would increase to around 2.0 million tonnes when all the DD work was complete. Although not high grade, that tonnage would be low-cost, mined through simple side-cut open pits.

Examination of recent operating statistics indicated that the catch-all MCF had increased from 0.85 to close to 0.9. We were all unsure why that was happening - perhaps less waste dilution, or a change from square-set mining to underhand and sub-level L/H stoping or? The Geological Department had commenced a geostatistical examination of grade-distribution bias using some Chilean software and the Compaq 386 computer. That would obviously produce a far more rigorous analysis than the previous work of grade-distribution of ore reserve blocks which were of widely varying size. After our earlier criticism of the 8.2% combined metals COG the mine was now working to a 6.2% operational COG - good. Provided the mine could deliver 2224 tonnes/day with that operational COG and maintain an 88% metallurgical recovery then Aguilar would meet its zinc concentrate contract with the Sulfacid smelter.

Over the past few months Ing Delfor, the Buenos Aires based Technical Manager, had been acting as de facto CME for Aguilar. He visited the mine every month and directed and coordinated all mine planning activities. In particular he was heavily involved in the mine expansion to 3,000 tonnes/day. He was the key link man with Wright Engineers over the preparation of the concentrator expansion study. Overall the expanded mine production would derive from 150,000 tonnes/year from open pits and 900,000 tonnes/year from underground thus providing 3,000 tonnes/day for 350 days/year. That schedule had considered daily outputs of 39t/d for C & F stopes, 24t/d for underhand stopes and 260t/d for sub-level L/H stopes. Praise the Lord, square-set stopes had been eliminated altogether. So Carlos and I had achieved something over the past 2.5 years - hallelujah!

Recent stoping performance had, in fact, declined in spite of the introduction of new Seco S250 jackhammers and longer drill steel. Apart from the increasing importance of underhand stoping at the expense of square-set the figures were disappointing. Overall TMS was down and the drilling yield was only 0.88 tonnes/m. The percentage use of ANFO in stoping was still less than 60%. Apparently the mine experienced problems loading prilled ANFO (from Chile) with the Portanol loaders. The prills were breaking down and coalescing, which blocked the venturi aperture, hence the continued use of ANFO-Aguilar home-made cartridges. Both the prills & loader needed modifying.

Although the number of stopes breaking more than 1,000 tonnes/month had increased that had been achieved by increasing the shifts worked per day whilst both drill and explosive yields had fallen. By contrast the trial sub-level L/H stope had regularly delivered over 400 tonnes/day with an output of 21.2 TMS and a drilling yield of 9.05t/m, almost a quantum jump improvement over cut-and-fill and underhand drilling yields. Although filling of the trial stope was not yet completed the initial Putzmeister pumped hydraulic backfill had produced good results. The bottom 5m sill with 9% cement gave 14.0 Kg/sq cm uniaxial crushing strength and the next 5m with 5.5% cement gave 7.3 Kg/sq cm, both at 56 days. To all intents and purpose the sub-level L/H stope and subsequent fill had demonstrated the veracity and production potential of the method.

For the 50% expansion project (2,000 to 3,000 tonnes/day) the mine had to complete 4750m of capital development comprising the ramp-decline, two vent declines, two vent raises and three fill raises for an estimated cost of US$ 2.0 million. Additional mining equipment was estimated to require a further US$ 6.2 million for electro-hydraulic drills (both L/H and jumbo),

LHDs, trolley locos, haul trucks etc. Since Wright Engineers did not appear to have upgraded the two small jaw crushers, the mine capital costs included two Rammer Breakers. Wright's estimate for the concentrator expansion was US$ 11.1 million including EPCM and contingency. With a further US$ 0.85 million for increased compressor capacity and an additional fill preparation plant the total cost of the expansion project was estimated to be US$ 20.2 million. All those costs included a 40% import tax on CIF value. Total Aguilar direct operating costs were estimated to be US$ 22/tonne mined and treated.

That wrapped up Carlos and my visit and we headed down to Jujuy for a session in the CMASA offices for some clarification on cost data. We stayed overnight and caught the early morning AA flight back to La Paz. Having deposited my "stuff" in the company flat I made my way up to the COMSUR office for an afternoon debrief with Jaime. As usual there was some good news and bad news. The good news was that the mine was now operating to a 6.2% combined metals COG and meeting it's zinc concentrate terms with Sulfacid. Also good news was that Ing Delfor from the Buenos Aires office was acting as CME for new projects and liaising with Wright Engineers. The sub-level L/H stoping method had proved suitable for the lower levels at Aguilar and slow and expensive square-set stoping was being phased out. A total budget for the expansion project was nearing completion. The bad news was the resignation of the Chief Geologist, Pablo, with no experienced replacement. There were serious shortcomings in front-line mine supervision since nearly all yardsticks for production performance had declined. All of these aspects were discussed in detail with Goni, Jaime, Jim, Mario, Stan, Carlos and myself over the next four days.

On the 3rd May I cleared El Alto airport for the short LAB flight to Lima and onto KLM's flight for Amsterdam. Here, as usual, I transferred to NLM City Hopper for Birmingham. Although I was only travelling with a permitted cabin bag (a Gladstone brief case) dear old Customs were waiting for me. I was pulled out of the arriving passenger line by name and taken into a small interrogation room. They wanted to take my bag off and examine it, but I said they should open it in front of me (obviously I'd watched some drug smuggling films - hey ho!). Well they went bananas when they discovered I had a small mirror in my sponge bag. Out came the dusting powder, presumably to see if I had "cut" any coke on the mirror's surface. Sounds exciting but it was pretty worrying, especially when one of the Custom's guys said as I left "we'll catch you out, Mr S". I was, I hoped, not becoming paranoid, but Customs were really starting to hassle me. Apart from anything it was seriously delaying my transit through the airport.

Over the next week or so I finished my report on Aguilar and sent it off to COMSUR by DHL Couriers. They had never let me down over the past ten years. I'd no sooner finished the Aguilar report when I had another call from John at the DTI in London. Could I join a DTI monitoring visit to Carnon in Cornwall next week? Yes, welcome to job No. 075. Gillian, who had now become a "bank" nurse at St Michael's Hospice, rather than a volunteer, managed to obtain a weeks leave. We drove down to Cornwall on the 14th May and I dropped her off in Mawgan Porth. I continued SW to the Greenbank Hotel in Falmouth. Here I joined John and also Neil from the government's Warren Springs Laboratory (WSL). Later Keith the BGS geologist joined us. Our broadbrush scope of work was an update on current operations at Carnon's WJ and SC mines and the WJ concentrator together with a review of direct operating costs.

Well things had certainly changed since our last visit six months ago. Carnon had made the decision to stop all development at WJ and allow the mine to flood to 15 level. At WJ mining was now concentrated on the remaining accessible higher grade reserves in the upper levels prior to a planned mine closure towards year end. The low tin price had forced Carnon to take drastic steps to reduce costs. The WJ mine workforce had reduced from 174 to 121 over the past six months. As noted on previous visits WJ was a wet mine pumping up to 13,000 gals/min, the actual tin lodes acting as aquifers. The action of air and water on the sulphide rich ore as mining took place ensured that the water was very acidic, around pH 3.0. Thus with the planned closure of WJ a major item to be considered was how to handle the mine drainage water. Carnon's current ideas as to what to do with the WJ site were somewhat ephemeral - a mining heritage site; all-weather tourist centre; light industrial site; hydroponics; underground water storage and heat-exchange. At this stage all pie-in-the-sky with no engineering or costing.

We stressed that the three urgent engineering aspects vis-a-vis mine closure were mine pumping, mill water supply and tailings disposal. Should mine pumping cease then the mine would flood to the County Adit Level (CAL) and if the WJ mill was still required then process water could be pumped from the CAL horizon. The underground hydraulic environment at WJ was complex and we thoroughly endorsed Carnon's inclination to approach specialist hydrological consultants Watermeyer Legge Piesold Uhlmann (WLPU) to examine the situation.

Likewise at SC all capital development has been stopped. That included the shaft deepening project at the 445 and 470 levels and associated facilities such as new crusher station and the new 400 level pump station. No further work had been undertaken to connect the Tuckingmill Decline to the 380 level by a vertical Alimak raise. That was also reflected in SC manpower figures, down from 230 to 201 over the past six months, but the latest SC ten year plan showed the SC mine workforce falling further to 179. In fact that plan showed SC delivering only 175,000 tonnes/year in 1991, to minimise operating costs, thereafter rising to 250,000 tonnes/year from 1996 onwards. Both the ore expectancy and total ore reserve position at SC could sustain that rate of production. Their plan envisaged using the WJ concentrator until 1993, whilst modifications/upgrading were undertaken to the SC concentrator. After 1993 the modified SC concentrator would be recommissioned with the tailings being pumped to a new Wheal Maid facility. Exactly what happened to the WJ mine site, plant and equipment after 1993 was unspecified. Obviously certain WJ plant, eg the standby diesel-generator sets, would find a welcome home at SC.

The SC ten year plan showed a direct operating costs for 1991 of £51.54/tonne mined & treated using the WJ concentrator. On those costs Carnon estimated a Breakeven tin price of £4133/tonne. However should the head grade drop to 1.4% Sn and metallurgical recovery to 80% the Breakeven price for tin would soar to £4700/tonne, well above the current market price. In a nutshell Carnon's long-term survival was slim and the DTI extremely unlikely to see any of its "investment" back. Hey ho, governments just should not get involved in mining. A prime example was the Zambian government nationalising RCM and Anglo to form the State company ZCCM, where the Copperbelt was going to hell in a handcart.

On that gloomy note John and Neil headed off for Truro station whilst Keith motored to Devon and I drove to Mawgan Porth to pick up Gillian. John had asked me to compile all the technical visit notes and to that effect both Keith and Neil had given me their outline hand written comments. Thus back at Gorsty the Monitoring Visit Report now expanded to twenty pages and took me the next week to compile. With nothing else immediately on the horizon I could get stuck in to the garden. We also went over to St Richards most Saturday afternoons to watch a school cricket match.

One particular Saturday in mid June could not be missed as it was the school first eleven versus the "Dads". The school batted first and made a reasonable score helped by some erratic fast-medium bowling from me. However the "Dads" batting was woeful and I tried to lighten the gloom by wearing Sproggs Devils hat when I went in to bat at No 7 or 8. At least it raised a surprised laugh from the school team, such that their bowling went to pot and I managed to score a boundary and a few singles. Having a swipe I was unsurprisingly stumped. As we had agreed before the match the "Dads" duly lost, but to be honest there was never any chance that we might win. Oh the arrogance of age!

41

Out of the blue Don, from Golder Associates (GA), called asking if I would provide some engineering input into a pumping problem their client, Ret-Ser Engineering Agency (RSEA), were experiencing in the construction of the Sungai Piah Hydro-Electric Project in Malaysia. In spite of my protestation that I was not a pump/pumping specialist Don said it was a straight forward de-watering job of an inclined access tunnel to the Lower Power Station. GA were advising RSEA on geotechnical conditions but RSEA were meeting much more ground-water than indicated in the civil excavation specifications issued by the National Electricity Board of the States of Malaysia. My feeling was "if it's so straightforward, why do they need me - a scapegoat or what?" I suggested GA should approach somebody like Weir Pumps for specialist advice. However Don said that for "face" reasons, or more probably "loss of face", GA, wanted a pump wallah to appear under their banner as an individual subcontractor and he felt I'd fit the bill. Somewhat reluctantly I said OK to job No. 076.

I left Heathrow on a Malaysian Airlines 747 for Kuala Lumpur (KL) on the 22nd June. At KL I had about a three hours wait for a connecting flight north to Ipoh. While waiting at the bar I was fascinated to note several German 747s full of package European tourists transiting to flights for the Penang beach resorts. When last at KL airport on my way to Manila in the early '70s there were very few tourists to be seen. The advent of the 747 Jumbo had dramatically increased mass package tourism. The 140 mile flight to Ipoh only took 45 minutes. I didn't see much of Ipoh, the centre of the Malaysian tin industry, as there was a RSEA ute waiting to drive me to Sungai Piah in the Cameron Highlands, which lay about forty miles east of Ipoh. The road climbed steadily through numerous rubber plantations, but above 1,000m altitude the plantations gave way to heavily wooded country. Many of the trees were tropical flowering varieties swarming with giant butterflies - very spectacular.

The RSEA campsite was pretty remote with PortaKabin type accommodation and a communal mess. The RSEA labour force was Taiwanese with the exception of some Malay drivers. The sum total of my Chinese speaking ability was zilch, but I eventually got it across that

I'd like to find the Project manager/Boss Man/Honcho/Jeffe/El Supremo etc. The driver took me to a double-deck office PortaKabin where I found the resident Canadian consulting engineer. He was a tall, scratchy fellow (unsurprising really the contract was behind schedule), who merely said "so you're the Golders pump expert. Well get those damn pumps sorted so we can get on with the construction work". I said I understood no Chinese could he find me a Malay with some pidgin English who could accompany me underground. He reluctantly agreed and I was dismissed. So no Commonwealth bonhomie there then.

In fact it was a fairly simple problem to solve. The Access Tunnel to the Lower Power Station (LPS) had been driven down-grade at minus 11.25% with dimensions 5.5m height by 6.2m width where it reached the LPS location, 1040m from the portal. Here it had been driven 16m horizontal (width of LPS cavern) and then a further 52m down-grade at minus 19% to the High Pressure Drop Shaft (HPDS). A pilot hole for the HPDS had been completed and back reaming was underway whilst side stripping of the LPS cavern roof continued. Average water inflow during development of the Access Tunnel was modest, around 50 litres/s whereas the maximum inflow specified in the contract was 35l/s. However total inflows were now about 120l/s or over 1500 gals/min and the existing pumping layout could not handle that quantity.

Two types of pump were in use - electric submersible sludge pumps and electric high speed single stage centrifugal water pumps. As the Access Tunnel was driven small sumps were excavated at approximately every 100m of linear advance and the low-head submersible sludge pumps handled the water by stage pumping from sump to sump. The submersibles were low-head pumps running on "snore" and handling dirty, gritty water, sand and sludge. Three types were in use, Grindex, Weda & Flygt with discharges ranging from 12 to 25l/s against heads of 25 to 55 m. They were driven by 220 volt, 50 Hz, 2900 rpm direct coupled 2 pole AC induction motors with abrasion resistant chrome alloy impellers. They were ideal for that initial job and had given very good service.

The problem was with the Ulysses model 125 x 80 - 315 centrifugal water pumps manufactured by CK Engineering in Ipoh. Those pumps were also fitted with 220 volt, 50 Hz, 2900 rpm, 150hp direct coupled AC motors with cast iron (CI) impellers. To date they had given very poor service with very short bearing and impeller life. That model Ulysses was rated at 50 l/s against a 110m total head. I calculated the theoretical velocity head of that pump to be 116 m, which indicated that the pump would be operating close to its limit. I examined about ten discarded Ulysses pump impellers that showed that none had worn out. They had all prematurely failed, half on account of poor castings (manufacturer's fault) and half through poor pump alignment and maintenance routines and/or water hammer and cavitation problems (RSEA's fault). Examination of pump records showed that many impellers had been discarded after only four to eight days!

The Ulysses was a water pump, not sludge, and thus needed to be fed with fairly clean water. So the first, major improvement would be the excavation of a 40m^3 capacity settling sump at circa 1090m from the portal by ramping down off the north side of the Access Tunnel to HPDS. That capacity would provide a residence time of over six minutes with a water inflow of 100 l/s, sufficient to provide a reasonably clean water overflow into the adjacent clean water pump sump. Then RSEA should ask CK Engineering to switch to bronze impellers with their closer quality control and higher mechanical tolerances. Unfortunately there were no operational or maintenance manuals for that Ulysses pump, which was, apparently, a copy of a UK manufacturer. A set of guidelines should be developed to ensure the correct axial location of the back liner and prevent over tightening of the casing bolts and/or incorrect shim packing.

Finally the centrifugal pump's pipework and layout needed radically changing. An intermediate "Water Tank" at 560m from the portal should be removed. All pipeline leaks should be stopped in particular faulty Victaulic gaskets. All extraneous pipe fittings should be removed and one should never throttle pumps on the inlet or suction side. It was apparent that RSEA had used throttling on the suction side and that had caused cavitation, damaging the pumps. To further improve the output of the Ulysses pumps compressed air (at plus 6 bar) could be introduced via a check valve into the 6" delivery line midway between 1090 and 560 and 560 to surface. Just four Ulysses pumps could handle all the inflow. One pair at the new settling sump/clean water sump at 1090 pumping direct to a small holding sump at 560, where the second pair of Ulysses pumps would then pump through to surface. Sounded complicated but, in fact, it was pretty simple. The key problems were poor CI impellers and incorrect assembly/maintenance of pumps plus the overriding aspect of feeding dirty water to a high speed centrifugal water pump.

After three days collecting data and looking at the installation I spent a final day in RSEA's office preparing a brief report and sketches of the Settling Sump and pipe fittings on both the delivery and suction sides of the pump. The sombre resident Canadian consulting engineer was not at all happy with my report. By heck he wasn't, he went ballistic! Hell no they couldn't "stop" to excavate a settling sump, or change all the incorrect or unnecessary pipe fittings. What did I think this was a holiday camp? I was taken aback at first, well you would be wouldn't you? Then I thought, hey I don't work for you Mister. I've found out what the problems were and what needs to be done to fix them. Over to you buddy, your problem, not mine to implement, I'm outta here. With that I exited, found my Malay driver and took off for Ipoh, leaving behind a fuming Canadian. I was glad my client was Golders and not RSEA or the Canadian's firm of power station gurus.

I caught the late afternoon flight from Ipoh back to KL and checked into the pleasant Regent Hotel for the night. The following morning I booked onto the Malaysian Airlines evening flight to Heathrow. I asked the receptionist what should I see whilst in KL for the day. She recommended the Batu Caves only ten miles from KL. So I took a taxi there and they were well worth visiting. As expected they were in limestone terrain and had strong Hindu religious connections. There was a huge (plus 120 ft?) gilt statue of Lord Murugan, said to be the largest Hindu statue outside India. The caves were certainly extensive but although in a spectacular location were spoilt (for me) by the thousands of tourists and Hindu worshipers. No matter, it made a pleasant jaunt for the morning leaving me to wander around KL on foot during the afternoon. It was a very pleasant, bustling, tropical city.

Back at Gorsty Gillian was very excited about the possibility of applying for the job of Practice Nurse at the Fownhope surgery a few miles south of Hereford. She had phoned an old nursing friend, Karla, who had some detailed documentation on what was required for the new role of Practice Nurse. Gillian sent off the application plus, of course, a resume of her SRN qualification and nursing experience in Truro, Stoke, Tanganyika, Tasmania (twice!), Kent and now at St Michaels Hospice just outside Hereford. It was impressive hands-on experience. Gillian's biggest worry was that she would be considered too old, but I said one couldn't get that amount of practical experience as a twenty year old - think positively!

Anyway she was invited for an interview at the surgery in Fownhope. I drove her down and then went for a walk. Afterwards we had lunch in the nearby Mordiford Bridge pub. Gillian felt the interview had gone alright and the Doctor was very impressed with the "stuff" on Practice Nurse protocols. So impressed that he asked Gillian if he could make some copies. They told Gillian that they would let her know, yes or no, by mid August. I made the decision to buy a second car. I placed an order with Steels of Hereford for a new 2 litre Honda Accord. Our existing 1.6 litre hatchback Accord was now nine years old, but still gave reliable service. Whilst awaiting news of the Practice Nurse job I had a call from Jaime of COMSUR asking me to visit both the Porco mine in Bolivia and the Aguilar mine in Argentina in the second week of August.

It was still summer holiday so Sproggs was at home. There had been a bit of trouble at school so we had decided that after two years boarding he would spend his final year at St Richards as a day boy again. In fact he quite looked forward to the school run on the back of the Honda 400/4 motorbike when Gillian needed the car to go to the Hospice. Gillian with Sproggs drove me to Birmingham to catch the NLM flight to Schiphol. As usual it was KLM to Lima and then LAB to La Paz. The COMSUR driver took me to the Plaza Hotel as the new company flat had two other people staying there. In the afternoon I joined Mario, Carlos and Edgar for a meeting with Jaime. Basically our brief was to estimate the mining potential of the Porco mine as well as comment on various mine engineering requirements such as underground haulage, hoisting, ventilation and compressed air.

The next morning the COMSUR plane flew us down to Potosi airport, where a couple of utes drove us SW on the tortuous dirt road to the mine. As usual Mario and I started off by looking at the latest Industrial ore reserve summary. That had been compiled at the end of June and showed 1.5 million tonnes at 16.1% Zn, 1.41% Pb and 2g/t Ag. There were additional Possible reserves at slightly lower grades. The gross Porco reserve was thus 2.96 million tonnes at 16% Zn and 1.2% Pb. However if the correct marginal ore reserve COG of 6.13% Zn were used the tonnage-grade curves indicated a total reserve tonnage of 3.3 million tonnes. All in all a healthy position, but it got better. The mine had used an in situ bulk density figure of

3.0 t/m³, whereas at the average ore reserve grade a better estimate of bulk density would be 3.4 t/m³. At a stroke this increased the total ore reserve tonnage by a further 13%.

Just under 1.0 million tonnes of the Industrial reserves was above the main San Cayetano adit level. The balance was below and must, therefore be hoisted. The three largest veins each had an ore expectancy (OE) of 1,000 t/vm. The Porco veins were narrow width, 0.7 to 1.4m only, steep dipping, circa 70 degrees with typical pinch and swell on both strike and dip directions. However the wall rocks were competent dacite tuff enabling shrink stoping to be used. The fifteen largest veins had a combined OE of 13,810 t/vm. Considering an extraction rate of 10% OE for the three largest veins and 7.5% OE for the other, smaller veins suggested a sustainable mining rate of 1,185, say 1,200 tonnes/day. Taylor's Rule suggested 1158 tonnes/day, which provided a close check. That also assumed that ore loss through an 85% mine recovery was offset by 17.5% waste dilution. Porco's mining potential was estimated to be 1200 tonnes/day and all engineering requirements were based on that output.

Data from two deep DD holes and information on other veins indicated that the vein's depth extent were up to 100% of their strike extents. The main SAP vein had a strike length of 1km and a depth extent of at least 600m was conservative. The San Cayetano level, the lowest adit level, was already 250m below the SAP vein's outcrop. There was thus a strong probability that the SAP vein would continue for 350m below the San Cayetano level. In fact the deep DD holes had intersected good vein structure at the -240 and -275 levels. Past experience at Porco had shown that the other veins virtually doubled the OE of the SAP vein. Thus the total projected tonnage below the San Cayetano level was 2.3 million for an ore expectancy of about 6,000 t/vm. That would sustain a mining rate of 600 tonnes/day. Allowing for waste (10%), moisture (5%) and a design margin (10%) gave a requirement to hoist 765 tonnes/day. With an allowance for a loading box below and a dump bin above, the total hoisting spec for a new shaft would be 435 m.

The mine was currently producing 900 tonnes/day. Current performance was 28 tonnes stope/ day, so that at an expanded 1200 tonnes/day a total of 38 stopes would be needed if single shift working continued. COMSUR should make every effort to operate Porco stoping on at least two shifts/

day, preferably three shifts/day. That would have a huge beneficial effect on requirements for compressed air and ventilation.

The current development yield was 37 tonnes/m at a payability of 65%. However many of Porco stopes commenced off the main level rather than a sub-level driven 5m above rail height. The requirement for stope sub-levels would reduce the development yield to 26 tonnes/m. With an average development advance of 45 m/mth that would require 26 headings. Assuming three shifts/day working the estimated quantities of ventilation air below the San Cayetano level would be as follows:-

Location	No.	Section (ft²)	Velocity (fpm)	Quantity (CFM)
Headings	5	35	150	26250
Active Stopes	7	16 (manway)	300	33600
Loading Station	1	-	100	5000
Pump Chamber	1	-	100	5000
Battery Charge Stn	2	-	150	15000
Store/Mtce shops	2	-	100	10000
Total	-	n/a	n/a	**94850**

Thus circa 100,000 CFM was estimated as the ventilation requirement below the San Cayetano level. With five levels in operation that implied an intake of 20,000 CFM per level. In turn that indicated an air velocity of 425 fpm (2.16 m/s) in each 2.2m by 2.0m main level. With a daily mining rate from below the San Cayetano level of 660 tonnes (inc waste) the total ventilation air intake was about 150 CFM per daily tonne mined. That was the right sort of order. With 85 to ninety workers underground on day shift that would provide more than 1,000 CFM/man, well above the statutory minimum level.

Unsurprisingly it was that ventilation requirement which determined the minimum size for the new No 2 Shaft. Since that shaft would handle men, the downcast air velocity should not exceed 600 fpm (3 m/s). The shaft section must be increased by 30% to provide the effective cross section desired ie. 100,000 (CFM)/600 (fpm) x 1.3 = 20.1 m² or 217 ft². Although a circular shaft would be preferable on most counts, there was no experience of such shafts in Bolivia and I felt it would be prohibitively expensive to bring in overseas shaft sinking contractors. Thus a conventional timber framed rectangular section of 6m by 3.5m was suggested.

The requirement to hoist 765 tonnes/day from 435m depth on a two shifts/day basis required a double-drum rock winder of circa 350hp pulling balanced 2.5 tonnes capacity skips at 6m/s full speed. Those size skips still left room for a large (3m by 2m) single cage and counterweight suitable for handling a 3.5t battery locomotive and lowering the full day shift workforce in under ten minutes. Cage full speed 3m/s only and power requirement about 230hp.

Although a detailed RMS calculation was not undertaken a good approximation was:- Power (kW) = 2 x Net load (t) x g (9.81 m/s/s) x rope speed (m/s). The use of twin skips rather than a large single skip and counterweight was to minimise major hoist components for underground installation. Of course one drum should be clutched to enable hoisting to be undertaken from multiple loading stations. Duty specifications should be sent to winder manufacturers for their detailed recommendations. Nevertheless it was the ventilation duty that determined the correct shaft size.

For the main San Cayetano haulage level COMSUR were contemplating using second-hand rolling stock from the Huari Huari mine. That comprised an 8t trolley locomotive and 4.1m^3 capacity Granby mine cars running on a 61 cm gauge 30 Kg/m rail. The haulage level was graded at 1 in 200 down to the portal and distance from the new No 2 Shaft to the surface grizzly dump was 1200 m. The normal drawbar pull of the 8t loco was 1720 Kg and the maximum 2270 Kg. Under those conditions a full rake would be seven granbys for a net ore load of nearly sixty tonnes. Over 2 shift working the haulage capacity would be 1320 tonnes/day.

The existing Compressor Plant contained three Atlas ER7E (piston) units derated to 1000 CFM each at the San Cayetano adit level, plus one Joy RCS (screw) derated to 930 CFM. A total effective plant output of 3930 CFM. When mining 1200 tonnes/day the maximum compressed air demand would rise to 5840 CFM, a shortfall of over 1900 CFM. Average demand would be 4400 CFM. For good plant operation/maintenance routines the mine should purchase three new ER7E Atlas units, whence average demand would be nearly 65% of installed capacity and maximum demand 84% capacity. Well that wrapped up the first part of job No. 077.

The second part commenced when we retuned to Potosi. Here we were joined by COMSUR's exploration geologist, Jim, for an underground visit to the famous Cerro Rico mine of COMIBOL which lay on the flank of that iconic mountain. In fact the less said about it the better. The mine was in a complete state of dilapidation, to the extent that many main drives had collapsed and we only visited one overhand stope to realise that it would be foolhardy to visit any more. I certainly wasn't game to go down any sinking winzes. A brief walk through the concentrator showed a veritable junk heap of crushing and milling machinery. We rapidly made our escape - definitely not for COMSUR.

Jim, Carlos and I now had yet another assignment to visit the Aguilar mine. From Potosi we took a small diesel rail car due west some eighty miles to Mulatos station on the main Bolivian rail line. Here we boarded the ENFE southbound international train passing through Uyuni and crossing the Bolivian border at Villazon and La Quiaca on the Argentinian side. We finally detrained at Tres Cruces (yes, the very same) where a CMASA ute was waiting to take us on up to Aguilar. At the mine both Jim and Carlos joined consulting geologists, Merwin and Paul (both Americans based in Chile) for a "think tank" on the exploration potential of Aguilar's surrounding area. I went to the geological offices to review the current ore reserve position. Those offices now sadly lacked the stimulating presence of Pablo, the recently departed Chief Geologist.

The reserve position had not changed since my last visit in April. Consulting geologist Paul had pointed out that the hornfels, as well as the quartzite, provided a favourable stratagraphic horizon for mineralisation. That was an important observation since there was thus the possibility of additional mineralisation in the hangingwall, to the west of the present mine workings. Unsurprisingly that area was a major target for the exploration "think tank".

Utilising recent metal prices and operating cost data indicated an economic breakeven grade of 9.5% combined metals and an ore reserve marginal COG grade of 6.8% combined metals (based on 50% mining costs and 50% Jujuy, Buenos Aires & Mendoza costs). At a protracted management meeting it was decided to "round" the formula, such that the marginal COG became 6.2% combined metals, the same as that used for the past two years. Certainly that would simplify comparisons of specific changes in different parts of the mine. The MCF had continued to increase from 0.85 in 1988 to 0.90 in 1989 and had now settled at 0.92 in 1990 and that was the value selected for the COG calculations.

The historical ore expectancy was 31,900 t/vm over a vertical extent of just over 900m and the sustainable mining potential of Aguilar was thus believed to be 3,000 tonnes/day. That implied a 50% expansion from the present mining rate. However the rapidly increasing direct operating costs (part caused by the unrealistic Austral/US$ exchange rate) would effect the viability of that expansion. A further disturbing technical occurrence was that the main ramp-decline face below the 22 level had encountered poor hornfels ground when good strong quartzites were expected. The ramp-decline was thus stopped until a reappraisal of the geology had been undertaken. Another problem for the geological "think tank".

No progress had been made on recruiting a CME plus additional mining engineers to handle all the mine planning activities such as stope scheduling; ventilation; backfill; services; work study especially on stope production indices etc. The present open-pit operation was totally unplanned and, in fact, had turned into a high-grading operation, which, of course, would now have sterilised lower grade material in the pit walls. One despaired.

The trial sub-level L/H stope had now been completely filled with Putzmeister pumped hudraulic cemented fill to the stope crown, 3m above 18 level. The 56 day crushing strength when using 5 - 6% cement was a little over 7.0 Kg/cm^3. All these testwork results needed to be analysed by Peter, the geotechnical consultant. The price of cement from the Jujuy plant was four times the "normal" price and Ing. Vlad from the planning section was to be congratulated on using locally dug clay from the quebrada below the concentrator to reduce cement in rock fill from 5 to 3% with the addition of 7% clay to 90% surface detritus.

The biggest operational problem was the steadily declining output from cut-and-fill and underhand stopes. All stope indices were down - TMS;t/m drilled; t/Kg explosive etc. Perhaps the most worrying was the decline to a mere 19.4 m/JH/shift. That was appalling. It was only possible to break tonnage by drilling shot-holes within the stopes and the lack of stope drilling had been hidden by working a greater number of stopes up from 69 to 87! That was obviously the wrong approach. One should maximise production from the larger stopes by using two jackhammers when the stope width was over 4m and increase the number of shifts worked per day. In turn that would reduce the total number of stopes required for a given output.

The final Feasibility Study of the Expansion Project had still not been delivered by Wright Engineers, so no comment could be made. Talking to the resident Wright's guy over a beer or two it appeared that several alternatives to their base case had been requested by RTZ Technical Services (RTZTS), although not sanctioned by COMSUR. The presence of Wright Engineers and RTZTS at Porco in Bolivia got me thinking that my consulting days for COMSUR would soon be over. After eight days at the mine it was time to go.

The exploration "think tank" around Aguilar was still in full swing so I made my way back to Jujuy by ute and caught the evening AA flight back to La Paz. This time the driver dropped me off at the company flat. Next morning I headed up to COMSUR's offices on the main drag. I ran through the main points with Jaime and he asked me to draft up my report as he had a meeting with Goni later in the week. Everyone was getting nervous about the economics of the Expansion Project at Aguilar, and with good reason - productivity was down and costs were sky high. COMSUR also feared they might be getting a "gold plated" concentrator from Wrights at "gold plated" prices. That, he said, was why RTZTS was involved. It made sense to have an independent opinion.

After four days running up a draft for Fanny and the girls to type I departed from El Alto by LAB for Lima on the 30th August. From Lima it was the regular KLM flight to Schiphol followed by NLM to Birmingham. By now the usual "going over" by Customs followed Immigration. The Customs guys were disappointed that I was only carrying a cabin bag. They went through it with a tooth comb (surprise, surprise), which delayed me, as usual, by twenty minutes or so. I determined to talk to my MP about these guys continually hassling me. All that was forgotten meeting Gillian and Sproggs outside the Arrivals area. Gillian had got the Practice Nurse job at Fownhope and, of course, was very excited about it. We all were and stopped for a celebratory drink just outside Bromsgrove on the way back to Gorsty. Not just the Fownhope job though, the garage, Steels of Hereford, had called saying that the new Honda Accord was ready for collection (and payment!) on the 8th September. The timing was perfect since Gillian would be starting the new job at the end of the month.

Sproggs was starting his fourth year at St Richards as a day boy again, so for the first few days I ran him to School and picked him up again on the 400/4 Honda bike. He had his own crash helmet which created some interest from his school mates. On the car collection day we drove to Steels in the old Honda, did the business, and drove back to Gorsty. We had agreed that Gillian would use the new Accord, whilst I could use the old Honda for running Sproggs around, taking the dogs up to Bircher Common and running myself to Birmingham airport if more work should turn up. Right on cue I had a call from Edwin, Director of Corporate Planning at ZCCM asking me to join Ian, President of Mineral Resource Development (MRDL) for comment on ZCCM's five Year Plan. Naturally I said that I must first check with the World Bank to see that there was no conflict of interest vis-a-vis my previous work on the Copperbelt for the WB. The WB said "absolutely no conflict whatsoever" and, in fact, welcomed my involvement with ZCCM. So welcome to job No. 078.

42

In the third week of September I drove myself to Birmingham airport and left the old Honda in the Long Stay Car park. Unlike at Heathrow that car park was only 200 yards from the terminal's main door. I caught the BMI service to Heathrow Terminal 1 from where there was a special shuttle bus to Terminal 4 enabling checked-in passengers to go straight in to the main airside departure hall. Excellent, it avoided the Heathrow hassle. Here I caught up with Ian of MRDL. I had first met him nine months ago in their Project Office at Konkola. The over-night BA flight stopped at Harare before the short hop to Lusaka arriving around 9 o'clock. As usual we took a taxi to the Pamodzi Hotel. Over a few beers on the terrace Ian explained MRDL's involvement with ZCCM. Currently that entailed preparing a Feasibility Study of reopening the No 3 Shaft mine at Konkola, but Edwin, the ZCCM Director of Corporate Planning, was using him (Ian) as a de facto internal consultant on geological, mining and metallurgical matters. Edwin had said to Ian that he felt my outsiders knowledge of Copperbelt mining's problem, through my involvement with the WB Missions, might help MRDL's analysis.

That afternoon we went to see Edwin at the ZCCM Head office in Lusaka. He made clear we had two objectives. Firstly commenting on ZCCM's corporate strategy for exploiting its ore reserves and secondly a critical appraisal of their current Five Year Production Plan - was it achievable or pie-in-the-sky? Both Ian and I realised that we must tackle the second objective first as a prime input to addressing the strategy question.

The next day we caught the early morning RoanAir flight to Southdowns airport in Kitwe. We had decided to first go through the latest ore reserve figures and then look at ZCCM-wide development performance and grade factors - the relationship between mined ore reserve grades and measured mill head grades. We thus started at the Technical Services office in Kalulushi. After that we would visit each of the four Divisions - Nchanga, Mufulira, Nkana and Luanshya. The total ZCCM ore reserves were a massive 404 million tonnes grading 3.10% Cu. Those gross figures indicated a huge ore resource, but it was the dramatic fall in the Fully Developed reserve category which range alarm bells. Over the past nine years that category of reserves had fallen 51% at Nchanga, 56% at Mufulira, 58% at Nkana and 32% at Luanshya from the 1980/81 figures. It was the nub of all the mine's "squeezed" position as they struggled to maintain output. The Fully Developed reserves had now stabilised at fourteen million tonnes, but that represented only seven months cover of ground ready for stoping against ZCCM's present mining rate of 23 million tonnes/year. The shortage of developed ground was most acute at the Nchanga Open Pit (NOP), Mufulira and Baluba.

Developed reserves, of course, required, in the mining sense, development. The quantity of development required at each operating unit to sustain a given rate of production, the ore reserve replenishment rate, was affected by mining method/layout and the respective orebodies characteristics - width, strike length, dip etc. Development yields ranged from only 28 tonnes/m at Chibuluma to 130 tonnes/m at Mufulira. Across the Copperbelt the average development yield was 84 tonnes/m, which with ZCCM mining 23 million tonnes/year implied an enormous 274,000 metres, or 274 Km, of development/year to merely replace the ore mined. It should, of course, be more than this to increase the Fully Developed reserves to improve the "squeezed" situation. The importance of development was paramount and yet that key activity was still largely carried out by slow, inefficient jackleg machines drilling short length rounds rather than using modern electro-hydraulic jumbos. That had definitely got to change for ZCCM to achieve the development advance required to meet their production forecast.

Grade Factors ranged from a high of 0.81 at Nchanga to a low of 0.58 at Luanshya. Both Mufulira and Nkana were also very low at 0.61. The ZCCM average was 0.71. The basic reason for low Grade Factors was waste dilution introduced into the ore stream. The main reasons for this were 1) poor ground control; 2) open stoping followed by hangingwall caving; 3) down-dip caving method at LOB; 4) insufficient developed reserves ahead of stoping; 5) delays in completion of major mine infrastructure and 6) poor, inexperienced front-line supervision following nationalisation of Anglo and RST. An average Grade Factor of 0.71 implied a waste dilution (at zero % Cu) of 41%, defined as 0.41 tonne waste for each tonne of ore mined. Considering the form and disposition of the Copperbelt orebodies and the inherent competent ground conditions that was excessive. Certainly with good ground control, hangingwall support and the introduction of cemented backfill methods it should be entirely feasible to reduce waste dilution to circa 15 - 20%, equivalent to a 0.85 Grade Factor. The impact on ZCCM's copper outturn would be enormous. For example last years' average milled head grade of 2.27% Cu would rise to 2.71% Cu for an additional 85,000 tonnes of finished copper. ZCCM management should apply a great deal of effort in that area.

At Nchanga, the company's largest copper producer, the shortfall of waste stripping at the NOP was the major constraint on output. That in turn was primarily caused by poor/low mechanical availability of the large haul truck fleet. There were also scheduling problems removing the TD1 tailings dam which overlay the A Block reserves. An associated problem had been the shortfall in production of acid soluble copper from the TLP which had only achieved 41% of the planned throughput of 9 million tonnes/year. In addition to mechanical difficulties with the belt filters and thickeners in the TLP the main constraint was lack of sulphuric acid for leaching the dumps. ZCCMs own acid production from copper smelting was 31,000 tonnes short of that required. The acid shortfall had to be bought in at a high cost. An acid production/consumption balance was not expected until 1994/95.

In comparison to NOP and TLP outputs, the underground LOB mine met its production target as well as being ZCCMs lowest cost per pound Cu producer.

The Mufulira mine output was restricted by lack of developed reserves ahead of stoping and a very low Grade Factor (0.61). The MAD project was more than a year behind schedule and hoisting on the new Musombo SV1 shaft was only achieving 75% of that planned. All parts of the below 1040 level development were seriously delayed. Unfortunately the Mufulira management still would not accept that the greatly reduced ore expectancy at depth would not permit the mine to sustain their planned output of 4.2 million tonnes/year. Between the 1040 and 1540 levels there were 39.6 million tonnes of reserves outlined; an ore expectancy of about 80,000 t/vm. My 10% OE rule suggested a mining rate of 8,000 tonnes/day, which over 330 days/year indicated a mining output of 2.64 million tonnes/year, less than 63% of Mufulira's target. Their planned output was just not tenable.

At the Nkana Division mines the Fully Developed reserves had increased at Mindola, Central and SOB as a consequence of development targets being met. Although the Mindola shaft deepening project was delayed, generally all three mines were in better shape than two or three years ago. The introduction of modified VCR stoping (reduced the quantity of development) followed by post cement backfill had improved both output and grade. Those improvements had been introduced by Redpath Engineering from Canada. The Nkana smelter was being refurbished with CMT technology from Chile and that was expected to improve the availability of sulphuric acid for the Nchanga TLP leach plant.

The Luanshya mine was a very old mine and was just managing to maintain tonnage and grade. By contrast the newer Baluba mine was struggling to meet its tonnage and grade targets. It was seriously squeezed for lack of developed reserves, now down to just two months! As noted before the Baluba No 1 shaft had shaft steelwork problems which reduced the planned hoisting output. Another difficulty was the rapidly flattening dip of the orebody with depth, such that conventional sub-level open stoping would not be applicable. A project team was appraising flat dip mining methods.

Ian and I repaired to the Kalulushi offices in Kitwe and spent a couple of days working up our production estimates. We predicted finished copper metal production of 438,000 tonnes for 1990/91 then stabilising at around 420,000 tonnes/year for the next four years. Of course those outputs were considerably less than the ZCCM estimates. However in meetings with the technical guys in Kalulushi and the management guys in Lusaka we argued our case with no major points of contention. I guess the ZCCM ethic was optimistic whereas Ian and I had a more pragmatic/realistic approach. Of course it was easier being "outside" ZCCM. Importantly, Edwin seemed pleased with our Five Year Production Plan. He said he felt he could believe what we were telling him - no axe to grind, or backside to protect.

After ten days in Zambia I left Ian who went back up to Konkola whilst I flew back to Heathrow, where I transferred to BMI for the short hop to Birmingham. The old Honda waited in the long stay car park and duly took me back to Gorsty via the M42, Droitwich and the back roads to Tenbury Wells. All was quiet at Gorsty, apart from excited dogs who burst out of the external store. It was the first week of October and Gillian was in her first week as Practice Nurse at the Fownhope surgery. Sproggs was still at school so I took the dogs up to Bringsty Common for a run and blow-through before returning to St Richards to collect Sproggs. He was surprised to see me. He said it was OK being back as a day boy, but really he missed the fun of being a boarder. Gillian came back around 6.30 in the new Accord. She said the car was "alright" but boring and preferred the old Honda Hatchback. However all the talk was about her new Practice Nurse job and that was absolutely "tickety-boo". She had her own room/office and was totally self contained. Very importantly she had a good working relationship with Dr Patrick.

I'd only just completed writing up my five Year Production Plan for ZCCM when I had a call from Arthur my old friend from Riofinex days. He was now Technical Director of the Europa Minerals Group. They had taken over the small coal mining properties of Mineral Search Ltd. He wanted me to have a look at their Draycott Cross colliery near Cheadle in Staffordshire. We arranged to meet at the colliery in three days time - job No. 079.

Thus on a cold, blustery day I drove north up the A49, around Shrewsbury and turned NE onto the A53 for Stoke-on-Trent turning SE onto the A50 for Draycott in the Moors a few miles south of Cheadle. Arthur was already at the site office with Ken, GM of the Coal Division. The mine entrance was unusual. We entered through an abandoned British Rail tunnel and about 200 yards in entered a much smaller decline which intersected the BR rail tunnel side wall. Hey presto we were in a typical narrow coal seam dipping SW at 1 in 8. As we progressed down-dip in crouch mode, headroom was, perhaps 4ft only, it became progressively wetter and wetter. Arthur commented that the water emanated from the overlying Triassic (Bunter sandstones). At the bottom of that now very wet, decline we reached the southern mining boundary formed by an east-west striking fault dipping south at 75 degrees. Quite correctly Draycott had sited a drainage drift some 20m from and parallel to the fault extending towards the western boundary.

The mining plan was to extend that drainage drift ahead of any mining activity so that it would drain the up-dip coal measures. Thereafter development was to comprise up-dip 3m wide headings which would later be widened to 9m by taking 3m off each heading side as one retreated south to north up-dip. However it had not worked out like that. The drainage drift had not been kept far enough ahead of coal extraction. Thus the coal was not dewatered and extraction headings had now to be driven down-dip in appallingly wet conditions. The water naturally exacerbated the weak seat-earth floor. All in all it was a complete pig's breakfast and not in a suitable state to contemplate mechanisation. The brief visit in very wet low workings was hard enough let alone having to work in those conditions. Fairly obviously the mine had been starved of capital.

Thankfully back in the site office, Ken gave me a copy of a 1986 Wardell Armstrong (WA) report on the mine. From that it was apparent that the fundamental problem at Draycott was coal quality. Analysis of two drill holes by WA showed the coal quality to be Ash 8%, Sulphur 2.4%, Moisture 10% with a Calorific Value (CV) of 11,480 Btu/lb for rom coal. A CV of 11,480 Btu/lb was understood to be 26.66 giga-Joules/t (gJ/t). Apparently the minimum CV requirement for power station feed was understood to be 23.8 gJ/t and it was originally thought that Draycott could easily meet that. However Ken advised that, in fact, Draycott's CV was circa 20.5 gJ/t with Ash 8%, Sulphur 2.4% and a Moisture content of 11 to 17%. Thus it did not meet the power station minimum CV, which, bluntly, was the nub of the problem. To meet that minimum CV spec it was necessary to blend Draycott (and the Acres Nook & Durham pits) rom production with high CV imported Colombian coal. That took place at the Tideswell blending yard in Cheadle. Thus Europa's pits were acting as "Fillers" or "Extenders" for imported Colombian coal. Ken said that everyone in the industry knew what was going on, including their main customer - Meaford power station.

The economics of operating the Draycott colliery and the Acres Nook and Durham pits was inextricably linked with the economics of importing/transporting/blending and distributing Colombian coal. With the planned privatisation of the electricity generating industry there would be more freedom for the generators to purchase coal at the cheapest possible price, which would be open-pit mined, imported Colombian, Australian or Canadian coal. Europa's local small mines, with a basically unsaleable product, looked extremely exposed. Certainly my underground visit showed that there was little hope of Draycott producing a rom coal that would meet the minimum 23.8 gJ/t CV criteria of the power generators.

In truth both Arthur and Ken felt that that also was the case, but wished to have a non-coal industry opinion. I said I would check all the CV calculations & prepare a brief report, but the key aspect for Europa was to look at the overall economics of coal supply in the UK from small mines which were unable to meet the minimum CV specification. I agreed to bring my report to Europa's London office at the beginning of next week. After a beer or two with both Arthur and Ken in a nearby hostelry I set off for the drive back to Gorsty.

There was a message from John at the DTI asking me to join a DTI monitoring visit to Carnon in Cornwall early next month. I phoned back and confirmed I would be available for the visit - welcome to job No. 080. Whilst reworking the Draycott CV numbers I received a call from Frank of RTZTS asking if I could come up to London to discuss the Aguilar operation of CMASA in Argentina. He had received a fax from COMSUR in Bolivia suggesting that they (RTZ) discuss the Aguilar operation with me. I said yes subject to getting the all clear from COMSUR, and that I would be up in London early next week - job No. 081.

On the following Monday I drove myself to Great Malvern station to catch the early morning Cotswold Line train to Paddington. There was plenty of free parking at Malvern, unlike Worcester, which had very limited parking space. I took the tube to Knightsbridge and easily found Europa's office on the fourth floor at No. 197. Both Arthur and Richard (ex Mineral Search) were moderately relaxed about my conclusion that Draycott colliery was just unable to meet the minimum CV requirements of the power stations. They felt that the only viable solution for their small mines was to attempt to increase the percentage of lump coal in the rom which could be sold as house coal. That commanded a price of £60/t ex-pit head as against £36/t ex-pit head paid by the power generators. However, at present Draycott produced only 15% of lump. They were also going to examine the economics of buying, shipping, transporting and delivering Colombian coal.

After lunch I went to RTZ's offices at 6 St. James's Square to meet Frank of RTZTS. In fact it was not a technical discussion, per se, on the Aguilar mine, but an off the record talk on CMASA's management. It was evident that Goni, owner of COMSUR, was in essence getting into bed with the RTZ group. With COMSUR's increased zinc concentrate production from Porco and Quioma in Bolivia plus surplus Aguilar production (over the Sulfacid contract) in Argentina the RTZ's group CRA zinc smelter at Avonmouth, Bristol was looking for concentrate. It all made sense. A number of RTZ/CRA personnel were being seconded to assist in managing COMSUR's Bolivian operations and they wanted to know the management score at CMASA in Argentina.

I gave my opinion that both the GM in Buenos Aires and the Mine Manager and Underground Manager at Aguilar needed replacing since those individuals (ex St Joe Lead) were totally un-cooperative with the directives of their owner COMSUR, dismissively known by them as "the mountain men"! From my own experience as COMSUR's mining consultant on Aguilar over the past three years we had had little support from either Buenos Aires or Aguilar mine management to the changes requested. Well that was it really, no report, nothing written down merely a personal opinion. It was my briefest professional job - No. 081.

At school Sproggs had taken an interest in learning a musical instrument. He had first started, unsurprisingly, with the recorder. However the music teacher had felt his embouchure was more suited to a reed instrument and we had bought him a second-hand clarinet. He was making slow, but steady progress with the clarinet. To encourage him further Gillian had bought a second-hand flute and together with my (poor) efforts on the tenor saxophone the three of us used to frighten the cattle in the fields surrounding Gorsty. The school had a number of pupils who played in the Bromyard Wind Band and we were delighted to learn that Sproggs had "made the grade" and would be playing at a Christmas concert in Bromyard church.

In mid November, with Gillian working and Sproggs at school I drove myself to the Greenbank Hotel in Falmouth, Cornwall to join John from the DTI, Keith from the BGS and Neil from Warren Springs for a monitoring visit to Carnon. Our observations were restricted to the South Crofty (SC) mine, although Neil visited the Wheal Jane concentrator. At SC the total mine reserves were 3.7 million tonnes at 1.50% Sn. Carnon's production forecast was for 200,000 tonnes at 1.54% Sn in 1991 rising progressively to 235,000 tonnes at 1.55% Sn in 1995. That seemed entirely reasonable since the seven largest lodes had an ore expectancy of 15,000 t/vm and could thus easily sustain that rate of production. Metallurgical recovery at the Wheal Jane concentrator was predicted to be 83% when treating SC ore. Thus payable tin metal was forecast to rise from 2456 tonnes in 1991 to 2993 tonnes in 1995. A direct operating cost of £46.40 was predicted.

Operation	£/t mined & treated	Comment
South Crofty Mine	27.00	Current performance
Wheal Jane Concentrator	13.00	Reduced tonnage
Technical Services	2.15	70% YTD average
Baldhu/Wilson Way	4.25	70% YTD average
Total	**46.40**	

For 1991 the direct gross operating cost per tonne payable tin metal was estimated to be:- 46.40/ 0.154 x 0.822 x 0.97 = £3779 Those were cash costs and did not include depreciation, financing charge, interest payments, redundancy or other one-off costs.

Realisation costs for smelter charges, insurance and freight were £662/t Sn metal which meant that the NSR was only 81.1% of the tin metal price. Other overheads and royalties added £73/t Sn metal. Thus Carnon's breakeven tin price was estimated to be (3779 + 662 + 73) = £4514, which was virtually identical to our estimate earlier in the year.

Because of cash flow problems Carnon had halted several major capital projects. Those included the SC 400 Pump Station; Mine Deepening; New Crusher; Ore Handling; Surface Rationalisation; Cooks Kitchen Shaft/ Winder Upgrade; Tuckingmill Access/Raise Bore. Altogether these savings would be equivalent to £2.5/t mined.

We looked at a "rape" or high-grading operation, where all development was stopped and all peripheral activity ceased. At a 200,000 tonnes/year production under those conditions the direct operating cost became £2610/t payable tin metal. With similar smelter, freight and insurance charges the breakeven tin price was £3300, still £226 more than the current £sterling price of tin metal. Thus even under a rape scenario the SC mine lost money. Conclusion - Carnon was unlikely to survive without further large cash injections. It was an unprofitable undertaking at current tin prices. On that gloomy note John and Neil took the train back to London, Keith drove to Devon and I returned to Gorsty.

The next job, No. 082 was already on the stocks. A request from Jaime of COMSUR for me to visit the Quioma mine in Bolivia followed by another regular visit to the Aguilar mine in Argentina. Thus a few days after returning from Cornwall I drove myself to the Long Stay car park at Birmingham airport to catch the faithful NLM flight to Schiphol, Amsterdam, where I transferred to the KLM flight to Lima, Peru. Another transfer to the LAB flight to El Alto airport, Bolivia. COMSUR's driver picked me up in the trusty Range Rover for the drive down in to La Paz. Again I stayed at the company flat. Jaime was not at the COMSUR office that afternoon so I took the opportunity to look around central La Paz. Exiting the impressive cathedral I browsed the adjacent local Indian street market, where I was inveigled to purchase any number of llama foetus. Just couldn't see how they would blend into an early 18th century Herefordshire farmhouse so settled for a pair of thick Bolivian sweaters for Gillian.

The next day Jaime asked me to make a swift visit to Milluni with Mario to check on the progress of breast hole drilling in the flat-back cut-and-fill stopes. The fifty minute drive up to the mine was as stimulating as ever. Both local mountains, Huayani Potosi and Chacaltaya were snow covered above 5,000 metres. It was cool at Milluni (4500 metres) so it was great to get underground where the ambient temperature was around 10 degrees C. The mine had definitely reduced waste overbreak by the switch from back-stoping to breast-stoping, but both the drilling and explosive yields were still too low. For the first time Mario agreed that there was better control of the stope contacts - so, at last a convert - but, he said my Spanish was even worse as I now had an Argentinian accent, which was considered beyond the pale in Bolivia.

Jaime then had two further properties he wanted Carlos and me to visit, the Bolivar mine and Carguaycollo mine, both in the central Oruro district. The drive to the Bolivar mine took just over three hours. We spent the rest of that afternoon tramping over the surface outcrop and later working through the geological and ore reserve plans with the mine geologist. We spent the night in the euphemistically called "guest house", it really was very basic, but nonetheless the goat stew was acceptable. It was a small, 200 tonnes/day mine developed through a series of adits into the steep, barren hillside. A typical steep dipping, narrow vein Zn deposit, which now required capital for an internal shaft to develop the vein below the lowest adit level. The owner had consequently approached COMSUR to see if they were interested in investing/taking a stake. Our underground visit showed that it was a strong vein structure with good competent host rocks permitting shrinkage stoping to be used. Although a reasonable structure of 1000m strike, 1.5m average vein width, plus 75 degree dip the payability was only 45%. That implied an ore expectancy of just under 2,000 t/vm. Assay values on the lowest level were very patchy and overall payability on that level was barely 40%. There was no information on vein continuity at depth. Both Carlos and I gave it the thumbs down.

However the Carguaycollo mine was not just a dog, it was a dead dog! Again it was a small adit mine, but this time ground conditions were very poor. The vein appeared to occupy a shear zone with much chlorite and clay present. The mine was not currently working but had, apparently been producing between 100 and 150 tonnes/day of rom Zn ore which was trucked to a COMIBOL plant for toll treatment. After a full morning on surface and underground we likewise gave it a definite thumbs down. That afternoon we drove south and then east to spend the night in our usual central hotel in Cochabamba. It was good to wash the dirt and muck of Carguaycollo and Bolivar off before repairing to our favourite bar for a few beers. Up early to catch the narrow gauge train for the three hour trip eastwards down the Rio Misque valley to the Chaguarani sidings where a ute from the mine was waiting to take us across the ridge and down into the Quioma valley.

As usual Carlos and I started in the Geological Office. Industrial reserves were now 877,000 tonnes at 11.29% Zn and 8.1% Pb. Over the past two years the Industrial reserve had grown by 54% although both Zn and Pb grades had fallen. However the main change had been brought about by development on the Triunfo vein west of the Giezecke fault on the Zero level. Below the Zero level the Triunfo vein had an ore expectancy of 3,000 t/vm relating to a strike length of 650 m, an average width of 1.4 m, a payability of 100% and a bulk density of 3.4. The Candelaria vein had similar ore expectancy. A small footwall vertical shaft had been sunk 167m below Zero level and three levels developed at - 40, -80 and -120 m. All three levels were showing both good grades and widths. Consideration of those physical characteristics had led the mine, correctly, to use cut-and-fill stoping utilising waste rock from surface glory holes. All those factors suggested a sustainable output from the Quioma mine of 10% OE of the main veins Candelaria/Triunfo or 600 tonnes/day. Taylor's Rule also suggested 600 tonnes/day output.

The present back-stoping should be converted to breast-stoping with jackleg machines. The 10hp air scrapers were too small to effectively work 40m length stopes. They should be changed to 15hp electric scrapers. Future production should be obtained from 15 cut-and-fill stopes at 34t/d = 510 tonnes plus 6.2 m/d development = 90 tonnes, a total of 600 tonnes/day. Ground conditions were not great and the use of split sets and chicken wire should be replaced by cement grouted rebar. Ing Vlad from Aguilar should come and train up the ground support crews at Quioma

For that production from below Zero level a ventilation duty of 85,000 CFM was estimated. That quantity could be handled by a short rectangular vertical shaft of dimensions 3.5m by 5m. The daily tonnge and hoisting distances were similar to the new Porco shaft and COMSUR should consider utilising similar shaft layouts and hoisting equipment. Again the main lateral haulage on the Zero level was similar to that at the Porco mine and standard 6t locos pulling 5t Granby cars in 8 car rakes should be used. On the compressed air supply side a new Atlas ER7E was required to bring the installed capacity up to 3700 CFM.

After a very hectic three days at the mine Carlos and I took the ute back to Chaguarani to pick up the narrow gauge train back to Cochabamba followed by a long, dusty drive back to La Paz, finally collapsing into the company flat for an early night. The following morning Carlos and I briefed Jaime on the status quo at Quioma. The COMSUR office was radically changing with the presence of a number of Australians from CRA in senior management positions. At present those CRA people were mainly concerned with the Porco expansion project and working with Wright Engineers on the concentrator modifications.

However it was as plain as a pikestaff that my days as a mining consultant to COMSUR were strictly numbered. On the qt Carlos said as much and Stan, the office manager, had recently resigned and returned to the USA. More importantly the owner of COMSUR, Goni, was now heavily involved in politics. He was currently Minister of Planning in the government of President Victor Paz Estensoro. He was also the MNR's candidate to run at the presidential elections due in 1993. As a consequence his direct involvement with running COMSUR had diminished. It was generally understood that he had persuaded the RTZ group to take a one third stake in COMSUR, so the presence of a CRA team was no surprise. Hey ho onwards and upwards for one last hurrah at Aguilar.

Carlos and I caught the late AA flight to Jujuy and checked into a town-centre hotel. Here we met up with CMASA's Technical Manager, Delfor, who had just flown up from BA to join us on our visit to the mine. A mine twin cab ute picked us up at 7.30 for the three and half our drive up to Aguilar. As usual in the afternoon all three of us went to the Geological offices. The total reserve was 9.52 million tonnes at 6.9% Zn. 4.1% Pb and 97g/t Ag. Those reserves considered a 6.2% combined metals marginal COG. That was a large increase over the 1989 reserves brought about firstly by the lower COG and secondly by reinterpretation of surface reserves by Paul, the consulting geologist.

The mine Accounts section now produced detailed costs for each stope - a very necessary and welcome improvement. Because of low metal prices the mine was currently operating at a loss. To combat that the operational mining COG had been raised to 8.2% combined metals and individual stopes were modified/or stopped. However Aguilar had high fixed costs (eg schools, hospitals, markets, transport, housing, fuel etc) and the economic analysis showed quite clearly that the concentrator must be kept full to minimise unit costs and cash losses. In October 1990 direct costs were US$ 43.31/tonne mined and treated. That rose to US$ 48.12 adding the 10% Regalia for the Province of Jujuy. The direct costs of running the Jujuy, Mendoza (exploration) and Buenos Aires offices added a further US$ 9.44 giving a total cash cost of US$ 57.56/tonne, excluding depreciation, interest and financing charges. The average value of the reserve grade at mid December 1990 was US$ 46.44/t indicating a gross operating loss of US$ 11.23/t ore treated or US$ 0.6 million loss/month. It was obvious that CMASA was facing a very serious economic squeeze.

Both Carlos and I provided some geological and engineering input into the initial design of an open-pit based on vertical, transverse cross sections. That gave 367,000 tonnes of ore at 6.8% combined metals and 954,000 tonnes waste for a 2.60 to 1 strip ratio. The grade was well above the estimated open-pit COG of 4.8% combined metals. It certainly demonstrated how the mine's unplanned open-pitting had sterilised payable ore in the pit walls!

Although no CME had been appointed yet, Ing Delfor from Buenos Aires office had supported excellent work by Ing Vlad in producing a good backfill from surface glacial detritus, plus locally dug clay and 3%

ordinary Portland cement to replace the pumped hydraulic fill. They had also introduced bulk-blown ANFO in place of the Aguilar ANFO cartridges which was a win-win in increasing productivity & reducing costs. Stope productivity was still very low, but finally Aguilar had instigated some basic Work Study to determine what was or was not going on in the stopes. The trackless mine, below 18 level, was now engaged in an extensive diamond drilling campaign to determine ore outlines before the ramp-decline and main levels were positioned accordingly.

After six days at the mine Ing Delfor and I drove down to Jujuy. Here we caught the midday AA flight to Buenos Aires where I stayed overnight in the "noisiest hotel in the world". That evening we went out for a slap up Argentinian steak and a few glasses of Malbec at a little place which Ing Delfor knew. The food/drink was superb and the sea-level air terrific after the rarefied air of Aguilar. Next morning we had a debrief meeting with Miguel, the GM. We had never seen eye-to-eye on how to develop and improve Aguilar, but now he had an entirely new worry other than the owner, COMSUR - the ever increasing presence of RTZ/CRA personnel. He was not a happy bunny. I took the early afternoon direct flight back to La Paz and stayed that night in the company flat. I had a similar debrief meeting with Jaime the next day. He confirmed that CRA were taking an active role in COMSUR's management of Bolivian operations and expected them to extend that to CMASA and Aguilar in Argentina. I also got the impression that he was unsure about how the RTZ/CRA presence impinged on his role as GM of COMSUR.

I left La Paz on the 17th December following my usual route, LAB to Lima, KLM to Amsterdam and NLM to Birmingham, where the trusty Honda awaited. The M42 was now a lot busier than it used to be, but still a lot less stressful than fighting the M4 around Heathrow. Apart from that it was a pleasant, rural drive taking less than an hour and half. I was glad to be back just in time to go with Gillian to the Bromyard Wind Band's Christmas concert in the town's parish church. We were both very proud to see Sproggs there blowing a mean clarinet. He had certainly made progress with the instrument to the extent that it galvanised Gillian with the flute and me with the alto sax to practice. In truth the "Gorsty Wind Trio's" practicing was almost drowned out by the dog's howling. Good job our nearest neighbours were 150 yards away across the field.

The early part of January 1991 was spent compiling detailed reports of the visits to the Quioma mine in Bolivia and the Aguilar mine in Argentina. In addition I had to prepare brief notes on breast-stoping at Milluni and visit notes on the Bolivar and Carguaycollo mines. As there was no immediate work in the pipeline I made a rail trip up to London to visit a few contacts at Mackay and Schnelmann, British Mining Consultants (BMC) and Seltrust Engineering. Brian, the boss at BMC, did, in fact offer me a full-time job with his outfit, but I valued my independence and certainly didn't want to return to being London based.

I then made a train trip up to Doncaster to see Cementation Mining out at Bentley. Here I caught up with Stuart, who I had last been in contact with on the Parys Mountain job in Anglesey four or five years ago. This time I was looking for second-hand double-drum winders that might be suitable for COMSUR's expanding mine at Porco. I took the details of two sinking winders that were no longer needed by Cemco. Stuart also gave me the name of a NCB contact in Doncaster who was handling their surplus plant. I arranged to see Jim at the NCB the following day and found that they also had a couple of winders that were of interest.

On my return to Gorsty I duly sent a fax to Jaime in La Paz outlining the technical specifications, history and price of the four winders. I was a little put out by his return fax which said "don't bother, RTZTS are looking for winders". Well yes. He had asked me to look for winders on my last visit to La Paz, but obviously the RTZ/CRA take over of COMSUR had speeded up.

43

During early March I received a call from Roger of Hatch Associates Ltd (HAL) based at North Cave in East Yorkshire. HAL had been working at the nearby RTZ tin smelter, Capper Pass. HAL had been approached by the Ugandan Development Bank (UDB) and asked to carry out a survey of the dormant tin and wolfram districts of western Uganda. My old friend Nick, Capper Pass's Commercial Director, had mentioned my name to Roger, hence the telephone call. Would I be interested in undertaking that survey/review work? I said "yes, but I need to know a little more". Roger then invited me to come up to East Yorkshire to talk things over. A week later I caught a Marches line train from Leominster direct to Manchester Piccadilly. There I joined a trans Pennine train for Leeds and Hull. I disembarked at North Cave station about fifteen miles west of Hull. A short taxi ride took me to HAL's offices.

The scope of work for the UDB was both large and somewhat vague. There were believed to be six wolfram and seven tin properties. Few had been worked since the mid 1970s when the war to overthrow Idi Amin took place. Most of the mining area was remote in far western Uganda, along the Kagera river towards the Virunga mountains on the Rwanda/Zaire border. HAL had a local agent in Nairobi, Kenya who would arrange transport and had a support offices who could obtain local cost data. The Ugandan Ministry of Mines would also provide a Ugandan geologist to act as guide. The UDB required an assessment of the production potential (tin or wolfram) of each of those thirteen properties and preliminary economics of developing them. The time scale appeared to be three to four months.

After spending all afternoon going through the Terms of Reference Roger drove me to an hotel in central Hull. Later we had a good dinner overlooking the Hull Marina. He picked me up the next morning and we returned to his offices in North Cave. I said that provided his agent in Nairobi could obtain all local cost data I felt that I could tackle the job with a team of three - geologist, miner and metallurgist. Both the geologist and metallurgist would be my subcontractors. I felt the scope of work was too ill defined for a fixed, lump-sum quote, but would undertake the job on a Schedule of Rates contract. Roger wasn't sure that the UDB would accept that, but could I provide the relevant consulting rates plus CVs and an overall Budget Estimate of likely total cost? I reluctantly said yes and agreed to get back to him by the end of the week. With that Roger dropped me off at the station for the return rail trip to Gorsty.

That evening I phoned Ross in Scotland. He was the geologist I had worked with before in both Saudi Arabia and Ghana. He was now running a second-hand furniture business, but was more than happy to do the occasional geological job. He said he was interested and gave me a daily rate. The following morning I phoned Chris, who lived in North Wales. He was a mineral processing engineer who had previously worked at South Crofty in Cornwall and later Robertson Research International, natural resource consultants. He also was interested and gave me a daily rate and promised to mail me his CV. I already had one for Ross. I went back through my notes of the UDB scope of work and came up with a Budget Quote with an elapsed job time of five to six weeks. I sent the Quote and CVs by fax to Roger, who said he would incorporate that into HAL's bid to the UDB. He anticipated the UDB awarding a contract within three months.

Gillian had settled in as Practice Nurse at the Fownhope surgery, working four days per week. As Sproggs had had his 14th birthday in early April we decided we must go and look at schools for him to move to in September. We looked at Hereford Cathedral and Belmont Abbey, but neither seemed suitable. We then went out to Bedstone College at Bucknel in Shropshire which had a lovely setting, but, again didn't "click" with us. We thought about Shrewsbury School but that was still boys only. I felt Sproggs would do better at a co-ed school. Somebody said try Wrekin College at Wellington, near Telford. We looked the school up in the Schools' Handbook, liked the sound of it and duly arranged an interview with the Head. We drove up the A49 to Shrewsbury and had a pleasant lunch at the Prince Rupert Hotel in the town centre before driving out to Wellington. We liked the Head very much and the School itself had a good feel, not too big, four boys houses and three girls. Sproggs was quiet, but came across OK and was certainly impressed by the sports facilities. We duly "booked him in" for the September term.

In late April Roger phoned to say that HAL had been awarded the UDB job. Hurrah. Could I mobilise Ross, Chris and self to meet in their North Cave offices for a day before heading for Nairobi on the 15th May? I contacted both Ross & Chris and we arranged to check in to a central Hull hotel on the 13th May. At the meeting with Roger the next day I was nominated de facto leader for the Ugandan site visit. However Roger joined us on the BA flight to Nairobi, where we checked into the Hilton Hotel. That evening HAL's local agent, Pete, joined us for a lively, bibulous dinner. In the morning we went to Pete's office and prepared a list of likely mining and metallurgical consumables for which we would need local prices/costs. We also needed data on local labour rates, import duties, port charges at Mombasa, Mineral Export taxes, Royalties, rail freight charges for a standard 20ft container from Kampala to Mombasa, road haulage costs in Uganda etc. Pete took it in his stride as an experienced expat agent and promised to have most of that stuff ready by our return to Nairobi following the Ugandan site visit.

Pete came to the hotel early next morning and said our transport, a long wheel base Toyota Land Cruiser, would pick us up at the hotel after lunch. With the morning off I had a quick wander around the centre of the city - wow, how it had changed since I was last there 29 years ago with Gillian after our stint at Tangold Mining Co in, what was then, Tanganyika. All I recognised was the outside Thorn Tree coffee shop and the updated colonial style Norfolk Hotel. As promised the Toyota turned up driven by Freddie, a large very cheerful Kenyan. As the drive to Kampala was about 450 miles and with the international border to cross Pete had arranged for us to stop overnight at Nakuru. We drove NW out of Nairobi soon dropping down the escarpment into the eastern rift valley. A short stop at Naivasha to look at the pink flamingoes on the eponymous lake. What a stunning sight. Then on to our night stop in the sizeable town of Nakuru. I noticed that both Ross and Chris had no trouble adjusting their thirst buds to the local Tusker beer.

Early next morning we drove westwards stopping at Kisumu, the port on the NE corner of Lake Victoria. Here Freddie filled up the Toyota with diesel and all four jerry cans. His told us that not only was it much cheaper in Kenya but there was often a shortage in Uganda. From Kisumu it was a 75 mile drive NW to the border crossing at Busia. The Ugandan border guards were polite and meticulously stamped all our passports. Now in Uganda we drove first west then SW and about eighty miles from Busia we crossed the start of the Victoria Nile at the Jinja power plant. Continuing for a further ninety miles or so through to the capital, Kampala, which was as shambolic and run-down as Nairobi was new, shiny and modern. In fact we were booked into the very pleasant Lake Hotel out in Entebbe. We met Roger in the hotel. He had flown to Entebbe from Nairobi two days previously for meetings with the UDB in Kampala. He told us we all had a meeting with the UDB in Kampala next day.

The meeting with the UDB officials was a bit of a non-event. Really it seemed that they just wished to meet us and ensure that if they were paying for three minerals industry specialists there actually were three of us! The most useful thing was that we met Sam, a Ugandan geologist from the Ministry of Mines, who was to be our guide in the field. He also organised our visit to the Geological and Mines offices. We spent the next two days there working through old plans and reports of the various tin and wolfram properties in the SW part of the country. Much to my surprise I noted that some plans, dated in the 1950s for the small Ruhiza wolfram mine had been signed by Alan, the mine surveyor. He was later the Chief Surveyor at the Kiabakari gold mine of Tangold Mining Co and in fact was my boss when I worked there from 1960 to 1962.

In the morning driven by Freddie we set off SW for the ninety mile trip on a reasonable road to Masaka following around the NW shoulder of Lake Victoria. Here we turned west for the similar length journey to Mbarara, Thereafter the road deteriorated, now dirt, as it climbed and twisted on its way SW to Kabale. On the way climbing one steep scarp we burst out of heavily wooded country onto a cleared ridge. There was a magnificent vista of the volcanic Virunga mountains in Zaire (Congo) stretching down towards Goma on Lake Kivu. Although wild and spectacular country I was surprised to see intensive hillside cultivation southwards to the Rwanda border. The total 270 mile trip from Kampala to Kabale took over eight hours and we were all pleased to check in to a compact, clean hotel which was to be our base for the next three days. It was a small market town at the junction of roads from Rwanda to the south and Zaire from the west.

Our first visit was to the Kirwa mine site, which was now completely deserted. One could still make out old open pits along a spur, but already secondary bush was reclaiming the area. The only sign of mining equipment was a vintage Holman Rotair portable compressor, a scraper and some small side tip mine cars. According to the records Kilembe Mines undertook underground development in 1955 and later Anglo American resampled. A resource of two to three million tonnes at 0.13% wolfram was outlined. Of course that was totally uneconomic at today's price of US$ 60/t unit.

Later we visited the Mutolere/Mugumbero mine area close by the White Fathers mission. A more encouraging sign was that some tributors were working a small quarry with primitive hammer and moil mining - damn hard work! There was no mining or treatment plant. The Mines Department records indicated a wolfram grade of 0.1% only. Thus the first two sites were distinctly discouraging.

The next day we visited the Nyamulilo site. Here commercial mining had ceased in 1984. Now the mine was owned by Continental Ore Ltd and the Uganda Development Corp. About twenty tributors were working the remnants of some elluvial deposits whilst three men were working a quartz vein underground with hammer and moil. Again there was no mining plant. Ground conditions were poor underground with host rocks of siltstone and phyllite. The records showed low wolfram grades of 0.16%. A better prospect but a long, long way from a viable mine.

After three days at Kabale we drove west to the small town of Kisoro close to the Zaire (Congo) border. The splendid extinct volcano Muhavura 4127m (13,540ft) dominated the town. Although only 48 miles from Kabale the drive took three hours in the Toyota and we were really happy to have 4-wheel drive. The dirt road was very badly rutted on account of considerable heavy transport to and from the Congo. We checked into a very primitive "guest house" where our three white faces created quite a bit of interest. Sam went down to see the local Chief of Police (CoP) to see if it was considered safe for us to visit the Bahati mine, right on the Rwanda border. There had been some shooting nearby apparently ethnic problems between the Tutsi and Hutus. The CoP advised against a visit today, he would check in the morning. Next day, still no message from CoP, and as team leader I had to make a decision whether to visit or not. The Mines report indicated that the Bahati mine was likely to be the most encouraging wolfram mine in

Uganda. We'd come all this way so I took the decision for a rapid visit. Nothing untoward happened, but we could all hear repeated gunfire from across the adjacent border.

All commercial mining had ceased at Bahati in 1975. Now six tributors or illegal miners were working the vein outcrop by hammer and moil. We traced the vein outcrop for 250m. It was a strong vein with little pinch-and-swell on strike or dip. Host rocks were massive siltstones giving good underground conditions. Two adit levels were accessible. The vein had been completely mined-out from hangingwall to footwall over the entire strike length. The open stoping method was overhand-onto-stulls as evidenced by the stull timbers remaining in place. Vein width averaged 0.8 metre. Main mine development was an incline shaft of variable inclination and strike drives driven in from the side of the valley. The old development showed a vertical vein extent of 105m or 45% of the known strike extent. Level interval was 21 m. The lowest accessible level (No 3) was also the drainage level. On our underground visit by flashlights we had to be very careful not to stumble into several flooded winzes which penetrated the level floor - quite scary. The presence of numerous bats in the old workings added to the entertainment.

The veins ore expectancy was about 550 t/vm at 90% payability. The tonnage of ore extracted over a vertical mining depth of 90m would have been nearly 50,000. The Mines Department reports quoted an in situ grade of 1% wolfram and allowing for waste dilution and a 70% metallurgical recovery would indicate a total output of 490 tonnes wolfram (65% basis). The mine had started in 1949 and records showed a production of 270t of wolfram over an eleven year period. That crudely checked with our total mine output estimate. Bahati thus had the potential to be a small wolfram mine utilising shrinkage stoping. At the urging of Sam and Freddie we made a swift exit and drove back to Kisoro.

Next morning we headed north into the Impenetrable Forest in Kigezi District looking for the Ruhiza mine. The approach road in the Forest was in a very poor state of repair and the Toyota barely made seven mph for the final thirteen miles. The mine site was completely deserted. The invading jungle had reclaimed the whole mining area. In fact the jungle was so thick we were unable to find the mine! Fortunately with the invaluable assistance of a local miner, complete with panga, the lowest No 7 level, just above a stream, was located. We did not enter it as it had water and foul smelling air. The No 6 main haulage, identified from the plans was totally blocked by fallen ground. We entered both the No 4 and No 1 adits to note that the host rock was heavily sheared graphitic phyllite. All crosscuts and drives off those adits were blocked by fallen ground. The old assay records indicated average grades of 0.2% to 0.4% wolfram on individual veins up to 70m length. All mining and processing plant had vanished in the jungle. With the current site conditions and low wolfram grades it could be classified as a non-starter. I looked forward to talking to Alan about Ruhiza on our return to the UK. So we began our very slow, rough ride back to Kisoro, which, by comparison with Ruhiza, was beginning to look very civilised and cosmopolitan. As that was our last night in the Kisoro guest house the owner had been down to the local market and suitably armed with some of our Ugandan dosh had rustled up a very imaginative "stew". I had no idea what it contained (and didn't ask), but it tasted excellent.

In the morning we turned east and headed back to our first base in Kabale. In the afternoon we repaired to the local Mines Offices and looked at the plans and production records for the Kaina, Mwirasandu and Kikagati mines. That evening Sam took us to a Kabale restaurant to try some of the local cuisine. A lot of that seemed to involve green bananas, known as matoke, which could be fried, steamed, baked - you name it. We had already discovered another use for matoke. Outside Kampala/Entebbe none of the hotels or guest houses had showers and the baths were always missing plugs. Yes a squashed, moulded matoke made a great, water tight bath plug!

Next day we drove thirty miles east towards Mbarara and turned north to the nearby Kaina mine. At present four tributors were mining the quartz mica veins with hammer and moil. The mineralisation outcroped along the northern flank of the Kaina-Ruhega ridge. From the gully between the two hills strike adits had been driven in short distances. The Geological Survey offices indicated a strike length of 125m but a depth extent of only 45 m. The main activity now was the movement of thousands of bats who had taken possession of the deserted tunnels and stopes. The adit portal was knee deep in bat droppings - ugh. Underground host rocks were strong and the steep dip of the 1 to 2m wide quartz veins indicated that shrink stoping was possible. However quoted grades were a miserly 0.31% Sn - so no viable tin mine here, but a sure source of guano!

The following day we headed east again towards Mbarara and then turned south towards the Rwanda/Tanzania border junction with Uganda. The Mwirasandu mine was previously the largest tin mine in Uganda. Between 1926 and 1956 production was recorded as 5716t of cassiterite. The operator was Kagera Minerals in which the Dutch company Billiton had a major interest. Through the '20s and '30s production was obtained from surface elluvial deposits grading 1.1% Sn. During the '40s and '50s underground mining took place but grades were low at 0.35% Sn. The area was looted during the 1979 war. Now thirty tributors were working outcropping quartz veins with hammer and moil. The old records indicated that the underground mine had a vertical extent of 182m and numerous deposits extended over 3.6 Km. The main Mwirasandu vein had a strike of 670 m. Through a 2ft by 2ft rat-hole we accessed the old No 7 drainage level and located the flooded No 42 and 53 shafts which accessed the deeper levels. The mine appeared profitable in the early days when working the high grade elluvials. During the 1940s the underground mine's output was around 225 t/day and in spite of the low grade it remained profitable. However the tin price collapse in the 1950s was terminal for the operation. Any future? Doubtful, the in situ grades were too low.

Back at Kabale we checked all the geological, mining and production data in the Mines Office for both Mwirasandu and Kikigati. After much chat between Sam and the local Mines office staff it was agreed that it would be easier to access Kikigati from Mbarara rather than Kabale. Thus in the afternoon we duly drove east to Mbarara, where we spent the night in a pleasant colonial style hotel. The mine lay just north of the Kagera river, which in turn formed the Uganda-Tanzania border. Kikigati town and the surrounding area were totally destroyed by the late 1970s war which ousted Idi Amin.

Close by at Murongo a small cable ferry crossed the Kagera river into Tanzania. Arguably the Kagera river could be considered as the main headwater of the River Nile. Its source was Lake Rugwero in Burundi whence it flowed north to form the Rwanda and Uganda borders with Tanzania before flowing into Lake Victoria 25 miles north of Bukoba. As a consequence of the war and border tensions the area was very sparsely populated with no infrastructure whatsoever. The "main road" (euphemism!) from Mbarara was scarcely passable by jeep. Transit time Mbarara to Kikigati was 3.5 hours for 45 miles. Thank goodness the Toyota had a powered logging winch complete with steel cable on the front to pull us out of immense muddy ruts otherwise we'd still be there.

The deposit comprised a swarm of quartz veins ranging from 0.3 to 3m width hosted in hard, competent quartzite. The veins were strong with very little pinch and swell. The veins cut obliquely across a steep spur which descended to the Kagera river. The "main road" from Mbarara to Kikigati curved around the nose of the spur about 25m above and 70m distant from the river. The deposit was originally mined through a number of elongated open pits on the spur. Thereafter two strike adits were driven from the NE side and a crosscut adit was driven into the spur at the main road elevation. That adit was partially blocked at the portal, flooded and swarming with mosquitoes and bats - it was not entered! According to a British Geological mission (1965 - 1968) the deepest workings were 45m below the "Road" adit level. The top of the spur was 175m above the "Road" adit implying a vertical extent of 220 m. Total recorded production was 1250 tonnes of cassiterite. The competent ground, strong veins and steep dip were plus points which would enable shrink stoping to be employed, but the reported in situ grade of 0.2% Sn would not permit a viable underground mine to be developed.

We departed the spooky deserted town of Kikigati and made our slow, bumpy drive back to Mbarara for the night. Next morning we headed east towards Masaka, but turned north after a few miles to the isolated Buyaga deposit. One miner was working with hammer and moil at the base of a 50 degree incline which extended below the base of a small ragged open pit. Again the deposit was a swarm of quartz veins hosted by heavily altered schists exhibiting alteration minerals such as sericite, chlorite and kaolin. Ground conditions were thus poor. There was no information on grade or past production. All in all it appeared a small deposit suitable only for artisanal working.

So after fifteen eventful days in the SW Ugandan bush we headed for Masaka and on to the Lake Hotel at Entebbe. We really enjoyed the hotel's luxury and downed plenty of Tusker beers sitting out on the hotel's verandah overlooking Lake Victoria. The next two days were spent in the Geological and Mines offices checking through what little data was available concerning all the properties we had visited. Then one final day in Kampala giving a wrap-up briefing to the UDB. Certainly the best wolfram deposit was Bahati, where it might be feasible to develop a small underground mine. As far as tin was concerned the best possibility was a smallish open pit at Mwirasandu. It was impossible to give a positive spin on the other properties. In reality they were dead in the water as commercial properties, suitable only for artisanal mining. I guess it wasn't what the UDB wanted to hear but potential mines require suitable ore reserves and there was a paucity of those in SW Uganda.

We said goodbye to Sam at the Geological Office and also Freddie as he was driving the Toyota back to Nairobi whilst we took the EAA flight from Entebbe to Nairobi. The next two days were spent with Pete going through all the local cost data he had collected. He had done an excellent job and used his initiative on getting quotes for alternative materials to those I'd specified. On our last day in Nairobi Pete told us that Freddie, driving back from Uganda, had been "done over" at the Busia border crossing into Kenya. He was unharmed but had been robbed of all his own possessions. Fortunately Freddie had filled up the Toyota in Kampala so had enough fuel to make it back to Nairobi.

It was good that we had now finished the field visit as Ross and Chris were getting a bit scratchy with each other. I had no idea why or over what, but it was definitely time to be going their separate ways. We took the BA direct flight back to the UK. I had agreed with Roger that it would be simpler if they each invoiced him direct rather than through me. I also reiterated at Heathrow that they should send their respective geological and metallurgical reports direct to Roger asap. With that Ross went to Terminal 1 for a flight to Scotland and Chris caught the tube into central London to catch a train to North Wales. I caught the RailAir coach to Reading, then train to Worcester and taxi to Gorsty.

Over the next few days I completed my field visit notes for the six wolfram and seven tin deposits and despatched those to Roger. Towards the end of June he contacted me again to say that they HAL had had further discussions with the UDB, who now wished them to comment on the "Rehabilitation of the Ugandan Tin and Wolfram Mining Industry". Finally they wanted an indication of the required in situ breakeven grades for both a tin and wolfram operation. Could I rustle up something by yesterday? Yes, can do as part of job No. 083.

The wolfram and tin deposits currently identified in SW Uganda were all small in extent and low grade in tenor by international standards. There was nothing to suggest that additional "grass-roots" exploration would disclose anything significantly larger or higher grade than those deposits already known.

In essence both the wolfram and tin fields were the province of the small-worker or artisan miner. The deposits were not of sufficient size or grade to warrant the attention and costs of a fully self contained commercial mining operation. Apart from the main road Kampala-Masaka-Mbarara-Kabale, basic infrastructure was totally lacking. Away from those main towns the road network was minimal, generally poorly maintained murrum tracks. Telecommunications, power and engineering facilities did not exist. Unfortunately much of the infrastructure in and around Masaka, Mbarara and in particular Kikigati was almost totally destroyed during the late 1970s war. Even today, 1991, there was unrest in the Kagera river area where the Rwanda Patriotic Front (RPF) were waging a guerrilla action against the Rwanda government. That obviously involved both sides of the border and many of the mining properties were sited within one to two miles of that border.

Taken together, the small, low grade "spotty" deposits, virtually zero infrastructure and continuing civil unrest would not support, let alone attract a commercial mining operation. We suggested that the UDB assist and expand the incumbent small-workers or artisan miners by setting up a Small Mines Unit (SMU). That would provide:-

Technical Advice (geology, sampling, mining, processing, engineering)

Mobile Equipment (truck mounted compressor, jackhammers, explosives, pumps etc)

Wolfram and Tin concentrate purchase and marketing

How to manage that SMU? The Geological Survey/Mines Department (GS/MD) was now totally run down with only a skeleton staff. In the absence of a viable GS/MD it could be attached to the government controlled Kilembe Mines operating up in the Ruwenzori. Already Kilembe had an agreement with the French BRGM to study processing of stockpiled cobalt rich pyrite concentrate, so a precedent had been set.

With regard to breakeven grades I considered a hypothetical 250 tonnes/day underground tin mine and a hypothetical 1000 tonnes/day open-pit wolfram mine. Based on mid-1991 prices the breakeven grade for the underground tin mine was 1.56% Sn and for the open-pit wolfram mine 0.70% WO3. None of the tin mines and only the small Bahati mine had grades anywhere near those values. It should also be noted that those breakeven grades had only considered direct operating costs. Much higher grades would be required to provide a return on capital to develop those mines. The estimated cost to develop the 250 tonnes/day underground tin mine was US$ 4.8 million with an operating cost of US$ 13/t mined. The estimated cost to develop the 1000 tonnes/day open-pit wolfram mine was US$ 8.7 million with an operating cost of US$ 2.5/t mined. All of that second report was despatched post haste to Roger by mid July.

All in all that fascinating Ugandan job had kept me fully occupied for two months. In truth I felt that we, HAL, Ross, Chris and me were the most likely people to benefit from the UDB study rather than the indigenous people in SW of Uganda. On that sobering thought I felt that a chat with Alan, the Mine Surveyor at Ruhiza during the 1950s, might assuage any disquiet I felt about the pertinence of our work for the UDB.

Although we had exchanged Christmas cards for many years I hadn't spoken to Alan since he had been working in Ireland. He was amazed to learn that I had recently been at Ruhiza in the Impenetrable Forest. His recollection of the mine was that it was a very small wolfram mine with patchy mineralisation and poor, weak ground conditions. He said that in the 1950s production was only a "few tens of tonnes/day". He agreed that a supported stoping method would be required. However like us he felt it was merely a deposit for artisanal miners. When I described the state of the access road and that the jungle had completely reclaimed the site he agreed it was a no-no. In fact he felt that our practical, down to earth conclusions on the non-viability of the tin and wolfram prospects in SW Uganda would bring a sense of realism to the UDB "suits" in Kampala who lived in cloud cuckoo land and dreamt of a "Californian gold rush".

Finally Gillian and I managed to go and watch Sproggs playing in a cricket match at St Richards School on the last weekend before the summer holidays. Unfortunately I had missed a lot of the matches in May and June whilst away in East Africa. Back home for the summer holidays Sproggs and I went to a Sports shop in Hereford and bought a steel framed back-up net, which enabled us to play our own cricket matches in the Gorsty garden. With all the recent practice he'd had at school I didn't win many matches. However to counter that I took him to the new Leominster Leisure Centre and still, just about, managed to beat him at squash. He also continued to go swimming with the Leominster Kingfisher Club and had developed a strong back crawl.

44

Around the middle of July, much to my surprise, I received a call from Jaime of COMSUR. He told me he had been appointed a director and he would like me to visit Aguilar with Carlos and meet the new Mine Manager, Robin, from RTZ. I said yes to job No. 084, but with some reservations, as it was obviously "changing of the guards time" and I was firmly associated with the pre RTZ/CRA days when Goni called the shots. Still work was work and there had not been a lot of that this year. As usual I drove the old Honda to Birmingham. Then it was the regular NLM flight to Schiphol, KLM to Lima and LAB to La Paz. The COMSUR driver picked me up for the drive down into La Paz - destination the company flat.

At the office in the morning Jaime was very straight forward and said that he wanted me to join Carlos and Delfor, CMASA's Technical Manager, in ensuring that Robin, the new Mine Manager, was aware of our joint technical concerns about the Aguilar mine. Carlos and I duly caught the afternoon AA flight to Jujuy and checked into a downtown hotel, where Delfor joined us later after flying up from Buenos Aires. We left early in the morning for the three hour drive to Aguilar. As usual after a snack lunch we rallied in the Geological Office to get up to date with the latest exploration results. Robin turned up after a while and I realised I had met him before, either at Tara Mines in Ireland or Neves Corvo in Portugal. Neither of us were sure where.

Recent diamond drilling below 18 level had increased the Possible reserves by over 600,000 tonnes at similar grades. However those holes had disclosed much more interbedded hornfels and much flatter dips than originally projected from the earlier, wide spaced drilling. It certainly emphasised the importance of close spaced drilling before stope planning commenced. The recent recalculation of the Possible reserves below 18 level provided the opportunity to examine the grade-frequency distribution of those samples. The skew log-normal distribution demonstrated that the use of an arithmetic mean would introduce an overvaluation bias of about 15%. The mine should cut all Possible ore reserve grade estimates by a factor of 0.85 to avoid over optimistic metal production forecasts. Those new ore outlines did not appear suitable for cheap, productive transverse bulk mining. Unfortunately the more costly less productive method of longitudinal cut-and-fill stoping would seem more applicable.

A new mining planning engineer has been appointed and with the assistance of the SURPAC mine planning programs, recently acquired by COMSUR, and the Compaq 386 computer he should be able to drastically improve Aguilar's (non-existent) mine planning process. At last, after three years of cajoling, Aguilar had a mine planning capability.

With the uncertainty of ore continuity below 18 level CMASA had decided to stick with a short term production schedule of 2,200 tonnes/day for 300 days/year, or an annual mine output of 660,000 tonnes. They had also hired an experienced open-pit planning engineer from Peru to sort out the present anarchic high-grading of certain open-pit areas.

There had been improvements in current stoping. Specifically the use of bulk-blown ANFO had finally reached 83% and both the drilling and explosive yields had increased. However the Sindicato, local labour union, took exception to the the commencement of Work Study in some selected stopes. An all out strike was threatened and Aguilar had stopped that vital work. As usual in those cases it was a question of who runs the mine - management or unions? At the moment the Sindicato had the whip hand. It would be interesting to see how the new Mine Manager, COMSUR and ultimately RTZ/CRA deal with the impasse. Overall stope output of 9.63 TMS was slightly up, but the majority of the increase was due to open-pit output! You cannot break rock unless you drill holes was an old maxim. It was certainly relevant to Aguilar. Unfortunately without the necessary Work Study, management did not know what did or did not go on over the complete breaking and filling cycle. That was essential data to increase TMS outputs and decrease cost.

Current direct operating costs were US$ 36.1/t mined and treated a welcome decrease from the US$ 43.3/t recorded for October 1990. However the operation was still losing money on account of the very low metal prices. After twelve days at the mine I left for Jujuy and took the afternoon AA flight back to La Paz. Next morning I had a short meeting with Director Jaime and confirmed that I had passed on all my concerns about the Aguilar operation to the new Mine Manager. As expected we agreed that "that was it - my services were no longer required" since RTZ/CRA were now firmly in the COMSUR driving seat.

I caught the afternoon LAB flight to Lima and the night KLM flight to Schiphol and the NLM flight to Birmingham. Here the regular hassling by Customs took place, but I thought with my exit from COMSUR work I would not be troubling their computer with "nefarious" cross-border journeys in South America.

In truth I was very sorry to lose COMSUR as a client. I had worked for them for over ten years in Bolivia, Peru, Argentina, USA and UK. In particular I had really enjoyed working for Goni. He had such a clear, incisive mind and as it was his company he made the decisions straight up without interminable committee meetings. Now, of course, he was a politician and no longer directly involved with COMSUR. Let's hope the new RTZ connection did not stultify the decision making progress. But, hey that was no longer my problem.

Back at Gorsty Gillian had started getting things ready for Sproggs move to Wrekin College during September. The School had told us that he would be in Tudor House and that all his clothes had to have "T S labels" (for Tudor House/Stoakes). Getting plenty of those labels was the easy bit - it was the sewing into the clothes that took the time. Earlier in August, before I went to Bolivia, we had taken Sproggs up to London to the John Lewis store on Oxford Street to sort out the required Wrekin College school kit. In the Leominster Antique Market we found an old steamer trunk which seemed ideal for all Sproggs clobber. So out with the paint pot and it was duly daubed with T S------. Most of his sports kit was pretty grubby but nothing a good scrub couldn't fix. At least his rugby gear should survive one more term.

Towards the end of August I received a call from Paul, a geologist with the WB. He asked me to join a WB mission to ZCCM in Zambia from the middle of next month. With no other work on the horizon I was glad to welcome job No. 085. The timing was good since I was able to take Sproggs and clobber up to the Wrekin for the start of the winter term. Here the old hatchback Honda came into its own with the split rear seat. We managed to get the steamer trunk, tuck box and various odds and ends in as well as all three of us. He had a good room in Tudor House for four pupils. We met two of his "room mates", one of whom, Dan, was to be the room head honcho. He seemed a good sensible lad from a military family. We met some of the other parents over tea and buns and felt more relaxed about leaving him there as a boarder. Sproggs, of course, was away with the other lads and couldn't wait for us to go. We also met David who was the assistant housemaster and the important one for keeping an eye on the year's new intake to Tudor House.

A week or so later I drove the old Honda up to Birmingham airport and caught the BMI flight to Heathrow. On the excellent BA flight (how BA had improved since being privatised) I managed to have a good sleep before we landed at Harare in Zimbabwe. Wandering around the transit lounge I encountered Paul. It was good to see him again from the last WB mission. Paul, now an American citizen, was originally English from the north-east. We used to chat about boats. He lived in Washington DC and had a yacht on Chesapeake Bay. By contrast my old canal narrow boat seemed very provincial. We had something in common, which made us laugh, we each carried a photograph of our respective boats in our wallet, alongside a photo of our wives as well (natch)! Paul confirmed that we were booked into the Pamodzi Hotel and suggested we all join up for a beer on the terrace after we had checked in.

It was only a short flight on to Lusaka and, of course, the WB guys were long gone by the time I cleared Immigration and Customs. No matter by the time I arrived on the Pamodzi terrace the WB guys were only on their second beer. Paul confirmed that our principal objective was the preparation of a new Five Year Copper Production Forecast. Our first two days were spent in Lusaka in discussions with officials from the Ministry of Mines, Maamba Collieries Ltd and, of course, ZCCM. Thereafter we flew with RoanAir up to Kitwe and established ourselves in the Nchanga Directors Lodge cum guest house.

Over the next nine days I visited various operating units at all four divisions of Nchanga, Mufulira, Nkana and Luanshya. At each division we had talks with the General Managers and their respective geological, mining and metallurgical staff. On the last day we had discussions with ZCCM Consulting Engineers and the Corporate Planning Unit in Mutondo House in Kitwe.

Since the last WB visit in December 1989 copper production had gone from bad to worse. As before the problems were in the mines. Too little developed ground ahead of stoping and too little waste stripping ahead of open-pit production. Overall FD ore reserves had fallen sharply to an all time low of 12.2 million tonnes. That represented just over six months cover for the present ZCCM mining rate of circa 23 million tonnes/year. The squeezed position was demonstrated at the NOP open pit. On the day of our visit the pit was "snowed in" with all face shovels digging waste with no pre-stripped ore available for loading. As bad as that was it got worse at Mufulira where FD reserves had fallen 2.7 million tonnes over the past year. As a consequence planned production for Mufulira for this current year 91/92 had been reduced by over 1.3 million tonnes to 3.4 million tonnes/year. Unsurprisingly the predicted rom head grade for Mufulira had declined sharply - a double whammy.

The WB had been warning Mufulira for several years that their planned extraction rates were incompatible with the mine's rapidly reducing ore expectancy below the 1040 level. Now the chickens had really come home to roost. All Mufulira's thoughts of mining 4.2 million tonnes/year from below 1040 level must, absolutely must, be abandoned. We, the WB, believed that Mufulira could only realistically sustain an output of 2.65 million tonnes/year from below 1040 level. As if the reduced ore expectancy wasn't enough constraint, the heavily delayed MAD project was the final nail in the coffin.

Another production disaster area was the TLP output. Designed to handle 9 million tonnes/year it was still only managing 3.5 million tonnes/year, due to shortages of sulphuric acid and mechanical failures of belt filters and lack of thickener capacity. With a ZCCM average development yield of around 75 tonnes/m, an annual underground mining rate of 16.5 million tonnes required a yearly development advance of 220 Km. That was a huge amount and ZCCM were still using antiquated jackleg face drilling!! It beggared belief. They should introduce modern, electro-hydraulic multi-boom jumbo drilling as soon as possible, preferably yesterday. Naturally that would also require experienced operators to train the local miners. Again the WB had been highlighting that for several years.

A final problem affecting copper outturn were the very low grade factors. Across the four Divisions the average mill head grade was only 58% of the average FD ore reserve grade, which implied a "zero grade" waste dilution of 72%, defined as an additional 0.72 tonnes of waste for each tonne of ore. That level of waste dilution was unacceptable. It was caused by 1) poor ground control practice; 2) mining methods based on open stoping followed by hangingwall caving; 3) insufficient developed reserves ahead of stoping; 4) delays in completing major mine infrastructure; 5) poor, inexperienced front-line supervisors.

The net result of those cumulative problem areas was that our Five Year Copper Production Forecast was way, way lower than we had forecast only 21 months ago. For the financial year 91/92 we estimated only 375,000 tonnes finished copper, progressively rising to 395,000 tonnes in 95/96. In short it all looked very bleak for ZCCM. In discussion with their senior management in Lusaka, everyone finally accepted that the company was in deep trouble. Their only defense was that the BoZ had been slow to release foreign exchange for essential equipment and plant purchases. For the first time we encountered talk that the Zambian government might contemplate selling off certain parts of ZCCM to the private, international mining sector. From what I had seen of nationalised mining outfits the sell-off couldn't come quickly enough to save a foundering industry.

We headed out of Zambia in early October. At Heathrow Paul asked me to have my write-up into his hands no latter than the 20th of the month. With that the WB guys headed for a Washington DC flight and I headed for home.

Gillian seemed very pleased to see me. Although she had been busy as the Practice Nurse at Fownhope surgery, she said that it felt very quiet at Gorsty after Sproggs had left for boarding at the Wrekin. She was also glad that I could take over chopping logs for the wood burner, yet another task where she missed Sprogg helps. Apart from the nursing, looking after the home and walking the dogs, she had been busy on the mining secretarial front. Stewart from Cementation Mining wanted me to call him and John from the DTI had sent a package of documents for my comments. I rang Stewart and he had some queries on the Parys Mountain project on Anglesey. He would send me the Anglesey Mining Prospectus, (AMP) could I comment? Welcome to job No. 086, I'd reply asap after receipt of the Prospectus.

In the meantime I continued with my write-up and Five Year Copper Forecast for the WB. The AMP turned up the next day and I produced a two page response for Stewart. Basically after AM (Anglesey Mining) had spent nearly £9 million on 300m of shaft sinking, about 900m of lateral development and 8,000m of underground diamond drilling the ore reserve base had shrunk, rather than grown! The reserve was still "drill indicated", Probable only and thus anything but secure. In fact the Probable reserve tonnage had shrunk to 60% of the original estimate by Robertson Research International (RRI) after an extensive underground exploration programme. To me that was a real danger signal. The structural geology was incredibly complex and the proposed mining rate of 1,000 short tons/day was incompatible with an ore expectancy of 5,500 t/vm. It was not tenable. Finally it struck me as curious that AM kept changing engineering consultants - Davy, Wright and now Kilborn. In answer to Stewart's question I said Parys Mountain was not a project to invest in - supply services only.

I phoned John at the DTI and said that I would review the Carnon business forecast early next week after I had completed my work for the WB. That was OK for him, so welcome to job No. 087. The Carnon package included a South Crofty (SC) ore reserve summary of July 1991. It showed that the Demonstrated reserves had fallen to 193,000 tonnes or 15 months cover for the 150,000 tonnes/year mining rate. With an average development yield of 50 tonnes/m, the requirement for development would be 3,000 m/year or 250 m/month. It was disturbing to note that SC were achieving less than half that amount. Axiomatically SC would have difficulty in sustaining a 150,000 tonnes/year mining rate at a head grade of 1.7% Sn if the Demonstrated reserves fell to only six months cover. Direct operating costs had improved to around £35.5/t mined and treated from plus £40/t during 1990.

Metallurgical recovery at the Wheal Jane (WJ) concentrator had stabilised at 83.5% and the breakeven price was estimated to be £3395/t Sn metal. All capital expenditure had been stopped, including the planned second exit via the Tuckingmill decline and Alimak raise. Thus Robinson's shaft was still in use and the ground conditions were being closely monitored by both SC and the CSM. A warning was raised that the mine water in the flooded Wheal Jane mine was now only 10m below the Great Country Adit overflow into Restronguet Creek. Carnon were monitoring that, but did not specify their plans to handle/neutralise the eventual overflow.

For 1992 we estimated a gross operating cost per tonne payable Sn metal of £3569 and with royalties of £97/t and £376/t for freight and treatment charges indicated a breakeven price of £4042. However the current tin price was US$ 5590, which with an exchange rate of 1.705 indicated a sterling value of £3278 or a loss of £764/t payable tin metal to Carnon. Thus in spite of all the cost savings made Carnon would still lose £1.48 million in 1992. There seemed little else the mine could do to reduce operating costs and only a major hike in the sterling price of tin metal would make Carnon profitable.

On the family front we went up to the Wrekin on most Saturdays to see Sproggs playing either rugby or hockey. He had settled in well and was enjoying himself. After the games we went for the usual tea and buns and a natter with some of the other parents. Both Gillian and I really liked the ambience at the Wrekin. At home I had to face the inevitable. Poor old Luke, the Old English sheepdog, was on his last legs. Although of good pedigree from the same kennels as Matt he had never been anything like as robust. By early December he was obviously in pain, so I took him to the vet, who agreed that the kindest thing was to put him down. This was quickly done and although fully expected I was very upset. The old dog had only lived for ten years which didn't seem a very good innings, whereas Anjon, the bitsa at fifteen years old was still going strong and had now outlived both sheepdogs. The old farmhouse now felt really empty without the sheepdog and Sproggs, away at the Wrekin.

I had no mining commitments during December so it was on with the DIY and internal painting. On Gillian's day off on Wednesday we used to take off on an "away day", generally to somewhere in deepest Wales. We liked the weekly Wednesday street market in Machynlleth and invariably bought three or four second-hand books before retiring to the very pleasant Wynstay Arms for lunch. In the afternoon we'd have a walk alongside the beautiful Dovey estuary before we drove home via the upper Teme valley to Knighton and on to Leominster.

I had kept in touch with Pablo, the ex-Chief Geologist from the Aguilar mine and had sponsored him for membership of the UK's Institute of Mining & Metallurgy (IMM). Nevertheless I was surprised to receive a fax from the Ecuadorian company Cia Minera Gribipe SA (CMG). It was from Pablo, who was now Operations Manager at CMG. That company now had an option on a RTZ exploration gold prospect at Macuchi, in Cotopaxi Province about eighty miles SW of the capital, Quito. Pablo wanted me to come and do a rapid valuation of the property, which was being offered for sale. I replied saying I could visit in early January 1992. Welcome to job No. 088. My friend down at Thomas Cook in Hereford said there was the regular service by KLM to South America, one of which had an intermediate stop at Quito on its way to Lima. For me it was a no-brainer with NLM from Birmingham then KLM direct to Quito.

At the end of the first week of January I drove to Birmingham airport to catch the NLM flight. I wondered if "my friends" at Immigration and Customs had noted that I was on a South American run again. No doubt I would find out on my return to the UK. We landed at Quito airport in the early morning. I was pleased to see a CMG 4-wheel drive vehicle outside the arrivals terminal. We set off south from the city down the wide, open valley steadily climbing from around 2750m to well over 4000m as we passed the towering Cotapaxi volcano (5896m). Well into the central spine of the Andes the dirt roads became very rough around Macuchi. The jeep was a short wheel base Vauxhall Vitara and incredibly uncomfortable. My backside felt absolutely hammered after the four hour journey.

CMG had a primitive exploration camp, but a cup of mate de coca seemed to cure all my aches. I had not realised that the RTZ gold prospect lay in the hangingwall of an old copper mine. In the CMG office we examined old records of the Cotopaxi Mining Company (CMC) from the 1940 - 1950 period. Although CMC had been primarily a copper mine there were significant gold values. A plot of the gold values indicated a positive skew log-normal grade-distribution. RTZ's gold values were likely to be overvalued by circa 15%. The RTZ resource of 270,000 tonnes at 7.0g/t Au and 1.6% Cu lay in the hangingwall of the previous mining operations and the gold mineralisation appeared to be associated with the main shear structure rather than the massive sulphides of the old CMC mine.

The ore expectancy of the RTZ resource was only 3 to 4,000 t/vm. Examination of the RTZ drill logs, surface outcrop and the old CMC No 1 level indicated that ground conditions in the immediate hangingwall of the old workings would be poor on account of the clayey gouge associated with the shear structure. A max mining rate of 300 tonnes/day for 330 days implied a production potential of 100,000 tonnes/year. Cut-and-fill appeared the obvious mining method and I allowed for 15% waste dilution. There was no pertinent metallurgical testwork so I assumed a bulk sulphide float to recover Cu, with pyrite depression, followed by regrinding, then pachuccas for agitation and cyanidation for gold recovery. Guesstimated recoveries would be 70% for Au and 80% for Cu.

There was very little to see on site. We camped in the office overnight and set out for our bumpy ride back to Quito in the morning. We had a couple of hours at Quito airport before taking the short, 150 mile flight down to Guayaquil on the coast. CMG had booked me in to a town-centre hotel a short distance from their offices. Next morning it was good to catch up with Pablo. He had been in Ecuador for two years now, the first nine months on his own before bringing his family up from Argentina. He was interested to hear the latest news about Aguilar, not least the presence of RTZ/CRA in COMSUR and the new CMASA management team. When I told him I had been discarded by COMSUR, he laughed and welcomed me to the ex-Aguilar Club.

Over the next three days I worked up notional mining operations for the Macuchi project, utilising my current Bolivian small mine experience, since there was no suitable data available in Ecuador. I estimated a direct operating cost of US$ 35/t comprising US$ 17/t for mining, US$ 8/t for treatment and US$ 10/t for services/administration and overhead. However after much discussion with CMG we settled on US$ 40/t mined & treated. Total revenue per tonne treated was estimated to be US$ 60.5 comprising US$ 42 for gold and US$ 18.5 for copper. That gave a gross operating margin of US$ 20.5/t mined and treated. After deductions for regalia and other taxes we arrived at a net operating margin of US$ 16.4/t mined and treated. With a 100,000 tonnes/year treatment rate that would give a net cash flow of US$ 1.64 million/year. CMG advised that their cost of capital was 12% and that discount was used to ascertain a ten-year NPV of US$ 9.27 million. I had to point out that a ten year life required an ore resource four times larger than that RTZ figure!

The estimated capital cost for a 300 tonnes/day operation was US$ 10 million, which gave a project DCF rate of return of 10.2%. The obvious conclusion was that the RTZ resource base did not provide a viable project. However Pablo considered the Macuchi geological potential good. Thus CMG could take a nine-month option in an attempt to locate "another

Cotopaxi" orebody. That work could cost US$ 300,000 and if successful offer RTZ US$ 1 million for the property. Later discussion with Sr Estefano, CMG's GM indicated a preferred approach of offering RTZ around US$ 250,000 for the property "unseen", since that secured the property as a tangible asset whatever the outcome of the later CMG exploration. That certainly made excellent sense to me.

That wrapped up my work. I had managed to see a little of Quayaquil, a port town on the estuary of the Rio Babahoyo. It was quite a threatening town at night quite unlike the relaxed ambience of the capital, Quito. I was more than happy to board a Delta airlines flight for Miami where I transferred to a BA flight for Heathrow. There was no trouble with Customs and I transferred to Terminal 1 for the BMI shuttle flight to Birmingham. As that was a domestic arrival I didn't see any sign of my Brummie Customs guys - thank goodness. The old Honda awaited for the regular hour and a half run back to Gorsty.

Gillian was busy at the Fownhope surgery four days per week and Sproggs was back at the Wrekin for the Winter Term. At home now it was just Anjon and me and although fifteen years old he still enjoyed a good walk each day. Apart from log splitting there was nothing to do in the garden yet. During the week I continued with re-decorating one or two of our inside rooms. We'd been at Gorsty for twelve years now, which seemed to be the trigger for lots of things to wear out. I drove up and back to the Wrekin several times a week to support Sproggs playing either hockey or rugby and towards the end of term, cross country running. One Saturday evening Gillian and I went up to see him playing his clarinet in a school concert. We spoke to his Assistant House Master, David, who said that Sproggs was getting "involved in everything" and seemed to be a natural at any sport. The news on the academic front was OK, but less encouraging. From our viewpoint the great thing was he was enjoying school life.

In the early part of March I had a call from Ernst of the World Bank (WB) asking me to join yet another mission to the ZCCM mines of

Zambia. Welcome to job No. 089. On the penultimate day of March I followed the usual travel route of car to Birmingham, BMI to Heathrow and BA to Lusaka. A taxi took me to the Pamodzi Hotel where I caught up with the WB guys on the terrace. The objective was similar to that of the last mission in September 1991, namely a Five Year Copper Production Forecast. The visit followed the usual WB format. We spent the first two days in Lusaka in discussions with the Ministry of Mines and ZCCM followed by eight days on the Copperbelt and a final three days in Lusaka again with the Ministry and senior ZCCM management.

As usual I visited each of the four operating Divisions, Nchanga, Mufulira, Nkana and Luanshya as well as the Kalulushi Operations Centre in Kitwe. Unsurprisingly there were very few significant changes from our last visit, a mere six months ago. The most encouraging aspect was the marked improvement in waste stripping in the NOP. That had been achieved by increased mechanical availabilities of major open-pit equipment, especially the haul trucks. The Mufulira mine was still in very poor shape due to ZCCM's past policy of over-mining whilst paying scant attention to the matching development requirement. Its mining output should steadily be reduced to circa three million tonnes/year. All three major mining projects at Mufulira, Mindola and Baluba were falling further and further behind their respective schedules. The TLP was still running (staggering?) at 3.6 million tonnes/year as opposed to the designed throughput of 9 million tonnes/year. At the Copperbelt's largest concentrator, Nchanga, metallurgical recovery had fallen by 5% over the past year. The departure of many experienced mining supervisors was highlighted by the almost complete absence underground of adherence to or understanding of basic safety rules - very alarming.

All operations were "squeezed" through inadequate ground available for stoping. Thus tonnage was down, rom grade was down and subsequent metallurgical recovery was down - a triple whammy. Finished copper metal recovery now represented only 45% of the metal content of the Developed ore reserves. We estimated that ZCCM might just maintain production at 395,000 tonnes/year until fiscal 1996/97. Cobalt production was expected to continue at about 4,800 tonnes/year.

Average direct operating cash costs over the whole of ZCCM were estimated to be 99.4 US cents/lb Cu. Current three months copper was

£1263/tonne which at the present exchange rate of 1.78 was equivalent to 102 US cents/lb, indicating a gross operating surplus of 2.6 US cents/lb or slightly better than cash breakeven. A back calculation using attributable downstream mining costs indicated a direct cash cost of 71 cents/lb which indicated a recovered copper grade of 0.86%. In turn that implied a mill head grade of 1.1% Cu and and an ore reserve marginal COG of 1.9% Cu and that would be the breakeven grade! Under those conditions it was clear that ZCCM's ore reserve COG of 1.0% Cu was much too low. The future was definitely bleak.

Again the parlous state of the industry became apparent in the WB's wrap-up meetings with ZCCM's senior management in Lusaka. Everyone now felt that an independent management consultancy should look at the company and see how it could best be organised. Certainly there was a body of opinion that favoured a return of ZCCM to the private sector almost exactly ten years after Anglo and RST's Zambian operations had morphed into the government owned ZCCM. Once again the past ten years had demonstrated that "governments didn't do mining". With that we all headed for the airport and the evening Lusaka - London BA flight.

I completed my report for the WB towards the end of April and was really pleased to be home to enjoy the rest of the Spring weather. Gillian was still busy at the Fownhope surgery and Sproggs, now 15, was, unsurprisingly, both enjoying cricket at the Wrekin and the burgeoning interest of some of the girls! It was Spring and the sap was rising. On Saturday afternoons we went up to the Wrekin to watch a cricket match. Later, over tea and buns, we chatted to other parents and all agreed that it was "the girls who made the running". Not, I think, that Sproggs or any of the other lads were complaining.

45

In early May Derek from the DTI called and asked me to join a DTI visit to South Crofty (SC). Welcome to job No. 090. As usual we were booked in to the Greenbank Hotel in Falmouth. I repaired to the bar where I found Keith from the BGS and Neil from Warren Springs but as yet no one from the DTI. After our third beer we decided to have dinner. Later, in the bar for a post prandial drink Derek turned up with Danuta, an economist from the DTI. He said they had already eaten on their drive down from London. They joined us for a drink and Danuta, who was Polish, blonde, and attractive, definitely livened up our rather predictable "mining yarns". We all noticed a certain frisson between Derek and Danuta and none of us were at all surprised that they were extremely late for breakfast the following morning!

At SC we did a three way split. Neil went off to appraise the Wheal Jane concentrator whilst Derek and Danuta went to the Carnon Head office and Keith and I headed underground. In an attempt to increase the rom grade the mine had concentrated stoping activity in the Roskear A and B lodes, west of the Great Crosscourse. Mine production was now from two L/H stopes in A lode and three L/H stopes in B lode. The Demonstrated reserve grade of the A and B lodes was 1.95% Sn appreciably higher than the overall average reserve grade of 1.57% Sn. SC were thus "over-mining" or "high-grading" the mine in an attempt to stay afloat at the current low £sterling tin price. Obviously that would have a detrimental effect on the grade of the remaining reserves.

SC had restarted limited development again after the almost complete cessation of that crucial activity during 1991 (to cut costs). It was now running at 160 m/month. In the first quarter of 1992 total direct operating costs were £37.75/t mined and treated. However that was artificially low through an increase in tonnage to offset the low (1.6% Sn) head grade. A realistic operating cost of £43/t allied to a head grade of 1.6% Sn and a metallurgical recovery of 83.5% indicated a breakeven price of £3771. Current price was US$ 6075 for tin metal and an exchange rate of 1.8145 gave a value of £3348, implying a loss of £423/t tin metal produced, a loss of nearly £0.85 million/year. Yes, it was an improvement (mainly due to the tin metal price rise), but Carnon was still unprofitable.

Keith and I had a final day with Andy, SC's Chief Geologist, developing a tonnage-grade curve for SC's Demonstrated reserves. In essence that showed that raising the COG from 1.0% to 1.4% Sn reduced the tonnage from around 1 million to 500,000 tonnes whilst increasing the grade from 1.57% to 1.95% Sn. QED the rationale for the present SC high-grading policy in an attempt to stay alive. With that the engineers, Keith, Neil and I went our separate ways to Devon, Stevenage and Herefordshire whilst the DTI couple motored back to London.

In late May Gillian took some holiday from the surgery and we went up to Whixall to take Toadflax for a chug up the Llangollen canal. Now with only one small dog, Anjon, we took him with us. Much to my surprise he was very well behaved on the boat and was in seventh heaven with the smells along the towpath when I went to work the numerous locks. However both Gillian and Anjon stayed below in the cabin when we crossed the Chirk and Pontycysyllte aqueducts. That would be our last run up that canal as I had received news that finally a mooring berth in Stourport Basin would be available for Toadflax at the start of the next cruising season. That berth would halve the traveling time from Gorsty to the boat and introduce us to the Staffs & Worcester, Trent & Mersey and Birmingham Canal Navigation (BCN) waterways of the Midlands.

Sometime in June I had a call from Ian of MRDL asking if he could include my name in their list of personnel being submitted to SRI for a bid that SRI were making to ZCCM. I contacted the World Bank (WB) to check that that was OK and was duly cleared. Apparently ZCCM had requested international management consultancy outfits to bid for a complete review of, in effect, "What to do with the Zambian copper Industry". That was hardly a surprise to me following my recent involvement with the WB Missions to ZCCM. Ian was quite confident that MRDLs exposure on the Copperbelt with the Feasibility Study they had undertaken at Konkola No 3 mine would add good weight to SRI's bid. After all ZCCM's business was mining and metallurgy and that was also MRDL's speciality. Apparently bids had to be in by August with a decision expected early November.

Things were definitely quiet on the work front. Also from Ian's enquiry about a SRI bid to ZCCM, it would appear that the WB would no longer be having regular visits to Zambia. For me another disappearing client. At present the good old DTI's monitoring of the government's investment (!) in Cornish mining at South Crofty (SC) was my only active consulting work and the financial plight of SC foretold a fairly imminent cessation of work there as well. Hey ho, what to do? After the usual round of telephone calls and fax messages to various mining contacts I decided to do some serious hill walking in central and southern Wales. Gillian was still busy four days/week at the Fownhope surgery, but knew enough about the "mining business" to act as my secretary/back-up in following up any calls left on the answer-phone.

Towards the end of July Sproggs was back home after completing his first year at the Wrekin. He had very good reports on all manner of sporting activities, but not too many positives on the academic side. Still, not too worry, he had improved his social skills and demonstrated a real talent for moving ball games and above all he was enjoying life. While at home he played cricket at the Luctonians Club at Kingsland and continued with both tennis and squash at Leominster. Sproggs continued to beat me at our own Gorsty-style cricket one-on-one. My only success related to cycling, but then I had a full size bike with ten gears whilst Sproggs had a small-wheel folding bike with three hub gears. In fact that worked out as a suitable handicap to give me a chance to win at something!

Gillian's sister Pat and husband Tony came up to stay for a few days. Sproggs was still in awe of Tony, who wouldn't let him get away with any poor manners - good stuff. One Sunday Tony and I decided to walk into Leominster to buy the papers. It was a round trip of about seven miles. Normally Tony could walk me off my feet, but I noticed that he was much slower than me on the return journey up Gorsty hill. At the time I didn't think much about it.

With still no work around I was pleased to take Sproggs back to school for the winter term, and Gillian and I could go up to the Wrekin most weekends to watch both home and away (at Ellesmere, Newport or Monmouth) rugby matches. At tea and buns after one of the matches, Dave, assistant house master, asked us if we were coming to a school concert/show in three weeks time? Spoggs hadn't told us about it (surprise, surprise). When we found out when the concert was we said yes, we'll be there. Back home I phoned Ollie, my old walking mate and asked him if he could help me bring Toadflax down the Llangollen and SUC canals to Brewood for overwinter mooring just before the canal system closed for winter dredging and lock maintenance? He agreed and together with Gillian we organised the movement of Toadflax so as to arrive at Cheswardine, three miles south of Market Drayton, on the day of the Wrekin concert.

Just over a week before the concert Gillian drove Ollie and me to the Whixall Marina. Gillian returned home and thence to the Fownhope surgery. Ollie and I worked old Toadflax out of the Marina and down the Llangollen canal to Hurleston Junction where we joined the Shropshire Union main line. It was slow going through the Audlem and Adderley flights as British Waterways Board (BWB) had already reduced water supply to those locks. However we made Market Drayton the night before the concert and were pleased to find Gillian ensconced in a town-centre hotel. After a good dinner we agreed that Gillian would meet us the following day at Cheswardine by 5pm. Here we moored Toadflax and all three of us then drove the eighteen miles to Wrekin College in Wellington. The concert was good fun and it was very encouraging to see Sproggs puffing his cheeks on the clarinet. After the concert we drove back to Cheswardine where Ollie and I reboarded Toadflax and Gillian returned to the Market Drayton hotel.

Next day we had an easy lock-free 18-mile run to Brewood, where BWB had allocated us an over-winter mooring. Gillian had a much later start from Market Drayton but was waiting for us as we chugged into Brewood - the car being somewhat quicker than Toadflax's regular cruising gait of 3.5 mph. We secured the old boat for her six months "winter holiday" mooring, packed our gear into the car and headed back to first Gorsty and then Hay-on-Wye to drop Ollie home.

There were two pieces of good news on the work front waiting at Gorsty. Firstly a packet of "stuff" from Carnon and a message from Derek at the DTI, now the Steels, Metals & Minerals Division, asking me for comments on the latest Carnon stuff. Welcome to job No. 091. Secondly there was a fax from Ian of MRDL saying that SRI had been successful and could I be ready to join the SRI/MRDL team in Zambia in early February? Yes I could and that would be job No. 092.

The Carnon reports showed that during the first nine months of 1992 production at South Crofty (SC) had risen nearly 17% to 126,600 tonnes and that had largely offset the decline in head grade to 1.45% Sn. However it was disturbing that those results had been achieved whilst SC was following a deliberate "high-grading" policy. The implication was that if SC had been mining to the average Demonstrated reserve grade the resulting mill head grade would have only been 1.24% Sn, a disaster. The lower average mill head grade, of course, gave rise to a lower metallurgical recovery of 82.5%. Monthly development advance was now over 700m which was getting close to the ore reserve replenishment rate of 850 m/month. The current gross operating cost per tonne of payable tin metal was £3416 and with freight and treatment charges the breakeven price was £3906/t Sn metal. The current Sn metal price of £3770 ensured a loss of £136/t Sn metal or about £280,000/year. Much, much better, but Carnon was still haemorrhaging money. The old tax payer was never going to get his money back.

In late November I received a telephone call from Paul of the WB who said that Mike, a director of the reactivated RTZ Consultants (RTZC), who had been canvassing work from the WB, was casting serious slurs on my professional integrity concerning my inclusion in the successful SRI/MRDL bid to ZCCM. His contention was that I was involved with ZCCM via the WB in appraising the bids for the management consultancy contract. Absolutely untrue. The following day Ernst from the WB and Frank, an independent financial consultant I knew from London, telephoned to say they had also heard Mike slagging me off over the SRI contract. Well I went ballistic. I telephoned Keith, the RTZC MD, and asked for an explanation. He stone walled, said he would speak to Mike who was in the USA at present. I wrote requesting a written retraction of those slurs. Again RTZC stone walled. I then contacted the Secretary of the Institute of Mining & Metallurgy (IMM) and lodged a formal complaint against Mike personally and the company RTZC.

Over the next few weeks the IMM professional misconduct committee also stone walled (the IMM was a major beneficiary of RTZ generosity) to the extent that I engaged Tom, my local solicitor, to pursue my complaint. That was quite time consuming and ugly over the next few months culminating in a meeting in the IMM London offices when Tom and I fronted up to an RTZ Group lawyer and the IMM Ethics Committee. The arcane rules of the IMM meant that Mike (and RTZC, the company) could only give me a written retraction and apology if I withdrew my accusation! (no, I don't follow the "logic" - if I withdrew, what was there to apologise for?). Anyway that was how it played out. Tom, my solicitor, was fantastic. He had the RTZ's lawyer's guts for garters. Finally after seven months or so I received a fulsome apology from Mike, as a director of RTZC. Yes victory, but I sure wouldn't be getting any further work from the RTZ group.

We were expecting Pat and Tony to come and spend Christmas with us, but a week or so before they cancelled as Tony was unwell. In early January Pat phoned to say Tony had been taken to hospital with bowel cancer. Wow what a shock. As soon as Sproggs went back to the Wrekin, after the Christmas break, we drove down to Pat's house at Mawgan Porth in Cornwall. The next day we visited Tony at the Penzance hospital. He looked terrible and one just knew that he wouldn't live for long. In fact he died on the 17th February, a mere six weeks after going in to hospital. He would be sorely missed.

At the end of the first week of February I had a fax from Ian asking me to join his MRDL team in Kitwe, Zambia working as mining subcontractors to SRI. I duly drove to Birmingham airport and caught the BMI flight to Heathrow. Then it was the overnight BA flight to Harare and Lusaka. Now the routine was different. No Pamodzi Hotel for mere subbies. I walked across to the Lusaka Domestic Terminal and caught the first RoanAir flight to Kitwe's Southdowns airport. Here I was met by Ian, driving himself in a small Datsun sedan. We made our way to a single mens mess, Cassia House which became my home, on and off over the next year. After dumping my gear in my small but adequate room, Ian drove us the short distance to the SRI Project Office. He introduced me to the SRI Project manager and his Assistant and then to the other MRDL guys, Brian, John and Cliff. They'd only just started working on the SRI job so I wasn't far behind. Besides that I knew a fair bit about the Copperbelt mines from my work for the World Bank.

Ian explained that SRI required detailed costing of all mining methods and development at each of the five operating Divisions. ZCCM had hived Konkola off from the Nchanga Division which now included just the NOP and LOB. Brian was MRDL's open-pit mining engineer and he was thus handling Nchanga costs with help from Cliff on the LOB caving mine. John was looking after the three separate shaft mines at Nkana. Ian, obviously, was updating Konkola costs from their recent Feasibility Study as well as Luanshya and keeping an eye on the rest of us. That left me with Mufulira and Baluba, which Ian felt was sensible on account of my previous engineering work on both mines' main shafts.

First though, ZCCM and MRDL (with input from SRI) had to agree a five year and tentative ten year copper and cobalt production forecast. That was where I came into my own as I had had to produce those forecasts for the WB over the past three years. Obviously we had input from ZCCM's consulting staff as well as each Division's GM, Chief Geologist, Chief Mining Engineer and Chief Metallurgist - an awful lot of Chiefs! We (MRDL) achieved a production forecast consensus after a week and that provided the starting point from which to estimate each mine's requirements for development, stoping, haulage and hoisting crews and equipment. John, a feisty South African, absolutely did not agree with my estimate for Mufulira's mining potential. He definitely sided with the mine's unrealistic plus four million tonnes/year figure. He pooh-poohed my 10% ore expectancy "rule" and feigned not to have heard of Taylor's Rule, which, in fact, confirmed my 10% estimate. Ian intervened and sent John back to Nkana and left me to get on with Mufulira. Nevertheless John came back to it time and again when we were (attempting) to relax with a beer or two. His experience was mainly obtained in the South African gold mining industry where the very flat dipping banket reefs had totally different characteristics to steep dipping tabular deposits. In the end we just plain disagreed.

Over the next three weeks I worked up detailed costs for bench-and-fill mining in the lower levels of Mufulira. That entailed all drilling, blasting loading and support costs for both top overcut and bottom undercut development followed by the same for the actual bench mining and subsequent filling with de-slimed tailings. The mine's Accounts people provided cost information on lateral haulage, hoisting, ventilation, engineering services (sampling, survey etc). In addition to those generated costs they also provided factual cost data on major consumables such as power, diesel, ANFO, gelignite, drill steel, LHD tyres etc. I often found that my synthesised total cost per tonne for, say, bench-and-fill mining from basic labour rates and consumables was often higher than the mine figures. A lot of that difference appeared to be due to re-allocated overhead costs. We also made an effort to split our individual cost centres into fixed and variable elements. That would obviously make it much easier to recalculate costs for different tonnage throughputs.

By early March we had completed the initial costing exercise and SRI called a break and I (attempted) to return to the UK. For anyone who believed that international travelling was glamorous and fun I quote in full the fax I sent Ian at MRDL's office in San Mateo, California when I finally reached Gorsty:-

"Travelling back from Zam, yes, well it took 58 hours door-to-door, no kidding! It was a complete cock-up. Left office Tuesday 4.30pm. RoanAir does not land at Southdowns (storm); at 6.15pm advised it had gone to Ndola, mad rush across I cadge lift with Guy (Haulpak agent) as John does not see too well in dark! Southdowns contacted Lusaka Air Traffic saying there were eight passengers for BA flight please hold (some hope!). At Ndola no Roan plane - couldn't land (storm) had returned to Lusaka as fuel low. They sent message, Challenger jet was coming up it arrives Ndola 7.55pm & we eventually arrive Lusaka 8.55pm. I gallop across to International - BA flight already left - hoping to switch to UTA Paris flight due out at 9.40pm. Terminal deserted. UTA flight has been cancelled. Take taxi to ZCCM Kwacha Lodge for night. Wednesday check flights and switch to QZ etd Wednesday evening at 10pm. Watching TV at 6pm in Kwacha Lodge news flash QZ London flight delayed until 9amThursday, hey ho (the DC 10 was still in Bombay). Lousy flight with QZ arrives late at Heathrow, 4.45pm takes fifty mins to get bags (hey not lost - the good news) & as a consequence I just miss 5.55pm BMI flight to Birmingham (with seats). Next BMI flight & last 8.40pm, but don't worry no seats huge WL. Shit. Thus hire car & drive 120 miles to Birmingham to retrieve my car from Long-term Park. Car won't start. Jump leads the lot, no go. Call AA spend further forty mins in freezing weather (now circa 10.30pm) they can't fix it, tow to nearby garage. I give up retire to hire car (again) and drive home arrive one minute to midnight - stuffed. Great trip!"

As it happened I only had ten days at home before SRI requested further mining input from MRDL and I duly drove to Birmingham Airport on the 15th March en route to Heathrow, Lusaka and Kitwe. The work was more of the same detailed costing, but this time for various development activities - haulage level; sub-levels; scram drifts; draw points; raises; winzes etc. There was a wide difference between the Division's costs. As before I concentrated on the Mufulira and Baluba mines. We had that tranche of work wrapped up by the first week of April. That time my trip back to the UK with BA went like clockwork with an elapsed time of nineteen hours from Kitwe to Gorsty - fantastic.

I had just missed Sproggs 16th birthday, but as he was now home for the Easter holidays I had an interesting trip planned - moving Toadflax down to Stouport basin. Over the weekend Gillian drove us up to Brewood where the boat had over-wintered. She helped us stock up with easy-cook grub before she drove back to Gorsty, complete with Anjon for company. I had had enough nous to take Toadflax's batteries back to Gorsty for charging, so we had plenty of power for lights and more importantly grunt to start the old Petter PH2W engine. We got Toadflax underway early next morning with Sproggs steering on the five mile lock-free run down to Autherley Junction to get used to the boat again. At Autherley we turned south onto the Staffs & Worcester canal almost immediately passing the BCN main line junction at Aldersley. Thereafter Sproggs was busy working the three locks at Compton and Wightwick. He very soon got the hang of it and as it was early in the new boating season the canal was really quiet. We fairly flew along (well, for a canal narrow boat!) with only a small glitch at the Bratch three-lock staircase before mooring up at Stourton Junction around 6pm having travelled eighteen miles and worked through eighteen locks. We'd been on the go for just over ten hours. It sounds slow but in canal speak that was good going.

We collapsed into the Stourton Arms for beer and fish and chips around 7.30. Shortly afterwards a gang of young (late teens & twenties) girls came into the bar, obviously on a girls night out. Well their language would have made a hardened navvy blush. Both of us were intrigued with the girl's "goings-on" as the language and gestures (don't ask) got more and more explicit. I thought the hard rock mining industry was fairly crude but it couldn't hold a candle to those girls. I was glad Sproggs was at a co-ed school.

The following day was much more relaxed as we were well ahead of my original schedule. We had a late start and moored up at Wolverley Court Bridge at just after midday having travelled seven miles and worked through seven locks in a little over four hours. After more pub refreshments we tackled the final five and half miles and six locks arriving in Stouport basin shortly after 4pm. I located the resident BWB gaffer who pointed out Toadflax's new berth. I found a phone and called Gillian asking her to come and collect us. Then the three of us went into the Tontine Arms, overlooking the River Severn, for a celebratory dinner. It was great to have a new mooring less than forty minutes drive from Gorsty.

There was no mining work on the horizon so it was full throttle on gardening and outside DIY (everlasting repairing and painting windows). Most weekends we'd go up to the Wrekin to watch Sproggs playing cricket followed by tea and chat to some of the parents. Notwithstanding the riotous "Stourton girls", or maybe because of it, Sproggs was obviously taking an interest in the fairer sex and vice versa. So everything normal there. As the long sumer holidays approached I told Sproggs we were going to take Pat, Gillian's sister, to Portugal for a holiday. Would he like to come, bringing a Wrekin mate (stressed mate!) with him? Yes he would and thus we met up with his parents for them to vet us. All sorted.

It was a bit of a squeeze for five of us in the grey Honda Accord for the run up to Heathrow. It seemed years since I had driven there. I'd booked a Long Stay parking slot for the car. A minibus took us to Terminal 2 for European flights. We flew TAP to Lisbon and caught a taxi to a Holiday Inn (HI) a short distance from the city centre. I knew Lisbon a little from previous work visits and found it a pleasant relaxed city after manic Madrid. The HI was good for the youngsters as there was a rooftop pool. It was good for us as well. We did the usual tourist "things" such as the Castle St Jorge; waterfront; Jardim Botanico; tram rides; Gulbenkian Museum; Rossio restaurants; Barrio Alto and Alfama including an evening fado session. Further afield we visited the Belem Tower and made a day trip

In early February Ian called telling me that the next phase of the SRI study was starting. MRDL were now required to revamp the NOP pit production schedule and new underground mining methods, such as VCR, bench & post fill and variations on drift mining all needed detailed planning and costing. Thus mid-month I headed for Birmingham and the BMI flight to Heathrow. In the departures lounge at Terminal 4 I caught up with Ian, Brian and Cliff who had transited from a San Francisco flight. The overnight BA flight delivered us into Lusaka around 7.30 in the morning. That time we did head for the Pamodzi Hotel since the MRDL guys were knackered after more than twenty hours flying. However by early evening they reappeared on the terrace to build up their strength with a beer or two.

The following morning it was the early RoanAir flight to Kitwe where we dumped our gear in Cassia House before heading for the SRI Project Office. Ian split up our work in a similar manner to last year whereby I "won" Mufulira and Baluba. Thus I spent the next week at the Mufulira mine working through all the recent geological data, in particular the DD logs from below the 1040 level, to ensure that I was au fait with the latest orebody outlines. Then I worked through all the maintenance records for development jumbos, LHDs, stope L/H drill rigs and haul trucks. I ignored jackhammer records as, finally, Mufulira had introduced modern trackless development methods. I also collected the last three months detailed production and performance records for all major items of mining machinery. Back at the SRI Project Office I used all that basic data to plan in detail how to mine the ground below 1040 level.

At Mufulira we had decided to stick with blast-hole open stoping with post-filling. In an attempt to cut down high waste dilution we opted for a full width overcut and parallel down-hole benching to a trough-undercut with flank drawpoints. The flattening dip with increasing depth dictated down-hole benching rather than the traditional ring drilling layout. Benching would also produce cleaner stope contacts which would reduce dilution.

I completed the Mufulira exercise by mid March and followed a similar approach to basic data collection at Baluba. That was a more challenging job since the very much flatter dip of the main orebody meant that we were unable to continue with traditional sub-level open stoping with ring drilling. Instead we developed a variation on drift-and-fill stoping similar to that employed at the Neves Corvo copper mine in southern Portugal. In essence that involved driving a full size crosscut from hangingwall to footwall then slyping 3m of each side working from footwall to hangingwall and immediately filling that 10m wide horizontal slice with de-slimed hydraulic fill. The next 10m crosscut/slype was sited adjacent to the already filled primary cut thus leaving no pillars or nasty abutments to aggravate ground conditions. My experience with the trial open stope at the Aguilar mine in Argentina plus the advice then of their geotechnical consultant, Peter, was invaluable in determining the details of the Baluba drift-and-fill stoping system.

By mid April we had completed the Baluba stoping layout and associated operating costs, which wrapped up my work on job No. 094. On the final weekend Ian took me up to have a look at the Konkola project. In the afternoon he drove us across the Zaire (Congo) border into the town of Kasumbalesa to, as he said, sample some Katangan beer. From the greetings he received from the barman I gathered that was not his first visit. Although less than twenty miles from Konkola both the bar and town had a different feel from Zambia. Unsurprising, I guess, since everyone was speaking French or pidgin English!

Ian was staying on in Zambia as he had set up a local MRDL subsidiary to handle all the geological and mining work they were doing for both ZCCM and SRI. I flew back to Lusaka with RoanAir, stayed overnight in Kwacha Lodge and caught the mid-morning BA flight back to Heathrow.

A few days after I got back a Mr Donovan from Benfleet in Essex called regarding a gold project he was investigating in Tajikistan! Well yes I thought, pull the other leg it's got bells on it. He said Mike, from Zimbabwe, had recommended me. I racked my brain then remembered that I had worked with Mike on the Harry Winston job in Sierra Leone back in 1988. That also was a small prospect. Mr Donovan asked me to come down to his place in Essex where he had established an office for the Tajikistan Gold Project. Could I make it next week as the Donovan Group, were planning a site visit in early June? I said yes, I would come to Benfleet. the following Monday.

I sent a fax to Mike's Geomet analytical laboratory in Zimbabwe, asking him to confirm that he was working on a Tajik gold prospect for Donovan. Also, was he getting paid? Mike replied saying yes and yes. So what's not to like I thought. I looked up the Donovan Group and found several different companies operating in the fields of refuse disposal, earth works contracting and supplying quarrying equipment to North Africa.

On Monday I caught the very early train from Worcester to Paddington, then the tube to Liverpool Street station and finally a train heading for Southend. At Benfleet I detrained and took a taxi for the five mile ride north to the Towerfield property of Donovan. It comprised a largish farmhouse with several barns, old and modern, close by. I was duly directed to the Gold Project office, which comprised an engineering/geological office plus secretarial facilities. It was now mid-morning as I was ushered into Mr Donovan's office, so a coffee was very welcome. He seemed a straight forward, middle aged business man. I told him my experience and daily fee rate and that was that. We shook hands and after a little over fifteen minutes he took me in to the project office to introduce me to an independent consulting geologist, Scot and left. As it happened that was the first and last time I saw Mr David Donovan.

Scot had been retained by Donovan for several months and had already visited the Tajik site with Mike. They had collected several samples which had been sent to the Zimbabwe laboratory for analysis and subsequent metallurgical testing. There were rudimentary geological/assay plans of the existing underground workings as well as a small open pit. The geologist confirmed that the mine site was quite remote with virtually no infrastructure, situated about 25 miles SE of the small town of Kairakkum. That town lay just south of the Kairakkum hydro reservoir and was noted for carpet weaving. Never having been to that part of the world it all sounded fascinating. Of course, up until the fall of the Berlin Wall in 1989 and the subsequent collapse of the USSR in 1991, places such as Tajikistan were largely unknown to Westerners. With the removal of central Russian control of natural resources many of those deposits were now available for development by foreign investors, hence Donovan's interest. Overall it all seemed to make sense and my initial caution vanished as I welcomed job No. 095. I went to say goodbye to Mr Donovan but he was out. The secretary ordered a taxi to take me back to Benfleet station.

I duly caught a Liverpool Street train crossed to Paddington by tube and fought my way onto a rush hour train bound for Worcester arriving there at close to 8.30pm. Finally back to Gorsty after a total of eleven hours travelling and waiting for just over four hours at Donovan's place. That didn't seem a very good return, but at least I now had a job lined up for early June.

With May clear Gillian took some time off work from the surgery and we decided to take Toadflax for a run up the Staffs & Worcester canal as far as the Great Haywood junction with the Trent & Mersey canal. We moored up at the northern end of Tixall Wide after four days cruising in which we covered 43 miles and forty locks. Gillian had become a very good steerer and found the boat much easier to control after she (the boat!) had been lengthened to 45ft Although there were many locks there was only the three-lock Bratch staircase to tax ones ingenuity. Some of the locks had quite a savage by-wash which thumped the old Toad around taking off a bit of paint. We walked up to the junction and turned south down the Trent & Mersey towpath to the magnificent NT property of Shugborough Hall. We enjoyed both the house and lovely gardens.

On the way back we took things a little more slowly stopping at Teddesley Boats in Penkridge so the lads could admire their handiwork on the boat's refit. We also moored overnight at the pleasant little town of Kinver and had a half day exploring Kinver Edge and the sandstone cave dwellings. On our return to Stourport it really felt like a proper canal boat mooring.

Towards the end of May I had a call from Mr Donovan's secretary asking me to join the "Tajik gold team" at the Uzbekistan Airlines (UA) check-in desk at Terminal 3, Heathrow on the 5th June. So, slightly to my surprise, the Tajik project was about to commence. For some reason BMI had suspended their shuttle flights between Birmingham and Heathrow so I arranged for a local Leominster taxi service to drive me to the airport. I eventually found Scot, the independent geologist together with John, the Donovan project jeffe and Svetlana our Russian interpreter. I was really pleased to see the interpreter as I was certain neither Scot nor I, nor John as it transpired, knew any Russian other than da! Apart from anything Svetlana was lively and very amusing. The UA check-in worked well, but the actual plane, a re-flagged Aeroflot discard did not inspire great confidence. But hey, after nearly eight hours we landed at Tashkent in one piece.

We stayed overnight in a vast, empty, hotel with a daunting babushka stationed on each floor to ensure there was no decadent western hanky-panky (fine chance). Svetlana certainly came into her own sorting out the very limited menu for us in the largely deserted dining room. In the morning John and Svetlana went off to collect an UAZ Russian jeep plus driver for the 140 mile trip south to Kairakkum. We reached the border crossing in seventy miles. The Tajik border guards were fully armed with AK47s and not at all friendly. Again we were all very happy to have Svetlana who, with the aid of various letters, permits and female guile persuaded the guards to let us through. A warm welcome to Tajikistan it was not. A further hitch occurred on arrival in Kairakkum - hotel shut! Enter Svetlana again, who after interminable discussions with all sorts of town officials, saw us ensconced in a carpet factory! That was the good news. The bad news was no food. Forward Svetlana and together we all went down to the main town market and bought anything/everything that looked faintly edible. A supply of local beer was also found. The market traders were definitely not a barrel of laughs and even Svetlana found the going tough. We also had to buy rough and ready crockery and cutlery.

Back at the carpet factory they had set aside a supervisor's room for us to use as a dining area. Suitably "wined and dined" Svetlana retired to the factory's guest bedroom and John, Scott and I retired to bunks in a carpet finishing room. The Uzbek driver had disappeared into the town. Well bunking down in a carpet factory was a new experience.

Next morning we shopped for hard hats and heavy duty torches and with the return of the Uzbek driver set off for the 25 mile drive to the gold prospect. The UAZ jeep certainly earned its keep on the dirt road as we climbed steadily up a valley. Some thirty miles ahead we could see the snow capped Pamir mountains rising to 5621m (18,442 ft). It was extremely remote country. By contrast the old mine site was unexceptional. It lay alongside the small river and was accessed by a series of adits into the side of the valley. At the southern, or downstream end of the outcrop a small side-cut open pit lay abandoned. The whole area was deserted. Scot and I scrambled around the surface looking for old trenches and surface scratchings in an attempt to guesstimate strike length, average width and dip of the quartz schist zone.

We took an early lunch break of sandwiches and beer before heading underground. Svetlana insisted on coming too. In turn I insisted on going first and testing (lighting matches) that the air was OK. In fact it was good. There were old raise connections through to the surface. Obviously we had a good look at the ore zone and I could get a better handle on strike length by using the high-tech method of pacing along the vein drives! Scot had already done some historical research that indicated that the long disused, dilapidated treatment plant had utilised a sulphide processing route. Mike, in Zimbabwe, was currently continuing metallurgical tests on several ore samples that he had collected last year. We collected several more samples from underground. Back out in the sunlight it was possible to distinguish pyrite with the aid of a hand lens. Svetlana was convinced it was gold we were looking at.

The next day was spent in and around Kairakkum collecting basic information on availability and cost of labour from the town officials and later visiting the nearby hydro power company to ascertain availability and details of supply. Of course Svetlana was absolutely key in that work as the Tajiks and us were deaf, dumb mutes to each other. She was brilliant handling queries on MVA capacity, frequency Hz, bus voltage, tariff kWhr etc. I was impressed. No surprises then when she told us that she had studied engineering in Russia before coming to the UK and becoming an interpreter. There was absolutely zero infrastructure at the old mine, so we started, in effect, with a clean slate. My biggest problem would be trying to generate realistic capital and operating costs for a new mine. However that all depended on whether Scot felt he could "develop" an ore reserve of some sort, given the very limited sample/assay data available.

Apart from an evening looking around the town there was really nothing more to be done except to enjoy another night in the carpet factory. The drive back to Tashkent went smoothly, well as smoothly as a UAZ jeep would allow, until the inevitable delay at the Tajik-Uzbek border. That time the Uzbeks seemed slightly less aggresive than the Tajiks since they had shouldered their own AK47s. It was almost welcome back to Uzbekistan. Another night in the deserted Tashkent hotel and then it was out to the airport. Those ex-USSR countries definitely do not make international passengers, either in or out, feel welcome. Of course the UA plane was three hours late, but we heaved a sigh of relief when it eventually left the tarmac bound for Heathrow. There my waiting driver had run up a sizeable coffee bill.

I had only been back three days when I had a call from Patrick of Mineral Research Development Inc (MRDI) a UK subsidiary of Ian's MRDL concerning a desk study of the Taror gold project in Tajikistan. Just like buses they came along in pairs. Welcome to job No. 096. Thus for the rest of June I was busy on Tajik business. Scot sent me a summary of his geological report and ore reserve calculation. Using that as a basis I developed a notional small underground gold mine and sulphide treatment plant together with the necessary infrastructure and services. I prepared crude capital and operating costs and despatched my mining report down to Mr David Donovan in Essex.

On the Taror job, Patrick sent me a copy of MRDI's Geological Report and some Mining Notes prepared by Paul of Robertson Research. It appeared to be a fairly compact gold orebody with an ore expectancy of 19,600 t/vm implying a sustainable mining rate of 600,000 tonnes/year from a transverse SLC mining method. I prepared order-of-magnitude capital and operating costs for a Taror operation of that size. Because of the low in situ gold grade of 5.5 dwt/t and the high dilution SLC mining method such a project would only just have a positive gross operating margin. I sent brief fax reports to Patrick in Norwich and Ian in San Mateo, California.

No sooner had I finished the "multiple Tajik reports" to Donovan and Patrick than a Swedish gentleman from the European Commission telephoned inviting me to come and discuss a mining job in Botswana. I drove to Birmingham, left the car, and caught a shuttle flight to Brussels. I had visited the EU Commission once before when working for ZCCM. It was a monstrous bureaucratic organisation to strike fear into ones heart. There seemed to be miles of interminable corridors that all looked identical. In the Swedes office he explained that the EU was considering providing funds for the rehabilitation of the Selibe-Phikwe copper-nickel mine. The EU required a technical assessment of the operation. Could I handle the mine? I did my usual selling spiel and the Swede seemed happy. I then went with him to see his manager and signed an "Engagement Contract". That specified a starting date in the third week of August. Daily fee rates were agreed and that was that. Welcome to job No. 097. Amazingly the contract formalities were concluded swiftly and I caught a late afternoon shuttle flight back to Birmingham.

Sproggs was home again for the summer holidays. He was now playing cricket for the Lucktonians on their rugby ground over at Kingsland. He was OK as a lower order batsman, No 5 or 6 and a very occasional change bowler. However his main forte seemed to be fielding where he had a very good, accurate throwing arm. Speaking of which we came to chancing his arm. He had arranged for his Wrekin girlfriend, Emma, to come and stay. Being old-fashioned Gillian had arranged for Emma to be in the spare room in the guest end of Gorsty. Of course the kids had other ideas once the "dreaded parents" had gone to bed. However old farmhouses have their advantage (for parents) - the old elm floorboards creak! Well we had to step in, after all Emma was only 15. It caused much bemusement since, as Sproggs said we both want to "do it", so what's the problem? Using the argument of "she's underage" somehow didn't sound very convincing, but that was that. So I bundled them both in to the Discovery and took Emma back to join her mother who was staying with her new man, having separated from Emma's father. Yes, by George it was a tricky meeting and I was made to feel about two inches tall as an irresponsible father! Sproggs and Emma sat in the kitchen saying nowt. By comparison the "new man" felt I had done the right thing. It was a long, silent drive back to Gorsty with Sproggs.

In mid August the EU Commission phoned and said the Botswana visit was delayed by a week or so. I replied no problem. Early in September I took Sproggs back to the Wrekin for the winter term. I sought out David, the assistant Tudor housemaster and told him of the "affaire Emma". He looked at me in amazement and said "well what did you expect in 1994, they are both mid-teens and the girls always carry a pack of condoms for the boyfriend"? To be honest I was gobsmacked, how things had changed since I was a teenager in the early 1950s. I had already had a sex talk session with Sproggs, stressing the need for condoms and now expanded that to "please, only girls over 16". Well as they say, there you go, the joys of boarding in a co-ed school. You can't knock it, it's an essential part of education and growing up.

I phoned the EU Commission up to be told that the Botswana job had been further delayed for a few months. No new start date. I was beginning to get a bad feeling about that non-job. In the same vein it was now eight weeks since I'd submitted my invoice to Donovan for the Tajikistan job - nothing. I submitted a Statement of Account requesting payment. Yet another bad feeling. Amazingly another mining job in Central Asia turned up in early October when Chris of Commodities Research Unit (CRU) in London asked if I could accompany him to Uzbekistan to look at a number of gold mining operations. I said when? He replied next week for about a ten-day visit. Unsurprisingly I said yes and welcomed job No. 098.

Later that same week I had a call from the Swede at the EU Commission saying that they wished to start the Botswana job next week. He was a little surprised when I said that their Botswana job would not now involve me as I was committed to a job in Uzbekistan. I pointed out that I was self-employed and could not sit at home twiddling my thumbs waiting for the EU to call for a job which had been delayed for three months and then expected me to drop everything at a weeks notice. I made a note, don't bother with the EU as they were totally unreliable and a difficult client. Who needed them?

My Leominster taxi service took me up to Heathrow, Terminal 3 on the 18th October where I met Chris at the now familiar UA check-in. It was the same old clapped out ex-Aeroflot discard plane but I could reassure Chris that only a few months ago it had got me to and back from Tashkent in one piece. He was not reassured. Nevertheless it did the business and we duly checked into the same vast, empty hotel. The following day, complete with Uzbek driver, we headed 260 miles SW to the famous Silk Road city of Samarkand. Here we were booked into another large, empty hotel. We seemed to be the only Westerners staying there. The city, a UNESCO, World Heritage site was considered to be at the crossroads of different cultures. After a very early dinner/late lunch we set out to look at some of the marvellous architecture. For me the Lions Gate at the Sherdar Medressa, covered in ceramic tiles, was a really impressive sight as the sun set. There were many more but I cannot recall specific names. Chris and I agreed we needed a week rather than the three hours we had for tourism.

Next morning we headed NNW of Samarkand for 1.5 hours on a sealed road to the town of Zarmitan, where we visited the Charmitan underground gold mine. The deposit comprised a swarm of steep dipping quartz veins in a host rock of metamorphosed Silurian sediments. Strike length of the veins ranged from 300m to 1km with an average width of 2m. There was little folding or faulting, but plenty of pinch-and-swell of the veins on both dip and strike. Ore reserves were quoted as 15.8 million tonnes at 10g/t Au and 18g/t Ag. Two exploration shafts had shown mineralisation to 350m depth. The current production shaft, 4.3m diam concrete with RSJ buntons and wooden guides, was 210m deep. Ore was hoisted in 2t mine cars in balanced cages by a 450 kW AC winder built in Donetsk, Ukraine. Oldish, heavy design, badly maintained. Present output was about 100,000 tonnes/year although it had been 350,000 t/year in 1990/91.

It got worse underground where the housekeeping was non-existent with rubbish everywhere. Fortunately ground conditions were strong, otherwise it would have rated as one of the worse, unsafe mines I'd visited. The stoping method was shrinkage with breast hole drilling with medium weight jacklegs. Underground trackwork, compressed air lines and ladderways were in complete disrepair. Ventilation was non-existent. Ore recovery from the shrinks was by air driven overshot loaders to the 2t box cars hauled by 5t DC trolley locos. A big plus point was the absence of ground-water. Both Chris and I were extremely glad to get back to surface without mishap. An underground nightmare. The so-called surface infrastructure - admin building, lamproom, changehouse, winder house, compressor building were all an absolute disgrace. The management's response, via an interpreter, was always "shortage of everything - no money".

Without doubt it was one of the most depressing mines I had visited and I was glad to get back to Samarkand, which immediately raised my spirits. Chris, who was a minerals economist not a mining guy, took everything in his stride and seemed somewhat surprised when I said the Charmitan mine was an appalling shambles. I said I hoped some of the other mines we were visiting were "good ones" and he would see the difference. After another quick look around the city we retired to the hotel and chatted to an English speaking local over very strong Turkish coffee. Inevitably the talk turned to the break up of the USSR and what future now for an independent Uzbekistan?

In the morning we headed ENE for 45 miles to Majanbulak, the concentrator site. Here the Charmitan ore, brought in by truck, joined that from three Majan open pits. Present plant capacity was stated to be 0.5 million tonnes/year. The plant was designed for free milling gold ore so that the arsenopyrite from Charmitan was causing problems with cyanide consumption. Well the least said the better. If the Charmitan mine was bad the Majanbulak plant was downright awful. The worst, most hazardous mineral concentrator I'd ever visited. Overall metallurgical recovery was quoted as 80% with a tails grade of 0.4g/t Au. Taking those figures at face value would imply a head grade of only 2g/t which did not seem compatible with a Charmitan reserve grade of 10g/t Au. Something didn't add up, but just about anything could happen in that plant. The 70% gold cathodes from the electrolysis section were sent to the Almalyk metallurgical complex. Since CRU's interest in those Uzbekistan gold operations was in essence a preliminary due diligence exercise for a Swiss banking group I had to prepare a metallurgical flowsheet, which in that plant required a modicum of guesswork and imaginative thinking. What a nightmare.

We left immediately after a "lunch" of disgusting, unchewable, unrecognisable lumps of meat in a greasy gruel accompanied by rock hard black bread. Fine dining it wasn't! We headed back east for the long drive back to Tashkent, where the menu in the hotel's deserted dining room had one positively salivating. The next day, Friday, was a religious holiday so Chris and I did some tourism in Tashkent. Of course there was a lot of heavy Russian architecture and much of the city was laid out on a grid pattern, but the streets were wide with green/fawn trams running down the centre. Although the city was on the Silk Road very little of the old traditional architecture remained. It was quite clearly a Russian built city dominated on the outskirts by gaunt, grey apartment blocks that put fear into ones heart.

The next day we drove for 1.5 hours ENE of Tashkent to the Angren gold mine at Kzilalmasai, about thirty minutes from the huge metallurgical complex at Almalyk. That was a newish gold mine developed over the past three years. There were two orebodies about 90m apart dipping at 70 degrees within Ordovician sediments and porphyry. Strike lengths was up to 600m with average true widths around 22 m. There was little folding or faulting. Total ore reserves were quoted as 17 million tonnes at 8.4g/t Au. The mine had been developed by a 5m diam concrete lined shaft furnished with RSJs and wooden guides. A double-drum winder with twin, 630 kW AC drive hoisted two balanced cages with 2.2t capacity mine cars over a full depth of 410 m. There was also a 12m² section 1 in 8 ramp-decline. Level interval was 55m. Current output was 100, 000 tonnes/year with a planned output of 350,000 tonnes/year. Certainly the current daily hoisting output of 400 tonnes was way under the hoist's capacity.

The stoping method was transverse SLC, retreating from hangingwall to footwall, with a 12m sub-level vertical interval. Our underground visit showed that ground conditions throughout the mine were weak. Of course SLC stoping required weak host rocks, especially on the hangingwall, so that the ground caved readily and a relatively strong orebody so that the brows of the sub-level extraction cosscuts remained firm and did not wear/collapse producing uncontrolled dilution. At Angren the orebody was very weak such that all mine development was 100% supported by steel arches, concrete slabs and round timber. Because of the support it was extremely difficult to observe "pristine" rock, but in one or two places where the local support had failed the ground appeared to be a loosely cemented conglomerate. Drilling utilised lightweight jacklegs and mucking was by small rubber tyred auto loaders, similar to an Atlas T2G or Cavo 310. The choice of an SLC stoping method was quite incompatible with the weak orebody. That seemed confirmed by the very low grade of ore delivered to the concentrator, as a consequence of high dilution.

Underground haulage was by 380 volt DC trolley operating on 45 lb rail. Ventilation was passable (SLC was notoriously difficult) and mine services were reasonable. Surface infrastructure was much better than the Charmitan mine, but inadequate by western standards. Through an interpreter the Mine Manager confirmed that the main problem was weak ground conditions and the lack of money to buy consumables. Nothing new there then.

There was just time for a "sort of filled black bap" for lunch (phew thank goodness no more gruel) before we had a real bums rush around the concentrator. Here the rom ore from Kizilalmasal and other mines was picked up from ground storage by a rope shovel to a conveyor feeding a silo. From there it was extracted by a vibrating feeder to an Autogenous Mill. Curiously there were no primary nor secondary crushers at all. From the Mill trommel oversize passed to a ball mill in closed circuit with cyclones whilst the under size passed to Humphrey Spirals and shaking tables. The overflow passed to a flotation section from which a final dried concentrate was loaded into rail wagons for haulage to the nearby Almalyk metallurgical complex.

After leaving the Angren mine, Chris had somehow wangled a visit to the Almalyk complex, which was only fifteen miles away. With the help of a secretary who spoke excellent English we got in to see one of the senior managers. He seemed more than happy to talk to us (also spoke perfect English) and insisted on showing us one of the nearby open-pit copper mines. Well, what a surprise. It was absolutely vast. I would guess three times larger than the Nchanga open pit in Zambia. It had obviously been a rail haulage strip mine initially, but as it had got deeper had switched to a shovel/truck operation. For a bit of mining tourism (or is that an oxymoron?) it was out of the top drawer. I was quite overawed at the scale of operations. It seemed a quantum jump from the rather sad little underground gold mines we had visited elsewhere in Uzbekistan.

One last night in the hotel and we said goodbye to our ever watchful babushka. Tashkent airport was it's usual messy self but we got better acquainted with it when UA announced that their London flight was delayed - "technical problems". To me that announcement was filled with foreboding for the chances of the Aeroflot discard making it to Heathrow in one piece were not high. Three hours later, hurrah, UA announced that the flight would now be handled by a DC8 borrowed from another airline as their own plane had been taken out of service. That really was a splendid outcome, as the DC8 was infinitely preferable to a Tupolev or Antonov or whatever it was. Finally airborne Chris and I celebrated with a vodka or two.

My Leominster taxi guy had used his head and checked arrival times with UA so he had only been waiting an hour. I had agreed with Chris that I would write up and fax him some Visit Notes in the next few days. Those notes were somewhat delayed since, as I said to Chris, "to put it bluntly I have been keeping within five yards of the loo & today visited the Doc as it seems to be mild amoebic dysentery - curtesy of the Tashkent Airport cafe"!

Two days after I had faxed the Visit Notes to CRU, Chris phoned and asked me to prepare capital and operating cost estimates for both the Uzbek mines as if they were now being developed by a western company. He wanted these asap. For Charmitan the costing was based on an output of 2200 tonnes/day over 300days/year or 660,000 tonnes/year. Mining was by conventional shrink stoping providing a mill head grade of 8.4g/t Au and a metallurgical recovery of 88% in a new, gravity concentrator and CIP plant.

Area	US$ millions (mid 1994 basis)
Mine	37.83
Mine EPCM Fee (7%)	2.65
Plant & Surface Facilities	47.00
Concentrator EPCM Fee (13%)	6.11
Contingency (8.6%)	8.05
Total	**101.64**

say US$ 102 million

That figure excluded Working Capital, which based on four months operating costs, would require a further US$ 9.9 million.

The total project capital cost was equivalent to US$ 154/annual tonne of ore treated. That was 20% higher than the average underground mine/plant capital cost quoted by the Mining Journal of US$ 128/annual tonne throughput based on recent western developments. However Charmitan costs would be higher on account of it being a narrow vein deposit, hence very low development yields and an Uzbek location with high freight/procurement costs.

Total direct operating costs were Mining US$ 26; Treatment US$ 14; Service /Admin/Overhead US$ 5 giving a total direct operating cost of US$ 45/tonne mined and treated. An additional US$ 2.5/tonne should be added for Capital Replacement.

With a current gold price of US$ 383/oz each gram was worth US$ 12.3 and the Charmitan ore was thus worth US$ 90.5 providing a gross operating margin of US$ 45/t mined and treated, or a gross revenue US$ 29.7 million over a full year.

For Angren the basic mining plan was to use longitudinal two pass cut-and-fill stoping for No 1 orebody and transverse SLC for No 10 orebody giving a total mine output of 4300 tonnes/day or 1.29 million tonnes/year at a mill head grade of 6.4g/t Au and a metallurgical recovery of 88% in a new gravity and CIP plant.

Area	US$ millions (mid 1994 price)
Mine	58.24
Mine EPCM Fee (7%)	4.08
Plant & Surface Facilities	66.00
Concentrator EPCM Fee (13%)	8.58
Contingency (9%)	12.57
Total	**149.47**
	say US$ 150 million

That figure also excluded Working Capital, which, based on four months operating costs would require a further US$ 15.8 million.

The total project cost was equivalent to US$ 116 per annual tonne of ore treated. That was about 9.5% lower than the underground mine/plant capital cost quoted by the Mining Journal.

Total direct operating costs were Mining US$ 18; Treatment US$ 12.5; Sevice/Admin/Overhead US$ 3.5 giving a total direct operating cost of US$ 34/t mined & treated. An additional US$ 2.3/tonne should be added for Capital Replacement.

With gold at US$ 383/oz the Angren ore was worth US$ 69/t providing a gross operating margin of US$ 35/t mined and treated, which, over a full year mining 1.29 million tonnes yielded a gross revenue of US$ 45.1 million. The cost of gold production would be US$ 189/oz, almost identical to Charmitan.

Finally clear of the Uzbekistan job I noted that I had still not been paid by Donovan for the work in Tajikistan. I called their offices in Essex, but, unsurprisingly neither Donovan nor their "Office manager" was available. I decided to phone Scot, the geologist, to see if he had been paid. No, he had not and the previous week he had been laid off. The stink was getting stronger. I next sent a fax to Mike in Zimbabwe and by return had a reply saying his lab, had also not been paid, what was going on? As my invoice was now outstanding for five months I contacted Tom, my local solicitor and asked for his advice. He advised me to collect all relevant paperwork and make representation to the Debtors Court in Hereford. That I duly did. I was told that the Court would pass judgement on my case early next year. You can't hurry the legal system.

We were now into December and Sproggs was heavily involved in both hockey and rugby up at the Wrekin. His latest girlfriend (one of many according to David!) had pooh-poohed playing a musical instrument, so that was the end of Sproggs interest in learning the clarinet. I could cheerfully have strangled her, but really it was no contest - a clear come-on from the fairer sex or persevere with scales. Again I noted that it was the girls who made the running. He had been in a bit of trouble at school since he and a number of mates (and girls) had been caught out of bounds down in Telford drinking. They were all now "gated", but that didn't seem to stop in-school fraternal activity between girls and boys boarding houses. Because Sproggs was in the Wrekin's first rugby and hockey teams he seemed to be dealt with fairly leniently. Both Gillian and I enjoyed watching both home and away matches in both sports, but there were no more concerts to attend.

Not long before Christmas I had a call from an old ex-RTZC mining guy, Terry, now with the consulting outfit Brook, Hunt & Associates (BHA) down in Surrey. Did I fancy a trip to Kazakhstan to look at some lead-zinc mines and gold mines? They, BHA, were advising a German bank, on the likely value of those ex-USSR mineral assets now the property of the independent Kazakh government. Hard to believe yet another Central Asian job, but that part of the world was obviously flavour of the month. Welcome to job No. 099. Terry expected the visit to take place in early January (1995). It would definitely be cold so be prepared. With that advice ringing in my ears I headed off to Shephards Surplus Stores at Ivington, a few miles west of Leominster. I settled for two pairs of long johns, thick socks for my working boots and some fur lined gloves. On a try out, kitted up at home with the long johns, thick fisherman's sweater, hiking waterproof, topped off with my Chinese fur hat I could hardly move! Gillian and Sproggs killed themselves laughing at me waddling around the kitchen.

47

On the 8th January my faithful Leominster taxi driver drove me down to the BHA offices in Addlestone, Surrey. Terry introduced me to his Kazakh team which comprised Phil, (BHA project engineer); Mark (BHA geologist); Umit (independent metallurgist) and Natasha (independent economist and interpreter). I supplied the mining input. A couple of senior managers from the German firm, MG, also took part in the team's briefing. MG and some German banks were BHA's ultimate client. In effect our brief was to undertake a rapid appraisal of the Malieva lead-zinc deposit and the Vasilkovskoye gold deposit to ascertain if they were sufficiently attractive to invest in their development. As with my previous work in Central Asia that was all a consequence of the collapse of the USSR in 1991.

In due course a minibus delivered us to Terminal 3 at Heathrow. We were flying Kazakhstan Airways (KA) to Almaty. As expected the plane was an ex-Aeroflot reject in that case a Tupolev TU 154, narrow bodied, rear three-engined jet. Well it got us there with a minimum of on-board cabin service and a couple of Heathrow plastic meals. I had put on a pair of long johns at Heathrow as the check-in staff had warned us it was cold in Almaty. They were spot on the money it was bloody cold. At the airport we were met by what could only be called some "heavies" from the Zyrianovsk Lead-Zinc Combinate who steered us through to the Domestic part of the terminal to purchase tickets to Ust Kamenogorsk. The flight to Ust K took just over one hour flying in an ancient Yak 40 tri-jet.

Ust Kamenogorsk was an unpleasant, dirty city dominated by mining and a huge lead-zinc-copper smelting complex on the river Irtysh. Everywhere was covered with filthy, coal-dust blackened snow. We piled into a Russian version of the VW Kombi for the four and half hour drive ESE on rough tortuous roads to the town of Zyrianovsk. It was bitterly cold in the "Kombi" as several of the doors/windows let in an icy blast. The Combinate's house where we stayed was warmish with blazing open fires. The town was covered in snow with snow-ploughed roads. There were three mining centres. Grekhov and Zyrianovsk were both old underground mines and the new Malieva mine, which was a high grade, massive pyrite hosted poly-metallic deposit, currently under development. A central, differential flotation concentrator was located at the Zyrianovsk mine.

Our target was the new Malieva mine about 25 miles from Zyrianovsk. The massive sulphide orebody (cf Iberian Pyrite Belt) sub-outcropped 250m below surface and extended to a depth of 650 m. Strike length was 550m with an average width of 90m and a dip of 75 degrees. Developed reserves were quoted as 43.2 million tonnes at 7.7% Zn, 2.5% Cu, 1.2% Pb, 0.6g/t Au and 80g/t Ag. Ore expectancy was 72,000 t/vm. The hangingwall rocks were quartz porphyry whilst the underlying sediments comprised shales, mudstones, siltstones and sandstones. There was little folding or faulting and ground-water was minimal. Underground ore exposures showed that the massive sulphides were strong, competent Class 1 ground. Both the quartz porphyry and footwall sediments were less strong, probably Class 3 ground. My old 10% ore expectancy rule would indicate a sustainable mining rate of 7,000 tonnes/day, which over 300 days, would imply a production rate of 2.1 million tonnes/year.

The mine was still under development and stoping had not yet commenced. The Combinate were planning to use a transverse version of drift-and-fill. They appeared paranoid about ground conditions, planning for small stope spans with rapid placement of very high strength cemented backfill. That was hard to understand. The orebody dimensions and ground conditions seemed to me entirely suitable for bulk mining utilising sub-level blast-hole open stoping or VCR. Either method would utilise a primary/secondary stope layout with post backfilling. If the hangingwall porphyry was consistently weak and caveable then transverse SLC would be an obvious low-cost stoping alternative. The orebody was strong, an essential pre-requisite for successful SLC.

Four vertical monolithic concrete lined shafts had already been sunk to the full depth. Those ranged from 5.5m up to 7.5m diameter. Main levels connecting those shafts had been completed on three levels at 4m x 4m size. Present production was 200,000 tonnes/year, the rom ore being trucked 25 miles from the headframe bins to the central Zyrianovsk concentrator. Ore was hoisted in small mine cars by cage, but skip winding was planned. A final production rate of 1.0 million tonnes/year was projected for 1998. Firstly, that production rate would seriously undermine the deposit and secondly, a further four years for that to be reached seemed excessive when the major mine development (ie shafts and main levels) had already been completed.

On surface the main mine infrastructure had been completed, apart from new double-drum winders for two of the shafts. Power was adequate, derived from hydro-electric plants on the river Irtysh and lake Buchtamar near Zyrianovsk. All underground mining equipment was either electric (DC trolley), electro-hydraulic or diesel thus there was no need for a surface compressor plant. Other supplies such as diesel, cement, explosives were readily available from sources in the Ust Kamenogorsk/Zyrianovsk corridor.

Later in the afternoon we drove back to Zyrianovsk and caught up with Umit who had been working his way around the differential flotation concentrator. In fact we were just in time for the most entertaining bit of the day. Attached to the concentrator change house there was a senior staff sauna, yes, really. So with no more ado four Brits and six Russians stripped off and started sweating (well it made a pleasant change from shivering). In spite of much cajoling from the Russians, Natasha declined to come and join us (sensible lady). I was somewhat apprehensive about the adjacent cold water plunge tank, but apart from knocking one's breath out and, somewhat alarmingly, shrinking one's tackle to microscopic size, we survived. The final coup de grace was the appearance of several large shots of vodka which, of course, had to be downed in one. Mind you, the grim winter climate in that part of the world made daily vodka an essential for survival.

After a morning meeting with the Combinate's management we set off in the dreaded icy cold "Kombi" for the four to five hour drive back to the airport at Ust Kamenogorsk. In fact our driver insisted on giving us a quick tour of Ust K. Away from the metallurgical complex it was not quite so bad, but in truth pretty awful as the pollution and dust from the smelter stacks covered everything, not least the piles of ploughed snow. The return flight to Almaty was by another ancient ex-Aeroflot Yak 40 plane. The heavies again met us and took us to a very pleasant, well run small hotel. I asked Natasha what was the reason for the heavies. She said that apparently some western employees of a local company had been taken hostage as a bargaining tool by another local competing company. The Combinate, very thoughtfully, had decided that they did not want that to happen to us. We all agreed.

We had some of the next day to do a little sight seeing. Almaty, being the capital of Kazakhstan was a big bustling city situated in the south-eastern part of that enormous country just 25 miles north of the Kyrgyzstan border along the towering Tian Shan mountains which rose to nearly 5,000m

(16,000 ft). Natasha had sussed out that we ought to take a cable car ride up Kok Tobe, an 1100m hill (small mountain really!) on the cities southern boundary. All five of us went for this exhilarating ride accompanied by two heavies (armed bodyguards), which either gave one a feeling of security, or anxiety, because the heavies might attract attention. To be honest no one seemed in the least bit interested and like us everyone was admiring the spectacular view. On return to the city proper we visited Panfilov Heroes Memorial Park and the amazing wooden construction Zenkov Cathedral.

Then it was back to the hotel to collect our bags and catch an afternoon KA flight to Kokchetau. The plane was, yet again, an ancient ex-Aeroflot Yak 40 rear-engined tri-jet. After de-bussing and waiting to mount the central rear stairs I noticed that the wings were fairly heavily iced up. I hoped someone in the crew would notice that as well. Faint chance. When the pilot or co-pilot boarded through the cabin he was cheerfully carrying a bottle of vodka! Everyone seems to carry a bottle of vodka - it was one of life's essentials in Kazakhstan. It got better, my seat (yes, we had seats) had no back rest stop. If I leant back on it I ended up on the lap of the passenger behind. Nil desperandum, the take-off from Almaty and landing at Kokchetau were perfect. The 800 mile flight NNW from Almaty took just over two hours.

On deplaning onto the tarmac at Kokchetau the cold was so intense it made ones ears and nose feel brittle. The ambient temperature was minus 40 C. Two four-wheel-drive utes travelling over hard packed snow took us into a small town-centre hotel. It was a large town, apparently 150,000 population and everywhere giant (3 or 4ft diameter) lagged pipes distributed central heating from the town's coal fired power plant cooling system. In spite of that the temperature inside the hotel was still below freezing! All of us, now fully clad against the cold, took a quick, unsteady (because it was extremely slippery underfoot) trip around the main town square as the light was fading, before reassembling in the hotel bar, where we now had company. Word had gone out that westerners were in town and half a dozen or so ladies of the night appeared to peddle their charms. Practically it was a non-starter for us. Firstly it would take an age to find one's tackle through the layers of clothes (long johns included) and secondly the cold had a hugely diminishing effect. Natasha was convinced that Brits would not last long in northern Kazakhstan and that comment had nothing to do with sex.

The Vasilkovskoye gold deposit lay about eleven miles NW of the town. The whole area comprised flat, featureless steppe country covered with hard packed frozen snow at the time of our mid-January visit. Winter here lasts from October to May and temperatures were said to drop to minus 50 C on occasions. Another aspect was the chill factor brought on by strong winds which whipped across the flat steppes. The deposit comprised a mineralised granodiorite and gabbro diorite sliced by a major fault structure. The bulk of the free gold was associated with the granodiorite whilst some was combined with minor sulphides. The primary deposit was overlain by a 50m deep oxide zone. The deposit had been extensively probed by diamond drilling (DD) where core recovery in the competent diorites was in the 80 to 90% range.

From 1969 to 1983 there was extensive underground development from two vertical shafts. Levels were developed at -60 m, -120m & -180m depth. Now all of that development was inaccessible due to flooding. However we were able to examine the old level plans. The Canadian company, Placer Dome had made four visits and was currently putting down a DD to 800m having already completed another DD to 600m depth. The Australian company, Dominion also spent several weeks on site. The crude reserve data indicated an increase of grade with depth but reducing tonnage. The Kazakhs were quoting 41 million tonnes at 3.6g/t Au down to -360m depth and 12.7 million tonnes at 4.3g/t Au from -360m to -600m depth. What was immediately apparent was that there was not "an ore reserve", there was a suite, a tonnage-grade curve, the actual ore reserve selected totally dependent on the cut-off grade (COG) applied. Unfortunately no tonnage-grade data was forthcoming and it appeared that, in fact, the Kazakhs had not done that analysis. With an ore expectancy of 132,500 t/vm above the -360m horizon an open pit could easily sustain a mining rate of four million tonnes/year.

Most of the main open-pit area had been pre-stripped and the oxide ore stockpiled. That was now being trucked to a heap leach/resin plant about 6Km distant. A conventional shovel-truck pit was planned based on 15m benches in waste and 7.5m benches in ore. The lower bench height in ore was to enable greater selectivity in handling internal pit waste. Some of the stripped waste diorite was passed through a crushing and screening plant for the preparation of aggregate for either concrete or roadstone use. The Kazakh's project envisaged a 1.2 million tonnes/year operation but recently that had been scaled back to only 600,000 tonnes/year due to lack of money.

Of course that was a ludicrously low output for a deposit of that size, but as so often in those old USSR countries lack of investment funds was the key.

All pit equipment was, unsurprisingly, Russian. A 300mm diam rotary drill, 5m^3 rope face shovels and forty tonne capacity Belaz trucks and assorted track dozers. We were wandering around the open pit for thirty to forty minutes only, but my feet, in spite of thermal socks and heavy mining boots, were frozen solid. Much civil construction work had been completed at the nearby plant site - primary crusher building; conveyors; crushed ore silos; grinding bay; maintenance shops and administrative building. There was also an enormous quantity of equipment and stores just dumped outside onto the steppe with little or no protection from the severe weather! In fact as we drove in from Kokchetau a km from the plant two grinding mills were visible just lying alongside the branch railway line. With a temperature range of minus 40 C to plus 30 C degrees much of the electrical and rotating machinery (bearings etc) would be damaged beyond repair. Some of that machinery had been lying on the steppe for five to ten years! Projects in Kazakhstan seemed fraught with difficulty.

The cold hotel seemed like a tropical paradise after the freezing open pit. It took thirty minutes to thaw out my feet in the wash basin water. Just after lunch we headed out to Kokchetau airport. I have no idea what the problem was, but the KA flight to take us back to Almaty did not turn up. After a two hour wait and numerous visits to the airport manager, we were bundled into a minibus and set off on a two and half hour drive to Atbasar/Akmola where there was another airport. The only thing I noted of interest across that interminable frozen steppe was an arctic fox lopping along close to the road. Much to my amazement, we had no sooner arrived at Atbasar airport than we were hustled onto the inevitable Yak 40 which immediately took off for Almaty. That time I had a seat with an adjustable stop on the backrest - such luxury.

Our last night in Almaty was uneventful under the watchful gaze of the heavies. Next morning they seemed really happy to deliver us to Departures at the airport, but not so ecstatic that any of them cracked a smile. Central Asia, what a place. Cold, heavy Slavic atmosphere. Give me South America or SE Asia anytime, warm climate and warm friendly people. Yes an interesting experience, but I was glad when we lifted off the Almaty runway for the eight hour haul back to Heathrow and yes, we did sample some vodka and beer en route. At Heathrow I caught the CoachAir rail link to Reading where I transferred to the Cotswold Line for Worcester. As it was late Gillian was there to meet me for the drive back to Gorsty.

Over the next five days I prepared Visit Notes for both mines and sent them by fax to Terry at BHA. Two days later he phoned and asked me to prepare cost estimates for a notional 2 million tonnes/year underground mine at Malieva and a notional five million tonnes/year open-pit mine at Vasilkovskoye and yes, MG wanted those asap. I completed those notional mine costings over the following week and a half. The Malieva two million tonnes/year underground mine capital cost came to US$ 70 million and the direct operating cost estimate was US$ 14.5/tonne mined. The average mill head grade was 7.2% Zn, 2.3% Cu and 1.1% Pb. The Vasilkovskoye five million tonnes/year open-pit capital cost was US$ 145 million and the direct operating cost estimate was US$ 6.3/tonne ore at a 5.8 to 1 strip ratio. The cost per tonne moved (ore & waste) was US$ 0.93. The average mill head grade was 2.6g/t Au. The good news was that BHA and more importantly MG seemed satisfied with those estimates.

Once I was clear of the Kazakhstan job I contacted my solicitor, Tom, again about the non-payment of my invoice by Donovan. He said he had been informed by the County Debts Court in Hereford that I had been awarded "the case" against Donovan. However the Hereford Court had been in contact with the Essex County Court as Essex was the (apparent) domicile of various Donovan companies. From the inter-County Court discussions it had emerged that Barclays Bank was a large creditor of Donovan. Barclays had financed the purchase of some quarrying plant being supplied by Donovan for export to a Tunisian company. As collateral Donovan had put up the Deeds of his Essex farmhouse complex. When push came to shove it appeared that Donovan had switched ownership of the farmhouse into his wife's name, unbeknown, of course, to Barclays. The Hereford Court had suggested to Tom that I get in contact with Barclays and that we exchange all/any information we had on Donovan.

I first contacted Scot, the independent geologist, and told him what I had learnt. I asked him to let me know which Donovan company had been paying his monthly retainer. The Court had already told Tom, my solicitor, which branch of Barclays was dealing with the "Donovan problem". I phoned Barclays, explained who I was and that I was also an unsecured creditor of Donovan. I confirmed that I had been awarded the case against Donovan, but that it would now be necessary to sue him to get the money owed. Barclays was in the same position (owed more than £1 million) and asked if I could come up to their offices to exchange background information on Donovan. We agreed to meet at their offices the day after next.

It was a Wednesday, Gillian's day off from the surgery, so she ran me over to Worcester to catch an early train to Paddington. From there I took the tube to the Bank station (of course) and eventually located the desired Barclays branch. They made me feel very welcome even though they appreciated that I was only a one-man creditor owed a few thousands compared to their plus £1 million outstanding. They were interested in the bank details of the Donovan company that had been paying Scot, the geologist and also that Mike's outfit in Zimbabwe had been paid by telegraphic transfer from a Donovan company based in Gibraltar.

The Barclays chappie said his investigators were delving into the complicated web of Donovan companies and perhaps I might like to join Barclay's action against Donovan. Obviously I welcomed it as Barclays had the wherewithal to pursue Donovan through the Courts. I said I would contact Mike in Zimbabwe to ascertain how much he was owed and if he also would like to join Barclay's action. If so, for him to send fax copies of outstanding invoices direct to Barclays own fax. They were not optimistic that any money would be recovered since the beneficial ownership of Donovan's UK based companies appeared to be held by a Gibraltar registered company, which was outside UK jurisdiction. Hey ho, it was comforting to learn that I was not the only mug taken in by Donovan.

In late February I had a call from Ian of MRDL could I come back to Zambia to do some more work on Mufulira? Of course I said yes, welcome to job No. 100. On the 6th March my old school mate Oliver drove me up to Heathrow depositing me at Terminal 4. I caught the usual BA overnight flight to Harare with a short hop on to Lusaka. At the airport I switched to the Domestic Terminal and boarded the early morning RoanAir flight to Kitwe. Ian collected me from Southdowns airport and took me to Cassia House to drop my gear before going on to the SRI project office. There were a few familiar faces from a year ago but most of Ian's mining guys had gone having finished their costing work. He explained that SRI wanted another opinion on the proposed sub-vertical rock hoisting below the 1040 level at Mufulira. Fortunately I had brought a copy of my own 1984 report on that topic undertaken for Zambia Engineering Services. Obviously some things would have changed but much of the basic engineering data would still be relevant.

The following day Ian and I went to Mufulira for a briefing on the status quo by the Underground Manager, Chief Geologist and Engineering Manager. Due to the lengthy delays in the sinking of the Musombo SV2 shaft by the contractor Mowlem-Fry, much of the original mine development plan had been compromised. In addition a South African contractor, SAMAT, had fallen way behind on primary development on the 1140, 1240 and 1340 levels, such that ventilation in the 1360 Crusher and Pump Station was very poor. How to quickly overcome that was the nub of the problem. In essence it would require rescheduling the raise borer vent holes between 1340 & 1240 levels. The temporary waste rock handling system was also well under design capacity.

After supper that evening at Cassia House I turned in early as I was not feeling too good. The following morning, if anything I felt worse with a fever and headache. I stayed in bed and later in the day Ian popped in to see me. Next day I felt really ill and fortunately Dave, one of the ZCCM project engineers, poked his head round my door and said "oh no, we must get you up to the hospital". They whizzed me up to the Nkana Mine Hospital where if one went left it was malaria or to the right it was AIDS. I went left and into a pleasant private room complete with bathroom. A doc came and did various tests and they dosed me up with some chloroquine. In fact I had been taking Lariam as the preferred prophylactic in Zambia. Whatever, by now my headache was really, really bad. It seemed as if I had a chainsaw running around my head. Sometime in the night I staggered off to the loo and that was the last thing I remembered until I came to sometime in the morning surrounded by docs and nurses with various drips attached here and there, feeling awful. The pain in my head was excruciating and I really felt as if I was dying. The staff continued to pump me full of chloroquine over the next few days. Ian came to see me and joked "well you really had us fooled, we thought you were a gonna".

For what its worth so did I. They kept me in the hospital for ten days. The headache abated and fever disappeared along with more than a stone and half in weight. Yes cerebral malaria, for that's what it was, was more effective than a Weight Watchers campaign. I realised just how lucky I had been since the Nkana Mine Hospital was used to dealing with malaria cases and knew just what to do. I felt as weak as a kitten on discharge and both Ian and the SRI Project manager agreed I should return to the UK for some R&R. Ian came down to Lusaka with me, which was much appreciated, and made sure I got on the BA flight for Heathrow. Gillian met me at the airport having driven up with Sproggs and boy was I pleased to see them.

I did next to nothing over the next three weeks other than try to build up some strength. Then with some trepidation it was back to Zambia. All the lads up at Cassia House gave me a great welcome back. They gave me a giant paper bag and said "see if you can punch your way out of that". I spent the following three weeks up at Mufulira working on the ventilation network to improve working conditions in the Crusher and Pump Chambers. With the Mufulira engineering guys we modified the skip dumping scrolls. That was it for me on the SRI project and I said goodbye to Kitwe and headed down to Lusaka. No problems with malaria that time, nevertheless I was glad to get on the Heathrow bound plane.

Sadly I had to take old Anjon to the vet for him to put the old dog down. The randy old bitza had reached the grand old age of 18, but was now virtually blind and unable to eat. I was very very upset and brought his body back to bury in the Gorsty garden under an ancient damson tree. The old farmhouse seemed very empty with no dogs around. With Gillian working at Fownhope surgery and Sproggs away at school I could only manage two days on my own. Come the weekend Gillian and I went first to Blackwardine Kennels to see if they had any "Rescue Dogs" looking for a home. No such luck, but they suggested the RSPCA rescue centre at Tibberton, just to the east of Worcester. We drove across the same afternoon. They had a large selection of dogs of all shape and sizes housed in large caged runs. Eventually we found a smallish terrier cross (Lakeland and Border) looking like a fed-up teddy bear propped up at the back of his run. They provided us with a long lead to take him, yes a dog although castrated, for a run around an adjacent field to see how we got on. Well he went bananas, quite wild, full of energy charging around everywhere.

That was it, we paid our £40, signed a form and agreed a day when the RSPCA could come and inspect "the dog facilities" at Gorsty. Fortunately we had a dog guard for the back of the Disco otherwise that mad terrier would have been in the front seat. Not sure how or why but we called him Bosworth, which of course shortened to Boz. It took me six months of dedicated morning and afternoon walking Boz on a lead before he became trained to a whistle or call. Because all our local footpaths ran across farmland with both sheep and cattle flocks Boz just had to be trained. He was an inveterate "hedger &and ditcher" and used to come up with the occasional rabbits and once a pheasant. These he would bring back to Gorsty in triumph only dropping them when bribed with a lump of cheese.

In June I went up to the Wrekin to watch a Saturday afternoon cricket match. David, Tudor's assistant house master collared me after tea and said they had been having trouble with Sproggs and "the latest" girlfriend (over 16, phew!) who were just pushing the limits too far. We knew that girl, Becky, as we had taken her and Sproggs out to lunch on a Sunday and her Mum, Dad and sister had visited Gorsty a few months ago. Well I sought out Sproggs and read the riot act - that's it, one more complaint from the school and you're out.

Of course they (the kids) never believe you. The following Friday I had a call from David - Becky had been found in Sproggs bed. So I drove up to the Wrekin. Found David the assistant housemaster, said sorry for the troubles and went to find Sproggs to tell him to collect and pack all his things into the Disco NOW. I went to see the Headmaster and Tudor Housemaster to thank them for their efforts and hoped that things would be better for them without Sproggs. The Head confirmed that Becky was also being taken out of College. All Sproggs said to me in a slightly aggrieved voice was "we weren't even doing anything"!

I didn't rant and rave I was just furious, what a wasted opportunity. On the way home, half way down the slope to the river Severn at Buildwas I stopped the Disco in a lay-by. I turned to Sproggs and said "you've got three choices - you can get out of the car now and bugger off; you can come home and get a job or you can start at the Hereford Technical College in September". He was, after all, aged 18. After a short pause he said he'd prefer to go to the Hereford Tec. We drove home in silence. Poor Gillian was so upset. It was not a great Saturday evening supper.

I calmed down, but felt upset that he'd mucked up on his chance to get some A levels and go on to Uni, if he'd wanted to. Well that was out for the immediate future. He and I went down to the Hereford Tec next week and booked him in for a GNVQ course related to sport starting in September. I had noticed that the new Leominster Leisure Centre was advertising for temporary staff and suggested that Sproggs might apply as a possible summer holidays job. Keen to please (!) he wrote up a sports oriented CV on my computer and biked down to the Centre with it. The young Assistant Manager and he just clicked and having explained that he was going to do a sports GNVQ at Hereford in September they gave him a job, which was great for his morale and our peace of mind. He could be independent as well, since he could bike to and fro as the Centre was only four miles away. I was really pleased that he had got the job with an immediate start.

48

On my work front things were very quiet after the rush of work in Central Asia. However I had obviously appeared on the radar screen at BHA since I got a call from Terry asking me to help them with a review of the Centromin operations in Peru. Their client was the American Bank, First Boston, who were advising the Peruvian government on the privatisation of Centromin. It was deja vu again, just like the Zambians. A socialist government nationalised the private sector mining industry and then, ten years down the track realised that a government company (in that case Centromin) did not have the expertise to run a complex mining business, so privatise it! The good news, of course, was that the nationalise/privatise routine provided plenty of work opportunities for natural resource companies and individuals like me. Welcome to job No. 101.

So at the end of July Clive drove me up to Birmingham airport, where I caught the NLM City Hopper to Schiphol airport, Amsterdam. One of the reasons I liked that airport was that all departure gates were accessible from one terminal. No mucking about with transfer buses as at Heathrow or Frankfurt. The NLM plane was nearly an hour late arriving and I had to scuttle through the terminal to catch the KLM flight for Lima by the skin of my teeth. That flight had started from Heathrow and my ex-RTZ mates, Arthur and Umit plus Ken from BHA were already ensconced in business class.

At Jorge Chavaz airport in Lima, Centromin had sent a car to pick us up which cut out the hassle of getting a taxi. Having the longest legs I ended up in the front seat the other three guys in the back. I was more than a little taken aback when I spotted a compact hand gun lying on top of the console between the driver and me. He laughed when he saw my reaction and said "por El Sendero Luminoso". Apparently that guerrilla group had recently been active around Lima suburbs as well as the reign of terror that they had spread up in the high, remote Andean villages. He drove us to the downtown Lima Sheraton Hotel, otherwise known as The Jail since it had a similar internal layout to that of a classic jail. In the bar we met Cliff, a large genial American project banker from First Boston, who would be the leader of our group. He had already been talking to the Centromin top brass here in Lima and had arranged for an introductory meeting and lunch tomorrow.

The meeting in the Centromin offices was attended by the Peruvian Minister of Mines as well as Centromin's General Manager of Operations. The four of us from the UK had to introduce ourselves together with some background information. We all used English although both Umit and Arthur spoke pretty good Spanish, whereas Ken's and mine was not great. It didn't seem to matter as all the Peruvians spoke an American version of English. For my part, unsurprisingly, I stressed my mining experience in Bolivia, Argentina, Ecuador and, of course, Peru, where I mentioned Quiruvilca, Raura and San Rafael. That Peruvian mine experience went down well as all three of those mines were sizeable operations and known to Centromin staff.

First Boston's overall scope of work was to advise Centromin of the likely Present Value of their company as "a going concern" in order to gauge the value of any buy-out bids. In turn BHA had to provide First Boston with the necessary technical input to estimate cash flows from each of Centromin's operating units. Brought down to technical essentials it was ore reserves; mining rates; head grades; metallurgical recoveries. It was a technical due diligence exercise for the owner. Centromin would provide detailed operating cost data for each of their operating units/mines. There were severn operating mines and two large open-pit projects. Of course there was also the huge La Oroya smelting complex, but the valuation of that was being handled by another engineering/banking group. I could see we were going to be very busy with a lot of travelling in the high Andes.

The next morning we set off in two 4 x 4 vehicles heading ENE up the Rimac river valley towards Vitarte and Chosica. After only fifteen miles or so we emerged from the perpetual Lima dank, grey pall (the Inca's revenge) into glorious sunlight. As we steadily climbed, the valley sides closed in until it looked doubtful that a road would be able to continue, let alone the railway which was running alongside. At one point where the valley had become a gulch between vertical walls we passed under a "stack" of three bridges where the railway disappeared into a tunnel on one flank to reappear at a higher elevation to cross a bridge to the other flank. Obviously it spiraled around inside that flank as it climbed to the next bridge crossing to repeat the exercise to the third bridge. An amazing piece of railway engineering. The valley widened a little after that gulch pinch point and the railway could be seen steadily climbing via a switch back on the western flank. The railway eventually reached a height of over 4700m (+15,000ft on its way to Huancayo.

Higher up the valley we passed both the Casapalca and Morococha mines on our way to the filthy smelter town of La Oroya, which lay in the Rio Montaro valley. A small, somewhat dilapidated hotel in that grim town was to be our base. The pollution from the copper, lead and zinc smelters and refineries was horrendous. The town was surrounded by stark bare mountainsides totally devoid of any vegetation. It reminded me of the moonscapes in Queenstown, Tasmania and Sudbury in Canada. La Oroya was definitely not going to become a major tourist attraction in the high Andes. That afternoon we went to the Centromin general offices in the town and met the Operations General Manager. Cliff and Ken sorted out an itinerary of visits to the various mines and concentrators with him. In turn, to my surprise, he emphasised that we must be alert to the threat of terrorism from the Sendero Luminoso (Shining Path) guerrillas. Whilst travelling to the various mine sites we would be accompanied at all times by fully armed Peruvian Army personnel. It seemed unreal, but after my experience at the San Rafael tin mine near Pune definitely a "good thing". The GM said that there had been incidents at Cobriza and Andaychagua.

Next day we headed north for the original Cerro de Pasco mine. The open pit was delivering 1.57 million tonnes/year and the underground mine 0.73 million tonnes/year. The open pit's remaining life was 5.5 years. It had been a large open pit and was nearing completion. By contrast the much newer underground mine had more than twenty years reserves and below the 1600 level the ore expectancy was 60,000 t/vm, which could support a much higher rate of extraction. However the main shaft hoisting capacity was limited to 90,000 tonnes/month. Some underground production was being obtain via a ramp-decline developed from the 4200 level bench in the open pit.

Cut-and-fill stoping, both overhand and underhand, was in use, the latter method being used in the weaker ground areas. There was a lot of ill matched mining machinery - development and stope drilling with jackleg units whilst mucking used 3.5 cu yd electric LHDs. Also the surface Volvo and Scania trucks required a huge 25m2 section tunnel to operate in, whereas custom built Toro 25D or Jarvis Clark 25t units only required a 15m^2 section, a huge saving in development waste and cost. All in all we could see plenty of potential at Cerro de Pasco to increase tonnage and reduce costs.

Much to my surprise both Arthur and I suffered from quite severe siroche although Cerro de Pasco was only a little over 4300m (14,100ft) elevation. I put it down to too much beer the previous evening. At any rate we were both glad to get back to La Oroya further down the Mantaro valley at only 3700m elevation and we both had a night off the cerveza in our small hotel.

In the morning we headed south for sixty miles to the Yauricocha mine situated at 4600m elevation some 35 miles SW of the Huancayo rail terminal. It was an underground operation mining irregular shaped querpos and and steep dipping veins. Ground conditions were reasonable to poor and stoping methods were overhand and underhand cut-and-fill, shrinkage and square-set. Current production was 354,000 tonnes/year from a reserve of 2.7 million tonnes. The Central mine area had been developed by a 470m deep small vertical shaft. The lowest level, the Klepetco tunnel was both the mine's 3.5km drainage and haulage adit to the Chumpe concentrator. There were satellite mines at Exito and Ipillo connected to the main Central mine by tortuous, narrow dirt roads up to 13km length. Most of the mining machinery was old and there appeared little upside potential at Yauricocha.

Mine number three was San Cristobal located 25 miles SW of La Oroya near Yauli. It was an underground mine developed through several adits and a ramp-decline. Current production was 647,000 tonns/year from a reserve of 5.7 million tonnes. The reserves were distributed 66% in veins, 19% in mantos and 15% in querpos. Mining method was by overhand cut-and-fill and shrinkage. The ramp-decline and much of the development was grossly over sized due to the use of surface Scania and Volvo trucks. Ore expectancy on the main vein was 40,000 t/vm, which could sustain a much higher rate of production than the current 2,200 tonnes/day. There was upside potential.

There was an urgent need to rationalise mining operations at San Cristobal. It was crazy to truck crude ore from the Toldorrumi pit (at San Cristobal) 10 km down the valley to the Andaychagua mill and then truck the concentrates back past San Cristobal on their way to the railhead at Mahr Tunnel. The adjacent Volcan private mine should be combined with San Cristobal and adjacent open pits into a combined 5,000 tonnes/day operation. There was also a proposal to extend the Victoria drainage tunnel 5.5km towards Andaychagua. That would have great importance for draining the Andaychagua mine at depth and prospecting the ground between the two mines for parallel vein structures.

Reserves at Andaychagua were 1.5 million tonnes and current production was only 160,000 tonnes/year. It was a strong, steep dipping vein with a strike length of 3Km in the upper level and an average width of 6 metres. However the main vein was also the mine's main aquifer and groundwater was seriously curtailing production now that operations were well below the lowest adit level. In winter the mine was pumping 4,000 gals/min, which at present rates of production was between 50 and 60 tonnes of water per tonne ore hoisted. That would place the mine in a "very wet" category. The Victoria tunnel extension from San Cristobal would intersect the Andaychagua workings at circa 4275m elevation. Once the main vein was pre-drained it would be feasible to replace the present cut-and-fill stoping with sub-level long-hole bench-and-fill mining. With an ore expectancy of 15 to 20,000 t/vm the mine could easily sustain an output of 1,500 tonnes/day more than 2.5 times the present production rate. Again, plenty of upside potential.

Next day we headed further south down the Rio Mantaro to Huancavelica. Our Peruvian army guards became much more twitchy as the Sendero Luminoso guerrillas had been active hereabouts. The large underground Cobiza mine was developed through a series of adits driven into the steep western bank of the Rio Mantaro. Current ore reserves were over 19 million tonnes although 7.5 million tonnes were sterilised in pillars supporting the spiral ramp-declines. The orebody comprised one large manto with a strike length of 5Km, an average thickness of 14m and a dip ranging from 30 to 65 degrees. Mining was by trackless overhand cut-and-fill producing 2.1 million t/year. The ore expectancy of 130,000 t/vm could easily sustain the planned throughput of 9,100 tonnes/day or 2,7 million tonnes/year. It was an easy orebody to mine and the current shortfall in tonnage was caused by low availabilities on electro-hydraulic jumbos, 8 and 13 cu yard LHDs and 27t low profile trucks. Most were fifteen years old. Re-equipping the mine would enable its full potential to be easily achieved. Definitely a good prospect.

The old Morococha underground mine lay alongside the Lima to La Oroya road. The mine delivered 305,000 tonnes/year from a reserve of 3.3 million tonnes. However the reserves were widely scattered and contained in both narrow veins and replacement bodies (querpos). Average width of the veins was only 1 m. The main mine infrastructure was very run down and most of the machinery and plant well past its sell-by date. One of the Ingersoll Rand compressors was a collector's item dating from 1917! The veins were mined by shrinkage and the querpos by a trackless pillar and stall method. All drilling used simple jacklegs. Mine drainage was handled by the 10 km Kingsmill Tunnel which exited close by the Mahr Tunnel concentrator. The mine was struggling to make tonnage, and failing, the shortfall being met by the adjacent Toromocho open pit. The future for Morococha did not look propitious.

The new Toromocho open pit lay at an altitude of 4700 to 4800 m. The orebody size ranged from 300m by 300m up to 900m by 900 m, depending on the cut-off grade (COG) selected. That was demonstrated by a series of tonnage-grade curves at various COGs from 0.5% Cu to 1.1% Cu. Present production was small and variable merely making up the shortfall from the underground mine. For our review Arthur selected an ore reserve of 75 million tonnes at 0.98% Cu at a COG of 0.7% Cu. The average ore expectancy was 250,000 t/vm and the ultimate pit depth would be 335m at a 2.7 to 1 strip ratio. A mining rate of 17,000 tonnes/day or 5.1 million tonnes/year would give a project life of fifteen years. It would be a conventional shovel-truck pit using heavy duty rotary blast-hole drills (type BE 49R) putting down 250mm diam holes 16.5m deep on 15m benches.

Production loading would be by 17m^3 electric rope shovels (type P&H 2300) loading 120t capacity dump trucks (type Dresser WABCO, 1000hp twin axle). The order-of-magnitude capital cost for a new five million tonnes/year open pit would be US$ 70 million. the direct operating cost would be US$ 1.02 per tonne moved (ore and waste) or with a 2.7 to 1 strip ratio US$ 3.77/t ore mined. An operation of that scale would add greatly to the Centromin sales portfolio.

Our final night at the La Oroya Hotel involved a fairly rowdy dinner with senior Centromin managers. We had one more mine, Casapalca, to visit on our way back down to Lima plus an expedition by Arthur and me to the remote Antamina project. The Casapalca mine was only 25 miles from La Oroya. Current production from that underground mine was 618,000 tonnes/year from a reserve base of 6.2 million tonnes. The mine was developed by many adits into the valley sides of the Rio Rimac. Stoping was by cut-and-fill and shrinkage methods. Much of the mining plant and equipment was old and past its economic life. All drilling was by jacklegs only, no jumbos of any description were used. Loading was by Cavo 310 and 510 pneumatic LHD units. Overall housekeeping was good and the modern (1981) ASEA 2 rope friction skip winder and 4-rope friction cage winder on the underground Pique Central Shaft were excellent & well maintained.

The mine was wet. Upper levels were drained by three adits, but the bulk of the mine water was handled by the 12km long Graton Tunnel situated 420m below the deepest workings. Drainage discharge from that tunnel was quoted by Centromin as 4.77m^3/sec which was absolutely enormous. If correct that would be 412,000m^3/day or 200 tonnes of water for each tonne of ore hoisted. Thank goodness that quantity of water didn't have to be pumped! It was understood that the Graton Tunnel discharge comprised the major part of the Rio Rimac's flow. With low in situ grades, narrow veins and high dilution the economic future of Casapalca looked poor.

On the way back down to Lima we stopped at San Mateo, below the Graton Tunnel portal, to look at the Rio Rimac. It was certainly quite a sizeable river already, but how much bigger than the suggested mine discharge of about 63,000 gals/min I couldn't say. As expected, fifteen miles from Lima the sun disappeared into the grey murk that continually covered the city. One imagined that all the residents had a Vitamin D deficiency. Back at the Sheraton Hotel we luxuriated in plenty of oxygen after ten days at high altitude. The Peruvian Army guys looked pleased to be back, but probably disappointed that they were not required to demonstrate their fire power to the gringos. We went out for a few beers and dinner to make up for the loss of appetite up in the Andes.

We had a meeting with Centromin in the morning to discuss our findings. Unfortunately Umit was sick having picked up a stomach bug from last night's dinner so we didn't talk about metallurgy. Cliff, the First Boston guy was our team leader and he stressed that all the mines had fully cooperated with us and all mine units had provided full operational cost data. Arthur ran quickly through the geological and ore reserve data. I then described the mining potential of each mine confirming that those outputs and head grades via a metallurgical recovery (from Umit) would be the basic input to the economic NPV calculation for each mine. Adding all those together would provide an estimate of the value of Centromin as a "going concern". We also pointed out that we had established a notional open-pit operation at Toromocho. At that point the GM said that we had not yet visited the Antamina project site. After a rapid team discussion Cliff said that only Arthur and I would visit. It was then arranged that we would fly up to Huaraz that afternoon.

Out at Lima airport we boarded a private 6-seat Beech aircraft for the 180 mile flight almost due north to the town of Huaraz. The landing at the airstrip in the early evening was uneventful, but the view of Huascaran mountain, 6768m (22,205 ft), 25 miles to the north lit by the low western sun was spectacular. We stayed overnight in a small, clean hotel. There the elevation was 3100m and did not pose a problem for either of us. We had an early start tomorrow as the Antamina project area was very remote.

I was glad we had a rugged, reliable 4 x 4 for the trip. The site was almost inaccessible. It took us seven hours to cover the 161km to the project site over appalling, tortuous dirt roads. Antamina was located on the eastern side of the Andean watershed. The site was isolated with zero infrastructure at an elevation of 4200 m. The topography was amazingly precipitous with the adjacent valley sides rising 700 - 800m sheer.

The orebody comprised a mineralised skarn and took the form of a flat lying half moon shape occupying an area of 36 hectares with a vertical thickness of 150m. The deposit was on the lip of a glacial corrie hemmed in between near vertical limestone walls merely 700m apart. The valley drained SW towards San Marcos then north into the Rio Mosna. The deposit had been explored by surface trenching, 16,000m of diamond drilling and 6300m of underground development. As usual with that type of deposit there was no single ore reserve, but a suite of tonnage-grade curves dependent on the COG selected. For the purpose of our review Arthur selected a reserve of 155 million tonnes at 1.3% Cu, 1.9% Zn, 13g/t Ag and 0.04% Mo at a 0.2% Cu equivalent COG.

Examination of both DD core and the underground development showed good, competent ground conditions with little ground-water. Average ore expectancy was over 1 million t/vm. A mining rate of 30,000 tonnes/day or 9 million tonnes/year was selected to give an average descent of only 9 m/year and a mine life of 17.5 years with a 95% extraction and 7% dilution. It would be a conventional, shallow, shovel-truck pit with ultimate pit slope of 50 degrees and a very low 0.65 to 1 stripping ratio on account of the orebody disposition, lack of overburden and the terrain.

The estimated capital cost for the 9 million tonnes/year mine was US$ 46 million plus US$ 25 million for a new access road and US $6 million for a power line, a total of US $ 77 million. A direct operating cost of US$ 1.02/tonne moved (ore and waste) with a 0.65 to 1 strip ratio gave an overall cost of US$ 1.68/tonne ore mined. It would be a relatively simple mining operation, once a decent access road had been built. The only major difficulty would be the supply of raw water to the 30,000 tonnes/day concentrator as none of the local streams were adequate. That would be a problem area for Ken and Umit to consider.

After five hours roaming around the surface and exploring the old underground development with the aid of powerful torches we repaired to the old, deserted exploration camp as nightfall came. We assisted the driver in collecting some old timber, mainly ruined core boxes, to get a fire going. The temperature fell rapidly at that altitude once the sun disappeared. The Antamina project geologist from Huaraz had brought a "picnic" with him and had thoughtfully included a case of beer. The picnic and beer went down a treat in front of a roaring fire. It was a chilly, fairly sleepless night spent wrapped up in all ones clothes curled up on a basic cot. Hey ho, the joys of Andean mining projects. We were underway by 7.30 for the bone jarring jeep ride back to Huaraz. By 3pm we were at the town's airstrip where the little Beech plane was a welcome sight. Just under the hour for the flight and we were back at the Lima Sheraton by 5pm. A quick shower and repair to the bar to bore the pants of the other guys for further tales of the high Andes.

We had a final wrap-up meeting with the Centromin management then out to Jorge Chavaz airport for the KLM flight to Schiphol, Amsterdam. Here I split from the London bound guys and transferred to the Birmingham bound NLM City Hopper flight. Much to my amazement dear old Customs did not pull me over. It was four years since I had last been in South America and Customs had obviously lost interest in me. I had called Clive from Schiphol and he was waiting for me at the airport. The drive back to Gorsty was a lot more comfortable than the dirt road to Antamina. It was a Thursday and Boz, left loose to run in the garden, went bananas when I came in the gate. That's the great thing with a dog they're always pleased to see you and never grumble if your late. I guessed Sproggs was still down at the Leisure Centre and sure enough he turned up around 5 o'clock, puffing a little after cycling up Gorsty Hill. Gillian arrived in the Disco around 7 after another busy day at the surgery.

Sproggs would start at the Hereford Tec in another couple of weeks. Gillian would drop him off in the morning at the College at the top of Aylesford Hill on her way to the surgery at Fownhope. On Wednesday, her day off, Sproggs would cycle into Leominster station and catch the train to Hereford. It only took twenty minutes. There was a secure cycle rack at the station. I was busy for the next week or so writing up all my Centromin mine Visit Notes and preparing cost estimates for the Toromocho and Antamina projects. I sent all those by fax to Terry at BHA in Surrey. That was finished as we moved into September. That was usually the last month of the year when it was still feasible to do outside window repairs and painting before the early morning mists descended making that an unrewarding activity. It wasn't a problem since there was plenty of internal DIY jobs to keep me out of the pub.

49

Just before the end of the month I had a call from John of the World Bank (WB) in Washington. He wanted me to join yet another WB mission to Zambia next month, was I available? Well I tried not to bite his hand off and said yes, I could squeeze that work in - welcome to job No. 102. When I had started as an independent consultant I had said to myself that I would stop when I completed my one hundredth job. I didn't do that as the adoption of Sproggs and his education had had a major influence on our finances. Thus I had determined to keep going, if I could secure any work. However now that Sproggs would not be going on to university with their huge costs, I had had yet another rethink. Clambering up and down ladders in the high Andes with guys 35 years younger than me had started to lose its appeal. Couple that with the ghastly food and intense cold in northern Kazakhstan and retirement was coming into focus again. What I really would have liked was two or three jobs a year in Southern Spain! Dream on. So, dear old Zambia again. At least it would be warm and the food was OK.

Clive was busy with his livery work so my Leominster taxi driver drove me up to Heathrow just before the end of October. It was the regular BA flight from Terminal 4, arriving in Lusaka at 7.30 the following morning. I saw nothing of the WB guys until I'd checked into the Pamodzi Hotel and repaired to the terrace. I had met John before on my visit to the Bank in Washington. Although a long-term WB staffer John was a straight-talking, practical guy who didn't do bullshit. The WB scope of work this time was more in the nature of a due diligence, looking at current operating costs tied to a finished copper and cobalt production forecast. That made sense since the government owned ZCCM had indicated their wish to privatise the operations and would welcome an independent "valuation" from the WB.

We flew straight up to Kitwe with RoanAir next day. It was a really tight schedule for the technical guys. Paul on geology, me on mining and Dick on metallurgy. We had one week only and my own schedule was as follows:-

nchanga division	nop open-pit mine/a block open pit/ chingola c open pit
	lob underground mine
mufulira division	underground mine (musombo sv area)
nkana division	mindola underground mine
luanshya division	baluba underground mine (flat area)
konkola division	no 3 shaft underground mine
	kdmp planning team

At Nchanga the NOP open pit was virtually "snowed in" with very little stripped ore available for loading. For the next two years production would be down nearly two million tonnes/year as a direct consequence of insufficient waste stripping capacity primarily due to low mechanical availability on the haul trucks. The NOP was a difficult trench-like pit on account of the flat dipping sediments and the current cuts had a huge stripping ratio of 13 to 1! The original production schedule called for an ore output of 6.8 million tonnes for that year, which required the pit to shift over 37 million BCM. The mine physically could not move that quantity of material with the current drill/shovel/truck fleet and long waste haul cycle times. Thus contained copper output would be down a staggering 60,000 tonnes. It would only pick up again in three years time with the purchase of new haul trucks. Direct mining cost was US$ 0.9/t moved (ore and waste) or US$ 10.1/t ore

The LOB underground continuous down-dip caving mine had for years maintained a contained copper output of 90,000 tonnes/year. however for the next few years output would be down about 8,000 tonnes/year on account of interface difficulties with the mining of A Block in the hangingwall of the NOP. That in turn had been caused by delays in removing the overlying TD1 tailings dam, itself due to lack of throughput in the Tailings Leach Plant. The direct mining cost at LOB was US$ 11.2/t ore, the lowest underground mining cost and also the least mechanised mine on the Copperbelt.

Thirty years ago Mufulira was easily the largest underground mine on the Copperbelt, mining over six million tonnes/year. Today, finally, ZCCM had accepted that it was now only a 2.6 million tonnes/year mine commensurate with an orebody strike length of 2Km compared with the previous 6Km. As a member of the WB team of eight years ago we had warned ZCCM that the Mufulira production forecast in the MAD project of 4.2 million tonnes/year was unachievable. At last the mine now had a realistic production forecast. Although the mine was the most mechanised its direct mining cost was high at US$ 20.0/t ore. It was also noted that the mine's power consumption at over 100 KWhr/t mined was excessive and that the compressor load was more than double an acceptable consumption rate. Perhaps those power and compressed air consumptions were a reflection of the old output of six million tonnes/year? Major cost savings must be made in conjunction with a reduction in waste dilution (reflected in increased rom grade) to make Mufulira a profitable mine again.

The less said about the Mindola section of the Nkana Division the better. The Mindola Shaft re-deepening project was the major piece of mine infrastructure for that division. Apart from being way behind schedule both the new 5360 Crusher Chamber and Loading Station were an absolute disgrace. They were patently unsafe with rubbish, discarded mining gear, wire ropes etc littered everywhere. General mine housekeeping and safe working practice were entirely absent. There was no ventilation in the new 4440-4180 stope block and the whole area was unkempt, unsafe and with no discernible front-line, middle or senior management in evidence. Supervisors had no plans nor idea of what was supposed to be done. Had a Mines Inspector been present he would have shut the mine forthwith. The direct mining cost at Mindola was US$ 14.8/t ore mined.

At Luanshya, the oldest mine on the Copperbelt, the original Roan Antelope mine, was now virtually a remnant mining operation spread out over several kilometres. The direct mining cost was US$ 13.2/t ore mined. Baluba, by contrast was the newest mine on the Copperbelt having originally been developed via a ramp-decline from surface. The near surface steep flanks of the plunging syncline had been mined by conventional sub-level blast-hole open stoping. Now mining was concentrated in the keel, or "Flat" area. That project was also well behind schedule and experienced ground support difficulties. A variety of stoping methods were now being used, eg drift-and-fill; post pillar cut-and-fill and room-and-pillar. That was the first "flat mining" operation on the Copperbelt. It was still in the nature of trial mining and direct mining costs were high at US$ 16.4/t ore mined.

Close to the Zaire/Congo border were the two Konkola mines No 1 Shaft and No 3 Shaft. They were mining the same orebody around the nose of an anticline but operated as separate entities. The mines were very wet, pumping circa 300,000m^3/day equivalent to 46,000 gals/min. In summer the Konkola mine water discharge made up more than 50% of the Kafue river flow. Sub-level blast-dip open stoping was used at both mines. Down-dip from the No 3 Shaft lay the Copperbelt's major undeveloped ore resource, the Konkola Deep Mine Project (KDMP). That would be a flat mining area and Baluba's experience of those flat ore resources would be extremely useful. Direct mining costs were US$ 21.3/t ore mined at No 1 Shaft and US$ 17.0/t ore mined at No 3 Shaft. At No 1 Shaft direct costs were greatly influenced by 40MW of power being absorbed by pumping alone.

We then went to the Operations Centre at Kalulushi for discussions with the Operations Director, Technical Director and company Consultants. Everyone agreed that the delay in waste stripping at the NOP would have the largest effect on copper outturn. No one seriously challenged our estimate of a 60,000 tonnes/year copper shortfall from the ZCCM forecast. They also accepted that Mufulira was now a 2.65 million tonnes/year mine. All talk of 4.2 million tonnes/year had finally vanished - yes, at last! All aghast and very defensive about underground conditions at Mindola. However there was a consensus that everything possible should be done to reduce waste dilution to increase the grade of rom ore sent to the concentrators.

We all flew back to Lusaka and spent the next two days in the Pamodzi Hotel working up our numbers before a final meeting with ZCCM's Chief Executive, Directors, Consultants and Divisional General Managers. It was quite a tense meeting since our copper and cobalt production figures were significantly (minus 15%) down on ZCCM's own forecast. However John, the WB team leader put our position across strongly. With detailed support on geology (reserves), mining (output and grades) and metallurgy (recoveries) we were able to justify our estimates. The unsafe working conditions underground at Mindola created considerable consternation and the Nkana GM was obviously heading for a justifiable roasting.

The following morning we all caught the BA flight back to Heathrow. The WB guys transferred to a trans Atlantic Washington flight, whilst I went out of Terminal 4 looking for my Leominster taxi driver. He was there and we had a steady three hour drive back to Gorsty via the M4 and A419/A417. It was now nearly mid November and my first job was log splitting for the woodburner and Franklin stoves. Thereafter it took me four days to check calculations and write up my report for despatch to Washington by DHL Couriers.

Sproggs seemed to be getting on alright at the Hereford Tec, but I got the impression that he wasn't really enjoying it. More in the nature of "keep the old man happy". Oh well it was only the first term. Gillian was still working at Fownhope surgery four days per week. She felt that the Gorsty bathroom really needed an upgrade after fifteen years and I was in agreement. We perused Yellow Pages and visited three or four company premises. At least three showed an interest, but being close to Christmas, none could come to measure up and quote until the new year. So no rush then, but at least interest.

In early January 1996 I had a call from Ian, ex-MRDL, but now CEO of American Resource Corp of Greenbrae in California. They, American Resource Corp, owned the Bissett gold mine in Manitoba, Canada. As the new CEO, Ian was concerned about an expansion plan proposed by Tonto Mining and rubber stamped by a Simon Engineering feasibility study of last year. Could I take a look at the mine? He said he very clearly remembered my reservations on the Mufulira mining rate! I said yes and welcomed job No. 103. Ian asked me when I could go and I replied anytime. He said he'd talk to the Mine Manager and get back to me.

Over the next couple of weeks we had visits from three different kitchen firms. We quickly picked out Ray from Hereford as he was a "can do" sort of guy. Both of the other firm's chaps saw nothing but problems and difficulties, which did not inspire confidence. Ray had come at the weekend as he was busy during the week. We agreed a probable start in early April, so not too long to wait.

Ian called back and asked me to meet the company President, Jim and GM, Fred at the Holiday Inn at Winnipeg airport on the 30th January. Both Jim and Fred would accompany me to the mine the following day. After that it was up to me how long I stayed. He warned me that at that time of the year it would be very cold. I contacted my friend at Thomas Cook in Hereford and asked him to book me flights to Toronto and on to Winnipeg to arrive there on the 29th January. Well it was a good job I had kept the old long johns and gloves from the Kazakhstan visit.

From Heathrow Terminal 3 I had a very comfortable flight with Canadian Pacific to Toronto. It was eight years since I'd been to Toronto and the airport seemed so much busier than I remembered, but then that was the main gateway to Canada. I expected it to be cold, but, of course inside the airport is was pleasantly warm. I had a four hour wait for a connecting flight to Winnipeg. That was a three hour flight in a modern turboprop plane and made me realise just how big Canada was. I checked with the Information desk that the Holiday Inn was only a short taxi ride away. The cab rank was in a fully enclosed area and it was only when I got out of the taxi at the Holiday Inn that I realised just how cold it was. The cabbie said about minus 35 C and it felt like it as I scuttled into the hotel. There was a message waiting, asking me to join the Bissett Mining guys at 10am tomorrow in one of the hotel's conference rooms. I didn't venture outside but from my room's window noted that all the parked cars were "plugged in" to individual power posts. Obvious really as with those low temperatures most cars would fail to function after a three or four hours non-use.

After a good breakfast I duly found the correct conference room. There were five guys there, three more than I expected. It was pretty sticky for a while when I felt the general feeling was "who the hell is this Limey to tell us what to do". It really was tricky as they were senior long-term Canadian mining types. Besides Ian, as the new CEO of their ultimate owner, American Resource Corp was a naturalised American and Cannucks are not overly fond of Yanks, let alone their Limey chums. So for the first half hour or so I had to do a personal selling job, telling them that I'd worked (for a short while) as a machine miner at Algom Quirke and had done consulting work at INCO and Falconbridge in Sudbury and Kidd Creek in Timmins. That broke the ice, but the clincher was ten years with RTZ Consultants, the last five years as Director of Mining. RTZ was well known in Canadian mining circles with its involvement in the Elliot Lake uranium field (Algom Nordic and Quirke), the huge Lornex open-pit copper mine in British Columbia and the Churchill Falls hydro-power project in northern Manitoba. Then, of course, I had to go through my gold mining experience. Fortunately I could run off fifteen or so mines/projects I'd worked on and everyone had heard of the famous Ashanti mine. By the time for a coffee break Jim had thawed out and was prepared to talk about their Bissett Mine with me.

Fortunately Al, GM of Exploration & Acquisitions, had brought a set of mine plans with him and a copy of the Simon Feasibility Report so I was able to ask some specific questions. For me ore expectancy (t/vm) for steep dipping tabular deposits was the key to determining sustainable mining rate. The Simon report stated that the production rate would be 1,000 short tons/day. There was no back-up justification. When I quizzed the guys on that fundamental parameter, no one had an answer. Phew, at a stroke I established some mining credibility. We had a sandwich lunch and by early evening were ensconced in the bar, where I learnt a lot about Canadian Molson beer, Red or Blue. Not too much as we were flying up to Bissett early in the morning.

There were four of us, Jim, Al, Fred and me as we drove the short distance to the private side of the airport. We quickly boarded a small, 6-seater light aircraft for the fifty minute flight NE to the small settlement of Bissett. For me it was another first as the plane landed on the frozen Rice Lake and taxied to the lake edge, no more than seventy yards from the main mine headframe. Fred drove me round to a small hotel where I dumped my gear and then we went on to the mine office. Bejesus it was so cold! One's breath froze and ice appeared on one's eyebrows. At the office one of the guys cheerfully announced that the temperature was minus 48 C. With that in mind we got underground pronto, where it was a great deal warmer.

It was a typical steep dipping shear vein structure with associated stockwork veins. Average width of the shear veins was only 1.2 m. Ground conditions were competent with a regular steep dip and conventional shrink stoping was practiced. Although stockwork areas were limited the average assay width was 6m, but both dip and strike directions exhibited excessive pinch-and-swell. The mine was using shrink stoping here, but I felt the stockwork should be mined by cut-and-fill to reduce excessive dilution. The bulk of the reserves, 3.2 million tonnes were located below 26 level with the balance, 0.55 million tonnes in the A, B & C shaft areas. It soon became apparent that the mystical 1,000 short tons/day production rate emanated from a 1993 report by Tonto Mining. They had merely selected that rate!

Unbelievable, and Simon had just accepted it. The size and distribution of the reserve between 26 & 33 levels had an ore expectancy of 6,500 t/vm only. Thus on the present, known ore reserve base the sustainable output was no more than 700 st/day. Of course a concerted exploration programme could increase that if it should find additional strike tonnes. Additional down-dip tonnes merely extended mine life and did not affect the average mine ore expectancy. So 1,000 st/day output was not tenable.

The next problem area was the inadequate shaft sizes. Those shaft sections could just handle 140,000 CFM of ventilation air, which was just adequate for a mining output of 500 st/day. It was a deep mine, 5,660ft from collar to lowest level so that ventilation had already become a constraint to increasing production. There was also insufficient haulage capacity between the sub-vertical shaft and the main shaft. After a full day underground I was not looking forward to facing the icy blast on surface.

The next day I spent in the engineering office calculating ore expectancies and ventilation quantities and hence shaft cross sections required to downcast and upcast those amounts. I finally followed that up with power calculations for the main shaft double-drum winder following a detailed discussion with their electrical engineer on the security of supply from Manitoba Hydro. He agreed that the DC winder should be fitted with Ward Leonard close loop control rather than thyristors as those might cause secondary harmonic problems with the existing spur feed line.

So that was it. In a nutshell only a 700 st/day mine at best. Both major shafts required stripping to a larger size and re-equipping to provide sufficient cross section to double ventilation capacity. The main double-drum winder needed up grading to 1,000hp for handling six tonnes capacity skips. I'm afraid I didn't make too many friends at Bissett, but then my client was Ian, the CEO of their owner, American Resource Corp. The light aircraft flew me back to Winnipeg for another lengthy wait before flying to Toronto, where I was just in time to catch a midnight, red-eye shuttle to Heathrow. I'd called Gillian from Toronto and she'd arranged for Kevin, the Leominster taxi guy, to pick me up. He was there and we had a smooth run back to Gorsty, which felt nice and warm after Bissett, although it was now early February.

50

Back in early January I had received a call from Peter an old colleague from Golders days. Peter was now with Bechtel International in Perth, Western Australia. He asked me to fax him copies of my CV and recent work experience. Apparently Western Mining Corp (WMC) had invited Bechtel, and several other engineer-constructer outfits, to bid for a Feasibility Study of an expansion project at the Olympic Dam copper/uranium mine in South Australia. He said that if Bechtel were successful the work would probably be handled by their main office in San Francisco, but it could be useful to have some local engineering know-how in his Perth office. With the arrival of the Bissett job in Canada I had forgotten about Peter's enquiry. A couple of days after I returned from Canada Peter called again and said Bechtel were short-listed for the Olympic Dam job, but WMC had queried Bechtel's experience of planning a plus 10 million tonnes/year underground hard rock mine. What about me? I told him that I did not have first hand experience of such a large underground operation. In fact I said there were very few such operations that sprang to mind. LKAB in Sweden; El Teniente in Chile; Magma and San Manuel in the USA and Philex in the Philippines. Apart from LKAB all the others were block-caving mines, a totally different mining system to that in use at Olympic Dam.

The biggest mine I had experience of was Mufulira in Zambia, which was hoisting six million tonnes/year in the early eighties. I had completed a design exercise for Zambia Engineering Services of the proposed Musombo SV2 shaft capable of hoisting 4.2 million tonnes/year and downcasting $190 m^3/s$ of fresh air. Most of my experience had been with medium sized underground mines in the 1 to 3 million tonnes/year category. Peter asked me to fax all that background to him asap, which I did.

Ten days later Peter called to say Bechtel had been awarded the job and a guy called Kevin from Bechtel Mining & Metals, San Francisco would call me to set up the timing for the visit to South Australia. Kevin duly rang two days later and asked me to front-up to the Majestic Hotel on Rundle Street, Adelaide on the 5th March for about a two week stay. Welcome to job No. 104. Well you just never knew where the work would come from. With Sproggs not going to university, Hereford Tec instead, the financial pressure had been removed for me to work, work, work. Thus I had enrolled with the Open University to do an Art's degree, which would exercise the grey cells as I wound down the mining work and headed for retirement. I felt that an art course would be stimulating and mind broadening after forty years of working in the mining industry.

In early March I boarded a Singapore Airlines (SA) jumbo for the long flight to Singapore's brand new Changi Airport. That was my first visit to that airport and wow it certainly made Heathrow seem old-fashioned and staid. It was, of course, vast, with huge waterfalls, tropical gardens, umpteen restaurants and bars and a cinema. Oh yes and lots of departure gates. I had about half a day there before catching a SA plane for the 4.5 hour flight to Perth, Western Australia. There I transferred to the Domestic Terminal for the final 3.5 hour flight by TAA to Adelaide. I took a taxi for the short, twenty minute, drive to the Majestic Hotel. I phoned Kevin's room, no reply, so left a note in his pigeon-hole at the front desk. Around 7pm he phoned and suggested I meet him in the bar to catch up on the visit programme.

Kevin was there with three other Bechtel guys. Apparently they had arrived a day ahead of me. Kevin, a mining engineer, was project leader of an eight man team, including me. Three of the other guys were out on the town. The plan was to all fly up to the mine at Roxby Downs early tomorrow and spend three days on site before returning to the WMC Project Office here in Adelaide to work through all the documentation. It had been a long trip, around thirty hours elapsed time from Gorsty, so after a couple of beers I went back to my room and crashed out.

After an early breakfast a couple of cabs took us to the private side of the airport where we boarded a small charter plane for the 350 mile flight NW towards Andamooka. On the way we passed close to the Woomera rocket range. The existing Olympic Dam mine complex was no shrinking violet. It was a large integrated underground mine feeding a copper concentrator and associated uranium treatment plant. My scope of work for input to the Bechtel Feasibility Study was quite specific, namely, the mine plan; mine materials handling and hoisting; mine underground facilities and mine backfill. After dropping our gear at the Single Mens Bunkhouse four of us went to the Underground Manager's office to sort out mine visits over the next three days.

We spent time underground with WMC's geotechnical guy. Generally both the ore zone and host rocks were good Class 1 ground. In addition the mine was virtually dry. There was a lack of basic geotechnical data, to the extent that regional pillars were not designed due to a non-systematic mining sequence which was driven by a high-grading production schedule. The principal horizontal stress was normal to the ore zone's strike, so that the transverse orientation of stoping was correct. The mining method was sub-level open stoping for primary stopes followed by a secondary stope sequence with post cemented aggregate fill. Dilution at 13% was higher than one would expect in that strong ground. There were definite signs of drill and blast damage on both hangingwall & footwall contacts. Our suggestion to WMC would be to consider bench-and-fill where parallel hole drilling down ore contacts would surely reduce overbreak dilution. However our main concern was that the non-systematic mining sequence, driven by grade (Cu output and Cu/Sulphur ratio) made it difficult to verify whether the desired development schedule would be met.

I was particularly concerned that the main Robinson shaft deepening and headframe/winder recommissioning schedule was unlikely to be achieved. There were delays on driving the ramp-decline to access the new shaft sump position. The Robinson shaft itself was to be deepened 266m by raising and subsequent slyping. None of that could start until the ramp-decline was completed. All level development was huge, 6.8m wide by 6.0m high to accommodate 50 tonnes capacity open-pit type trucks. We discovered another constraint at the underground primary crusher dump bin. That was a single side dump bin only. At the proposed 8.5 million tonnes/year production rate that meant that a 50t truck would need to dump every 2.7 minutes. With reversing, dumping, lowering body and clearing the dump bin there was bound to be truck congestion. The crusher station required modifying for double side dumping.

However the main problem area was the Robinson shaft. The nominal hoist rate was 1100 tonnes/hour which exactly matched the concentrator throughput. There was no allowance for moisture (3%) and no design margin, say, 10%. WMC also suggested a RAM of 0.9 for the main rock hoist, ie the hoist would be available 24 x 0.9 = 21.6hrs/day, 365days/year. That was absolutely not tenable considering - unscheduled breakdowns; no power; no operators; no ore; ripped belts etc. Also it was not a stand-alone hoist, it was integrated with fine ore bin feeders, conveyors, loading station flasks, skip winder itself, headgear bin, feeder and overland conveyor to concentrator. An achievable RAM would be 0.8, or 19.2hrs/day. Considering moisture, design margin and a 0.8 RAM indicated a design hoist rate of 1375 tonnes/hour, a massive 25% increase over WMC's proposed hoisting rate.

The Robinson shaft was small, 5.3m diameter only which ensured that the skips had a small cross section to maintain adequate separation and running clearance with the proposed rope guides. Also the proposed winder full speed of 16m/s was higher than the optimal 45-50% Vmax. Finally the skips tare weight at 100% of the net load was excessive. I believed that the designers had done that to maintain a reasonable T1/T2 ratio for the friction winder. A well designed, bottom dump skip should have a tare weight of 75% of the net load, no more. All in all a pig's breakfast. The whole of the Robinson shaft hoisting complex exuded a design "fudge" to enable 8.5 million tonnes/year to be hoisted up a small, 5.3m diameter shaft. Many aspects were not designed to normal good engineering practice. For example the T1/T2 ratio was close to the limit (for slippage) such that additional dead weight had to be added to the skips. The full speed was higher than the optimum to minimise power requirements. The skip dumping time of ten seconds for a 28 tonne load was hopelessly optimistic for the long, narrow skips and above all a RAM of 0.9 was completely unrealistic. Kevin was really quite excited by my comments and called the Robinson shaft, the link between underground and the concentrator, as the "fatal flaw" in the WMC expansion proposal.

There was no detail whatsoever on underground maintenance facilities which was obviously a serious omission since the mine was highly mechanised. There was also insufficient testwork on desliming the concentrator tailings by cycloning for use as mine backfill. However all those other aspects paled into insignificance with the Robinson shaft hoisting constraint.

Back in Adelaide after the three day site visit we spent the following ten days working up our comments in discussion with the WMC expansion project team. On the Robinson shaft hoisting problem, WMC requested detailed justification (impossible in my view!) from their hoisting consultants, Sinclair Knight Merz (SKM) of Sydney, for skip dump times, skip cross section, skip tare, hoist full speed, hoist a & r rates, T1/T2 ratios and the lack of consideration of the coriolis effect to minimise twisting of the friction winder's tail rope. In honesty their reply wasn't worth a row of beans. To be fair (why?) to SKM it was apparent that WMC had lent on them to "get 8.5 million tonnes/year up the Robinson shaft". It couldn't be done. WMC did finally agree with us that a 0.9 RAM for hoisting round the clock, 365days/year was too high. They accepted 0.8 as more practical and accepted that they had made no allowance for moisture nor incorporated a design margin. The outcome was that it looked like a brand new main hoisting shaft or split hoisting duties between the Robinson shaft and the Whenan shaft, currently handling men and materials.

WMC had calculated a mine capital cost of Aus$ 132.34 million, but that excluded any underground development. Apart from that the Robinson shaft "fudge" would incur considerable further expenditure to fix. Direct operating cost was estimated to be Aus$ 15.9/tonne mined. Kevin asked me about capital costs for a new shaft and I produced budget figures based on Cementation experience for sinking a 7.3m (24ft diameter shaft equipped with twin balanced skips and large cage and counterweight). I suggested they (Bechtel) contact major winder manufacturers such as GEC, Siemens, Nordberg, GHH etc, with the hoisting requirement of 1375 tonnes/hour from a depth of 838 metres requesting budget quotes.

On our first weekend back in Adelaide three of us had a browse round a South Australian vinyard and winery. It all seemed very organised with masses of stainless steel everywhere, a very far cry from Westons cider plant at Much Marcle. On both Sundays I stayed in my hotel room beavering away on my Open University (OU) TMA (Tutor Marked Assessment) for my first years course "The Shape of the World". It was a shame to be shut inside, but I was afraid to get too far behind with my OU work. In fact it required sixteen hours/week study. However on our final Sunday I visited the Adelaide Natural History museum which was superb - really enjoyed it.

That wrapped up our Australian work. I opted to fly east with TAA to Melbourne where I transferred to a Qantas jumbo for the short hop to Sydney, then Singapore, Bahrain and finally Heathrow. There was no doubt about it, the Anti-pods were a long way from Europe and civilisation! My faithful Leominster taxi driver, was waiting to collect me for the three hour run back to Gorsty. He was the best, smoothest driver I've ever travelled with. His ability to anticipate what other motorway drivers might do was quite uncanny. Really it was possible to relax.

Back home I had about six days writing up notes. Those I faxed to Kevin just before the end of March - job done. A new doctor had joined Patrick's practice at Fownhope and Gillian was no longer enjoying her work there as much, so she was thinking about retiring after her birthday in September. It made sense to me. I had met that new doctor/partner and could see how Gillian and he didn't gel. He was so different from Patrick who had established a personal relationship with all his patients over many years.

My next engineering job was giving Sprogg's bike a complete overhaul! His class from the Hereford Tec were going on a cycle touring jaunt in Holland during the up and coming Spring holiday. Sproggs was great at all form of sports but practical bike maintenance was not one of his skills. About twelve of them were going together with their tutor. However it transpired he wouldn't need his own bike (pulled a fast one on me there) as they would hire some in Holland when they got off the ferry. In fact my real contribution was not bike maintenance but a few "readies". Sproggs trip to Holland worked out well as Ray from Hereford turned up in early April to do a complete bathroom makeover. It also involved new hot water pipework from the Aga and a new airing cupboard in the bathroom. Ray did everything and had the whole job finished in a week.

In July we went down to Cornwall to stay with Pat to celebrate the OW's (their father, Lofty's moniker for their mother - the Old Woman) 90th birthday. It was a glorious sunny day and plenty of friends from St Mawgan and Mawgan Porth turned up, including sister Sue's previous husband, Patrick, and her new version, Shanta. It was all OK though helped along by plenty of champers. By great good fortune the Red Arrows did a fly-past that afternoon over RAF St Mawgan, which was just across the valley from Pat's house. As Lofty had had a lifetime career in the RAF it couldn't have been a better present for the OW's birthday.

Sproggs had finished his course at the Hereford Tec and passed a few exams. It had not been a great success, he wasn't really interested in the course. One day whilst shopping in Leominster Gillian noticed that the Talbot Hotel was advertising for staff. She went in to get the details, met the Manager and liked both him and the hotel's atmosphere. She told

Sproggs and sent him down to the Talbot for interview. He was accepted and started on Monday as general roustabout and barman. Well it was a start in a real, paid job. Not ideal but he had to start somewhere.

In the middle of August I had another call from Peter of Bechtel International in Perth. He had been approached by WMC asking if I could go and assist them in writing specifications for ITBs for a new shaft and winder at Olympic Dam. I said of course I'd be happy to do that, but what about their, Bechtel's involvement? He said it was quite OK by them for me to work directly for WMC. They, Bechtel, would not be bidding for either sinking a new shaft or building/supplying a new friction winder; that was not their business. He said I should contact Charlie directly at WMC to arrange things. This I did and welcomed job No. 105.

Thus on the the 25th August Kevin, my local taxi man delivered me to Heathrow Terminal 4. This time I flew with BA direct to Bombay then on to Perth. As before I transferred to TAA for the flight to Adelaide. Overall that London-Adelaide routing was more than six hours quicker than interlining at Singapore. That time I was booked into the Richmond Hotel, only 400 yards from the Majestic, but two stars rather than three. No one from WMC was in the hotel so I phoned Charlie at the WMC Project Office and he told me to come to that office tomorrow at 8.30.

I spent the next ten days in that crazy, frenetic WMC Project Office. My time divided neatly into five days with the project mining guys determining the shaft size and layout to hoist 1375 tonnes/hour in twin bottom dump skips. After much discussion it was agreed that the shaft guidance system would be fixed steel squashed pipe buntons and RHS guides. With the high ventilation air volume to be downcast those were felt to be more suitable for 35 to 40 tonne capacity skips rather than rope guides. It also enabled a larger skip cross section to be used whilst minimising running clearance from the shaft walls. My final five days were spent with the engineering guys, both mechanical and electrical. At the start it was agreed that a friction winder was desirable to reduce power demand. The hoisting depth was fixed so that the full speed of the winder should be no more than 50% Vmax, say 13 m/s. To limit costs WMC preferred to opt for a ground mounted friction winder. A T1/T2 ratio of 1.5 (static) should not be exceeded and was largely controlled by acceleration (a) and retardation (r) rates with an upper limit of 1 m/s/s. A drum/rope, D/d ratio of 120 was preferable for locked coil head ropes.. Finally the specific rope pressure on the friction drum grooves should not exceed 2.0 Mpa and that would determine how many head ropes would be required. After all those permutations were considered we arrived at a minimum shaft diameter of 7.5 m. The electrical guys felt that a DC skip winder with either Ward Leonard or thyristor control was required. In all circumstances it would be a very large winder with a RMS power rating of 5500 to 6000 kW. After much discussion we agreed it should be left to the winder manufacturers/supplies to make their own recommendations for the skip winder to meet WMC's hoisting duty specifications.

Well that was it. I'm not sure the Olympic Dam management was particularly pleased that we had all, finally, trashed the Robinson shaft proposal, but it was now agreed that that shaft was incapable of sustaining an 8.5 million tonnes/year hoisting rate so, of necessity there had to be a viable alternative. Couldn't spoil the boat for a ha'porth of tar.

51

With that I packed my bags, said cheerio to Oz and headed for Perth and the BA flight back to Heathrow. As usual Kevin was there to deliver me back to Gorsty. It was now early September, so I was going to be busy finishing off outside DIY window repairs and painting plus getting the grass, hedges and ditches tidied up for approaching winter. Sproggs was still busy working at The Talbot Hotel in Leominster and seemed to be getting very "friendly" with Kate, who was one of the live-in staff. Sproggs said that Kate would like to move out of the Hotel and perhaps they could move into a rented place.

I went around all the local estate agents and eventually located a place at 28 West Street, Leominster, about fifty yards from the Talbot Hotel. Gillian and I weren't sure it was a "good idea", but, decided to go for it. I stood surety for them and signed a six-month lease on their behalf. The first floor flat was a bit of a mess, so I asked Ray (he of our bathroom update) if he could come and upgrade the kitchen and bathroom plumbing/fittings. That he did in short order and Gillian and I completed wall repairs in living room and bedroom and repainted the flat. Thus after two weeks Sproggs and Kate were able to move in. A Kimbolton neighbour lent me a horse box which I hitched to the Disco and with Sproggs and Kate on board drove up to Kate's parent's house in Droitwich.

Like Gillian and me they felt the Sproggs/Kate tie-up was a little precipitate, but ....let's give the kids their head. With no more ado we loaded up the horse box with Kate's things and headed back to Leominster. So in a matter of a month and a half Sproggs had left home and set up in his own flat with Kate. All of a sudden Gorsty seemed very quiet again. Not for long though. Gillian decided to retire as Practice Nurse at Fownhope surgery. The surgery put on a splendid farewell dinner for her at The Wheelbarrow Castle in nearby Stoke Prior. Gillian also decided to start an OU Art History degree as a stimulating project for retirement.

In the first part of November I had a call from Bob, a consultant with Golders. They were retained as geotechnical advisers to the underground limestone Middleton Mine near Wirksworth in Derbyshire. Bob felt that the existing methods of underground pillar-and-stall mining might require significant modification as the workings moved in to the Hopton section where the useful limestone beds were considerably thicker. Could I come and have a look at the mine? Never known to turn down an interesting assignment I said yes and welcomed job No. 106. Early the following week, having telephoned Darren the Manager at Middleton Mine, I drove first north to Ludlow and turned NE to Much Wenlock, then around Telford and on to Stafford passing the huge JCB factory just outside Uttoxeter. From there it was into the Peak District at Ashbourne and up and over down into Wirksworth. The mine was a mile or so further north.

We first studied the geological and mine working plans in the adjacent mine office before donning boots, helmets and lights and walking the short distance into the mine portal at the side of the steep valley. It immediately reminded me of the bedded deposits I had worked in. Gypsum at Robertsbridge in Sussex; salt at Winsford in Cheshire and potash at Cardona and Llobregat in Spain. The main truck haulage adit was 6m high by about 8m wide and as we moved into the main limestone mining area the height increased to 12m and the width to 20m or more. It was very very spacious. In the current room and pillar mining area Darren pointed out the occasional steep dipping voids left from previous lead vein mining activities. We walked into the steep dipping Hopton area, where the ground conditions were excellent. There was no water and no folding or faulting. It looked ideal ground for mining by sub-level open stoping or SLOS.

Back in the mine/engineering office I sketched out how one could mine that Hopton limestone by SLOS based on 20m wide stope between 20m pillars. That would comprise an upper drill drive sited alongside the pillar line with an intermediate drill drive, placed centrally, 40m below. 35m below that there would be a centrally placed trough drive. Inclined drawpoint crosscuts would be driven into the trough drive at 15m intervals on both sides. A slot would be developed over the full 80m stope height by long-hole blasting into the initial slot raise on the NE limit. The stope face would advance SW, blasted ore being extracted from the trough-undercut by LHDs operating in the flank drawpoints. A typical SLOS stope of that size would yield just over 0.5 million tonnes. The development yield would be 423t/m, the stope ring drilling yield would be 9t/m and the blasting yield would be 4.1 t/Kg ANFO.

Basic equipment would be a Tamrock SOLO 606 single boom L/H drill rig which would drill off over 400,000 t/yr and a Toro 400D LHD which would load circa 135,000 t/yr. However I had to point out that those outputs were very low on account of their practice of only working one shift/day. Most hard rock metal mines operate three shifts/day, six days/week, 300days/year to maximise utilisation of expensive capital equipment. Under those operating conditions the Tamrock rig would drill off 1.2 million tonnes/year and the Toro would load plus 300,000 tonnes/year.

Darren was aghast at the concept of operating the limestone mine on a three shifts/day basis for 300days/year. He said the Union would never accept it. I merely pointed out that with a round-the-clock basis the cost advantages of SLOS mining versus room and pillar mining should be demonstrated to the Middleton mine owners. It would be crazy to have expensive capital equipment lying idle for 70% of the time. Basically the UK quarrying industry only worked one shift/day and the Middleton mine was, in reality, being worked as an underground quarry.

Darren asked me to present a write-up with detailed calculations of drilling and loading rates as if the Middleton SLOS stope was being operated on three shifts/day basis. That would then be his starting point in talks with management and owners. We wrapped up our discussions and repaired to a splendid pub in Wirksworth for a couple of beers before I began the cross country drive back to Gorsty. I completed the report and detailed calculations over the next three days and faxed all the data through to Darren. He replied a week later and said, in effect, "good stuff", but the management and Unions were never going to agree on three shift working, but if management really want to reduce operating costs that was the way to go.

Bob, the Golders consultant, phoned and asked me to send him details of a trial 40m (ie half size) SLOS stope for the Middleton limestone mine. That was a variation on the work I had completed for Darren before Christmas. I had to use the mine's existing equipment, comprising a Boart-Komatsu jumbo, DTH quarry drill rig, a Komatsu FEL and Terex 30t haul trucks. I had to switch to down-hole benching with 64mm diameter holes 20.5m deep on a 2m by 2m burden/spacing pattern. The drill jumbo was then used to drill 45mm fan up-holes to form the underlying trough. The maximum length of those fan holes would be 15.5 m. I produced detailed sketches of drilling layouts plus ANFO loading rates. I produced a development and stope blasting schedule so that Bob could then examine the geotechnical impact within the overall, existing Middleton mine.

Sproggs and Kate invited both sets of parents to Christmas lunch in their flat at No 28 West Street, Leominster. In fact Kate's Mum did most of the cooking/organising but it was a chance for us all to get to know each other. It was a good happy day. As Gillian had retired and I had almost retired, we had decided to have a celebratory retirement holiday at the world famous Reids Hotel in Funchal, Madeira. We had persuaded Pat to come with us. We planned to go early in the new year when there was the Funchal Winter Carnival and Fireworks display. We picked Pat up in Cheltenham from the cross country train service from Penzance. After a couple of nights at Gorsty I drove to Birmingham airport and left the car in the Long Stay park. The Monarch Airways flight to Funchal took three hours and from there a coach took us to the hotel.

Reid's has a marvelous position high on the cliffs overlooking Funchal harbour. The hotel itself was very friendly and luxurious. The food and service were impeccable. One evening we had a formal dinner in the main dining room. Both Gillian and Pat were dressed up to the nines and I wore a white Tuxedo! In the adjacent cocktail bar the pianist lent over and whispered to me that I was a very lucky chap with two elegant ladies in tow. Well there you go - a smidgin of La Dolce Vita. We did all the usual tourist things around Funchal. As Madeira is the top of a large submerged volcano, there are no beaches, the surrounding water deepening very swiftly. For this reason there were few family holiday makers, making it an ideal destination for the older generation. The Carnival and Firework Display were spectacular and seemed to go on all night - Rio eat your heart out.

We only stayed a week and all agreed we needed longer to have a look around the rest of the island. No matter, the girls managed to make sure we arrived back at Birmingham airport with a lot more luggage than we set out with. Pat stayed for a few more days at Gorsty before we drove her back to Cheltenham to catch the train back to Cornwall.

All was not going well with Sproggs and Kate. Apparently the Talbot Hotel bar manager still took a shine to Kate and Sproggs was still being chased by Becky from the Wrekin. The 28 West Street flat idea seemed doomed to rapid failure. With the initial six month lease expiring at the end of March I had a session with Sproggs and said I'd give notice to the agent that we would quit the lease. Kates' parents collected her things and we parted on good terms accepting that it just hadn't and wasn't going to work. C'est la vie.

Sproggs moved back to Gorsty, but as it happened, not for long. Somehow, on the hotel grapevine, he had heard of a hotel staff vacancy at the famous Feathers Hotel in Ludlow. He applied, was interviewed and accepted. He gave the required one month's notice to the Talbot Hotel and started at the Feathers in June. One of the attractions of the Feather's job was that it included accommodation in a company owned flat in Broad Street, Ludlow. We moved him and his clobber into the Feathers flat over a weekend. The old Disco and my small trailer were more than adequate for the job.

Sproggs job at the Feathers seemed to be as a useful pair of hands for whatever needed doing. After a while his main job was serving in the Comus bar, where, of course, his bar experience from the Talbot Hotel was put to good use. We went up to have a drink in that bar and catch up with his news. More of the same really, since another girl, Helen, who worked at the Feathers, but was currently living with her parents in Ludlow, decided to move in with Sproggs in the company flat! At least I wasn't putting up a surety for leasing a flat, perhaps a step in the right direction - for me, anyway.

Gillian then surprised me and said she'd like to have her own car. I imagined a small VW Polo or similar. Wrong. She fancied a Jag, an XJS. Once I'd got over the shock I offered only two pieces of advice - do not get the V12 model and if it comes from a second hand dealer get the AA to vet it. We went up to Birmingham to view a 3.6 litre manual one, which she quite liked although the garage looked pretty iffy. We paid the AA to inspect it and they systematically damned it. Phew. Next we visited the main Jag dealer in Cheltenham. They had nothing suitable at present, but Jason, their Sales guy said he'd keep looking. Two or three months later he called saying he had a 1993 four litre XJS automatic, were we interested? Later that week he brought it over to Gorsty. It was a lovely sapphire blue with the old AJ6 twin OHC engine coupled to a ZF automatic box, with only

23,000 miles on the clock. Gillian and Jason took it for a spin down the Leominster by-pass. Although slightly more than she had budgeted (twice as much!) Gillian fell in love with L299JOP. There were only two previous owners, the first a director of Jaguar Cars, the second a lady whose name was also Gillian. The XJS was designed by Lawson, Gillian's maiden name. All those aspects helped clinch the deal. As part of the sale Jason took the car back to the Cheltenham garage to give the XJS a comprehensive service as they had only just acquired it to sell on commission.

We sorted out comprehensive insurance cover for Gillian, plus me as named driver and a week later drove over to Cheltenham in the Disco to pick up the XJS. Jason gave Gillian a full run through on all the controls etc, the money was paid, documents and log book exchanged and we headed (fairly gingerly) back to Gorsty. I lead the way in the Disco with Gillian following a discrete distance behind in the XJS. It certainly made the Gorsty yard seem busy.

As we had all enjoyed the visit to Reids in Madeira I had booked a ten day stay for February. Pat came up from Cornwall by train and, as before, I drove to Birmingham airport, where we again caught the Monarch Airways flight to Funchal. Well the island looked just the same, but what a shock at Reids. The hotel's ownership had passed into German hands and much to our amazement the service and ambience had really crashed. The staff now seemed perpetually grumpy and of course the place was (unsurprisingly) full of Germans. Yes it was true you had to get down to the pool very early to "bag" a sun-bed before the arrival of large groups of loud Germans. Fortunately our room opened directly onto the lovely garden, so if the pool area was "verbotten" we could relax in the sun in the garden. However the loss of hotel ambience lead me to hire a car so we could explore the rest of the island. It was very mountainous in the central part and the road along the northern coast was very hair raising. It was a good holiday, but the Reids ambience we had known had vanished completely.

April the 3rd was Sproggs 21st birthday. I collected him and Helen from their Ludlow flat and with Gillian we drove down to Steels Garage in Hereford. On the forecourt there was an azure Honda Civic 3-door Bali hatchback - his birthday present. It was second-hand but low mileage and in nice condition. I think the kids were quite blown away. Anyway they headed back to Ludlow in it after we'd had a celebratory lunch and game of bowls at the new Ten-Pin Bowling club close by the station.

In spite of climbing numerous ladders underground I managed to miss my footing transferring from ladder to scaffold tower when doing some DIY work on Gorsty chimneys. I fell 15ft onto the surrounding slab path. Fortunately my right shoulder connected with a horizontal strut of the tower as we hit the ground which prevented me from splitting my head open. However it completely dislocated my right shoulder. I had no idea how painful dislocations were. I really didn't want to move. Gillian called A & E and an ambulance took me to Hereford hospital. I was very lucky that afternoon as I went straight in and a young Indian doctor, using his foot as a brace jerked my shoulder back into place. Gillian collected me a couple of hours later with me looking, she said "as white as a sheet". Well as a first hand (or shoulder) experience of NHS A & E treatment it was first rate, it could not have been better.

With my right arm in a sling it prevented me from joining Arthur, my independent geologist mate, on another new mining project in the Iberian pyrite belt. I was very sorry to miss that opportunity as Arthur was always great company and southern Spain was one of my favourite places. However yet another project hove into sight. Sproggs, who had now been at the Feathers Hotel in Ludlow for a year, had been offered a transfer by the Regent Hotel group to their Lion Hotel in Shrewsbury. Good stuff. The only downside was it didn't include accommodation. So forward Dad. With Sproggs we ended up at Pooks letting agency in the town. Yet again I provided surety for a nice little flat on Coton Hill, less than a 100 yards from the river Severn. Helen's Dad set up a job for her at Briggs shoe shop in Mardol. So things looked promising, both with jobs, nice central flat and a new(ish) motor. What's not to like.

I had finished my second year OU course on the English Language and was pleased to learn, just before Christmas that I had achieved a pass. Gillian meanwhile was continuing with her Art History course. To obtain further hands-on art experience she and sister Pat flew to New York on a package Art History tour. They both enjoyed the experience and Gillian was particularly pleased to see that in the Museum of Modern Art (MoMA) in pride of place was an E-type Jaguar. OK not an XJS but a classic British sports car. In July they went on yet another art tour to Paris. That time they went by Eurostar from Waterloo. It included visits to the Louvre and the Musee d'Orsay. However coming back on the Eurostar was a shambles. The train in front broke down and the operators placed all those passengers on to their train, which was consequently jammed. It was the hottest day of the year and the train's air conditioning system was not working. Everyone was frazzled.

Earlier in the year we had suffered a total breakdown of the old Disco on our way up to Shrewsbury. Fortunately Shukers of Ludlow rescued us fairly rapidly and provided a courtesy vehicle. The Disco had a failure of the main drive shaft in the transfer gearbox. It was an expensive repair made all the more annoying by the fact that Land Rover knew of that "problem" with the Mark 2 Discovery, but failed to recall them for modifications. Grrr. I determined to get rid of the Disco as soon as possible. I visited my old friend at Steels Garage in Hereford and asked him if he had anything suitable for us and whether he would take the Disco as a trade-in. Yes he had a ready buyer for the Disco and what about a second-hand Subaru Impreza 5-door hatchback? He test drove the Disco and Gillian and I went for a buzz in the Subaru. That was that; the deal was done apart from exchanging log books, MOT certificates and service records. After the truck-like Disco the Subaru felt very light and fleet.

Sproggs had told me that he really wanted to see the 2000 Olympic Games in Sydney, but he and Helen were finding it quite hard to save up in Shrewsbury, so they had decided, if it was OK with respective parents, to get a local job whilst living at home, Helen with parents in Ludlow and Sproggs at Gorsty. They had completed twelve months in the Coton Hill flat, so at least I was able to terminate the lease with not too much financial damage. Both appreciated that living at home was a lot cheaper than renting a flat! Helen planned, courtesy of her father, to get a job at Briggs shoe shop in Ludlow. Sproggs had nothing specific lined up, but by extreme good fortune, met some of his old Luctonian rugby and cricket mates in one of the Leominster pubs, who told him that the Salutation Inn in Weobley was looking for experienced bar staff. He drove over, saw the Manager and hey presto he had a new job.

The OW had not been too well recently so Gillian decided to drive down to Cornwall in the XJS to give Pat some support. I thought that that would be a good time for me to finish off my Offa's Dyke walk from where Ollie had twisted his ankle. Sproggs did not start work at the Salutation Inn until 11am so I asked him to run me up to the Dyke path just west of Clun. It was a grey misty day after overnight rain as I hitched my rucksack on and headed north for Mainstone & Clun Forest. On the climb out of the river valley I caught up with another lone walker and we continued together into the little town of Montgomery, just to the west of the Dyke path. Although now mid September it was quite difficult to obtain B&B accommodation. Eventually one of the pubs came up with a bare attic room and bed. It was OK, dog tired I crashed out. In the morning after breakfast my walking companion was on his way, whilst I had a look around Montgomery.

The day was bright and sunny with glorious walking over the Long Mountain as I dropped down to Buttington and crossed to the left bank of the river Severn. There it was easy level walking beside the river, overlooked on the other bank by Rodney's Pillar on the Breidden Hills. As the river turned east I walked NNW and found a pub in Four Crosses for the night. After an early breakfast I was underway by 8 o'clock and in a few miles passed the old quarries and lead workings on Llanymynech Hill. Thereafter it was very up and down through Nantmawr, Craignant, to Bronygarth near Chirk Castle. There I shared a static caravan at a small holiday camping site. Another early start and I was walking over the famous Pontcysllte Aqueduct on the Llangollen canal, followed by a steady climb over Ruabon Mountain to Llandegla, where I stayed in a very comfortable, up-market B&B. It was just as well I slept and ate well as the next day was really strenuous walking over the Clwydian Hills, including a climb of Moel Famau, 555m (1820 ft). The pub in Bodfari was a welcome stop for my fifth night. I finished the final eleven mile walk into Prestatyn by 1pm the following day. There I had a quick walk on the beach, to finish the Dyke walk in style and returned to the station to catch a train to Crewe, then a Marches Line train to Leominster. I phoned Clive and he came to collect me. His first words were "you look knackered" and he was spot on. I was, but happy that I had, finally, completed Offas Dyke walk from the Severn Estuary to Prestatyn.

In March 2000 Gillian drove Ollie and me to Kington, where we set out on the thirty mile long Mortimers Way. Ollie had a full pack as it was a trial run for his upcoming walk on El Camino, the pilgrims way from Roncevalles in the Pyrenees to Santiago de Compostella in NW Spain. On our first day we walked seventeen miles through to the Riverside Inn at Aymestry. Day two took us out of the Lugg valley, up onto Yatton Ridge and over our old dog walking ground, Bircher Common and on into Ludlow. Here I managed to raise Sproggs, who was at Helen's parents house, to run us back to Leominster. It was a great walk through beautiful border country. Easy for me with only a light day pack, definitely hard going for Ollie with a full 30 Kg pack.

In April we drove Sproggs up to Heathrow where he joined Helen for their flight to Thailand. They went to the island of Ko Samui off the east coast.

In early May Gillian and I drove the Jag down to Plymouth to catch the Britanny Ferries, boat Val de Loire, bound for Santander in northern Spain. Much to my amazement both of us and the Jag were given a full intensive search whilst waiting to board the ferry. I had never had that before on leaving the UK and could only assume that dear old Customs at Birmingham airport had flagged us as potential drug smugglers, again!

We motored westwards and stopped for the night at the Cangas de Onis Parador. The following day we drove up to Covadonga, birthplace of the movement to retake Spain from the Moslems. Then we climbed higher into the spectacular Picos de Europa. Back at Cangas we had to get a new heavy duty battery for the XJS. A little later than planned we headed further west, along superb new roads (thanks to EU funding) to another Parador at Ribadeo. We then headed SW for the lovely walled city of Lugo. Parked outside, then walked on top of the medieval walls - fascinating. After lunch in Lugo's central plaza we drove west to Santiago de Compostela where we stayed at the Hotel Reyes in the shadow of the cathedral. The hotel was a notable ancient monument with masses of objects d'art but, unfortunately, zero service for patrons who seemed to be invisible to the hotel staff. The bedroom and food were also lousy.

On the way south to northern Portugal we stopped in Pontevedra. There was a pleasant central plaza with a lovely, friendly ambience. We crossed the Rio Minho into Portugal and, wow, how the roads and driving manners deteriorated. That night we stayed in Viana de Castelo where the Pousada hotel Monte De Sta Luzia was excellent. From there the roads to Canicada were terrible and the low slung, long wheelbase Jag took quite a hammering. The Pousada at Canicada was a friendly ranch style hotel with a great location overlooking a beautiful lake. Then down to Pinhao on the river Douro where the Taylors' Vintage House Hotel was the best of the holiday. The river was in spate, an orange-brown colour, so a boat trip was off the agenda. Instead the arrival at the hotel of the Rolls Royce 1922 Tour of the Douro, when 32 vintage/classic RRs plus 70 participants rather took over the place. No matter Gillian's Jag was in pride of place by the front door surrounded by all the RRs! It made a great photo.

We continued eastwards to the Spanish border and stayed in the Miranda Pousada, overlooking a gorge and hydro dam. It was a little weird as we were the only guests in the hotel. Needless to say the service was excellent! Next morning we crossed the border and drove SE into Salamanca. What a glorious city with a magnificent central plaza, university and cathedral. Here for the first time the Jag created a bit of interest. Generally though, both the Spanish and Portuguese were uninterested in "motors" unlike the Italians. Unfortunately we were not staying in Salamanca, but we agreed we would definitely come back again and stay. We headed north for the Parador at Benavente. Both the hotel and town were without merit. We left early next morning heading ENE for Burgos and the delightful Landa Palace Hotel, which lay just south of the city. Here we had a surprise. The receptionist said that a parcel had been left for us. It had been left by my old mate, Oliver, as he trudged westward on El Camino, the pilgrims route to Santiago. I was convinced it would be dirty clothes and various unwanted items, discarded from his rucksack. I did him an injustice as he'd included an "offering" of French brandy!

Our ultimate stop was the San Ramon hotel in Escalante, near Santona. It was quiet and peaceful set in beautiful gardens with an eye catching metal statue of Icarus falling to earth. We had a short drive west to Santander to catch the Val de Loire ferry, due to leave at 10.30. As before we had a good, amidships outside cabin and that evening we had an excellent meal of succulent lamb chops. Hard to believe on a ferry, but the best lamb we'd ever tasted. Eat your heart out Wales.

When we got back to Gorsty there was a message from Helen's parents saying they had heard that the kids couldn't get a flight to Australia. By all accounts they loved Thailand and seemed reluctant to leave. I sent an email to Sproggs hotmail address and gave him the hustle-up to get down to Singapore airport and wait-list for flights to Darwin, Australia. Surprise, surprise they were soon in Darwin. They worked there for a while before making their way to Sydney via Ayers Rock. In Sydney they ended up in a Bondi beach house with a group of Aussies they'd met in Thailand. The

2000 Sydney Olympics were fantastic, according to Sproggs. They stayed on in Sydney working in an insurance call centre. Then moved down to the Murray river region to do some fruit picking, but found that really tough going and quickly moved on to Melbourne and more call centre work.

In late September Ollie and his wife Marjatta joined us for a trip on Toadflax. As we chugged across Stourport basin to lock down onto the river Severn it started to rain. It rained steadily all day as we passed through Worcester arriving late afternoon at the Avon lock at Tewkesbury, where we moored. It rained throughout the night. We locked up early and set off up the river Avon. The old Toad seemed to be struggling. I checked the weed hatch - nothing on the prop. By the time we eventually reached the old bridge at Pershore, it was obvious that the river was now in spate. We only just managed to pass through the centre arch with the old Petter PH2W on full throttle, barely making half a mile per hour against the surging river. With great relief we moored up on the Pershore recreation ground.

Next morning I walked the towpath to the next lock, Wyre, to see if it was OK. It seemed passable so we set off battling against the river with the old Petter working overtime. We got through Wyre lock reasonably well but the next lock, Fladbury, was almost under water and we were forced to call a halt in the lock itself. There we remained, virtually marooned, for two days until the river levels fell two to three feet. We still had 23 miles and ten locks to work through before we could escape the surging river Avon into Stratford basin. It took us a day and a half on full throttle and I was as glad as the Petter was to reach the calm and safety of the canal. Rivers in spate are definitely no place for a narrow boat.

In Stratford whilst Ollie and Marjatta went shopping, Gillian found a Toni & Guy to have her hair done and I went to the Municipal Pool for a swim. Well I was so wet from our incessant soaking on Toadflax it was a real busman's holiday. Afterwards I went to Toni & Guy to collect Gillian, but didn't even recognise her with the new hair do! In the evening we got seats for The Other Place theatre to take on some culture.

It was an early start next day as we were so far behind our planned schedule. We had thirty miles and over thirty locks to navigate up the Stratford canal and the Birmingham & Worcester canal joining the BCN at Worcester Bar. After two full ten hour cruising (misnomer?) days we moored up close to the International Convention Centre by Brindley Place.

The girls ditched the boating jeans, broke out the make-up and went off to the ballet at the Hippodrome. Ollie and I went to a super Japanese restaurant, just off the canal in Brindley Place serving Teppanyaki cuisine. We collected the girls from the Hippodrome in, you guessed it, pouring rain.

Unbelievably it continued to rain for the next three days as we navigated the fifteen miles of the BCN to the Aldersley junction with the Staffs & Worcester canal, which included descending the 21 lock Wolverhampton flight (so no rest there). Then it was a steady 25 mile run with 28 locks to our home base in Stourport basin. Ollie and Marjatta took off in their car at once as they had a prior engagement at their Hay-on-Wye house. Gillian and I went to the Tontine Hotel for a late lunch and agreed then and there that that was enough narrow boating. What could, or should, have been a lovely trip was almost completely washed out by incessant rain. In the pub I learnt that that was one of the wettest Septembers ever and large swathes of the country were flooded. Back at Gorsty I composed a For Sale notice for Toadflax and contacted Waterways World, the narrow boat magazine, to place the ad. On my next trip over to Stourport I put a For Sale notice up in the resident BWB officers hut. Like me he felt it would be unlikely to sell until the thc new season opened in late March.

Early in 2001 Gillian's mother died at the age of 95. There was a moving service at St Mawgan Church where she had been a regular helper for years. The three sisters, Pat, Sue and Gillian put on a lovely wake at Pat's house in Mawgan Porth. The OW would have been pleased as it was a lively gathering of old friends helped along by plenty of bubbles. One local acquaintance said she hadn't been to such a good party for years - stopped - said Oh I suppose I shouldn't have said that - but really the OW would have agreed. It was definitely a celebration of life.

Old Toadflax sold in early March. We did the deal over pints of beer in the Tontine Hotel. We had owned her for 14 years and seen a lot of the Midlands from a canal viewpoint. I had found canal boating a very peaceful way of relaxing from the fairly frenetic, stressful business of continual flying to isolated mine sites hither and yon. After last September's complete washout both of us agreed we should head for the sun, but no flying. In early April I emailed Sproggs to remind him that they should use their RTW air tickets before the twelve months was up at the end of the month or they would be invalid. Surprise, surprise they were still in Oz at the end of the month. However there was good news in April when I received my degree from the Open University. Hurrah, a BA to go with my ACSM.

In May it was the Britanny Ferries Val de Loire ferry from Plymouth to Santander again. That time we turned east from Santander and stopped in the little fishing town of Castro Urdiales. Here the seafood was exquisite especially the prawns, fried squid and lobster. We then headed further east to the French border, crossing at Irun and climbing to the small village of Sare in the Pyrenees. The following day a long drive north through Gascony to Bordeaux then east to Bergerac. After a night stop it was a short drive up the Dordogne valley to Meyssac where we stayed with my geologist mate, Ross and his wife Sheelagh.

That was our base for five days and we visited the Lascaux Caves and the towns of Brive, Martel, Beaulieu and Aurillac. I could see why so many Brits had settled in the Dordogne region, it was very pleasant, rolling countryside. We then drove south through Figeac to the town of Albi on the river Tarn. It was an attractive pink town with many fine medieval buildings. Of course two hours were spent wandering around the Toulouse-Lautrec museum. From there it was a short drive SW to the city of Toulouse, where we stayed in a central hotel. The central square of the city was magnificent and we found a good bistro close by. We walked out to the Canal du Midi, so much bigger (wide beam) than the English canals and marvelled at the facade of the main railway station.

From there we drove SW to Arreau and then up steeper and narrower roads as we climbed the Pyrenees to the Bielsa tunnel and crossed into Spain. There we stayed at the mountain chalet style Bielsa Parador, which was not far below the snow line. Next day we headed south into the quiet, hot, dusty town of Huesca. From there we headed NW to Ayerbe then west through Ejea, past hundreds of wind turbines and down to Tudela in the river Ebro valley. Then we headed NW along the Ebro to Logrono where I had booked a town-centre hotel. I was interested to see if the hotel had a reservation for "Es toe ack ees" since, to try out my Spanish, I had booked the hotel over the telephone from the Bielsa Parador. In spite of my dubious accent, they had a reservation - success. Logrono was the capital of the Rioja region.

Encouraged by my " Spanish phone prowess" I booked a small inn in the town of Enciso, which was due south of Logrono. Again, the booking worked, and we checked into that family hotel, which was barely open for the new season. They did not do an evening meal so we drove a few miles to the local town of Arnedillo. We went into a local bar for a drink and to ask where we could get a meal. The local owner was exceptionally friendly and suggested the local Health Centre/Spa or Balneario, as the place for a good meal. He was spot on, it was. Attached to the Health Spa was a large restaurant which provided great food and drink to all comers, not just health bunnies. Apparently throughout Spain those Balnearios were renowned for serving good food.

After an early breakfast in our Enciso inn we drove a few miles to the Parque Jurasico. On a gently sloping hill above the river that was the site of one of the largest finds of dinosaur fossils and footprints in Europe. Apart from interpretation plaques alongside the excavations there were several full size plastic dinosaurs dotted around the landscape. In the early morning sunlight it was quite surreal. We left the Jurassic Park by 11am and headed due north for the Basque Country. We stopped in Guernica, but found the atmosphere unfriendly, almost threatening. The same was true of the port of Lekeitio, a few mile from where we stayed at a fine old inn in Guizaburuaga. Next morning we headed west to Bilbao and went to the fantastic Guggenheim Museum alongside the river Nervion. Bilbao used to be a heavy industrial city based on coal and iron mining and steel making. Definitely one of Spain's least scenic cities. Frank Gehry's super modern titanium clad Guggenheim building and a new Metro system had led the transformation of the city. The Museum exhibits were disappointing and the internal facilities not people friendly, but the actual building itself was very striking.

In fact I was glad to leave the unfriendly Basque country and return to friendly Castro Urdiales in Cantabria. We had another night there, enjoying the marvellous sea food before heading further west to the Bahia Hotel in Santander. A full day of shopping and seeing the sights before we caught the ferry for Plymouth. One thing we both agreed on was that the Subaru lacked air conditioning and we had really felt the heat in Huesca, Logrono and Enciso. On return to Gorsty I contacted the Subaru agent in Cheltenham to see if they had a modern demonstrator car available. Yes, they would have a green, two litre, non-turbo, 5-door hatchback available at the beginning of September. Also they would take our old car as a trade-in. Of course the new car would have excellent air conditioning.

Finally in late August we had a call from Sproggs saying that he and Helen had nearly saved up enough money to buy air tickets back to the UK, before they got deported by the Oz authorities for overstaying their twelve-month visas. They expected to be back by mid September. He also said that he and Helen were interested in doing a photography course. So I asked around and contacted various Colleges that ran photography courses. Of course it was now late in the academic year and most were fully booked. The only available option was Doncaster, whose course began in the third week of September. I filled out all the enrollment forms on Sproggs behalf; sent a monetary deposit and said he would report to the college no latter than the 22nd (I quietly crossed my fingers).

Gillian and I drove over to Cheltenham and picked up the new Subaru. We were amazed at how the fairly basic design of our original Subaru had improved. The agent was especially keen to demonstrate the new keyless entry, but wasn't too sure how it worked! At home I made sure Sproggs little Honda Civic was "ready to go" for the expected return of the prodigal son. Everything went on hold on the 11th September after the heinous attack on the Trade Centre towers in New York. We wondered if the kids would still be able to fly back. In fact they advised arrival at Heathrow by Emirates Airline on the 15th September. The airport run was the first lengthy journey we'd made in the new Subaru. At the Arrivals gate in Terminal 3 much to our bemusement Sproggs went one way and Helen the other. Well that was it, apparently. Their seventeen month trip to the Far East and Australia had confirmed that they were not going to be a unit. Well I guess it was a good way to find that out. Sproggs looked unchanged, merely a little older at 24.

After a day to unwind we sent him down to Hereford in his car to buy some clothes and essential student "stuff" that he'd need for Doncaster College. Gillian had already prepared a suggested list for him as well as purchasing duvets, towels and such like. I spent a day with him going through all the paperwork to apply for a loan from the Student Loan Company as well as over-signing the College bumph. We just had a couple of days to look through some of the numerous photos he taken on their trip before we loaded up the Honda Civic and he headed north for Doncaster. In fact I think he was slightly blown away at the speed with which things had happened. He'd only been home for six days, but that was all the time available before the photography course started. We said we'd come up and see him in a months time after he'd settled in.

In late October we drove up Corve Dale to Much Wenlock and on to Newport, Stone, Leek, Buxton, Glossop to Tankersley Manor where we stayed. The College was set on a lovely wooded hill overlooking the Dearne valley, about five miles west of Doncaster. It made a very pleasant, quiet contrast to the surrounding South Yorkshire coalfield towns. He had a good, simple bed-sit, complete with shower cubicle. There was a communal laundry room in his building and a refectory, common sitting room and library in the main admin block just across an internal quadrangle. In addition there were tennis courts and a nine hole golf course. I was really impressed, let's hope the teaching was as good. We drove into nearby Doncaster to have a pub lunch with him and then went to a supermarket to buy "stuff" to top up his fridge. We visited the Great Northern pub where Sproggs had got friendly with the bouncer, Jonny. Once he'd got the photography course sorted out he hoped to make some extra cash by working in the pub at weekends.

For me it was absolutely fascinating to see how Doncaster had changed from 1958, when I first went to Cementation Mining's offices in Bentley. Then it was a bustling coal mining and railway town plus the huge British Ropes factory. Now, 44 years later, all that heavy industry had disappeared. With the help of EU money the town had been gentrified. I only recognised three iconic landmarks - the parish church, the Danum Arms and the Railway Station. However, more to the point, we were very happy to see how Sproggs had settled in to the Doncaster College scene and was enjoying himself. He came back to Gorsty for Christmas, but returned after a few days to earn some cash doing bar work at the Great Northern pub.

In May we took the ferry to northern Spain again. That time it was a rough crossing with high winds and driving rain. The old Val de Loire was 75 minutes late docking in Santander. We drove due south on the N623 and soon encountered brilliant sunshine as we climbed the Cantabrian Cordillera. Near the top of the climb we stopped for a coffee and noticed that the Subaru was covered in salt (from sea spray). When loading at Plymouth the Subaru had been up the front on one of the car decks close to the bow doors, hence the salt covering - scary! Our first stop was Burgos, home of El Cid and Franco's base in the civil war. The following day we drove south-west to Segovia, a lovely city, with a magnificent roman aqueduct.

After two days we headed south up in to the Guadarrama mountains (1880 m) and eventually down into the walled city of Avila. Then we continued west to my favourite Spanish city of Salamanca where we stayed for four days in the delightful hotel Rector. We then headed north through Zamora to Astorga where there was a fascinating Gaudi facade overlooking the small plaza. From there we drove east to the city of Leon, staying in the magnificent San Marcos Parador. The stained glass windows in Leon cathedral were superb. The following day we headed north, on the Oviedo road as far as La Robia, then turned east and north climbing into the mountains to the spectacular Valporquero Caves. We had a 1.5 hour visit enlivened by a good guide and an amusing Egyptian tourist.

We spent that night at the run-down, mock Swiss chalet Cervera Parador. Not a great choice. Away quickly in the morning heading north through spectacular mountain scenery to Potes. Then down the Rio Deva Hermida gorge to Panes and finally into Castro Urdiales and the Las Rocas hotel, where the manager greeted us like long lost friends. We stayed two days sampling the superb sea food in the Meson Merino and Segovia restaurant. It was noticeable how Castro had changed. As it was the weekend the town was full of Spanish tourists with poser cars and designer dogs, presumably from Bilbao. The following day we drove to Santander to stay at the Bahia hotel. Next day it was another rough crossing, very rough indeed, the ferry was 3.5 hours late docking in Plymouth. The three hour drive back to Gorsty was uneventful.

Out of the blue I had a call from a Mrs Dickie. Could I come and have a look at the stability of her house in Broseley, Shropshire? Apparently she was trying to get a mortgage on the house and, since Broseley was an old coal mining and clay working area just across the river Severn from Ironbridge, she had been advised to get "a ground stability survey". She had obtained my name as a competent person from South Shropshire Council. Well I said yes and welcomed job No. 107.

I drove up to Broseley on a cold, early December day. The property was part of a relatively modern terrace development on the ENE side of the B4375 road. I had already studied the IGS map, Telford SJ60, which indicated that the sub-soil was boulder clay, a short distance south of the lower coal measures contact. The major Broseley Fault lay 400m away to the north-east. That fault strikes NW and dipped steeply NE. Ergo Mrs

Dickie's property was sited on the stable footwall rocks. The closest old mine workings were two old coal mine shafts (now filled in) approximately 150m from the property, but sited to the west of the B4375 road. Those shafts thus had no influence on the stability of the property. About 35m due east there was an area of backfilled or made ground. That was understood to be the site of former clay workings. That area was also stable as evidenced by the footings of a large pylon carrying the overhead, high voltage transmission line from the Ironbridge Power Station. There were no signs of shafts/subsidence within the property or its immediate neighbours. I was thus happy to give Mrs Dickie's property a clean bill of health for stability.

On the drive home I stopped for a pint at the George & Dragon pub in Much Wenlock. Enjoying my pint in front of a blazing open fire I had a thought - yes, I do get them occasionally! Time to stop this mining consulting malarkey. I was coming up 67 years old and had been actively engaged in the mining industry for over forty years. Things seemed to have come full circle. As a qualified engineer I started in Doncaster in 1958 and now Sproggs was a student at Doncaster College. Besides, I had said to myself that I would stop when I had completed 100 projects as an independent consultant. Mrs Dickies assignment was job No. 107. Hence, to labour the point - job done. I could now retire with a clear conscience.

I always wanted to see the world and hard rock mining provided opportunities to do so in spades. I had been part of 125 mining projects in 37 different countries across the globe. It had been a fascinating experience and I'd enjoyed (nearly) all of it. When I hear people sounding off against mining I wonder if they realise that it's products are everywhere in their life - energy, cars, TVs, mobile phones, food production, packaging and so much more. In fact, although the basic industries are always quoted as Farming, Forestry and Fishing, the fourth is Mining.

www.ingramcontent.com/pod-product-compliance
Lightning Source LLC
Chambersburg PA
CBHW060747230426
43667CB00010B/1470